הרובע
היהודי
מגדל
דוד

Where Heaven Touches Earth

Where Heaven

Jewish Life in Jerusalem

Dovid Rossoff

Touches Earth

from Medieval Times to the Present

GUARDIAN PRESS
Jerusalem

Revised Edition

First published 1998
Second printing, November, 1998
Third, revised printing, May, 1999
Forth, revised printing, September, 2001
Fifth printing, November, 2002
Sixth, revised printing, February, 2004

Copyright © 1998 by Dovid Rossoff
02-651-8054
שנת ציון וירושלים (תשנ״ח) לפ״ק

ISBN 0-87306-879-3

All rights reserved
No part of this publication, including all original graphics (pp. 165, 240, 260, 277, 293, 305, 311, 347, 387, 467, and front endpaper) and photographs taken by the author (i.e., excluding photographs from archives) may be translated, reproduced, stored in a retrieval system or transmitted, in any form or by any means, electronic, mechanical, photocopying, recording or otherwise, without prior permission in writing from the publisher and the copyright holder.

Edited by Eli Linas

Graphics by Zvi Mordechai Chiappetta

Photo credits: All recent photographs are by the author. Special thanks to Shaarei Zedek Hospital for use of their photographs.

Published by
GUARDIAN PRESS
POB 5437
Jerusalem

Distributed by
FELDHEIM PUBLISHERS
200 Airport Executive Park
Nanuet, N.Y. 10954

POB 35002
Jerusalem

Printed in Israel

צילום ולוחות "פרנק" ירושלים.

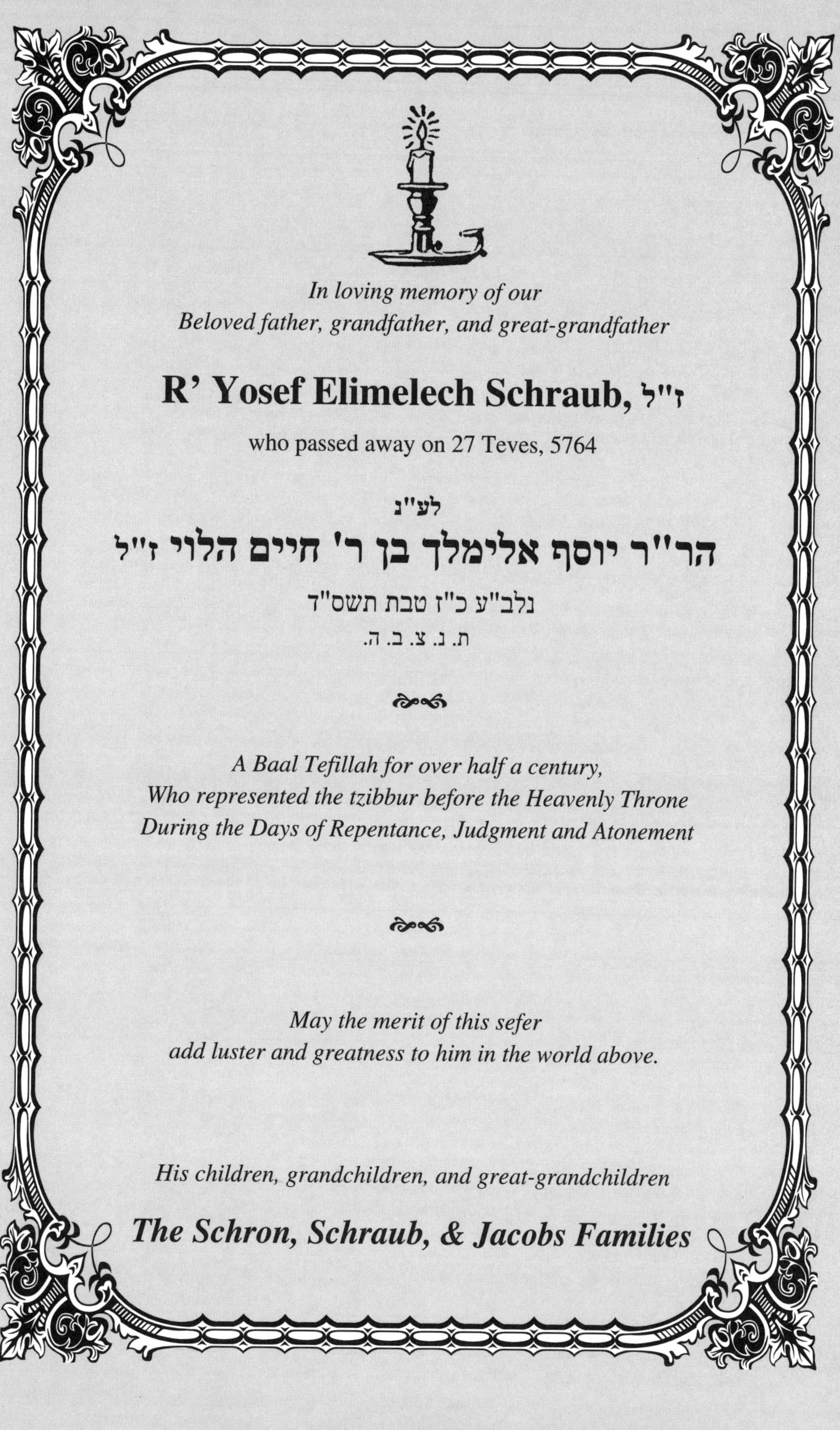

In loving memory of our
Beloved father, grandfather, and great-grandfather

R' Yosef Elimelech Schraub, ז"ל

who passed away on 27 Teves, 5764

לע"נ

הר"ר יוסף אלימלך בן ר' חיים הלוי ז"ל

נלב"ע כ"ז טבת תשס"ד

ת. נ. צ. ב. ה.

A Baal Tefillah for over half a century,
Who represented the tzibbur before the Heavenly Throne
During the Days of Repentance, Judgment and Atonement

May the merit of this sefer
add luster and greatness to him in the world above.

His children, grandchildren, and great-grandchildren

The Schron, Schraub, & Jacobs Families

In memory of

Maurice M. Rothman ז״ל

and

Golde N. Rothman ע״ה

לחמו מלחמות ה׳

"who lived and fought for Torah-true Judaism"

Published through the courtesy of the
HENRY, BERTHA and EDWARD ROTHMAN FOUNDATION
Rochester, N.Y. • Circleville, Ohio • Cleveland

This book
is dedicated to the memory
of all the tzaddikim of Jerusalem,
both those mentioned and unmentioned
— from the renowned scholar to the small infant —
who breathed the air of the Holy City, and,
by their very presence, words, prayers, deeds, and Torah studies;
in times of joy and in times of need and desperation,
were builders of Yerushalayim, guardians of the faith,
and genuinely beloved by the Almighty.

May their souls shine
with the splendor of Yerushalayim,
and may they return to rejoice in the rebuilding
of the final Temple on Mount Moriah,
soon in our days.

In loving memory of

Sherman 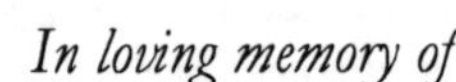 **שבח בן ר׳ יעקב Shapiro, ע״ה**

who passed away on 23 Iyar, 5758 (1998)
Endeared to the many who knew him for his deeds of loving-kindness.
May the merit of this *sefer* add luster and greatness
to him in the world above.

His children, grandchildren, and great-grandchildren

Contents

Foreword i

Preface iii

Introduction vii

Overview xi

Who's Who in Jerusalem / Prayer and Study Houses / Leadership / Inauguration of Rishon l'Tzyon / Homesteading / Water: The Source of Life / Standard of Living / Livelihood / Chalukah System / Palace of the King / Custodians of Eretz Yisrael / Discrimination Against the Minority / Pilgrimage Season / Touching Stones

12th – 16th Centuries: Upholding Jerusalem's Dignity

The Buried Legacy 3

The Long Endurance / "Holy Wars" / Saladin's Reconquest / End of Crusader Period / The Jewish Legacy / The Baalei Tosefos / The Ramban's Imprint / The Ramban Synagogue / The First Researcher of Eretz Yisrael / The Silent Years

Great Names in the Holy City 16

Rav Ovadiah of Bartenora / The Turn of the Century / The Spanish Expulsion / The Ottoman Conquest / David's Tomb / The Last Naggid

Jerusalem as the Center of the World 25

Ralbach: Rav Levi Chaviv / Birth of the Ari Zal / Semichah: Reinstating Ordination / Rav Yaakov Berav / Ralbach's Stand / The Middle Years / The End of the Century / Rav Bezalel Ashkenazi / Rav Menachem Lunzano / Sheik al-Yehud

Notes 36

Bygone Days (Stories) 38

David HaMelech, May He Live Forever / The Hidden Treasure / Mishmeros / The Ari Zal's Roots / The King's Ultimatum / The Miracle Worker

17th Century: The Silent Fervor

Shelah versus a Despot ... 51

The Prince of Prague / The Rav of Jerusalem / The Sultan's Empire / A Despot Usurps the Crown / Farouk's Reign of Terror / Reaction from Damascus / The Trap / Insurrection / Farouk's Fatal Error / The End of a Tyrant / Rebuilding Shattered Lives

The Rise of the Yeshivah World & the Fall of the Wicked ... 65

The Era of Spiritual Growth / Rav Meir Paparish / Tzaddik and Leader / Troubled Times /A Glimmer of Light / The Rosh Yeshivah / The False Messiah / The False Prophet / A Traitor to His People / Jerusalem's Stand / The Aftermath / Repurcussions / City of Torah / Rav Galante: Rishon l'Tzyon / Scholars of the Holy City / Hard Times / Rav Moshe Chagiz and Rav Moshe Chaviv / The Pri Chadash / Rav Silva and the Torah World

Notes ... 86

Bygone Days (Stories) ... 88

The Unforgettable Shabbos / The Tug of War / The Missing Boy / A Glimmer of Light / At the Tomb of Zechariah / Shabbetai Tzvi at the Tomb of Shmuel HaNavi / May His Name Be Blessed / The Torah's Honor / "I Am Black Yet Comely" / The Day of Rain

18th Century: The Ancient Legacy Renewed

The Aliyah of Rav Yehudah HaChassid ... 111

A Legend in His Own Time / The Domino Effect / The Wheel of Fortune / A Tzaddik from Italy / Rebellion / Shots in the Dark / Churvas Rav Yehudah HaChassid / Shock Waves / The Reign of Terror / The Yoke of Galus

The Light of Kabbalah ... 125

Threshold of a New Era / A Pure Light / A Time of Striving / The Karaite Scheme Foiled / The Ohr HaChaim's Passing / A Lion in the Grave / Stones for the Future / Midrash Chassidim / Revelation of a Tzaddik / Beis El / Enduring Legacy

Forging Onward ... 138

Two Extremes / From the Very Depths / Rav Yom Tov Elgazi / The Mount of Olives / Rav David Pardo / A Personal Loss / At the Turn of the Century

Notes ... 145

Bygone Days (Stories) ... 147
The Snowstorm / The Dogs / The Miracle / The Paper Note / The Inner Circle / A Hairsbreadth from the Redemption / Statues of Flesh and Blood / Kill Me Too! / The Bottle of Wine

19th Century: From Napoleon to Beyond the Walls

Part 1:
The Era of Suffering: 1800–1840

Face to Face with Napoleon ... 163
Napoleon's Scheme / Napoleon's Decision / A Breathing Spell

A Foothold in Yerushalayim ... 168
Vision of Zion / Breaking the Ban / Era of Perushim / Perushim: Two Sides of the Same Coin / Era of Suffering / Revolt from Within / Death of the Righteous / Sir Moses Montefiore's First Visit / The Water Breakthrough

Under Egyptian Rule ... 182
Internal Strife / High Hopes for the Yishuv / The Long-Awaited Building Permit / Rav Zundel of Salant

End of the Beginning ... 188
Earthquake and Its Aftermath / Deep Introspection / Troubles upon Troubles / The Last of the Original Leaders / The Ultimate Breakdown

Notes ... 194

Bygone Days (Stories) ... 196
The Hidden Light / The Immovable Stone / The Courageous Decision / Passover Miracle / Montefiore's Dream / The Fountain of Salvation / The Poisoned Cup / In Search of the Lost Tribes / The Granddaddy of Mussar

Part 2:
Bound within the Walls: 1840–1870

The Turning Point ... 211
Return to Ottoman Rule / The Maggid Speaks / Uplifting the Yishuv / An Added Dimension

The 1840s 216

Chacham Bashi / Rav Avraham Gagin / The Beck Publishing House / Sir Moses' Humility / Amending the Chalukah System

The Right of Self-Identity 222

The Moroccan Congregation / The Moroccan Tzaddik / A Leader of His People / The First Chassidic Dynasty / The Lelover Dynasty / The Chassidic Community

Pillars for the Future 232

Torah from Zion / Etz Chaim Yeshivah / A Brilliant Idea / The Lemel School / Alternative Education / The Great Churvah Synagogue / The First Jewish Hospitals

Archeological Finds 244

The Tomb of the Kings / Zedekiah's Cave / First Excavations around the Temple Mount

The Silence before the Storm 250

The Jewish Predicament / Sir Montefiore's Plan / Avraham's Vineyard / Battei Machse / Two Lights of the Yishuv / The Plague of 1865 / Tiferes Yisrael Synagogue / The Emperor's Visit

Notes 262

Bygone Days (Stories) 264

Jerusalem Blood Libel / The 2,500-Year-Old Apology / Saving a Soul / A Proud People / The Wonder-Worker / Wheat from Heaven / Rav Schwartz Meets the Archduke / Birth of a Tzaddik / Gunpoint / Yoma d'Pagra / The Fiery Torah / The Emperor's Gift

Part 3:

Beyond the Walls: 1870–1900

Mapping the Future 281

Givat Yerushalayim / Mishkenos Sha'ananim / Battei Yehudah Touro / Machane Yisrael

Nachalas Shiva 288

Bonei Yerushalayim / Land Acquisition / The Seven / Stone Houses and the Lone Pioneer / Price Tag / Beis David

Meah Shearim 297

The Hundred Signers / Vineyard of Cadcod / Building a Fortress / Founding Fathers / The Polluted Marshland / The Rivlin Plan / Settlers of a Different Brand / Suburbs of the 1870s

Montefiore's Final Mission 308
The Two-Man Commission / The Disputation / Montefiore's Last Trip / The Wonder of Yerushalayim / The Feud / The Montefiore Testimonial Fund / Sir Moses' Legacy

Jerusalem Faces the World 315
The Jewish Press / Danger Signs / The Rav of Brisk / A Historical Perspective / The Battle Cry / The First Library / The Diskin Orphanage

Sacred Places 330
The Western Wall / The Place of the Deshen / The Cave of the Prophets / The Cave of Shimon HaTzaddik / The Cave of Shmuel HaNavi / The Tomb of Rachel

Greater Jerusalem 339
A Survey / New Suburbs / Jewish Presence in the Old City / The Yemenite Community / The Close of the Century / The Centennial Crossroads / Scanning the 19th Century

Notes 357

Bygone Days (Stories) 359
Needs of the Hour / The Biographer / Blast of the Ram's Horn / The Miser's Roundabout Present / The Saving Hand / The Report / The Cosigner / By the Work of Your Hands / For the Sake of the Holy Shabbos / The Hidden Treasure / Glimpses of Rav Salant / The Innocent Thief / The Wealthiest Jew in the City / The Book Dealer / The Maggid's Illness / The Passing of a Gaon

20th Century: Birth Pangs of the Ancient City

Part I:
The Decline of Turkish Rule: 1900–1918

Jerusalem Enters the 20th Century 383
The Sultan's Half-Jubilee / New Neighborhoods / Shaarei Zedek Hospital / Beis Strauss / A Growing City

Signs of Danger 396
The Last Chacham Bashi / Shepherds of the Yishuv / The Untimely Death of the Aderes / The Yerushalmi Maggid / Parallel Forces / Reaching Out / Eve of the First World War / The Crisis of the First World War / The Catastrophe / A Fearful Premonition

Notes 410

Bygone Days (Stories) 411
The Sundial / The Tailor and the Rav / The First One in Heaven / The Telegram / A Jerusalem Archivist / The Homeopathic Cure / A Chassidic Segulah / The Tefillin Maker / Hideaways / The Draft Dodger / Jamil's Reign of Terror / The Father-Son Relationship / In Honor of the King

Part 2: The British Mandate Period: 1918–1948

Post-World War I 433
The Jewish World after the First World War / The Era of British Rule

For the Sake of Jerusalem 439
The Rise of Zionism in Eretz Yisrael / Weizmann versus Rav Zonnenfeld / Torah and Eretz Yisrael / Lovers of Zion / Rav Kook and Rav Zonnenfeld / Assistance from Abroad / Dr. Yaakov DeHaan

A City in Flux 453
Growing by Leaps and Bounds / Arab Unrest / In the Halls of Torah / The Sabba Kaddisha / A New Leadership / The 1930s / Influx of Chassidic Rebbes / The Second World War / End of Mandate Rule

Notes 477

Bygone Days (Stories) 479
The Abominable Movie House / The Gerrer Rebbe's Blessing / Not for All the Money in the World / Funeral of a Righteous Woman / Nothing in Order / The Wallach Hospital / Donkeys and Bicycles / The Hundred-Year-Old Message / The Security Deposit / Rebbe Shlomo of Zweille / Father of the Prisoners / Paralysis and the Pledge / Two Halves make a Whole / Forty Days Straight / From the Depths / The K'vitel / The Rav and the High Commissioner

Part 3:
Rebirth of a Nation: 1948–1998

Birth Pangs of an Ancient City 507

The Siege / The Jewish Quarter Falls / Surrender of the Old City / A Divided City / The Jewish Capital

The Maturing Years 519

Blossoming of Yeshivos / Vaad HaYeshivos / The Chassidic World / The Six-Day War / The Three-Day War / A United City

Metamorphosis in the Holy City 535

The Yeshivah World / The Teshuvah Movement / A City of Many Colors / Sephardic Influence / Rabbis from the Last Generation / For the Sake of Jerusalem / Recent Archeological Finds / In the Footsteps of the Ancient One

Notes 549

Bygone Days (Stories) 550

A Heavenly Sign / A Letter Home / The Mandelbaum Gate / A Parable for All Times / The Bar Mitzvah Drash / To Be or Not To Be / The Chida Lives On / The Legendary Finkels / Place Your Trust in God / A Day in the Life of a Mohel / In Honor of Aharon HaKohen / The Dream that Came True / Mountain View, Jerusalem / From a Knock at the Door / Embedded in the Kosel

Epilogue 577

Triumph of Time / Mount Moriah / The Smallest Letter / The Eye of the World / Zion and Jerusalem / The Untouchable Temple and the Indomitable People / The Master Plan

Tables 585

Table 1: Rishon l'Tzyon

Table 2: Jerusalem Suburbs: 1855–1998

Table 3: Chassidic Dynasties in Jerusalem

Heroes of Jerusalem 593

Bibliography 608

Glossary 611

Index 613

FOREWORD

by Rabbi Nachman Bulman

Locations where Jews have lived since our Father Avraham's time, have dotted the globe. But one Place remains central from beginning to end — Yerushalayim, the heartland of Hashem's People.

Its evocations are vast beyond words: *Even sheseeya* (the Foundation Stone); at its center point, the altar where Yitzchak Avinu was bound; Yaakov's ladder connecting Heaven and Earth; Dovid HaMelech's lyre. Here Yeshaya and Yirmiya spoke; here our People "see and are seen" three times a year; here conquerors destroy but no one else rebuilds; here the Shechina remains, even after its withdrawal. From the endlessness of Exile, Jewish prayer breaks through all barriers to arrive here.

In the last two hundred years, Yerushalayim's children have begun to return home. Enemies leave no stone unthrown to erase their return. Misguided brothers seek to come here, while attempting to undo Yerushalayim's eternal character. Magnets draw children of our People here with deep, sometimes subconscious, pangs of love.

The heart of our People trembles over the fate of Yerushalayim in fear and hope, such as no other People could ever know.

We seek words to express something of what Yerushalayim means to us.

R. Dovid Rossoff has written earlier works about Eretz Yisroel in general, and certain cities in particular. His works have been well received. But it is as if his earlier efforts were introductory to his present great work — *Where Heaven Touches Earth* (Jerusalem from Medieval Times to the Present).

His panorama is extensive. In general portrait and painstaking detail, R. Rossoff illuminates his theme. To many, who are pained by the "secularization" of the Holy City and the lack of eloquent voices in English to sing its real song, R. Rossoff's work will be a balm and a healing — with the help of the One Above Whose Presence dwells here.

Written with yearning for Yerushalayim's holiness, and in gratitude to those who express its essence.

ב׳ ניסן תשנ״ח פה עיה״ק ת״ו

נחמן בולמן

PREFACE

The aim of this book is to fill the gap in the knowledge of what transpired to the Jews in the Holy City of Yerushalayim over the last thousand years. Many Jews know bits and pieces of the role our forefathers played in building Jerusalem, but like isolated fragments they lack the overall picture. There is definitely a continuum of the Jewish presence starting around the time of the Ramban all the way until today. The full picture allows us the opportunity to better fulfill the role we must take as inheritors of the efforts made by our forefathers.

This book has been divided into two paths. The first is historical and the second is narrative. They are intertwined like the body and the soul. The body, with its well-defined limbs and organs, is like the historical facts of any time period. Each era has its lay and religious leaders, its righteous and wicked persons, its tragedies and miracles, its time of war and peace, and its momentum to stride forward in time. Yet that body, generally called its history, falls short of depicting the full picture of the times. Therefore, true stories, like the soul which is hidden inside the body, reveal the inner pulse of the times. These stories may be of unknown characters, or of small incidents, which have no room in the "history" of that period; yet, they were real, human, and meaningful. Together the two paths merge and we can begin to fathom what our forefathers were experiencing.

The history of Yerushalayim is unique from that of other cities of the world in several ways. Firstly, Jerusalem is God's City. He chose it as His capital on this planet and entrusted it to the Jewish people. He commanded us to build a Temple for Him there – and nowhere else – so that He could rest his Divine Presence in His Holy City. No other city in the world can claim that.

This leads us to a second unique factor about the history of this city – it is the city where God's eyes and heart are, always gazing first and foremost on the Jews living there. *Chutz LaAretz* is His forest, Eretz Yisroel is His garden, and Yerushalayim is God's palace. Those fortunate to live in the Holy City seek to serve their Father in Heaven from as close a proximity as possible. Surely God is sincerely concerned about His children who live in His palace. He gave it to us as guardians of the city, a place to feel elevated spiritually.

Today, we cannot compare our sense of elevation with that of our forefathers. For instance, we have no conception how our Jewish forefathers felt in the time of the Temple on the Seder night while eating their paschal lambs. We can study and dream about it, but the reality is far from our grasp. Likewise, the *avodah* of Yom Kippur in the Temple is more like a dream than a reality.

During the long exile after the destruction of the Second Temple, most of the Jews who lived in Jerusalem chose to live there of their own volition. They were not, for the most part, people who stumbled upon this city, and out of default agreed to stay and make it their home. Instead, they carefully planned to make *aliyah* and, be it as it may, suffered for the sake of preserving the Jewish presence in the Holy City and seeking its spiritual essence. No one came with the hope of striking it rich in Jerusalem.

Therefore, this book portrays the *Jewish* history of Yerushalayim. Everything else is secondary, including the Moslem and Christian influence. If in God's eyes Jerusalem is close to His heart, then it is natural that likewise we should feel bound up with Jerusalem. There is no better way to do this than to understand its roots. The ancient history of Yerushalayim, the chronicles of the First and Second Temple eras – though not part of the scope of this work – will one day soon become a dream-come-true with the *Mashiach* and the Third Temple. The history of Jerusalem-in-*galus*, which *is* the theme of this book, is the lifeline that will make that dream come true. Only when Yerushalayim is built up by Jews can this happen, as our Sages say (*Tannis* 5a): Hashem said, "I shall not enter the Heavenly Jerusalem until I enter the Earthly Jerusalem." Thus, once we can better appreciate the work that the Jerusalemites-of-old did, we will be armed with the tools to forge on with the goals which they set before themselves. May we be privileged to be numbered among those who sacrificed for the glory of Yerushalayim, the Holy City.

We cannot fathom the greatness of the *tzaddikim* mentioned in this book. They were living on a standard far above the ken of the everyday Jew. Regrettably, we have not been able in these pages to depict their true image. It may be well for us to keep in mind what happened at the funeral of Rav Yosef Chaim Zonnenfeld. Rav Yerucham Fishel Perlow, of whom Rav Yosef Chaim said, "He is a living Torah," lived next to Rav Zonnenfeld in Battei Machse for seven years. During the eulogies, Rav Perlow turned to a friend and said, "Why are they eulogizing him? Did they really know him? Did they really grasp his true stature?"

Besides not being able to qualitatively convey the true stature of the *tzaddikim*, it has been impossible to quantitatively write about all of them. Yet in the Heavenly chronicles of the Holy City, every *tzaddik* has a place, as well as every Jew who lived in the Holy City. Each one laid another stone in the annals of the history of Yerushalayim.

The words of Rav Ishtori HaParchi, author of *Kaftor VeFerach*, are applicable to the author of this book. He writes (Ch. 11), "I humbly come forward to present to my fellow Jews what I have found in my searches. My findings do not stem from a greater depth of knowledge that others; rather, I have simply spent more time investigating this subject than they have and feel duty bound to share the fruits of my research with the public."

Without the personal assistance of a number of friends and rabbanim, this book would not have reached fruition. Rav Nachman Bulman read through parts of the manuscript and discussed vital issues with me. I thank Rav Gershon

Kitzis for opening his vast library to me, and Rav Binyomin Kluger, who has authored important books on Jerusalem, for discussing many pertinent points with me. Thanks go the editor, Eli Linas, for his discerning eye, and to Tzvi Mordechai Chiappetta, for his masterful artistry. Also, Mrs. Zusman was very helpful with her wide experience as a tour guide, and Mrs. Feuchtwanger graciously took me through the Moslem Quarter to those places I had researched but not seen. Furthermore, Avinoam Kahan and Menashe Hus helped provide important research material.

Many lovers of Yerushalayim also assisted me during the writing and production of the book. Especial thanks go to my dear friend, Ruby Schron, as well as to my father-in-law, Mr. Sherman Shapiro, may he rest in peace, for their encouragement and support. May all the others as well be recorded in the Heavenly chronicles and blessed for their part in helping me make this dream come true.

Lastly, but first in thought, the culmination of all this work is in the merit of my wife, may she be well until 120. And may we live to witness the coming of the *Machiach* and the building of the Temple, speedily in our days.

Yerushalayim
Elul, 5761 (2001)

Due to the wide appeal of this *sefer*, it was translated into Hebrew two years ago, with fifty pages of new material. *Baruch Hashem*, the Hebrew edition was warmly weclomed, and many Jerusalemites, realizing how it deepened their knowledge of the Holy City, praised it highly. In fact, the author was interviewed on Israeli radio a number of times.

This new edition includes two new stories, "In Honor of Aharon HaKohen" (page 569), which depicts how the the famous *Birchas Kohaim* ceremony at the Kosel first came into being. The second story, entitled "The Dream that Came True" (page 571), ties together two generations of the distinguished Auerbach family.

May we all, wherever we may live, fill one chamber of our hearts with an intense love of Yerushalayim. By so doing, we are continuing the process of rebuilding Yerushalayim, and, *b'ezras Hashem*, will be privileged to see the *geula* in our lifetime.

Yerushalayim
Shevet, 5764 (2004)

Introduction

JERUSALEM. It is a name that conjures up associations for every Jew. Some relate it to the city of antiquity, which served as the capital of King David and King Solomon, and of the Maccabean and Herodian dynasties which followed centuries later. Others relate to it as the present-day capital of the modern state of Israel. Still others relate to it on the supernal plane, in which it represents the spiritual heart of the Jewish people.

The purpose of this book is to review the dramatic events which led to the building of the permanent and numerically dominant settlement of Jews in the Holy City, known as the *yishuv*. The *yishuv* — or the Old Yishuv, as it is commonly referred to — is generally considered to have taken root after the earthquake of 1837, when thousands of fugitives from Safed and Tiberias crowded into the city. In the decades which followed that catastrophic event, the city's demographic balance became markedly altered in favor of a Jewish majority — a majority which has been maintained ever since.

However, the Old *Yishuv* did not appear out of a Jewish vacuum. Rather, it was planted on the foundations laid by earlier pioneers who had struggled up Jerusalem's precarious mountain slopes in order to maintain a vital Jewish presence in the Holy City. Historians generally credit the Ramban, Rabbi Moses Nachmanides, with founding the *yishuv* several hundreds of years earlier, at the close of the Crusader period in the thirteenth century. Therefore, this book opens with the Crusaders' conquest of Jerusalem, and the seeds which the Ramban planted when the last of the European invaders left the country.

This book is *not* a chronicle of the development and history of Jerusalem at large. The Moslem and Christian churches and mosques, their architectural styles, and their diary books of life have been well documented and dramatized by their own historians. What *is* lacking is an unadulterated depiction of the true scope of Jewish strivings, sufferings, and struggles for survival in the city which God chose for the capital of His nation. Our modern heritage is grounded on the foundation stones which our forebears labored to establish for us.

Furthermore, the only genuine and permanent — albeit invisible — imprint in the City of God is the spiritual one left by those hardy Jewish settlers for all subsequent generations.

The question arises, why has such a unique group of people with such a

← Jews lingering at the Cotton Gate entranceway to the Temple Mount. Since the destruction of the Second Temple, the Temple has been in alien hands. Jews always sought to glimpse into the holy area into which they were prohibited access until the time of the Mashiach.

rich and varied history been passed over by the historian's magnifying glass? Simply put, the historians did not find any Jewish contribution to the outward decor of the Holy City. The stories of the settlers' lives and their struggles for survival did not fill the experts' criteria for significance. Their measure of historical importance was based on visible, tangible relics — be they buried or standing. According to them, man's physical heritage is what takes center stage in relating the story of the past. Therefore, the ruins of a Crusader church overlooking the Temple Mount make an ideal tourist stop, and the Roman Cardo is a "must see." Similarly, the Dome of the Rock is an architectural feat of the ancient Moslems not to be missed.

Yet, it is was the small but indomitable Jewish people who were the real titleholders to the city. It is true that their contribution is not visible to the eye. However, it is they who built up the inner soul of Jerusalem, and this is the city's true beauty.

There is no doubt that God cared deeply about what was happening to His children in the courtyard of His terrestrial palace. Their prayers, Torah study, and even the everyday ebb and flow of their lives, were under the watchful eye of God. Why then, we wonder, did He treat them so harshly? They were princes of the King, and yet they were constantly under the thumb of foreign rule — occasionally benign, but usually brutally oppressive. Their freedom was stifled and their spirit attacked; in almost every generation they found themselves harassed simply because they were Jews.

In *Shaarei Yerushalayim* (Gate 4, *Yishuv HaAretz*), the author raises this very question: "How can I describe the hardship of *galus* (exile) which our brethren here in Eretz Yisrael have borne from time immemorial until today [1847]. It is beyond belief...."

He then provides us with an answer: "...Yet this is precisely what our Sages forecast when they said (*Berachos* 5a): 'The Lord gave the Jewish people three special gifts, and each of them is acquired by virtue of their suffering: Torah, the World to Come, and Eretz Yisrael.'" Thus, the Land only truly becomes ours through suffering for it — for perhaps then it becomes more precious to us.

Additionally, the jagged wound left by the destruction of the two Temples has not been healed through all the eons of *galus*. Our forefathers, who fell away from serving the Almighty properly, caused its destruction and incurred the curse of *galus*. Thus the Land fell into the strict and unforgiving hands of foreign custodians, who maintained control of their temporary charge for a seeming eternity. Throughout this time, however, a small number of select Jewish souls felt compelled to cling to the city's stones and breathe her dust. Their tenacity constituted a poignant expression of longing for the end of a torturous phase of our history. As we shall see, this special group included some of the most sublime souls in Jewish history.

The goal of the book is to unravel the story of our people in Jerusalem, so that we may gaze upon the inner beauty of the city. In this way, we will gain a new impetus to discover our present role as Jerusalemites (and lovers of Jerusalem). This, in turn, may speed up the process of which the prophet foretold: "Torah will come out of Zion, and the word of God from Jerusalem."

* * *

Wherever possible, the author has relied on firsthand reports or recorded testimony by men living close to the period of time being discussed. Undoubtedly, many *chachamim* and tzaddikim of Jerusalem have gone unmentioned in this book. The author asks their forgiveness. Each deserves a separate volume of his own, for in a sense, the story of Jerusalem is incomplete without them.

For the Record....

This book, faithful to the sources upon which it is based, is inherently limited by the material available. Tracking down the sources relating to the earlier generations was relatively simple since only a moderate number of books and manuscripts exist which treat those eras. But with the turn of the twentieth century, an overwhelming amount of source material exist, enough to fill many bookcases. Moreover, the issues which stirred the fires of controversy then are still burning hot today. It is beyond human intelligence to fully reckon the meaning of those events and influences of personages who lived so close to our times. Suffice it to quote the words of the Chazon Ish: "The reason why there are so few religious Jewish historians today is that one must be equipped with insight which is unique to *nevu'ah* (prophesy) to know what to write!"

Therefore, the guidelines followed in this work lead the reader to the edge of the burning coals, but no further. In this way, the book remains a historical documentation of major events in the annals of Jerusalem without becoming a political forum for a certain cause.

Overview*

SCANNING THE annals of history, one can find a large array of patterns which remained stable throughout most of the period covered in this book. From the thirteenth century until the mid-nineteenth century, there were no quantum leaps in science, engineering, travel, and communication. People traveled by horse and wagon, lived in simply built houses without gas and electricity, and were without modern medical advances. During this entire period, the most revolutionary invention to make its debut was arguably the printing press, which had a radical impact on the course of civilization and the dissemination of ideas and information. But for this lone, albeit significant, advancement, people's lifestyles did not change drastically for hundreds of years. Only with the onset of the industrial revolution in the early 1800s did a deluge of technological and scientific discoveries and breakthroughs change western civilization. As we shall see, even after discoveries were made and introduced to the world at large, it often took considerable time before they made their way to Eretz Yisrael. To give but one example here, the railroad, introduced in America in 1830, did not make its inaugural run in Israel until 1892.

To focus in on life in Jerusalem, we must take many factors into consideration: the types of people who comprised the community, where they lived, the synagogues in which they prayed, the communal hierarchy, and the interplay between the religious and lay leaders, to name but a few. At the most basic level, we must try to understand the daily living conditions with which they were confronted. How did they manage to make ends meet? How did they succeed in imbuing their children with a Jewish education? Also, these Jews lived under a capricious gentile ruling power that was very often indifferent to their needs and concerns. Such a lifestyle was fraught with dangers, uncertainties, and difficulties — both long-standing and unanticipated. On the other hand, these people had very little day-to-day contact with their Moslem and Christian neighbors, and very rarely made lasting friendships with them, which was a blessing in disguise. Most of all, the hand of God measured the faith of His people with natural calamities such as drought, famine, war, and epidemics, as well as miracles and instances of personal and communal salvation.

* Much of this material is culled from firsthand reports: *Chorvos Yerushalayim,* published in the 17th century; *Elei Masei*, *Sha'alu Shalom Yerushalayim,* and *Likutim,* written at the beginning of the 18th century; and *Shaarei Yerushalayim* and *Sha'alu Shalom Yerushalayim* (by Rav Kahanav), written in the mid-19th century.

Who's Who in Jerusalem

From early medieval times until the nineteenth century, the Jewish population of the city rarely exceeded three hundred families. Yet, qualitatively speaking, the Jews who settled in the Holy City throughout this period were some of the greatest Torah luminaries in history. Men like the Ramban, Rav Ovadiah Bartenora, the Ralbach, the Radvaz, Rav Bezalel Ashkenazi, the Shelah HaKodesh, Rav Yaakov Tzemach, Rav HaMagen, the Pri Chadash, Rav Yehudah HaChassid, the Ohr HaChaim, the Chida (he, of all those mentioned here, was a native Jerusalemite), Rav David Pardo, Rav Menachem Mendel of Shklov, Rav Shmuel Salant, Rav Meir Auerbach, Rav Yehoshua Leib Diskin, Rav Yosef Chaim Zonnenfeld, just to mention a few. We have already discussed in the introduction what caused these people to gravitate to Jerusalem. But it was Jerusalem that guided them to what they ultimately achieved.

There were three types of Jews who settled in the city: scholars, widows, and the elderly. Scholars came to enrich their souls at the spiritual hub of the universe. Widows, among them *agunos,* chose the Holy City as a way of expressing their eternal love for God. Indeed, there were periods when the population of these women numbered over five hundred! The elderly came to breathe their last breath in the city that would one day be rebuilt, and whose Temple would one day shine forth its light to the whole world.

We can loosely classify world Jewry into two basic categories: Sephardim and Ashkenazim. This categorization held true in Jerusalem and Eretz Yisrael as well, with one exception — the Morishkas (or Mostarbim). These Jews were indigenous to the Land of Israel from the time of the destruction of the Second Temple. Over the generations, they alone were fluent in Arabic, and their dress was similar to the attire of the native Arabs. The mother tongue of the Sephardim who immigrated to

Eretz Yisrael was generally Ladino (Judeo-Spanish), and their dress varied slightly from the indigenous peoples of the land. In general, the Sephardim comprised the largest group and the Ashkenazim the smallest. However, there were several periods when the Morishkas were in the majority (for example, in the mid-seventeenth century). The nineteenth century heralded a shifting of the scales, as the influx of Ashkenazim caused a major shift in the ethnic demography of the city, both in relation to the Sephardim and the gentile populations, as will be discussed later.

Prayer and Study Houses

In keeping with their individual characters, each group prayed in its own synagogue. Until the nineteenth century, the Sephardim used the Talmud Torah Synagogue (later called Eliyahu HaNavi Synagogue), the Zion Synagogue (renamed the Rabban Yochanan ben Zakkai Synagogue), and later, in the mid-eighteenth century, the Middle Shul and the Istanbul Shul. The Ashkenazim used, at different time periods, the Ramban Synagogue and the Rav

Rabban Yochanan ben Zakkai Synagogue, as it appeared for hundreds of years

Yehudah HaChassid Synagogue (later called the Churvah). Finally, the Morishkas also had a shul of their own in earlier generations, but by the mid-eighteenth century they assimilated completely into the Sephardic community.

Generally speaking, the educational system differed somewhat from that of modern times. In place of a cheder, there was a *hesger*, in which children were all lumped together so that the teacher taught six-year-old boys together with nine-year-olds. The same building which housed the *hesger*, housed the yeshivah where married men studied Torah. (Today the word yeshivah refers to the place where teenage boys learn Torah, and a *kollel* refers to a place where married men study.) In the 1600s there were eight *melamdim* (teachers), and over a hundred and fifty children. The basic goal of this system was to impart a fundamental appreciation of Judaism and its laws and rituals to the children. The tender years of youth were critical for their Jewish identity, as most teenagers went to work — if a job could be found. Throughout the years, innovators appeared who strove to deepen and expand the scope of the educational system, such as Rav Yaakov Chagiz in the mid-seventeenth century, as will be discussed later in the book.

The most famous Talmudic academies of the seventeenth century were the Beis Yaakov Vega Yeshivah and the Beis Yaakov Ferira Yeshivah. The latter continued to function for hundreds of years into the twentieth century.

Leadership

The spiritual and lay leaders of the people acted as a bridge between the community and the outside world. In addition, they kept a watchful eye on communal affairs. Depending on which generation he lived in, the Sephardic leader was called Chacham, Rishon l'Tzyon, Nasi, or Chacham Bashi. The Sephardic leader was highly respected — not only by his Jewish flock, but even by the non-Jewish community. For example, in 1705, a series of anti-Semitic decrees was promulgated by the Turkish *kadi* (chief Turkish judge). During this time, the Nasi was imprisoned without cause. Prominent Arabs were shocked and rioted against the *kadi*. Ultimately, they freed the Nasi and forced the *kadi* to flee for his life! The Ashkenazic leader was known as the Rosh Beis Din (Chief Rabbi) and/or Rosh Yeshivah. Of course, both groups had *dayanim* (religious judges) and a *beis din* (rabbinic court) of their own. The first Ashkenazic Chief Rabbi was Rav Ephraim Fish, who lived in the mid-sixteenth century.

There were two prominent lay leaders. The *parnas* (literally, "the provider") dealt with community affairs, controlling incoming funds for the *chalukah* (distribution of funds from the Diaspora for the scholars and poor people of the city), borrowing money for the *kehillah* (community) when necessary, and caring for the needs of the scholars. He was generally a wealthy and respected individual who did not receive remuneration for his services, being voted into office by the sages of the city. As we will see, he hedged a narrow line with the authorities, who always took advantage of the wealthier Jews. The other lay leader was the Sheik al-Yehud ("the Chief of the Jews"). He was a prominent Jew who dealt mainly with bilateral issues between the ruling power and the Jewish community. As opposed to being selected by the community, he was appointed by the Ottoman *kadi* in a public ceremony. Although the duties of the *parnas* and Sheik al-Yehud were quite distinct, in fact, both offices were often invested in the same person.

Inauguration of the Rishon l'Tzyon

The Rishon l'Tzyon, a title conferred on the leading Sephardic Rav of each major Sephardic community in the Mediterranean basin since the late seventeenth century, stood as the spiritual leader of Jerusalem (until the mid-nineteenth century, when prominent Ashkenazic rabbis shared equal status). His voice was heard throughout the Sephardic world.

The post of Rishon l'Tzyon was assigned through a vote by the Sephardic sages of Jerusalem. The position was a lifetime appointment, which generally came about by a unanimous vote, except in one or two isolated cases.

The coronation ceremony, unique and memorable, began in the Baalei Battim Yeshivah on Misgav Ladach Street (later, due to lack of space, the inauguration ceremony was conducted in the Rabban Yochanan ben Zakkai Synagogue). The Rishon l'Tzyon-elect sat on the *bimah* with some of the leading rabbis of the community, one of whom gave a speech in Hebrew mixed with Ladino. After this speech, the Rishon l'Tzyon-elect would speak, promising to follow the illustrious tradition of his forefathers, and ending with a *drash* (Torah exposition) based on the Talmud and the commentaries. After his address, one of the notables would bedeck him with a new embroidered cloak that had been purchased from the communal fund.

Beginning in 1842, the post of Rishon l'Tzyon received official government recognition. From that time onward, a delegate from the Sultan's court attended the inauguration ceremony and would present a *firman*, an official statement of recognition (bearing the additional title of Chacham Bashi and granting him special privileges), together with a mantle lined with a silver and gold design.

Leading a procession of the entire Jewish community, the Rishon l'Tzyon walked from the synagogue to his house. Before he entered, a *shochet* (ritual slaughterer) would slaughter a goat in the courtyard. Taking some of the blood on his fingers, he would paint a picture of a hand with five fingers on the Rishon l'Tzyon's doorpost, which symbolized a special protection for the new leader against the evil eye. The goat's meat would then be distributed among the poor.

Before taking leave and entering his house, the Rishon l'Tzyon would visit the Turkish mayor and *kadi*. Subsequently, the Rishon l'Tzyon would regularly meet with these government representatives on official holidays. In turn, the

Moslem leaders accorded him great respect.

As Chacham Bashi, he was escorted by a Turkish guard wherever he went. This obviously enhanced his prestige with the populace, especially with the gentile inhabitants of the city.

Homesteading

To say that the Jews lived solely in the Jewish Quarter would be an oversimplification. It is true that for most of the period covered in this book, the Jews lived primarily there. However, with the influx of the Perushim (disciples of the Vilna Gaon) in the first half of the nineteenth century, renting from Moslems became a necessity as overcrowded living conditions in the Jewish

New immigrants approaching the Jaffa Gate

Quarter forced them to look elsewhere. Scattered around the city, Jews tried to rent or buy an enclosed courtyard (*chatzer*) which contained a number of apartments. Some of these courtyards were used for prayer and study as well. Should a wealthy Jew own the courtyard, he would dedicate one of the apartments for that purpose.

To be outside the city walls after nightfall was to court almost certain death. Indeed, traveling outside the city walls was a risky affair even by day. Bedouins and marauders lurked everywhere, and they were infamous for their ruthlessness. No one ventured outside alone, not even the Arab inhabitants of the city. Once, in the 1820s, a band of these robbers captured a caravan of Ashkenazic immigrants on their way from the Jaffa port to Jerusalem. Fortunately, their plot was foiled by a clever scheme.*

* See story, "The Courageous Decision," in *Bygone Days: 1800–1840*.

By the mid-nineteenth century, there was an acute housing shortage that escalated beyond the danger point, with blatant overcrowded conditions being directly responsible for some diseases; yet expansion outside the Old City wall was forbidden by decree from the Ottoman capital in Constantinople. There were attempts to build more housing inside the walls, such as Battei Machse, but these efforts could not markedly reduce the pressure. The Sultan finally retracted the decree in the 1860s, and the first suburbs outside the city walls were inaugurated with a tremendous wave of enthusiasm. However, those who chose to live outside the walls were exposed to new dangers that their brethren within the gates never had to face. The first suburbs, like Nachalas Shiva, suffered from Bedouin attacks.* The dangers of living outside the walls quickly sobered the hearts of those who chose to live there. In the first years it was not unusual for the residents of the new neighborhoods to return to the walled city every night to sleep! It was only in the last quarter of the nineteenth century that the process of expansion outside the city gates solidified and ushered in a new era.

As we mentioned above, living conditions barely changed throughout the millennium. The houses, designed with courtyards, were made entirely of stone. Few were more than two stories high. The courtyard of a block of houses was not initially intended for privacy or to provide a play area for children (though, in fact, they also served these purposes). Buried underground beneath the courtyard lay a huge cistern that collected and stored one of Jerusalem's rarest commodities — water. This pit was the size of a cellar room and was completely sealed with waterproof lime mortar to prevent seepage of the precious liquid into the ground. A single opening allowed a pitcher to be lowered

Cistern cover in Nachalas Shiva. The hand pump became popular in the 1890s.

* See story, "Blast of the Ram's Horn," in *Bygone Days: 1870–1900*.

by rope and bring up the water as needed. During the rainy winter months, rain was collected from the roof via a gutter, and fell into the cistern. Some courtyards had two cisterns: one for drinking (via the roof gutter), and one for washing and laundry (via the floor of the courtyard). When used wisely, the cistern supplied enough water to last through most of the summer. As we shall see, water was very hard to come by in Jerusalem. Because of its scarcity and the difficulty in obtaining it, water was recycled to be used as much as possible: bathwater became detergent water to wash clothes, which then was used to wash the floor. Every drop was used sparingly and judiciously. After Passover, people would begin to supplement their supply, buying some fresh water from Arab water carriers. Rav Malki, a *dayan* and physician at the turn of the eighteenth century, wrote: "This water [from the cisterns], because it sits so long, is heavy and difficult for the body to assimilate, leading to intestinal problems." However, poor as its quality might have been, it was nevertheless life-saving.

The Temple Mount possessed dozens of cisterns. The largest one was nineteen meters deep and held 12,000 cubic meters of water, probably the size of a small swimming pool. In 1850 there were 950 cisterns in Jerusalem, and by the end of Turkish rule seventy years later the number had grown to over 6,000 (including, of course, the New City). These cisterns continued to function long after water was piped in. Indeed, they were destined to come to the fore once again in the city's history. During the War of Independence, they saved the lives of the Jewish residents of Jerusalem when their water was cut off during the Arab siege of 1948.

Water: The Source of Life

The problem of water was more acute in Jerusalem than in other important centers of Jewish settlement, like Safed and Hebron. The latter, unlike Jerusalem, had natural springs within their city limits. In contrast, Jerusalem lay completely under the eyes of God and was dependent solely on the rains that He sent.

While there was a spring outside the city walls — that of Shiloach, in the Valley of Kidron — its waters were salinated, and it was used as a laundry site. The closest freshwater source was the Well of Yoab, called also Ein Rogel, further down the valley to the south. Arab water carriers had a monopoly over this well, which left the Jews entirely at their mercy.

During the Second Temple period, water was "pumped" from Solomon's Pools, located twenty-seven kilometers south of Jerusalem via a sixty-kilometer-long aqueduct. These three enormous pools, replenished by rainfall and natural springs, were built during the Herodian period. The aqueduct, however, had long fallen into disrepair and lay broken and unusable for over a thousand years. Sections of the stone aqueduct were discovered as recently as 1997.

Ein Rogel, the closest source of fresh water, is located two kilometers south of the city

Another source of water during Temple times came from the Arrub springs, located still further to the south, beyond Etzion. These springs stood at 820 meters above sea level. Their waters were brought to Jerusalem (750 meters above sea level) via a winding, hundred-kilometer-long aqueduct, built with a one percent gradient, illustrating another daunting feat of engineering in the world of ancient technology. However, this source of water, too, had long been defunct, as it fell into disrepair before the period covered in this book.

Once, in the beginning of the eighteenth century, a wealthy and altruistic Moslem decided to use his wealth for the good of the city. He designed and built a waterduct system that would bring fresh water from kilometers away. To protect it from damage and pollution, he had the water piped underground. Unfortunately, not long after its completion some lowly Arabs foiled his project. They dug up the clay water pipe in a certain spot, broke it open and stuffed it up, and then reburied it. Now it was impossible to find the spot, thus crippling the entire project. Decades later, the famed Jewish philanthropist Sir Moses Montefiore also proposed to build a waterduct system, but Arab water carriers foiled this plan as well.

There were two other reservoirs around the Holy City. The Mamillah Pool, located east of Independence Park, was built during the Temple period. Six meters deep and 60 by 90 meters in size, its waters were transported via an aqueduct into another pool, called the Pool of Amygdalon, inside the Old City near the Jaffa Gate. The second reservoir was called the Sultan's Pool (or the Serpents' Pool). Located in the Valley of Hinnom below Mount Zion, it dates back to the Mamluk period when the Sultan built it in the mid-fourteenth

Mamillah Pool, one of the most ancient reservoirs of Jerusalem, is located near Agron Street. Today it is empty. An Arab cemetery borders one side of the pool.

century. Repaired several times by later rulers, the pools, which collected rainwater, were primarily used as large water troughs for animals.

The Rosh Yeshivah of Etz Chaim Yeshivah, Rav Moshe Nechemiah Kahanav (1814–1887), wrote about the perennial water crisis: "Every summer, when the cisterns dry up, we are forced to buy water at high prices. Last year (1875), it did not rain until very late in the month of Shevat, so the prices soared even more. The poverty-stricken cannot afford water and are compelled to drink salinated water, and even foul water, which can lead to sicknesses."

Stagnant water, pooled in inaccessible ruins throughout the city, became the birthplace of malaria and cholera. Epidemics easily got out of control, and a state of emergency ruled whenever contaminated people brought a new epidemic into the city. One of the worst epidemics took place in the summer and fall of 1865 when some sick Arabs from Transjordan came to Jerusalem. The death toll for the Jews reached over a thousand. After the introduction of the railroad in 1892, water was sent to the Holy City by rail, but that, too, was not a permanent solution.

Thus it was that the preoccupation with obtaining water played a vital role in the lives of the city's residents. This would only change in the twentieth century, when the British piped water into houses from reservoirs (and to a smaller degree by the Turks before the First World War). As we know, the twentieth century was the age of miracles within the physical world, an era in which many new standards would replace the outmoded and dangerous norms of the past.

Standard of Living

Food was readily obtainable in Jerusalem, except, of course, in times of famine or war. The variety of fruits was much the same as today, except that oranges, bananas, avocados, and other modern imported fruits and vegetables were not available. There were bakeries which supplied round *pitos*, similar to those one finds today in the Arab *shuk* (marketplace). Since most households did not have private stoves for baking or cooking, ovens were located at various street corners and in larger bakeries, all run by local Moslems. There, one could bake his own loaf of bread or cook his meal. Because wood was prohibitively expensive, the ovens were first heated with charcoal, after which small stones were laid on top of the coals to retain the heat. The bread was then placed on the stones to bake. Smaller ovens were heated with sun-dried animal manure, a common source of fuel in times past.

These ovens were also used to keep people's *cholent* hot on Shabbos. Each Jewish household would bring their pot of *cholent* to a corner oven shop Friday afternoon. Sometimes, the oven would be packed with fifty or more pots, one stacked on top of the other. Shabbos morning everyone would return to the shop, collect his pot, and take it home. The pots people used give us an insight into their stations in life. Most pots were made of brass. However, the Ashkenazic followers of Rav Yehudah HaChassid (1700) lived in grinding poverty and were happy to have even simple earthenware pots. "One Shabbos morning," a disciple of Rav Yehudah tells us, "I went to bring the *cholent* home. In my pot were beans and sheep meat (the loins, which are the cheapest cut). I rejoiced, since I usually cannot afford meat. However, when I opened the pot, I realized that someone else had taken my pot by mistake. His had only beans in it."

Though beef was nonexistent in Jerusalem, sheep and goat meat were in ample supply. The Jewish *shochet* went to the Arab slaughterhouse, where he slaughtered and examined the animal. If it was halachically disqualified, it was sold cheaply to the Arabs. This in turn caused kosher meat to be sold at a high price in order to offset the losses, often leaving the poorer Jews happy to afford the least expensive part, the bones.

As in all cities before the advent of modern plumbing gave people the luxury of their own private baths, Jerusalem had public bathing facilities. Arab bathhouses were called *hamam*, and the Jews had a number of kosher *mikveos* (ritual baths), a vital necessity of any Jewish community. To illustrate how important a *mikve* was to the pioneers of yore, in the beginning of the thirteenth century, three hundred Baalei Tosefos (French Talmudists) came and settled in Jerusalem. The first thing they did was to build a *mikve*. When the Moroccan community came into its own in the 1850s, its leader, Rav David Ben-Shimon, made sure to have a *mikve* built as soon as possible.

No one in Jerusalem, not even the wealthy Arabs, had a private heating system in his house. Instead, on cold days they would place hot coals in a pot and set it up in the middle of the room, where they would huddle around it to keep warm.

Though people generally dressed according to the customs with which they were raised and according to their means, there was one major exception: wealthy Jews were very careful never to flaunt their status in public. The reason for this was quite pragmatic: once the authorities realized that so-and-so was in a higher financial bracket than his Jewish brethren — the Jewish community was generally pictured as living below the poverty line — he was liable to be arrested on trumped-up charges, which would bring a handsome sum of ransom money into government coffers.

Livelihood

Making a livelihood is one of the most time-consuming enterprises of man throughout the world. This task was complicated for a variety of reasons in Jerusalem. While the native-born Morishkas had certain advantages that allowed them relative freedom in pursuing a livelihood, most Ashkenazim and Sephardim were limited in what they could do. Besides a few positions such as scribes, *shochatim*, teachers, and the like, there were very few job opportunities during most of the millennium. Most Jews were not fluent in Arabic, and if they wanted to open a shop, they had to be prepared to accept Arab thievery as part of their daily business. This was due in large part to the fact that police and judicial authority was in the hands of corrupt Turks, and there was no justice when an Arab blatantly entered (or broke into) a Jew's shop and stole whatever he wanted. Smart Jewish shopkeepers took an Arab partner into the business to safeguard against thievery.

On the other hand, the Morishkas blended so well into the Arabian surroundings that they were free to travel as peddlers from village to village. This they did, using the ubiquitous Middle Eastern mule. They would sell their wares and barter or buy with it grains and fruit to sell in the Holy City. Nevertheless, most of them remained poor, as was the lot of most peddlers.

Only in the mid-nineteenth century did more job opportunities open up, in direct proportion to the population boom and the expansion beyond the Old City walls.

The Chalukah System

The main source of income, especially for the scholars, came from the *chalukah* system. The Jews in the Diaspora were asked to donate money to support the Torah institutions in the Holy Land. This was considered a mitzvah of the highest order, with a historical precedent dating back to Talmudic times. The four major cities — Jerusalem, Hebron, Safed, and Tiberias — each sent emissaries to represent them in the Diaspora. Ashkenazic and Sephardic *shelichim* (emissaries), usually Torah scholars of repute, had the arduous task of traveling long and dangerous routes for extended periods of time. It was not uncommon for a *shaliach* to be on the road for a number of years. He would give sermons and speak with lay leaders and philanthropists, encouraging people to contribute to the *chalukah* fund. Among the most famous *shelichim* were the Pri Chadash, Rav Moshe Galante, the Chida, Rav Yisrael of Shklov, Rav Moshe Nechemiah Kahanav, and Rav Shmuel Salant.

The *shaliach*'s task was made more complex by the problem of ensuring that the money he collected actually reached the Holy Land. Banks as we know them today did not exist until the nineteenth century. Thus there was no assurance of funds reaching Eretz Yisrael. Traveling with cash was very risky, easy prey for marauders and hijackers. Once, Rav Yisrael of Shklov, who traveled during the Napoleonic Wars for the Perushim (disciples of the Vilna Gaon living in Eretz Yisrael) of Safed, decided to ship wheat rather than money. In Eretz Yisrael it would be sold and the cash would be used for the community. However, the ship ran into a turbulent storm and sank in the Mediterranean Sea.

The Ashkenazim attempted to organize a collection system throughout Europe. Beginning in the seventeenth century, charity boxes were distributed locally and then collected annually. A *gabbai* (treasurer) of a large city would collect the boxes from the towns and villages in the area, and pass the money to the "Nasi of Eretz Yisrael" in a major city like Warsaw, Vilna, or Amsterdam. The Nasi, in turn, would be responsible for guarding the money until it could be sent to Eretz Yisrael. To lend authority to the system, the Nasi was usually a renowned sage, such as Rav Shimshon Wertheimer and Rav Yisrael Friedman (the Ruzhiner Rebbe). The system was only partially successful and did not supplant the personal efforts of an emissary from the Ashkenazic community of Jerusalem.

Each community had its own system for distributing the funds. Generally, the *chalukah* was divided into three portions: communal needs (taxes, upkeep of synagogues and yeshivos, etc.), stipends for scholars who were completely dependent on the *chalukah*, and subsidies for the poor to increase their meager earnings. Nobody ever became rich from what he received from the *chalukah*. World Jewry lacked a succinct awareness of the needs of their brethren in Eretz Yisrael until well into the nineteenth century, and often European communities were fraught with their own economic problems. At best, the money helped people subsist just above the poverty line.

In the mid-nineteenth century, the Ashkenazim subdivided their members according to their place of origin, and each district in Europe had its counterpart in the Holy City. Thus, names like Kollel Galicia, Kollel Warsaw, and Kollel Vilna came into being. The Perushim organized a Central Committee (Vaad HaKlali) to channel its funds and ensure that they would be used to maximum benefit.

The tradition and mitzvah of collecting and channeling funds to the Holy Land did not end with the demise of the old *yishuv* (settlement). Some of the *kollelim* still function today. Furthermore, representatives of institutions in

Eretz Yisrael still travel abroad to collect for their yeshivos, orphanages, etc. Therefore, in one form or another, the *chalukah* system has supported Torah and the *yishuv* in Eretz Yisrael for hundreds of years.

Palace of the King

Living in the Jewish homeland under foreign rulers left the Jew feeling like a stranger in his own home. In Jerusalem, the Palace of the King, this feeling was magnified many times over. The pain of seeing the Holy City overrun by heathens and administered without any sensitivity to its true sanctity only reiterated the prophesy that this *galus* (exile) would be the bitterest in our long history.

Under Moslem rule, Jews and Christians were forbidden entrance to the Temple Mount and the Machpelah (burial place of the Patriarchs and Matriarchs). An early eighteenth-century scholar, Rav Gedaliah, notes, "The Moslems gave this reason [why Jews were forbidden into these sites]: No other faith is fit to enter such a holy spot [except the Moslems]. The Jewish people, though once the chosen of God, had sinned. God left them, and chose instead the Moslems."

Later in the book we will discuss the fact that the Kosel (Western Wall) was lost for many centuries and not rediscovered until the medieval period. However, let us note here that from the time of its rediscovery, it was difficult to

approach. Poor Moslem residents had built slum-type houses to within a few meters of the Wall. Nearby stood the impressive courtyard of the *kadi*. Thus, no more than a mere slender stretch of the Wall was accessible to Jewish worshippers, who made their way there against a backdrop of heckling from Arab children. At times, that relatively harmless backdrop gave way to more aggressive anti-Semitic behavior by the Moslem inhabitants of the city.

Until the nineteenth century, it was customary to pray at the Kosel on the eve of *rosh chodesh*, Tisha b'Av, and other fast days, when the Arabs generally respected the Jewish presence there. At these times, Rav Gedaliah noted, "The Arabs did not disturb us, even when the women wailed near the Moslem homes. Occasionally, an Arab boy would make trouble. We would give him a sewing needle [inexpensive yet valuable to a child] to leave us alone. If an adult Arab noticed him first, he would scold him for disturbing us." Ironically, in other generations the Moslems chose those same days to vent their anger against the Jewish worshippers.

Custodians of Eretz Yisrael

Except for a two-hundred-year period (1099–1290), Eretz Yisrael was ruled by Moslems until the beginning of the twentieth century. However, this does not mean that the same group maintained its hegemony for this entire period. The term "Arab" is almost as all-inclusive as are the words European or Christian, and Arabs may be subdivided into several different nations and religions. The breakdown of governorship of Eretz Yisrael is as follows:

Ruler	*Year (C.E.)*	*Jewish Population of Jerusalem*	*Total Population of Jerusalem*
Arab	638 – 1099	small	unknown
Crusade	1099 – 1250	nonexistent, then small	unknown
Mamluk (Egyptian)	1250 – 1517	300 – 2,000	c. 3,000 – 6,000
Ottoman (Turkish)	1517 – 1840	2,000 – 5,000	6,000 – 13,000
	1840 – 1870	5,000 – 10,000	15,000 – 20,000
	1870 – 1900	10,000 – 32,000	20,000 – 50,000
	1900 – 1914	32,000 – 50,000	50,000 – 75,000
British	1917 – 1939	30,000 – 80,000	58,000 – 110,000
	1939 – 1948	80,000 – 100,000	110,000 – 165,000
Israel	1948 – 1967	100,000 – 196,000	165,000 – 265,000
	1967 – 1996	196,000 – 420,000	265,000 – 595,000

In general, both the Mamluk and Ottoman rulers of Eretz Yisrael were tolerant towards their Jewish subjects. However, such vast empires, spanning the entire range of the Middle East, could not always keep a close eye on the doings of small provincial cities like Jerusalem. During both reigns, Damascus was the provincial capital of the area, while Jerusalem, with no strategic or commercial significance, was a minor backwater. It was only in the 1840s that the city received the status of *sanjak*, provincial capital.

Because of Jerusalem's insignificance and anonymity in the eyes of the empires that ruled over it, unscrupulous Moslems were apt to take advantage of their semi-independence. As a result, they often wrought havoc in the lives of the innocent residents of the city, especially the Jews. This is precisely what happened to the Shelah HaKodesh, who settled in the Holy City in the 1620s and was ultimately forced to flee for his life when a tyrant usurped control of the city. This was just one example of a phenomenon that recurred repeatedly over the course of the millennium.

As in all times and places, taxes were a standard feature of life. Unfortunately, as is also often the case, bribery was as well. The Jews suffered exceedingly from the latter, being forced to pay exorbitant fees to prevent illegal imprisonment. This led them into greater and greater debts. The quickest way of exhorting money from the Jews was to imprison one of their leaders. Thus, in 1625, the Shelah sat in a dungeon for two weeks until he could be redeemed, and Rav Menachem Mendel, leader of the Perushim in the 1820s, was likewise illegally imprisoned.

Similarly, the bureaucratic hierarchy had to be pampered in order to get anything done. For instance, when Rav Yehudah HaChassid purchased his synagogue in 1700, he sought permission to expand it. Only after handing over an exorbitant sum to the *kadi* did he receive the necessary permit.

Discrimination against the Minority

The Moslem rulers sought to segregate their Jewish subjects whenever possible. Most of their decrees applied to Christians as well, yet the Jew felt the tough hand much more forcibly. No Jew was allowed to ride a horse in Jerusalem. Throughout most of this period, Jews were permitted to dress as they pleased, with the exception of wearing anything with the color green in it. That was reserved for the Moslem sheiks. Also, walking outside one's house at night without permission was a punishable offense, and even by day a lone woman could be abducted by sadistic Arabs. At one time, at the beginning of the eighteenth century, Jews were forbidden to wear metal heels on their shoes and they had to walk to the left of an oncoming Moslem.

Humiliation was the lot of the Jews until the mid-nineteenth century, when the industrial revolution altered mankind's view of the world, and internationalism spread to the Middle East. Also, foreign embassies opened to protect

The Jewish Quarter in the late nineteenth century. The two domed synagogues, the Churvah (right) and the Tiferes Yisrael (center), rise high over the Holy City.

the rights of their citizens living in the Holy City. In *Shaarei Yerushalayim*, the author tells of an incident that happened to Rav Yeshaya Bardaky, one of the great leaders of the Perushim in the first half of the 1800s. One day while innocently walking down the street and minding his own business, he was suddenly attacked by a group of Arabs. They beat him and tore his clothes, and then dragged him off to prison on trumped-up charges of making sacrilegious statements about Islam.

Building permits were difficult to obtain, and numerous bylaws interfered with Jewish plans for expansion. Among the bylaws was a prohibition against building over a certain height. Both the Churvah Synagogue and the Tiferes Yisrael Synagogue, among the tallest structures in the Old City, had to get a special permit directly from Constantinople in order to bypass the ordinance.

Living in a generally hostile environment, the Jews kept mainly to themselves, minimizing their associations with their Moslem and Christian neighbors. This, in turn, led them to put their trust in God, and to spend their time studying Torah and keeping the mitzvos.

Pilgrimage Season

Aside from the holidays, the biggest event in the Jewish calendar in the Middle East was the *yartzeit* (anniversary of the date of death) of Shmuel HaNavi (Samuel the Prophet), on 28 Iyar. On that date, thousands of Jewish pilgrims would converge upon Jerusalem, coming from as far as Egypt and Damascus. Since it fell ten days after Lag b'Omer, some went first to Meron for the festivities at the cave of the Tanna Rabbi Shimon bar Yochai. Then they traveled south to Jerusalem for the *yartzeit* of Shmuel HaNavi.

This annual event was important for all strata of Jerusalem society. The pilgrims, who often stayed many days, markedly increased commerce in the city. Furthermore, the Turkish authorities levied a tax on the pilgrims, and the local Jews received donations from wealthy pilgrims. The event was both a spiritual and social happening, depending on one's position in life. The event was uplifting for everyone.

In the mid-eighteenth century, the Moslems took control of the prophet's burial cave and tried to disband the yearly event. In the mid-nineteenth century, the Sultan's court finally realized that accommodating Christian and Jewish pilgrims was to their advantage. In order to accommodate the influx of visitors, certain previously closed gateways into the city were reopened, and a minimal attempt was made to improve the conditions of the city.

In recent years, there has been a tremendous reawakening by Jews everywhere to honor the different tzaddikim buried in Eretz Yisrael and Europe. On 28 Iyar, thousands travel to Rama outside of Jerusalem to pray by the cave of Shmuel HaNavi.

Touching Stones

The bottom line for the Jews of Jerusalem was, is, and always will be to touch the stones of the city. Whether the forecast is for rain or for drought, for benevolent rulers or demonic ones, for healthy times or fierce epidemics, for freedom to express Judaism openly in shul, home, and at the Wall, or its denial, the Jew longs for the spiritual and physical closeness to God that comes with living in the Holy City.

In the following pages, we will see how our ancestors who inhabited the city weathered every conceivable combination of the above. They felt that struggling in Jerusalem was a Divine call to act as guardians of the city. We today are able to inherit the fruits of their selfless deeds. Likewise, may our deeds today be the seeds for the next generation to harvest.

12th – 16th Centuries

Upholding Jerusalem's Dignity

אֶזְכְּרָה אֱלֹקִים וְאֶהֱמָיָה,
בִּרְאוֹתִי כָּל עִיר עַל תִּלָּהּ בְּנוּיָה,
וְעִיר הָאֱלֹהִים מֻשְׁפֶּלֶת עַד שְׁאוֹל תַּחְתִּיָּה,
וּבְכָל זֹאת אָנוּ לְיָ-הּ וְעֵינֵינוּ לְיָ-הּ.

סליחות לעשרת ימי תשובה

I recall God and wonder,
How every city is well built,
Yet the City of God is cast down to the utmost depths,
Nevertheless, we are for God, and our eyes are unto God.

Slichos

The Buried Legacy

For over a thousand years, from the time of the destruction of the Second Temple until the time of the Ramban at the end of the thirteenth century, Jerusalem lay devoid of its grandeur. After such a rich and splendorous past, when kings and prophets walked her streets and the Temple service was carried out in all its glory, an acute spirit of desolation lay over the city, shrouding it in darkness. The annals of this unprecedented vacuum in the history of Jerusalem must go unwritten, though it is known that there was a small community during most of that time.

In truth, even the two-hundred-year period (1267–1488) between the Ramban and Rav Ovadiah of Bartenora is sparsely chronicled. However, as we noted in the introduction, historians generally credit the community established by the Ramban as the beginning of the yishuv from which the present settlement is descended, and it was from this time that the historical record of the city reappears. The Crusaders purged the city of its Jewish residents, and the Ramban rekindled the Jewish presence. From that point onward, there has been an unbroken chain of Jewish occupancy in the Holy City.

The Long Endurance

When the Ramban passed over the threshold of the Holy City in Elul, 1267 (5027), his eyes filled with tears. The city which captivated every Jewish heart was in semi-ruin, barren and nearly desolate. Since the Crusader conquest of the city nearly two hundred years earlier, the picture of Jerusalem reminded one of the destruction of the Temple. Five times the Crusaders marched from Europe, and a number of counter "holy wars" by the Moslems left the city devastated.

"What can I tell you about the Land?" lamented the Ramban. "The desolation is everywhere, and the destruction is great. The guiding principle is: The holier the place, the greater the destruction. Jerusalem was devastated the most, next Judah and next the Galilee."[1]

An overview of the general history of medieval times provokes mixed feelings about the humanitarianism of great powers and religious faiths. As the center of a bitter controversy between the great nations and faiths of the world, Jerusalem was buffeted by several turbulent and devastating wars over a span of hundreds of years. In that time, unspeakable atrocities were committed by the warring factions, both against one another and against innocent bystanders as well. Yet through it all, a small but indomitable band of Jewish settlers cleaved to the dust of the Holy City and survived. Unnamed martyrs gave their blood for the honor of the city, and unknown settlers stretched all rationality in their desire to dwell near her holiness. The lives of only a few rabbis that lived during this period were chronicled for posterity. However, above them all shines a pattern of almost incomprehensible self-sacrifice for the opportunity to live near the place of God's glory.

"Holy Wars"[2]

In the year 1095 (4855), Pope Urban II sermonized at the Council of Clermont and set the Crusades in motion. At the time, few realized the implications of his action. In effect, he had launched the biggest bombshell of medieval times. As a result of his designs, many tens of thousands of men, women, and children — Moslem, Jew, and Christian — lost their lives. Indeed, rivers of innocent Jewish blood were shed well before the Christian armies even left European soil and engaged the Arab hordes. The hysteria of fanatic Christians on the march to Jerusalem, proudly and zealously waving the cross as their banner, left whole Jewish communities massacred throughout the Rhineland and onward.

The Crusaders reached the Holy Land in 1099 (4859) after a major victory at Antioch and proceeded with their attempt to wrest the country from Arab control. The siege of Jerusalem took place in the summer of 1099. The Crusader army numbered 40,000 men (according to others, 12,000), with over a thousand mounted knights. The Moslem population of Jerusalem proper stood at 30,000. Additionally, another 10,000 Arabs from surrounding villages jammed into the walled city for safety. The Jewish inhabitants, numbering in the hundreds, gathered in their synagogue.

On 15 July, after a five-week siege, the Crusaders succeeded in breaching the wall. In a single day, they annihilated almost the entire populace of the city. The lanes and corridors of the city were strewn with corpses, and blood flowed ankle-high. The synagogue in which the Jews congregated was locked and set ablaze. Not one person — Jew nor Arab — escaped alive. Except for a thousand Arabs who were sold into slavery (after being forced to bury the dead), the Crusaders had purged the city of all "heathen" influences. The Dome of the Rock, built by the Moslems in 691, became a cathedral. A golden cross was bound at its top like a banner of victory. For decades to come, not a single Jew or Moslem lived in Jerusalem.

Events were equally momentous from a geo-political point of view. After more than five hundred years, absolute Moslem rule of Eretz Yisrael came to an end. The Crusaders' stunning victory was partially aided by an ongoing feud between the Seljuk Turks (Sunnites) and the Fatimids of Egypt (Shi'ites). The Seljuks came from the central steppes of

Asia and in the early 1050s had conquered Baghdad from the Abbasid caliphate. From there, they expelled the Fatimids from Eretz Yisrael and Jerusalem in the 1070s. In 1098, a year before the Crusaders assaulted Jerusalem, the Fatimids regained control of the city. Confronted with the dissension fostered by this inter-Arab conflict, Jerusalem was ill-equipped to face the threat presented by the Crusader forces.

The first major Egyptian counterattack against the Crusaders, which took place at Ashkelon, proved to be a disaster for the Fatimids. The Crusader leader, Godfrey of Bouillon, who successfully conquered Jerusalem, stunned his enemy and repulsed them. After his death, he was succeeded by Baldwin I, who proudly proclaimed himself King of Jerusalem. He strengthened the Crusaders' control of Eretz Yisrael in victory after victory until 1118, when he died in battle against Egypt.

For nearly a hundred years the Crusaders had autonomous control over almost all of Eretz Yisrael. However, their rule was far from peaceful. Throughout the entire period there was internal strife between different Christian sects, as well as constant wars with the Moslems. In 1148 the second Crusade marched on Damascus with over 50,000 troops, but was defeated outright. As for Jerusalem, it remained a Crusader stronghold for decades, and only Christians were allowed to live there. However, by the 1150s, realizing that it was impossible to live in a vacuum, the Crusaders allowed some Moslems and Jews to return to the city. Not being indigenous to the country, the conquerors needed local help to conduct commerce and to grow and acquire food.

Saladin's Reconquest

As we noted previously, the Moslems never reconciled themselves to their defeat at the hands of the Christian forces. Shortly after their ignoble defeat, the Arabs called for a *jihad* (a holy war) to "purify Jerusalem from the pollution of the cross." Still, the Sunnites and Shi'ites remained at odds. At one point, a Sunnite named Zengi, and his son, Nur al-Din, began a counterattack. Zengi captured the Crusade stronghold of Edessa. Overall, however, they were unsuccessful at driving the Crusades out of the country. But the Christian hegemony was not to last forever, and very soon they would experience crushing defeats at the hands of their implacable enemies.

In 1171 (4831), Saladin, a Moslem of Kurdish descent, rose to power in Egypt, strongly opposing the Isma'ili Shi'ism. Though the Crusaders defeated him at Gezer in 1174, he managed to escape unscathed. That same year the Crusader leader Amalric died. Eventually, Saladin was successful in uniting the country behind him. Facing both united opposition and internal dissension, the Crusader forces would not maintain their control of the country for much longer. In July, 1187, Saladin overwhelmed them at the Battle of Hattin, near Tiberias, capturing King Guy of Lusignan and Prince Arnat of Karak. A few months later Jerusalem fell into Saladin's hands, when the Crusader leader

Balian of Ibelin surrendered. Fifteen thousand Christians were sent into slavery, while others fled, some leaving the country. Immediately, Saladin ordered the church towers torn down and the churches converted into horse stables. After eighty-eight years of rule, the Christians were vanquished. As we shall see, it would take another hundred years, and much more bloodshed, until the last Crusaders left Eretz Yisrael, due to a new wave of Christian warriors coming from Europe. However, Jerusalem never again came under their grasp for more than a few brief periods of time.

Saladin eagerly beckoned Moslems and Jews alike to settle in the city, and the people responded to his call. In particular, the Jews of Ashkelon, a large Jewish settlement during this period, heeded his call.

In 1191, King Richard the Lionhearted of England and King Philip II Augustus of France led the third Crusade. They defeated the Egyptians at the Battle of Akko and gained control of the coast between Jaffa and Akko, but they never reached Jerusalem. A fourth Crusade in 1202 never reached Eretz Yisrael.

Quite apart from all the man-made hardships that characterized this period, the Almighty, through the agency of natural disaster, also contributed to the general turbulence. In Sivan, 1202 (4962), an earthquake shook the western Galilee, destroying most of Akko and Tyre. This, in turn, was the cause of a general famine and plague that overran the country.

In 1211, in the midst of all this tumult and strife, some three hundred Baalei Tosefos came from France (and England). What prompted them to immigrate is speculative, some believing it as reaction to Louis IX's burning the Talmud and the resultant tense environment in France. Their presence had a tremendous impact on the Jewish inhabitants of the land, as we shall discuss later.

The End of the Crusader Period

In 1219, Saladin's nephew, Al-Mu'azzan, commanded that the walls of Jerusalem be demolished. The Citadel of David, however, remained untouched. His decree was prompted by news that the Christian army of the fifth Crusade had landed in Egypt, and he was afraid of a Crusader victory. The act of destroying the walls, for whatever reason, was nearsighted, since the city would remain unwalled for three hundred years. However, his fears were not unfounded. Jerusalem fell later that year, and all non-Christian "infidels" fled or were killed. Most of the Jewish fugitives resettled in Akko, including the Baalei Tosefos. The following year the Moslems recaptured the city.

In 1228, Emperor Frederick II of Germany signed an agreement with Sultan Al-Kamil of Egypt in which Frederick became King of Jerusalem. In exchange, Frederick promised to help the Sultan defeat his brother in Damascus. When his brother suddenly died, the Sultan honored his promise on condition that the Crusader king would not rebuild the walls of the city. Frederick's rule lasted until 1244, until it was usurped by another group of fierce invaders — the Mongol hordes.

Hailing from Asia, a migration of Mongols headed by Genghis Khan reached the Middle East in the 1240s. Known as Tatars, they captured Jerusalem in 1244 from the Crusaders. With this defeat, the Crusaders lost control of the Holy City forever, but they retained a presence in Eretz Yisrael until 1291.

When the Sultan of Egypt suddenly died in 1249, there was a fight over the succession to the throne. In the end, a court revolution brought the Mamluk mercenary soldiers of Turkish descent into power. The Mamluk king, Baybars, became the new Sultan. After consolidating his rule, Baybars turned his attention to the foreign invaders that occupied parts of his kingdom. First he defeated the Mongols in a battle in the Galilee in 1260, and later in the decade he began a major offensive against the Crusaders, wresting Eretz Yisrael from their hands forever. The last of the Crusaders left the country in 1291 when the Mamluks captured the port city of Akko. At the Battle of Ein Harod, the Mamluk victory over the Mongols brought Syria and Damascus under Egyptian rule as well. The Mamluk rule, passive and generally benign to its Jewish subjects, would continue for 250 years, until 1517, when the Ottoman Empire burst onto the world's stage.

The Jewish Legacy

In spite of the terror, carnage, and general uncertainty that marked the two centuries of Crusader domination of Eretz Yisrael, people sought to maintain the rhythms of a normal lifestyle. For the Jew, this meant that Shabbos was still Shabbos, Pesach was still Pesach, and Rosh HaShanah was still Rosh HaShanah. If Jewish life was impossible to live in Jerusalem, then it would continue in Ramla, Akko, Hebron, Ashkelon, or Gaza, or other places.

A fascinating record of life in those days comes down to us from Rav Binyamin of Toledo, Spain. This intrepid wanderer gained fame as the first international Jewish traveler to keep a journal of his odyssey.[3] His decade of traveling (1165–1173) took him along the Mediterranean basin, through France, Italy, Greece, Turkey, Lebanon, Eretz Yisrael, Damascus, the Arabian desert, Egypt, Sicily, Germany, Russia, Paris, and back to Spain. In his journal, he recorded his observations about the Jewish life in each community he visited.

In each of the cities of Tyre, Akko, and Ashkelon, he found 200 Jewish families, which constituted a sizable

Title page of "The Travels of Rav Binyamin of Toledo"

community in those times. Beruit and Tiberias had 50 families apiece. Damascus, with 3,000 Jewish families, was by far the most densely populated city in the Middle East. Interestingly, he did not record any Jews living in Safed or Hebron.

He visited Jerusalem in 1170, while it was yet under Crusader sway. Besides the obvious Christian presence, there was a sizable Moslem population. The Jewish presence was limited to a mere four individuals living next to the Citadel of David. The ruler of the city, Amalric, gave them exclusive rights to make and sell dyes in exchange for a large cut of their profits.

When Rav Binyamin made his journey, the exact location of the Western Wall was unknown. With the passage of years, the successive destruction and rebuilding of the city, and the generally precarious position of Jewish life, its whereabouts was forgotten and would remain undiscovered for many generations.* Thus, Rav Binyamin, like all Jews in Jerusalem for centuries before him and after him, prayed by the eastern gate of the Temple, called the Gate of Mercy. He wrote: "Here Jews gather to pray before the wall of the Temple courtyard."

In the year 1140 (4900), some thirty years before Rav Binyamin's arrival, the author of the *Kuzari*, Rav Yehudah HaLevi, arrived at the Holy City. He first fulfilled the halachah of rending his garments. Then, as he walked barefoot on the ground, he raised his voice in a chant, in fulfillment of the verse (*Psalms* 102:15), "Your servants cherish her stones, and her dust they favor." He recited one of his most famous poems, ציון הלא תשאלי, about the yearning for Jerusalem. As his voice rose and he lifted his arms in cleaving to God, a heathen riding on horseback galloped over to the tzaddik and trampled him to death.[4]

Though the Rambam, Rav Moshe Maimonides, passed through Eretz Yisrael around 1165, when he and his family were fleeing from persecution, it is not difficult to understand why he chose to continue on to Egypt. At the time, conditions were not right in the Holy Land for him to fulfill his great task in life

The Rambam, as printed in Venice, 1744

* See story, "The Hidden Treasure," in *Bygone Days: 12th–16th Centuries.*

there. He spent three days in Jerusalem with his family, where he mourned not only the ancient destruction of the Temple, but the modern one that gripped his eyes. Though he did not live in the Holy Land, the Rambam is buried there, in the city of Tiberias.

The Baalei Tosefos

We noted before that the year 1211 (4971) saw an aliyah of Baalei Tosefos from England and France. This group of pious settlers was welcomed by the Sultan of Egypt, who permitted them to settle in Jerusalem and allowed them to build a synagogue and a yeshivah. One of the Frenchmen, Rav Yechiel ben Yitzchak, built a *mikve* in his house. He wrote: "It is good that the *mikve* is located in our house. This way, we can teach the women the laws of immersion."[5] One of the Baalei Tosefos by the name of Rav Yonasan HaKohen of Luniel, who wrote a commentary to the Rif on Tractate *Eruvin* before leaving Europe, arrived soon after the main contingent. He headed the community. We are told that during his lifetime, a severe drought descended upon the country, and Rav Yonasan was responsible for leading the communal prayers begging for relief. In the merit of the Jews' prayer, the Almighty responded with a bountiful blessing of rain.

The Baalei Tosefos' sojourn in Jerusalem was not long enough to make a permanent impression. In 1219 they were forced to evacuate the city when the cross-bearers reconquered it. Most of the survivors resettled in Akko, which, although controlled by Christians, permitted Jewish settlement.

Later, other Baalei Tosefos joined them. Among them were Rav Shimshon ben Avraham of France, and Rav Yosef, whose opinion is quoted by Tosefos in the gemara *Nazir* 10a. Another member was Rav Moshe d'Lyon, who discovered the *Zohar* (primary text of Jewish mysticism, written by the Tanna Rabbi Shimon bar Yochai) hidden in a Galilean cave and brought it to Europe for publication. Another was Rav Yitzchak bar Shmuel of Akko, the Ramban's chief disciple, who wrote *Meiros Einaim*, a work that unraveled the secrets which the Ramban had hinted to in his commentary on the Torah.

Yet the most famous Jew to reach the Holy Land during this period was undoubtedly the Ramban himself.

The Ramban's Imprint

At seventy years of age, Rav Moshe Nachmanides, known by his acronym, Ramban, stood at the pinnacle of life. As the greatest sage of his generation, he was in communication with all the leading Torah scholars of his time. A prolific writer from his youth (he wrote *Milchamos* at the age of nineteen), the Ramban stood equal with the Rambam as one of the greatest Early Authorities.

Yet at a time in life when most people look forward to being comfortably settled, he was forced to take up the wanderer's staff — the result of his successful debate against a Jewish apostate turned Christian priest by the name of Pablo

חדושי התורה לרב רבינו
משה בר נחמן תנצב״ה ::

Ramban's commentary, printed in Lisbon, 1489

Christianni before the King of Spain. Some time after the debate, the venerated sage set his compass for Eretz Yisrael. In those times, travel was precarious at best, and at his age — old even by today's standards — there was no certainty that he would survive the difficult voyage. Yet he was bold and determined.

He reached Eretz Yisrael in 1267 (5027). After landing in Akko, he traveled to Jerusalem, Hebron, and then back to Akko, where he finally settled. Thus, while he was responsible for the reestablishment of Jerusalem's Jewish community, he himself did not actually live there for more than a short period of time. He continued writing after he settled in the Holy Land. In addition to several letters to his sons in Spain and the text of a sermon he gave in Akko that have come down to us, he worked on his famous commentary to the Torah.

Following is an excerpt of a letter the Ramban wrote to his family.[6]

May Hashem bless you, my son Nachman, and may you see the goodness of Jerusalem. May you live to see your grandchildren. And may your table be like that of the Patriarch Avraham.

I am writing you this letter from Jerusalem, the Holy City. With praise and thanksgiving to the Creator I managed to arrive there in peace on the ninth of Elul, [1267 (5027)], and remained there until the day after Yom Kippur. Then I went to Hebron for the Holiday [of Sukkos]. I prayed by [Machpelah] the burial place of the Patriarchs and sought to purchase a burial plot for myself.

What can I tell you about the Land? So desolate and forsaken! In a nutshell: The greater the holiness of a place, the greater the destruction. Jerusalem suffered the most, the portion of Yehudah more than the Galilee. Yet, even in this state of destruction, it is still very good.

There are nearly two thousand inhabitants [in Jerusalem], including three hundred Christian fugitives from the Sultan's sword. There are no Jews since the Tatars came, forcing the Jews which they did not kill to escape. Only two Jewish brothers [remained in the city], dyers by trade, buying the dyes from the ruler. On Shabbos, they have to gather a minyan in their house [probably including Jews from outlying areas].

We encouraged them and found an abandoned building built with marble pillars and a lovely arched ceiling. As every place in the city is ownerless, we took it for ourselves and made it into a synagogue. Anyone can claim a deserted house as his own. We freely set about fixing up the place. In the middle of the renovations, a message was sent to the city of Shechem to return the Torah scrolls which were sent there from Jerusalem when the Tatars came.

At last the synagogue stood, and there people prayed. Many come regularly to Jerusalem from Damascus, Aram Zovah, Egypt, and from all parts of the Land to view the Temple and weep over its [destruction]. One who is fortunate to see Jerusalem in her desolation will see it when she will be rebuilt, when God will place His glorious Shechinah there.

May you, my son, and your brothers and your families, be worthy of the goodness of Jerusalem and the consolation of Zion, as the wish of your father, who worries and sighs, sees and rejoices, Moshe bar Nachman.

Mention me well, my son, to my disciple, Rav Moshe bar Shlomo, your uncle. Tell him that I climbed up the Mount of Olives. It is situated opposite the Temple Mount. Between the two there is only the valley of Jehoshafat. There, across from the Temple, I recited verses with great emotion.

May the One Who rests His Name on the Temple watch over you and extend to you abundant peace, together with the congregation of your renowned city for all eternity. Amen.

The Ramban Synagogue

The Ramban Synagogue, as it was called, was the first synagogue established at the end of the Crusader period. It flourished for hundreds of years, and both Sephardim and Ashkenazim prayed there. However, just before Rav Ovadiah

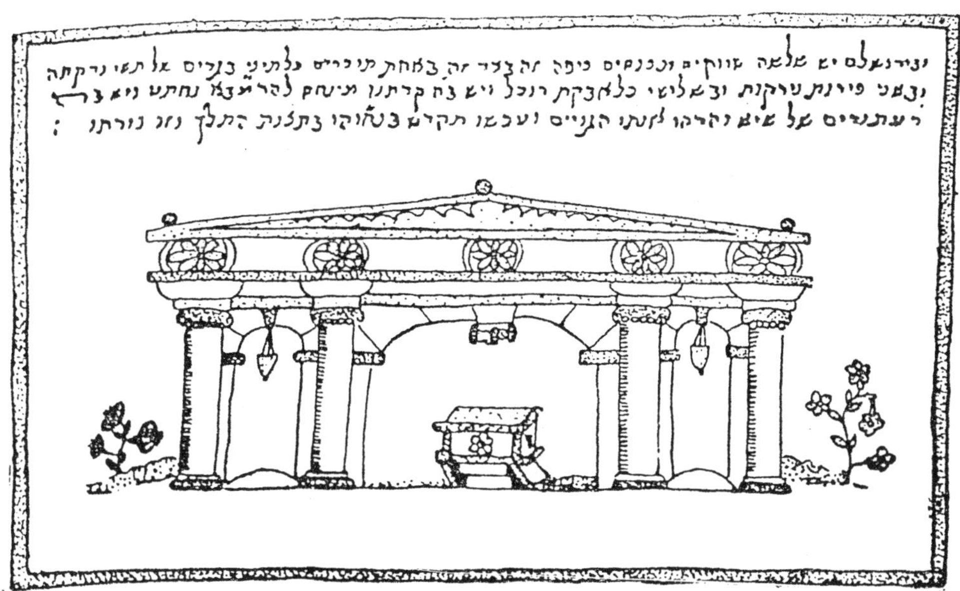

Ramban Synagogue, as depicted in 1598

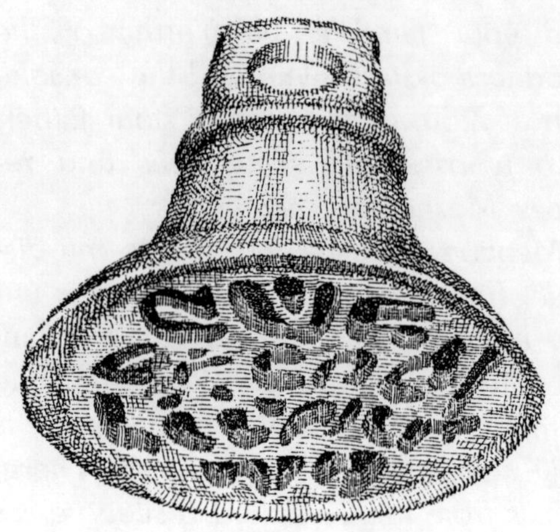

The Ramban's Seal, discovered in 1972

Bartenora came to Jerusalem in 1488, the Jews were forcibly evicted from it. At that time, unscrupulous communal "leaders" sold it to Moslems, who subsequently turned the building into a warehouse. Until the twentieth century it continued to be used as a wheat storehouse.[7]

Most, if not all, of the Ramban's commentary to the Torah was written in Eretz Yisrael. The only commentaries existing in his time were those of Rashi and the Ibn Ezra. The Ramban, standing at the culmination of a lifetime as a teacher of Torah, felt a tremendous need to leave behind him an in-depth approach to understanding and unraveling the mysteries of the Torah. The powerful and lasting impact of his commentary testifies to his accurate perception of the need for such a work. Throughout the generations, until today, Torah scholars have studied it and labored to understand it.

In 1972, a small bronze seal was discovered near Akko.[8] About 2.5 centimeters in diameter, the stamp reads:

Moshe	משה
bar	בר
Nachman	נחמן
n'n	נ"נ
Granada	גירונדי
Chazak	חזק

The n"n (נ'נ) is an abbreviation of נוח נפש, meaning "the deceased." In this case, it is referring to his father, Nachman.

Whether or not the stamp was actually used by the Ramban is a matter of speculation. While it seems clear that it was commissioned by him, we have no correspondence or manuscript from him that actually bears its mark.

Legend has it that the disciples whom the Ramban left behind in Spain begged him to give them a sign whereby they would know of his passing. Being separated from their mentor was hard enough, but not being able to mourn his death would be even more difficult. The Ramban acceded to their request and before setting out from Barcelona told them, "On the day I die you will find the tomb over my mother's grave split in two. Inside you will see a drawing of a candelabra."[9]

According to the legend, his words came true. In any event, we know that he died in 1270, at the age of 76, three years after his arrival in Eretz Yisrael. At that time, all Jewry mourned the passing of one of the greatest lights of Jewish history. Though the exact location of his burial site is unknown — opinions varying as far apart as Akko to Hebron — his imprint on the Jewish world has remained alive.

The First Researcher of Eretz Yisrael[10]

In the fourteenth century, after two hundred years of upheaval, Jerusalem experienced a desperately needed period of stability. The Mamluk dynasty had established deep roots, and the Sultan in Cairo stood at the head of a vast Middle Eastern empire. Damascus was the provincial capital, headed by a governor. On the other hand, Jerusalem was merely one of many cities under Damascus's jurisdiction, headed by a mayor. As if to reinforce Jerusalem's minor status, the city remained unwalled.

In 1313 (5073), a French scholar of repute arrived in the Holy Land — Rav Ishtori Parchi. In his mid-thirties, he had a tremendous grasp of both the Babylonian and Jerusalem Talmuds, as well as the whole body of Midrashic literature. He first settled in Jerusalem, where he lived for a year studying with the scholars of the city. One of the leading rabbis, Rav Baruch, became his lifelong companion. Among other topics, he delved into a study of the Temple courtyards and gates. These findings would later be incorporated into his magnum opus, *Kaftor v'Ferach*, which we shall discuss shortly.

His motive for coming on aliyah was an unusual one for the times. He planned to survey the land of our forefathers, find the exact location of every town mentioned in the Bible, and map the boundaries of Eretz Yisrael according to Joshua's conquest and Ezra's settlement.

Cartography, of course, is both an art and a science. However, in those days it was unheard of as an occupation. What would a Torah scholar, a *rishon* (Early Authority), be doing camping out for weeks at a time trying to pinpoint forgotten places? Yet, it is obvious that he found his chosen task both compelling and fulfilling, as well as very important. He writes: *"Searching for the location of different historical sites in Eretz Yisrael was more precious to me than an astronomer's scanning the sky to map the stars.... Each of the stellar bodies is constantly circling around us, and most people know nothing about them. And even among astronomers, only a few are capable of discerning the motion of one constellation from the other. How aptly this describes the task of locating places in Eretz Yisrael! People are in movement, much like the stellar bodies, without knowing the unique histories of these very special places."*[11]

The following year, 1314, he moved to Beis Shean, south of Tiberias, where he would reside for the rest of his life. He spent two years investigating the

Galilee and another five researching the rest of Eretz Yisrael. In 1320 he began writing his masterpiece, *Kaftor v'Ferach*. Its subject matter included everything about Eretz Yisrael — from the laws of *terumah* and *maaser* (the priestly tithes), *shemitah* (the seven-year sabbatical of the land) and *yovel* (the fifty-year Jubilee), to calculating the *molad* (the appearance of the new moon) and identifying the different flowers and trees of the Land. He also identified the locations of hundreds of towns mentioned in the Bible and the Talmud, as well as revealing a great deal of information concerning the layout of the Temple and its courtyards. His method was clearly that of a *rishon*, based on Talmudic sources which were at his fingertips.

In 1322 Rav Parchi returned to Jerusalem with the first draft of a 700-page manuscript. He wanted Rav Baruch and other scholars to first review it before signing his name to it. Based on their comments and discussions he had with them, he added some parts, deleted others, and changed still others. He also added a table of contents. At the end of the chapter on Jerusalem, he composed the following poem, probably meant to be recited near the Temple environs:

The One and only Master of this House [i.e., the Temple]; the Light of the world,

Here is a meek [Jew] calling out, pouring out his heart, releasing the bitterness,

Crying, soaked with tears, arms spread out,

Opposite You, unto the name of Your Presence,

Standing in the open thoroughfare, facing the multitude of hardships from those who hate us,

And the gentile, who is not from Your people, is great in the House.

There is no one from those who belong in the House, in the House,

With Your faithful kindness, my Lord, rebuild Your House as it once was,

Bring the redemption, redeem Your precious nation,

Our exile has been to quiet Your wrath,

Unto Your Holy City, in the chamber of the magnificent fortress,

You will bring him in kindness and mercy, and upon Your altar he will offer

אוצר ספרות ארץ ישראל

ספר א׳

כפתור ופרח

מאת

הרב אישתורי הפרחי ז״ל

הוצאה מוגהת ומתוקנת, עם הערות והוספות רבות, תולדות המחבר, ועוד.

מאת

אברהם משה לונץ

עורך הירושלים ולוח ארץ ישראל.

כרך ראשון

פעיה״ק ירושלם תובב״א

תרנ״ז

בדפוס ובהוצאת המו״ל.

Title page of the second edition of Kaftor v'Ferach *(Jerusalem, 1897) a sacrifice,*

When You will give it to him for Your Name's sake.[12]

Written before the invention of the printing press, very few copies of the work were produced. We know that at the time, at least two copies existed, but none survived. Indeed, the tale of how the original book came down to us is quite remarkable. Had the *naggid* (literally, 'prince,' referring to the leader of the Jewish community) of Egypt, Rav Yitzchak Sholal, not discovered it in the Cairo *genizah* (burial area for discarded Torah literature), no one would have known of this masterpiece or its author. For two hundred years the work lay hidden from the eyes of man. In subsequent centuries its tremendous value was recognized, and such towering authorities as Rav Yosef Karo and the Rama quote from it to draw halachic conclusions concerning Eretz Yisrael.

Rav Parchi wrote: "I humbly come forward to present to my fellow Jews what I have found in my searches. My findings do not stem from a greater depth of knowledge than others; rather, I have simply spent more time investigating this subject than most people have and feel duty bound to share the fruits of my research with the public."[13]

The Silent Years

For the next hundred and fifty years, until the arrival of Rav Ovadiah of Bartenora in 1488, a curtain of silence once again descended on the history of Jewish Jerusalem. In terms of general history, we know that in 1277, Sultan Mohammed built up the city to a much greater degree than his predecessors had. The most impressive and lasting of his projects was the Sultan's Pool, outside the (current) wall and below the Jaffa Gate. The purpose of the pool was to retain rainfall which could be used as drinking water for camels and horses. Water for human consumption was collected in underground cisterns throughout the city.

Jewishly, the only thing known for certain about this time is that there was a benevolent Mamluk rulership over Eretz Yisrael, and a growing Jewish element in the Holy City. In general, however, the shroud overlaying this period has not been penetrated. Without a doubt we can say that there were men and women of vision who braved the vicissitudes of fortune to come on aliyah. There were scholars who studied Torah for its own sake, pushing away sleep in order to study late into the night. There were simple weavers and silversmiths who recited Psalms by heart while they worked, as well as many others who were privileged to live out their lives in the Holy City. Their stories, although untold, shine before the Heavenly Throne.

Great Names in the Holy City

As is the way of the world, the Ramban, the Baalei Tosefos, and their generations were consigned to the dust over the course of time. However, the small yishuv they left behind survived — although it could not be said to have thrived. The community was struck a particularly hard blow in the late 1400s, when the entire country was overrun by a ravaging epidemic, and experienced a severe famine as well. At that time, the yishuv lost its physical and spiritual nucleus when a few ignoble community "leaders" sold the Ramban Synagogue to some Moslems for personal profit, as we mentioned previously. Fortunately, the gloomy picture was destined to brighten, for it was just at this low ebb that the Almighty sent a man of high caliber to uplift the community and infuse it with new life. He is known to us as Rav Ovadiah of Bartenora.

Rav Ovadiah of Bartenora[14]

Sometime in the beginning of the year 1488 (5248), news reached the Holy City that a most prominent rabbi was on his way from Egypt to Jerusalem. His name was Rav Ovadiah, and he came from the Italian city of Bartenora. Though his famous commentary on the Mishnah would only be completed a few years later in Jerusalem, he was already well known in the Jewish world, and his renown had preceded him to the *yishuv*.

The city in the mountaintops thirsted for nobility, and genuine nobility meant Torah excellence. In addition, the tiny Jewish enclave, numbering around seventy families, was desperate for leadership and a sense of direction. Thus Rav Ovadiah, combining all three qualities, was a true Godsend to Jerusalem, just in its time of need.

In the years prior to this exceptional man's arrival, the community had been shattered by a series of calamities — both natural and man-made. First, corruption at the highest level of the communal leadership weighed heavily on the communities' financial resources. Ruthlessly extorted, several residents fled to Hebron and Egypt. Secondly, a devastating epidemic, accompanied by a severe famine, ravaged the area, bringing sickness and death in its merciless path. This too caused people to flee for their lives.

In contrast to this bleak situation, Cairo, where Rav Ovadiah had arrived before undertaking the last leg of his journey to the Holy Land, was a bustling metropolis. There were plenty of jobs available, in both wholesale and retail trade and in money-changing, and all the amenities of the big city. Boasting over seven hundred Jewish families, the community was served by two ancient synagogues. The *naggid*, Rav Nasan HaKohen, acted as an emissary between the Jewish community and the Mamluk authorities. Yet despite an attractive offer to settle in Cairo, and fully aware of the hardships that would face him in the Holy Land, Rav Ovadiah bid farewell to the Egyptian city and set his eyes on Eretz Yisrael.

On his way to the Holy City, he stopped in Gaza and Hebron. As he approached Jerusalem, he recorded that, "At a place of descending steps, we saw the praised city, the city of our joy. There we tore our garments in accordance with Jewish law. And when we came a little closer and saw the ruins of our holy and magnificent Temple, we tore our garments yet again."

Street in Cairo

Rav Ovadiah tells us:

We arrived at the gates of Jerusalem and entered at noontime on the thirteenth of Nisan, 5248 [1488]. On that day, "our feet stood within your gates, O Yerushalayim!" [Psalms 122:2]

We were met by an Ashkenazic Rav who had grown up in Italy, Rav Yaakov Colombano. He brought us to his home, and we stayed there with him for the Passover holiday.

Most of Jerusalem is in ruins, and it goes without saying that there is no wall about it. According to what I was told, a total of four thousand families live in the Holy City. However, of these, only seventy are Jewish, and they are the poorest of the poor, earning no money. Almost everyone lacks even the basic necessities, and if someone has enough food for the year, he is considered wealthy. There are many old and lonely widows, both of German and Spanish descent, and of other origins as well, seven women to a man.

At present, the land is quiet, because the elders [Sheik al-Yehud] regret their previous actions, seeing that nothing is left and that they themselves have lost money. Now they encourage people to return to Jerusalem. They apologize profusely for having done what they did, saying that they had only been interested in punishing those who had tried to take power away from them...

When I first came to Jerusalem there was a great famine. One meal's worth of bread cost a derham (which is the same as a bolognino) and it still did not satisfy a person. But I was told that this famine was not as bad as the one they had experienced the previous year.

Many Jews died in that famine. A day or two before their death, they would ask for bread but there would be none to give them. The next day they would be found dead in their homes. Many people had to wander through the fields and eat the grass.

I rented a house close to the [Ramban] synagogue. It is an upper-story room, built into the wall of the synagogue. The courtyard that my house faces has five other inhabitants, all of them women. The one exception is a blind man, whose wife I have hired to serve me.

I give thanks to the Almighty for keeping me in good health, for all the people who came here with me fell ill. In fact, most people who come to Jerusalem from distant lands become ill. This is due to the change of atmosphere, and also because of the rapid changes in temperature, from cold to hot and back again.

All of the winds in the world blow through the Holy City. It is said that before a wind goes to its destination, it first comes to bow before the Lord in Jerusalem. Blessed is the One Who knows the truth.

The Turn of the Century

Slowly, with each passing month, more Jews returned to the Holy City. By 1495, the Jewish community comprised some two hundred families. Rav Ovadiah, as the city's Rav, led them with vigor and royalty. His dynamic personality and total command of Torah knowledge blended together seamlessly to unite the community under one head.

As a teacher concerned with the propagation of Torah, the Rav's activities consisted of teaching a few select students and writing his prodigious commentary to the Mishnah. There was no antecedent to his novel idea other than the Rambam's commentary, whose brevity beckoned a fuller elucidation. Rav Ovadiah felt a Heavenly blessing at being able to compile a commentary on the Oral Law in such a succinct and lucid form. It was published by his nephew in Venice in 1548, years after Rav Ovadiah passed away. History has validated the Rav's instinct that such a commentary was necessary, and some five hundred year later, his work remains the standard commentary on the Mishnah.

The Radvaz, who lived in Jerusalem in the generation after the Rav, wrote: "The man's wisdom was proverbial, and he stood at the head of the sages of Jerusalem. He studied under Ashkenazic *rabbanim* and had a clear grasp of all the writings of the Early Authorities. Though there were others in Jerusalem who were his seniors, they all sat meekly before him."[15]

Rav Ovadiah, a superb *darshan* (public speaker on Torah topics), chose to speak only on the holidays. Throughout the rest of the year, an elderly rabbi by the name of Rav Zechariah spoke, usually for a short time after the evening and morning Shabbos services.

The grave of Rav Ovadiah of Bartenora, jutting out from a small cave near the Shiloach Spring

When a young Venetian Jew arrived penniless to the city, Rav Ovadiah personally took him under his wing, telling him, "I shall watch over you as my own dear son."

This student described Rav Ovadiah with the following words: "He is a great man and has a lot of influence. No one [in the Jewish community] will do anything without his consent. Jews come from distant lands to seek him, and they heed his every word. From as far as Egypt and Babylon his decrees are enforced. Even the Moslems honor and fear him. I even heard that he once killed a wicked man by whispering something. He is very humble, and he mixes easily with people. Everyone praises him, saying of him that he is not of mortal flesh."[16]

Rav Ovadiah passed away sometime in the early decades of the sixteenth century and was laid to rest in a small cave in the Kidron Valley. He left an eternal legacy of his succinct commentary to the Mishnah, which became a classic throughout the ages, as well as a commentary on the Chumash.

Generations later, in the 1880s, Rav Yehoshua Leib Diskin delved into Rav Ovadiah's commentary to *Seder* (Order of) *Zeraim* with one of his disciples. They spent a month studying a single chapter. Rav Diskin commented, "In these laws which pertain to the Land of Israel, we must analyze each word of the Rav Bartenora, since he was the leading sage of Eretz Yisrael, and surely he was elucidating these laws for the generations to come."[17]

The Spanish Expulsion

By the mid-1490s the tragic news of the Jewish expulsion from Spain had reached Jerusalem. Hundreds of thousands of Jews had been cast out into the elements to suffer every manner of privation. In the Inquisition itself, many died a martyr's death at the stake, while others elected to convert. Some of the latter eventually regretted their decision and became Marranos, who secretly kept their Jewish identity. In the 1530s, the sages of Eretz Yisrael would try to help these secret Jews return fully to their faith, as we shall see.

The Spanish expulsion, followed by one from Portugal, would trigger a definite shift in the Jewish world. At first it was too early to tell how and where Torah authority would surface. However, in the coming generations it would shine forth from Eretz Yisrael, in ways unexpected to everyone.

The Ottoman Conquest

In the year 1516–1517 (5277), Selim I conquered the vast area from Syria to Egypt in a series of victories against the Mamluk army. A number of factors contributed to this dazzling success which doubled the size of the Ottoman Empire and made it the wealthiest and most powerful country in the world. The Ottoman army was well organized and used modern weaponry, such as cannons and gunpowder, while the Mamluks fought with spears and arrows. Due to growing internal strife, a large number of Mamluk officers defected to the Ottoman forces in return for new positions in the reorganized government. The general population, too, favored the security offered by the Ottoman rule, rather than the state of anarchy which had prevailed over the last century.

Suleiman the Magnificent

When Selim I died in 1520, his son Suleiman replaced him. Sultan Suleiman (1520–1566), called the "Magnificent," stood at the helm of one of the largest empires known to man. It stretched from Turkey in the east across the whole of North Africa. Though most of his subjects were Arabs, and therefore loosely identified as Moslems, they were actually subdivided into numerous sects, some of which even warred against each other, as we mentioned earlier during the Crusade period.

The Sultan's relationship with his new Jewish subjects in Eretz Yisrael was a direct outgrowth of his earlier relationship with the Jewish community of Constantinople. There, in his court, he was served by Rav Moshe Hamun, his personal physician. The Sultan, wise and benevolent, sensed the grandeur of his physician's faith. In the course of time, he asked Rav Moshe to translate the Bible into Arabic so that he could better appreciate this ancient, monotheistic religion. Above all, he enjoyed reciting Psalms. A second physician, Rav Tam, was a member of the Sultan's inner circle. Thus, Suleiman's personal experience favorably predisposed him towards his Jewish subjects.

In general, the Mamluk kings had displayed a neutral attitude toward the Jews living under their rule. On the other hand, the Ottoman presence had a definite, positive impact. Overall, life improved for all the empire's subjects, as the old and corrupt Mamluk dynasty gave way to the dynamic leadership exhibited by the young Ottoman Empire. One major cause for this improvement was an increase in the attention given to protecting the roads. As the highways were made safe from marauders, commerce increased proportionately. In turn, more and better job opportunities became available. Concerning the Jews specifically, the most dramatic demonstration of the new era was seen in Jerusalem. In 1527 (5287), under the guidance of his master architect, the Sultan initiated the construction of a wall around the Holy City. For 308 years the city had stood exposed, completely stripped of all the ancient dignity she rightfully deserved. Under the beneficent ruler, a small measure of her grandeur would be restored. Though the Jewish population of Jerusalem itself was negligible, the Sultan's gift had tremendous symbolic significance to the multitudes of Jews throughout his realm. Suleiman's

Wall of Old City with Jaffa Gate, built by Sultan Suleiman the Magnificent between 1527–1542

Tomb of David surrounded by early Christian and Moslem shrines

great present was completed fifteen years later, in 1542. Its circumference was nearly four kilometers long; its height reached to over twenty meters in certain places, and its ramparts were three meters thick. Practically speaking, the city would never require the impressive defenses offered by the wall during the entire Ottoman period. However, it was, and remains, an imposing tribute to the high esteem in which the Sultan held his Jewish subjects. The empire engaged in building projects in other areas of the country as well, such as the rebuilding of Tiberias's city wall. All of this activity testified to the vitality of the Ottoman Empire and the concern it showed for its subjects during its flourishing golden years.

David's Tomb

In 1522 (5282), a small but very significant incident occurred. As we noted in the story section for the 12th–16th centuries, Mount Zion has always been revered as the burial place of the kings of the house of David. The source for this belief can be traced to the Bible, where it says, "So David slept with his fathers and was buried in the city of David" (I *Kings* 2:10), which the commentators note is a reference to Mount Zion. During the Crusader period the Christians controlled the area, building a church there. During the Mamluk rule (1291–1517), the Tomb of David was declared a holy Moslem site, and all Christians and Jews were forbidden to enter. However, in the time of the

Ottoman Empire, Franciscan monks regained access to the site by purchasing more and more space in the building which contained the tomb on its ground floor.

Concerned for the future of the tomb, the Jews decided to take action, albeit in a roundabout fashion. In 1522, an emissary was sent to meet with a high-ranking religious Moslem who had a voice with the new Turkish government. The emissary presented the following claim against the Franciscans: The growing annexation of Mount Zion by the monks through the private purchase of property on the mountain posed a threat to the new government. Mount Zion, strategically overlooking the entire city, could secretly be made into an army base, from which a revolt might be launched. The Turkish authorities accepted this claim, and in 1523 an edict arrived from Constantinople ordering the Franciscans to return all the property they had purchased. Thus, besides losing David's tomb, they also lost their so-called Cenacle (the room where the "Last Supper" was held), which was on an upper floor of the same structure. In this way, the tomb of King David remained out of Christian hands from that time onwards.[18]

Mount Zion, whose location was of strategic importance, was mysteriously not included within the new wall which the Sultan had commission. When Sultan Suleiman heard of the engineer's oversight, he was outraged and ordered him to be executed. Interestingly, the engineer's body was buried just inside the Jaffa Gate.

Yet, there would come a time in a later generation — 1948–1967 — when Mount Zion would play a strategic role for the Jewish people precisely because it lay outside the walled city. Then, it became a military outpost, as well as a shrine where devout Jews could pray to God that in the merits of King David He would be merciful to us, unite the Holy City, and bring us closer to the time of the Mashiach.

The Last Naggid[19]

Rav Ovadiah's influence had a lasting imprint on the Jewish community of Jerusalem. By the time he passed away, there were over three hundred families there. More importantly, the city was left in the hands of top *rabbanim* after his death. Two of them, *gedolei ha'dor* (Torah giants and leading scholars of their generation), put Jerusalem firmly back on the map of the Jewish world.

One of them, Rav Yitzchak Sholal, was the last *naggid* of Egypt. The title *naggid* designated the official leader of the Jews during the Mamluk dynasty (1203–1517), a position similar to the *reish galusah* in Babylon. His power extended beyond that of any other Jew in the realm. Once the Ottoman Empire took control of the Middle East, the post of *naggid* was abandoned.

As we mentioned in the first chapter, it was Rav Sholal who accidentally discovered the only surviving manuscript of *Kaftor v'Ferach*, written over two hundred years earlier by Rav Ishtori Parchi. He immediately recognized the significance of the work and ordered scribes to make copies of it so that it could be sent to Italy for printing.

Sometime between 1514 and 1520

he moved to Jerusalem. He brought with him all of the nobility attendant to his office, as well as great wealth. He personally supported the scholars in two yeshivos of the city. In addition, he was influential in having the scholars exempted from paying government taxes. Encouraged by Rav Sholal's largesse and the favorable conditions prevailing in the city, scholars flocked from Egypt and Safed to settle there. In a very short time, the streets of Jerusalem reverberated with the sounds of Torah study. Rav David Shushan became Rosh Yeshivah. One of the most celebrated *chachamim* in the city was Rav Avraham HaLevi, author of several kabbalistic works.

Rav Sholal also instituted *mishmeros,* special contingents of Jews who agreed to pray and fast for the sake of all Jewry. Jerusalem was the spiritual antenna of the world, and a dedicated core of Jews in the Holy City could awaken Divine mercy for Jewry everywhere. There were two *mishmeros*, each fasting one day a week.*

In 1523 (5283), Rav Sholal had a brief encounter with David Reuveni, one of a number of infamous false messiahs, who claimed to be a descendant from the royal house of King David. Reuveni presented himself as a messenger from the lost Tribe of Reuven — hence his appellation, Reuveni. The king of that tribe, he said, had told him that it was time to reveal himself and promulgate the redemption. Reuveni claimed that by removing a certain stone from the Wailing Wall, he would be removing the very object which was preventing the redemption.

The *naggid*, upon meeting him and hearing this story, openly repudiated the young man. It was preposterous, claimed Rav Sholal, and Reuveni was clearly an instigator against Torah, the Jewish people, and the Almighty. The *naggid* had letters sent to the world's major Jewish communities in order to warn them about this impostor.

In the fall of 1524 (5285), a devastating plague struck Jerusalem. In those times, of course, there was no known remedy for the scourge of pestilence that periodically swept the populace of cities and towns the world over. The only way to survive was to flee to another town until the plague ran its course. Thus, Rav Sholal, together with the most of the residents of the city, left for safer ground. Unfortunately, of all the *rabbanim*, he was struck with the dread disease, dying on 1 Kislev. He left no writings, but the leaders of the next generation — the Radvaz, the Ralbach, and Rav Yosef Karo — quote him in their responsa.

* See story, "Mishmeros," in *Bygone Days: 12th–16th Centuries*.

Jerusalem as the Center of the World

Sixteenth-century Jerusalem experienced the vicissitudes of fortune. The passing of leaders like Rav Bartenora and Rav Sholal, coupled with abject poverty, brought the Jewish inhabitants to a record low. Unable to alter their economic situation, they were privileged to have new leaders come and instill them with fresh courage.

It was with the coming of Rav Levi Chaviv, a renowned sage in his own right, that the status of Jerusalem as the center of the Torah world came into the forefront. The confrontation between him and the sages of Safed, concerning semichah d'oraysah, is the theme of this chapter.

The Ralbach: Rav Levi Chaviv[20]

The other leading rabbi at this time was Rav Levi Chaviv. As a child, he was a refugee from the Spanish Expulsion, together with his family. After settling in Thessaloniki (modern-day Salonika), he grew to be an outstanding Torah scholar. At a relatively young age he became one of the leading *rabbanim* in that city, which was famous for the quality of its Torah scholarship. At the age of twenty-four, he wrote an exhaustive study on calculating the date of the Sabbatical year. When his father passed away before finishing his sefer *Ein Yaakov*, a collection of all the Talmudic *haggados* with his and other commentaries, Rav Levi completed it.

At the age of forty-five, Rav Chaviv, known by the acronym Ralbach, ranked as a well-known sage in the Torah world. It was at this stage in his life that he decided to settle in Jerusalem. Around the year 1524 (5284), he moved to the Holy Land, stopping for a short time in Safed before proceeding on to Jerusalem. While recuperating from an illness there, he had ample opportunity to become acquainted with the leading sages of the city, including Rav Yaakov Berav, whom we shall meet shortly.

Rav Chaviv moved to Jerusalem around the time of the plague which took the life of Rav Yitzchak Sholal. Upon settling in the Holy City, he set as his first priority the study of the laws pertaining to Eretz Yisrael. Of particular concern to him were the laws of *kiddush ha'chodesh* (the determination of the lunar calendar and leap years). Some of his studies were to have practical ramifications that still affect us today, hundreds of years later. Based on his calculations, Shushan

Purim (15 Adar, when Purim is celebrated in Jerusalem) fell on Shabbos in the year of 1527. He had never had an occasion to be faced with this halachic question while living in *chutz l'aretz*. The problem with Purim coming out on Shabbos is that the Megillah may not be read on that day. This was (and is) a precautionary law. It was instituted by the Sages thousands of years ago for fear that one might accidentally come to carry on the Shabbos by bringing a Megillah to the synagogue. As 14 Adar — Purim throughout the world except Jerusalem — never falls on Shabbos, no precedent existed to direct the community as to how they should conduct themselves. Therefore, the Ralbach delved into the law and concluded that the Purim feast should be on Shabbos, as well as exchanging presents of food with friends. The gifts to the poor and the Megillah reading, however, should be on Friday. His views, though quoted by some of the later authorities, is not the accepted halachah today.[21]

The following years were difficult ones for the *yishuv* of Jerusalem. In 1529–1530 the population dwindled to less than a minyan of adult men, partially due to the passing of Rav Sholal and the closing of his yeshivos. Rav Chaviv wrote: "The living conditions for the scholars of the city are not simply a question of forgoing delicacies. Their material means are small, and if one should have enough money to buy the head or intestines of a goat for Shabbos or Yom Tov, then he feels that he has been freed from the house of bondage."

Slowly, with each new year, the population grew. Still, it would take decades for the city to reach the size it had attained during the 1520s.

Birth of the Ari Zal

In 1534 (5294), a very inconspicuous, and, in the great scheme of things, seemingly minor event occurred in the city. Rav Shlomo Luria Ashkenazi became a father.* His son, Yitzchak, grew up in the Holy City until he was eight years old, at which time his father died. Shortly thereafter, his mother sent him to live with his uncle in Cairo. There, Yitzchak Luria spent the next thirty years engrossed in his studies. In 1570 he moved with his family to Safed, and he began disseminating the wisdom of the Kabbalah to a select group of students. Included among them was his chief disciple, Rav Chaim Vital, who would later commit his master's words to writing. Known by the acronym Ari Zal, Rav Luria scaled heights in the understanding of the mystical Torah that were unsurpassed by nearly any other Jew in history.

Rav Luria's imprint on Judaism — whether in Halachah, Kabbalah, or Jewish customs — was greater than almost any other individual since his time. A glimpse at his greatness may be ascertained from the words of his contemporary, Rav Yosef Karo. After the engagement party of his son with the Ari's daughter, Rav Karo commented: "I never would have imagined what fortune was

* See story, "The Ari Zal's Roots," in *Bygone Days: 12th–16th Centuries*.

in store for me tonight when I listened to such profound words of Torah as emanated from the mouth of the saintly Rav Yitzchak Luria. It is absolutely unimaginable that a human being has such depth of perception. Even an angel does not know what he knows. Truly, his soul must be descended from one of the early prophets, for even the greatest of Talmudic Sages could not attain that which he has. And yet, on that very account I am greatly afraid for him. Our generation has fallen too low to absorb the radiance of his saintliness, and I fear that he might be taken away from us all too soon."[22] His fear was not unfounded — the Ari was taken from this world at the relatively young age of thirty-eight.

Semichah: Reinstating Ordination[23]

In 1538 (5298), the sages of Safed, led by the renowned Rav Yaakov Berav, reinstated the highest form of rabbinical ordination, *semichah d'oraysah*. This exalted office had been defunct for over a thousand years. Now, the sages of Safed felt the time was propitious for its reinstatement. As we shall see, however, they faced strong opposition from their counterparts in Jerusalem. In order to fully appreciate the disagreement, let us first briefly review the history of *semichah*.

From the time of Moses until three hundred years after the destruction of the Second Temple, there existed an unbroken chain of ordained rabbis. The power invested by this ordination far surpassed that which rabbis have today: Rabbis with *semichah* were empowered to judge monetary cases, punish a guilty party with lashes, sentence a criminal to death, and declare the new month and the leap year.

In the fourth century, Rav Hillel the Younger (not to be confused with his illustrious forebear, Hillel the Elder, who lived several centuries earlier), a direct descendant of Rabbi Yehudah the Prince, was the leading sage in Eretz Yisrael. He foresaw the dangers of a widening Diaspora that would separate Jewish communities from one another, playing havoc with the Jewish calendar. When *semichah* existed, the new lunar month could only be proclaimed based on eyewitnesses before a *beis din* of ordained rabbis. However, with the Diaspora so far flung, there would simply not be enough time for the messengers of the *beis din* to reach every Jewish community between, say, Rosh HaShanah and Yom Kippur to inform them of the proper time. Were this to happen, an individual community would be forced to set the new month based on its own calculations, which might differ from the *beis din*'s "witness set" proclamation by a day. As a result, the distinct possibility arose that one Jewish community might celebrate a holiday on a different day than another one did. To prevent this from happening, Rav Hillel, together with his *beis din*, calculated a predetermined calendar. Thus, Rav Hillel and his *beis din* purposely did not continue the 1,500-year-old tradition of granting *semichah d'oraysah* to leading rabbis of the next generation, and with them the unbroken chain came to an end.

What added to the immediacy of Rav Hillel's introduction of the set calendar was a Roman decree of a death sentence to any newly ordained rabbi. In such a situation, there was no way to physically continue the ancient *semichah*.[24]

Rav Yaakov Berav

In the sixteenth century, feeling that the time was right for this great institution to be reintroduced, Rav Berav and his *beis din* took action. They did so by invoking a law stated in the Rambam's *Mishneh Torah* (*Hilchos Sanhedrin* 4:11) which apparently permitted the reinstatement of *semichah*: "Should all the rabbis living in Eretz Yisrael agree to appoint judges and ordain them, then their declaration of *semichah* is official. These newly ordained rabbis have the power to judge cases of fines, administered lashes, and also to ordain others."[25]

Based on this seemingly explicit Rambam, Rav Yaakov Berav reintroduced *semichah*. In an impressive ceremony in the Bannai Synagogue in Safed in 1538, he was ordained by all the rabbis and immediately ordained four other rabbis: Rav Yosef Karo (author of the *Shulchan Aruch*), Rav Moshe Tarani (known as the Mabit), Rav Moshe Galante, and a young genius by the name of Rav Moshe Cordovero. It was a momentous occasion in the history of Jewish spiritual revival.

The reason for Rav Berav's move was altruistic. A teenage fugitive from the

The Bannai Synagogue of Safed

Spanish Expulsion of 1492, Rav Berav personally empathized with the sad predicament of his Spanish brethren. Many, like himself, had been cast penniless out of their homelands. The devastating disruption to these peoples' lives and the struggle for simple survival that followed, very often drove spiritual considerations far, far away. Simply rebuilding their shattered physical existence was the most that many of them could focus on. Only the most exceptional of men, like Rav Berav and Rav Levi Chaviv, clung to the tree of Torah life regardless of the circumstances. Recognized as a brilliant scholar in his youth, Rav Berav became Chief Rabbi of Fez, Morocco, at the age of eighteen. Later, in Egypt, he was a member of the Cairo Beis Din. Eventually, he settled in Safed, where he open-ed a yeshivah.

One of the most unfortunate outcomes of the Spanish Inquisition was the predicament of Jews who succumbed to threats of torture and became Marranos, Jewish converts to Christianity. Many only renounced their faith in order to remain alive, but continued to cling to Torah practice clandestinely. As the years passed, some of these converts left Spain and desired to openly return to their faith. According to Torah Law, the sins they committed while living in Spain as Marranos were punishable with Divine excommunication (*kares*). The transgression of such grave prohibitions cannot be atoned for even by the most sincere and wholehearted repentance. There is only one method of ameliorating the effects of this dire sin — lashes (*malkus*). The Mishnah (*Makos* 3:15) states, "Anyone who deserves *kares*, once lashed by the court, is freed from his Divine punishment, as the verse says, 'Then your brother shall be dishonored before you' — once he has been dishonored by receiving lashes, then he is your brother." Thus, such punishment freed the offender from Divine retribution. However, as we mentioned previously, one of the powers which disappeared with ordination was the ability to administer lashes; only a *beis din* of ordained rabbis can convict a person and determine how many lashes may be given as an atonement for someone who is, Heaven forbid, liable for *kares*.

Rav Yaakov Berav was eager to annul the decree that hung over the heads of his brethren. Finding the answer in the *Mishneh Torah* quoted above, he proceeded to mobilize the sages of Safed to aid him in his quest to bring relief to these unfortunate Jews. However, these illustrious sages did not anticipate the repercussions that their act would have in the Torah world.

The Ralbach's Stand

Immediately after the completion of the ordination ceremony, Rav Berav sent a dignified emissary to the Holy City with a letter personally conferring *semichah* on the Rav of Jerusalem, Rav Levi Chaviv. The Ralbach, however, refused the ordination, claiming it was invalid. Rav Chaviv's dissension led to a disputation between these two *gedolei ha'dor*, expressing two sides of a Torah issue with far-reaching ramifications. In a series of responsa, each of these giants substantiated his own view with proofs from the Talmud. Ultimately, there was a stalemate between the two sides, with neither one being convinced by the proofs and refutations of the other. Yet, so basic were the issues — such as the power to declare the new month with eyewitnesses — that for generations afterwards scholars have delved into the matter, many writing long treatises on the topic.

As for the ordained rabbis of Safed, there is no record of them having used their newly gained ordination to actually inflict lashes or penalize someone with a fine. It must be noted that the ordination did not end with the first four appointments. Rav Yosef Karo went on to ordain Rav Moshe Alshich, who in turn ordained the Ari's leading disciple, Rav Chaim Vital. However, after a few generations, the granting of ordination quietly ended.

Part of the controversy between the Ralbach and Rav Berav pertained to the holiness of Jerusalem over other cities in Eretz Yisrael. The Ralbach contended that the sages of Safed erred when they reintroduced *semichah* without consulting the sages of Jerusalem. Claimed the Ralbach: when the Rambam wrote that *all* the sages in Eretz Yisrael must agree to ordination, this certainly included Jerusalem. The fact that the sages of Jerusalem were a minority was immaterial.[26] As further substantiation, he quoted the verse, "From Zion comes forth Torah, and the word of God from Jerusalem." Jerusalem should never be inferior to Safed or any other city, even during an era when most of the sages do not reside there.

The Middle Years

After Rav Levi Chaviv died, around 1542, Rav Shlomo Sirilio became the new Sephardic Rav of Jerusalem. (The city would not have an Ashkenazic Rav until decades later.) This great man was the first person to write a commentary on the *Talmud Yerushalmi*, completing Tractate *Berachos,* together with the rest of *Seder Zeraim*. His views on the laws of *shemitah* are highly regarded by today's scholars. He died in 1558.

He was followed by Rav Yosef Zaya, who presided over the community during a very difficult period in the city's history when there was simply nothing to live on. So severe were the times, that he had to leave the city and spend his last years in *chutz laAretz* (Diaspora). He corresponded with leaders of Safed and published a number of works, including *She'eris Yosef,* and *Even HaShoham*.

Around 1552, the Lion of Egyptian Jewry, Rav David ben Zimra, came to live in the Holy City. Known as the Radvaz, he had spent the last forty years leading the Cairo community, where he continued the high standards set by Rav Sholal. For Jerusalem, it was a great honor to have such a distinguished rabbi in her midst. The mentor of Rav Bezalel Ashkenazi (author of the *Shitah Mekubetzes*, whom we will discuss shortly) and Rav Yitzchak Luria (in the revealed Torah), he was one of the leading rabbis of his time. Close to ninety years old, the venerated sage lost no time in his self-appointed task of strengthening Torah in the Holy City.

His fifteen years in Jerusalem were not quiet ones. Most of the trouble came from the Arabs, as he wrote: "I left the security of my home in Egypt to ascend to Jerusalem to seek hope in my final years. But I was not allowed to enjoy my old age in peace, due to constant harassment and anxiety [from the Moslem residents of the city] — they [the harassments and anxieties] are uncountable. I reacted by turning to the Almighty and uttering, 'Haven't I suffered enough!'" [27]

Yet even in his old age he retained his vigor and vitality. Indeed, so commanding was his personality that his presence was enough to redirect certain wayward Jews back to the Torah. As is true in most Jewish communities, the level of observance by individual members varied greatly, with some more observant and some less. Many people accepted the Radvaz's words of *mussar* and returned stronger to the fold.

In 1567, the venerable sage left Jerusalem to spend his last years in Safed. As he approached the Galilean city, the entire Jewish community came out to meet him. A measure of the respect accorded the elderly sage can be ascertained from the fact that the revered, eighty-year-old Rav Yosef Karo, together with members of his *beis din*, stood first to greet him. The Radvaz dwelled in Safed for a number of years, dying sometime between 1573 and 1580. He was buried in the ancient cemetery of that city.

Just before the Radvaz left Jerusalem, the first Ashkenazic Rav of the city settled there. Rav Ephraim Fish, the grandfather of the Shaar Ephraim, moved to the Holy City around 1566 and led the Ashkenazic community until his death in 1596.

The End of the Century

Two celebrated Torah personalities lived in Jerusalem during the end of the sixteenth century: Rav Chaim Vital and Rav Bezalel Ashkenazi.

Rav Chaim Vital, a native of Safed, began his Torah career as a disciple of Rav Moshe Alshich, who granted him ordination. (As we noted earlier, Rav Alshich himself had been ordained by Rav Yosef Karo.) In his early twenties, Rav Chaim studied Kabbalah under Rav Moshe Cordovero, a brilliant mystic who lived in the city until his death shortly after the arrival of the Ari Zal (and, the reader will recall, was also a recipient of *semichah* from Rav Yaakov Berav). When Rav Cordovero died in Tamuz, 1570 (5230), Rav Chaim became the disciple of Rav Yitzchak Luria, the Ari Zal, who initiated him into the deepest secrets of Kabbalah. In fact, the Ari made it clear that his only reason for moving to Safed was to reveal all that he knew to Rav Chaim Vital. Rav Chaim was then to have sole responsibility for recording and disseminating his master's teachings. After his mentor passed away in 1572, Rav Chaim spent the next fifty years committing the Ari's teachings on the inner world of mystical Judaism to writing, and elucidating them, until his death in 1620.* His works include the

* The precedent for having one's teaching written down by leading disciples is an ancient one. The *Zohar*, written in Talmudic times, was authored by Rabbi Shimon bar Yochai, yet penned by his disciple, Rabbi Abba. Modern examples include the writings of the Baal Shem Tov and the Vilna Gaon.

Shemonah Shaarim (Eight Gates of Supernal Wisdom), as well as the prodigious *Etz Chaim*. Recognized by all as the faithful, accurate, and definitive rendering of the Ari's teachings, these influential volumes were responsible for a complete reorientation in the study of Kabbalah for all ages to come.

זה השער לד' צדיקים יבואו בו

זה ספר

שער הכונות

השער הששי מהשמונה שערים אשר חברם הרב המפורסם המקובל האלקי רבינו מוהרח"ו זלה"ה כפי מה שקיבל מרבו איש האלקים קדוש הוא המקובל האלקי, בוצינא קדישא האר"י ז"ל זיע"א אשר קבל מפי אליהו ז"ל שלהיות כי השער הזה צדיקים יבואו בו שיד הכל ממשמשים בו ונתוספו ספסלי ומה שנדפסו מעט מזעיר מדפוס סאלוניק ומה שנדפס בירושלם עה"ק חלפו והלכו. כי עד בן העיר ד' את רוחינו ונתן בלבנו הח"ם לזכות את הרבים למען ילמדו ישים רבים להדפוסי הדרה מכיסנו וממטתנו בדפוס נאה ומשובח כתבנית של הנדפס בירושלם עה"ק ודף על דף לא תחסר כל בה. ובתוספת מרובה כמבואר בההקדמה. ואנחנו נברך יהי רצון שתשרה שכינה במעשה ידינו. ויהי נועם ד' אלהינו עלינו זכות הרבנים הקדושים הנזכר יגן עלינו להבין ולהשכיל סודות תורתנו. נא גל עיני ואביטה נפלאות מתורתך ונזכה לעבוד את ד' בשמחה ולא ימוש ספר התורה הזה מפינו ומפי זרעינו וזרע זרעינו מעתה ועד עולם כיר"א. כעתירת הכו"ל

מנחם מענבין הײלפרין | שלמה מוסאיוב | דוד סיפי | יצחק נחום לעווי

פעה"ק ירושלם תוב"א

הוצאת מקור חיים

לזכרון עולם על שם הבחור הנפטר בק"ו"ש
הרב חיים עטייה נ"ע

נולד ר"ח חשון תרצ"ה, נלב"ע ה' תשרי תשכ"ג
תנצב"ה אמן

Title page of Shaar HaKavannos *by Rav Chaim Vital*

At least twice during the last decades of the sixteenth century Rav Chaim Vital lived in Jerusalem. Sometime after the passing of the Ari Zal, he moved to the Holy City and lived there until 1576. After sojourning in Egypt for a couple of years, he returned to Jerusalem until around 1585. While it is unclear why he decided to leave and where he went upon leaving the city, we do know that before returning there in 1588, he spent a few years in Egypt.

Rav Chaim Vital's saintliness and superior character were recognized by everyone, and despite his personal modesty and humility, his fame spread, until even the gentiles knew of this holy man. When the new Turkish governor, Abu Sipin, arrived in Jerusalem in the mid-1580s, he sought to increase the city's water supply by reopening the source of the Shiloach spring. It had been sealed in the time of the First Temple by King Hezekiah, when the city was under siege by Sennacherib. Sipin was told that Rav Vital was a saintly man who could determine a method to unlock the spring. He gave the Jew an ultimatum: open the spring or lose your life. For reasons unknown to us, Rav Vital chose to flee the city.[28]* Incidentally, Abu Sipin, according to gentile accounts, earned the epithet of a "witch in human form," due to his behavior towards his Jewish subjects.[29]

* See story, "The Pasha's Ultimatum," in *Bygone Days: 12th–16th Centuries*.

Rav Bezalel Ashkenazi

In 1588 (5348), Jerusalem was blessed with a Rav of the highest caliber. After living in Cairo for over fifty years, Rav Bezalel Ashkenazi moved to Jerusalem. He would remain in the Holy City for eight years, until his death in 1596. In Egypt, Rav Ashkenazi had earned a reputation as a first-rate *talmid chacham*. For seven years he studied together with Rav Yitzchak Luria, when the latter was still in Egypt.[30]

Rav Bezalel's legacy to the generations was his commentary on the Gemara, the *Shitah Mekubetzes*, published today in seven large volumes. The genius of the Shitah lay in his sifting through the commentaries of the early authorities and then weaving them together into a commentary of his own, using their exact words. To accomplish this, Rav Bezalel scrutinized all the existing Rishonim, some still in manuscript form, and chose from this one on a certain piece of Gemara, and from another one on another piece of Gemara, tying them all together with his own introductory sentences. Thus, as opposed to a cut and paste of every commentary on every topic in the Gemara, or a digest of opinions on selected topics, or a mere anthology of all existing commentaries, the Shitah gathers together the key opinions on a given topic and quotes them verbatim. So popular was his work, that it remains a standard classic in every Jewish library until today. In addition to his masterwork, he also published a volume of his responsa addressing all facets of Halachah.

Rav Bezalel Ashkenazi was a strong leader and highly respected by both the Sephardic and Ashkenazic communities. Rav Ephraim Fish, the Ashkenazic Rav, bowed to his authority. Even the Turkish authorities recognized him as the sole spokesman for the Jewish settlers.

A major goal of Rav Ashkenazi was to foster a sense of community among the disparate elements of the city's few Jewish residents. One of his achievements in this area was his success in instituting a decree by which the Ashkenazic community would give a sixth of the funds they received from *chutz laAretz* to aid the impoverished Sephardic community. Throughout most of the period covered in this volume, the Sephardic community's large and well-established network of *shelichim* ensured more funding for them than their Ashkenazic counterpart. Yet at this time, the reverse was true. Rav Ashkenazi accomplished instituting this decree by securing the support of Rav Ephraim Fish, who agreed with his efforts to strengthen the solidarity of the Jews of the Holy City.

One of Rav Bezalel's disciples during his time in Jerusalem was Rav Shlomo Adani. Rav Shlomo was left an orphan at sixteen years of age. In those times, when the head of a household died, the result was catastrophic for the other family members, who, without a welfare system, were literally left to starve. For several years the unfortunate youth lived in abject poverty, until a newcomer to the city, Rav Moshe Alchami, took him into his home. During the five years Rav Shlomo lived with Rav Alchami, he blossomed into an outstanding *talmid chacham* and began writing a commentary to the Mishnah. Shortly thereafter, he moved to Hebron. Several years

Jerusalem, viewed from Mount Scopus

later, in 1624, he finally completed the manuscript of his commentary, entitled *Meleches Shlomo*. However, right at that time, word reached him of Rav Yom Tov Heller's newly published commentary on the Mishnah, the *Tosefos Yom Tov*. Realizing that the two works attempted to elucidate the Mishnah in a similar fashion, and feeling that his work was therefore redundant, he abandoned the idea of printing it. The work would remain in manuscript form for two hundred and fifty years, until 1886. At that time, it was published by the famous Ram publishers of Vilna, who recognized its genius and included it in their complete edition of the Mishnah.

In 1594 (5354), a very special man visited Jerusalem. Rav Yosef Tarani, known as the Maharit, sojourned for a short time in the Holy City. He wrote of his visit: "Since I was privileged from on High to stand in the courtyards of Hashem's [palace]... I committed myself to the study of the Temple in great detail, concerning its location and all its physical elements. Isn't it known that as long as one is studying about the Temple, it is as if he is rebuilding it? Therefore, I set forth to write down whatever I discovered about the Temple."[31] He called his work *Derech HaKodesh*.

Rav Menachem Lunzano

There was one other Jew who stood out during the time of Rav Bezalel Ashkenazi. This was Rav Menachem Lunzano. Though he was employed as the community's scribe, his true nature, full of depth of soul, aspired to increase the honor of the Torah. Poet, author, *chazan* (cantor), *talmid chacham*, and lover of his fellow Jew: all were aspects of Rav Menachem Lunzano.

A native Jerusalemite, Rav Menachem was a superb Torah scholar, who humbly accepted his lot of constant impoverishment. One seemed to play on the other: Whereas the Mishnah in *Pirkei Avos* (*Ethics of the Fathers* 3:21) tells us that "If there is no flour [sustenance], there is no Torah," the worse Rav Menachem's physical plight became, the more he seemed to grow in Torah scholarship. His magnum opus was a work called *Shetai Yados* (Two Hands), which was actually a combination of ten separate works. Some of these dealt with the *mesorah* (literally, "tradition," here referring to cantilation, paragraph placement, etc.) of the *sefer Torah* and the translation of strange words found in the Talmud. Some used poetic license to instruct in Halachah and *mussar*.

Concerning the interplay of Torah study and *mussar*, Rav Lunzano wrote: "As one toils more and more in Torah, his soul becomes illuminated and his fear of Heaven increases. The more one toils in Torah, the less he needs to read books of *mussar*. But should he become lax in Torah study, then reading *mussar* books will have very little effect on him."[32]

With the passing away of Rav Bezalel Ashkenazi in 1596, a vacuum was created in the leadership of the Holy City. Rav Ephraim Fish, too, passed away at this time. No great Torah personalities came forward to lead the flock, neither in the Sephardic nor Ashkenazic communities. Of course, there were scholars in Jerusalem, and basic queries from her residents could be answered. However, complex questions from around the world no longer made their way to the city, and in fact, if exceedingly difficult questions arose in Jerusalem itself, they were sent to the *rabbanim* in Safed and Egypt. With all this, though, the spiritual legacy of Rav Chaim Vital and the leadership provided by Rav Ashkenazi provided strength and stability for Jerusalem for years to come.

Sheik al-Yehud

While Jerusalem could not boast of having scholars of the caliber of Rav Ashkenazi and the like at the end of the sixteenth and in the early seventeenth centuries, it was served by God-fearing individuals who were genuinely concerned for the welfare of the community. One of these men was Rav Gedaliah Cordovero, the son of the great kabbalist, Rav Moshe Cordovero, who was a *rav* in the city at the turn of the century. In addition to his post as *rav*, he had been selected by the *kadi* to serve as the Sheik al-Yehud — the Jewish elder who officially represented the community to the Ottoman authorities. As spokesman to the government for his people, Rav Cordovero did everything possible to better their lot.

As we noted before, Rav Gedaliah's father was the pre-eminent mystic in Safed in the period before the Ari's arrival. A prolific writer whose works are still popular today, his writings remained in manuscript form for many years after his death. His wife sold her husband's colossal commentary on the *Zohar*, *Ohr HaYakar,* to an Italian scholar, Rav Menachem Gazariya, himself a noted kabbalist, who recognized the value of the work. Thirty-five years after Rav Moshe's passing, many of his manuscripts were in the possession of his son, Rav Gedaliah. While in Jerusalem, Rav Gedaliah sold his father's commentary on *Sefer Tikunim* and his commentary on the Siddur called *Tehillah L'Moshe*, to Rav David Costro. Though both works together were valued at two hundred *grushim*, a fantastic sum, Rav Gedaliah accepted one hundred and twenty *grushim* — still an impressive amount of money, sufficient to support an average family for over a year.[33]

As we mentioned in the Overview, the Turkish overlords of Jerusalem generally perceived their Jewish subjects as impoverished. Even if a Jew had some means, he was careful to disguise the fact, for whenever the Turks sensed that a Jew had money, they devised schemes to force it out of him. This required a precarious balancing act: on the one hand, the Jews were careful not to dress and act ostentatiously. On the other hand, they had to make sure they were not too inconspicuous, for then the Turks would suspect that they had something to hide. The trick was to be inconspicuously inconspicuous. Thus Rav Costro, afraid that the authorities might discover that he was wealthy, carefully hid the manuscripts away and made sure not to drop completely out of public sight.

Rav Gedaliah published two works of his father: *Ohr Ne'erav* and *Zivchei Shelamim*, and his own commentary on Hebrew and Aramaic words, entitled *Cheshek Shlomo*. He was close to the Maharit, Rav Yosef Tarani, several years his elder. Indeed, of the scant information we have of this period, one detail that has come down to us is the fact that Rav Gedaliah and the Maharit once had a lengthy discussion concerning the halachic status of Eglon. This was a town in Transjordan, and the question arose as to whether the Jews who lived there were required to keep two days Yom Tov or not.[34]

Although we don't know with certainty, Rav Cordovero most likely died sometime in the early 1620s. It was right around that time that the Shelah HaKodesh came to the City of Glory. With his arrival, the gates of Divine beneficence would reopen, and the grandeur of Torah and the holiness of Jerusalem would blend together once again.

Notes

1. Letter of Ramban, pub. *B'yemei HaBinayim*, pp. 135–136.
2. History of Crusade period culled from various sources, including *The Crusaders in the Holy Land, B'yemei HaBinayim,* and *Toldos Chachmei Yerushalayim*.
3. *Otzar Masa'os*, pp. 15–44.
4. See also *Seder HaDoros*, year 4900.
5. *Tevuos HaAretz,* p. 443.

6. Letter of Ramban, pub. *B'yemei HaBinayim*, pp. 135–136.
7. *Luach Eretz Yisrael*, vol. 9, p. 123.
8. Essay by Yeshaya Shachar, *Chosmo shel HaRamban*, published in *B'yemei HaBinayim*, pp. 137–142.
9. *Seder HaDoros*, 4954 (p. 215).
10. Based on biographical sketch by Rav Avraham Lunz, published in Introduction to *Kaftor v'Ferach*, pp. xxii–xlii.
11. *Kaftor v'Ferach*, chap. 11, pp. 282–283.
12. Ibid., p. 114.
13. Ibid., p. 283.
14. Based on Letters, *Otzar Masa'os*, pp. 111–121.
15. *Toldos Chachmei Yerushalayim*, vol. 1, p. 27.
16. *Otzar Masa'os*, p. 128.
17. *Betuv Yerushalayim*, p. 326.
18. See *HaKehillah HaYehudis b'Yerushalayim b'Meah ha-17*, p. 79.
19. *Toldos Chachmei Yerushalayim*, vol. 1, pp. 25–38.
20. Ibid., pp. 38–45.
21. Today, we have the festive meal and gifts of food to friends on Sunday (*Shulchan Aruch, Orech Chaim* 688:6). Cf. Magen Avraham's commentary where he discusses why we do not follow the halachic decision of the Ralbach.
22. *Shivchei HaAri*.
23. See *Iyr HaKodesh v'HaMikdash*, part IV, chap. 16; *Toldos Chachmei Yerushalayim*, vol. 1, pp. 48–51.
24. *Kuntras HaSemichah*.
25. *Mishneh Torah, Hilchos Sanhedrin* 4:11.
26. The reader might ask, if the Rambam said "*all*," wasn't it obvious to Rav Berav that he had to consult with the rabbis of Jerusalem? The answer is, "all," according to everyone means a *majority*. Thus, Rav Berav felt no compulsion to consult with the rabbis of Jerusalem. Since the rabbis of Safed were much more numerous than their counterparts in the Holy City, he knew that no matter what their opinion, they would be overruled. The Ralbach countered that while it is true that the majority rules, this does not obviate the necessity to consult the minority as to their opinion. Majority rule is only effective after all parties have been consulted and allowed to vote — even if the minority's opinion doesn't ultimately count.
27. *Toldos Chachmei Yerushalayim*, vol. 1, p. 73.
28. *Shem HaGedolim*, part I, *os ches*, no. 21.
29. See *HaKehillah HaYehudis b'Yerushalayim b'Meah ha-17*, p. 35.
30. Indeed, the Ari's sole writing in *niglah* (revealed Torah) was a commentary to Tractate *Zevachim*, probably an outcome of their joint studies. Unfortunately, this manuscript was destroyed in a fire in Izmir, Turkey.
31. *Toldos Chachmei Yerushalayim*, vol.1, p. 119.
32. Ibid., p. 139.
33. *Toldos Chachmei Yerushalayim*, vol. 1, p. 136 (n. 1).
34. Ibid.

David HaMelech, May He Live Forever

Mount Zion is revered as the site where King David and other kings of the House of David are buried. Today one can visit a modest hall on the ground floor of a larger structure which is said to be built on top of the actual burial cave. In this hall lies a marble slab, or cenotaph, marking the spot below which King David is buried. The entrance to the burial cave has been unknown for several centuries. The following story took place in the 1170s, at the time when the Crusaders were in control of Jerusalem. It was during that time that the Jewish traveler Rav Binyamin of Toledo passed through, and he recorded an eyewitness account of the episode.*

THE CHRISTIANS had constructed some kind of a large, elevated platform on Mount Zion. As time went by, one of the platform walls collapsed. The church patriarch called to one of his friars and told him to rebuild it, using stones from the ancient retaining walls of Mount Zion. The friar hired a dozen Arab workers and they began to remove the stones, one by one.

One morning, one of the workers invited his companion to feast with him before going to work. When they finally arrived at Mount Zion, the friar scolded them for coming late.

"Don't worry," said the Arab. "When all the other workers stop for the day, we will continue working."

As they worked alone late that afternoon, they took out a large stone, revealing the entrance to a cave.

"Let's crawl inside and see if there's a treasure there," whispered one breathlessly to the other.

Inside, they were able to walk upright. After a short passage, they found themselves at the entrance to a chamber built with marble pillars that were

* See "Sacred Places," in *From Napoleon to Beyond the Wall: 1870–1900*, for a historical synopsis of the Tomb of David.

overlaid with silver and gold. Before them they saw a gold table with a golden scepter and crown resting on it. That was the grave of King David. To the left, they saw the grave of King Solomon. Further away were the graves of other kings of Israel. Besides this, they noticed treasure chests with unknown contents.

Gathering their courage, they proceeded to enter. Suddenly, a turbulent wind struck them down on the ground. They lay there unconscious until nightfall. Then another wind whistled by them with a human voice screaming, "Arise! Get out of here at once!"

They scrambled out of the cave as fast as their legs could carry them. Petrified and in a state of shock, they dashed to the patriarch and told him everything that had occurred. Realizing that this was an ancient Jewish site, the church official thought that the Jews might help to unravel the mystery behind the Arabs' story. He therefore summoned Rav Avraham HaChassid of Constantinople, who was living in Jerusalem at the time, hoping that this saintly Jew could help explain the mysterious tale.

After hearing the Arabs' story, Rav Avraham said, "The cave is the burial place of the kings of the House of David. Tomorrow we will enter there with these Arabs and see for ourselves."

The next morning Rav Avraham and the patriarch waited for the two workers to arrive. When they failed to appear, the patriarch sent a messenger to bring them. The messenger returned and reported, "I found them lying dead in their beds!"

Shivers rippled over the listeners' bodies.

"This is a sign and a warning," said the pious Jew, "that God does not wish to show this holy spot to any human being."

The patriarch agreed. He had the entrance to the cave sealed shut and the stones returned to their place.

(Masa'os Rav Binyamin)

The Hidden Treasure

The story of the rediscovery of the Western Wall, hidden under a mound of earth and rubbish for generations, was told to Rav Moshe Chagiz (1672–1744) by one of the elders of Jerusalem who heard it in his youth from another old man. According to this version, Sultan Suleiman the Magnificent was the central figure in the story.

There is, however, evidence that the Western Wall was visible sometime earlier than the Sultan's visit in 1540. For instance, Rav Ovadiah of Bartenora wrote shortly after his arrival in 1488, "The Western Wall, a part of which is still standing, is made of great, thick stones that are larger than any I have seen in buildings of antiquity in Rome or in other lands." In the book HaKosel HaMaaravi *by Rav Yitzchak Yehudah (pp. 71–73), the author concludes that the story, albeit true, took place generations earlier, in the time of Omar al-Khattab (638 C.E.).*

The version presented here is that of Rav Moshe Chagiz. The reader should mentally replace the Sultan's name with some other earlier Mamluk Sultan or Omar to have a truer historical perspective.

IN 1540 (5300), the Sultan visited Jerusalem. His masons were laying the last stones of the gigantic wall around the city (which still stands today), the building of which he had authorized as a gesture of affection and respect towards his Jewish subjects. During his visit, he stayed in the *kadi*'s courtyard, which was located in the Moslem Quarter on the western side of the Temple Mount.

One day he noticed a elderly gentile woman carrying a sack of garbage and dumping it on an open mound of dirt and rubbish that was adjacent to the *kadi*'s residence.

Incensed at this apparent lack of respect, the ruler had the woman brought to him in order to question her concerning her behavior.

"I am of Roman descent," she told him. "I live a two-day walk from Jerusalem and am merely fulfilling the ancient edict of my forefathers. They decreed that all their descendants living in the city must throw their garbage here every day; those living nearby must bring it here twice a week, and those living within a three-day radius must bring it once a month.

"The reason," she continued, "is that this was the location of the Temple of the Jewish people. When my forefathers were unable to destroy this one wall down to its foundations, they instituted this decree, so that the last remnant of the Jews' Temple would be covered over."

The Sultan ordered her to be arrested until he could investigate the matter further. He stationed guards near the site, and whenever someone came to throw his trash there, he was questioned about it. Everyone gave the same answer, and the woman was released.

However, the Sultan was not satisfied to merely verify the woman's account. He decided to take steps to rectify this affront to the city and to his esteemed subjects. He therefore sent a proclamation throughout the city and the surrounding environs, saying that anyone who wished to find favor in the Sultan's eyes should come to his residence, where he would be amply rewarded. When a crowd gathered, he walked over to the garbage heap. Taking a handful of small coins, he scattered them over it.

"Whoever wants the coins," he announced, "should take a shovel and a sack and fill it with the dirt and refuse from the mound."

All the poor people were delighted to work. The Sultan stood and gave more incentives. Moreover, at one point he actually joined them for a while and asked his courtiers to do likewise.

Every day the mound dwindled in size, until after a month's time the hidden Wall was revealed in its entirety.

Then, by authorizing the arrest of anyone who threw garbage there, he set fear in the hearts of those who thought to continue their old custom. Furthermore, he decreed that no one should profane the area and even forbade spitting near there.

Next, he met with the leaders of the Jewish community. He wanted to convince them to rebuild the Temple, and he told them that he would be willing to pay the entire cost, no matter how great.

"We thank his Highness for his gracious offer," they replied. "But we have a tradition that only when our redeemer will come can we rebuild the Temple."

They were hinting at the halachic problems facing them (and us!) which could only be surmounted by the coming of the Mashiach. One of the problems concerned the state of ritual impurity, which, according to Torah Law, deemed them forbidden to enter the Temple Mount. Only by having the ashes of a red heifer mixed with pure water sprinkled on them would their status change. Another problem concerned the exact spot of the sacrificial altar, which only a prophet would be capable of identifying.

"Alas," the Sultan sighed. "To where shall I pray? Does not King Solomon say in the Book of Kings, 'Concerning the stranger who is not of your people Israel.... When he comes and prays towards this House....' "

As they bid the Sultan farewell, the Jews grieved that the time was not ripe for the rebuilding of the holy Temple.

(*Elei Masei*, pp. 12b–15a)

Mishmeros

In the historical portion of this chapter, we mentioned that one of Rav Yitzchak Sholal's accomplishments during his years in the Holy City was the establishment of mishmeros, groups of Jews who would pray on behalf of their brethren throughout the world. The following narrative was written by an unknown disciple of the naggid, who belonged to one of these mishmeros.

AFTER PASSOVER, 1515 (5275), our master, the *naggid* Rav Yitzchak Sholal, exhorted us: "How long will we be lazy in returning to God? How long will we fail to wake up from our slumber? When will we be able to call out to Him with our whole hearts, return to Him, and see the redemption?"

His response to these questions was to institute *mishmeros* (watches). We would be divided into groups, each one responsible to pray and fast on certain days. Our task was to act as emissaries for all Jews in the Diaspora. We would beseech the Lord to free all of us, to protect us, and to show us mercy.

Each *mishmar* was assigned one day of the week.

The 26 of Nisan, 1515, the 11th day of the Omer (the countdown between Passover and Shavuos), was selected as the first fast day. Incredible as it may sound, we were granted a sign of the redemption on that first day. The day started normally; however, to everyone's surprise, it began to rain and thunder tempestuously. The raging storm was accompanied by fierce gales. Besides its awesome strength, what made it even more unique is the fact that it nearly never rains from after Pesach until Sukkos. Rain normally only falls during the winter months.

During Shacharis (morning prayer service), while reciting the *U'vo l'Tzyon* portion of the prayer service, we heard a great and fearful noise. None of us had ever heard such a loud and eerie sound. Simultaneously, a ball of fire fell down from heaven. It landed on the church of the Holy Sepulcher and partially destroyed it. There is an ancient tradition that a destructive fire has never descended on Jerusalem. Therefore, everyone was amazed. Surely this was a sign of the redemption, and we must strengthen ourselves!

(*Toldos Chachmei Yerushalayim*, vol. 1, p. 36)

The Ari Zal's Roots

In the historical section, we noted that Rav Yitzchak Luria, the holy Ari, was born in Jerusalem and spent his early childhood there. Following are some details and stories about his birth and the monument that remained in the city after he left.

LIFE IN the Jerusalem of 1534 (5294) was quiet and uneventful. The dynamic policies of the youthful Ottoman Empire had benefited most strata of society. The future looked bright, with a promise of increased peace and prosperity for all. Only seven years before, the new government had commenced the historic project of building a vast and imposing wall around the ancient city. It would take another dozen years to complete, but the populace waited patiently for the sense of security that the new wall would provide. Furthermore, the Sultan had a benevolent relationship with his Jewish subjects.

At that time, a Jew by the name of Rav Shlomo Luria lived with his wife in the Holy City. He was a saintly man. His wife, too, was virtuous and devoted.

When Rav Luria's wife became pregnant, Eliyahu HaNavi appeared to him while he was alone in shul.

"I have been sent by God to inform you that your wife will bear you a son. You are to call him Yitzchak. He will save many Jewish souls from the grips of the *kelipos* (destructive spiritual forces) and will rectify many other souls. Furthermore, he will be a vehicle for God to reveal the hidden wisdom of Kabbalah.

Continuing, Eliyahu HaNavi warned Rav Luria: "Beware of one thing. On the day of the bris milah, do not commence the ceremony until you see me standing beside you in the synagogue. There I shall be the *sandak*." With these words, Eliyahu disappeared.

Rav Shlomo Luria, alone in the synagogue, fervently prayed, "Please, O Lord, let the words of your prophet Eliyahu come true. Don't let any of my sins prevent this wondrous blessing from reaching fruition. I am so insignificant and undeserving, and I ask You to do it for Your sake, not mine."

Eight days after the birth, the couple brought the baby to the shul at the appointed time. Rav Shlomo's friends and *rabbanim* were present, as was the *mohel*.

Rav Shlomo looked nervously around, but Eliyahu HaNavi was nowhere in sight. With no plausible reason not to continue with the ceremony, Rav Shlomo devised excuses to stall the proceedings.

He managed to delay the ceremony for more than half an hour. At that point though, people were becoming agitated and beginning to grumble. Rav Shlomo, known for his unpretentious and straightforward manner, was not acting like himself at all.

Soon a commotion started, and some individuals began to vehemently voice their feelings. Still, Rav Shlomo would not permit the *mohel* to begin. He began to cry, thinking that since Eliyahu did not come, it was a sign that — due to his own sins — this was not the child the prophet had referred to.

Suddenly, unnoticed by everyone except Rav Shlomo, Eliyahu appeared.

"Don't cry, dear servant of the Lord," said the prophet gently in Rav Shlomo's ears. "Come forward to the altar and bring your offering to God. Sit on the chair and hold your son on your lap."

Eliyahu stood beside him and placed his hands under the baby. The *mohel* performed the ceremony, believing that Rav Shlomo was the *sandak*.

As soon as the *mohel* finished, Eliyahu slipped his hands from under the baby.

"Take your son," said Eliyahu HaNavi. "From him shall shine forth a great light that will illuminate all of Israel and the entire world." With that, the prophet suddenly disappeared.

As Eliyahu had commanded, the child was named Yitzchak. *Mazal tov*'s resounded around the synagogue, and blessings for the child's future were given by all. Miraculously, by the time the baby was brought home, the scar from the circumcision had completely healed.

Yitzchak grew up in the Holy City, his house in the present-day Moslem quarter. It was obvious to all that he was a wonder child. His grasp of Torah was unbelievable, and his thirst for wisdom insatiable.

In 1542, when Yitzchak was eight, his father passed away, and soon afterwards his mother sent him to Cairo to live with his uncle. There he studied with Rav Bezalel Ashkenazi, and at the age of fifteen he married his uncle's daughter. Some twenty years later, at the request of Eliyahu HaNavi, he moved to Safed, where he initiated Rav Chaim Vital into the world of Kabbalah.

During the two and a half years that he lived and taught Kabbalah in Safed, Rav Yitzchak Luria, known as the Ari Zal, brought a light of Divine wisdom into the world not seen since the time of Rabbi Shimon bar Yochai.

After the Ari passed away, the house in which he was born and lived during his early childhood was regarded as a holy place. Efforts were made to ensure that it remained in Jewish hands. No one was allowed to act there in a lightheaded manner, and married couples were not allowed to live there. The Chida, who lived over two hundred years after the Ari Zal, wrote that he was privileged to see it. Some believe it was in the courtyard of the Ohr HaChaim Synagogue. Others say that it was located somewhere else, where it was used as a *beis midrash* for the study of Kabbalah, but was finally destroyed by the Arabs in 1948.

(*Shivchei Ari* and *Toldos Chachmei Yerushalayim*, vol. 1, p.101)

The Pasha's Ultimatum

We saw that Rav Chaim Vital sojourned in Jerusalem at different times, the last period ending when he fled for his life because of his refusal to carry out a command by the pasha (governor), Abu Sipin. Following are the details of that story.

EVERY FRIDAY at noontime, the Turkish sentries shut and bolted the gates of Jerusalem. No one could enter and no one could leave. This was done as a precautionary procedure to safeguard the Moslem inhabitants of the city. At that time, almost without exception, every male Moslem would enter the Temple Mount, where, due to our many sins, a giant mosque stood. There they would pray. From inside the mosque, water could be heard flowing underground, a small amount of which trickled out from the spring of Shiloach.

In the early 1580s, a new pasha was sent to rule the city. His name was Abu Sipin. When he ascended the Temple Mount to pray, he became curious to know more about the underground spring. He was informed that centuries earlier, in the era of the First Temple, Jerusalem was besieged by Sennacherib of Assyria. With a vast army of 180,000 men, Sennacherib prepared to destroy the city. In an attempt to weaken the enemy, the Jewish king, Hezekiah, ordered that the gushing spring of Shiloach be sealed, cutting off a vital source of water from the enemy. In addition to their mundane, earthly preparations and efforts, the Jews of ancient Jerusalem turned to their Father in Heaven in prayer, beseeching Him for Divine mercy against the fearsome enemy. Scripture testifies that God hearkened to their cries. At night, an angel descended on the enemy camp and smote the entire army dead. Sennacherib fled, only to be assassinated later by his sons. The Jews of Jerusalem rejoiced at this miraculous victory, yet they never unsealed the spring. Only a small trickle seeped through and came out into the pool of Shiloach.

Pool of Shiloach

When Abu Sipin heard this story, he was intrigued. As pasha, he was aware of the acute water shortage which constantly plagued the city. In addition to dogging the current residents, the lack of a convenient and viable water source was responsible for limiting the city's growth. Were there a way to open the spring to its full strength, he would be able to solve one of Jerusalem's oldest and most pressing dilemmas.

Turning to the communal leaders of the city, he inquired if perhaps there was someone who could reopen the spring. He was told in reply that there was a very wise Jew by the name of Rav Chaim Vital who could surely do it.

That Friday afternoon, Rav Vital was brought before the governor.

"I order you," Abu Sipin said in no uncertain terms, "to unseal the spring which your king plugged up, so that there will be fresh water for the inhabitants of the city. You have as much time as it takes me to go to the El Aqsa mosque and pray. I am told that you have the power to do it. Therefore, your failure will cost you your life!"

With these words Abu Sipin marched towards the Temple Mount.

Rav Chaim Vital returned home and contemplated his choices. It was true that as the leading kabbalist of his time he had the power to open the spring. Yet, to do so would entail making use of holy Names, which he was extremely careful not to utter unless absolutely necessary. On the other hand, the locked city gates made escape seemingly impossible.

With each passing minute, the threat to his life grew stronger. In the end, Rav Vital devised a means to escape from Jerusalem, despite the sealed gates.

When the pasha returned and found the spring of Shiloach unopened, he sent for the Jewish wise man. To his surprise and dismay, Rav Chaim Vital had managed to escape the locked city without anyone knowing of his whereabouts!

That night, safely in Damascus and away from Abu Sipin's clutches, Rav Chaim Vital fell asleep. In his dreams, his master, the Ari Zal, came and scolded him.

"Why didn't you open the spring? Didn't you know that the governor was none other than a reincarnation of Sennacherib!? Abu Sipin in Arabic means 'the father of destruction' and *cherib* also means destruction. And attached to your soul is a spark of the soul of King Hezekiah. You were presented with a golden opportunity to rectify an error which the Sages attribute to King Hezekiah. The Mishnah *Pesachim* states at the end of chapter four, 'Six things King Hezekiah did, on three of which the Sages agreed with him, and three of which they disagreed with him.' One of the three on which they disagreed with him was sealing the spring of Shiloach. He should not have done it since the prophet foretold the downfall of the enemy, and there were other sources of water which he could not dry up that the enemy had access to.

"You had the chance to rectify the error that the Sages ascribed to 'you' at that time. By doing so, you would have ushered in the beginning of the long-awaited redemption."

"But I wanted to refrain from using holy Names," protested Rav Chaim.

"I would agree with you," said the Ari Zal, "had you not come to Damascus by using those same holy Names. But since you chose to use them to escape from Jerusalem, you should have used them instead to open the spring. By doing so, you would have sanctified the name of God in the world and caused a Divine rectification."

"If so, I'll return now to Jerusalem and open the spring."

"Alas." The Ari Zal lowered his head. "It is too late. The auspicious time has passed."

(*Shem HaGedolim*, part I, no. 21)

The Miracle Worker

SOMETIME IN the mid-sixteenth century, an Ashkenazic Jew by the name of Rav Kalonimus, son of Rav Yaakov, lived in Jerusalem. He was a saintly man as well as a Torah scholar of repute. Everyone in the community respected him and honored him accordingly.

One Shabbos morning, the congregants of the Talmud Torah shul, which stood next to the Rabban Yochanan ben Zakkai Synagogue, were shocked by the sight that greeted them in their house of worship. A Moslem child lay dead on the floor! Before they could assess the situation, a squad of Arab soldiers sent by the *kadi* arrived. The Jews were accused of kidnapping the youth and murdering him.

Within minutes Jews were being rounded up and arrested. An Arab mob started gathering, the Moslems darkly murmuring and yelling out, "Murderers!" The tension mounted, and violence threatened to erupt. Jewish women cried out, "My husband is innocent." Men tried to escape, some into the synagogue, some down the alleyways. The serene beauty of Shabbos had been shattered to the core.

As a number of suspects were dragged off for interrogation, the crowd dispersed from the courtyard of the shul. Quickly, Rav Kalonimus entered the shul and approached the corpse that was lying in the aisle. He turned to the few people in the synagogue and asked them to leave him alone with the dead child. He walked over to a cupboard, and took out a quill and parchment. He wrote some holy Names on the parchment, and through a kabbalistic meditation, he revived the child. He spoke to the Arab boy and compelled him to reveal his murderer. He then made the child swear to tell the truth to the *kadi*.

Rav Kalonimus took the boy by his hand and led him through the streets of the city to the house of the *kadi*. An angry mob of Arabs stood outside the *kadi*'s house, demanding death to all the Jews. When they saw the bloodstained child walking by the side of an old Jew, they froze in silence.

Rav Kalonimus entered the house and stood before the *kadi*.

"What is this?" demanded the *kadi* dumbfoundedly.

"Here is the dead boy!" Rav Kalonimus's voice rang out. "Ask him yourself who raised a knife and killed him last night!"

The *kadi*, shocked by presence of the dead boy before him, weakly managed to command the boy to speak.

The child's parents and other Arabs had entered the house and were watching. Speaking in a low voice, the boy described the events of the previous night, and how in a fit of anger, so-and-so, a Moslem had hit him and stabbed him to death. Turning slowly, he pointed to the murderer and cried out in a chilling voice, "He killed me!"

The Arab tried to escape from the house, but was immediately apprehended by the *kadi*'s soldiers. With his hysterical confession, the spell over the boy was broken, and once again he left the land of the living. Immediately, the *kadi* ordered the release of all the Jews.

With his quick and decisive action, Rav Kalonimus had successfully diverted what might have been a genocide of the entire Jewish population of Jerusalem. However, whereas the Jews felt that they had been miraculously saved, Rav Kalonimus was upset and agitated. In order to save the community, he had had to profane the Shabbos by writing. True, the imperative of saving a life overrides the laws of Shabbos, but the necessity of having to break those laws troubled him for the rest of his life.

When he passed away, he was buried at the foot of the Mount of Olives. Shortly before his death, he requested that for the next hundred years, anyone passing his grave should throw stones on it. By voluntarily forsaking his honor and submitting himself to such a degrading and contemptuous act, he hoped to atone for his "sin."

Over the generations a custom developed concerning the stones over his grave that anyone going overseas should take one of them with him. It was a *segulah* (charm) that he would have a safe journey and would return to the Holy City.

(*Toldos Chachmei Yerushalayim*, vol. 1, pp. 98–99)

A Jew reciting Psalms at the foot of the Mount of Olives in the Kidron Valley. According to tradition, the grave of Rav Kalonimus, whose location is unknown today, is not far from where the man is sitting.

17th Century

The Silent Fervor

Adam was created holy and placed in the Garden of Eden. When he sinned and was exiled from the Garden of Eden, his rectification came about through the Jewish nation, who are collectively called "Adam" in the Torah.

They were given the Holy Land, whose sanctity is similar to that of the Garden of Eden, as the verse says in Ezekiel (36:35), "This land will be like the Garden of Eden."

Even now, in its destroyed state, it nevertheless has holiness, and is the land which God seeks to know its tidings.

The Shelah

Shelah versus a Despot

The seventeenth century was a period of tremendous spiritual growth and development for the Torah world at large. In Jerusalem, the imprint left by Rav Bezalel Ashkenazi and Rav Chaim Vital would remain visible for decades to come. In the early 1620s, the legacy of their Torah leadership would be revitalized by a Torah giant from Europe — Rav Yeshaya Horowitz, the Shelah HaKodesh.

The Prince of Prague[1]

In 1620 (5380), Rav Yeshaya Horowitz left Prague for Eretz Yisrael. At the time, he stood at the zenith of success — both worldly and spiritually. After serving as rabbi of Lvov, Posen, Cracow, Vienna, and Frankfurt, he became Chief Rabbi of Prague, the crown jewel of European Jewry. Wherever he went he opened a yeshivah and raised new disciples, disseminating Torah to followers who drank his words thirstily. By 1620, at the age of sixty, his status and reputation as an outstanding Torah sage ranked him alongside the greatest of all the generations.

Rav Yeshaya had harbored a desire to ascend to the Holy Land for many years, but was unable to do so because of his myriad communal and familial responsibilities. When he felt the time was right, he began making his preparations. Realizing that the community would exert tremendous pressure to try and convince him to stay if word of his plans got out, he proceeded very discreetly. In fact, almost no one knew of his intent until shortly before his departure. One of his highest priorities was to entrust a repository of his wisdom as an everlasting legacy to the children and grandchildren he would be leaving behind. Thus, one of his preparations, undertaken long before divulging his aspiration to move to Eretz Yisrael, was to write a compendium of Torah wisdom, *mussar* (guide to ethical conduct and character perfection), and *hashkafah* (Torah worldview). He entitled it *Sh'nei Luchos HaBris* ("Two Tablets of the Covenant"), known by its acronym, *Shelah*. Though he wrote it for his children and grandchildren, it has long since become the property of the entire Jewish people, a legacy and testament of man's quest to strive for perfection and acquire knowledge of God. Unable to complete it before his departure, Rav Horowitz finished it in Jerusalem.

Shortly before leaving Europe, perhaps somewhat regretful over the impending separation from his family and aware of the great difficulties about to face him on his long trip, he nevertheless told his son, "What can I do, my son? This move has been decreed from on High."[2]

His journey by land and sea took many months and entailed great dangers for himself, his wife, and their personal attendant. While at sea his ship was attacked by pirates. "The Lord saved us," he testified, "for He sent a strong wind from the south and we were able to sail speedily along, while their ships lingered behind." On their arrival in Syria, they traveled by caravan inland to the city of Aleppo, near the Turkish border. From there they headed south to Hamath and then continued on to Damascus. In each city, the Jewish community honored the rabbi in a manner befitting one of his stature and beseeched him to remain with them. However, he was single-minded in his determination to reach Eretz Yisrael.

The news of his approach aroused great excitement throughout Eretz Yisrael, especially in Safed and Jerusalem. Since the time of Rav Levi Chaviv a hundred years earlier, the two cities had vied for newcomers. Rav Horowitz was certainly no ordinary Jew, and each city realized that his presence would give a dynamic boost to the spiritual level of the community.

"A two-man delegation from Safed came to me while I was in Damascus," he wrote. "They greeted me and implored me to settle among them. In the name of the city councilors, they offered me the position of Chief Rabbi.

"'Am I not on my way to Safed?' I answered them evasively, not wanting to reveal to them my secret desire to settle in Jerusalem. 'Upon my arrival we will discuss the matter fully.'"

The following day Rav Horowitz set out from Damascus. On the way, he was met by an emissary from Jerusalem, a respected rabbi of European descent. The rabbi presented him with an official letter signed by all the rabbis of Jerusalem that earnestly requested him to accept the post of Chief Rabbi of the Holy City. They also granted him special privileges, including free living quarters and other subsidies.

Rav Horowitz considered the positions he had been offered. Whereas Safed did have a larger Jewish population, Jerusalem's population was by no means insignificant — the Sephardic community alone comprised some five hundred families. More importantly for the European Rav Horowitz, Jerusalem had more Ashkenazic Jews than Safed. Jerusalem seemed to be a better choice from a purely material standpoint as well. Her inhabitants were well protected from invaders by Suleiman's magnificent wall, built seventy-five years earlier, while Safed was open and more vulnerable to attack. Finally, there was the not insignificant fact that basic commodities were more readily available in Jerusalem than in Safed.

The Rav of Jerusalem

"I accept your offer," he declared to the emissary from Jerusalem. "May the Almighty give me life and good health so that I may guide the Jerusalem community according to Torah law. As a loyal shepherd, may I be granted the strength not to stand as a silent witness to the transgressions which undoubtedly caused so much destruction in the past. My goal will be to establish and intensify the inherent truth of Torah in each and every aspect of life in the city."[3]

Rav Yeshaya Horowitz entered the Holy City in Cheshvan, 1621 (5382). The *parshah* of the week was *Vayetzei*, where Scripture states: "How awesome is this place.... This is the gate of Heaven" (*Genesis* 28:17). He was respectfully greeted by all the *rabbanim* of the city, Sephardic and Ashkenazic alike, with all the honor due both him and his position. An apartment near the Ashkenazic synagogue became his new home.

With bright hopes for the future, he immediately set to work on all fronts, including communal involvement and writing. At that time he began his commentary to the Siddur, which he called

Title page of Sh'nei Luchos HaBris *by Rav Yeshaya Horowitz*

Shaar HaShamayim (in commemoration of his first Shabbos in Jerusalem). Furthermore, he completed his *Sh'nei Luchos HaBris*. As Chief Ashkenazic Rabbi, and also a compelling *darshan*, Rav Horowitz naturally integrated into the community on every level.

The year after his arrival was *shemitah*, the Sabbatical year. In those days, produce was not always readily available, and most people lived at or below the poverty level. With the advent of *shemitah*, produce would become even more scarce, and prices would skyrocket. Under such circumstances, many residents of the city were inclined to follow the most lenient opinions concerning the laws of *shemitah*. Rav Horowitz, however, felt differently. "I thought to myself: I am obligated to fulfill this mitzvah more than they. If need be, I must be willing to sell the coat off my back. Didn't the Almighty tell me: 'Why did you come from a land where you were exempt from this mitzvah to a land where you are obligated?' Furthermore, everyone who immigrates to Eretz Yisrael is doing so in order to sanctify himself."[4]

Within two years Rav Yeshaya completed his commentary on the Siddur. The first edition appeared with the approbation of Rav Yoel Sirkish, known by his acronym, the Bach, who wrote: "When we read his [Rav Horowitz's] writings, we feel a holiness from on High descend into every one of our limbs. This is a sign that his books were written for the sake of Heaven in order to aid the coming generations."

The Sultan's Empire

At this juncture in history, calm reigned in Jerusalem. The relations between the Jews and their Moslem and Christian neighbors were relatively peaceful, and law and order prevailed. The Ottoman Empire, as vast as it was,

Constantinople, capital of the Ottoman Empire

established a hierarchy of power which somewhat guaranteed a sense of security and stability throughout the realm. The center of the empire was in Constantinople, where the Sultan and his royal court resided. Surrounding him was the imperial court, called the Upper Gate. The Vizier was his chief minister, and he had a chief of staff as well.

The empire was divided into geographical areas, or provinces, each of which had a royally appointed governor who was directly responsible to Constantinople. These governors were appointed for indefinite periods of time. While they were ultimately answerable to the capital, they nevertheless had a high degree of autonomy and wielded a great deal of power. The provincial capital of the Middle East was Damascus. From the provincial capitals, deputies were dispatched to govern the individual cities and townships. These deputies, or pasha's, were appointed by the governor, and like him, they served for indefinite terms.

Parallel to, and independent of, the executive branch, there was a judicial branch, or more precisely, judicial network. It was comprised of civil judges called *kadis*. Unlike the mayors, who owed their allegiance to the governor, these judges were appointed directly by the Sultan. Also, in contrast to the mayors, the *kadis* generally served one-year terms. All of the major cities enjoyed the presence of a *kadi*, even those that were not capitals. Their job was both to administer the empire's law code and adjudicate cases. The local *kadi*'s word was the law, and there was no recourse to a higher court. Barring intercession from the executive branch, the *kadi* was the only and final authority for the dispensation of justice. Unfortunately, the entire system did little to discourage graft and corruption, and abuse of office was far from uncommon. The *kadi* in particular was open to bribery — being appointed for such a short time meant that he was never settled in a community long enough to become sympathetic to it. As a result, he was usually more interested in accruing as much personal benefit as he could during his brief tenure. This was not to say he had a completely free hand — if his excesses went too far, the Sultan would not give him another appointment — but there was still ample room for illicit activities. If stuck with a particularly crooked *kadi*, the populace could always hope that his replacement would be an improvement.

Kadi

In addition to all the above, the Sultan himself maintained a nominal presence throughout the empire by having a small garrison of imperial solders stationed in each major city. These garrisons had no military or police status;

rather, their function was to remind the citizens that they lived under the authority of the Ottoman Empire. In Jerusalem the garrison was stationed in the fortress of Migdal David (Citadel of David) located just inside the Jaffa Gate.

Each year, when a new *kadi* arrived in Jerusalem, the Jewish leaders welcomed him to their city and gave him a customary gift of thirty *grushim*. They then gave him ten more each month. The local Moslems and Christians did likewise. The same applied with a new mayor sent from Damascus.

A Despot Usurps the Crown[5]

Although far from perfect, this system of government served the empire well. However, in the early seventeenth century, a tyrant would descend on Jerusalem and play havoc with both the system and with people's lives. At the end of Teves, 1625 (5385), a ruffian by the name of Mohammed Farouk entered the Holy City. Backed by three hundred armed soldiers, he deposed the mayor and declared himself absolute ruler of Jerusalem. Unfortunately, there was no recourse to Damascus, for Farouk had bribed the governor of Damascus himself to grant him rulership of the Holy City! In effect, the governor had consented to the establishment of an independent fiefdom within his province. The token force of the Sultan was also of no help, being vastly outnumbered by Farouk's mercenary army.

From day one Farouk instituted a reign of terror, demanding bribe money and threatening anyone who refused to obey him with imprisonment. No one — neither Jew, Moslem, nor Christian — was spared from his greed and threats, aimed at anyone with money or precious valuables. He threatened, beat, tortured, and imprisoned — whomever and whenever he wanted. For well over a year, he subjected the citizens of Jerusalem to unbearable servitude.

Within the first month, the one-eyed Farouk succeeded in extorting a record 3,000 *grushim* from the Jewish community alone.

During this time, the city was at least fortunate to have an honest *kadi*. In vain the *kadi* tried to reprimand the tyrant, initially using a soft-touch approach. Finally, in a burst of anger, he publicly scolded the tyrant. Infuriated, Farouk drew his sword to smite the *kadi*, and only quick action by the judge's attendants prevented him from doing so.

Next the *kadi* ordered the courthouse closed for two days. He hoped that his action would provoke the local Arabs to kill Farouk or exile him from the city. But to his dismay, the Arab leaders sought to act as mediators between him and the tyrant.

With his tenure up, the *kadi* left the city without even waiting to greet his replacement. The new *kadi*, an elderly man whose arrival had been delayed, sent a deputy to temporarily officiate in his stead.

In the interim, Farouk designated his brother-in-law, Ibrahim Aga, as second-in-command. Aga's first "duty" was to oppress the Jerusalemites mercilessly. He and his soldiers entered the Arab *shuk* (marketplace) and arrested various well-to-do Arab merchants and imprisoned them. They were only released after a large ransom was paid.

When the Arabs heard of the arrests, some sought to flee from the city. When he found this out, he locked the city gates and had them guarded by soldiers. With this action, no one could escape his clutches and notify the world outside about the atrocities being committed in the city. Thus, the Jerusalemites were captives within their own city, prisoners of a ruthless despot. Unable to get a message to the governor in Damascus or to the imperial court in Constantinople, the residents of the city were entirely at Farouk's and Aga's mercy.

Farouk's Reign of Terror

When Adar began, Ibrahim Aga sent for the leaders of the Jewish community. In the name of Farouk, he demanded an immediate payment of 5,000 *grushim*. They pleaded with him to withdraw his outrageous demand. The destitute community was simply incapable of paying such an exorbitant sum. Miraculously, Aga somewhat softened his stance and granted them one night to come up with a counter-offer.

After a long meeting, the group returned and proposed to pay half the amount originally demanded. Aga consented, but placed heavy pressure on them to pay almost immediately, which was nearly impossible. Each new day was filled with fear of sudden reprisals. It was dangerous to walk freely in the streets and alleyways of the city, and all the city's residents went into hiding.

In Nisan, the new *kadi* finally arrived. Instilled with new hope, the Jerusalemites came out of hiding and pleaded their case before him.

Mohammed Farouk also came out to greet the new *kadi*, welcoming him with great fanfare and bribing him lavishly. He then had the commander of a squad of soldiers hand a forged imperial document, or *firman*, to the *kadi*. The news in the "*firman*" was grim indeed — a supposed decree from the Sultan to expel all but forty Jews from the Holy City!

Shocked at this turn of events and unaware of the duplicity, the panicked and powerless Jews frantically tried to appease all those involved with bribes. The *kadi*, the commander, and Farouk all received large sums of money to overlook the "imperial" decree.

In Iyar, Ibrahim Aga called one of the important leaders, Rav Shmuel Tardiola, to appear before him. His son Rav David, fearful of what might befall his father, volunteered to go in his stead. Together with one of the elders of the community, Rav David went to face Aga.

"Where is your father?" Aga demanded.

"If it pleases my lord, my father, your servant, is very preoccupied with earlier requests which you have ordered him to fulfill. I, too, am at your service, ready to do whatever you request."

Aga looked at the elder. "And you! Why did you complain to the *kadi* against me?"

"I never uttered a word," he protested.

Ibrahim called one of his captains and ordered him to beat and torture the two hapless men. Rav David was publicly flogged, mercilessly beaten until he was almost dead. Only when Aga was promised 2,000 *grushim* was he released.

The situation had reached critical proportions. The danger of being arrested forced everyone to go into hiding. The yeshivos were forced to close their doors, and services in the synagogues ceased. The soup kitchen for the poor no longer functioned. Jews were forbidden to go the Western Wall. Great rabbis like Rav Yeshaya Horowitz were living in cramped quarters, subsisting on a meager diet of vegetables and water. Fortunately, Rav Horowitz had completed his *Sh'nei Luchos HaBris* and shipped it back to Europe before the days of evil threatened his life.

A visiting Italian Jew wrote: "They [Farouk and his minions] promise, but do not fulfill. When they are in a rage, they are like a wild bull from which one must flee. Things grow worse daily, and it seems that they have been given power to destroy and victimize, *chas v'shalom* (God forbid), whatever and whomever they please."

Reaction from Damascus

News of what had befallen Jerusalem finally reached the ears of the governor in Damascus. In order to dislodge Farouk and question him concerning his activities, he contrived to lure him to the capital. In a cunning attempt to appeal to the tyrant's vanity, the governor commanded him to come to Damascus in order to lead an army against the Persians, with whom the Ottomans were at war at the time. At first Farouk refused, sensing a trap. However, the *kadi* reasoned with him: Do not be afraid. You must go because the governor is your superior, and if you defy him, he will certainly send an army to overthrow you. I will write him a letter praising you as a sincere leader. This will disprove any testimony which he might have heard about you.

On 9 Tamuz, 1625 (5384), Mohammed Farouk left Jerusalem for Damascus, with Ibrahim Aga at his side. He left his second brother-in-law, Ottman Aga, in command.

After a few weeks, Ottman summoned the Sheik al-Yehud, Rav Shimon Cohen, and informed him that as temporary ruler in Farouk's absence, it was fitting for him to receive 1,000 *grushim* from the Jewish community. He spoke in a soft, gentle voice. In the end, Ottman agreed to the "mere" sum of 500 *grushim*. The community rejoiced, thinking that although Ottman was no angel, he was at least more reasonable and easier to deal with than his wicked brother-in-law.

The Trap

Over the next month, the quiet that prevailed in the city seemed to bear this hope out, and throughout the month of Av, a sense of stability returned to the city. Still, no formal activities were resumed.

On Shabbos, 11 Elul, the Jews felt safe enough to pray in their synagogues. Unfortunately, their all-too-brief and fragile sense of security was to be momentarily shattered. In the middle of services, Ottman and his army suddenly stormed into the shuls and arrested fifteen of the community's leaders. Among them were Rav Horowitz, Rav Shmuel ibn Sid, and Rav Yitzchak Chavilio.*

* See story, "The Unforgettable Shabbos," in *Bygone Days: 17th Century*.

Immediately after Shabbos, the shell-shocked community dispatched an urgent message to Damascus deploring the beastly act. Aside from this, the hard-pressed populace attempted to collect ransom money to secure the release of the hostages. With communal and individual funds depleted, they turned to their Arab neighbors, who lent them the money at a 50% interest rate. Within two weeks all but six were freed, and by Rosh HaShanah they were released as well. In all, Ottman Aga netted 20,000 *grushim* in exchange for the fifteen leaders.

Migdal David

Insurrection

Tensions remained high throughout Tishre and Cheshvan.

On 2 Kislev, Mohammed Farouk returned from Damascus, having successfully pacified the governor and allayed the suspicions against him. With much trepidation, the communal dignitaries approached him and gave him the customary donation of 30 *grushim*. Claiming that most of the money in his coffers was depleted due to his recent military campaign against the Persians, Farouk demanded 1,000 *grushim*. This time he reassured them that no other demands would be placed on them.

Three weeks later, Farouk gained entrance to the fortress of Migdal David, with the intent of overcoming the Sultan's soldiers who were stationed there. With drawn swords, he and his men drove the imperial forces out of the city and took control of the fortress.

His move was a declaration of insurrection against the Sultan, and now he was in great danger. However, whatever his mad designs, the megalomaniac found himself well supplied. The citadel contained stockpiles of weapons — both light artillery and cannon — as well as storerooms full of wheat, barley, and other produce. On the other hand, the oppressed populace felt themselves in greater danger than ever. They were utterly defenseless and completely at the madman's mercy.

Farouk prepared for war, securing the fortress and fortifying the city walls. When Damascus got wind of his insubordinate actions and sent a communique questioning his behavior, he answered in a very cunning fashion. He claimed that he had seen that the fortress was improperly run and had therefore decided to expel the incompetent Turkish garrison and replace it with his own men. The *kadi* added his own letter substantiating Farouk's claim.

At the end of Teves, one of Farouk's henchmen burst into the house of Rav Yitzchak Gaon, a wealthy scholar and one of the leaders of the community.

"Where is he?" the thug shouted. "He promised me 10 *grushim*!"

"He's not here," Rav Yitzchak's wife answered.

At the time, Rav Yitzchak actually was home, studying in a room upstairs. Upon hearing the commotion downstairs, he quickly locked the door to the attic, climbed out a window, and jumped into a neighbor's courtyard.

The henchman searched the house. When he saw the locked attic door, he broke it open with a hatchet. Fortunately, Rav Yitzchak had fled to safety.

However, the thug was not to be appeased. Leaving Rav Yitzchak's house, he made his way to the residence of Rav Yaakov ibn Amram, the Jewish physician. Rav Yaakov was apprehended and locked up for ten days, at which time he was ransomed for the sum of 3,000 *grushim*.

The situation in the city was intolerable, and there did not seem to be any immediate relief in sight. Under such hopeless circumstances, many Jews, like their Arab neighbors, fled from the city. Despite the guards Farouk had set around the city's gates, escape was not completely impossible. At first, only a few left. But as the dangers escalated and starvation set in, more and more people successfully snuck out of the city.

For the leaders and wealthier members of the community, the question was not so simple: were the leaders to desert the city, it might precipitate a mass exodus. With no Jewish presence, all property — including the yeshivos and synagogues — would be prey to Arab vandalism. If the wealthy Jews fled, Farouk would crush the impoverished remnant. Furthermore, the city's Arab residents, to whom the entire community owed vast sums of money, might interpret their decision to leave as an attempt to renege on their obligations and attack them in a fit of rage.

Facing unbelievable pressures, Rav Yeshaya Horowitz and the Ashkenazic rabbis decided to flee from the lion's den. Confronted by imminent danger of capture and imprisonment, they fled for their lives, leaving whatever possession that remained them behind. Rav Horowitz went to Safed and later to Tiberias, while others went to Ramla.

Farouk's Fatal Error

For twelve full months, Jerusalem had been turned upside down and shaken to the core. Mohammed Farouk's heart never softened to the plight of his pathetic subjects. His megalomania had no boundaries, and his one-track mind knew no consideration other than personal aggrandizement.

His fatal error came when he overran the fortress and earned the epithet of insurgent. Although he succeeded in fooling the governor in Damascus, the Sultan was not so naive.

Around the time all these events were unfolding, the Sultan's commander-in-chief was on a military campaign against Persia. Farouk, knowing that he stood on shaky ground, decided to take the initiative and visit the commander in order to defend his takeover of the fortress. Ibrahim Aga accompanied him to the Persian front. Upon presenting himself, Farouk was immediately imprisoned on charges of insurrection, for an indefinite period of time. Aga, making himself out to be a simple subordinate, managed to remain free.

In a display of fealty to the Sultan, the governor in Damascus sent an army against Ottman, demanding his immediate surrender. Ottman's answer was to prepare for battle. The gates were barricaded with rocks, cannons were positioned on the walls, and red flags of war were raised over the city. Additionally, he stole food supplies from the city's residents in order to supplement the reserves from the fortress.

The legions from Damascus remained in Ramla for two months, hoping Ottman's resolve would crumble under the imminent threat facing him. However, Ottman stood firm, and in the end, the governor's forces left. The entire episode served to strengthen Ottman's arrogance, and he prided himself as the victor in a battle of nerves.

In the meantime, the *kadi* received a threatening letter from Constantinople, where his conduct had come under suspicion. Realizing the danger that faced him, he left the city so as not to be implicated as an accomplice to Ottman's insurrection. On 15 Adar, 1626, the date of his departure, Jerusalemites rejoiced.

The new *kadi* refused to enter Jerusalem. Instead, he demanded that Ottman relinquish his hold on the fortress and come to him in Ramla. Refusal, he said, would force him to return to Constantinople where he would denounce Ottman to the Sultan. The self-styled warlord refused to budge.

True to his word, the *kadi* returned to Constantinople. Upon his arrival, he found that two rabbis from Jerusalem were trying to get an audience with the Sultan. Rav Shmuel ibn Sid and Rav Shmuel Tardiola had been sent by the desperate community to plead on their behalf to the imperial court. The *kadi* confirmed their words and added the latest news.

Hearing of Ottman's incredible audacity, the enraged Sultan immediately dispatched an army to Jerusalem to crush the rebellion.

At the end of Sivan, before the Sultan's forces crossed into Eretz Yisrael, Ibrahim Aga returned from Persia with a high-ranking Turkish officer. Eager to free his brother-in-law, Aga had struck a deal with the commander in chief. As he explained to his brother Ottman, if the city were to be relinquished to the Sultan, Farouk would be liberated from prison.

Ottman, however, was enjoying his reign and was more concerned for his own gratification than the welfare of his brother-in-law. He therefore convinced Aga to join him, regardless of what would become of Farouk. By trickery, they managed to keep the Turkish officer in the city, all the while treating him royally.

The End of a Tyrant

Shortly after all this transpired, Farouk successfully escaped from prison and made his way to Jerusalem. When he heard of his brother-in-law's self-coronation, he burst in on Ottman in the upper tower of Migdal David and slew him. Ibrahim apparently managed to weasel his way back into Farouk's good graces, although nothing more is mentioned of him in the historical record.

All that summer, tensions were high. Arrests and floggings continued, and some women even were imprisoned.

On Hoshannah Rabbah, two of the communal leaders, Rav Yaakov ibn Amram and Rav Yitzchak Gaon, were arrested for no reason and thrown in jail without bond. The following day, Simchas Torah, the despairing Jews were unable to rejoice because of their tremendous sorrow. The climax to this bitter episode came eight days later, when the two "criminals" were publicly flogged inside the synagogue. Not content to merely lash them, their tormentor placed a spiked metal ball between their clasped hands before tightly binding them.

Offering to free the unfortunate men if enough ransom was paid, Farouk laughed when he saw the "precious" items brought by the people to redeem their beloved leaders — kitchen pots and simple saucers. The Jews were penniless.

Soon after this, Farouk received a final ultimatum from Damascus: Leave Jerusalem or the Sultan's army will destroy you.

On the night of 12 Kislev, Farouk had a nightmare. He dreamt that an old, well-dressed man stood before him. The man reached over and started to strangle him. Farouk screamed and asked, "Who are you?"

"I am David HaMelech!" he answered. "You will surely die if you sleep another night in this city!"

Farouk woke up, distraught and shaken over the intensity of the vivid dream. He immediately ordered several camels to be laden with the plunder he had managed to extract from the residents of Jerusalem during his reign of terror. Within a few hours he deserted the city forever, and nothing more is known of him.

The twelfth of Kislev remained a day of rejoicing in the Holy City for years to come.

Rebuilding Shattered Lives

The aftermath of Farouk's heinous ransacking of lives and possessions left the Jewish community shattered. Its population was depleted by two thirds, and only a thousand souls remained. The tyrant's insatiable greed had drained the populace of what little wealth they possessed, and mountainous debts had accumulated — more than 50,000 *grushim*, a sum worth a million dollars today. Children had been without schooling for over a year and a half, and basic necessities were lacking, causing malnutrition and sickness. Also, the psychological trauma engendered by the brutal subjugation would take years to heal.

The most pressing issue facing the community, and one which would dog them for years to come, was the prodigious debt they had incurred trying to pacify Farouk and Ottman. Large amounts had been borrowed from Arab neighbors who were now clamoring for repayment. With interest rates as high as fifty percent, the impoverished Jews felt overwhelmed and desperate.

Emissaries were sent to Jewish communities in Italy's city-states, Bohemia, Bavaria, Netherlands, Poland, and Austria. A fifty-page chronicle of the tragic period, called *Chorvos Yerushalayim*, was printed in Venice. Written by an anonymous scholar and resident of the Jewish community, its authenticity was attested to by the *rabbanim* of Jerusalem. The booklet was circulated throughout Europe in order to encourage fellow Jews to lend a helping hand. The Shelah HaKodesh, too, wrote letters to Prague and to other communities.

Unfortunately, European communities were facing their own problems at the time, and were unable to help to any significant degree.

One consequence of the titanic debt was a rift that formed between the communities of Safed and Jerusalem. Before the economic genocide in Jerusalem of 1625–1626, unspecified funds sent to Eretz Yisrael from the Diaspora were divided into twenty-four portions. Safed received ten, Jerusalem seven, Tiberias four, and Hebron three. After the disaster, the *rabbanim* of Jerusalem felt a new apportioning of the *chalukah* was in order. Shortly before his death in 1630, Rav Horowitz, now living in Tiberias, was asked to arbitrate over this delicate issue.

His *sh'tar pasharah* (judgment of compromise) allocated an increased percentage to Jerusalem. However, the *rabbanim* of Safed refused to accept his ruling and forced the Jerusalem community to agree to less favorable terms.

Safed

As a result, there was a tense state of affairs between the two cities that would not be ameliorated for decades.

In 1633 (5393), an Ashkenazic Jew from Safed, Rav Yaakov Philip, moved to Jerusalem. He attempted to help make peace between the two cities. Rav Yaakov succeeded in persuading the Jerusalem leaders to agree to a new compromise. However, Safed flatly refused to budge, regardless of how convincingly he worded the agreement to their side.

In the end, he wrote to Safed: "What do you expect me to do? Am I forced to beat them [the Jerusalem community] until they agree to do what is unrealistic from a logical point of view?"[6]

Only much later, in the 1660s, did a more reasonable solution come about. This was the result of a new demographic reality in the country: for years, the Jewish community of Tiberias had been dwindling, until finally not a single Jew was left there. At that point, Jerusalem asked for three of the four portions allotted to Tiberias, and Safed agreed.

During the 1660s and 1670s there would be other demographic changes in the Jewish populace of Eretz Yisrael as well, as more and more scholars moved from Safed to Jerusalem. As we shall see, a major cause for this movement was the news of outstanding Torah personalities assuming leadership and opening yeshivos. The Chief Rav of Jerusalem in those days was Rav Moshe Galante, who, because of the shifting numbers, was able to get even more favorable terms for the Holy City, achieving a totally new division of the *chalukah*: Jerusalem received thirteen portions, Safed eight, and Hebron three.

The Rise of the Yeshivah World & the Fall of the Wicked

Slowly, a new era began to unfold for the small community of Jerusalem. The predominance of Torah scholarship, after suffering drastically at the hands of a tyrant in the 1620s, emerged in the 1640s with a small, yet intense, group of sages. Later in the century, other notable rabbanim would open some of the most important yeshivos of the time, producing world-famous rabbis.

The Era of Spiritual Growth

In the early 1640s (5402) a Jew came to Jerusalem who would subtly initiate a spiritual awakening among his brethren. Though his personal work was confined to the Holy City, his teachings would eventually spread forth until they reached the entire Jewish world.

Rav Yaakov Tzemach came from Damascus in 1642. He brought with him eighteen years of intense study of Kabbalah under Rav Chaim Vital's son, Rav Shmuel Vital. His whole being was dedicated to synthesizing and selectively teaching the works of the Ari Zal. To this end, he opened a yeshivah, supporting it and himself through his work as a physician.

Born half a century before to a Marrano family in Portugal, Rav Yaakov eventually made his way to Salonika, Greece. It was there that he first began learning about his Jewish heritage. From Salonika he traveled to Safed. Concerning his time in the mystical city he writes: "For six years I studied Gemara, Rambam, Beis Yosef, and the Levush. I sold all my gold and silver, and purchased *sefarim*, especially the writings of the Ari Zal.... From the time that I began to study his works and realized the greatness of his wisdom, I began to arrange indices and tables of contents."[7]

From Safed, Rav Yaakov went to Damascus. There lived Rav Shmuel Vital, who had inherited all of his father's manuscripts after Rav Chaim died in that city in 1620. Guarding the manuscripts zealously, Rav Shmuel literally never allowed them out of his sight. Based on instructions from his father, he toiled to organize the writing into eight "Gates." Furthermore, Rav Shmuel taught a select few disciples the Kabbalah of the Ari Zal, among them Rav Yaakov Tzemach.

Rav Yaakov's brilliance lay not only in his deep grasp of Torah, but also in his ability to arrange and synthesize the vast body of knowledge of the mystical worlds. By the time he came to Jerusalem he had already written a few works of his own on the subject.

After his first year in Jerusalem something very extraordinary occurred. He writes: "At the end of my first year in Jerusalem, I received a number of writings of the Ari Zal which had never been published before."[8] These writings comprised thousands of folios, each handwritten by Rav Chaim Vital. Inquiring of his teacher, he discovered that Rav Shmuel Vital knew nothing about them.*

These new revelations essentially consisted of several different versions of Rav Chaim's elucidations of the Ari Zal's teachings. Arranged topically according to expositions on the various supernal worlds, these writings covered the whole gamut of Kabbalah. Although the different versions were substantially the same, each contained some new ideas and references that the other ones did not.

After their long burial, they were completely unorganized and were in very poor condition. Rav Tzemach wrote: "When I got them, they were difficult to read, smudged and torn from the passage of time. Everything was in disarray. With Hashem's help, I was able to organize them and arrange each one in its proper place. I divided them into five volumes, each with its own name."[9]

Rav Meir Paparish

Rav Yaakov's prime disciple, Rav Meir Paparish, described the task of organization as follows: "My mentor, Rav Yaakov Tzemach, found the pages torn and withered away. It was only due to his astute wisdom that the fragments were pieced together into a coherent whole."[10]

This labor of love on Rav Tzemach's part took years to finish. A scribe was hired to rewrite the organized folios. Rav Tzemach then went over them, adding marginal notes. Before the end of the decade, Rav Moshe Zechos of Italy had received some of these writings. From Italy they spread throughout Europe.

Later on, Rav Meir Paparish took the various versions and collated them into one large whole, in unabridged form. Thus, whereas someone referring to what Rav Chaim said on a given topic from Rav Tzemach's work would have to consult several manuscripts in order to compare the different versions, Rav Paparish's work presented all the writings on a given section all together. The work was entitled *Etz Chaim*. Reams of commentary have been written on these subtle differences, and the work became the classic text over which all later kabbalists have toiled.

* The story behind these writings is quite mysterious, and even today puzzles remain. They were unearthed either from the cemetery in Safed or from next to the grave of Rav Chaim Vital in Damascus. Exactly why their author commanded them to be buried is open to speculation. What we do know is that Rav Avraham Azulai, the grandfather of the Chida and a saintly man in his own right, received permission from Heaven to dig them up. From there they came into the hands of Rav Yaakov Tzemach, although it is also not clear how they reached him.

Tzaddik and Leader

Rav Yaakov Tzemach's yeshivah was as unique as its Rosh Yeshivah. One of his disciples wrote: "Everyone who thirsted for this lofty wisdom [Kabbalah] came to him [Rav Tzemach], and studied from him the *Zohar* and the writings of Rav Yitzchak Luria."[11] Indeed, the leading personalities in Jerusalem flocked to him to learn the Torah's mysteries.

Rav Yitzchak Gaon, one of the leaders of Jerusalem during Farouk's reign of terror, survived the harrowing ordeal and remained in the city until his death many years later. He studied Kabbalah, and was a close associate of Rav Yaakov. Rav Yitzchak also supported another *beis midrash*, where the revealed Torah was studied. Rav David Conforti, the author of *Korei HaDoros*, also studied in Rav Yaakov's yeshivah. Additionally, the Ashkenazic Chief Rabbi of Jerusalem, Rav Nasan Shapiro, became very close with Rav Tzemach, his mentor in Kabbalah, and later wrote a number of books on the subject.

The Rosh Yeshivah was "a *chassid* and was humble, a disseminator of Torah, as well as a top physician." Though he held no formal position, he was looked upon as the leading Rav of the city, and his influence was felt for years after his passing, sometime after 1665. His son, Rav Avraham, sat on the *beis din* of Rav Moshe Galante.

זה השער לה' צדיקים יבואו בו

דבק ספר טוב

קורא הדורות

כשמו כן הוא.

כי הוא קורא ומכריז שמות רבני הדורות ראשי ישיבות ומנהיגי הדורות. מאסף לכל המחנות מעת שנסתם התלמוד שלשלת היוחסין מרבנן סבוראי עד זמן הגאון המחבר ז"ל, עם ביאור מספיק וראיות נכונות מהש"ס והפוסקים ז"ל במיעט המחזיק את המרובה.

חיבורו וגם הקרו הגאון המהולל החכם השלם מיקירי ירושלים עה"ק

כמוהר"ר דוד אשכנזי זלה"ה.

תלמיד מהר"ם קלעי וחבירו של מהר"ש אלגאזי זכרונם לברכה.

בהוצאות בית מסחר הספרים של

ה' יענטע אלמנת המנוח ר' מרדכי ז"ל קנאסטער

בוארשא ברחוב פראנציסקאנער 39

פיעטרקוב

בשנת תרנ"ד לפ"ק

ДЕВЕКЪ ТОВЪ

часть II

Title page of Korei HaDoros *(1894 edition). The author wrote his "modern" history of the Jews, listing scholars and their works, and published it in Venice at the end of the 17th century. Today, it can be found on archival CD-Rom.*

Troubled Times

The middle of the seventeenth century heralded troubled times for Jewish communities the world over. Eastern Europe in particular was suffering from the infamous Tach v'Tat (1648–1649) pogroms at the hands of Bogdan Chmielnicki, the infamous Cossack insurgent of the Ukraine. The massacres perpetrated by this demonic fiend had ramifications extending to Eretz Yisrael as well. With a major part of the Jewish world in turmoil, a vital source of funding for the *yishuv* dried up. This brought terrible repercussions on the already destitute Ashkenazic community in the Holy City. In 1655, as a result of mounting debts to the Arabs, the Ashkenazic shuls were forced to close. As the situation deteriorated, rabbis were imprisoned. Things became so serious that some people even starved to death.

At this point, the pasha, a Turk by the name of Sanjak, made the Jews a generous offer — with one catch: he would lend them enough money to pay off all their debts, on condition that the Jews would repay him half of the total amount — interest free — within two years. Payment for the second half would then be staggered over the course of the next several years, with interest. However, if they failed to repay the first half within the allotted two years, they would become his slaves. In desperation, the community agreed to his terms.

Rav Nasan Shapiro was immediately sent to Holland to collect funds to repay Sanjak. Though the times were difficult everywhere, he was surprised and gratified to find a helping hand extended by people and from places that he least expected. Even some non-Jews gave generously. The most notable was an English priest, Henry Jessey, who wrote a pamphlet for Rav Shapiro to help him explain his cause. His mission a success, he returned with enough money to redeem his fellow Jews.[12]

Rav Shapiro would later return to Europe — both to collect for other causes in Jerusalem and to seek sponsors to help him publish his writings. He eventually settled in Rigo, Italy, where he lived out the rest of his days.

After Rav Shapiro, the post of Ashkenazic Chief Rabbi in the Holy City was held by Rav Uri Shraga Feivish, who remained in the position until his death in the late 1660s. One of his famous halachic decisions concerned the validity of the use of the word "Ohr" (אור) as a name, similar to the name Uri (אורי). Another case involved a Sephardic man who sought to marry two Ashkenazic women. Rav Feivish permitted the marriage on the grounds that the ancient decree of Rabbeinu Gershon which forbade polygamy among Ashkenazim applied only to Ashkenazic men, and not to Ashkenazic women. Rav Yaakov Chagiz, a prominent Rosh Yeshivah of Jerusalem whom we shall meet shortly, agreed with his decision.[13]

A Glimmer of Light[14]

Throughout the last half of the seventeenth century, the residents of Jerusalem lived between the extremes of spiritual exaltedness and physical destitution. Sometimes the crushing poverty engendered desperation, and led to imprisonment and even death. In the year 1656 (5416), a mysterious event took place that would provide a spark of hope to those whose physical plight was so desolate.

In that year, a fantastic letter reached the civilized world, electrifying Jewry with its amazing tidings. It seemed that a *shaliach* from Jerusalem, Rav Baruch Gad, had been on an extended trip in Moslem lands. At one point in his journey, he got lost somewhere in the Arabian desert. Suddenly, a fierce warrior on camelback attacked him. Rav Baruch raised his voice and cried, "*Shema Yisrael...*," and prepared to die.

Hearing these Hebrew words, the warrior stopped and asked him who he was and where he was from. When he heard that Rav Baruch was from Eretz Yisrael, he immediately left and went to the encampment of the ten Lost Tribes of Israel! These tribes, of course, had been exiled by the Assyrians over two thousand years earlier and had not been heard from since. The warrior returned with two bags of gold and a long letter from the King of the Lost Tribes. The larger bag was a present for the Jews of Eretz Yisrael, and the smaller one was for Rav Baruch.

Rav Baruch returned to Jerusalem and presented the letter and the gold to the Ashkenazic Chief Rabbi, Rav Nasan Shapiro. The authenticity of the letter and the validity of the *shaliach's* testimony were attested to by the leading rabbis of Jerusalem, who wrote an epistle concerning the event. Signatories to the letter included Rav Yaakov Tzemach, Rav Nasan Guta, and Rav Yitzchak Biton. Later, the Chida vouched for the signatures.

At this low point in our history, when the darkness of persecutions and abject poverty ensnared the lives and souls of Jews everywhere, a glimmer of light seemed to shine through the lattice. Excited questions were on everyone's lips: was this the beginning of the ingathering of the exile? Was this the long-awaited preamble to the redemption?

Even though there were no further developments in this mysterious episode, it touched a deep chord in people's souls. Jews became tenacious in their faith in God, and strengthened in their resolve to stand by the tenets of their forefathers no matter what the consequences.

The Rosh Yeshivah

In 1658 (5418), one of the premier rabbis of Europe, Rav Yaakov Chagiz, settled in Jerusalem. Hailing from Leghorn (Livorno), Italy, he brought with him his newly published commentary on the Mishnah. Entitled *Etz Chaim*, this six-volume masterpiece was studied throughout the Torah world. His goal in coming to Eretz Yisrael was to disseminate Torah to a new generation of scholars in Jerusalem. Ultimately, he would be responsible for a spiritual revolution that swept the Holy City and brought renewed commitment to God and His Torah in its wake.

Young *talmidim* (students) thronged to Jerusalem to study Torah at the feet of the master. He opened a yeshivah called Beis Yaakov, under the patronage of the Vega brothers, famous philanthropists from Rav Yaakov's hometown of Livorno. Scholars of rank also flocked to Jerusalem, at least in part due to the dynamic personality of the recently arrived Torah sage. At the age of thirty-eight, Rav Chagiz was one of the leading sages of his generation. As his son would later write, "He was as great in his generation as was the Rambam in his. He was thoroughly versed in all aspects of the Torah."[15]

In those days, the educational system was organized along different lines than it is today. Children learned in a *hesger* (equivalent to the *talmud Torah* and yeshivos of our times), and then in a yeshivah (*kollel*) for married men. Both the *hesger* and the yeshivah were cen-

Rav Yaakov Chagiz's commentary to the Mishnah, called Etz Chaim. *The six-volume set was pocket-size, clearly printed, and leather-bound.*

tralized in the same building, which also functioned as the seat of the *beis din* and was a meeting place for the community as well. Having one central building simultaneously serving so many functions both made economic sense and helped foster unity among the small community.

The Rosh Yeshivah's goal was not to surround himself with brilliant students. He had a genuine desire to see every *talmid* grow up with a thirst for Torah, and he took a active part in each level of a child's education. Boys studied Tanach (Bible) until the age of seven, at which time they would be divided into two levels. The brighter boys began learning Gemara, continuing in their studies until they reached twenty years of age. They studied whole tractates, emphasizing clarity of *peshat*, the simple meaning of the Gemara. Special prizes were awarded for knowing a tractate by heart.

The rest of the boys continued learning Tanach, and started Halachah (Jewish law), Aggadah (homiletic teachings), and Mishnah with the commentary of Rav Bartenora. At thirteen years of age, they began studying Gemara with Rashi.

Rav Chagiz understood the needs of his students. In those times, pressed by economic circumstances, many boys would go off to work at a relatively young age. Realizing this, the Rav strove to instill in them the minimum requirements that would help ensure they became good, faithful Jews. It was these boys who generally began studying Gemara after their bar mitzvah. This was because if they began studying only Gemara from the age of seven, they would end up taking very little with them into adulthood.

He spared nothing to see that each *talmid* reached his maximum potential. Monetary rewards were used as an incentive to achieve excellence. If a student preferred Halachah, he motivated him to become an expert in Torah Law. Some wanted to study Gemara all day, which he welcomed wholeheartedly, encouraging them to know it by heart. Rav Yaakov guided each student according to his talents.

The importance and effective usage of time played a critical role in his teachings. He wrote: "One should ask himself: 'For what purpose has God given me this hour of life? And what does He expect of me? Surely, since He has given me life, it is in order to perform His will.' By thinking this way, one will never waste time."[16]

He instituted a custom that on Friday mornings, everyone in the *beis midrash* would study the *parshah* (Torah portion) for that Shabbos. Some learned Chumash (Pentateuch) with Rashi's commentary, others learned Midrash, and a select few, the *Zohar*. The students were given a question on the *parshah*, which they would discuss among themselves, and then write down their answers. On Shabbos, the Rosh Yeshivah would center the first half of his sermon around the question he had raised to the students Friday morning. The second half would consist of a discussion on halachic aspects of current public issues, designed to encourage the more senior scholars.

He mixed well with all types of Jews. On one occasion, some lay members of the community asked him how to concentrate in prayer. They worried so much about making a livelihood that their *tefillos* (prayers) were mere rapid-fire lip service. Rav Chagiz answered: "Your question reveals a lack of understanding. Think — what will you gain by worrying during prayer time? In fact, you will only fall deeper into anxiety and confusion. Let me illustrate this with a parable:

"Once there was a man who wanted to make a special request of the king. He received permission to get an audience before the monarch on such-and-such a day. As he traveled to the capital city, he concentrated on how to best present his petition, rehearsing his words over and over again. When he entered the palace, his apprehension grew. His success depended on his presentation. His wholeheartedness and sincerity were crucial factors.

"Thus it is with our prayers before the King of Kings," concluded the Rav, "Whether you are rich or poor, you must realize that everything you have and everything you ask for are from God. If you pray with the same intentions as you would before a human king, then your prayers will be set properly before Him and He will hearken to them."[17]

Rav Yaakov's first wife had passed away before he left Italy, and shortly after arriving in Jerusalem, he married the daughter of Rav Moshe Galante. In the year 1672, she bore him a son, Moshe. Soon after the child's birth, Rav Yaakov left for Constantinople to publish a new book of his.* Carrying out his personal business and acting as a representative of Jerusalem, he remained in the Ottoman capital for two years. His

* The history of the Jewish printing press in Eretz Yisrael will be discussed in *Bound Within the Walls: 1840–1870*. Until then, authors had their writings published in such places as Leghorn, Amsterdam, and Constantinople.

physical constitution was always very frail, and he passed away there at the age of fifty-four.

When news of his *petirah* (death) reached Jerusalem, everyone felt both a personal and a communal loss. However, his legacy to the Holy City endured well after his passing. Other great Torah figures had lived in Jerusalem and had raised disciples there, but with their passing, the glory of their Torah went with them. Rav Yaakov Chagiz, in the course of the sixteen years he lived in the Holy City, managed to establish it as a major Torah center that flourished long after he was gone.

The False Messiah[18]

One of the most earth-shattering episodes in Jewish history is the story of Shabbetai Tzvi, who became one of the most infamous false messiahs of all time. In the span of two years, from his "coronation" in Eretz Yisrael in 1664 until his conversion to Islam in 1666, Shabbetai Tzvi was responsible for a major upheaval throughout the Jewish world. At the time, he posed a major threat to Judaism from within, and the repercussions of his actions are still being felt today, hundreds of years later.

When Shabbetai Tzvi came to Jerusalem from Izmir, Turkey, in the summer of 1662 (5422), he was completely anonymous and quietly became a part of the community. Much later it would come out that he had been banished from Izmir and from Constantinople because of his outlandish behavior, but at the time, no one had reason to suspect him of anything. In fact, the opposite was the case, and he was very careful not to behave in a manner that would cast aspersions on himself. As was true of most settlers, Shabbetai was known to everyone in the small Jewish community, and he made a good impression as a scholar. He spent a good deal of time fasting in seclusion and would often wander in the Judean hills, meditating. He was thirty-six years old then, tall and handsome, with a distinct presence about him. His speech was lofty and passionate, and he loved to compose and sing songs.

After the High Holidays of 1663 (5424), the Sephardic community asked him to go to Egypt and collect for the *kehillah*. They chose him because he had stayed in Cairo before coming to Jerusalem and had become friendly with the wealthy and influential Rav Raphael Yosef, who was also unaware of his past. As the Jelebi, the highest post a Jew could hold in the Egyptian court, Rav Raphael Yosef was a leading figure in Egypt. Shabbetai Tzvi accepted.

On his way, Shabbetai Tzvi passed through Hebron and stopped at the Cave of Machpelah, where the Patriarchs are buried. He prayed there with tremendous fervor, attracting much attention. A group stayed up all night with him, mesmerized by his tremendous charisma. One of them, Avraham Conki, became one of his most dedicated followers.

During his extended stay in Egypt, Shabbetai Tzvi collected close to four thousand rials, a significant sum. He lived in the courtyard of the Jelebi and continued his close relationship with Rav Raphael Yosef.

In the spring of 1664, news reached

Cairo of a young seer in Gaza named Nasan Ashkenazi. Rav Raphael sent some students to investigate the authenticity of the supposed visionary, and the report he received was very positive. He related his findings to Shabbetai Tzvi, who decided to travel to Gaza and meet him in person. He told Raphael Yosef that he was going to the seer to request a *tikun* (spiritual rectification) for his soul.

The False Prophet

Nasan Ashkenazi was born in Jerusalem, around the year 1643. His father, a man of impeccable character, had emigrated from Europe and had spent extended periods of time in *chutz laAretz* as an emissary for the Jerusalem community. He studied Kabbalah and published the second half of *Maggid miYesharim*, Rav Yosef Karo's record of his conversations with his Heavenly *maggid* (angelic mentor).

Nasan himself studied in the Beis Yaakov Yeshivah and was one of Rav Yaakov Chagiz's foremost students. An acknowledged genius, Nasan's grasp of Torah was phenomenal. As a teenager he had memorized half of Shas (the Talmud), and his depth of learning was remarkable. Many people saw greatness on the horizon for the young man, believing that he was destined to become a *gadol baTorah*.

When a wealthy Jew from Gaza spoke with the Rosh Yeshivah about a match for his daughter, Rav Chagiz pointed to Nasan as the best prospect. As a result of this fortuitous match, Nasan would be able to concentrate on his studies without any financial distractions for the rest of his life. The only stipulation that his father-in-law made was that he live in Gaza. This was not an untowardly demand, for Gaza had a sizable Jewish community at the time. Everyone agreed, and the young couple moved to the coastal town around 1663.

At that time, the Rav of Gaza was Rav Moshe Najara, the son of the famous Rav Yisrael Najara, who composed the song *Kah Ribon Olam*. The town had also hosted Rav Avraham Azulai twelve years earlier, after that saintly man had fled there from an epidemic in Hebron. Rav Avraham, it will be recalled, was the pious scholar who had received Heavenly permission to unearth Rav Chaim Vital's buried writings. While in Gaza, he completed his book, *Chesed l'Avraham,* an important compendium on mystical topics.

While in Gaza, Nasan discovered the world of Kabbalah and steeped himself in its study. Although he initially understood it in the proper fashion, he unfortunately came to misuse it due to reasons we will discuss shortly. Soon he was having visions and was conversing with what were, unbeknownst to him, damaging angels. Meanwhile, word of the "holy man" began to spread, and people far and near were drawn to him for spiritual healing.

One day while fasting, Nasan suddenly felt an unearthly spirit come upon him. Trembling, he saw before him what he thought was a vision of the Heavenly Chariot. He would later write: "From that moment I began to prophesy like one of the prophets: Thus says the Lord, 'Their savior is coming; his name is

Shabbetai Tzvi..., who will succeed against his enemies.'"[19] Thus Nasan of Gaza was irrevocably set on the road to destruction that would bring so much damage, sorrow, and grief in its wake, all the while believing in the righteousness of his cause.

When Shabbetai Tzvi entered Nasan's house, the false prophet fell at his feet and begged forgiveness for not going to him first. He revealed to him their respective appointments as prophet and messiah.

The Jews of Gaza soon fell under the spell of these two charismatic figures, and the momentum of their movement quickly began to spread to the rest of the Jewish world. Soon the two took to the road to proselytize, first going to Hebron. On the way, Shabbetai Tzvi's prophet gave full reign to the spirit bubbling within him, and everybody was caught up in his frenetic intensity. Walking past a stone in a field, he would announce that it was the heretofore unknown grave of a particular tzaddik, in a manner seemingly similar to that of the Ari Zal decades earlier. He even claimed to be in communication with these dead souls. When they arrived in Hebron, the community was electrified by the news.

At the time, the fast of 17 Tamuz was close at hand. Nasan sent letters to the major cities in Eretz Yisrael announcing a decree to annul the fast. This would be the beginning of the redemption, announced the missive. In Gaza they rejoiced on that day and sang Hallel. Many people in Hebron also followed the decree.

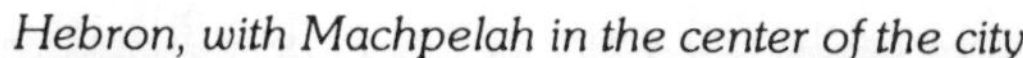

Hebron, with Machpelah in the center of the city

When the two reached Jerusalem, they faced one of their biggest tests. Could they convince the *rabbanim* who resided there of their mission? Besides Rav Chagiz and the kabbalist, Rav Tzemach, there was Rav Moshe Galante, Rav Avraham Amigo, and Rav Shmuel Garmizan.

A Traitor to His People

When Jerusalemites saw Nasan and Shabbetai Tzvi and their entourage, they could hardly believe their eyes. Children taunted them, saying, "You left as a *shaliach*, but you returned as a *mashiach*."[20]

Shabbetai Tzvi was undaunted by his less than enthusiastic reception. Audaciously, he planned to offer sacrifices on the Temple Mount, choosing one of his Gazan followers to be High Priest. When the *rabbanim* of Jerusalem heard of this, they rent their garments. Such an act, besides being a *chillul Hashem* (desecration of God's name), could incite the Moslems to react with force and punish the entire Jewish population.

A message was dispatched demanding that he not follow through with his plan. With a sigh, the false messiah acquiesced, saying, "Woe, just when we were about to do this mighty thing, it was denied us."[21]

Shabbetai Tzvi was no fool. He had accumulated a lot of Torah knowledge during his youth and knew how to make an impressive presentation. Rav Moshe Galante recalled later: "In the beginning, although I did not believe in him, I was not openly against him. It was only after I saw a letter he wrote to one of his followers that I realized how dangerous he really was. He signed the letter, 'I am the Lord your God, Shabbetai Tzvi' — spelling Hashem's Name as it is written in a *sefer Torah*."[22]

Next, he openly declared that forbidden fats (*chelev*) were now permissible. Also, he composed a special blessing to be recited over them — "Blessed are You...Who permits the forbidden."

With this blatant attempt to abrogate Torah law, Shabbetai Tzvi drew the firm opposition of the rabbis upon himself. Openly attacking him, they went before the civil authorities and accused him of embezzling some of the funds which he had collected. Furthermore, they claimed, by calling himself the *mashiach*, he was rebelling against the Sultan.

Under the spell of Shabbetai Tzvi's magnetic personality, the *kadi* and his court freed him of all charges. The "messiah" and his followers were ecstatic with the news, calling it an open miracle. The *kadi,* in a bizarre turn of events, permitted Shabbetai Tzvi to be led around the city on horseback, a privilege no Jew was permitted under Turkish law.*

Deeply disturbed over Nasan's behavior, Rav Chagiz asked his renegade disciple what had caused such a great change to come over him. Nasan answered him openly. He said that the kabbalist Rav Avraham Chananiah of Hebron had been in Gaza recuperating from an illness. When Rav Avraham Chananiah was about to return to Hebron, Nasan stole a private manuscript on practical Kabbalah from him, which explained how to invoke celestial beings and communicate with them. With this book, he succeeded in soliciting powers from the spiritual worlds.

* See story, "Shabbetai Tzvi at the Tomb of Shmuel HaNavi," in *Bygone Days: 17th Century*.

Jerusalem's Stand

Realizing the dangerous threat posed by Nasan and Shabbetai Tzvi, Rav Chagiz threatened them. In the time of the Sanhedrin, Nasan would have been convicted of being a false prophet, and sentenced to death. The same fate would have befallen Shabbetai Tzvi. Barring that possibility, Rav Chagiz had the authority to excommunicate them, a formidable punishment in itself, which would exclude them from the Jewish community. His words, however, fell on deaf ears. Thus it was that the *rabbanim* of the city, under the leadership of Rav Yaakov Chagiz, who declared a *cherem* (decree of excommunication) on them. They were banished from the Holy City, never to return, at the beginning of Av, 1664 (5424). Though they were only there for about a week, in that short time they succeeded in arousing the hostile feelings of nearly everyone in the city.

Although Shabbetai Tzvi heeded the *rabbanim*'s injunction, he was infuriated by it and cursed them. Later, however, when he met a group of Jewish pilgrims on their way to Jerusalem, he sent an apology.

Rav Chagiz was unmoved. "See how empty this *mashiach* is!" he said mockingly. "He obeys my *cherem* and is afraid of me."[23]

Immediately after issuing their proclamation, the *rabbanim* sent letters to all the world's major Jewish communities, warning them of the false messiah.

However, despite the strong wording of their eyewitness report, the force of this messianic movement was very difficult to arrest. The local populations throughout the Ottoman Empire (and some rabbis) were swept away by the turbulent happenings. Soon, news of the *mashiach* and his prophet had spread like wildfire throughout the world. Even the Pope in Rome sent a delegation to Jerusalem to get a firsthand report about him. By the time his representatives arrived there, the false messiah and his prophet were long gone. However, the strong impression they had made on the city lingered. The local priests told the papal nuncio that Shabbetai Tzvi and Nasan were men who performed miracles. The two of them claimed that they would return and build the Temple, and that the time of redemption of the Jewish people had come. If so, continued the churchmen, they (the Christians) would leave Jerusalem. The priests were manifestly afraid of them and what the ultimate consequences for the Gentile people would be.[24]

The Aftermath

The aftermath of Shabbetai Tzvi's brief but eventful stay in Jerusalem was hard to measure. Trying to entirely snuff out his influence, the rabbis forbade the practice of any customs he had instituted and firmly censured public allegiance to his messianic cause.

One of the most obtrusive of Shabbetai Tzvi's new *minhagim* (customs) was the annulment of the four major fast days which commemorated the destruction of the Temple. Claiming that he came to usher in the light of the *geula* (redemption), and not to perpetuate the darkness of *galus* (exile), he said they were no longer necessary.

Shabbetai Tzvi left Jerusalem several days before the fast of Tisha b'Av. In other towns, like Gaza and Hebron, many people marked the day with a festive meal. In Jerusalem, the *rabbanim* implored everyone not to break away from tradition and halachah.

On that Tisha b'Av, Rav Yaakov Chagiz spoke to the congregation. He wanted to give them words of inspiration in the wake of Shabbetai Tzvi's claim to being the *mashiach*.

"Why," he asked, "do we say *v'Ata Kadosh* at the end of the Maariv service on the night of Tisha b'Av?"

Continued the Rosh Yeshivah, "I heard an answer to this question from Rav Yosef Malko, may he rest in peace. He quoted a statement in the Talmud (*Sotah* 49) which says that the world is sanctified by the saying of Kedushah.

"We know that on Tisha b'Av we are forbidden to study Torah. The problem is, we also know that Torah study helps maintain the world. What, then, insures the existence of the world on Tisha b'Av? From the Talmud's statement, we now understand that by saying this prayer of Kedushah we are helping to maintain the existence of the world."[25]

These words were meant to instill hope in the real *geula*, since the ultimate level of *kedushah* which mankind can attain will be in the messianic times. Also, Tisha b'Av is traditionally known as the birthday of the *mashiach*. By reciting *v'Ata Kadosh*, we are praying that the Mashiach will be born and redeem us, which is the ultimate aim of the existence of the world.

In a large measure, the *rabbanim* were successful in minimizing Shabbetai Tzvi's influence in Jerusalem. However, it was impossible to completely wipe out the impression he had made, and some individuals continued to clandestinely practice the impostor's customs.

Repercussions

Due to the Jerusalem *rabbanim*'s vigilance and decisive action, the local community's brief encounter with the false messiah left it relatively unscathed. However, the same could not be said for the rest of the world. The momentum of the movement created by Shabbetai Tzvi and Nasan of Gaza was intense and out of control, presenting a very real peril to the entire Jewish nation. The danger was twofold: Shabbetai Tzvi, as "Mashiach," stood as a direct threat to the Sultan. Every gentile realized that the redemption of the Jewish people meant the termination of their reign in the world. Confronted with this possibility, the Sultan might very easily interpret the mass movement as a rebellion by his Jewish subjects. In his wrath, he could decree genocide for the Jews throughout his kingdom.

The second danger was internal, within the ranks of the Jewish people. The *gedolei Yisrael* had disclosed him as an instigator against the Torah and her people, and anyone who followed him would become an accomplice to his crime. Thus, the "messiah" would be responsible for a terrible rift within the Jewish people.

Thankfully, the first danger never materialized. However, as history has so sadly proven, all too many people followed Shabbetai Tzvi into apostasy and forsook their Jewish heritage.

It would be over two years, until the beginning of 5427 (Fall, 1666), before Shabbetai Tzvi would stand before the Sultan and, presented with a choice to convert to Islam or die, would choose to apostatize. However, even this shocking news did not completely extinguish the blaze he had started. With characteristic audacity, he claimed that this was merely a climactic stage in the redemption process, hinted at in the holy books. Incredibly, many Jews converted with him, including his old benefactor, Raphael Yosef, the Jelebi in Cairo.

Though Shabbetai Tzvi personally came to an ignoble end, the movement which surrounded him would not die out for decades after his passing. Rav Chagiz's son, Rav Moshe Chagiz, one of the foremost opponents to the Shabbetian movement — just as his father had been to the "messiah" himself — wrote: "We see from this how God watches over the Jewish people with a special supervision. This whole episode should stand as an example and a reminder to us. If the nations of the world stood in fear over the flurry of a false *mashiach*, then how much more so when the true *mashiach* will come and redeem us!"[26]

City of Torah

The Jews of Jerusalem in the latter part of the seventeenth century were not blessed with wealth, but the vast majority of them aspired to spiritual heights. More than eighty scholars lived and studied in the Holy City, a phenomenal number for those times. Torah and *avodah* echoed in the lanes of the city.

In 1668 there were nine yeshivos in Jerusalem, the most famous one being Beis Yaakov Yeshivah. Another two, Zion Yeshivah and Talmud Torah Yeshivah, had a long history. Founded earlier than the Beis Yaakov Yeshivah, they outlived it by hundreds of years. All three were Sephardic houses of study.

The Zion Yeshivah was also called Rabban Yochanan ben Zakkai Synagogue. It stood until 1948 when the Arabs destroyed it. Later, in 1967, it was rebuilt on the same site.

The Rabban Yochanan ben Zakkai Synagogue was long and narrow. On festivals, when the synagogue was filled to capacity, the overflow spilled out into the courtyard to pray. When the *sefer Torah* was lifted up, the holder would carry it around the shul while it was open, so that everyone could have an opportunity to see the script. He even carried it out into the courtyard.

Talmud Torah Yeshivah was also called Eliyahu HaNavi Synagogue, where Rav Yaakov Chagiz customarily prayed. Like the Rabban Yochanan ben Zakkai Synagogue, it served the community until 1948.

The Ashkenazic shul, later known as the Churvah Synagogue, stood next to the Ramban Synagogue. It functioned until the beginning of the eighteenth century when it was destroyed by the Moslems. Rebuilt one hundred and fifty years later, it continued to serve the Ashkenazic community until 1948 when it was demolished by the Arabs, along with all the other synagogues, during the War of Independence.

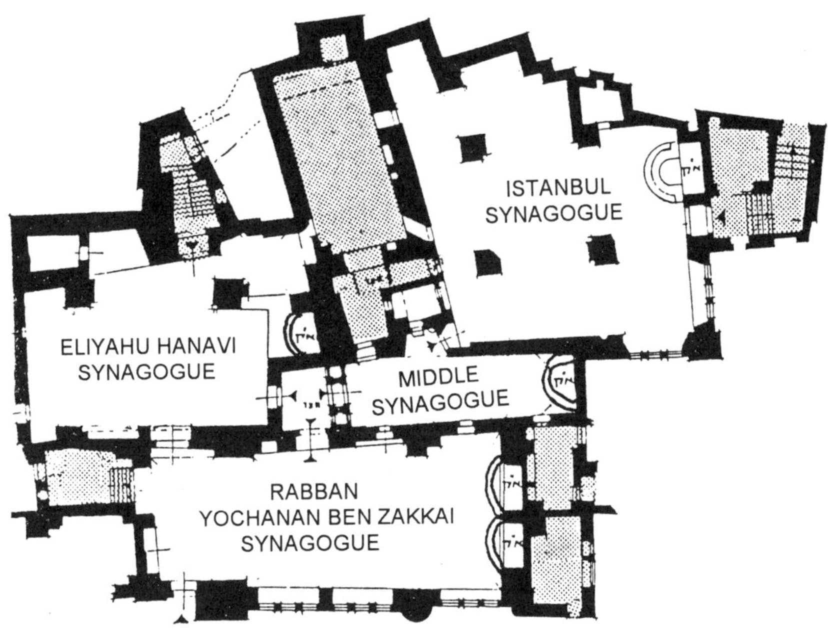

The four Sephardic synagogues were the center of religious activity for hundreds of years. Although built at different times, they stood clustered together in the Jewish Quarter.

Rav Moshe Galante: Rishon L'Tzyon

When Rav Yaakov Chagiz died in 1674 (5434), Rav Moshe Galante replaced him as Rosh Yeshivah, remaining in that capacity until his death in 1689. In addition, he sat at the head of the *beis din*. Although Rav Galante was the official Rav of Jerusalem throughout this period, he declined the title out of humility. For this reason, he became known as the Rishon L'Tzyon. At the time this was an unheard-of title, but in succeeding generations it became the designation for the leading Sephardic sage of Jerusalem.

Rav Moshe Galante was born in Safed in 1620 (5380) into the renowned Galante family. His grandfather, also named Moshe, received *semichah* from Rav Yosef Karo when he was but twenty-two years old. Indeed, so esteemed a scholar was the elder Moshe Galante that he succeeded Rav Karo as the Rav of Safed.

Rav Moshe Galante was the undisputed *gadol ha'dor*. His knowledge of Torah included all four levels of *pardes* (the four levels of Biblical exegesis), and his humility was proverbial. Of him it was said: "The Holy Spirit constantly hovered over the yeshivah of Rabbeinu."[27] His grasp of worldly sciences stunned even the most knowledgeable gentiles, as we shall see in the story section.* He was called Rav HaMagen after the name of his responsa, *Elef HaMagen*. He also authored numerous other works, both on homiletics and Halachah.

Rav HaMagen moved to Jerusalem sometime in the 1650s or early 1660s. One of his closest colleagues was Rav Yaakov Chagiz. The same age, they

* See story, "May His Name Be Blessed," in *Bygone Days: 17th Century*.

were both outstanding Torah personalities. When Rav Galante gave his daughter in marriage to Rav Chagiz (whose first wife had died in Italy), he expressed his joy with these words: "How privileged I am to give my daughter to a person who possesses the finest of qualities. I am enamored by him, his knowledge of Torah, and his superior character." Only someone of similar rank could truly discern the nature of his peer.

When Rav Chagiz suddenly died in 1674, he left a two-year-old son, Moshe. Rav HaMagen personally supervised his grandson's education and strove to infuse within him a love of Torah. Not disappointing his grandfather's expectations, Rav Moshe Chagiz would grow to be a formidable scholar in his own right.

The communal leader during this period was Rav Aharon Pardo. Wealthy and influential, Rav Aharon was responsible for the needs of the community, especially bilateral relations with the Turkish authorities. Rav Pardo worked in close consultation with Rav HaMagen, to the degree that the verse "Like sheep You led Your people, through Moshe and Aharon" (*Psalms* 77:21) was used to describe their relationship.

Every year on 28 Iyar, Rav HaMagen would lead a procession of Jews by foot to the grave site of Samuel the Prophet, a few hours north of Jerusalem. On that date, the *yartzeit* (anniversary of the day of death) of the prophet, Jews came from as far away as Egypt and Damascus to pray at his tomb. Indeed, thousands of men, women, and children would typically be congregated there at that time.

Rav Galante would stay up that entire night and teach Torah. One of his *talmidim* wrote: "This halachic *chiddush* (novella) came to our master [Rav Galante] at the cave of Shmuel HaNavi.... How fortunate we were."[28]

Scholars in the Holy City

During Rav Galante's time in Jerusalem, the city was fortunate to boast other notable scholars as well. Rav Shlomo Elgazi the Elder was a *rav* in the city from as early as the 1630s or 1640s. When the rabbis issued a public proclamation, he signed first (a mark of distinction), followed by Rav Shmuel Garmizan, and then by Rav Moshe Galante and Rav Yaakov Chagiz. Rav Elgazi lived until sometime after the Shabbetai Tzvi debacle reached its height at the end of the 1660s. A staunch opponent of the false messiah, his life was once in grave danger when he went to Izmir to publish one of his books. At the time, Izmir was a hotbed of Shabbetean influence, and due to Rav Elgazi's outspoken views against Shabbetai Tzvi, he had to flee for his life.

Another *rav* in the city was Rav David Yitzchaki. He served on the *beis din* of Rav Galante. Rav Yitzchaki was the son-in-law of Rav Avraham Azulai (the grandfather of the Chida). Rav Moshe Chagiz described him as "a brilliant *rav*, an angelic being." Rav Yitzchaki, like Rav Elgazi, was the first in a long line of prominent *rabbanim* in Jerusalem for generations to come.

After the Ashkenazic Chief Rabbi, Rav Uri Shraga Feivish, died around 1670, the Ashkenazic community was left without a distinguished leader. As coveted a post as it was, it was not easy to persuade a prospective European *rav* to uproot himself and bear the inevitable hardships of living in Eretz Yisrael to become Chief Rabbi of Jerusalem. Finally, in the year 1678, Rav Ephraim HaKohen, father-in-law of the Chacham Tzvi, accepted the position and made plans to travel to Eretz Yisrael. Rav Ephraim was originally from Vilna, but for the last several years had been Rav of Budapest, Hungary. Before leaving for Jerusalem, he wanted to prepare his book, *Shaar Ephraim*, for publication. At this time, his oldest son died suddenly, at the age of thirty. As if this were not enough, while Rav Ephraim was sitting *shiva*, his only living son, Rav Yehudah Leib, fell ill and lay in critical condition.

Rav Ephraim poured out his heart in fervent prayer for his son's recovery. However, with each day, Rav Yehudah Leib's son's condition remained ominous. Finally, Rav Ephraim raised his hands heavenward and asked that his life be taken in his son's stead. Immediately, he became stricken and Yehudah Leib began to recover. On his deathbed, Rav Ephraim instructed his son to publish his book, and then passed away.

Rav Yehudah Leib fulfilled his father's wishes. First, he traveled to Jerusalem, arriving in 1685, after many hardships. There, he spent a year preparing the manuscript for publication. Additionally, he wrote supplementary material, which he called *V'zos laYehudah*. Rav HaMagen wrote a *haskamah* (approbation), as did other members of the *beis din*.

Bumpy roads like this one leading to Haifa were part and parcel with the travelers' hardships

Hard Times

On Friday, 21 Shevat, 1689 (5449), Rav Moshe Galante returned his soul to his Maker, at the age of sixty-nine. He had been a *magen* (shield) for his people during the lean, hard times and was a beacon of Torah, tolerance, and humbleness throughout his lifetime.*

Though Rav HaMagen left many *talmidim*, Jerusalem was at an invisible crossroads of events that would bring residents to his grave to pray for Heavenly assistance. The hard times began a few weeks after his death. Rainfall was scarce that winter, and instead of a plentiful harvest, it brought famine in its wake. Not only was produce scarce, but even wheat — which is typically stored and therefore keeps for a long time — was also in great demand. This was bad enough for the general food situation. However, with the Passover holiday arriving shortly, the members of the Jewish community who were careful to only eat *matzah shemurah* (matzah made from wheat that is guarded from water from the time of harvesting) were in a double quandary. This group included such luminaries as Rav David Yitzchaki, Rav Aharon Hivon, and Rav Yosef Malko. The situation was so difficult that they had to ask to be released from their vow of stringency.

Other troubles beset the community as well. Rav Yaakov Chagiz's yeshivah, Beis Yaakov, which opened in 1658, had been maintained by the philanthropic support of the Vega brothers of Livorno, Italy. When the Vega brothers passed away, they were careful to stipulate in their will that an endowment fund for the continuation of the yeshivah be set up. Unfortunately, unscrupulous people diverted the money to other places. With no other funding, the yeshivah was forced to close its doors.

The collapse of the yeshivah was a heavy blow to the city. A number of *rabbanim* who received stipends from it suddenly found themselves without livelihood. Having no other source of income, they were quickly impoverished.

Rav Moshe Chagiz and Rav Moshe Chaviv

The Chagiz and Galante families also came upon hard times. Rav Moshe Chagiz was seventeen years old when his grandfather, Rav HaMagen, died. While Rav Galante was alive, he had invested money in Egypt for the future welfare of his daughter. After his death, his daughter — Rav Moshe's mother — lived off these dividends. However, in 1692, the income ceased to be sent. By 1694, her situation was desperate, and Rav Moshe agreed to go to Egypt and try to reinstate the funds. In the interim, his young wife had suddenly passed away and, when he could not find a suitable match, he had to accept the *takanah* that a bachelor was forbidden to live within the walls of the Holy City for any long period of time. Thus he left the city of his birthright for Egypt, not realizing that he would never return to Jerusalem again.

Rav Chagiz was unsuccessful in his mission to help his mother. However, he

* See story, "The Day of Rain," in *Bygone Days: 17th Century*.

did build a relationship with an Egyptian philanthropist by the name of Rav Avraham Nasan. The latter agreed to back a new yeshivah in Jerusalem, to be called Chesed l'Avraham. In the end, however, the yeshivah failed to get off the ground.

Leaving Egypt, the young scholar traveled to his father's hometown of Livorno, Italy. Armed with letters from the rabbis of Jerusalem and Egypt, he hoped to settle the dispute over the Vega funds for the yeshivah in Jerusalem. However, despite superhuman efforts, he failed here as well. Rav Chagiz wrote: "I tried with all my might to expedite the funds for the scholars — my dear friends — in Jerusalem. Alas, I did not succeed... until a heavenly wind will change the course of things, and the evildoers who funneled the sustenance for the holiness of Eretz Yisrael into useless pits unfit for Torah will change their ways."

With all the city's material and spiritual woes, things were not all dark. Shortly after the death of Rav Galante, Rav Moshe Chaviv replaced him as Rishon l'Tzyon. Rav Chaviv had come from Constantinople a few years earlier, under the patronage of Rav Moshe Yevush, a well-known philanthropist who lived in the Turkish capital. The distinguished scholar had already earned a name for himself with his first work, *Get Pashut*. When he arrived in the Holy City in 1687, the yeshivah was studying the Gemara *Rosh HaShanah*. Each year, for the next three years, he sent his *chiddushim* back to Rav Yevush, who printed them. On Tractate *Rosh HaShanah* he wrote *Yom Teru'ah*; on *Yoma*, *Tosefos Yom HaKippurim*; and on *Sukkah*, *Kapos Temarim*. These works became classics in the Torah library. Rav Chaviv also fought the remnants of the Shabbetean messianic movement which existed in Eretz Yisrael.

Unfortunately, the Holy City was not destined to enjoy its newest prodigy for long. Rav Chaviv passed away at the age of forty-two, at the height of his Torah leadership. His grandson, Rav Yaakov Kuli, who conceived the popular *Me'am Loez* series, was responsible for preparing his other works for publication.

There was one more figure who would uplift Jerusalem in the midst of all her troubles. He was a ray of light that would burst forth and serve as a lighthouse of Torah for generations to come. The name of this fiery genius was Rav Chizkiah Silva, better known by the name of his halachic masterpiece, *Pri Chadash*.

The Pri Chadash

When the twenty-year-old Chizkiah arrived in Jerusalem from Livorno in 1677, he quickly unpacked and made his way to the *beis midrash*. Within minutes he was engrossed in a halachic debate with the Rosh Yeshivah. Everyone was amazed at the young man's grasp of Talmud and *poskim*. They were all at his fingertips. His words were like lightning bolts.* The Rosh Yeshivah, Rav Moshe Galante, sensed the young man's sincerity and longing for truth. They immediately formed a close relationship that would continue until the Rosh Yeshivah's death in 1689.

Rav Chizkiah Silva personified the

* See story, "The Torah's Honor," in *Bygone Days: 17th Century*.

Rav Chizkiah Silva (1657–1696), author of the Pri Chadash

greatness of Torah excellence, and his clarity and sharpness dazzled everyone he came in contact with. He viewed Halachah from a totally new standpoint. In those times, while the Talmud and the Rishonim (Early Authorities) were studied, the accepted method of arriving at actual halachic conclusions was to carefully scrutinize the words of the Acharonim (Later Authorities). Rav Silva's method was the exact reverse. He carefully examined every law from its source in Chazal and the Rishonim, and drew his conclusions without much regard for the Later Authorities. In fact, his conclusions were quite often at odds with them. Rav Chizkiah's refusal to bend to the honor of famous Acharonim would engender much controversy and would later force him to contend with antagonistic influences.

In the introduction to his commentary on the *Shulchan Aruch,* which he entitled *Pri Chadash* (literally, "New Fruit") he wrote:

At the age of twenty-two, I married

[the daughter of Rav Raphael Mordechai Malki]. From then onwards my learning was pure, and I was transformed from Heaven with a pristine spirit which enshrouded me. The mask of blindness was removed and I was able to discern between good and bad.... I realized how vain my life had been until then. Strengthened, I removed the garments of laziness and put on the mantle of salvation.

For some time I felt lowly and fervently prayed with tears to find favor in God's eyes, as its says, "God is close to all who call out truthfully to Him."

He answered my prayers at once, illuminating my eyes and giving me strength... From then onwards I achieved a level of true avodas Hashem [worship of God]... To show Him honor, I thirsted to write a commentary to all four parts of the Shulchan Aruch.

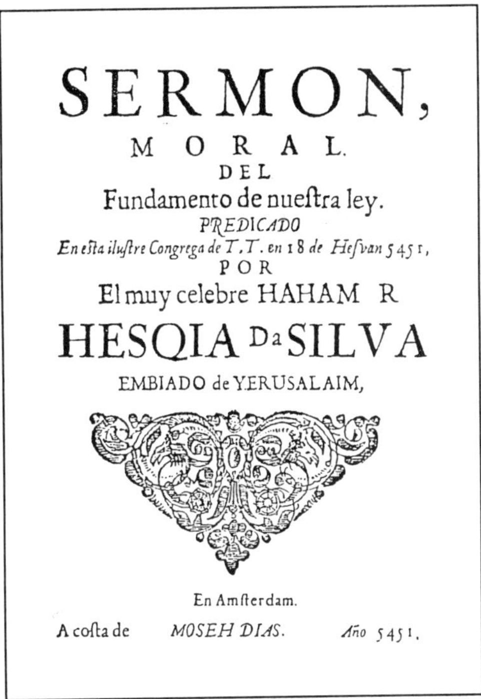

SERMON,
MORAL.
DEL
Fundamento de nueſtra ley.
PREDICADO
En eſta iluſtre Congrega de T.T. en 18 de Heſvan 5451,
POR
El muy celebre HAHAM R
HESQIA Da SILVA
EMBIADO de YERUSALAIM,

En Amſterdam.
A coſta de MOSEH DIAS. Año 5451.

Title page of the sermon delivered by Rav Silva in Amsterdam, 1691

After his mentor died in 1689, Rav Silva went to Amsterdam in order to raise funds for the Jerusalem community. He took with him folios of his manuscript, which he hoped to have published there.

In Amsterdam he was welcomed and honored as a true Torah sage. He gave a sermon in Ladino (the Sephardic vernacular at the time, equivalent to Yiddish for the Ashkenazim), which was later published. There he found backers for his book, and within a year the first volume of *Pri Chadash* (on *Yoreh Deah*) was printed.

While in Amsterdam, Rav Silva was faced with a personal decision that would affect the rest of his life. Two job offers were presented to him. Rav Yaakov Ferira, a genuine lover of Torah and philanthropist, had been supporting a yeshivah in Hebron for many years, and he now wanted to open one in Jerusalem as well. He asked the *Pri Chadash* to lead the new yeshivah.

The second offer came from the notables of the Sephardic community, who offered him the position of Rav of Amsterdam. The present leader, Rav Yitzchak Ahuhav, was aging and wished to retire.

Rav Chizkiah carefully considered both options. In the end, he consented to become Rav of Amsterdam, on two conditions: First, his halachic decisions could not be vetoed or contended by any other *rav*. Secondly, he demanded twice the normal salary.

When they consented to his conditions, Rav Silva announced the full breadth of the authority he expected. Were he to find any wayward Jew in the community, he would publicly make his sins known. There would be no exception — neither wealth nor position in the community would affect his leadership. Upon hearing the sweeping scope of his terms, the communal leaders hesitated. Reconsidering their offer, they decided to look for another candidate. Now Rav Silva was free to accept Rav Ferira's proposition.

Rav Silva and the Torah World

On his return to Eretz Yisrael in 1693, Rav Chizkiah passed through Egypt. His *Pri Chadash* had already reached the great Torah centers, and in some places it was received with much controversy. Egypt was one such place.

As we mentioned before, Rav Silva's system of analyzing halachic sources was unique, focusing primarily on Chazal and the Early Authorities. He treated all the Later Authorities — even the most preeminent among them, such as Rav Yosef Karo — as equals, and often differed with them. The rabbis of Egypt banned his *sefer*, claiming that he had no right to slight the honor of such *gedolim,* especially since he tended to hold a more lenient view. They were careful, however, not to ban him personally. Rav Silva weathered the storm and continued to his home in Jerusalem.

For the next few years, the Pri Chadash threw himself into the task of establishing and running the new yeshivah, called Beis Yaakov. Three of his most outstanding disciples were Rav Shlomo Elgazi, Rav Avraham Yitzchaki, and Rav Yitzchak HaKohen, author of *Battei Kehunah*. He also toiled to prepare the rest of his commentary for publication.

On 28 Kislev, 1696 (5457), at the age of thirty-nine, he passed away suddenly and was buried at the foot of the Mount of Olives. He had instructed that his kabbalistic writings be buried after his death. In the commotion that followed his passing, his commentary to the laws of Shabbos were accidentally buried as well.

The controversy that surrounded Rav Silva's *Pri Chadash* during his lifetime did not continue long after his death. Shortly after his passing, the *rabbanim* in Egypt looked on his writings in a different light. Rav Avraham HaLevi, the Rav of Egypt, wrote a long treatise in which he apologized for the ban. Ironically, the next Rav of Egypt was no other than the Pri Chadash's disciple, Rav Shlomo Elgazi. Rav Elgazi, who held that position for nearly fifty years, used his mentor's halachic decisions as law in the very land which had interdicted them a few years before.

The importance of the Pri Chadash cannot be underestimated. In the words of the Chida: "All scholars thirstily drink his words."[29] His revolutionary way of thinking, coupled with his zeal for truth, affected students' approach to Torah for generations to come — until the present day.

Rav Yaakov Ferira remained committed to supporting the yeshivah he started in conjunction with the Pri Chadash. Soon he asked Rav Yaakov Malko to act as Rosh Yeshivah. More classes were opened. In the merit of its founding Rosh Yeshivah's outstanding holiness, Beis Yaakov (Ferira) Yeshivah flourished and continued to serve the community for over two hundred years. It became the link between the established past of the Pri Chadash and the ever-changing future of each new generation.

Unfortunately, even with the establishment of the new yeshivah and its continued existence, Jerusalem's troubles were not over. Towards the close of the decade, in 1698, a devastating epidemic ravaged the Holy City. Rav Raphael Mordechai Malki, a physician and one of the survivors, described it: "Today, Eretz Yisrael feels desolate. Who would ever have dreamed that thirty-six *rabbanim* would die within a short time? Within another two years, even more scholars than that passed away. Now, Eretz Yisrael is barren of *rabbanim*."

The Holy City's dwindling population, frail and forlorn, was unaware of one of the largest mass-immigration movements to Eretz Yisrael. Starting from Europe, the aliyah of Rav Yehudah HaChassid and his numerous followers would breathe new life into the *yishuv*.

Notes

1. Based on *Letter of Shelah,* quoted in *Eden Tzyon,* pp. 103–106.
2. Ibid.
3. Ibid.
4. Ibid.
5. Based on the eyewitness report, *Chorvos Yerushalayim,* published in 1627.
6. *HaKehillah HaYehudis b'Yerushalayim b'Meah ha-17,* p. 267.
7. Introduction to *Kol b'Ramah.*
8. Ibid.
9. Ibid.
10. *Toldos Chachmei Yerushalayim,* vol. 2, p. 38.
11. *Korei HaDoros,* p. 90.
12. See also *HaKehillah HaYehudis b'Yerushalayim b'Meah ha-17,* pp. 55–56.
13. *Toldos Chachmei Yerushalayim,* vol. 2, pp. 46–47.
14. Ibid., p. 37 (footnote).
15. Ibid., p. 62.
16. *Zichron l'Bnei Yisrael,* p. 30.
17. Ibid. p. 40.
18. Based on *Toras HaKina'os and Mashichei HaSheker u'Misnagdeihem.*
19. *Toras HaKina'os,* p. 18b.
20. Ibid., 17b.
21. *Mashichei HaSheker,* p. 142.
22. *Toras HaKina'os,* p. 19.
23. *Toldos Chachmei Yerushalayim,* vol. 2, p. 63.
24. *Toras HaKina'os,* p. 7b.
25. *Hilchos Ketanos,* part II, no. 139.
26. *Toras HaKina'os,* p. 19.
27. *Toldos Chachmei Yerushalayim,* vol. 2, p. 57.
28. *Korban Chagigah, Parpa'os l'Chachmah,* 50a.
29. *Shem HaGedolim,* part I, *os ches,* no. 3.

Bygone Days

The Unforgettable Shabbos

THROUGHOUT THE spring and summer of 1625 the situation for the Jews of Jerusalem turned from grim to desperate. The tyrant Mohammed Farouk had ruled the city with an iron hand since Teves, and illegal arrests and sudden imprisonment were the rule of the day. His thirst for money was insatiable. Anyone of stature and wealth — even if he was an Arab citizen — was liable to be snatched and jailed until his brethren would redeem him.

The Jewish community especially suffered from the tyrant's greed. Drained of all resources, they had to borrow money at exorbitant interest rates from local Arabs in order to meet Farouk's ransom demands. Leaders of the community, along with common folk, were cruelly beaten and even tortured. Slowly, more and more families fled from the city to Ramla, Gaza, Hebron, and the Galilee. However, there were others, especially the leaders, who felt obligated to remain and guard the Jewish presence the Holy City.

All public activities had ceased for several months. The *hesger*, yeshivah, and public places of worship were closed. People did not venture into the streets unless compelled by necessity. Food supplies were rationed, and many went hungry.

In Tamuz, Farouk temporarily left to command a legion for the governor of Damascus, leaving his brother-in-law Ottman in change. At first Ottman seemed to adopt a more humane attitude to the city's populace. He spoke softly to the communal leaders, and although he requested a donation of one thousand *grushim*, he willingly agreed to accept half that amount.

As the weeks passed, the Jews began breathing easier, and people started to come out of hiding. Shops opened. No one was seized and arrested. Yet, it was felt that public functions were too risky. Although seemingly benign, Ottman still presented an ominous threat. His authority was not based on the rule of the law, and no one knew what he might do next.

At the beginning of Elul, 1625 (5385), the stirring sound of the shofar and its call to repentance fostered new hope in the hearts of those within the city walls. Many yearned to pray once again in the synagogue, especially on Shabbos. There they would unite and sing praises to their Creator.

Secret meetings were held by the communal leaders, such as Rav Yitzchak Gaon, the physician Rav Yaakov ibn Amram, and other rabbis. If Ottman was just playing possum, then the dangers were very great indeed; but if he was sincere, as he had appeared to be until now, then there was no reason not to conduct public services again. Each day the pendulum swayed back and forth, for and against.

Finally, it was agreed to pray in two of the several synagogues in the city, one Ashkenazic and the other Sephardic. Services would resume on Shabbos *Ki Tetze*, 11 Elul.

When the momentous day arrived, the humble congregants quietly began the Shacharis service. Everyone rejoiced over the resumption of the communal prayer service. The streets outside were nearly empty. It seemed that they had made the right choice.

Suddenly and without warning, soldiers brandishing swords stormed into the two synagogues. Everyone froze in his place. They were trapped. Women screamed, children cried. There was no escape.

Ottman strutted around, pointing to various people and shouting, "Arrest him! Arrest him! And him!"

The despot's cunning strategy had paid off well. He had before him all the wealthy members of the community, and most of its dignified rabbis as well. Within minutes fifteen of the most honored members of the community were bound and taken away. Among them were the prince of Prague, Rav Yeshaya Horowitz. Others included Rav Shmuel Sid, Rav Moshe Tarinsky, and Rav Menachem Nahar.

As the prisoners were shoved out the synagogue door and into the street, they did not know if they would ever return again. There was certainly no redress to the court, as the *kadi* was in league with the tyrant. There would be no hearing, no defense attorney, no trial, no civil rights outcry. As they were herded to their new destination, they caught a glimpse of sunshine — a symbol of freedom and hope — for one last time before the darkness set in.

They were apparently imprisoned in the Kishle compound, located near Migdal David. It would be charitable to call the dungeon primitive. The air was heavy and dank, and the only light came from a lantern set near the top of the arched ceiling. Beds were non-existent, sanitation was crude, and food was meager, especially since the prisoners all kept kosher. Worst of all, however, was the feeling of separation from the community and the uncertainty over the schemes of their tormentors.

Rav Horowitz, in his mid-sixties, uttered words of encouragement to his fellow inmates. This was a time of sanctifying the Name of God — even unto death. The Lord was refining them and cleansing them from their past sins. Surely, everything was for their good.

Outside, Rav Yoel HaLevi — one of the few rabbis of the community to be spared — subjected himself to great personal danger by going to the Ottman's residence and requesting to speak with him. He was accompanied by the

Sheik al-Yehud.

Ottman sat drinking with his friends. His daily routine consisted of getting drunk, sleeping it off, and then drinking some more.

"What do you want?" he laughed maliciously, enjoying himself immensely.

"I have come to inquire concerning the fate of the captives," Rav Yoel answered.

"I'm planning to torture and kill them all."

"Heaven forbid!" cried Rav Yoel.

"If you want them back alive, you'll have to put 20,000 *grushim* on the table. Are they worth that much to you?" Ottman chuckled to his companions.

Medieval Turkish weaponry

Rav Yoel returned to the synagogue and reported the tyrant's demand. People wept and cried. Shabbos, *parshas Ki Tetze*, had turned into a day of mourning.

Some of the wives of the prisoners ran to the *kadi*'s house. They begged him to do something, but his ears and his heart were closed to their pleas.

The following day, the community sent a messenger to the governor in Damascus, denouncing Ottman and his actions. However, precious time would be lost before a response arrived. Meanwhile, Rav Yoel returned to Ottman and informed him that the community would be able to pay 11,000 *grushim*, but that it would take time. Ottman "generously" agreed to these terms.

On the eve of Rosh HaShanah, the communal leaders presented Ottman with 10,200 *grushim*. After fifteen days of darkness and subhuman living conditions, all but six of the prisoners were released. These six would be held until the final 800 *grushim* were received. Rav Yeshaya Horowitz was among those to see the light of day. However, although he was free, he immediately went into hiding. It was not beneath Ottman to rearrest him, since he was Chief Rabbi of the Ashkenazim and worth a lot of money to the wicked oppressor.

In the meantime, the message sent by the community arrived in Damascus. The Jewish leader of that city, Rav Chaim Shiriz, read the letter to the governor. Rav Shiriz and his fellow Jews rent their garments and beseeched the governor to act immediately.

The governor dispatched a directive to Ottman, ordering him to release the prisoners. He backed up his words by sending a captain with thirty soldiers.

The captain arrived on the first day of Rosh HaShanah, 1625 (5386). He went directly to the *kadi's* house and demanded that the remaining Jews be released. Hundreds of Jews came forward and begged the captain — as representative of the Ottoman Empire — to also retrieve the 10,200 *grushim* which Ottman had illegally taken from them.

Both the *kadi* and the captain reassured them that everything would be corrected once and for all.

Ottman was informed of the captain's demands and promised to release the six prisoners at midday.

The captain, accompanied by a number of Jews, met with Ottman on the second day of Rosh HaShanah. The captain was shocked to hear the *kadi* reverse everything he had promised to do for the Jews! Ottman, knowing how money talks, had bribed the corrupt and greedy *kadi*.

While waiting to speak directly with Ottman, an elite unit of Ottman's soldiers entered the room with drawn swords. In the name of their leader, they ordered all the Jews to return to their homes, and the captain to leave the city immediately. If not, the blades of their swords would be felt.

The captain, shocked and fearful, left the city at once, and the Jews fled to their homes.

The following day, Ottman sent a messenger to the captain. The tyrant, afraid of the governor of Damascus' reaction to his high-handed treatment of his officer, sent bribe money to the captain, plus 5,000 *grushim* for the governor.

Thus, the Jews of Jerusalem were left once again at the mercy of the capricious despot. True, their beloved rabbis were free, but as long as they did not pay the remaining 800 *grushim*, the remaining six languished in jail, and the community was in danger of new reprisals.

On Hoshannah Rabbah, they sold their spare clothes in order to pay the wicked Ottman and succeeded in securing the release of the last remaining captives. Although their situation was still oppressive, they rejoiced with the Torah on Simchas Torah. A life of Torah and mitzvos, fulfilled in the Holy City, was worth more than all the gold and silver in the world.

(*Chorvos Yerushalayim*)

The Tug of War

WHEN A certain scholar by the name of Rav Chaim moved from Safed to Jerusalem in the first quarter of the seventeenth century, he was greeted warmly. Within a short time, Rav Chaim opened a small *beis midrash* and accepted four scholars to study with him. The money to support the *beis midrash* came yearly from a trust fund in Budapest that had been established for this purpose by a wealthy relative of the scholar.

Rav Chaim conducted the affairs of the *beis midrash* in keeping with the wishes of his deceased relative. The will stipulated that a hundred *grushim* would be sent annually to support four *talmidei chachamim*, two Sephardim and two Ashkenazim. It did not, however, specify where the yeshivah had to be located in Eretz Yisrael.

At the time Rav Chaim's relative set up the fund, Rav Chaim was living in Safed, and thus he naturally established the *beis midrash* in that city. However, after several years, a disagreement over a certain matter arose between him and the city leaders. As a result, the scholars at his yeshivah chose to leave and study in different institutions. With the yeshivah empty and the feud between him and the communal leaders at the point of "who can live with this deadly snake at my heels," Rav Chaim moved to Jerusalem.

For three years the yeshivah flourished in Jerusalem. In the fourth year, the communal leaders of Safed summoned Rav Chaim to *beis din*. In front of Rav Yeshaya Pinto and his colleagues, they charged that Rav Chaim had no right to move the yeshivah out of Safed. Once Rav Chaim had opened the yeshivah in their city, they claimed, the Jewish community of Safed had earned the right to have the inheritance money come there. He could not relocate the yeshivah as long as funds continued to be sent. Rav Chaim vehemently disagreed, declaring that he had the authority to open a yeshivah anywhere in Eretz Yisrael.

Rav Pinto ruled in favor of Safed. He explained that since the inheritance had been sent to Safed for several years, the yeshivah could not be relocated to any other city. Rav Chaim's power, he said, lay solely in accepting scholars into the yeshivah and supervising its daily needs.

The Jerusalem community, shocked at Rav Pinto's decision, asked Rav Shmuel ibn Sid of Jerusalem and Rav Eliezer ibn Archa of Hebron for a halachic ruling. After hearing both sides, they gave their decision.

Rav Sid, who moved to Jerusalem from Egypt in 1619, concluded that the move from Safed to Jerusalem could not be construed as altering the original wishes of the deceased. "Moreover," he said, "such a change is only for the better. Jerusalem is 'before Hashem,' and even today the Holy City possesses a higher spiritual standard than Safed."

Rav Archa endorsed Rav Sid's ruling. He even denounced the *rabbanim* of Safed for succumbing to jealousy and acting brazenly against Jerusalem.

News of the controversy reached the ears of the committee in Budapest that oversaw the disbursement of the fund. They agreed with the Jews of Safed and ordered their emissary to forward the money to the Galilean city. The emissary traveled with the funds via Egypt and passed through Jerusalem. While there, he conferred with Rav Chaim and the elders of the city, and it was decided to keep the money in the Holy City.

The elders sent a letter to Safed, and in return received a very forceful letter ordering them to forward the funds at once to Safed. The reply was silence.

The years passed and the yeshivah continued to function in Jerusalem. Safed suffered spiritually and economically during the following decades.

Some of her best scholars left. Rav Binyamin HaLevi, a *talmid* of the Ari Zal, and his disciple Rav David Chavilio traveled first to Jerusalem, but shortly thereafter moved to *chutz laAretz*. Rav Yosef Malko moved to Jerusalem and watched his son Yaakov grow up to be one of the *chachamim* of the city.

The dwindling community of Safed took their claim to a rabbinical council of seven rabbis in Turkey sometime in 1682. One of the rabbis was Rav Yosef Elmoshnino, who himself had studied in the Beis Yaakov Yeshivah of Rav Chagiz. *Shelichim* from both communities were present.

"Without any doubt," he announced, "the funding must be returned to Safed. It is immaterial whether more scholars reside in Jerusalem than in Safed. Even if ten Jerusalemite *chachamim* are willing to accept the same stipend that four would receive in Safed, the funds are to remain in Safed."

The only way the inheritance could be moved to Jerusalem would be if four scholars could not be found in Safed. This, he said, was impossible.

The tug of war between the two great Torah centers in Eretz Yisrael swayed back and forth for over half a century. The final outcome is not recorded. In any case, the noble intentions of the giver remained viable throughout the duration of the dispute. Those many *chachamim* who were privileged to study Torah, funded by a kindhearted Jew, gave honor to the Almighty and Eretz Yisrael.

(*HaKehillah HaYehudis b'Yerushalayim*, pp. 268–270)

The Missing Boy

IT WAS a spring day sometime in the 1630s. The date was 7 Adar, the day on which Moses was both born and died. Although most of the community went about their normal routine, some people fasted and others recited Psalms on this special day.

In the middle of the afternoon, a disturbance of some sort was heard coming from the Moslem Quarter, accompanied by shouting and screaming. At first it was unclear what the commotion was all about. However, one thing was certain: within a very short time, hundreds of Arabs had gathered together, some brandishing clubs and knifes. Within minutes the danger escalated as the mob set off towards the Jewish Quarter.

A Jewish boy burst into the yeshivah, out of breath.

"They're coming to kill us!" he screamed.

The *kadi* shouted for the mob to listen to him. He ordered them to stop, promising that the matter would be taken care of legally, and that if their charge against the Jews was substantiated, justice would be served and revenge would be taken. Thankfully, he succeeded in curbing the intended massacre, although some Jews suffered blows and even worse.

Soon the *kadi* ordered the Jewish communal leaders to come before him. His words were harsh, and the threat of annihilation was palpable in the air.

The innocent Jews, of course, had no idea what they had supposedly done to spark the barely averted pogrom. However, they had no need to comprehend the exact circumstances in order to realize the proper response. The corrupt *kadi* expected a sizable bribe — both as a reward for arresting the pogrom before it had gotten totally out of control, and to keep him from reinciting the mob. Rejecting their initial offer as not enough, he demanded five thousand *grushim*. With no choice in the matter, the communal leaders acquiesced to the astronomical sum.

Only then did he explain to them the reason for the Moslems' wrath: "They claim that a Moslem boy, so-and-so from Jerusalem, was murdered by Jews in Egypt. I have bought you time for the present. Now you must prove that he is alive or else pay the consequences — and then, even I will not be able to withhold the mob."

"That boy," answered one of the leaders, "is well known to us. He is a Jewish boy who was kidnapped and forced to become a Moslem. We tried to convince you and other authorities that he is Jewish and must be returned. But no one listened to us.

"It would seem that now he has fled to take refuge in Egypt. We are sure that he is alive and certain that no Jew has harmed him."

"Then you must do the following," the *kadi* said sternly. "You must send somebody to bring the boy back and prove that he is alive. If he is really Jewish, I promise that he will not be handed over to his Moslem family.

"But if you fail, then I cannot stop the Arab citizens from finishing what they set out to do today."

With a solemn look on his face, the *kadi* added, "As a guarantee, eight of you must be imprisoned until the boy is brought back."

The next morning a member of the community set off for Egypt to find the boy. Weeks passed until he succeeded in finding him — alive. He had indeed escaped from his Moslem family and returned to his faith. However, he patently refused to go back to Jerusalem for fear of being kidnapped again.

Finally, after many reassurances, the twelve-year-old boy agreed to return, especially in order to save the Jews of Jerusalem.

The two arrived in Jerusalem on the eve of the last day of Passover. Six weeks had passed since the beginning of the ordeal. Throughout the entire period a state of uncertainty hovered over the community.

Once the *kadi* and the Arab leaders saw the boy and realized that it was him, the decree was annulled and the eight hostages of the community were freed.

That night, *Shevi'i shel Pesach*, which commemorates the splitting of the Red Sea and the downfall of the Egyptians, became a night of freedom and *geula* for the entire Jewish community of Jerusalem.

(*Toldos Chachmei Yerushalayim*, vol. 2, p. 120)

At the Tomb of Zechariah

1639 WAS a lean year for Eretz Yisrael, as drought and famine covered the land. The ruler of Jerusalem, Mohammed Pasha, was desperate to divert the attention of a clamorous public from himself. He hit upon an age-old, and unfortunately all too successful, ploy — blaming the Jews as scapegoats for any problem, no matter how preposterous it might sound. He sanctimoniously proceeded to accuse the Jews of plotting the drought, and went so far as to threaten them with an ultimatum: produce rain or be exiled!

The Jews begged and bribed him to retract his threat, but he remained adamant, and allowed them three days to bring rain.

The leader of the community, Rav Emanuel Elbachari, requested permission for them to pray by the Tomb of Zechariah at the foot of the Mount of Olives, and it was granted. In those days, the Tomb of Zechariah was revered as much as the Ohr HaChaim's grave is revered today. However, were the entire Jewish community to go without permission, it would be interpreted as a ploy to escape en masse.

Men, women and children prayed by the tomb all day long. In the afternoon, clouds appeared and soon rain began to fall. The Jews had been saved by Heavenly grace. The ruler praised them, and acknowledged that the rain was due to their prayers.

(*HaKehillah HaYehudis b'Yerushalayim b'Meah ha-17*, p. 55)

The gigantic Tomb of Zechariah with its pointed roof is to the right. On the left is the Cave of Hezir, a burial cave for an ancient Cohen family of Jerusalem.

A Glimmer of Light

THE AFTERMATH of Farouk's tyranny left the hapless and victimized Jews longing for relief from the plight of *galus* more than ever. In the year 1631, ten *rabbanim* in Jerusalem sought to make an active attempt to hasten the Redemption. They did this by isolating themselves in a room for forty days in a row. There they prayed and wept before the Almighty to have mercy on the Jewish people. The bitterness of exile had reached the limit of human patience, they entreated, and Torah study and *avodas Hashem* had become weakened due to the constant economic threats and physical dangers faced by entire Jewish people. Each day they devoted themselves exclusively to beseeching God through prayer and Torah study.

At the end of the forty days, news spread throughout the city of a mysterious fire which had broken out in the Church of the Holy Sepulcher. The pious scholars interpreted the fire as a Heavenly sign that *avodah zarah* (idolatry) was about to be destroyed in the advent of the redemption.

Later, when the *geula* failed to materialize, they understood that the time for the redemption had still not arrived. There were just too many Jews who failed to keep the Torah and mitzvos as they should.

(*Maaseh Sh'haya b'Yerushalayim*, pp. 161–162)

Shabbetai Tzvi at the Tomb of Shmuel HaNavi

SHABBETAI TZVI was a person to reckon with. His personality was magnetic, especially after his prophet Nasan of Gaza revealed his "divine" mission as *mashiach* to him. His noble countenance, long black beard, and impassioned manner of speaking drew people to him. The day of his "coronation" was sometime in Iyar, 1665 (5425). In Tamuz he and his prophet went to Hebron and annulled the fast of 17 Tamuz. They then proceeded to Jerusalem, with a sizable entourage in tow.

Immediately the "Mashiach" set about to effect the purported redemption. Although it was not Passover, he felt compelled to offer a paschal lamb on the Temple Mount. *Baruch Hashem*, he acceded to the pleas of the *rabbanim* and did not bring it. However, he did publicly annul the prohibition to eat *chelev*, forbidden animal fats. He even formulated a special blessing that should be recited over it — *matir assurim* (permits the forbidden).

At one point he decided to visit the burial cavern of Shmuel HaNavi, a three-hour walk north of the Holy City. In addition to his personal entourage from Gaza and Hebron, some Jerusalemites also accompanied him. Among the group was a perverse man by the name of Shmuel Lubano, a man of very questionable character.

The party arrived at the cavern at nightfall. A large number of candles and lanterns were lit in the large underground cave. Most of the people went downstairs to pray by the tomb of the prophet. The group waited for their leader to come before beginning the Maariv service. However, Shabbetai Tzvi and a dozen of his followers did not want to *daven* just then. Instead, they went into the area called the *migdal*, where the Moslems prayed. There they sat down and ate and drank. The mood was frivolous, and time did not seem to matter.

When Shabbetai received a message that everyone was waiting for him by the tomb, he simply ignored it.

Finally, just before dawn, his followers succeeded in pressuring him to go down and lead the Maariv service.

Standing up to his full stature, Shabbetai Tzvi led his friends downstairs. When he entered the cave, he took a stick from the floor. He approached the tomb and began to strike it with the stick, once, twice, three times.

"Shmuel HaNavi!" his voice thundered. "I remove you from your position as prophet and replace you with my comrade, Shmuel Lubano!"

Evidently the hours of festivities coupled with heavy drinking had carried the *mashiach* away.

He turned and looked around him. Everyone stood silently and expectantly, waiting to see what he would do next. With stick in hand, Shabbetai began to smash the lanterns to pieces and knock over the candles.

People standing by the entrance to the cave scrambled to get out. Others

Tomb of Shmuel HaNavi as it appeared in the 19th century

moved to the side, so that Shabbetai would not accidentally hit them. Within a minute or two most of the hundred candles lay extinguished on the ground. Then he left and returned to his feast.

Somewhat shocked at his behavior, most of the men went to pray Maariv wherever they could. It seemed that their *mashiach* did not need to pray. Or maybe his acrobatics were his form of prayer.

(*Toras HaKina'os*, p. 25b)

May His Name Be Blessed

RAV MOSHE Galante, known as Rav HaMagen, left his beloved Jerusalem for Damascus as a *shaliach* for the community. While it is not known conclusively when he departed on this particular mission — since he traveled to Damascus several times — it might have been the one he is recorded as having taken in 1667 (5427).

While in Damascus, Rav Galante heard of an Arab sheik who was said to possess miraculous healing powers. Like Rabbi Chaninah ben Dosa, the sheik would say, "This one will live, this one will die," and his words came true. More than this, the sheik was said to be proficient in the so-called seven branches of worldly wisdom. Rav HaMagen, who was also well versed in the known branches of wisdom, was not phased by the sheik's grasp of worldly knowledge. However, he was intrigued by the sheik's seeming ability to decree something which was not in the realm of human hands with such certainty. Our Sages tell us that the key of life and death is not handed over to anyone — not even an angel; God retains that key for Himself alone. Even Rabbi Chaninah ben Dosa could merely sense whether or not an ill person would recover, but the actual key always remained in God's possession.

"Is this gentile so holy," Rav Moshe pondered, "that he is privileged to have the Book of Life and Death revealed to him? I serve Hashem, study Torah, and fulfill mitzvos all the time; why am I not granted this same privilege?"

Rav HaMagen's curiosity grew and grew. Determined to arrange a meeting, he sent the most influential Jew in Damascus, called the *parnas*, to tell the sheik that a very wise Jew from Jerusalem wished to meet with him.

The sheik, having previously heard of Rav Galante, was delighted to grant him an audience.

They met in the sheik's villa. Known throughout the city as a virtuous and pious man, the sheik rarely left the confines of his sumptuous residence. It comprised several courtyards, myriad rooms, and magnificent gardens.

The Rav's host quickly turned the conversation to the central issue. "I have heard that you are a wise man," said the sheik. "Is it true that you are knowledgeable in such-and-such a wisdom?"

"Yes, the Lord has granted me a little knowledge of this wisdom," Rav Galante answered.

In order to test him, the sheik commenced to ask Rav Galante a series of difficult questions. Rav Moshe answered each query in depth and to the point. The sheik was amazed to find him in complete command of such wisdom. Until now, the sheik had assumed that he alone had total grasp of this knowledge. Now he had found a comrade with whom he could relate as an equal.

"My beloved friend," smiled the sheik. "I have enjoyed your company immensely. I would be very pleased if you could come again, say once a week. I see that we have much to discuss."

Two days later, the sheik sent two of his servants to the Rav's residence with an invitation for another audience with him. They escorted the Rav on horseback to the sheik's mansion.

"Peace be with you!" said the sheik, embracing his dear friend. "Since you left here, I have been thinking a lot about our conversation. I could not wait any longer to see you again and therefore I sent for you now."

They sat down on cushioned pillows in one of the sheik's opulent lounge rooms. Again the sheik asked Rav Galante if he was versed in another one of the seven branches of worldly wisdom. And again he began to ask Rav HaMagen questions. Once again, he was astonished by the Rav's breadth of knowledge.

Approaching the city of Damascus

As the conversation drew to a close, the sheik asked his friend, "If I have found favor in your eyes, would you please come every other day to me?" Rav Galante agreed to his request.

With each new meeting, they discussed another one of the seven branches of wisdom. Each time, the sheik felt a greater bond with the Rav. He had never met any other person who possessed as much understanding as Rav HaMagen.

At last, the sheik confided in his companion. "To be truthful, my friend, I am lacking certain preparatory details concerning the last branch of wisdom. Without these, I am unable to fully grasp and use this branch. Do you have a comprehensive understanding of it?"

"Yes."

Falling at his feet, the sheik pleaded with Rav Galante to teach him everything he knew. He would pay any price to have Rav Moshe reveal to him this wisdom.

"Heaven forbid," Rav Galante responded. "This is not a salable item. However, I am willing to teach you, on condition that you teach me concerning another body of wisdom."

The sheik was dumbfounded. "What do you mean? You are wiser than me. How can there be a branch of wisdom in which you are not proficient?"

"There is a wondrous body of wisdom that you possess, of which I am wholly ignorant: you can pray for a sick person and see into the Book of Life and Death. I lack this wisdom.

"Therefore," concluded Rav HaMagen, "if you will reveal to me this wisdom, I shall teach you what you want to know."

The sheik returned slowly to his seat. "Your request is impossible to fulfill. It is forbidden for me to reveal it to any human being."

"Likewise," responded Rav HaMagen, "I cannot reveal what you so much desire to know other than by an exchange of wisdom."

After a silence, the sheik spoke. "My dear friend, the reason that I cannot reveal it to you is because I have sworn to my forefathers not to divulge the secret to anyone."

"I am also sworn not to teach this wisdom I possess to anyone else," countered Rav HaMagen. "Yet, I reckon that since it is of great benefit for me to acquire this new knowledge, it is permissible to do so and does not abrogate my oath. You should feel the same; remember, you are not selling it for money; you are exchanging and sharing wisdom. With this new knowledge you will be enlightened and have total command of all the seven branches of worldly wisdom."

Rav Galante's words were spoken with complete sincerity. The sheik sat quietly for several minutes, gazing out the window into the garden.

"I agree," he said softly. "But I am afraid, my friend, that the risks are too great for you."

Rav Galante's face shone. "I am prepared to do whatever you ask of me,

Public gardens in Damascus

no matter how difficult."

"In that case, listen carefully to me. Return to your abode. When the sun is about to set, take a vow to fast for two consecutive days. At your last meal, be sure not to eat meat or drink wine. After eating, immerse in a pool of water and dress in fine garments. Throughout the two days, meditate on repentance and immerse often. Then, on the third day, return to me."

"I agree to everything you say," answered Rav Galante.

"Go in peace." The sheik bid him farewell.

Rav HaMagen returned home and followed all of the conditions laid out by the sheik to the letter. At the beginning of the third night, Rav Galante decided to refrain from breaking his fast. He wanted to experience this secret wisdom in a true state of humility.

When Rav Galante appeared before the sheik the next morning, he immediately noticed how weak and feeble the Rav looked. "I see you have fulfilled everything I requested."

"Yes," answered Rav HaMagen. "I am still fasting now."

"Wonderful!"

The sheik then led his guest to a locked room to which he alone had the key. After they entered, the sheik locked the door behind them.

From there they came to a second locked door. This one opened into a magnificent garden. In the middle of the garden was a spring of fresh water. Butterflies danced in the air. The spring flowed into a pool before continuing along a narrow channel. Next to the spring was a bench with two white cloaks on it.

"We must first immerse here before dressing in these white garments," whispered the sheik.

Silently they immersed and donned the new garments. The sheik then led the *rav* through the garden. Rav Galante's curiosity was at its peak.

Finally, hidden behind a grove, they came to an edifice of exquisite beauty. The double doors of the structure were made of pure silver, with marvelous engravings on them.

"Beware," the sheik said in a hushed voice. "Follow after me with utter fear and trepidation."

The sheik opened the silver doors and entered. Upon beholding the extraordinary beauty inside, Rav Galante was spellbound. The fragrance was otherworldly. Before them was a chamber. In the entrance to the chamber hung a curtain with precious stones sewn in it. The sheik bowed on the floor seven times before the curtain.

Rav HaMagen froze in his place. Was there an idol inside? The sheik motioned for him to bow. His head began to swim.

He closed his eyes, and as if in a stupor fell on the floor and whispered, שִׁוִּיתִי ה׳ לְנֶגְדִּי תָמִיד, "I shall place God before me always." He had never felt such a state of awe in his life.

"Now," whispered the sheik, "you may enter, and there you will find the secret you seek."

Rav Galante stood up and pushed aside the curtain and entered the chamber. On the walls hung tapestries of gold and silver. On the wall facing the curtain hung an exquisite tablet with an engraving of a candelabrum. Above the menorah were four Hebrew words: שִׁוִּיתִי ה׳ לְנֶגְדִּי תָמִיד. The Ineffable Name of God was spelled out in large, bold letters.

Rav HaMagen was overjoyed to see this. He had not bowed in vain! He bowed again and retraced his footsteps into the antechamber.

Outside in the garden, Rav Galante inquired of the sheik, "You told me that inside the chamber I would find the answer. But more than what my eyes saw was not revealed to me."

"My dear friend, let me explain. The four large letters you saw in the tablet are the name of the Creator of the world. When I am asked to pray for a sick person, I immerse in the pool and enter into the chamber. Before opening the curtain, I pray wholeheartedly. When I open it and gaze at the tablet, I see one of two things. Either the four-letter Name is glittering and sparks of light seem to emanate from it, or it is dark and unclear. If it is shining, I know the sick person will live, and if it is cloudy I know he will die.

"With this, I have now revealed to you a secret that no other human being knows."

When Rav HaMagen returned to his residence, he wept and cried. "Woe unto us on the Day of Judgment," he lamented. "Look at this goy — because he honors the Name of the Creator to such an extent, he is privileged to have such Heavenly secrets revealed to him. But we, the Jewish people, what can we answer? We are even more qualified to have Hashem reveal this to us. Yet, look at us and how we approach the Name of our Lord!"

(*Matok m'Devash*, by Rav Yitzchak Parchi, ch. 5)

The Torah's Honor

JERUSALEM HUMMED with the sound of rejoicing. Simchas Torah in 1675 (5436) fulfilled the words of the Sages: A small sanctuary filled with holiness. The entire community joined together to dance before the Lord.

On the night of Simchas Torah, after Maariv, the Holy Ark was opened and one by one the Torah scrolls were handed out to different rabbis and laymen. Verses were recited, and a melody set the congregants dancing around the *bimah*. The *gabbai* placed a lit candle in the Holy Ark, symbolizing that the light of Torah — even when all the *sifrei Torah* are removed — never wanes.

As the singing and dancing continued, one of the congregants took a lit candle and joyously started dancing in front of one of the men carrying a *sefer Torah*. He faced the *sefer Torah* and danced backwards, singing and stretching his other arm high into the air.

Seeing this, one of the *bachurim*, Chizkiah by name, yelled out, "Stop! Stop at once!"

He pointed to the person holding the candle. "Yom Tov! It's Yom Tov, and it is forbidden to carry a lit candle in such a manner."

The commotion the young man had stirred up interrupted the dancing. One of the scholars of the community walked towards the *bachur* and declared, "How dare you speak up like that, young man? Don't you see that you are in a synagogue full of *talmidei chachamim*? Don't you know — even if you are right — that it is forbidden to state a halachah before the rabbinical leaders of the city?"

Twenty-year-old Chizkiah remained undaunted. Again he repeated himself, adding, "As he moves the candle, some of the wax is sure to drip. This inevitably causes the light to dim, and this falls under the prohibition of 'reducing the fire.' And even worse, due to the dancing, it is conceivable that the candlelight might accidentally be extinguished."

The scholar and the student were surrounded by a group of bystanders. An argument quickly ensued concerning the halachic issue: Is such an act forbidden on Yom Tov or not? More and more scholars entered into the dispute. The Rosh Yeshivah, Rav Moshe Galante, remained aloof on the side.

Eventually, the singing picked up again and things returned to normal.

One of the younger married men, Rav Chaim Abulafia, spoke warmly to Chizkiah. He recommended that the two of them leave the synagogue and go to the *beis midrash*. There, with access to *sefarim*, they could delve into the halachah properly.

They opened the *Shulchan Aruch*, the *Tur,* and the *Beis Yosef*, referring also to the Gemara in *Shabbos* with its commentaries. They discussed minute aspects of the halachah and finally concluded that carrying a lit candle in such a manner was forbidden on Yom Tov.

When they returned to the dancing, Chizkiah Silva beckoned the *talmidei chachamim* to come over to the side and listen to him for a minute. His comrade, Rav Chaim, stood next to him.

"Dear Rabbis, I want you to know that my outburst was in no way a sign of disrespect for you and the Rosh Yeshivah. I simply could not stand by and witness a blatant dishonor of our holy Torah."

The young man spoke passionately. Because he had only lived and studied in Jerusalem for a few months, not everyone was fully aware of his superb level of Torah knowledge. The Rosh Yeshivah and Rav Chaim Abulafia were among the few who recognized his greatness.

Rav Chizkiah summarized all the commentators on this particular halachah and reiterated his earlier *pesak* that it was forbidden.

"If there is someone here who disagrees with me," he said in a low but firm tone, "let him first ask himself to distinguish between two similar Shabbos acts, one of which Rabbi Shimon bar Yochai permits and the other he forbids.

"Rabbi Shimon allows *dvar sh'eino mishayein,* but forbids a *melachah sh'eino tzericha l'gufa*. There is a very thin line between the two acts, and if someone cannot explain the difference, then he is not qualified to dispute this halachah."

Everyone in the group regarded the young man with silent respect. Their acquaintance with Rav Chizkiah Silva began on the day when everyone rejoices over being granted a portion in the Torah. Rav Chizkiah's portion would not only light up the *beis midrash* in Jerusalem, it would illuminate the whole Torah world. Fifteen years later he published the *Pri Chadash*, one of the most highly respected commentaries on the *Shulchan Aruch*.

(Eyewitness account by Rav Chaim Abulafia, *Responsa*)

"I Am Black Yet Comely"

THE YEAR was 1653. Fentalio de Abiro walked aimlessly through the streets of Jerusalem, in no hurry to reach a specific destination. As a Christian pilgrim from Portugal, his itinerary was simply to visit his religion's shrines for a few months and then return homeward. Actually, this was his second visit, and the city almost felt like home to him.

Every day he unselfconsciously walked through the Jewish section. There he would linger outside the synagogue and watch the Jews pass by him. He was enamored of them. There was something about their mannerisms that attracted his attention.

One morning he stopped an elderly Spanish-speaking Jew and began a conversation. Though it was obvious from his dress that Fentalio was a Christian, the Jew replied briefly to his questions about Judaism.

"Why are you so curious?" asked the Jew.

"I'll be honest with you," Fentalio replied. "I'm descended from a Marrano family. Ever since I discovered this, I've had a growing fascination with the Jewish people."

"Yes, I understand," the Jew smiled. "It's only a hundred and sixty years since the Spanish Expulsion, and I have met several descendants of Marranos myself."

As their conversation continued, the elderly Jew became increasingly aware that Fentalio's motives were not pure. Throughout their conversation, the Christian was attempting to demonstrate the superiority of his religion. He spoke arrogantly, not ashamed to belittle the faith of the Jew to whom he was speaking.

The elderly Jew turned to go away.

"No, no! My friend, don't go away. Please listen to me."

The Jew did not even bother to turn back or utter another word. He just kept walking away.

Fentalio didn't take that as an insult. He just kept wandering around places where Jews were found. Several times his discussions with other Jews turned into heated disputes. Once or twice they actually ended in blows.

One day he stopped a young teenage Sephardic girl.

"Excuse me," he began. "Do you speak Spanish?"

"Yes."

"Were you born in Spain, my dear?"

"No. I was born in Egypt. My father's family was originally from Spain."

Again he explained his mixed heritage and displayed a seeming desire to know more about Judaism. She thought, like most of the others who had come in contact with him, that he was a potential proselyte.

"When I was in Venice last year," he proudly exclaimed, "I went to a different synagogue on each Sabbath out of curiosity. There I listened to the Rabbi's sermon. One, in fact, spoke about the Messiah."

Yet, inevitably, he turned the discussion into a diatribe against Judaism.

She turned to walk away.

"Just a minute!" His tone changed as he pompously pointed at her dress. "Look at you! Barefooted, and dressed in rags!"

Tears rolled down her cheeks. She dashed off.

Fentalio smiled. This time he had won.

The girl's mother consoled her. "Don't cry, my darling. If we have to suffer the ridicule of the gentiles, then it is only to remind us that we are still in the long night of the exile. Yet there will come a day, my darling, when our Temple will be rebuilt. Then we shall be the princes and princesses of the world, and all the nations will admire us."

(*Tevuos HaAretz*, p. 432)

The Day of Rain

THE LATE winter sky over Jerusalem reflected the same pristine heaven as yesterday and the day before — in fact, that of the week and the months before as well. Not a drop of rain had fallen in over three months. The winter was nearly over, and the weather was turning warm. The threat to the crops posed a serious problem, but the dry drinking wells posed a much greater dilemma. Indeed, the situation had reached critical proportions.

Jerusalemites of all faiths turned to prayer. Special services were conducted in the mosques and churches. The Jews also prayed, turning to God in their synagogues, by the Wailing Wall, at the tomb of King David on Mount Zion, and at the Tomb of Rachel near Bethlehem. Still the heavens remained sealed.

The pasha, desperate to find a solution, ordered the Chief Rabbi of Jerusalem to appear before him. The venerable Rav Moshe Galante, escorted by his *shamash*, entered the ruler's office.

"You are the guilty ones!" the pasha lashed out as he pointed to the Chief Rabbi. "The Jews of the city have cursed their gentile neighbors. That's why the rain have failed to come."

Rav Galante stood in silence. The pasha's authority allowed him to imprison whomever he wished, and even to put his enemies to death.

"You claim to be the chosen people. If so, when you beseech God in time of need, He should answer you. Therefore, I give you three days to pray and be answered. If there is no rain by then, all Jews will be exiled from the city!"

Rav Galante returned home. He proclaimed a three-day fast for all members of the community. They would only eat at night. The days dragged by slowly as the dry lips of faithful Jews uttered Psalms and supplications before the Heavenly court. Their somber faces and downcast eyes painted a picture reminiscent of Tisha b'Av. The Rav sat in his chair next to the Holy Ark and recited Psalms. Outside, the sun still shone as brightly as if it were a summer day.

As the third day began to wane, Rav Galante ordered every member of the community to follow him outside the Old City's walls to the cave of Shimon HaTzaddik. Perhaps in the merit of the holy tzaddik their prayers would be answered.

"Everyone, man, woman, and child, should follow me," his voice rang out. "No one should forget to wear his winter rain garb!" he added.

Some of the congregants laughed despairingly. "Is our *rav* a prophet, too?"

However, the Rav's solemn countenance brooked no discussion. He had meant what he had said.

Everyone quickly scurried home to put on boots, heavy winter coats, scarves, and rain hats. Soon, hundreds of Jews marched through the city towards the Damascus Gate.

Arab water vendors in the Old City, carrying their precious merchandise in waterskins

When the Turkish sentry saw the assembly dressed for a downpour, he laughed and mocked them. In short order, his scorn turned to hatred. He wantonly stalked up to Rav Galante and slapped him on the face. The Rav just kept walking in silence.

Outside the gate, the group turned to the right and followed the dirt road through Jehoshafat Valley until they came to the cave of Shimon HaTzaddik.

Without a word, Rav Galante fell on his knees and kissed the grave stone. Everyone poured out supplications to God from the depths of their hearts. The Rav whispered prayers with tears rolling down his beard. The sounds of weeping and wailing bounced off the rocks of the cave walls. The echoes spiraled out of the cave and into the parched sky.

Suddenly, gusts of wind began blowing and dark clouds raced across the heavens. The trees swayed to and fro. Everyone gazed upward, and within seconds heavy raindrops landed on their tearful cheeks. The exuberant Jews danced for joy.

Rav Galante remained in prayer. The downpour increased in intensity until

Tomb of Shimon HaTzaddik

rivulets of water flowed down the valley. The wind lashed the rain in every direction.

As the Jews rejoiced, the Turkish sentry, breathless, descended into the cave. He fell at the feet of Rav Galante and begged to be forgiven.

In honor of the miracle, the sentry personally carried the Rav home on his shoulders. They marched into the city as victors and princes before the nations of the world. For three consecutive days the rains fell, and for three consecutive days the people of Jerusalem were ecstatic. The Moslems and Christians had no choice but to admit that the miracle was due to their Jewish neighbors.

On the fourth day, the Turkish sentry entered Rav Galante's house. The miracle had been absorbed into his very flesh and bones. He asked to convert to the faith whose God performs open miracles, and was accepted. He became Rav Galante's personal servant for the rest of his life.

(*Sefer Ma'asios* by the Ben Ish Chai)

18th Century

The Ancient Legacy Renewed

השם כְּכָל צִדְקֹתֶךָ יָשָׁב נָא אַפְּךָ וַחֲמָתְךָ
מֵעִירְךָ יְרוּשָׁלַם הַר קָדְשֶׁךָ
כִּי בַחֲטָאֵינוּ וּבַעֲוֹנוֹת אֲבֹתֵינוּ
יְרוּשָׁלַם וְעַמְּךָ לְחֶרְפָּה לְכָל סְבִיבֹתֵינוּ

דניאל ט׳ ט״ז

O Lord, in accordance with all of Your righteous deeds,
pray let Your anger and fury
turn away from Yerushalayim Your city,
Your holy mountain;
for through our sins and the transgressions of our forefathers,
Yerushalayim and Your people are held in disgrace
by all who surround us.

Daniel 9: 16

The Aliyah of Rav Yehudah HaChassid

The tragic episode of the largest aliyah until modern times — that of Rav Yehudah HaChassid (the Pious) and his followers — and its ultimate collapse stemmed from the noble vision of a selfless man. Rav Yehudah of Shidlitz, Poland, labored mightily to become a vessel worthy of God's light, living a life of self-abnegation and devout Torah study. At about the age of sixty he realized that the only place where a Jew could truly perfect himself was in Eretz Yisrael. It was at that time that he began formulating a plan to ascend to Jerusalem.

A Legend in His Own Time[1]

Wednesday, 1 Cheshvan 1700 (5461), was a historic day for the Jewish community of Jerusalem. Everyone went out to the city gates in order to greet the European Rav and his thousand-plus followers. There had not been such a massive aliyah in thousands of years! The only other large-scale aliyah in all that time had been the thirteenth-century arrival of three hundred *baalei Tosefos*, which nowhere near approached this one in scope.

Rav Yehudah HaChassid was both a great *talmid chacham* and a charismatic figure. Wherever he went and spoke, he captivated his audience by the depth of his earnestness and sincerity. He spoke straight from the heart and his words entered directly into the heart. His theme was clear and to the point: we are God's chosen people and we must take on the holy tasks which we were created to fulfill. The time of the redemption is dependent on us rising to the occasion and dedicating our lives to the ultimate cause. Therefore, he told the people, we must all repent and cleanse ourselves. His ultimate message was that the Jews must go to Jerusalem, and there God would fulfill the words of His prophets.

In the spring of 1699 (5459), Rav Yehudah set out with a following of thirty families from the Polish town of Shidlitz, near Grodna. From there they traveled through Hungary, Germany, and Italy on their way to Eretz Yisrael.

News of the charismatic leader's journey spread like wildfire throughout Europe. *Gedolim* praised him, scholars and laymen hearkened to him, and a surprising number cast their lot with him. Many who chose to remain behind still donated handsomely to the cause.

The author of *Meoros Nasan*, Rav

Nasan Nata, joined the group. He described his impressions in these words: "A huge *kehillah* of uplifted Jews. Each God-fearing individual (including elders and scholars of esteem) stood with a luster shining about him. At their head was one full of wisdom, an angel of Hashem...Rav Yehudah....(they all were) with one intention: to go and ascend to Jerusalem, the place of our inheritance."[2]

Fifteen hundred men, women, and children had joined Rav Yehudah HaChassid along the way. Yet the grueling physical conditions of the journey by land and sea had taken their toll: some five hundred died over the course of the journey. Despite all the hardships and the loss they exacted, the enthusiasm of the intrepid group did not dampen. Right after Rosh HaShanah, 1700 (5461), one and a half years after starting out, they found themselves on the last leg of the journey — actually setting sail for Eretz Yisrael from Italy. Spirits were high, the winds were favorable, and the seventeen-day journey brought them to the Jaffa port.

Although the physical danger of the long and arduous journey abated with the group's arrival in the Holy Land, a pernicious spiritual danger still faced them. In fact, this danger would prove to be far more disastrous in the long run. It was precipitated by a sinister character by the name of Chaim Malach, one of the participants in the epic aliyah. Malach advocated the philosophy of Shabbetai Tzvi and secretly tried to indoctrinate others into it. One of the leading rabbis in Europe, the Chacham

The Chacham Tzvi (1648–1718)

Tzvi, had denounced him as a heretic, yet the noble Rav Yehudah did not take the warning to heart. Malach's divisive influence, together with the events we will now chronicle, would contribute to the ultimate collapse of Rav Yehudah's grand vision. What would unfold in the coming days, weeks, and months would result in one of the saddest episodes in Jewish history.

The Domino Effect

Between the Wednesday of the group's arrival and the following Shabbos, a whirlwind of events took place. As everyone arranged for living quarters, Rav Yehudah HaChassid mobilized his energies into purchasing a synagogue and courtyard in the Jewish Quarter. He also helped others rent dwellings, giving many an outright monetary gift.

By Friday he had signed an agreement to buy what would later be called "Churvas Rabbi Yehudah HaChassid." It comprised a synagogue and courtyard, surrounded by a forty-two room structure. The Arabs later called it Dir al-Ashkenaz.

That Friday afternoon, as Rav Yehudah immersed in the *mikve* and prepared to go to shul, he began to feel sick. After Kabbalos Shabbos and Maariv, he returned to his quarters and collapsed on his bed in a semiconscious state. He was delirious, muttering verses from the Torah. His son-in-law, Rav Yeshaya, was by his bedside.

Though the hour was late, he ordered that the famous Sephardic doctor, Rav Raphael Mordechai Malki, be brought to examine Rav Yehudah. At the time, the Moslems did not allow Jews to be out in the streets later than half an hour after dark. The only exceptions were for doctors and midwives. Dr. Malki, after examining his patient, concluded that there was nothing to be done for twenty-four hours and returned home with a heavy heart.

Miraculously, Rav Yehudah awoke feeling completely recovered on Shabbos morning. He joined the services and publicly apologized for causing his followers such anxiety the previous night. When he returned home he collapsed again, this time falling into a coma. On Monday, 6 Cheshvan, he passed away.

His *levayah* (funeral procession and burial) was held on the same day. The entire Jewish community gathered in the Ashkenazic courtyard to pay their last respects. The Sephardic cantor led the eulogy, in traditional Sephardic manner. Afterwards, the *levayah* mournfully proceeded to the slopes of the Mount of Olives, where the noble leader was laid to rest in a large cave. Within a year, his wife and only son died and were buried there as well.

The Ashkenazim were left like a flock without a shepherd. The state of shock induced by the sudden and traumatic event was impossible to overcome. As a series of other problems complicated life, some of the newcomers returned to Europe. In the following years, as the burden of poverty increasingly weighed on the settlers' spiritual and physical lives, more and more of them returned to their homeland. In the end, the whole community collapsed, and the dream of a true chassid and his followers never came to fruition.

The Wheel of Fortune

The remaining followers of Rav Yehudah eventually became impoverished, and accrued a tremendous debt to the local Arabs that was never paid off. The borrowers were identified as the Ashkenazic community as a whole. The indigenous Sephardic Jews were therefore not held responsible. As a result of this liability, for more that one hundred years Ashkenazic Jews dared not live in Jerusalem, since any arriving European Jew was immediately held responsible for his compatriots' large debt.

This well-known episode of the impoverished Ashkenazim being oppressed by cruel Arab debtors, though true, needs to be put into perspective. The most obvious question is, how could the community have fallen almost immediately into such arrears when they came with ample financial resources?

One of the foremost members of the group, Rav Gedaliah by name, wrote a detailed booklet of what transpired during this period, entitled *Sha'alu Shalom Yerushalayim*. Rav Gedaliah writes:

The cost of the synagogue and the adjacent rooms was much more than we expected. First of all, the kadi had to be bribed before he would permit us to build. According to Turkish law, it is illegal to make any changes in the size of the building, even after a building permit is issued. Since we wanted to enlarge the shul, the kadi demanded a much larger bribe. He reasoned like this: since a new Jewish synagogue must pay a tax of 500 talers per year for three years, it is only fitting that

שאלו
שלום ירושלים

הדור אתם ראו זה: דבר חדש אשר בו
יתבאר כל עניני ירושלים עתה
בחורבנ׳ סדר הבניין חומותיה שהוא מפואר מאוד ·
וגם כל המערות וקברי נביאים אשר סביב לה· וגם
מעשים נפלאים אשר נעשו בה בין מה שנעשו בימי
בין מה ששמעתי שנעשו בימים קדמונים · וכמה
גזירות אשר נגזרו מירושלים והש״י שמע את
צעקת בניישראל והצילם · וגם יתבאר מן הגלות
המר אשר סובלים עתה· וגם עניין פטירת מ״ו
המוכיח המפורסם כרודינו ה״ה ר׳ יודא חסיד סג״ל
זצ״ל · וגם יתבאר זירת וחיזוק לכבות לעזור את
דלי ציון · וגם מוסר לקונן על חורבן ירושלים ע״כ
אחינו בני ישראל אל תהוסו על כספיכם
כי הוא דבר פלא כאשר משים
תחזנה עיניכם ובזכות זה יקוי׳
כמו הכתוב כי עין בעין
יראו בשוב ה׳ ציון
ונגלה כבוד
ה׳ וראו
כל בשר כי פי ה׳ דבר :

נדפס בק״ק ברלין

לסדר ולפרט בעתן אחישנה לפ״ק :

Title page of Sha'alu Shalom Yerushalayim *(1716)*

an extra 500 talers per year be paid to him if an existing shul is expanded, for that is the equivalent of building a new structure. These taxes were unforeseen and caused us to go into debt. Moreover, as we had to pay bribery money for every little thing the Arabs did for us, our debts mounted further.

The yearly taxes of two adumim per adult male, though it applied to all citizens of the city alike, became increasingly difficult for us to pay. Everything snowballed after the unforeseen expenditures for the synagogue. Within no time the debts zoomed over our heads. As soon as we got out of the clutches of one Arab lender, we fell into the hands of another.

Before long, we were afraid to walk in the streets during the day, for fear that one of them would apprehend us. At home the situation was also appalling, and we lacked the most basic necessities. In truth, before immigrating, Rabbeinu (Yehudah HaChassid) had traveled throughout the Rhineland and had received assurances of financial backing. But what was unforeseen was the astronomical sums necessary to keep us out of jail. Imprisonment is the worst thing of all. Therefore, we were left stripped of everything....

Additionally, it was impossible for us to work, for several reasons: first, there was the language barrier, as none of us spoke Arabic or Ladino, and none of the city's residents spoke our language. Secondly, it is forbidden to sell them (Moslems) intoxicating beverages, like beer and wine (from which a few could have made a living). If someone is caught — because the Arab he sold to got drunk — he is flogged and penalized heavily. Lastly, no Jew — including the Sephardim who speak the language — can set up a business which involves long-distance traveling, because of the ever-present danger of highwaymen. Even the Arabs travel in caravans, which for a Jew may have many halachic problems.

There are a few Jewish storekeepers in Jerusalem. In order to protect themselves from Arab thievery, they take an Arab friend as a partner.

There is one group of local Jews, called Morishkas, who are fluent in Arabic and whose dress is similar to the local Arab dress. Indeed, sometimes it is difficult to distinguish between these Jews and the Arabs, since neither group shaves their beards. The Morishkas own donkeys and travel from village to village selling spices and other wares. They also buy wheat and other foodstuff to sell in Jerusalem. Still, most of them are paupers. If this is the lot of those Jews who speak the language and are engaged in business, how much more desperate is our plight!

A Tzaddik from Italy[3]

In Adar, 1702 (5462), a wealthy Italian kabbalist leading a group of twenty-five followers moved to the Holy City. Rav Avraham Revigo was a kindhearted man with an abiding love for those who studied Torah. In his hometown of Modena, he supported a yeshivah and propagated the study of Jewish mysticism. Though he never published anything, one of his disciples did. Rav Mordechai Ashkenazi wrote a commentary on the *Zohar*, which he entitled *Eshel*

Avraham, after his beloved mentor who supported him for many years.

Rav Revigo had planned to open a yeshivah in Jerusalem and proceeded to do so. However, within weeks of his arrival, tragedy struck the group. The wife of Rav Revigo's outstanding student, Rav Mordechai, died in childbirth, followed by his daughter, and finally Rav Mordechai himself, along with his two sons. Rav Revigo, devastated by this chain of events, drew solace from throwing his energies into building his new yeshivah.

Some of the remaining members of Rav Yehudah's group joined the yeshivah. Among them were Rav Yeshaya and Rav Nasan Nata. The latter found a soul mate to study with in the person of Rav Yaakov of Vilna. The two studied Kabbalah together and co-authored *Meoros Nasan*. Some years later, when Rav Nasan was forced to go on *shelichus* to Europe, he wrote: "...yet leaving Eretz Yisrael is so difficult, even for an hour."

Rav Avraham Revigo did more than "just" bring the spiritual light of Torah into Jerusalem during this dismal period of her history. He was also concerned with his brethren's physical well-being. Eventually he decided to leave the Holy City as a *shaliach* in order to collect for the community. He took one of his disciples, Rav Chaim Chazan, along with him. It is not clear whether he went once or twice as a *shaliach*. What we do know is that he passed away in Italy in 1713. His sole aim was to better the lot of his downtrodden brethren in the Holy City.

One of the outstanding leaders during this time was Rav Raphael Mordechai Malki. This unique individual was the epitome of a Torah sage who gave himself over to the community. He had moved to Jerusalem over a quarter of a century before and had built up a reputation as an outstanding scholar. His involvement in Jerusalem life extended to all areas — he was a *dayan*, a doctor, and a communal leader. He had lived through the good years of the 1670s and 1680s, and never considered leaving during the lean times of the 1690s and the early 1700s. His two sons-in-law were themselves giants in Torah: Rav Chizkiah Silva (the author of the *Pri Chadash*) and Rav Moshe Chagiz.

Rav Malki's unpublished commentary to the Torah included medical observations, a description of the times in which he lived, and ideas on how to better the spiritual and physical lives of his fellow Jews. Part of his writings were later published as an anthology entitled *Likutim*. He died around 1704.[4]

Rebellion[5]

In 1703 a rebellion broke out in Jerusalem. At that time an influential Arab by the name of Nakib, together with a couple of hundred comrades, took control of the city. When the imperial tax collector came in the spring to collect the yearly tax for the Sultan, he found the gates locked and squads of soldiers on the wall with drawn bows. The official retreated and sent a message demanding entry. According to Turkish law, it was forbidden to shoot arrows into the city, in deference to the city's holiness. The rebels, on the other hand, were free to shoot at anyone outside the walls, which they did without hesitation. After a few weeks, the tax officer returned to Constantinople.

The other residents of the city, though innocent, were trapped as pawns in the rebellion. Many of the rich Moslems went hungry during those weeks, and the impoverished ones starved. In an attempt to save themselves, the citizens of the city smuggled a letter to the Sultan begging for mercy. They were simply innocent bystanders, they pleaded. Nakib and his companions alone were responsible for the insurrection. In the end, this message would bring relief.

Nakib and his followers had picked an opportune time to stage their rebellion, as the attention of the Sultan and the energies of the empire were focused on other matters at this point. While Nakib's act was arrogant and irritating, the situation in Jerusalem did not present a strategic threat to the stability of the empire. Thus the Sultan could afford to divert his attention from this minor problem until more pressing issues were resolved. As a result, two years passed without a change in the situation, until the winter of 1705–1706. At that time, the Sultan was not to be put off any longer. He sent a commander with an army of Turkish soldiers to resolve the situation. The news of the approaching army gripped everyone with fear. The prominent Arabs of the city entered Migdal David for safety. Nabik and some of his followers entrenched themselves in his fortified house nearby. A feud broke out between the two groups, each side shooting arrows at the other. The city's influential Arabs, of course, wanted to prove to the Sultan's general that they were against Nakib. The pitched battle between Nakib and his enemies was going against him. Desperate to leave the fray alive, the wily insurgent hit upon a plan to pacify his opponents and buy him some time. Nakib called out to the Arabs in Migdal David that he would meet with the Turkish general and acquiesce to his demands.

The general sent a message to the influential Arabs asking their assistance in bringing Nakib to him alive. The Sultan wanted him brought before him before sentencing him to death. Somehow the message reached Nabik's ears. When he realized what awaited him, he escaped in the middle of the night with several hundred men.

The army entered though the gates the next morning. Though the residents were free of the charge of insurrection, they were forced to pay dearly for their liberty. In those days, nothing in the corrupt Turkish Empire was for free. The Turkish general expected payment for services rendered, and Arabs and Jews paid him handsomely. Wealthy members of the Jewish community, of course, were expected to pay more than their impoverished brethren. As a result of this onerous burden, some of the wealthy Sephardim left the Holy City.

Soon a new commander from Constantinople arrived who took up residency to ensure the peace of Jerusalem.

Shots in the Dark

The money that trickled in from the Diaspora could not alleviate the dire financial situation of the Ashkenazic community in the Holy City. It was vital that new sources of support be found. Two hopeful prospects centered around the Jewish community of Cairo.

The first prospect came to light through Rav Yaakov of Vilna, leader of the Jerusalem community during the first decade of the eighteenth century. He discovered a problem in the handling of consecrated property from wealthy Jewish Egyptian individuals. Over the past twenty years, profits deriving from this property had been legally designated for the Jewish community of Jerusalem. Unfortunately, unscrupulous Jews in Cairo had confiscated the property, and the funds were no longer forthcoming. When petitioned to release it, they offered to send the profits but not to sell the property outright. This was not satisfactory to the Jerusalem community, the rightful owners of the property, who now wanted to sell it in order to raise as much ready cash as possible. Rav Yaakov, after consulting with *rabbanim*, went to Egypt and forcefully sold the property. In this way, he was able to return with a substantial amount of money. The sale had provided a momentary breathing spell.[6]

The second source was initiated when, in 1711 (5471), Rav Moshe HaKohen of Prague, head of Jerusalem's Ashkenazic *beis din*, went as a *shaliach* to Europe. On the first leg of his journey he stopped in Cairo, and while there he managed to convince the Turkish authorities to annul the future interest leveled against Jerusalem's Ashkenazic community. More than this, he succeeded in having one third of the existing debt erased, on condition that the remaining two thirds be paid within three years. All this came at a price, however: the Arabs demanded that the Ashkenazim put up their synagogue and homes as collateral. This was a threat to Jewish property. Furthermore, if the terms were not fully met, the Arabs lenders would take the law into their own hands. This was a threat to human life.

Rav Moshe, after conferring with the head of the Cairo *beis din*, Rav Avraham HaLevi, decided that a special *takanah* be introduced. For the next three years, every European community would give their donations only to Ashkenazic *shelichim* of Jerusalem. The Sephardic *shelichim* from Jerusalem, Hebron and Safed were told not to go to any European city during that time. It was hoped that this measure would enable the community to pay off their burdensome debts.

With this enactment in hand, Rav Moshe headed for Europe. In his hometown of Prague, he collected a substantial 10,000 florins.[7] Nonetheless, in 1714, when all the collected funds were added up, the total did not meet the sum necessary to free the community.

Providentially, it seemed, a non-Jew by the name of Kasan Geyoni offered to lend them over 1,000 talers for a period of one year, with interest. This amount would help them to temporarily alleviate the problem, although it did not completely cover the amount. When Geyoni's loan came due and the community was unable to repay it, the leaders of the community desperately begged him to extend it. He agreed to an extension of three years, but only after doubling the interest. When that time also passed without payment, Geyoni met with the communal leaders and angrily demanded the principal and all the interest. After desperate negotiations, he agreed to another extension — along with a handsome interest fee that was twice the amount of the original loan.[8]

These efforts by the sages of Jerusalem were gallant attempts to save the Ashkenazic community. Every coin given to the community was a mitzvah of the highest level. Yet the catastrophe which loomed over the community could not be averted, and in the end, the Arabs did indeed take the law into their own hands.

Churvas Rav Yehudah HaChassid[9]

On Shabbos, *parshas Lech Lecha*, 8 Cheshvan 1720 (5481), the Arabs suddenly descended on the Ashkenazic synagogue. With no sensitivity to the sacredness of a house of worship, they set it ablaze. Benches were used as firewood and pages of holy books as kindling. One after the other, the Torah scrolls were thrown into the bonfire like martyrs at the stake, until all forty were set afire.

Had the synagogue been made of wood, there would not have been anything left but a smoldering mound of ashes. However, like all buildings in Jerusalem, the structure was built of stone. The Arabs rioters stopped short of demolishing the shul. Instead, it became a garbage dump, and the courtyard homes were converted into Arab shops.

The Arabs were not placated with the destruction of the synagogue. Leading members of the congregation were imprisoned, and everyone else was ousted from the courtyard rooms. However, they were also not satisfied with this, and they eventually called for the dissolution of the entire community. Thus it came to pass that all the Ashkenazim were banished from the city. Some of

Churvas Rav Yehudah HaChassid
(Photo is of the Churvah Synagogue [1864–1948], built on the site of Rav Yehudah's synagogue.)

them went to Safed, others to Hebron, and others returned to Europe.

From that point onward, no Ashkenazic Jew was permitted to dwell inside the walls of the Holy City. If one did enter and was discovered, his lot was imprisonment. In the coming generations, a few brave Ashkenazic Jews did manage to surreptitiously get into the city. Dressed in Sephardic garb, men like Rav Gershon Kitover and Rav Menachem Mendel of Shklov succeeded in dwelling there. However, these few individuals were the exception to the rule.

It would take a hundred years until the ruling government would once again allow Jews of Ashkenazic descent to officially reside in Jerusalem.

Shock Waves

Though the Arabs' wrath was directed at the European Jews, the desecration of the Ashkenazic shul left the Sephardic community in a state of shock. Not since the Crusader victory over six hundred years earlier in 1099 had there been such sacrilege by non-Jewish hands. At that time, the Christians had been the culprits, and the Arabs had also suffered. This time the defiling hands were those of their Moslem neighbors, with whom they had to live and deal in the marketplace. Powerless to protest before the governing body, the Sephardim clung to their precarious existence and remained thankful that the Arab wrath had not burned like a wildfire in their camp as well.

A few years before the tragedy, in 1715 (5475), Rav Avraham Yitzchaki returned from a decade of *shelichus* in the Diaspora. This outstanding scholar had a reputation as a *gadol b'Torah*, an arch enemy of the Shabbetai Tzvi movement, and a lover of his people. Rav Yaakov Emden characterized him with the following words: "A man of distinction, great in Torah and wisdom, he rises above all the people." The Sephardic community immediately crowned him as their leader, making him the head of the *beis din* and proclaiming him Rishon l'Tzyon.[10]

During his years of leadership, Rav Yitzchaki led the community faithfully. The times were difficult, especially from an economic point of view. This was due both to onerous taxes imposed by the Turkish authorities, and a general spirit of lawlessness that prevailed in the city. To give but one example, the famous *rav*, physician, and savant, Rav Tuvia Narel, moved to the Holy City around 1718. This accomplished individual stood at the pinnacle of success, in no small measure due to his acclaimed work, *Maaseh Tuvia*. In Jerusalem, he

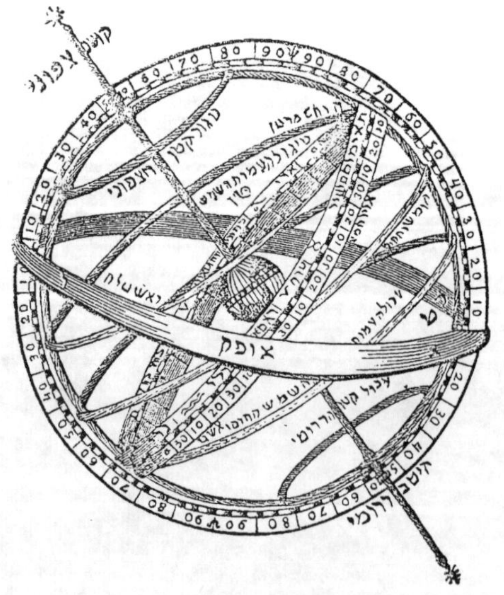

From Maaseh Tuvia

Portrait of Rav Tuvia Narel (1653–1729)

married off his only surviving daughter to Rav Avraham Meyuchas, author of *S'dei HaAretz*. However, Rav Tuvia's joy was diluted by a series of thefts, taxation, and oppression by high-handed Arabs which left him completely destitute. For a man of distinction, who had been honored by gentile kings in Europe and Turkey, this was a severe blow indeed.[11]

The winter of 1722 heralded a time of drought. Prices soared and children went hungry. Fast days were proclaimed and special prayers were recited with parched lips. After many weeks passed with no change in the weather, Rav Yitzchaki commanded every Jew to gather in the central square of the Jewish Quarter for a special communal prayer. Women and children cried openly. Rav Yitzchaki, with a *sefer Torah* in his hands, cried out, "Please, Hashem, hearken to the tears of these innocent children and bring rain." Immediately, clouds formed and rain descended.[12]

The Reign of Terror[13]

In the fall of 1722 (5483), an evil despot by the name of Yosuf Pasha took control of the city. Blatantly anti-Semitic, he immediately commenced arresting Jews at random, beating and flogging them mercilessly and demanding exorbitant ransom money for their release. To escape his clutches, the well-off and prominent Jews went into hiding.

After a few months, towards the end of the winter, Rav Moshe Meyuchas, one of the elders of the community, volunteered to stand before the despot and plead the Jewish cause.

The pasha ridiculed him and brought him before the *kadi*. Employing false witnesses, he accused the Jews of insulting Moslems through the use of derogatory epithets. Three times a day, he claimed, the Jews pray and depict the Moslems to be "like mules." He went on to insist that they deserved the death penalty for this outrage.

Rav Moshe hurried back to the Jewish Quarter and related the gravity of the situation to Rav Avraham Yitzchaki. A three-day fast was decreed. During this entire time Jews were indiscriminately flogged and imprisoned. On the third day, Rav Meyuchas was arrested and chained in a prison cell. The pasha cruelly proclaimed that on such-and-such a date the prisoner was to be put to death.

The communal leaders went to Yosuf to plead on Rav Moshe's behalf. The pasha ordered the prisoner be brought before him. As soon as Rav Meyuchas entered, the pasha erupted in a tirade of harsh words and accusations. The Jewish leaders cried out and begged for mercy. On the spot they offered to ransom the hapless prisoner for 91,000 *grushim*, a staggering sum. Suddenly, the pasha's expression softened. An agreement was written and signed, promising the full amount within three months.

The only way such a vast sum of money could be paid on time was by sending an emergency emissary to Constantinople. The wealthy Jews of the Turkish capital would understand the peril their brethren faced and would surely come to the rescue. A lottery was cast to see who would go, which fell to Rav Moshe's young grandson, Raphael Meyuchas.

The eighteen-year-old Raphael, later to become the Rishon l'Tzyon (in 1762), resolutely accepted the mission, and the next morning, not long before Purim, he set out for Jaffa port. However, time was short, and nothing less than a miracle would help him make the round-trip journey before the deadline. Incredibly, as soon as he reached the port he found a ship bound for the Turkish capital that was leaving on that very day. Favorable winds brought the ship into the Bosporus Straits within a record three days. That evening, Rav Raphael sat with Rav Yehudah Rosnis, author of *Mishneh l'Melech*, and explained the grave situation in Jerusalem.

Rav Rosnis called Jelebi Zonana, a high-ranking Jewish official in the Sultan's court, and asked for his aid. That night, Rav Raphael dreamt of three men warning him that all of the Jelebi's household were due to die of pestilence if they did not immediately flee the city. Even then, the only thing that would save them would be to give generously to the needy. Rav Raphael woke with a start, but quickly fell back to sleep. However, no sooner had he done so, than the dream recurred. Thoroughly disturbed at this point, Rav Raphael sent an urgent message to the Jelebi. Zonana hearkened to the dream and ordered his family to dress and leave the city in small rowboats. A single old lady refused to leave, and the next morning she was found dead in her bed.

The Jelebi, in gratitude for his life, donated the full sum to rescue Rav Moshe Meyuchas and the Jewish community. Thus, within a short time, Rav Raphael was on board a ship with a chest full of money.

The return trip brought him to Alexandria, Egypt. He stopped in Cairo for Purim and met with the Rav of the city, Rav Avraham HaLevi. From there he set out by camel across the Sinai desert. While alone in the desert, nomadic bandits attacked and robbed him of all his possessions, and tried to murder him. Miraculously, they were unable to kill him, and, overcome with awe, they returned the money to him. In memory of this miracle, Rav Raphael Meyuchas proclaimed that day as a personal Yom Tov for him and his descendants.*

Thus, Rav Raphael succeeded in his mission to save his grandfather and the Jewish community from the hands of a tyrant. When the Jews heard his tale, they all gave thanks to the Almighty for hearkening to their prayers and sending them a speedy salvation.

The Yoke of Galus

Though Rav Yitzchaki officially retired as Rishon l'Tzyon in 1722 (5482), a replacement was only sought out after his death in 1729. Rav Binyamin Ma'ali, who had served as a *rav* for many years in Egypt, was chosen, and he sat at the head of the *beis din* for two years, until his death around 1731.

In *Admas Kodesh* (by Rav Nisim Mizrachi, who served as Rishon l'Tzyon in the 1740s), several incidents which took place during this period are described.[14] In 1730 (5490), the community was forced to borrow large amounts from their Moslem neighbors, which they were unable to repay on time. Also, with the coming of the Turkish tax collector in the spring of that year, a number of Jews were thrown in jail for tax evasion. As a result, a *shaliach* was dispatched to Constantinople to collect emergency funds. The money he received was earmarked first to repay the debt and then to ransom the unfortunate Jews who had been taken captive. Unfortunately, this was only one example of several similar instances.

Another incident during this period concerned a Jewish woman who had illegally sold wine to two Moslems. While it was permissible for Jews to sell intoxicating beverages to one another, selling to Arabs was a dangerous thing to do, since wine is forbidden drink according to Islamic law. Should knowledge of such a sale become publicly known, the Jews could suffer for it. The problem was doubly compounded, for not only did the two Arabs get drunk, but one stabbed his companion to death. When

* See story, "The Miracle," in *Bygone Days: 18th Century.*

the pasha heard of the incident, he immediately ordered the arrest of *all* Jewish women who sold wine (since the one accused had disappeared). The Jews, stricken with panic over the possible repercussions, sent a delegation to the pasha. At first he was obstinate, but when offered a substantial bribe, he agreed to release the prisoners. As a result of this narrowly averted catastrophe, the *beis din* decreed that no woman could sell wine or beer.

In 1731 (5491), Rav Eliezer Nachum was appointed Rishon l'Tzyon. During the fourteen years in which he led the community, a number of Torah masters moved to Jerusalem, as we shall see in the next chapter. Rav Nachum wrote an in-depth commentary to all six orders of the Mishna. Entitled *Chazon Nachum*, the first two were printed during his lifetime. The last one, on *Seder Zera'im*, was recently published for the first time.

In 1733, a bizarre incident occurred when the governor of Damascus came to Jerusalem. One day, while standing near the mosque on the Temple Mount, he gazed across the rooftops of the Old City. In those days Jews rented dwellings in the Moslem Quarter, whose windows faced the Temple Mount. To the governor's surprise, he saw a number of Jewish women looking in his direction, probably wanting to get a glimpse of him. He was, after all, the second or third most powerful man in the Ottoman Empire. Outraged over what he deemed an immodest act, his first reaction was to expel all the Jews living in the area near the Temple, known as al-Sharaf. At first, the danger seemed very real and, in fact, many lost their homes and suffered greatly from the decree. Only later, through diplomacy, was the threat mitigated.

The outcome of this episode was an ordinance passed by the *rabbanim* of Jerusalem in 1737. The decree prevented Jews from renting housing from a gentile without prior permission from authorized Turkish powers.[15]

These incidents give small insight into the yoke of *galus* that weighed constantly on the Jews of Jerusalem and caused untold suffering.

The Light of Kabbalah

In the wake of the disaster of the Churvah and the expulsion of Ashkenazic Jews from the Holy City, a new era unfolded in which the hidden light of the mystical side of the Torah reigned in the Holy City. Some of the greatest kabbalists of all times — including Rav Chaim Attar and Rav Shalom Sharabi — lived and taught in Jerusalem. Their presence and their teachings provided a new dimension to the lives of the yishuv's guardians and tangibly strengthened the entire community.

Threshold of a New Era

In Elul, 1737 (5497), a middle-aged Italian *rav* moved to the Holy City. His name was Rav Emanuel Chai Riki, and he was a scholar and kabbalist of repute. He went quietly about his business, securing himself a house on a small, narrow lane in the Jewish Quarter. He captured his first impressions of the city with these words:

I reached Jerusalem, Baruch Hashem, eight days before Rosh HaShanah, 5498. I was forty-nine years old, and within no time everyone was asking me questions in Halachah. I walked around the city three times, counting the gates, both the open and sealed ones. Interestingly, they were exactly the same number as mentioned in the Book of Ezra. Apparently, this wall which the Turks built was constructed on top of the original foundations, with each gate parallel to the ancient ones. The stones which formed the doorposts are recent [from the Turkish rebuilding 200 years ago], but the lintel stone on one of the gates [Shaar Rachamim, the Gate of Mercy], engraved with flowers, is very ancient.[16]

Rav Riki built a house and *beis midrash* in a courtyard in the Jewish Quarter, and, with the patronage of friends in Livorno, he opened Chaverim Makshivim Yeshivah. One of the practices instituted in the yeshivah was that every *erev Rosh Chodesh* the scholars would gather in the study hall and learn throughout the night. When the morning prayers were completed they would then climb up on the roof of the yeshivah, which offered a view of the Temple Mount. There they would pray for the welfare of their Italian patrons.[17]

One of the foremost yeshivos during this period was Beis Yaakov Yeshivah, founded by Rav Chizkiah Silva in the early 1690s under the patronage of the Ferira family of Amsterdam. In the

1730s, Rav Yisrael Mizrachi was Rosh Yeshivah, and Rav Yona Navon was one of the *rabbanim*. Rav Yosef Chaim David Azulai (later known by his acronym, Chida), a youngster at the time, shone above his peers as the wonder child of Jerusalem. By the time of his bar mitzvah in 1737, he had completed a commentary on *Sefer Agur*. Rav Navon became his chief mentor, and Rav Yom Tov Elgazi (three years his junior) became his study partner and soul mate in Torah.

During the four years Rav Riki lived in the Holy City (1737–1741), he was known simply known as "the tzaddik." The Chida wrote that Rav Riki fasted every weekday for a period of twenty-two years. His masterpiece, *Mishnas Chassidim*, was a compendium of the Ari Zal's writings. Some compared his work in Kabbalah to the *Mishneh Torah* of the Rambam. Just as the Rambam compiled an encyclopedic review of the revealed Torah, Rav Emanuel Riki compiled one of the mystical Torah.[18]

When poverty interfered with his spiritual goals, Rav Riki chose to go to *chutz laAretz* and sell his books rather than to accept a subsidy from the *chalukah* system. From the profit of these sales he hoped to be able to return to Eretz Yisrael and continue to serve God wholeheartedly in the Holy City. Forebodingly, however, before taking his leave of Jerusalem, he dreamt that he would die a martyr's death while abroad. At the time he didn't reveal the contents of his troubling dream to anyone, although apparently he recorded it in his journal.

In 1741 (5401), Rav Riki reached the Italian city of Livorno on the west coast.

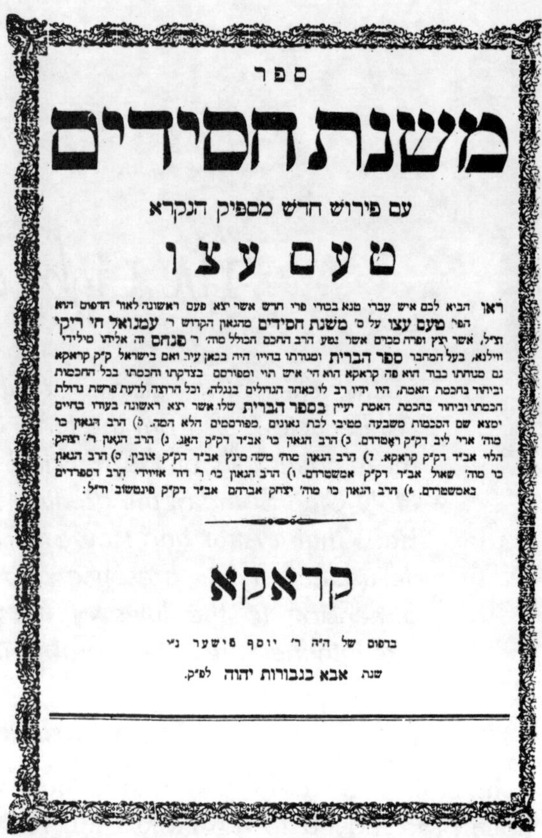

ספר

משנת חסידים

עם פירוש חדש מספיק הנקרא

טעם עצו

ראו הביא לכם איש עברי טנא בכורי פרי חדש אשר יצא פעם ראשונה לאור הדפוס הוא הפי' טעם עצו על ס' משנת חסידים מהגאון הקדוש ר' עמנואל חי ריקי זצ"ל, אשר יצץ ופרח מכרם אשר נטע הרב החכם הכולל מוה' ר' פנחס זה אליהו מילידי ווילנא, בעל המחבר ספר הברית ומגורתו בחייו היה בבאן עיר ואם בישראל ק"ק קראקא גם מנוחתו כבוד הוא פה קראקא הוא הי' איש תוי ומפורסם בצדקתו וחכמתו בכל החכמות וביחוד בחכמת האמת, היו ידיו רב לו כאחד הגדולים בנגלה, וכל הרוצה לדעת פרשת גדולת חכמתו וביחוד בחכמת האמת יעיין בספר הברית שלו אשר יצא ראשונה בעודו בחיים ימצא שם הסכמות משבעה מטיבי לכת גאונים מפורסמים הלא המה. א) הרב הגאון כו' מוה' ארי' ליב דק"ק ראטרדם. ב) הרב הגאון כו' אב"ד דק"ק האג. ג) הרב הגאון ר' יצחק הלוי אב"ד דק"ק קראקא. ד) הרב הגאון מוה' משה מינץ אב"ד דק"ק אובן. ה) הרב הגאון כו' מוה' שאול אב"ד דק"ק אמשטרדם. ו) הרב הגאון כו' ר' דוד אזוידי הרב דספרדים באמשטרדם. ז) הרב הגאון כו' מוה' יצחק אברהם אב"ד דק"ק פינטשוב וד"ל:

קראקא

בדפוס של ה"ה ר' יוסף פישער נ"י

שנת אבא בגבורות יהוה לפ"ק.

Title page of Mishnas Chassidim *(Livorno, 1727)*

There he found an open ear and purse wherever he went. It was at this time that he met Rav Chaim Attar, the author of *Ohr HaChaim*. Each praised the other's superlative qualities, and the two of them formed a close friendship.

On 2 Adar, 1742, he was ambushed outside of Modeno, Italy, by highway robbers, and killed. The murderers hid the body in the woods. Six days later it was discovered, and the following day he was buried. Everyone present, although grieved by the untimely passing of a great tzaddik, was amazed to see that his body had not deteriorated in the least. He looked as if he were asleep, though in reality he had lain dead under the open skies for a week.

Tiberias

A Pure Light

In a sense, Rav Emanuel Riki's presence in the Holy City might be considered as having set the stage for the renowned tzaddik, Rav Chaim Attar, who came to Jerusalem shortly after Rav Riki's death. Rav Attar moved into "the tzaddik's" house and there he opened his famous *beis midrash*.

Rav Chaim Attar settled in the Holy City in Elul, 1742 (5502), along with his family and disciples — altogether a group of some thirty people. Originally from Morocco, Rav Attar's fame had spread far and wide with the publication of *Ohr HaChaim*, his commentary on the Torah; *Chefetz Hashem* on the Talmud; and *Pri Toar* on *Shulchan Aruch, Yoreh Deah*.

Though he only arrived in Jerusalem in 1742, he had actually been in Eretz Yisrael for nearly a year before that time. He had delayed his ascent to the Holy City because, upon landing in Akko, he received reports of an epidemic in Jerusalem. Therefore, he reluctantly chose to stay in the port city of Akko and open a yeshivah, pending an improvement of circumstances in the Holy City. Furthermore, he used this time to make several excursions in the Galilee, to such places as Meron, Safed, and Tiberias.

While in Tiberias he met with the venerable Rav Chaim Abulafia, who had studied in Jerusalem with the Pri Chadash more than fifty years earlier. Now the revered sage was responsible for the reestablishment of the Jewish community in Tiberias in 1740. The sheik, Dahar al-Amar, governor of the Galilee, favored such a community and guaranteed safety for Jewish residents.

Rav Abulafia pleaded with the Ohr HaChaim to open his yeshivah there. Rav Attar seriously contemplated the offer, and went so far as to write his patrons in Livorno for their consent. In the end, however, he held to his original commitment and moved to Jerusalem.[19]

Rav Attar opened his yeshivah, called Knesses Yisrael, in the courtyard owned by Rav Emanuel Riki. He chose this location, he wrote, "both because no other option was free of gentile passersby, and every other site had Moslem owners who might cause trouble. Therefore, I chose (with permission from authorized parties) to open my study hall here, in the courtyard of Rav Emanuel Chai Riki, who had also made this his *beis midrash*. Even though it is of small size, we took it as a temporary quarters. It is hidden from public view, and there nothing evil should befall us, at least until I can find a larger, more suitable, place."[20] *

Rav Chaim Attar was a giant in both the revealed and mystical aspects of the Torah, who towered over even the formidable scholars of the Holy City. His stature, his Torah excellence, his noble qualities of character, and his total commitment to bringing holiness into the world were universally recognized.

Those who joined his yeshivah were granted a firsthand view of the new light of Torah which the Rosh Yeshivah brought into his Beis Midrash. The Chida, eighteen years old at the time, joined the yeshivah and captured the vibrant atmosphere with these words: "I was privileged to study in his yeshivah. I personally witnessed his greatness in Torah and his depth of perception, as well as his saintliness...which was beyond human grasp — it was as if an angel of God hovered over him throughout the day."[21]

Another of his new disciples was Rav Raphael Meyuchas. He depicted his mentor as follows: "We saw a great man come from the West [Morocco], filled with wisdom and understanding like a city which has everything in it.... He was more like a *seraf*, one of the Heavenly Host, clothed in mortal garments."[22]

During the ten months that he lived in the Holy City, Rav Attar offered his disciples a new approach to learning. He analyzed the Gemara as if there were no commentaries to it. Even Rashi's explanation, universally regarded as the basic commentary on the Talmud and relied upon by everyone, was held at bay until he had formed his own understanding. His book, *Rishon l'Tzyon*, a commentary on seven of the Talmud's tractates, was the outgrowth of his lectures in the yeshivah.

Concerning his book *Ohr HaChaim*, the Chida wrote: "In earlier generations, the *darshanim* [homiletical lecturers on the Torah] based their *chiddushim* on contradictory words of the Sages. Now, [due to the *Ohr HaChaim*] *darshanim* base their sermons on explaining relatively obvious statements. How many read the *Ohr HaChaim* every week, intrigued by his commentary, although it is built from self-evident premises!"[23]

A Time of Striving

It was Yom Kippur, 1742 (5503). The Ohr HaChaim wrote: "I saw a great light at the time of *Kol Nidrei*. When I opened the Ark, I genuinely felt as if I

* See story, "The Inner Circle," in *Bygone Days: 18th Century*.

had opened the gates of Gan Eden. The illumination was so powerful in the synagogue, that everyone was effected by it. Many burst out in tears, desiring to have the Temple rebuilt. Even the peasants (who came from the surrounding villages to pray in a synagogue on the High Holidays) reacted this way, giving further validation to what I experienced. I have never witnessed such a Divine illumination as I experienced at that moment."[24]

On such a note of promise the new year began, and throughout the coming months the city was vibrant with life. Rav Attar took his disciples to the graves of tzaddikim around Jerusalem. At the grave of the Pri Chadash, he lingered for a quarter of an hour by himself. "We understood," wrote the Chida, "that he was asking forgiveness for disagreeing with his halachic rulings [in his *Pri Toar*], saying that his sole aim was to arrive at the truth."[25]

שנת
בכתף ישאו לפ״ק ·
חלק ראשון
אור החיים
עם תרגום ופירשי ז״ל ·
בוויניציאה יע״א
NELLA STAMPARIA VENDRAMIN.
CON LICENZA DE SUPERIORI.

Title page of the first edition of Ohr HaChaim, *Venice (1739)*

The Karaite Scheme Foiled

Sometime later in the year, the Turkish mayor demanded that the Jews pay a special, inordinately high tax. An urgent, clandestine meeting was organized in the Karaite synagogue. As the fifteenth-century shul was literally built underground, everyone agreed that it would be the safest, most unobtrusive place to hold the meeting. At the appointed time, the leaders of the community filed down the steps, one after the other. As Rav Attar descended, he slipped and fainted on one of the stairs. The rabbis laid him on the floor and tried to revive him. Some reasoned that, due to his saintliness, he fainted in a place built by those who advocated a philosophy diametrically opposed to Judaism. The Karaites believed in the Written Law, but blatantly ridiculed any belief in the Oral Tradition. While waiting for Rav Attar to revive, the rabbis searched around the stair where he slipped. They discovered that underneath it had been placed a volume of the Rambam's *Mishneh Torah*, one of the pillars of the Oral Law. The Karaites had secretly planted it there so that the rabbis would unknowingly trample on it. When Rav Attar regained consciousness, he denounced them, and decreed that as punishment they would be responsible for paying the full tax demanded by the mayor. Furthermore, he cursed them that they would never have a tenth man to make a minyan. From that day on, whenever a newcomer joined their ranks, one of them died.[26]

Nearly a hundred years later, in 1834, twenty Karaite families immigrated to Jerusalem from Russia. As soon as they entered the gates of the city, all the men became deathly ill and passed away. People then recalled the curse which the Ohr HaChaim placed on the sect and gave praise to the Almighty that when a tzaddik makes a decree, God fulfills it.[27] The British Consul, James Finn, likewise recorded in 1853 that "it was a judgment from Heaven on the Karaites that they were never able to muster a prayer quoram."[28]

The Ohr HaChaim's Passing

To the sorrow of the community, the supernal light which Rav Chaim Attar shone was snuffed out on 15 Tamuz, 1743 (5503). He was forty-seven years old. At that same moment in Tiberias, the revered and venerable tzaddik Rav Chaim Abulafia was praying the *motzei Shabbos* service. Suddenly he fainted and did not regain consciousness for a quarter of an hour. When he awoke, he explained, "I was escorting Rav Chaim Attar — who just passed away in Jerusalem — to the gates of the Garden of Eden."[29]

That night Rav Avraham Meyuchas, author of *S'dei HaAretz*, who lived in the Holy City, dreamt a recurring dream. In the dream, it was pointed out to him that the numerical value of the word משיח (*mashiach*) was 358, almost the same as the numerical value of the word שליח (*shaliach*) (348), with the remaining 10 hinting at the ten Talmudic Sages who died a martyrs' death at the hand of the Romans.

The next morning, news reached the city of Rav Emanuel Riki's death, which had occurred five months earlier. Rav Riki, of course, had been traveling through Europe as a *shaliach*. Providentially, the news of his passing arrived on the very day that the Ohr HaChaim was buried. Many people understood from this that if Rav Riki was the *shaliach*, then the Ohr HaChaim was worthy of having been the Mashiach — if only the generation had been worthy.[30] Indeed, so universally recognized was the Ohr HaChaim's unique stature and greatness in Torah that he is one of a select few individuals in our history to be honored with the appellation of "HaKodesh" (the holy one) at the end of his name.

Rav Attar's yeshivah, Knesses Yisrael, flourished for decades after its illustrious founder's death. Rav Yona Navon, author of *Nechpah b'Kesef*, and Rav Yehudah Iyash were Roshei Yeshivah at different times. The seeds which the Ohr HaChaim had sown by opening the yeshivah resulted in a rich harvest of scholars who unreservedly took on the yoke of Torah.

A Lion in the Grave

Over two hundred and fifty years after the passing of Rav Chaim Attar, his grave site on the Mount of Olives remains a focal point for Jews. In fact, the trend to pray there has grown over the past decades. When the Shiniver Rav came to Eretz Yisrael in 1871, he prayed there on the tzaddik's *yartzeit*. He was baffled, however, by the fact that only a relatively small number of Sephardim came. He was told that, unlike the Ashkenazim and Chassidim, they simply did not recognize the extent of his greatness.[31] Today, however, the Sephardim

This photograph was taken on the yartzeit of the Ohr HaChaim (15 Tamuz), when thousands come to pray at his grave. The road above was built by the Arabs after the fatal accident.

are among the largest segment to hover by the tzaddik's grave and pray for their needs in his merit.

After 1948, when Jerusalem became a divided city, the Mount of Olives fell into Arab hands. In their utter brazenness, they not only desecrated graves, they even decided to build a road through the ancient cemetery. The planned road was to pass directly over the grave of the Ohr HaChaim. However, when the bulldozer came within inches of the grave, the engine suddenly sputtered and died, and could not be restarted. The next day, another tractor lunged towards the grave at full speed. As its forked steel shovel nipped the holy site, the bulldozer flipped upside down, rolled over and plunged into the Valley of Kidron. The driver was killed.

Paralyzed with fear, the Arabs immediately halted their plans for the road. They later resumed construction on it, but rerouted it to pass much higher up the mountainside. Even today, one can see how the original clearing went straight in the direction of the Ohr HaChaim's grave.[32]

Stones for the Future

The grandeur of Torah implanted by the Ohr HaChaim into the community bore fruit for years to come. A new generation of *gedolim* was enthusiastically studying all through the day and long into the night. Included among their ranks were the Chida and Rav Yom Tov Elgazi, Rav Raphael and Rav Avraham Meyuchas, Rav Yona Navon and Rav Nisim Mizrachi, Rav Gedaliah Chaiyun and Rav Shalom Sharabi, to name but a few.

After Rav Eliezer Nachum passed away around 1745, the new Rishon l'Tzyon was Rav Nisim Mizrachi. The new leader of the community served in the post for three years before his official inauguration, which took place in 1748. Actually, during the nineteen-year period between Rav Avraham Yitzchaki's death (1729) and Rav Mizrachi's formal investiture, no *rav* officially used the title.[33]

Rav Mizrachi's life was one of unrelenting poverty and affliction. As a prominent member of the community, he was often imprisoned by the greedy Turks, whom, as we have noted, would capture innocent victims and ransom them off to enrich their coffers. It was not unusual for these prisoners to have to endure having their legs chained together for weeks at a time while waiting for their fellow Jews to redeem them. Sometimes a captive had to wait for an extended period of time until money would arrive from Constantinople. As one who felt the humility brought about by a life of grinding poverty, Rav Mizrachi served as *chazan* on Rosh HaShanah and Yom Kippur, from beginning to end.

Nevertheless, this humble scholar prided himself on studying day and night in the Beis Yaakov Yeshivah. There, he studied with his brother, Rav Yisrael Meir Mizrachi. Both were first-rate *talmidei chachamim,* and they became known as the *Neros HaMizrachim* (the Eastern Candles). Rav Nisim wrote *Admas Kodesh* (responsa), and Rav Yisrael Meir wrote *Pri HaAretz* (halachah) and *Tiferes Yisrael* (expositions on the Torah).

Rav Nisim Mizrachi's rabbinical court

instituted a number of decrees which had far-reaching effects. The most dramatic one, promulgated in 1749, stated that no bachelor between the ages of twenty and sixty could live permanently inside the city walls. If, within a reasonable time, he did not secure a match, he was asked to leave. Though this law had been introduced in earlier generations, it was reinstituted at this time. A few years later, the ordinance was used to force Rav Gershon Kitover — the Baal Shem Tov's brother-in-law who had managed to live in Jerusalem surreptitiously disguised as a Sephardic Jew — to leave the Holy City. His wife had died, and the only available matches were with Sephardic women, whom he felt were unsuitable for him. He left and returned to Europe, remarried, and came back a year later. As a scholar and kabbalist, Rav Kitover felt Jerusalem to be his permanent home. He was known to pray at the Western Wall with such intensity that a number of times he fainted there.

The environment was not particularly friendly to Jerusalem's population during the years of Rav Mizrachi's tenure. In 1745 a pestilence of locusts devoured the crops. Three years later, the winter of 1748 heralded a drought. Forty days had passed since the first light rains of winter had fallen and water had become a scarce and expensive commodity. The *rabbanim* debated over the extent to which the people should fast, whether to be stringent or not. Rav Yona Navon opposed being stringent, while others voted against him. Suddenly, at the very hour of the debate, the skies darkened and a downpour of rain cascaded over the streets of the city. Of course, the debate ended with cheers of thanksgiving.

Midrash Chassidim

Rav Chaim Attar was not the only recognized kabbalist during this period. Already in 1737 (5497), Rav Gedaliah Chaiyun opened a yeshivah for the study of Kabbalah. He called it Midrash Chassidim — Beis El. The premises were located close to the Rabban Yochanan ben Zakkai synagogue.

Born and raised in Constantinople, Rav Gedaliah was already a *talmid chacham* of repute when he immigrated to Eretz Yisrael. He found himself drawn to the world of Kabbalah and devoted most of his energies to its study, carefully analyzing it with a select group of disciples. He led all the prayer services in Beis El, meditating on every word according to his understanding of the Ari Zal's writings. In the course of time, Rav Gedaliah became known as "Rabban Chassidim" — Leader of the Pious.

Once, during a time of drought, when the cisterns had dried up and the wells provided only a trickle of water, the special prayer services that were invoked failed to bring Heaven's blessing. When a fast day was proclaimed, a desperate crowd of Jewish men, women, and children congregated outside Rav Gedaliah's house, beseeching him to pray for rain. As he walked outside, the children cried, "Abba, Abba! Give us rain!"

With tears running down his beard, he raised his hands to the heavens. "Master of the Universe! Give us rain for the sake of these children who do not know the difference between 'Abba' who can bring rain and 'Abba' who cannot bring rain."

Immediately, strong gusts of wind blew heavy clouds over the Holy City, and minutes later large raindrops kissed the arid ground. Children danced, mothers cried for joy, and men recited a blessing of thanksgiving to the Almighty.[34]

Revelation of a Tzaddik

Rav Chaiyun's sole motive in studying Kabbalah was to arrive at the truth. The vast mystical worlds and their intricate overlapping influences, extending far beyond the reaches of the physical universe, demanded deep concentration and clarity of mind. Together with his elite group, Rav Gedaliah labored to unravel the mysteries of the supernal worlds.

Sometime in the 1740s, a young man from Aden, the capital of Yemen, asked to work in the yeshivah. In exchange for cleaning, serving, and generally keeping things organized, he would receive room and board. Rabban of Chassidim agreed.

Often, while Rav Chaiyun and his group studied, the young Shalom Sharabi sat off to the side and recited Psalms. No one thought of him as educated, let alone versed in Kabbalah. However, this impression would soon be revised.

One day Rav Gedaliah and his disciples were baffled by a certain secret mentioned in *Etz Chaim*, the official writings of the Ari Zal. They toiled for hours to untangle and solve the mystery, but were unsuccessful.

At the lunch break, everyone left the *beis midrash* to eat except Rav Gedaliah. He put his head on the table and dozed. In the meantime, young Shalom jotted some notes on pieces of paper and carefully inserted them in various places in the *Etz Chaim*.

When Rav Chaiyun awoke, he saw the markers and opened the book to read them. They were references to different places in the writings of the Ari Zal which, when joined together, answered the problem which had perplexed the kabbalists all

Entrance to the Beis El Yeshivah (left), as it appears today

Beis El Synagogue

morning.

Rav Gedaliah immediately realized who had penned the notes.[35]

"Admit to me," he called across the room to his aide, "admit to me that you wrote these annotations!"

"Yes," Rav Shalom replied, "but please don't reveal this to anyone."

"That I cannot do!" answered the tzaddik. "I see that from Heaven they want you to be revealed!"

So much did Rav Chaiyun esteem the young kabbalist's greatness, that he appointed him Rosh Yeshivah,[36] and gave him his daughter in marriage.

The revelation of Rav Shalom Sharabi spread quickly through the Holy City.* He was a true master of the writings of the Ari Zal, and he awed everyone with his clarity and depth of perception. After Rav Gedaliah passed away in 1751, Rav Sharabi moved into his apartment above the Beis Midrash. He spent the next twenty-six years developing and refining the Ari Zal's system of Kabbalah. Some said that his soul was that of the Ari Zal himself, in keeping with the Ari's prophesy before his death that he would return to teach and expand upon his mystical system.[37]

Beis El

The revolution engendered by Rav Shalom Sharabi in the Torah world was dramatic, and was even visible to the gentile population of Jerusalem. Beis El Yeshivah became a place of great repute, and some of the greatest minds of the generation flocked to study under the master, including Rav Chaim Roza, Rav Yom Tov Elgazi, the Chida, Rav David Majar, and Rav Gershon Kitover.

The *seder* of the yeshivah, broken into three *mishmeros,* went nonstop around the clock. Following the path of his predecessor, Rav Gedaliah, Rav Sharabi served as *chazan* for all the prayer services. Of the forty scholars, he chose twelve to be part of Chevras Ahavas Shalom, an exclusive group of kabbalists whose purpose was to bind themselves together with an everlasting bond.[38]

Interestingly, the Chida and Rav Elgazi were not initially admitted into the inner circle. Finally, the Chida asked Rav Sharabi point-blank, "In what way have I sinned? Why don't you wish to teach me?"

Rav Sharabi, known by the acronym

* See story, "Statues of Flesh and Blood," in *Bygone Days: 18th Century*.

Rashash, replied, "It has been revealed to me that you were not brought into this world to study Kabbalah. However," he continued, "I can promise you that if you first attain mastery in other areas of Torah, you will ultimately succeed in the study of Kabbalah as well."

So careful was the Rashash to not allow the uninitiated to study his writings — especially his siddur filled with permutations of the holy Names of God — that they were left in manuscript form for decades. Only in 1796, when his son went to North Africa, did his works begin to spread among the Sephardic sages throughout the rest of the world. His siddur, full of *kavannos* (mystical focuses of concentration), was not published until 1911. Together with the writings of the Ari Zal, they revolutionized the study of Kabbalah.

Chida, Rav Chaim Yosef David Azulai (1724–1806)

In the winter of 1753 (5513), the Chida suddenly took leave for Europe, never to return to Jerusalem, except for a brief period. The following story is told concerning the reason behind his abrupt departure: The Rashash felt that it was an auspicious time to bring about the redemption. He chose two disciples, the Chida and Rav Roza, to aid him in the endeavor. After fasting for three consecutive days, the three of them ascended to the roof of the yeshivah. There, they meditated deeply on special kabbalistic formulas. Suddenly a Heavenly voice was heard: "My sons, you do not have permission to force the redemption. However, you three tzaddikim together do have the power to bring it before its time. In order to prevent this from happening, you must be separated. Therefore, one of you must go into *galus* into the Diaspora." They took lots, and it fell to the Chida to be separated from his master and his city.[39]

The Chida, whose first twenty-nine years were spent completely within the physical and spiritual confines of the Holy City, spent the next fifty-three years of his life in *chutz laAretz* (except from 1758 to 1764). In 1779, he accepted a request from the Jewish community in Livorno, Italy, to settle there. He stipulated, however, that he would not accept any rabbinical post. He only wanted to write and teach. The only time he spoke in public was on the Shabbos between Rosh HaShanah and Yom Kippur, called *Shabbos Shuvah*. On that day, the whole community would escort him to the central synagogue, where he would deliver a sermon lasting hours to an enthralled audience. His profound influence continues to affect the Torah world today.

Enduring Legacy

The premises of Beis El Yeshivah remained in the hands of the leading kabbalists of each new generation. With the passing of the Rosh Yeshivah, a new leader inherited his apartment on the top floor. A partial list is as follows:

Rav Gedaliah Chaiyun	1737 – 1751
Rav Shalom Sharabi	1751 – 1777
Rav Yom Tov Elgazi	1777 – 1802
Rav Avraham Mizrachi	1802 – 1827
Rav Avraham Majar	1827 – 1842
Rav Avraham Gagin	1842 – 1848
Rav Yedidiah Abulafia	1848 – 1869
Rav Aharon Ezriel	1869 – 1879

On 11 Tamuz, 1927 (5687), an earthquake caused a serious crack in the tall building. People were afraid to pray there for fear that the roof might collapse. A month later, the British municipality ordered that the yeshivah building be razed. Cries of the yeshivah's *rabbanim* accompanied the sounds of the destruction. In that building, the leading kabbalists of Jerusalem had prayed and studied for nearly two hundred years. Not a single day passed without the sound of Torah study ascending to the upper realms, and not a single prayer service went unheard before the Heavenly court.

Immediately, plans to rebuild the yeshivah got under way. The new premises were finished eight months later, in Adar, 1928.

In 1948, when the Arabs took control of the Old City, the first group of soldiers to enter the premises were greeted by the ceiling caving in on them. They were killed on the spot.[40]

The Chida's tomb on Mount Menuchos

Forging Onward

The Sephardic community, small yet strong, would face a series of setbacks during the coming decades. A series of devastating natural disasters and famines threatened the people's physical well-being. Additionally, despite admirable and tireless efforts to collect funds, a lack of money was slowly strangling the yishuv. Yet through it all, rabbanim of high repute labored tirelessly to maintain their yeshivos, the tree of life, and to instill the love of Torah in the younger generation.

Two Extremes

Mirroring the situation in earlier times, the second half of the eighteenth century could be characterized as an era of two extremes. While the spiritual side of life remained exalted, the physical side became grimmer and grimmer.

The yeshivos bustled with scholars studying and writing holy works. There were over a dozen yeshivos in the Old City, three main synagogues and a handful of smaller houses of worship. Over a hundred scholars studied full-time, which was approximately one third of the (Jewish) male population of the city — a tremendous proportion. The most renowned yeshivah was Beis Yaakov. Below is a summary of the major yeshivos.

Yeshivah	***Founder***	***Rosh Yeshivah***
Beis Yaakov	Yaakov Ferira (Amsterdam)	Rav Raphael Meyuchas
Chesed l'Avraham	Rav Avraham Nasan (North Africa)	Rav David Pardo
Gedolas Mordechai	Rav Mordechai Talok	Rav Yona Navon
Magen David	David Pinto (Amsterdam)	
Knesses Yisrael	Rav Chaim Attar (Italy)	Rav Shem Tov Gabbai
Midrash Chassidim (Beis El)	Rav Gedaliah Chaiyun	Rav Shalom Sharabi
Kedushas Yom Tov	Yom Tov Baruch (of Istanbul)	Rav David Majar
Damascus Eliezer	patron from Istanbul	Rav Yehudah Navon
Neve Shalom	patron from Istanbul	Rav Moshe Bola

Rav Yisrael Yaakov Elgazi served as Rishon l'Tzyon from 1749 until his death in 1756. (Others say that Rav Yitzchak Rappaport, a disciple of Rav Chizkiah Silva and author of *Battei Kehunah,* was Rishon l'Tzyon during this period. Interestingly, both men passed away within a few days of each other). Rav Elgazi had moved to Eretz Yisrael in the early 1730s, and immediately entered the arena of *rabbanus* and communal affairs. In 1737, he fell seriously ill, and just when all hope expired, he whispered a vow: If God would heal him, he would publish one of his manuscripts. After his recovery, he kept his promise and published *Shema Yaakov*. His most famous work, however, was *Shelamei Tzibbur*, on the laws of prayer.

A number of decrees safeguarding the dignity of women were instituted during this period. As the Moslems were notorious for their indecent behavior, women were forbidden to enter a gentile shop to do business. Also, women under the age of forty were asked not to pray in the synagogue, except on Rosh HaShanah and Yom Kippur. These measures reflected the high standards which the Jews of Jerusalem were careful to maintain.

With Rav Elgazi's passing, Rav Raphael Meyuchas became the next Rishon l'Tzyon. This scholar's boundless love of Eretz Yisrael was reflected in the titles of his books, *Pri Ha'Adamah* and *Mizbeach Ha'Adamah*, which alluded to the Holy Land. As Rosh Yeshivah of Beis Yaakov, he was ideally suited for the role of Rishon l'Tzyon. Unfortunately, during his fifteen-year tenure, the community faced one crisis after another, both from within and without. In 1757, an epidemic of smallpox exacted a death toll of one hundred and fifty Jewish children. Nearly every home was in mourning. The following year, heavy rains and strong winds destroyed the Talmud Torah Synagogue. Fortunately, no one was injured.

Shortly before dawn on 9 Cheshvan, 1759 (5519), the tremors of a violent earthquake centered in the Galilee were felt in Jerusalem. No one was hurt in the Holy City, but when news of the disaster's extent reached there, a state of mourning was declared. The majestic city of Safed had been instantly transformed into a pile of rubble. Over two thousand inhabitants died, including one hundred and fifty Jews. The number of injured and crippled was even greater. "A few hours before dawn," wrote Rav Meyuchas, "we were suddenly awakened by the tremors of an earthquake. Later, when we heard [the details]...we lamented the disaster for a full week; eulogies were delivered and many cried openly."

In his eulogy, Rav Meyuchas spoke of a Talmudic tradition relating that Jerusalem is immune to such a catastrophe. Even if an earthquake should erupt directly under the Holy City, no human life would be lost.[41]

From the Very Depths

The communities in Eretz Yisrael lived on a narrow budget which left them hovering precariously above the bottom line. The slightest change could tumble them into an abyss. For generations, one of the mainstays of support for the *yishuv* had been the community in Constantinople, one of the wealthiest

Jewish *kehillos* in the Diaspora. At this time, however, there was a recession in the Turkish capital which resulted in a decline in philanthropic activities. The *yishuv* in Eretz Yisrael quickly felt the pinch. On the other hand, the situation in Europe was much better. On that continent, there was now more wealth concentrated in Jewish hands than in earlier times. Dedicated *shelichim* spent years canvassing for funds throughout Europe. Their success somewhat helped offset the reduction in funds from Turkey.

Despite the increase in funding from Europe, by the year 1765 (5525), spiraling debts put the impoverished community under a staggering burden. To make matters worse, the capricious Turkish overlords began passing evil decrees against their helpless Jewish subjects. The city's dungeons were full of innocent victims, and each day saw new atrocities committed. As the situation grew more intolerable, people fled the city, most relocating in Cairo and Alexandria. Concerning this period, a Jewish traveler, Shimon Gilriran, wrote: "Unbelievable! Besides the outstanding debts of the Ashkenazim, the Sephardim have accumulated half as much in debts — over 200,000 *pelorim*. Every day someone is arrested — either a *chacham* or a man of means. They beat him until he is ransomed.... All in all, some two hundred families have fled from the Holy City...."[42]

In 1771, just before Rav Yom Tov Elgazi — son of Rav Yisrael Yaakov Elgazi — set off to go abroad, Rav Meyuchas passed away. In his will, Rav Meyuchas asked that his son, Rav Mordechai Yosef, inherit the position of Rishon l'Tzyon. For whatever reason, the *rabbanim* overrode his wishes and elected Rav Yom Tov Elgazi instead. Obviously, Rav Elgazi had no part in the decision; however, this did not prevent tension from arising between the two sides. Shortly thereafter, Rav Mordechai Yosef's wife suddenly died, and Rav Elgazi unhesitatingly offered his daughter in marriage. With the joining of the two families, the two scholars became everlasting comrades.

The summer of 1772 proved to be a catastrophe for the inhabitants of Jerusalem. At that time, a famine, the likes of which had not been seen for generations, strangled the city. Within one and a half months, more than three hundred Jews died of starvation. Among the fallen was Rav Avraham Asher, a *dayan* and kabbalist.

Life in the Holy City finally began to ease somewhat in 1774, when a new Sultan, Abdul Hamid the First, came to power. As with all monarchies, the fortunes of the Ottoman Empire's subjects — in this case Jerusalemites — varied according to the abilities and attentions of the emperor. When the Sultan supervised and controlled the governor in Damascus, and he in turn controlled the pasha in Jerusalem, peace prevailed. However, when the Sultan was preoccupied with other affairs, those on the lower rungs on the ladder were left more or less to their own devices, and the result was often havoc. The new Sultan demanded obedience, and therefore a sense of normalcy returned to the realm.

With the new state of affairs, Jews began to return to the Holy City. By the end of the century, when the total population of Jerusalem reached about 10,000 inhabitants, the Jewish population was estimated at around 2,500.[43]

Rav Yom Tov Elgazi

Rav Yom Tov Elgazi served as Rishon l'Tzyon for over a quarter of a century (1771–1802). He earned a reputation as a world-renowned sage, both through his writings and from his travels as a *shaliach*. The Chasam Sofer wrote about him: "I met him personally when he came to Frankfurt. Though he was honored as a *chacham*, someone of his stature really deserved much more veneration."[44] Rav Elgazi's in-depth commentary to the laws of firstborn animals, called *Hilchos Yom Tov*, was included in the Vilna edition of the Talmud. He also wrote *Simchas Yom Tov,* on the laws of the festivals.

Rav Elgazi's lifelong confidant was Rav Chaim Yosef Azulai, the Chida. They studied as *chavrusos* (study partners) in their youth, learned Kabbalah together under Rav Shalom Sharabi in the early 1750s, and maintained a close correspondence during the long decades that the Chida lived in Italy. Their approach to learning (as revealed in their writings) were drastically different. Rav Elgazi wrote long, detailed halachic responsa, while the Chida wrote terse decisions. Furthermore, the Chida wrote works on all aspects of the Torah — both revealed and hidden. On the other hand, Rav Elgazi, while a kabbalist of the first order, wrote only concerning the revealed spheres of Torah in his numerous works.[45]

Rav Elgazi's mentor, Rav Shalom Sharabi, passed away on 10 Shevat, 1777 (5537). He had not been ill and was in complete control of all his faculties. With mystical insight, the fifty-seven-year-old kabbalist had known that his time was approaching and had donned his tallis and tefillin, completely ready to reunite with his Maker.

The news of his passing stunned the community. As the greatest innovative kabbalist in hundreds of years, his death was keenly felt. Fortunately, although no one could match the master's vast wellspring of mystical understanding, there was one person fit to replace him as Rabban of Chassidim. That person was the Rishon l'Tzyon, Rav Yom Tov Elgazi. He was a leading disciple of Rav Sharabi for a quarter of a century and was universally respected as a profound kabbalist himself. The humble Rav Yom Tov was reluctant to assume his master's mantle, but the insistent community left

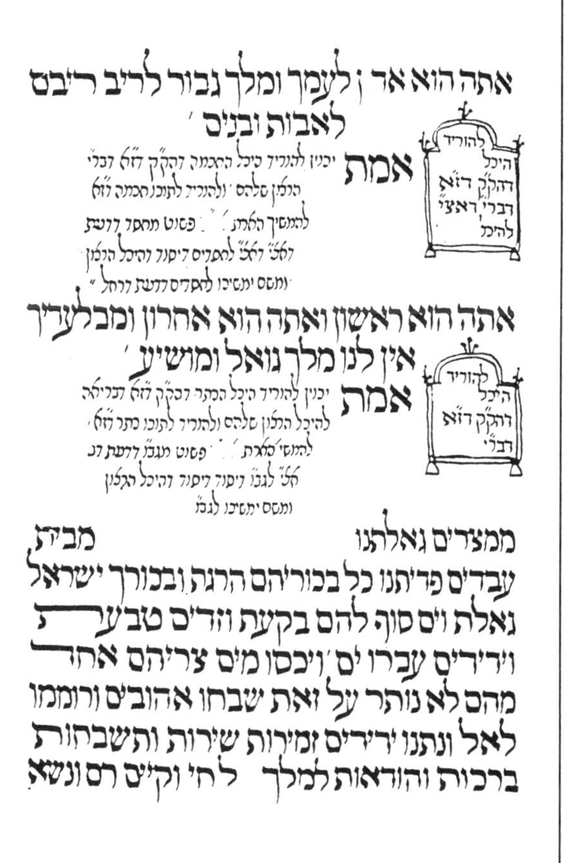
אתה הוא אד' לעמך ומלך גבור לריב ריבם
לאבות ובנים
אמת
אתה הוא ראשון ואתה הוא אחרון ומבלעדיך
אין לנו מלך גואל ומושיע
אמת
ממצרים גאלתנו מבית
עבדים פדיתנו כל בכוריהם הרגת ובכורך ישראל
גאלת וים סוף להם בקעת וזדים טבעת
וידידים עברו ים ויכסו מים צריהם אחד
מהם לא נותר על זאת שבחו אהובים ורוממו
לאל ונתנו ידידים זמירות שירות ותשבחות
ברכות והודאות למלך אל חי וקים רם ונשא

Handwritten page from the kabbalistic Siddur HaRashash, *as passed down by Rav Shalom Sharabi*

him no choice, and he finally acceded to their wishes. Rav Yom Tov led the Beis El Yeshivah until his death in 1802.

Rav Elgazi's duties as Rishon l'Tzyon and Rosh Yeshivah of Beis El filled his days and nights. Yet his heart opened to the destitute, and his home became a way station for all in need. When a fifteen-year-old boy suddenly became orphaned, Rav Elgazi took him in as a member of his family. The boy, Rav Yitzchak Parchi, author of *Tuv Yerushalayim*, would later write: "When my father died, I was fifteen years old. Immediately after the *shivah*, Rav Yom Tov Elgazi spoke warmly to me. When I burst into tears, he took a handkerchief and wiped the tears off my face. 'My child,' he consoled me, 'don't be afraid. I will be in your father's stead, and you will be to me like a son.'"[46]

The Mount of Olives

Throughout the ages, the Mount of Olives has been a choice burial sight for Jews the world over. In medieval and renaissance times, Egyptian Jews often chose to be buried there. Elderly Jews from the Diaspora would move to the Holy City in order to find a final resting place there. Our Sages said: "Anyone buried in Eretz Yisrael is as if buried under the altar, and anyone buried in Jerusalem is as if buried under the Throne of Glory."[47] The Mount of Olives stands directly opposite Mount Moriah, the Temple Mount. Tradition relates that at the time of the resurrection, those buried on the Mount of Olives will be among the first to enter the Third Temple. Today there are an estimated 50,000 to 80,000

Partial view of the cemetery on the Mount of Olives

graves on this sacred mountainside. In the late 1700s, the Turkish authorities in Jerusalem would try to take advantage of the Jewish people's connection to this holy place.

In 1782 (5542), the Turks instigated a new measure designed to squeeze money out of the Jewish community. The Mount of Olives, the undisputed burial site of the Jewish people for thousands of years, now stood with a "toll booth" at its entrance. No Jew could be buried there without first paying a tax.

The Rishon l'Tzyon wrote:

For an untold number of years, the Mount of Olives has been our sacred burial site, where thousands of rabbanim and gaonim lie. Recently, however, the ruling powers have inflicted a heavy blow upon us. They declared this holy mountain, where lie early prophets, a hazardous place for burial and forbade us to dig new graves. We were all thrown into mourning! How could we stand up against such a harsh decree?

With the payment of a substantial sum, it seemed like we succeeded in annulling it. Yet, this did not prove to be sufficient. Within a short time they again forbid us to bury our dead. This time nothing less than an official firman from the Sultan could stop them. But to get such a document would take time and lots of money. Yet every day we need to buy a burial plot from them.

Therefore, we are sending Rav Raphael Yosef Rubi as a shaliach to Constantinople....[48]

Rav Rubi was a scholar, author of *Derech HaMelech* on the Rambam, and an experienced *shaliach*. Together with influential Jews in Constantinople, a *firman* was secured — but only after long negotiations spanning several years. Finally, the burial tax was annulled.

This was not the first time that ruling authorities had interfered with burials on the Mount of Olives. In the mid-sixteenth century, the Radvaz asked the Egyptian Jews not to request burial there. The Moslems claimed that "imported" bodies were a cause of plagues. Such an association, although unfounded, had the power to bring dangerous reprisals against the Jerusalem community.[49]

In addition to interference by government authorities, the Mount of Olives also has a sad history of grave desecration throughout the generations. In the time of the Shelah (1620s), when the tyrant Farouk ruled, one of the reasons the Jews did not flee en masse from the city was to protect the graves. Without a Jewish enclave in Jerusalem, the Moslems would vent their hatred on the dead. Indeed, this is precisely what would happen after the War of Independence in 1948.

Rav David Pardo

Rav David Pardo immigrated to Eretz Yisrael in 1782, at the height of his career. This first-rate scholar, who had authored several halachic works and served as rabbi in several important cities, immediately impressed the leaders of Jerusalem's Jewish community with his profound Torah insights. Shortly after his arrival in the city, he became Rosh Yeshivah of Chesed l'Avraham Yeshivah, a position he would hold until his death in 1792.

Rav Pardo's elucidation of Rashi's commentary to the Chumash, *Maskil l'David,* became a classic. Over a hundred years later, when the Komarner Rebbe published his own commentary on the Chumash, *Hechal HaBerachah*, he chose to include Rav Pardo's commentary to be printed alongside his from among hundreds of others.

Besides serving as Rosh Yeshivah, Rav Pardo became close with the kabbalists of Beis El Yeshivah, especially Rav Avigdor Ezriel and Rav Yaakov Ninio. The latter published Rav Pardo's kabbalist exposition at the end of his book entitled *Sefas Emes*. Rav Pardo's commentary to the *Sifri* was completed in 1786.

מזמור לדוד

זמרו הנבונים וישירו המעיינים מזמור לדוד מ״ל לאור באור פני מלך חיי״ם הלכות ודינים · אלה דברי דוד האחרונים · יפה פרי תואר פריו קדש הלולים דברי הכמים כדר״ב בונים · ויהי דוד בכל דרכיו משכ״יל מצלי אודניה לגמרא שפתותיו שושנ״ים נצח ישראל ל״ו יסק״ר שיר למנצח במלאכת שמים עשה בונים · הנה הגבר הקי״ם ע״ל מכתם לדוד רוכב שפתי ישנים · הסדיו מרובים הסדי דוד הנאמנים · תני ספר״י דבי ר״ב בקרי״ת ארב״ע מקודש מקודש עונים · ארי שבחבורה שרשיו מרובים מרנא ורבנא הגאון המפורסם בשערים המצויינים גדול מרבן שמו והודו המו״ה כמוהר״ר דוד פארדו זצוק״ל וזכותו יע״ל ברוב הוני״ם לכל המתנדבים סגנים ואיתנים ונטעי נעמנים ושרי הנצבים אשר בח״ק מוהר הבתולו״ת כי הרבתה לתת מהר ומתן דמי״ם לעולם תהיה גברת מעולפת וספירים ·

פה ליוורנו יע״א

שנת והתענגו על ר״ב שלו״ם לפ״ק

ברפוס שמואל סעדון י״ץ

Title page of one of Rav Pardo's books

In an unusual occurrence during the winter of 1787, snow fell for three straight days and nights, from 4 to 7 Shevat. Drifts reached up to the top of the courtyard doors, and the city gates were unopenable. On Friday, the snow was so deep that no one ventured outside. Shabbos, *parshas Beshalach*, the synagogues were empty. Jerusalem was paralyzed. The Beis El Synagogue was unique in that it was several stories high. Upstairs lived Rav Yom Tov Elgazi, and with tremendous fortune he was able to secure a minyan.[50]

A Personal Loss

Elul, 1793 (5553), ushered in one of the darkest period's of Rav Elgazi's long and eventful career. At that time, an angry mob of Moslems demanded that he take responsibility for repaying the amassed debts of the Hebron community.

The affair had its roots in an incident that had taken place six years earlier. In 1787, the Jewish community of Hebron had asked Rav Elgazi to appoint Jewish officials to help manage their affairs, and he had willingly agreed. His son Yaakov was one of the appointees. The officials worked diligently to serve the community. When funds were short, they borrowed from wealthy Arabs at high interest rates. When the loan came due and was not repaid, the Moslems had some of the officers locked up in jail. After promises and delays, some money was forthcoming, but, with the ever-growing interest, it fell far short of the goal.

When the Arabs learned that one of the officials who had signed for the loan was the son of the leader of the Jerusalem community, they pressured Rav Elgazi directly. Their threats were not empty, and they nearly imprisoned him. Fortunately, Rav Elgazi persuaded them to extend the loan until letters could be sent and money brought back from the Diaspora.

Two years later, when the money was counted, it was still short of what was needed. Rav Yom Tov Elgazi, under renewed pressure, announced that he would personally travel to Constantinople to collect the necessary amount. The sixty-eight-year-old sage set out, and with the hand of God guiding him, he returned three months later with most of the funds.

But instead of finding smiling Jewish faces and content Moslems, he found himself face to face with a nightmare. Yaakov, his precious son, had been murdered by Arabs. The bloodthirsty Moslems had vented their wrath on an innocent man, mercilessly beating him to death with clubs and fists. Rav Yaakov left a number of small children orphaned, and Rav Elgazi took it upon himself to care for them.[51]

At the Turn of the Century

As the century came to a close, Rav Yom Tov Elgazi could look back over most of it with a sense of awe. His seventy-five years spanned a period in which a dazzling array of *gedolei Yisrael* had settled and built the spiritual Jerusalem. The Torah world would be forever enhanced by the contributions made to it by such tzaddikim as Rav Chaim Attar, Rav Shalom Sharabi, and Rav Chaim Yosef David Azulai, to name just a few.

The venerated Rishon l'Tzyon had lived through some of the most trying times that the Jewish community had ever faced. Poverty, famine, wicked decrees, murders, plagues, and more had all been meted out. The population had shrunk to the smallest of numbers and had grown again to new heights. Through it all, the needs of the community had been his primary concern, and both he and his flock had survived.

On the threshold of the nineteenth century, however, the city would face a new peril. Of all the trials and tribulations faced by the Jerusalem community, there was one which God withheld from them. They had never been attacked by a foreign power. Now, in 1799, three years before Rav Elgazi passed away, Napoleon marched with his army to conquer the Holy City. This, too, Rav Elgazi would witness and survive.

Notes

1. The whole episode is culled from the eyewitness report of Rav Gedaliah *(Sha'alu Shalom Yerushalayim)*, and *Toldos Chachmei Yerushalayim*, vol. 2, ch. 9.
2. *Toldos Chachmei Yerushalayim*, vol. 2, p. 142.
3. Ibid., vol. 2, pp. 100–102; *Maasef Tzyon*, vol. 6, pp. 61–69.
4. *Likutim*, Preface, pp. 2–11; *Toldos Chachmei Yerushalayim*, vol. 2, p. 107 (n. 1).
5. *Sha'alu Shalom Yerushalayim*, pp. 32–33.
6. *Toldos Chachmei Yerushalayim*, vol. 2, p. 87.

7. Ibid., p. 109.
8. Ibid., p. 86.
9. *Toldos Chachmei Yerushalayim*, vol. 2, ch. 9; *Tevuos HaAretz*, p. 471.
10. Ibid., pp. 153–154.
11. Ibid., pp. 113–119.
12. Ibid., p. 154.
13. *Megillas HaNess*, cited in *Gedolei HaDoros*, vol. 1, pp. 310–311.
14. *Admas Kodesh*, vol. 1, *Choshen Mishpat*, nos. 65, 67, 72.
15. See *Yerushalayim ben HaChomos*, p. 116.
16. Introduction to his book, *Adras Eliyahu*.
17. *Yerushalayim Quarterly*, 1950.
18. Ibid., p. 120.
19. *Toldos HaMechaber*, beginning of *Ohr HaChaim al HaTorah*, pp. 7–8.
20. Ibid., p. 9.
21. *Shem HaGedolim*, part I, *os ches*, no. 42.
22. Rav Meyuchas' *haskamah* to Rav Attar's book, *Rishon l'Tzyon*.
23. Ibid., part II, *os dales*, no. 62.
24. *Toldos HaMechaber*, beginning of *Ohr HaChaim al HaTorah*, p. 9.
25. *Shem HaGedolim*, part II, *os peh,* no. 143.
26. *Shaarei Yerushalayim*, Gate 10 (*Maaseh HaAretz*). Others say this incident occurred later in 1755, and that the Rav who tripped and fell was Rav Raphael Meyuchas. (*Toldos Chachmei Yerushalayim*, vol. 2, pp. 89–90.
27. *Yerushalayma,* p. 187.
28. *Stirring Times,* vol. 2, p. 57.
29. *Toldos HaOhr HaChaim HaKodesh*, p. 50 (n. 93). Some say he merely rested his head.
30. *Diglei Ahavah* by Rav Avraham Meyuchas.
31. *Masa'os Yerushalayim*, p. 95 (n. 9).
32. *Toldos HaOhr HaChaim HaKadosh*, p. 51 (n. 97).
33. *Nasi'im b'Yisrael,* p. 42.
34. *Toldos Chachmei Yerushalayim*, vol. 3, p.18.
35. There are several versions as to what happened at this point.
36. The Ben Ish Chai compares this to the story brought in the Gemara *Pesachim* 66a. Bnei Betera were stumped on an halachic question. Hillel the Elder arrived and succinctly answered it. They immediately placed him as head over them.
37. In the name of the kabbalist, Rav Chaim Shaul Deveik (*Chayei HaRashash,* p. 35*)*. See *Sefer Ahavas Shalom*.
38. The charter is quoted in *Chayei HaRashash*, pp. 18–28.
39. *Chachmei HaSephardim b'Eretz Yisrael*, p. 133.
40. Ibid., pp. 146–147.
41. *Pri HaAdamah*, part IV, p. 6.
42. Ibid., p. 52.
43. Ibid., p. 52., n. 25.
44. From his *haskamah* to Rav Elgazi's *Hilchos Yom Tov*.
45. *Toldos Chachmei Yerushalayim*, vol. 3, p. 115.
46. Ibid., p. 287.
47. *Tanna d'Rav Nasan*, ch. 26.
48. *Toldos Chachmei Yerushalayim*, vol. 3, pp. 122–123.
49. Radvaz, *responsa*, part 2, no. 611.
50. *Birchas Mayim, Orach Chaim* 135.
51. *Chachmei HaSephardim b'Eretz Yisrael*, p. 161–162.

Bygone Days

The Snowstorm

As we noted in the Overview, Jerusalem had no independent water source. Instead, every courtyard had an underground cistern that filled with water during the rainy winter months and provided for the residents' needs throughout the dry season. Thus, after the summer and fall, everyone would raise their eyes heavenward in hope, searching the skies for rain. By then, the cisterns were empty, and without rain to replenish their store, the situation would become critical.

THE WINTER of 1705–1706 (5466) threatened to usher in a year of drought. The Jewish community decreed fast days and special prayers during Kislev and Teves. In all, they fasted seven times, in accordance with the Mishnah, yet no rain was forthcoming.

The situation quickly deteriorated into a crisis of major proportions. The pasha hastened to declare a new policy. The closest freshwater supply was at the well of Yoab, a half-hour's walk down the Kidron valley to the south of the city. Until now, water carriers had a monopoly on the well, and no one was allowed to fetch his own water. The pasha, realizing the gravity of the situation, allowed anyone — including Jews — to go and bring back as much water as they wished. Anyone who prevented someone else from taking water would be penalized with the death sentence.

This measure helped to temporarily alleviate the immediate threat to the civilian population. Yet the water carriers still demanded a price for drawing up the water in buckets. Additionally, as bad as the situation was now, if no rain was to fall by the advent of spring, the situation would literally become intolerable.

The month of Shevat dawned very cold. At one point, the thermometer even dipped below zero, a very rare occurrence for Jerusalem. Then the skies filled with heavy, gray clouds that hovered silently overhead for days. One night, snow flurries started to fall as the wind whistled through the cracks in the windows. The following morning the snow fell in a steady stream and began to stick to the ground. As the children played in the snow, the adults col-

lected it in pots and pans and brought it inside to melt. Fresh water from heaven!

Another day of snow and still another day. For a full week it snowed, day and night, a storm the likes of which had never been recorded before. The joyous residents, snowbound, opened their cisterns and shoveled as much snow as they could inside.

No rain fell after the snowstorm that winter. The Lord had showered His mercy on His people in a very memorable fashion. Everyone turned to Him in thanksgiving.

(*Sha'alu Shalom Yerushalayim*, p. 12 a-b)

The Dogs

ONE YEAR during the first decade of the eighteenth century, the new Turkish *kadi* came from Constantinople. This wicked man delighted in devising schemes to make the lives of the Jews miserable (and some of his Moslem brethren as well). For example, he decreed that no Jew could wear white garments on Shabbos, nor could they put metal heels on their shoes. Additionally, the turbans worn by Jews had to be black, and the hat placed in the middle had to be high. All of these measures were designed to make the Jew stand out and be easily identified. The last ordinance was particularly troubling, for during the week, many Jews dressed with low turbans in a manner similar to the Arabs and were therefore not easily distinguishable. (In those days all male Arabs had long beards, as did the Jews.) This similarity had helped to reduce the hostility harbored by lowly Arab neighbors, and the new differentiation could only cause problems.

Next, the *kadi* sought to actively humiliate the Jews of the city. Jews were required to pass an oncoming Moslem by stepping over to his left side, and if one did not, he could be arrested and imprisoned. Often, an Arab would intentionally walk out of his shop in order to force a passing Jew to sidestep to the left. It was a new pastime for lazy Arabs. Yet, despite all the dangers, indignities, and inconveniences, the Jews persevered with their lives; after all, what else could they do? Thus life went on.

Shortly before Purim, the *kadi* discovered that a dog had entered the Temple Mount. Enraged that such a despicable creature should profane the holiness of the sacred spot, he ordered that all the dogs in the city be killed. To encourage Arab youths to fulfill his decree, he offered a monetary prize for each dead dog produced. They eagerly carried out his words and ran about the streets of Jerusalem in search of dogs.

The area beyond the outer wall facing Mount Zion had been designated as the burial site for the dogs. After collecting their reward, the Arabs would wait with the carcass for a Jew or Christian to pass by, and force him to take it outside the city. The Christians, mostly wealthy, were able to bribe the Arabs and avoid the obnoxious task. However, the poor Jews were at their mercy. Sometimes, after taking one dog outside the city, a hapless conscript to the task would meet another Arab on his way back and have to take yet another carcass. Along the entire way, Arab children would taunt and jeer at him.

The situation led to a self-imposed quarantine, as everyone stayed home to avoid the unpleasant business. This, of course, was a temporary measure at best, for one could not survive without the basic necessities of life. It was agreed that only the men should risk venturing outside to purchase household needs.

Before Passover, Rav Gedaliah, one of the followers of Rav Yehudah HaChassid, was grinding wheat for the baking of the matzos. He and some companions worked hard to finish the job. Suddenly they heard a group of noisy Arab youths dragging several dead dogs nearby. "We immediately shut the door to the shop and waited fearfully until the wicked Arabs passed us."

The situation persisted long after the Festival of our Freedom was over. Late in Iyar, on the *yartzeit* of Shmuel HaNavi, many members of the community went to pray at the prophet's burial cave. During the day, some latecomers informed the group that the *kadi* had just enacted a new twist to his decree. Since there were still dogs hiding in courtyards and abandoned ruins, every household was responsible for bringing one live dog to the wall outside of Mount Zion. There, an officer would kill the dog and present the man with a certificate. Those who did not have such a document within a certain amount of time would be arrested. This decree applied to Arabs as well.

When everyone returned home they realized the full impact of the decree. Dogs were scarce. Even the Arabs had a hard time fulfilling the *kadi*'s edict. An instant black market suddenly sprung up for the "precious" commodity as demand far outstripped the meager supply. Jews who had previously avoided the Arabs on account of the dead dogs now sought them out to buy live ones. Still, there were not enough.

After Shavuos, the *kadi* realized that the Jews had gone to the cave of Shmuel HaNavi without registering for a permit. Actually, every year permission was granted automatically by the *kadi*'s secretary, and a set fee was paid. But this *kadi* was an anti-Semite who thirsted for any excuse to harass the Jews. Without warning, he arrested the *nasi* (at the time, the term Rishon l'Tzyon was not in use) of the Sephardic community and placed him in detention. The Jewish community shivered at the news. A fast was decreed, and a communal prayer service held.

In the meantime, a number of prominent Moslems also indignantly responded to the arrest, albeit in a slightly more dramatic fashion. They, too, had a list of gripes against the *kadi* and were all too ready to put a stop to his mischief. The arrest of the *nasi* served to accentuate their feelings. The leader of the Jewish community was a highly respected man even in their eyes, and his imprisonment represented a breach of the honor afforded to communal leaders as a whole. They decided to take matters into their own hands.

On the second day of the arrest, an Arab mob forcefully freed the *nasi* from his imprisonment. At nightfall, they marched on the *kadi*'s house, out for blood. The *kadi*'s residence was inside a large fortified courtyard. The cunning judge knew what they wanted, and quickly wrote a note and threw it out to them. He meekly apologized for his actions and attempted to place the blame on someone else's unsuspecting shoulders. He claimed that his appointment was for a single year and, since he did not know the customs of Jerusalem nor the language (he spoke Turkish, and they spoke Arabic), he had relied on a Moslem advisor. That man, he said, was responsible for all of the actions he had taken.

The angry mob quickly sought out the advisor and slew him. However, their bloodlust was not satisfied, and they proceeded to throw rocks into the *kadi*'s courtyard. Had the *kadi* been standing there, he would have been stoned to death. As it was, he remained locked inside his house for a couple of days. One night he secretly escaped and returned to Constantinople.

(*Sha'alu Shalom Yerushalayim*, pp. 14b–15b)

The Miracle

FOR RAV Raphael Meyuchas, the day after Purim 1723 (5483) dawned warm and hopeful in Cairo, Egypt. The young scholar's urgent mission on behalf of the Jerusalem community had been blessed with success — he had raised the funds necessary to ransom his grandfather and other Jews from the hands of the wicked pasha. Rav Raphael had traveled by sea to Constantinople and worked his way home well within the three-month deadline. Now he was ready to set out on the last leg of his journey.

As he set out across the Sinai desert with his treasure chest and other provisions, the young man mused over his success. His boat had sailed from Eretz Yisrael to Constantinople in a record time of three days. Then he had received the entire amount needed to save the community within the space of a few days. The loving hand of God had truly been with him every step of the way.

The following day he was alone in the desert, with sand dunes stretching out on all sides as far as the eye could see. However, the arid wasteland didn't worry him; his water-skin was full, and in another few days he would be in sight of the Holy City.

Suddenly, nine Bedouin warriors swooped down on him, seemingly out of nowhere. Brandishing swords that glittered ominously in the brilliant sunlight, they began howling in an unearthly voice. Defenseless and frozen with fear, Rav Raphael was completely at their mercy. In short order, they killed his mount and demanded that he undress. Left with only his underclothes and his *tallis katan*, he was ordered to lay on the ground. Laughing and shouting, his cruel captors then proceeded to punch and kick him nearly senseless.

Suddenly, one of them raised his sword to strike a death blow. Rav

Raphael prepared to sanctify his life and began to whisper "*Shema Yisrael.*" Miraculously, however, as the metal blade touched his neck, the sword split in half. Bellowing with rage, another member of the band cursed his incompetent companion, and, roughly shoving him aside, tried his own hand — with the exact same result. With that, the remaining swordsmen all attempted to decapitate the terrified scholar, one after another, and each was left with nothing but a broken blade for his efforts.

"I felt," Rav Raphael would write later, "that my neck had stiffened as hard as granite."

Flustered and frightened at this strange turn of events, the bandits left Rav Raphael where he was and hurried off with their booty. The young man lay where he was in a daze. Not only was the ransom money lost, but he was left without so much as a drop of water.

In the meantime, the highwaymen were also in a state of shock. Who had ever heard of a sword forged in fire splitting in two over flesh and blood! Their victim was surely one of the righteous who enjoyed Heavenly protection. With each step they took, their fear of Divine retribution increased. They were soon gripped with a paralyzing terror and were physically unable to go on. They decided to return to the Jew and give him back everything they had stolen.

The marauders approached Rav Meyuchas slowly, unable to speak. The fear of a holy tzaddik and the mightiness of his God had shaken them to the core. Finally, one managed to blurt out, "Forgive us! Take back what is yours!"

As Rav Raphael nodded his consent, they were freed from the spell and dashed off, never to be seen again.

Collecting himself, Rav Raphael stood up and got dressed. The impact of the miracle raced through his body, bringing with it a heightened joy.

"Right then and there," recorded the tzaddik, "I took upon myself and my descendants to make that day, the sixteenth of Adar, a day of rejoicing; a feast day on which to praise the Almighty for miraculously saving my life."

However, this was not the end of the miraculous tale. As he repacked his remaining possessions and prepared to continue on his journey, a stranger rode by on a camel and stopped. The man's countenance was glowing; vibrant and alive.

"Where are you headed?" he asked.

"If God wills it, my goal is to reach the Holy City of Jerusalem," Rav Raphael answered.

The stranger looked kindly at the young man. "You need not be afraid. I shall escort you to your destination, and nothing dangerous shall befall you."

They started on their way, and Rav Raphael gazed ahead of him down the road. His eyes grew wide with surprise. Right before him lay Jerusalem!

Rav Meyuchas ended his chronicle with these words: "The Kingship is the Lord's; He is King of the whole world. His perfection and the perfection of His throne is situated in Jerusalem. Amen."

(*Megillas HaNess*)

The Paper Note

ONE DAY a destitute Jew came to the Ohr HaChaim to seek his blessing. It seemed that his whole world had suddenly turned upside down, and he was now without any source of income. The unfortunate man poured out his heart to Rav Attar, begging his forgiveness for having bothered him and explained that he had not come to speak to him until his situation had become desperate.

"Please," he entreated, "pray for me, and bless me with good fortune."

Rav Chaim Attar was genuinely moved by the man's heartfelt plea. He took a piece of parchment and began to write something on it in the script used by a *sofer* (scribe) for a Torah scroll. His quill tip darted between the small inkwell and the sheet before him.

When he finished, he waited for the parchment to dry and then carefully folded it over and over again until it was the size of a bean.

"Take this note," said the Ohr HaChaim. "Hold it firmly in your hand and go straight to the Wailing Wall. When you get there, look for a little niche between the holy stones and stick it inside. Then you can return home confident that your salvation is at hand."

Thanking Rav Attar profusely, the pauper took his leave and began walking swiftly along the lanes leading to the Wall. It was a brisk, windy day. As he turned a corner, a gust of wind caught the corner of his hat and sent it flying off his head. Though he naturally wanted to retrieve his hat, he realized that the success of his mission depended on fulfilling the words of the rav to the letter. Lurching forward against the strong wind, he put his left hand on his head to secure his *kipa*, while tightly holding the note in his right hand.

At another bend, the wind roared in his ears, and a split second later he lost his *kipa*. He instinctively lunged forward to grab it, but it hopped out of his reach. As he tried again, he momentarily loosened his grip in his right hand. A split second later the note was sucked out of his fingers and disappeared into the air. He searched for it, but it was nowhere to be found.

Broken-hearted, the pauper returned to Rav Attar.

"What can I do now?" the tzaddik muttered. "What can I do when Heaven has declared otherwise?"

Whether or not the Ohr HaChaim found another way to circumvent the decree is unknown. In any event, the note he had penned was found later. It was a letter to the Shechinah (a manifestation of the Divine Presence), which read:

My dear, beloved One,

I request You to please grant an abundant flow of parnasah to so-and-so, the son of so-and-so.

Chaim ben Attar

(*Masa'os Yerushalayim*, p. 94)

The Inner Circle

It is unclear whether Rav Gershon Kitover, the Baal Shem Tov's brother-in-law, actually met the Ohr HaChaim in person. They might have met in Jerusalem, or Damascus, or not at all. This uncertainty is due to a vague picture of Rav Kitover's exact whereabouts in 1742–1743. Thus the historical veracity of this tale is questionable. In the final analysis, however, it remains a story that is rich in meaning.

RAV CHAIM Attar, the Ohr HaChaim HaKodesh, opened a yeshivah in Jerusalem at the end of 1742. It was named Knesses Yisrael, and it attracted the finest scholars of the time. However, unknown to most people, he also had a second yeshivah for the study of Kabbalah, to which only a select few were permitted entrance. In fact, a guard was stationed outside the door to ensure that strangers would not enter.

Rav Gershon Kitover had been informed by his brother-in-law, the Baal Shem Tov, of the existence of this second yeshivah. He set for himself the goal of being accepted into this elite circle of kabbalists. First, though, he decided to ask permission to join Knesses Yisrael Yeshivah and prove himself as a top-notch scholar in the revealed Torah.

As time went by and his reputation as a *talmid chacham* spread, he began inquiring discreetly about the second yeshivah. However, no one seemed to know of its existence. One day he decided to ask Rav Attar directly.

"Who told you I have such a yeshivah?" the Ohr HaChaim asked.

"My rebbe, Rav Yisrael Baal Shem."

"I do not know him. Nevertheless, I can see that you are a worthy individual. Therefore, I will let you study in my *nistar* yeshivah."

After a few days of intense study there, Rav Kitover was denied permission from the guard to enter.

"Don't you recognize me?" prompted Rav Gershon, thinking that since he was relatively new, perhaps the watchman had forgotten who he was. However, the guard quickly disavowed him of this notion and informed him that the Rosh Yeshivah had given orders that he not be admitted.

Upset and confused, Rav Gershon asked for an explanation.

The guard replied, "Rabbeinu [the Ohr HaChaim] said to tell you that it is because you did not serve a master in a practical way."

Rav Gershon returned home and meditated on this turn of events. The message became clear to him, and he sought a means to rectify the situation. Later the same day, he saw the Rosh Yeshivah excuse himself to take care of his personal needs. Knowing that the Ohr HaChaim was accustomed to change all his clothes after he relieved himself, Rav Gershon raced to Rav Attar's house and brought him his shoes. Rav Attar smiled and said, "Yes, now you have served a master."

Ohr HaChaim Synagogue

The situation returned as it was, and Rav Kitover was readmitted to the yeshivah. However, a few days later he was again barred entry; only this time, no reason was given.

With no other recourse, Rav Kitover sought the Rosh Yeshivah.

"When you first mentioned the name of your rebbe," the Ohr HaChaim explained, "you forgot to call him Baal Shem Tov. In Heaven, this slight was deemed a very serious offense, and had the Baal Shem Tov not prayed for you, you would have been punished."

Humbled and grateful for his rebbe's intercession on his behalf in the upper worlds, Rav Gershon begged Rav Attar for forbearance in this world as well. Still, the Ohr HaChaim refused to allow him to join the select group of kabbalists studying in his *nistar* yeshivah.

(*Toldos HaOhr HaChaim HaKodesh*, p. 54)

A Hairsbreadth from the Redemption

On Hoshannah Rabbah, 5503 (1742), an incident occurred that had a profound effect on Rav Chaim Attar, as well as the future of world history. The Chida described the event as follows:

ON THE night of Hoshannah Rabbah, Rabbeinu stayed up and recited the traditional *tikun* (excerpts from Tanach). His face shone like the sun and rays of light emanated from his face. Dressed in white, he truly resembled an angel.

At midnight he went into his private chamber and replaced his white garments with black ones. Collapsing on the floor, he began to cry bitterly, not moving from that position throughout the night. When the morning prayers began, he rose and joined the congregation, but returned immediately afterwards to his study. For the rest of the day, he sat on the floor. In the afternoon, as the holiday of Shemini Atzeres was about to begin, he put on his white garments and joined the services.

After Yom Tov, I dared approach Rabbeinu for an explanation.

"That night," revealed the Ohr HaChaim, "I asked [before the Heavenly court] if the Mashiach could reveal himself, and consent was granted! But when the Satan saw that such a turn in history would mean his own annihilation, he deviously plotted to cause more people to sin, so that the permission would be rescinded. His scheme worked so well that he succeeded in denouncing the Jewish people and invoking a Heavenly decree against them. An edict of destruction was issued!

"When I saw this, I fell on the floor and made a desperate plea to avert the tragedy. In the end, I offered to let the Satan take me alone, and thereby save world Jewry."

Thus it was that Rav Chaim Attar died later that same year.

It was clear from his words that he was the Mashiach. He was ready to come forward and bring the redemption — only the time was not ripe.

(*Toldos HaOhr HaChaim HaKodesh*, p. 50)

Statues of Flesh and Blood

IN THE middle of the night, a number of Arabs living near the Western Wall were rudely awakened by the sound of a Jew crying at the top of his voice. This person regularly came to recite *tikun chatzos* (prayers uttered over the destruction of the Temple and the exile of the Divine Presence); but this night, in a spontaneous outpouring of emotion, his resonate voice tore the firmaments and echoed loudly through the silent streets of the city.

In the morning, the Arabs found out who the culprit was: Rav Shalom

Sharabi, the saintly Jewish mystic. As can easily be imagined, the Moslems living near the Kosel had a long-standing policy to disturb the lowly Jews who approached the Wall. They would throw stones and harass the hapless worshippers, sometimes even embarrassing Jewish women and girls. This time, however, it was *their* peace that had been disturbed by the accursed Jews. They were bent on taking revenge for their lost sleep.

The Mufti was one of those whose sleep had been shattered. The cleric proposed a scheme: that night some of his black servants, together with some of the neighboring Moslems, would hide on either side of the staircase leading down to the Kosel. When the Jew would pass by, they would attack him with clubs and fists, and thrash him to within an inch of his life, leaving him alive to tell the story.

That night Rav Sharabi set out from the Beis El Synagogue with his *shamash* (beadle). Rav Sharabi's nightly custom was to recite *tikun chatzos* by the Wailing Wall, be it summer or winter, rain or snow. He composed this lamentation to be said on such occasion:

Woe unto me — that the Shechinah is in galus.
Woe unto me — that the Temple is in ruins.
Woe unto me — that tzaddikim have been slain.
Woe unto me — that His great Name and holy Torah have been profaned.
Woe unto me — that the enemy prevails.
Woe unto me — that all the (spiritual) worlds are in suffering.
Woe unto me — that the Mashiach is distressed....

As the *shamash* led the way with a lantern, he suddenly panicked at the sight of the attackers.

"Don't be afraid of them!" whispered Rav Sharabi. "Just keep walking forward. Nothing will happen to us!"

The attackers stood frozen in their place. They did not even utter a sound as the Jews passed by.

After the tzaddik recited *tikun chatzos*, he returned home as usual.

When the next day dawned, the first Arabs to go outside were thunderstruck to see the Mufti's thugs frozen like statues, raised clubs in their hands. The Mufti was woken up, and within an hour the news spread like wildfire throughout the city.

Calling the Moslem leaders to his side, the Mufti went to the Jewish Quarter to speak with Rav Sharabi. Falling at the tzaddik's feet, he implored him for forgiveness.

Rav Shalom Sharabi, a mystic of the highest caliber, gently rebuffed the Mufti's pleas. "Whatever happened to them," he said, "was merely an act of Heaven. I had nothing to do with it."

The Mufti and his comrades continued to appeal to him. Finally, the tzaddik agreed to pray for the recovery of the ruffians. However, he first stipulated that the Moslems should unconditionally consent to allowing the Jews free access to the Kosel whenever they wished. Left with no choice, the Arabs agreed.

Rav Sharabi whispered a short prayer, and immediately the living statues were freed of their bondage.

(*Issachar v'Zevulun*, p. 37)

Kill Me Too!

ONE YEAR in the mid-1700s, the Turkish *kadi* leveled a special tax on the Jewish community. It was impossible for the poverty-stricken Jews to accumulate the sum by the appointed time. In order to "encourage" the impoverished Jews to raise the money, the *kadi* had three scholars arrested and imprisoned, threatening to kill them should the entire sum not be brought immediately.

The communal leaders went to the *kadi*'s house to beg him to retract his threat.

"If the money is not on this table by tomorrow morning," snarled the *kadi*, "then all three prisoners will be put to death!"

Rav Shalom Sharabi, the picture of composure, stepped forward and said, "If three are to die, then kill four!" (Rav Sharabi included himself in the decree, because he realized once he was in danger, his merit would save them all.)

The *kadi*, angered by his words, retorted, "As you wish! You shall be the fourth one! Take him!" he roared.

As the guards approached him, they quickly retraced their footsteps. The look in Rav Sharabi's eyes gripped them with fear. Suddenly, a veil descended over the Arabs' eyes, leaving them in a daze. In that instant, the Jewish leaders silently left the house.

That night the *kadi* awoke from a nightmare. He was so unnerved that he was unable to go back to sleep, and in the morning he ordered the release of the prisoners and the annulment of the tax.

(*Pri Etz HaGan*, pp. 13–14)

The Bottle of Wine

THE *SHAMASH* of the Talmud Torah Synagogue (also called Eliyahu HaNavi Synagogue) was a simple, God-fearing, Sephardic Jew. Late one Thursday night, after arranging the tables and siddurim for Shabbos, he returned home and went to bed.

His sleep was interrupted by a loud voice near his bedside. He immediately sat up and saw a complete stranger standing in front of him.

"Go quickly to the synagogue," the man uttered urgently. "Don't waste a minute! There are blood-red flames burning in the Holy Ark. If you don't hurry, *chas v'shalom*, the fire could spread to the whole synagogue and from there to the rest of the city!"

The experience was surreal, a dream, but its vividness and urgency compelled him to action.

Although it was dangerous to walk outside late at night, the *shamash* rushed to the synagogue, unlocked the door, and entered. In the dark, he quickly walked over to the Holy Ark and opened it. There was no fire. He felt around. All the Torah scrolls were in place. In one corner was the bottle of wine used for Kiddush on Shabbos night. He himself had placed it there last *motzei Shabbos*. But to his surprise, the bottle was not in the right place. His suspicion grew when he held it up to the moonlight and realized that it was not the same bottle which he had placed there. Gingerly, he poured some of the contents into a glass. It was blood. The dream had been a Heavenly message. He went outside and poured the blood on the ground and covered it with dirt. After disposing of the bottle, he replaced it with a bottle of superb, red wine.

Entrance to the Eliyahu HaNavi Synagogue

The next morning, the Shacharis service jarred to a standstill as the pasha entered together with a Greek Orthodox priest. The two grim figures were followed by other priests, a Greek citizen, and armed Moslems. There was a deafening silence, and a shiver of fear ran across the faces of the Jewish congregants.

"A Christian child was murdered yesterday," announced the pasha. "We have come to search for his blood, which the priests claim you use for sacramental purposes."

Soldiers searched under the tables and behind the benches, turning over cushions and taking books off the shelves.

"Open up the Holy Ark," called out a priest.

As soon as one of the soldiers picked up the bottle, one of the Greek civilians yelled excitedly, "See! Here is the blood of the child!"

The Greek Patriarch asked the rabbi what was in the bottle.

"It is a bottle of wine which we use on the Sabbath night to make Kiddush."

The Patriarch opened the bottle and poured some of its contents into a glass, and behold — it was fragrant wine! He passed the glass to the pasha, who passed it on to another priest. The aroma filled the synagogue, and it was obvious to all that the bottle contained only wine.

"I apologize," said the Patriarch to the rabbi. "It seems that this Greek citizen intended to provoke a blood libel against the Jews. He is obviously unsound and fabricated the whole story."

Turning to the pasha he said, "The Jews are completely innocent."

In a fit of anger, the pasha drew his sword and raised it to smite the Greek man.

"No!" shouted the Patriarch. "Don't spill blood in a synagogue. Wait until we are outside."

Outside, before being run through by the vengeful sword of the pasha, the Greek citizen confessed to everything.

The Jews, after hearing the tale of how the simple *shamash* had miraculously been warned and had acted decisively to save hundreds of Jews, proclaimed that day as one of celebration.

(*Shaarei Yerushalayim*, end of *Ma'aseh HaAretz*)

19th Century

From Napoleon to Beyond the Walls

Part I

The Era of Suffering: 1800-1840

הַרְחִיבִי מְקוֹם אָהֳלֵךְ
וִירִיעוֹת מִשְׁכְּנוֹתַיִךְ יַטּוּ
אַל תַּחְשֹׂכִי הַאֲרִיכִי מֵיתָרַיִךְ וִיתֵדֹתַיִךְ חַזֵּקִי.

ישעיה נד:ב

Enlarge the place of your tent,
and let them stretch forth the curtain of your habitations;
spare not,
lengthen your cords and strengthen your stakes.

Isaiah 54:2

Face to Face with Napoleon

Throughout the hundreds of years of Ottoman rule, Eretz Yisrael and Jerusalem had been generally ignored by the world at large. With the advent of the nineteenth century, however, this would abruptly change. The first European leader to focus his attention on the Middle East was Napoleon Boneparte (1769–1821), the ambitious French general who had ascended to power in the wake of the French revolution. Napoleon's brilliance in battle, coupled with a quick succession of decisive victories struck fear in the hearts of all who stood in his path.

In 1798 (5558), the daring military genius set his sights on conquering the Middle East. He wanted to strike at the source of Great Britain's wealth by occupying Egypt and threatening the route to India. His unexpected leap across the Mediterranean to Egypt and his subsequent success there served to reiterate his military prowess. Even after being defeated by the British Admiral Nelson at the Battle of the Nile in August, Napoleon's legions marched up the Sinai coast to Gaza in Kislev, and then to Jaffa in Adar 1799 (5559). In Jaffa, four thousand residents were killed, a staggering number for those times.

Napoleon's Scheme

Napoleon's swift, uncontested campaign soon brought him to a crossroad. From Jaffa he could either continue northward along the sea coast to the port city of Akko, or turn inland and ascend the Judean mountains to conquer Jerusalem. Both options had their attractions. Akko was the largest Turkish military base in Eretz Yisrael, and its downfall would effectively give Napoleon sovereignty over the whole country. Jerusalem, on the other hand, housed a small garrison of Turkish troops. Its defeat would make him little more than king of the Holy City — in theory a coveted prize of all Christendom, but in actuality a largely honorary title lacking substance.

Everyone in the country waited apprehensively to see which way he would go. In Jerusalem, plans for the city's defense were set in motion. There was a general call for everyone to help fortify the city walls. Trenches had to be dug, stones and mortar laid, and canons readied along the ramparts. The Jewish community pitched in along with the rest of the populace. Prayers were uttered in every synagogue, mosque, and church. This enemy had to be met with a united front.

However, despite the Jews' contribution, a suspicion persisted among the Moslems that they were in some kind of secret pact with the French forces. Napoleon had openly called on all Jews to side with him, offering them sovereignty over the Holy City in return. In particular, he tried to lure Chaim Parchi, the powerful court Jew of the pasha in Akko, to his side. While Napoleon's alluring call failed to sway the Jews' allegiance, it did cause sharp reprisals in the form of slander, abductions, and arrests. A contemporary Jew wrote: "From the time that Egypt fell [into French hands], we have been surrounded with untold tensions by wicked gentiles. They constantly contend with us and falsely accuse us, claiming that there are Jewish soldiers among the twelve thousand French armed forces with whom we have contact."[1]

Now, it seemed like the Moslems finally wanted to make peace. With the whole city facing the seemingly imminent threat of invasion, the pasha sent a message to the Jewish leaders, Rav Yom Tov Elgazi and his son-in-law, Rav Yosef Meyuchas, requesting them to convene special prayer services.

Sending a messenger in return, Rav Meyuchas angrily retorted: "Why does the pasha make such a request? Doesn't he know that our lives have been made miserable by the Moslem population! In addition to all the other indignities heaped upon us, whenever we try to go to

Napoleon as he appeared in 1797

our holy places, such as the Wailing Wall, we are prevented from praying there. How then can the pasha request something from us which he himself denies us!"

When the pasha received this message, he quickly revamped his policy and officially allowed Jews to pray at their holy sites, including the Kosel HaMaaravi. As a gesture of his sincerity, he cleared a wider area before the Wall for Jews to pray in. With this, Rav Meyuchas called for the special services the pasha had requested, and the Jews responded in kind, coming in large numbers to pray for the peace and safety of the city.[2]

There was another important result of the pasha's request, Rav Meyuchas's response, and the subsequent large turnout of Jews to the prayer service. Rav Meyuchas had been informed of a pogrom to massacre the entire Jewish community if and when Napoleon breached the city walls. His call to his brethren to help in the defense of the city mitigated this threat.[3]

Napoleon's Decision

In the meantime, Napoleon had come to a decision: Jerusalem. However, when he came to Ramla (or, according to others, Kiryat Yearim, which is three-fourths of the way to Jerusalem), he made a mysterious turnaround and headed north to Akko. To this day, the reasons behind his unexpected decision are unknown. Regardless of his motives, the populace of Jerusalem was relieved and joyous over this turn of events. It was clear that the Almighty was looking out for His city.

The siege of Akko lasted two months, during which time Napoleon fought a battle at Mount Tabor and passed through Tiberias and Safed in the Galilee. At Meron, he searched for a hidden treasure rumored to be buried in the cave of Hillel the Elder, without success. In Akko, a British fleet headed by Admiral William Sydney Smith, together with the large Turkish forces inside the walls of the city battled for their lives. By the middle of Iyar, Napoleon's troops, seriously weakened by an epidemic, were

Napoleon (1769–1821) on his campaign to the Middle East

forced to retreat south along the coast to Jaffa. After destroying the walls of the city (and poisoning his own sick and wounded soldiers), Napoleon returned to Egypt, and from there to France.

Europe and Russia would feel the impact of Napoleon's might for another decade and a half. The clamor for emancipation which he initiated for the Jews met with mixed feelings among the European Jewry. Rav Shneur Zalman, the first Lubavitcher Rebbe, vehemently opposed the French general and opted to support the Czar's government. In the long run, he understood that the "emancipation" heralded by Napoleon would undermine the tightly-knit fabric of Jewish life. Sadly, time has proven him all too correct.

One of the outcomes of Napoleon's campaign in the Middle East was a new attitude by the Turkish Sultan, Mohammed the Second. Coming to power in 1808, he looked to the European model of government for inspiration and adopted some reforms in his system of rule. Slowly and painfully, the empire began to modernize. Mohammed was hampered by a small but influential corps of troops spread throughout the empire, called Yanitshiri, that had dominated every Sultan for hundreds of years. After Mohammed had consolidated his rule, he disbanded the elite corps, and had over 100,000 men put to death. In Jerusalem, too, there were a small number of Yanitshiri who were executed.

A Breathing Spell

In contrast to the spirit of reform that gradually overtook the rest of the empire, the impetus to modernize was barely felt in Jerusalem. Life in the Holy City carried on much as it had for hundreds of years. Ruins, filled with pools of stagnant water, were scattered everywhere — a breeding ground for malaria and cholera. Bureaucracy, or the lack thereof, bottlenecked any drive to expand and refurbish either synagogues or homes. Outside the walls, lawlessness ruled supreme. This grim picture would only begin to alter in 1830, when the Egyptian pasha succeeded in rebelling against the empire and temporarily wrested control of the Middle East from Turkish hands. Although the Sultan would reconquer the area ten years later, the winds of change would prove to finally and irrevocably blow over this part of the world as well.

When Rav Yom Tov Elgazi died in 1802, the sixty-four-year-old Rav Yosef Meyuchas became the new Rishon l'Tzyon, a post he would hold until his death in 1808. Rav Meyuchas, a scholar of note from his youth, had a unique rapport with the Moslems of the city. A gentle and caring man, his mastery of the healing arts won the hearts of all whom he came in contact with. Many residents of the city owed their recovery and even their lives to his medical acumen, and he provided his services free of charge.

Between 1808 and 1820, four *rabbanim* served as Rishon l'Tzyon: Rav Mordechai HaLevi (known as HaRav HaMelitz), author of *Maamar Mordechai*, a work on Halachah; Rav Yaakov Iyash (who opened a yeshivah called Chaim v'Chesed in 1803); Rav Yaakov Korel; and Rav Yosef Chazan.

Rav Chazan's coronation as Rishon l'Tzyon was a singular event. In Iyar, 1818 (5578), the leaders of Jerusalem traveled to Hebron to announce their decision to the venerable sage, who was then serving as the *rav* of that city. The seventy-seven-year-old *rav*, who had immigrated from Izmir, Turkey in 1813, had purposely selected quiet Hebron as his home in order to dedicate his last years to undisturbed Torah study. However, he did not turn his back on this call of duty, and amidst a jubilant entourage he was escorted to the Holy City. As the group approached Jerusalem, the entire Jewish community came out to greet their new leader. Such a procession had never been seen before. Rav Chazan's eight-volume halachic work, *Chakrei Lev*, was compared to the acclaimed *Shaagas Aryeh* for its sharp, penetrating analysis of Halachah. His son, Rav David Chazan, would later follow in his father's footsteps, and become Rishon l'Tzyon in 1861.

Zion Gate

A Foothold in Jerusalem

While Napoleon and his call for emancipation rocked Europe and Russia, both physically and psychologically, Jerusalem was also poised at the threshold of a new era. In the early decades of the nineteenth century, thousands of European Jews were hoping and preparing to immigrate to the Holy City, and despite many obstacles — not the least of which was circumventing the century-old ban against Ashkenazim living in the city — they would succeed! Their presence would alter the ethnological balance of the city forever. The agenda of these Jews, who were followers of Rav Eliyahu of Vilna, the Vilna Gaon, was nothing less than to initiate the ingathering of the exile, and thereby activate the final countdown to messianic times.

Vision of Zion

The disciples of the Vilna Gaon, called Perushim, yearned to live in Jerusalem. The origin of their longing stemmed from the Vilna Gaon himself. On two different occasions, the Gaon had attempted to travel to Eretz Yisrael (1772 and 1782). Both times, however, he had met with Heavenly obstacles and was thwarted from achieving his heart's desire.[4] Although he himself never made it to the Holy Land, his disciples, infused with his fiery love, would fulfill their master's vision. Among them were Rav Menachem Mendel, Rav Ezriel (and his grandson, Rav Yisrael), and Rav Binyamin Rivlin (and his son, Rav Hillel), all of Shklov. All of these men were outstanding scholars, well versed in every aspect of Torah, and each one of them followed the unique approach of the Gra (acronym of Gaon Rav Eliyahu, the Vilna Gaon).

The group's activities were centered in the city of Shklov, 200 miles southeast of Vilna. As early as 1780, the Chazon Tzyon movement began propagating the idea of settling in Eretz Yisrael as part of the process envisioned by the Gra. In the year 1781, Rav Ezriel visited the country in order to gain a firsthand report on the problems and prospects that potential immigrants would face, and to establish preliminary contacts with the local population. He successfully returned from his mission, and everything seemed poised to move forward. However, with his subsequent death on a second journey, practical planning came

Rav Eliyahu of Vilna (1720–1797)

to a halt and would not resume for almost thirty years. In all that time, only a select few of the Gaon's students settled in the Holy Land. One of them was the tzaddik, Rav Shlomo of Talachin, a foremost disciple of the Gra. He ascended to Eretz Yisrael in 1797, shortly before his mentor's death. An inveterate wanderer, Rav Shlomo traveled between the four major cities of Eretz Yisrael, settling down to study wherever his spirit saw fit.

The Gra's vision, as disseminated by his disciples, contained three main elements:[5] ingathering of Jews, crowning Jerusalem as the Torah center of the world, and expansion of the *yishuv*.

These three themes can be summarized as follows: The envisioned ingathering would be similar to the one led by Ezra the Scribe at the beginning of the Second Temple period. At that time, the Persian king, Cyrus, permitted Jews to return and rebuild the Temple. Now, with permission from the ruling authorities, Jews from all over the world would move to Eretz Yisrael. There, they would farm the land and fulfill all the *mitzvos taluyos b'aretz* (mitzvos connected to the Land), which in itself would be a form of possessing the Land. This, in turn, would slowly lead to the messianic times, called *keitz ha'megulah.*[6]

The eminence of Torah would be heightened by its study in Jerusalem, whose very air is saturated with holiness. There, one would toil in Torah, including the mystical portions. Men of faith and learning would strengthen the inner fabric of Judaism. This would create another vehicle to allow the light of Mashiach to shine forth.

The cornerstone of the first two themes would be the third one — the expansion of the *yishuv*. The prophet's words were directed to this generation when he said: "Sing, O barren one [Jerusalem], you who did not bear [whose children were in exile], break forth into singing [now, at the time of the redemption].... Enlarge the place of your tent [build up Jerusalem and the rest of Eretz Yisrael]..." (*Isaiah* 54:1-2). Though settling anywhere in Eretz Yisrael was a mitzvah, expanding the *yishuv* in Jerusalem took precedence. Building Jewish homes in and around the walled city would directly affect the ongoing spiritual war with Amalek, who Chazal say has a sinister hold on the gates of Jerusalem.[7] These three themes were the momentum which inspired and guided the immigrants, and helped them persevere through the numerous hardships that faced them.

The first group of settlers left Europe late in the first decade of the nineteenth century, after a series of delays. With the Napoleonic wars raging in Europe, and a war between Turkey and Greece in the Mediterranean Sea, the times were distinctly not conducive to travel. These seventy brave souls reached the shores of Eretz Yisrael in 1809. They were followed by a second influx the following year, led by Rav Yisrael of Shklov. Over the next three decades, an average of several hundred Ashkenazim would immigrate every year, most of them Perushim.

Due to the ban on Ashkenazim in Jerusalem, the immigrants decided to settle in Safed. This move would turn out to be both a blessing and a misfortune. The mystical city, having recovered in large measure from the earthquake of 1759, provided a foothold in the Holy Land. However, severe economic problems, an ongoing housing shortage, and a disastrous plague that decimated the community in 1812 all did their share to discourage the intrepid settlers. Their leader, Rav Yisrael, lost his wife and children to the plague. Shortly thereafter, he himself became infected. On the verge of death, he swore that if God would heal him, he would write a book about the laws of Eretz Yisrael. That book, *Pe'as HaShulchan*, became a classic.[8]

Breaking the Ban

The disciples of the Vilna Gaon first began infiltrating into the Holy City in 1811. Rav Hillel Rivlin, dressed in Sephardic garb, came in Elul of that year, and after the Holidays another eight quietly settled in Jerusalem. They all came from Safed burning with an enthusiasm to fulfill their mentor's dream. Lacking one for a minyan, they used a *sefer Torah* as the tenth man.[9]

In Cheshvan, 1815 (5576), Rav Menachem Mendel of Shklov moved from Safed with his family, also incognito.[10] Rav Shlomo of Talachin, whom we met previously, also joined the group when he came to Jerusalem.[11] The Ashkenazim rented the old Ohr HaChaim Shul and prayed there clandestinely during the week. Unwilling to draw more attention to themselves, they joined a

Sephardic minyan for the longer and more vocal Shabbos service.

The rapport shared by the Europeans and the Sephardic community was good. Rav Hillel Rivlin taught *Toras HaGra* (Torah according to the approach of the Vilna Gaon) in his house, which was located near the Rabban Yochanan ben Zakkai Synagogue. Rav Menachem Mendel, a kabbalist of distinction, was accepted into the Beis El Yeshivah, headed by Rabbi Sharabi's grandson, Rav Avraham Mizrachi Sharabi. Rav Yisrael, who remained in Safed, corresponded with Rav Yosef Chazan on communal matters. The Sephardim, concerned with preserving the Sephardic tenor of the city, prevailed upon the tiny group of Ashkenazim to limit the number of immigrants. The Perushim agreed to the terms.

This small nucleus of idealists, together with another hundred European Jews who would move to the Holy City over the next decade, succeeded in unlocking the gates of the city for Ashkenazim. This task consisted of two parts: annulling the accumulated debts of the earlier generation and thereby making it legally possible for Ashkenazim to live in Jerusalem, and filing a claim that the Churvah Synagogue and the surrounding courtyard houses were stolen Ashkenazi property that must be returned. The Sephardim told them that the Moslems had all but forgotten the ancient debt. The creditors had long since died, and their descendants could not equate a buried debt to living strangers.

To accomplish their goals, the Perushim organized meetings with the *kadi* and other Moslem dignitaries. Naturally, they first sent gifts to influential Arabs. Next they sent Sephardic emissaries, fluent in Arabic, to explain the situation and convince the authorities of the innocence of the new European immigrants. Finally, leaders of the Perushim met face to face with the Moslem officials in order to appease them and help create an atmosphere of good will.

The first major breakthrough for the Ashkenazim's cause came in 1820, when the Sultan himself issued a declaration annulling all unpaid debts dating back forty years or more. This proclamation heralded the beginning of the community's salvation. Rav Menachem Mendel, the leader of Jerusalem Perushim, sent Rav Shlomo Zalman Zoref to Constantinople to procure a royal *firman* explicitly commanding the *kadi* of Jerusalem to enforce the declaration vis-a-vis the Ashkenazim. Rav Zoref was successful in his mission, and the document he secured provided undisputed proof of the Ashkenazim's freedom to homestead in the Holy City.

With this first gate unlocked, the second should have opened by itself. However, the descendants of the Arabs who had confiscated the houses in the courtyard and turned them into shops bluntly refused to relinquish their hold on the properties without full reimbursement as rightful owners. The same held true for the synagogue, still in ruin and used as a common garbage dump.

The struggle to reclaim the Churvah would enter several phases and stretch over decades. The first phase took nearly four years. Rav Moshe Sozin, Rishon l'Tzyon between 1824–1836 and a close friend of Rav Menachem Mendel, advised the Perushim to take legal action against the confiscation. However, no governmental office would listen to them without consent from the capital. This entailed another trip to Contantinople, where they succeeded in having their case heard and procured a directive ordering that the local officials in Jerusalem attend to the matter. In 1824, the *kadi* and his officials opened the case, and after a drawn-out investigation they concluded that the Churvah legally belonged to Ashkenazim from ancient times. As a result, the Arab squatters were forced to evacuate the Churvah courtyard. Most of them, however, refused to obey the court order. They would only be successfully removed a decade later, when Eretz Yisrael would temporarily fall under Egyptian control.

The Era of the Perushim

The Perushim's victory in their legal battle was overshadowed by a number of internal and external problems that faced the community. The Ashkenazim were impoverished, and their living conditions were abominable. Leaky roofs, poor ventilation and lighting, and dampness on the walls were the lot of many. Whole families lived in a single room. Several had Arab landlords who threatened their tenants with eviction if they did not pay their ever-escalating rents on time.

These problems, difficult as they were, had been perceived long before the immigrants had set out from their native lands, and were endurable. Much harder to bear was the threat to human dignity and life. Moslem lawlessness inside the city walls made a mere walk down the street dangerous. Simply going about their business, a woman might be abducted or a child molested. Even without such extremes, however, intimidation was a fact of daily existence. Sometimes, when an Arab owner found himself with unsold wares, he would plant them on the doorstep of a Jewish house. Then he would have the Jew arrested for failure to pay for the goods! The unfortunate Jew's plea that he had been framed would go unheeded, and he would be forced to pay for the goods.

Fortunately, the Jews did not find themselves with no recourse whatsoever in the face of these dangers and indignities. Beginning in the 1830s, the countries from which the Jews emigrated began establishing consulates to represent them in the Holy Land. Thus, the Jews had an address to which they could direct their grievances. In the realm of international politics, no self-respecting country would countenance the mistreatment of its citizens by another government. Thus a consulate would be sure to bring any injustice to the attention of the local authorities. The local populace, too, took a second look at their foreign neighbors, and in the smallest of ways had a more positive feeling towards them. Finally, not only did the consulates shield the Perushim, they also acted as a reliable means of transferring funds from Europe to Eretz Yisrael. At the onset, the closest consular offices were located in Akko and Beirut.

The embattled community faced official government discrimination as well. In the eyes of the Sultan, only the Sephardic community had official government recognition in Jerusalem. This had repercussions in many areas of life. For example, *shechitah* was controlled by

Beirut, where the first consulates were located. The British opened the first consulate in Jerusalem in 1839.

law, and only officially accredited Jewish butchers could work in the slaughterhouse. Therefore, the Perushim could not serve as butchers, which put the community in a very difficult position: the Sephardic butchers naturally followed the rulings of the Beis Yosef, which sometimes led to halachic problems for the Ashkenazim, who followed the rulings of the Rama. Furthermore, the Ashkenazim were required to pay a tax to the Sephardim for any meat that they bought. Additionally, the Sephardim also levied a burial tax, and all marriage and divorce documents had to be handled by Sephardic rabbis as well.

However, the above-mentioned problems between the two communities were overshadowed by the division of moneys coming from the Diaspora — the *chalukah*. Suddenly, the Sephardim found that they no longer held a monopoly over the control of these funds. This was a very delicate issue, as the *chalukah* system was the financial backbone of the *yishuv*. Every *kehillah* in the Holy Land sent *shelichim* to the Diaspora to collect for the scholars and impoverished Jews of Eretz Yisrael. When these funds were lost, stolen, or delayed due to wars or other reasons, Jews throughout the country found themselves in a critical situation. Some even starved during these periods. Fortunately, as sensitive a topic as this was, it was resolved over the course of time.[12]

Perushim: Two Sides of the Same Coin

Internally, the Perushim were split over the issue of where to homestead. Their spiritual mentor, the Vilna Gaon, had explicitly earmarked Jerusalem as the focal point of the new *yishuv*, yet conditions did not permit this when the Perushim first arrived in the country. Years later, when the ban was lifted and Ashkenazim were free to live in the Holy City, the Perushim were already well established in Safed, under the leadership of Rav Yisrael of Shklov. A second and much smaller group, led by Rav Menachem Mendel and Rav Hillel Rivlin, stood by the original wishes of the Gaon and moved to the Holy City. Rav Hillel had written a book about the Gra's vision of settlement in Eretz Yisrael, entitled *Kol HaTor,* which dramatically envisioned the settling of Jerusalem as the stepping-stone to the era of the Mashiach. Rav Hillel not only believed in this conception intellectually, he lived it and breathed it. It is told that whenever he helped a new immigrant renovate his house, he enthusiastically sang his own original songs of inspiration.[13]

The controversy between these two factions involved many complicated issues and continued until the earthquake of 1837, which leveled the city of Safed. Following this disaster, the remaining Perushim all moved to Jerusalem, rendering the point moot.

A communal body, called a *kollel*, was set up in the early years of the Perushim's settlement in Jerusalem. In 1821, the few Chassidim living in the city joined together with them.[14] The multifold functions of the *kollel* included absorption of new immigrants, distribution of monthly stipends from the *chalukah*, building water-storage facilities, maintaining a private security patrol (called *anshei gevardiah*), sending *shelichim* to *chutz laAretz* and corresponding with European rabbis and philanthropists, representing the Jewish cause before the Turkish authorities, redeeming ancient Jewish houses in the Old City, planning and building neighborhoods outside the walls, fighting missionaries, and organizing various societies such as *bikur cholim* and *vaad ha'achdus*.

The *kollel* Perushim, later renamed Vaad HaKlali (Central Committee), was the heart of the Ashkenazic community for over a century. Located first in the Churvah courtyards and later in the Beis David suburb, it was involved with nearly every important issue concerning the old *yishuv*. During the course of its existence, it was served by such spiritual giants as Rav Shmuel Salant and Rav Meir Auerbach.

From the early days of the influx of Perushim to Jerusalem, all disputes within the community were adjudicated by one central rabbinical court. A scholar of Halachah received the title of *chaver rabbanos*, which entitled him to an increased stipend. It also allowed him entry into a rotating schedule in which he would become one of the three rabbis on the court for a period of two years. This system, already established by the Sephardim, functioned for over half a century.[15]

Akko, a seaport fortress town, where the Turkish stationed a garrison and local governor

Era of Suffering

The first phase of the Perushim's settlement in Eretz Yisrael, from 1811 to 1840, became known as the era of suffering. With a backdrop of daily tribulations, nearly every year marked another crisis, natural disaster, or anti-Semitic act. In 1812 a plague struck the Galilee. Safed turned into a ghost town. Of the five hundred Perushim in the city, a third died, including almost all Rav Yisrael's family. His only surviving daughter later married Rav Yeshaya Bardaky, who would play an important role in the *yishuv* from the 1830s to the 1860s.

When a plague struck Jerusalem in 1819 (5579), many Jews fled temporally. Most of the Ashkenazim evacuated to a village, Beis Iksa, near the tomb of Shmuel HaNavi. Tents were set up, and the refugees were provided with just enough food and water to sustain themselves.

Other residents of the city reluctantly stayed. Both Rav Hillel and Rav Menachem Mendel refused to let all the cheder children leave the Holy City. They quoted the verse in *Lamentations* (1:6): "All of the beauty of the daughter of Zion has departed," referring to the exile of Jewish scholars and children from Jerusalem. Were every Jew to leave the city, it might endanger the very existence of the *yishuv*.

On the third night of the plague, the two leaders prayed by the Kosel. Physically and emotionally exhausted by the tremendous burden he was bearing, Rav Hillel dozed off. In a dream, the Gra came to him and told him he had made the right decision and that the plague would end faster in the merit of the children's learning.[16]

That same year, the *yishuv* learned of the assassination of Chaim Parchi in

Akko. As a powerful government official of the Turkish administration in Akko, Parchi was almost the de facto ruler of the Galilee for decades. As such, he stood in a position to aid his Jewish brethren. His success made him a friend of every Jew, especially the Perushim of Safed. His sudden death resulted in the arrest of Rav Yisrael of Shklov, who happened to be in Akko at the time of the assassination, along with many other Jews of the city, and the institution of a reign of terror in the Galilee.

A year or two later, a visiting Moslem pasha, on his way to Mecca, bribed the mayor into agreeing to his levying a personal tax from the Jews of Jerusalem. To show he meant business, he had Rav Menachem Mendel and his son, Rav Nasan Nata, imprisoned. The community, shocked at this turn of events, borrowed money in order to free their beloved leader.*

By the 1830s, an average of five hundred Ashkenazim were immigrating to Eretz Yisrael every year. The influx had a marked effect on the character of the Holy City. The earlier agreement with the Sephardim to limit Ashkenazic immigration had been invalidated once the Ottoman ruler permitted Ashkenazim to live in Jerusalem. Therefore, Jews from Safed and Tiberias, including Chassidim and disciples of the Chasam Sofer, chose Jerusalem as their new home. Housing became a major obstacle, as the tiny Jewish Quarter was simply too small to accommodate the crush of immigrants. In response, the Vaad HaKlali was forced to rent apartments in the Moslem and Armenian quarters. Additionally, precious water, an ever-present concern, had to be strictly rationed.

Revolt from Within[17]

In Tamuz, 1824 (5584), the Arab peasants revolted against the high taxation imposed by the pasha of Damascus. In order to oust the five-hundred-man Turkish garrison from the Citadel of David, they cunningly staged a fake war with the Arabs of Bethlehem. They then approached the leader of the Turkish legion and asked him to aid them against their Bethlehemite enemies. The Turkish commander agreed, and once he marched out of the city with his troops, the remaining skeleton staff in the Citadel was easy prey for the insurgents. The shocked commander was unprepared to attack the city and retreated to Damascus. Thus, Jerusalem fell without any blood being shed. Yet the Jewish community was pessimistic about the future.

When word reached Constantinople, the Sultan ordered Pasha Abdullah of Akko to quell the rebellion. His legions reached Jerusalem in Tishre, 1825, and surrounded the city. The Jews, innocent bystanders, were caught in the net and might be forced to pay the price with their lives. Prayer was the only weapon available to them, and everyone beseeched the Almighty for mercy.

Abdullah chose to attack the city from the east. He had a row of cannons set up on the Mount of Olives and besieged the city with cannon fire. People hid in

* See story, "The Passover Miracle," in *Bygone Days: 1800–1840*.

cellars and dried underground cisterns. Abdullah gave his soldiers explicit instructions to strike the marketplace and not the residential sections — his objective was to stop the rebellion, not to destroy the city. However, cannons had limited accuracy, and as a result, the whole city was endangered.

The bombardment took place on Sukkos, when most Jews lived in their sukkos, which they built on their rooftops. At a time like this, they were exempt from the mitzvah. One Jew refused to leave his sukkah during the shelling, and was injured in his leg.

The eerie sound of cannonballs whizzing overhead and crashing into courtyards and onto rooftops gripped the inhabitants of Jerusalem with fear. They cowered from the terrifying sound and prayed for deliverance. During one shelling, Rav Avraham Mizrachi Sharabi, the kabbalist of Beis El Yeshivah, sat down with his scribe, Rav Yedidiah Abulafia, and wrote various holy names and permutations on a parchment. He ordered his disciple not to move from his place while he concentrated on the holy names. It seemed that Rav Sharabi's prayers and meditations were effective. The damage from the shelling was extensive, but not a single human being was killed. At the end of the day, Rav Abulafia went outside to see what had happened. As soon as he started down one of the corridors, a piece of shrapnel struck him and left him limping for the rest of his life.[18]

When Abdullah realized that the hand of God was protecting the city, he offered to make a peace treaty. The rebels agreed to relinquish their hold on the city in return for safe conduct to escape. Abdullah consented and the following day entered with his legions. The Jews paid him homage as their emancipator and hoped to return to their normal routine. However, they would not get off scot-free. Before returning to Akko, Abdullah demanded a special tax from the Jews which burdened them tremendously.

Death of the Righteous

The deaths of two leaders and kabbalists in 1827 (5587) marked the end of an era. Rav Menachem Mendel and Rav Avraham Mizrachi Sharabi had enlightened the Holy City with their Torah and leadership for years. Their passing marked a crossroads for both the Ashkenazim and Sephardim of the Holy City.

Rav Menachem Mendel of Shklov towered as one of the closest and most devoted disciples of the Vilna Gaon. Indeed, most of the writings of the Gra were penned by Rav Menachem Mendel. After the Gra passed away during Sukkos 1797, his disciple began to organize and publish his works. At his mentor's request, Rav Menachem Mendel first published the Gra's commentary on Proverbs in 1798. Rav Menachem Mendel's commentary on the Haggadah was based on a Seder night he spent with the Gra. His commentary on *Seder Tahoros* (Mishnah) stemmed from their hours of studying the subject together. The Gra's glosses to *Seder Olam*, his commentaries to *Pirkei Avos* and *Sefer Yetzirah*, and his map of Eretz Yisrael and the Temple were all prepared by Rav Menachem Mendel. Together with others, he began the vast project of tran-

scribing the Vilna Gaon's glosses to the *Shulchan Aruch*. Rav Yisrael of Shklov had the distinction of preparing the work for press.

The first of the Perushim to arrive in 1808, Rav Menachem Mendel was the backbone of the group. One writer described his importance in these words: "Without him, the Ashkenazic community would have failed to take root in Jerusalem. Hashem sent him to build up the *yishuv* and guided him in the face of turbulent times."[19]

Rav Menachem Mendel was the mastermind behind every major decision for the community. Yet, his wholehearted dedication to Torah study remained unaffected. He wrote ten books, all on Kabbalah, but only one was ever printed.

During the twelve years he lived in Jerusalem, he recorded a number of other-worldly encounters he had with his mentor. As if in flesh and blood, the Vilna Gaon came to him and taught him Torah. Once it happened while crying at the Western Wall, another time at Rachel's Tomb, and another time while he was standing on the Mount of Olives by the burial plot which he bought for himself near the grave of Rav Chaim Attar. He also recorded that every Tisha b'Av he saw two black pillars hovering over the Temple Mount.

He wrote about his mission in Jerusalem:

Hashem brought me from Safed to Jerusalem, the heavenly city... There I organized programs of study and prayer at the Beis Midrash [Ohr HaChaim Shul]. Recently, Hashem helped me to liberate an abandoned ruin in the city that belonged to Ashkenazim well over a hundred years ago. Now, thank God, I extricated it from their [Moslem] hands.

*This is precisely what Chazal meant when they said [*Berachos *6b] that the reward for rejoicing before a bridegroom is as if one rebuilt a ruined place in Jerusalem. This [the fact that the comparison* *is made to Jerusalem and not to Eretz Yisrael in general] is a proof that building Jerusalem has precedence over other places in Eretz Yisrael.*

....Be'ezras Hashem, may I be worthy to build a synagogue — a small Temple — in the Holy City.[20]

His lofty soul was completely bound with the vision of his mentor.* He labored to free the Churvah from the Arab squatters and lived to see the completion of the first stage of the process. By the time he passed away on 1 Adar, 1827, the fruit of his toils were clear for all to see. Over a thousand Ashkenazim lived in the Holy City, and within a decade that number would double. In 1837, the community built its first synagogue. The Menachem Tzyon Shul was named after their noble leader and was built in the courtyard of the Churvah.

On the first day of Chanukah, 1826, Rav Avraham Mizrachi Sharabi passed away. The grandson of Rav Shalom Sharabi, Rav Arvaham Mizrachi, had inherited the leadership of the Beis El Yeshivah a quarter of a century earlier, in 1802, when Rav Yom Tov Elgazi died. Rav Sharabi's command of Kabbalah was matchless, and he radiated holiness to those around him. In addition to his duties as *rosh yeshivah,* he worked tirelessly on behalf of the community. He also authored a kabbalistic work, *Divrei Shalom.*

The Parchi family of Damascus, of which Chaim Parchi was a member, were wealthy and influential, and benefactors of the *yishuv*. Comparable to the Rothschilds' philanthropic generosity in Europe, the Parchis graciously spread their wealth throughout the Middle East. They supported the Beis El Yeshivah and maintained close ties with Rav Sharabi. Once, Raphael Parchi was imprisoned on trumped-up charges. By the time the news reached Jerusalem, he had already been sentenced to death. Rav Sharabi hastened to Damascus to try and save the unfortunate man. Arriving on Friday morning, he immediately sent a pair of *tzitzis* to Raphael, instructing him to wear them at all times. As Shabbos entered, he asked the Parchis to arrange a huge, festive third meal, because by then, Raphael would be sitting at the head of the table.

The next day, after Minchah services, Rav Sharabi was escorted to the Parchis' house for the third meal. As they sat down to eat, Raphael Parchi suddenly entered, beaming with joy. To the amazement of everyone, he explained that that day, the judge had decided to review the case and discovered that the witnesses had given false testimony. Without delay, Raphael had been set free.

The loss of these two great kabbalists dimmed the light of Torah in the world. Time and again the Gra emphasized the need to study Kabbalah in Jerusalem. While all Torah learning is compared to light, the study of Kabbalah is compared to a laser beam which can negate the efforts of the forces of evil that prevent the coming of the Mashiach.

The city, bereft of these masters, nevertheless forged onward. As the elder amongst the Ashkenazim, Rav Hillel Rivlin was looked upon as the spiritual leader of the Perushim. Similarly, Rav Moshe Sozin, the Rishon l'Tzyon, was the spiritual guide of the Sephardim. Temporally, Rav Menachem Mendel's son, Nasan Nata, together with Rav Aryeh Neiman, led the Perushim, and Rav Sharabi's son-in-law, Rav Avraham Gagin (who would serve as Rishon

* See story, "The Hidden Light," in *Bygone Days: 1800–1840.*

l'Tzyon in the 1840s), led the Sephardic community. Yet, a vacuum had been created, one which even these capable individuals could not entirely fill.

Sir Moses Montefiore's First Visit

Perhaps the only bright spot during this desolate time was Sir Moses Montefiore's first visit to the Holy Land, in 1827.* When he arrived, missionary groups sent Jewish-born converts disguised as observant Jews to confuse him and dissuade him from helping his brethren's cause. Fortunately, a meeting with the seventy-year-old Rav Rivlin forged a two-way link of trust between the British philanthropist and the Perushim. Indeed, the Perushim were also initially skeptical of Montefiore's motives and sincerity, and Rav Rivlin's positive impressions entirely dispelled the Jewish community's suspicions. Similarly, the nobility of the Perushim and the desperateness of their plight made a profound impression on Sir Moses, and moved him to become their patron and savior. In the coming decades, Sir Moses Montefiore would make six more trips to Eretz Yisrael — at a time when such journeys took months at a time, without modern amenities. On this first visit, which only lasted four days, the *yishuv* did not fully appreciate their illustrious visitor from England, but their impact on him would provide the impetus for his valiant deeds on their behalf over the coming fifty years.[21]

Sir Moses Montefiore's emblem
(all three banners say Yerushalayim)

* See story, "Montefiore's Dream," in *Bygone Days: 1800–1840*.

The Water Breakthrough

1829 (5589) was a drought year, and a number of families left Jerusalem for Jaffa and Gaza. The roadways leading from the city were littered with the carcasses of horses and mules that had died for lack of water. At the height of the summer, the despairing Perushim turned to their leaders and begged them to somehow come up with a solution. Through prayers and kabbalistic meditations, the desperate leaders pinpointed a spot west of the city where they believed water might be found underground. Digging was started at the spot, and almost immediately a gushing stream of water dramatically burst forth. The spectacular discovery proved a source of salvation for all the inhabitants of the city. For eight consecutive days, sweet water surged forth from the spring. The hour and a half's walk back and forth became a never-ending stream of happy people bringing water to their cisterns in the city. At the end of eight days, the spring dried up completely, never to flow again.[22]

As miraculous as the salvation from the draught was, its very temporary nature served to underscore the acute water problem. As a result, a new idea surfaced: to build water collection systems *outside* the walls of the city. At the time, the residents were unable to implement this novel idea. A few years later, however, when Rav Shemarya Luria and Rav Shemarya Zukerman arrived to bolster the *yishuv* with their wealth and expertise, the idea came to fruition. The two men bought plots of land outside the walls, and in some cases rented land for an extended period of time, and dug eleven cisterns with attendant collection systems. Colloquially called *mayim rishonim* ("first waters"), they later became the cisterns used in the first suburbs built on the land in the 1870s. In addition to being used for cisterns, the land was also utilized to cultivate wheat specifically designated for *matzah shemurah*.

This effort, daring and visionary as it was, did not provide a complete solution to the water shortage. Unfortunately, it would remain a major obstacle for decades to come. Yet, the initiative taken by the Perushim did provide some relief for the thirsty Jews of the Holy City.

Under Egyptian Rule

By the beginning of the nineteenth century, the Ottoman Empire had held total sovereignty over the Middle East for three hundred years. Despite numerous attempts, no major foreign power had succeeded in wrestling the Middle East out of Turkish hands, and, except for some minor local rebellions in Jerusalem and Tiberias, Ottoman sway was absolute. However, an Egyptian uprising that occurred in the 1830s would finally terminate that unbroken record.

Internal Strife

In October, 1831 (5592), the pasha of Egypt, Mohammed Ali, revolted against the Sultan, and marched across Eretz Yisrael and Syria. The flag that he raised flew over an area extending from Gaza to Izmir. His rebellion supplanted the apathetic Turkish attitude with a new spirit of law and order. Ibrahim Pasha, his stepson and deputy, governed Eretz Yisrael with a strong hand. The lawlessness that had prevailed previously was reigned in, and private tollbooths on the roads were abolished. In turn, this new security fostered increased commerce and vitality.

The Jews regarded this new rulership with curiosity and guarded hope. As Ibrahim consolidated his rule, conquering the Golan Heights, Beiruṭ, and the area northward to Izmir, foreign-born citizens were granted a state of immunity. The Jews generally felt safer and were eager to approach the pasha for the needs of the Jewish community.

In 1834 (5594), while Ibrahim was in Alexandria, angry Druse and Arab peasants rebelled against being drafted into

Mohammed Ali

the Egyptian army. They attacked the major cities of Safed, Jerusalem, and Hebron, venting much of their rage on the innocent and helpless Jewish communities. Hit hardest of all was Safed, where a reign of terror lasted throughout the month of Sivan. Jews were murdered, houses looted, shops ransacked, and synagogues pillaged. Rav Yisrael led the Perushim to the village of Ain Ziton for safety, while the Chassidim chose to hide in the courtyard of the *kadi*. Rav Nasan Nata, who was visiting Safed at the time, was caught and blinded in one eye. One of the ransacked businesses was the Beck Publishing House, which housed the first Jewish printing press in Eretz Yisrael. At the time, Rav Yisrael Beck was completing the typeset for *Pe'as HaShulchan*, and in an instant the painstaking labor of years was dashed to pieces. As a result, the first printing press in Eretz Yisrael closed before managing to produce even one book.

In Jerusalem, Rav Yosef of Laida, one of the Perushim, was murdered, and fears ran very high amongst the Jews for the safety of the entire community. With exorbitant bribes, the community managed to secure a promise from the rebels to spare their lives and property.

Ibrahim quickly returned from Alexandria and subdued and punished the malcontents. In Hebron, some Arab rebels hid in Jewish homes. Ibrahim, intent on crushing all vestiges of the rebellion, killed everyone in these homes, regardless of guilt or innocence. In Safed, thirteen Druse leaders were hung. Yet despite Ibrahim's zealous vengeance, very little of the booty plundered by the insurgents was ever found.

In that far-off time, there was no legal concept of restitution for such crimes. However, in the wake of the Druse rebellion, a lucky few did receive compensation. One of these was Rav Yisrael Beck, who received remuneration in the form of land outside of Meron. In those days, Jewish farms were completely unheard of, due in large part to the dangers posed by Bedouin marauders. In the sixteenth century, the Mabit recorded a number of Jewish farms producing wheat, barley, and cotton,[23] but since that time, no Jew had dared to live in such dangerous surroundings. Indeed,

Ibrahim Pasha chasing after Druse in the Galilee

Rav Beck himself was forced to close his farm and move to safer environs, shortly after Montefiore's visit in 1839. He settled in Jerusalem, where he reopened his publishing house and became one of the Chassidic leaders of the community.

High Hopes for the Yishuv[24]

Rav Hillel Rivlin's son-in-law, Rav Shemarya Luria, moved to Jerusalem with a party of forty followers during these momentous times. Rav Luria was wealthy, a lover of Zion, and influential in many circles. His arrival marked renewed expectations of better things to come for the fragile community.

When Ibrahim came to Jerusalem to restore order, Rav Luria arranged a meeting with him. Impressed by Rav Luria's presentation, Ibrahim lent a favorable ear to the needs of the Perushim. Of course, the wealthy Jew prefaced his requests with a large gift of money and with promises of more in the future. The pasha agreed to annex a large tract of land between Jerusalem and Jaffa upon which the Jews could build a colony with autonomous status.

Ibrahim's consent was sincere. He invited Rav Luria and the leaders of the Perushim to feast with him at his encampment north of the city near the tomb of Shmuel HaNavi. He also invited a number of sheiks from neighboring villages. Standing before his mixed audience, the pasha first introduced Rav Shemarya and his friends as well-to-do Russian Jews who had come to invest in the city. He wanted the Arab nobility to consent in theory to his plan. He announced that the land stretching from the tomb of Shimon HaTzaddik to Beis Iksa near the tomb of Shmuel HaNavi would be transformed into a Jewish colony called Yehudiah. Most of the area was government property, and Ibrahim declared he would sell it to Rav Luria and his companions. He also asked the Arabs who owned the remaining private land to sell it to the Jews. Once established, he said, this vast expanse of territory would bring new business enterprises and material wealth to Jerusalem and the surrounding environs. He concluded his speech with a prayer that a new relationship of confidence and friendship would build up between the Moslems and Jews.

The sheiks' initial reaction to Ibrahim's vision was positive. Later, however, a strong backlash to the idea developed among the Moslems of Jerusalem. Many Arabs were enjoying a new status as landlords due to the increased influx of Ashkenazim to the city. Should a new Yehudiah become available to Jews, their newfound income would be seriously jeopardized. These relatively few individuals incited the majority of neutral Moslems to their cause and threatened Jewish citizens with physical violence should they follow through with their plans. As a result of this agitation and opposition, the dream of Yehudiah had to be shelved. Forty years later, the Jews would face similar fears and threats from their Arab neighbors when they wanted to expand outside the city walls. However, at that time, they would finally succeed, and, under the leadership of Rav Hillel Rivlin's grandson, they would build to the west of the city, along the road leading to Jaffa.

The Long-Awaited Building Permit

The Egyptian rule over Eretz Yisrael was a blessing which capable men of vision could channel to their advantage. The novel idea of not facing the antiquated, insipid bureaucracy of Constantinople spurred them to act promptly. Still, wisdom and finesse were the secret keys to success.

As the first order of business, Rav Shlomo Zalman Zoref led a delegation to Egypt. Their goal was to have the plot of land called Dir Ashkenaz — where the Churvah was located — legally registered in the name of the Perushim, and to acquire a building permit. Though the Ottoman government had annulled the hundred-year-old debt in 1824, the Perushim requested that the new government reaffirm and uphold their ownership in light of the continued Moslem hold on the courtyard. They initially made contact with the Austrian ambassador, who gave a receptive ear to their request.

While the ambassador spoke with Mohammed Ali, Rav Shemarya Luria in Jerusalem bribed influential parties to side with the Perushim's cause. Furthermore, the owners of the shops in Dir Ashkenaz were informed that once the official registration was given by Egypt, they would receive a substantial sum for vacating the courtyard.

Back in Egypt, Rav Yosef Schwartz, a multilingual genius and author of *Tevuos HaAretz*, penned letters and requests to all the necessary parties. He wrote: "I was also there, and with the help of God, I wrote and composed requests in the most polished style possible."[25] The fruits of these efforts came in the form of a royal edict upholding the annulment of the previous debt and explicitly allowing the Perushim to build in the courtyard.

On Thursday, 19 Elul, 1836 (5596), the Jews began to clear away the rubble from the site. At first, only two or three Perushim volunteered to do the work, since vengeful Moslems threatened that "any Jew working there will be buried there." However, after a few days without incident, more and more joined, until soon everyone, including children, took part in what was felt to be a holy task similar to the work of Nehemiah in the time of the Second Temple.

The clearing project revealed a number of unknown historical facts. Besides the remains of the ancient synagogue, they discovered a *mikve* and some undamaged rooms. They also found some old documents dated 1579 (5339), signed by Rav Yisrael Najara.[26]

With the site cleared, construction was begun on the community's first synagogue. After much debate, it was decided to initially build a smaller shul on the edge of the courtyard, as opposed to rebuilding the Churvah itself. While the Churvah would eventually be rebuilt, this would not happen for some time. On the first of Shevat, 1837, the Menachem Tzyon Shul was inaugurated, a week before news of a major earthquake in the Galilee reached Jerusalem. A jubilant throng danced before the new Holy Ark with the *sifrei Torah*. The synagogue included a women's gallery and a *mikve*, and the *beis din* sat there during the early years of the *yishuv*. Rav Nasan Nata officiated as Rav of the shul that had been named for his father. In the

The Menachem Tzyon Synagogue as it appears today

forthcoming years, people would also refer to it as Beis Midrash HaYashan.

Rav Shlomo Zalman Zoref labored tirelessly to see that every last stone was in its place. He also battled negative forces which sought to interfere with the construction of the complex. Houses sprung up in the courtyard, and a new sense of vitality welded the community together.

The Sephardim, as well, took advantage of the Egyptian pasha's receptivity, and sent a delegation to Cairo. They sought a permit to expand the existing "Four Synagogues." Led by Rav Avraham ben Avraham, they too succeeded.[27]

Rav Luria attempted to purchase the houses near the Western Wall, but due to complications he was unsuccessful. After two years of dedicated work for the *yishuv*, Rav Luria returned to Russia, preferring to help from afar with money made from his business interests, rather than becoming impoverished in the Holy City.

Due to lack of funds, the main synagogue, slated to be built on the ruins of the Churvah Shul, would not be built for another twenty years. In 1864, the Beis Yaakov Synagogue would finally be inaugurated on the site, as we shall see later in the chapter "Pillars for the Future."

With funds sent from Akiva Lehren of Amsterdam, Rav Yeshaya Bardaky, the son-in-law of Rav Yisrael of Shklov, bought a courtyard and converted the upstairs house into the Sukkas Shalom Synagogue, where a *kollel* was started. The houses on the ground floor were rented to Perushim, the rent money going to support the men studying upstairs.

Rav Zundel of Salant

In 1837, a very unpretentious man moved with his family to the Holy City. Rav Yosef Zundel of Salant, one of the most prominent disciples of Rav Chaim of Volohzin, was asked to serve as Rav of the community, whose primary duty would be to answer halachic queries. He agreed on condition that he not receive any remuneration for his services. Throughout his life, Rav Zundel had worked to support himself in a manner that did not cause him to benefit from his Torah learning. Furthermore, he always preferred to mingle with simple Jews, shunning all distinction and honor. His knowledge of Torah was phenomenal. The entire Oral Law was engraved on his heart, and he would constantly review it in his mind. His primary concern was that there should be peaceful relationships between Jews. Rav Yisrael Salanter, the founder of the *mussar* movement, considered the eminent scholar as his mentor in this field. Now, as a *rav* of the Perushim, this humble man refused to alter his style of living. The Perushim happily accepted his terms. Both Ashkenazim and Sephardim came to pose their halachic questions to him.

Egypt maintained its control of the Holy Land for nine years, until the end of 1840. At that time, world pressure and Turkish guns forced Mohammed Ali and Ibrahim Pasha to retreat from the country. The turning point was the battle of Akko, in Tishre, 1840. The doorway of opportunity, which had cracked open for the Jews and let in some much-needed light and air, would close to a slit with the return of the Sultan and his regime.

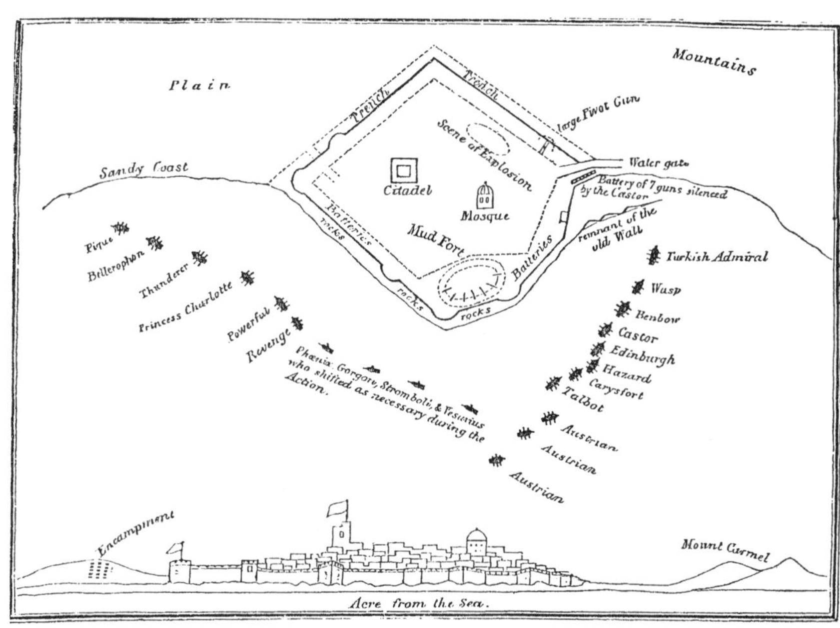

Plan of the Battle of Akko

In November, 1840, a fleet of twenty-one warships (mostly British) prepared for a siege of the strongly fortified town manned by an army of 6,000 Egyptian soldiers with 150 pieces of artillery. Within the first two days, shells from the ships' guns hit an ammunition dump, destroying part of the fortifications. The following day, Ibrahim Pasha and his troops retreated to Egypt.

End of the Beginning

The last years of the 1830s were the most grueling and painful of the thirty-year era of suffering (1810–1840). A series of natural disasters and internal bickering nearly caused the collapse of the young Perushim yishuv. Yet, the ever-watchful and loving hand of God guarded the yishuv and they survived all their ordeals.

Earthquake and its Aftermath

During the late spring of 1836 (5596), at the time when Rav Shlomo Zalman Zoref and his delegation were planning to go to Egypt, a storm of locusts descended on Eretz Yisrael and destroyed the wheat crop. In addition to the ensuing shortage of bread, wheat for the following year's Passover matzah had to be imported from Egypt.

Nine months later, another devastating catastrophe would occur. Sunday, 24 Teves 1837 (5597), would go down in the annals of Eretz Yisrael as a tragic day for the Jewish people. Late that afternoon in the upper Galilee, the earth's crust erupted in a violent earthquake. Tongues of flame leapt out of the Sea of Galilee. The city of Safed was leveled within seconds, and the walls of Tiberias fell. Shechem also suffered damage and casualties.

"The ground was jarred under our feet," wrote a survivor. "In a split second the entire city became a pile of rubble. The death toll was massive. As the darkness of night quickly fell, the piteous cries and moans of those trapped under stones and fallen rafters could be heard. The survivors were hysterical. 'Mama! Papa! Can you hear me?' 'My darling wife! My son! Where are you?'" [28]

The avalanche of debris turned Safed into a graveyard. Roads and walkways disappeared. Fully ninety percent of the population perished. Two thousand Jews died, and many more were injured and crippled. It was a long, dark night in the history of the mystical city.

Most of the men, praying in shul at the time, were buried alive. Rav Shmuel Heller, who would serve as the Ashkenazic Rav of Safed from 1840–1876, was standing under the lintel of the Beis Midrash Ari at the time of the disaster. He was found the next morning pinned in and buried up to his neck in fallen rock. He suffered multiple injuries, but eventually recovered completely. Rav Nachman Nasan Kornel, author of *Teshuvos HaGaonim*, newly married and happy father of a firstborn son, discovered his baby crushed to death,

The Bas Aiyn Shul in Safed

while his wife miraculously survived.

Rav Avraham Dov of Avritch, the Chassidic leader of Safed and close companion of Rav Yisrael of Shklov, was praying Minchah in his shul, Bas Aiyn, at the time. "Come to me!" he yelled to the congregants as he prostrated himself on the floor near the *bimah*. Over their heads, the domed ceiling hovered in mid-air as the walls shook under the jolting spasm. Suddenly, the empty half of the shul collapsed. Miraculously, the prayers of the tzaddik were accepted and everyone survived.

In Jerusalem, tremors stopped everyone for a long minute that Sunday afternoon. Two Arab houses collapsed, but no one was injured. In the immediate aftermath, no one realized the extent of the earthquake and the tragedy which struck the Galilee. At the time, communications in Eretz Yisrael were still primitive. Telegraph lines had not been introduced, and regular mail service to the Galilee only left once a week. In the Galilee itself, all major roads had vanished in the cataclysm, and reaching Akko and Sidon took days. It was not until two weeks later that news of the tragedy reached Jerusalem.

Rav Yisrael, in Jerusalem at the time of the tragedy, broke into tears. He immediately borrowed money from the Sephardim and set up an emergency fund. A team of rescue workers was sent to Safed with food, clothing, and medical supplies. Normally, the trip from Jerusalem to the Galilee took three days. However, due to the terrible conditions left by the earthquake, it took the caravan much longer to make the journey. In the meantime, the most seriously wounded victims, hovering between life and death, could hold on no longer and passed away. Later, when Rav Yisrael eulogized the victims at the Khal Tzyon Synagogue, he was overcome with emotion and fainted. This earthquake was a tragedy which broke the hearts of Jews around the world.

Rav Binyamin Navon eulogized the dead with such emotion that many burst out crying. That date, 24 Teves, became etched on the hearts of every Jew, and for generations to come, the anniversary of the tragedy was observed with mournful discourses and prayers.[29]

During the next weeks and months, a thousand survivors, among them many orphans and widows, flooded Jerusalem. These traumatized refugees, besides requiring the basic essentials of housing, food and clothing, needed a tremendous amount of personal attention, love, and sympathy.

The Jews of the Holy City mobilized themselves to extend a helping hand. A refugee house was set up for children, which later became Jerusalem's first orphanage. Urgent letters were dispatched to every major Jewish community in the Diaspora entreating them to send funds and clothing. The Jewish people, overwhelmed by the news, answered the call wholeheartedly.

Deep Introspection

Jews throughout the world pondered what could have been the cause of such a calamity. The wrath of God burned deep that night, and surely He wanted to shock His people into a deeper realization of some sin they had committed, whether knowingly or unwittingly.

The Perushim of Jerusalem interpreted the disaster as a Divine punishment against the refusal of the Perushim of Safed to heed the call of their mentor, the Vilna Gaon, and settle in the Holy City.

In Pressburg, Hungary, the Chasam Sofer eulogized the dead:

Psalm 79 opens with these words: "A Song of Asaf: O Lord, the nations have entered into Your inheritance, they have defiled the Sanctuary of Your holiness, they have turned Jerusalem into a heap of rubble." In Kiddushin 31b, the Sages ask: "Shouldn't this Psalm be called 'Lamentation of Asaf'?" They answer: "True, yet the word 'song' is appropriate in view of the fact that Hashem turned His wrath on wood and stone rather than destroying His people entirely."

And now we hear the heartbreaking reports of the earthquake in the Galilee. Woe! Had He only destroyed the synagogues, study halls, and the houses of the tzaddikim, it would have been enough of a disaster. Had He only taken some hundreds of lives, crushed to death by the weight of falling roofs, including innocent children, that too would have been enough of a disaster. And had He taken some chachamim, of whom Chazal say, the chachamim of Eretz Yisrael outweigh the chachamim of chutz laAretz by two to one, it would have been enough. Woe unto us, that He has taken them all, and more than we can ever imagine.

The survivors, destitute and broken, are more dead than alive. Orphans without parents, agunos, injured and crippled Jews living in pain. We must cry out bitterly over the horrendous scope of the tragedy.

Later in the eulogy, he spoke of a possible cause:

This earthquake is Hashem's way of showing His jealousy for Jerusalem... During the last hundred years, most [Ashkenazic] immigrants opted to settle in Safed, to be near the tomb of the Rashbi [the talmudic sage Rabbi Shimon bar Yochai] in Meron and the Ari Zal in Safed. Jerusalem, however, was utterly forgotten... Therefore, this tribulation has befallen us.

Rav Sofer concluded:

Just as we are lamenting and weeping over this catastrophe, so may we one day be worthy to rejoice over the ingathering of our people within her true borders, and participate in the rebuilding of Zion and Jerusalem.[30]

Rav Moshe Sofer (1763–1840)

In Warsaw, Rav Hillel Rivlin's son spoke in the central synagogue. Rav Moshe Rivlin was a well-known *maggid*, famous for his impassioned sermons concerning the rebuilding of Jerusalem and the ingathering of Jews to the Holy Land. Thousands came to hear him, among them Rav Yaakov Leib Levi, then a teenager. He described the speech: "My brother and I also came to hear the eulogy. Rav Moshe's voice resounded with such intensity that within the first few minutes thousands were in tears, and several hundred men and women fainted. After an interruption during which the needs of the listeners were attended to, he read the letter which he had received from his father in Jerusalem describing the tragedy and its aftermath in detail.

"During his four-hour speech, the *maggid* reaffirmed what the Chasam Sofer theorized as the source of the disaster. He then went on to speak about the importance of building up the *yishuv* in Jerusalem. He impressed everyone and succeeded in setting up a committee to help the community in the Holy City.

"My brother and I sat on the committee, and we lodged near Rav Moshe

Rivlin. He spoke with us at length about the Vilna Gaon's view on living in Eretz Yisrael and how we could help build the *yishuv*.

"Right then and there," said Rav Yaakov Levi, "my brother and I both vowed to go to Israel and settle in Jerusalem."[31]

The Levi brothers kept their word. Indeed, they would later marry Rav Moshe's daughters and become leaders of the Perushim.

Troubles upon Troubles

The collapse of the Ashkenazic community in Safed drastically altered the demography of both Safed and Jerusalem. In Safed, Rav Avraham Dov of Avritch struggled courageously to keep the remnant of the community together. Slowly, the few remaining survivors began rebuilding their lives, until the next year (1838/5598), when a Druse uprising against Ibrahim Pasha nearly demolished the Jewish presence in the mystical city. The sixty-eight-year-old Rav Avraham Dov was captured and about to die a martyr's death, when his captors heard that Ibrahim's soldiers were approaching. The Druse quickly abandoned the venerable scholar and fled. This episode was the last straw, and in its aftermath, there were many who wanted to move to Akko, Haifa, or Jerusalem. Only the charismatic personality of their leader held them together. As if in reward for their endurance, God sent an Italian philanthropist, Yitzchak Goyatos, to restore most of the synagogues to their former glory.[32]

In Jerusalem the situation was also difficult, albeit in a less harrowing fashion. Overnight, the Jewish population of the city jumped by one-third and now stood at 5,000. The demographic breakdown of the city's total populace, according to the Robinson-Smith report of 1838, placed the Jewish-Moslem population on equal standing, with the Christian population set at 4,000.[33] With the population bursting at the seams, everything seemed to be lacking for the Perushim, especially adequate living quarters.

There were a few bright spots scattered around the city. For some time, the Sephardim had a unique charity institution called Chayei Olam, headed by Rav Yitzchak Parchi, which distributed mezuzos, *tzitzis*, and tefillin at no charge to those in need. There is no doubt that at this time, many Ashkenazim gratefully availed themselves of this charity.[34]

Rav Shlomo Zalman Zoref, the emissary in times of need, had been among the first Perushim to move to Jerusalem. He gave his life over to the *yishuv* in every way possible and helped hold the community together. He passed away in 1837.

1838 (5598) marked a low point for the Jews of Eretz Yisrael. In the Galilee, the Druse peasants vented their animosity towards the Egyptian establishment on the Jews. In addition, the winter of that year was ominously dry. In Jerusalem, a communal fast day was declared. Rav Yisrael of Shklov led a group of Perushim to a spot outside the city to pray. On their return, the skies darkened and soon Heaven-sent rains cascaded down.[35]

Later that spring, an epidemic rampaged throughout the Holy City. A number of inhabitants were stricken and died. Among them was the father of the

Perushim, Rav Hillel Rivlin. The vibrant leader and lover of peace passed away on 9 Sivan, at the age of eighty. He had dedicated fifty-eight years of his life to the Chazon Tzyon movement, half in Russia and the other half in Eretz Yisrael. His last words were, "Be at peace, my children. So great is peace, that it will bring the *geula*."

His words were meant as a plea to the two branches of Perushim — those from Shklov and those from Vilna — to heal the widening schism between them.[36] There had been disagreements between the two groups for several years, and since the influx of refugees from the earthquake, the gap between them had greatly widened. Rav Hillel attempted to mediate between the two sides, but passed away before any real compromise could be reached. A few years later, when his son Rav Moshe the *maggid* arrived to lead the Perushim, the friction was ameliorated and unity was achieved.

Rav Hillel was buried at the foot of the Mount of Olives, next to the tomb of Zechariah. In 1948, gentile archeologists desecrated all the graves surrounding the tomb in an attempt to dig down and get inside the gigantic sepulcher at the site. They found nothing inside.

The Last of the Original Leaders

Rav Rivlin's death was followed exactly a year later by the passing of the last remaining leader of the Chazon Tzyon movement, Rav Yisrael of Shklov.

After the earthquake, Rav Yisrael moved to the Holy City. At the time of the tragedy he had been in Jerusalem, seeking a site on which to build a synagogue. Funded by the Dutch philanthropist Akiva Lehren, Rav Yisrael, together with his son-in-law, Rav Yeshaya Bardaky, purchased a courtyard and built the Sukkas Shalom Shul. It was colloquially known as the Chatzer, in order to distinguish it from the Churvah. Rav Yisrael spoke there every Shabbos. In time, Sukkas Shalom became known as "Rav Yeshaya's *chatzer*."

Attendance at the Sukkas Shalom and Menachem Tzyon shuls reflected the ongoing strain between the two factions of the Perushim. The two groups shared a common *talmud Torah, mikve*, and hospitality lodge. Yet tensions still persisted between the two groups. A visible manifestation of this was the fact that the Perushim from Safed gravitated to the Chatzer, while the Jerusalemite Perushim centered more around the Churvah complex.

In Sivan, 1839, Rav Yisrael traveled to Tiberias for health reasons. On 9 Sivan, the first *yartzeit* of Rav Hillel, he passed away, at the age of seventy. Rav Yisrael's death was mourned universally, but especially by all of the Perushim living in Jerusalem; his personal greatness put him far above any rivalry. His life, like that of Rav Hillel and of Rav Menachem Mendel, had been intimately bound with the dream of the Vilna Gaon. He lived to see the *yishuv* grow from seventy souls to thousands, and from two physical localities to a single one.

Rav Yeshaya Bardaky replaced his father-in-law as *rav* of Sukkas Shalom, and Rav Nasan Nata replaced Rav Hillel as *rav* of Menachem Tzyon. These two men were second-generation leaders who had never sat at the feet of the Vilna Gaon. Yet they had a clear vision of the master's goal: to bring the redemption by building up the *yishuv*.

The Ultimate Breakdown

The intense longing of the Perushim to effect the redemption never waned. Even during the last years of the 1830s, when confusion and darkness clouded the horizons, the fervent hope for a miraculous salvation was always close at hand. In their understanding, the process by which the Mashiach would come was alluded to in the *Song of Songs*. The verse says (2:12): "The flowers are visible in the land; the time of the singing has come, and the voice of the turtle dove is heard in the land."

In *Kol HaTor*, Rav Hillel Rivlin's monumental work, this verse is divided into three parts, each denoting a stage in the redemption: The flowers (הַנִּצָּנִים נִרְאוּ בָאָרֶץ) represent the acts of building the land — farming and living in Eretz Yisrael. The time of singing (עֵת הַזָּמִיר) is the auspicious time for the redemption, and the voice of the turtle dove (וְקוֹל הַתֹּר) is the people who help bring it about.[37]

The crushing physical conditions they faced only accentuated their inner conviction that the Mashiach was standing at the gates of the Holy City. The time, according to their calculation, was 1840 (5600). This was derived from the same verse, where the word turtle dove (*tor*, תר) has the numerical value of 600, hinting to the year 5,600.

For some members of the community, the fulfillment of this target date had life-and-death ramifications. When 1840 came and went with no sign of the Mashiach, the hopes of some of the Perushim were dashed. Missionary activists, although not new to Jerusalem, prepared to take advantage of these Jews' depression and mounted an intensive campaign to save some "fallen souls." Bishop Michael Alexander, professor of Hebrew at Kings College, England, was sent for this special mission. An apostate who knew the Jewish mentality firsthand, he was well groomed for the job. He immediately succeeded in enticing a number of Jews in the city. Within a couple of months, he had "saved" three souls of the community. In general, of course, the Perushim remained steadfast to their faith. In fact, there were many protests against the presence of Alexander and his ignoble deeds. However, all of the demonstrations could not redeem these shattered souls and return them to the flock. After this stunning success, the bishop traveled to Egypt. Although not old or ill, he mysteriously died on the way.[38]

This backlash to the broken expectations of the Perushim was one of the saddest episodes in the history of the *yishuv*. It stood as a warning to Jews everywhere not to invest undue energies in anticipating an exact date for the redemption, but rather to cleave to God and place their whole faith solely in Him and His Torah.

Notes

1. Letter in *Yerushalayim* (Journal), Jerusalem, 1928.
2. *Toldos Chachmei Yerushalayim*, vol. 3, pp. 184–185.
3. *Yerushalayim Bein HaChomos*, p. 186.
4. Some say his soul had a spark of Moshe Rabbeinu's soul, and just as Moshe was not allowed into Eretz Yisrael, so he was prevented from traveling there. Another explanation is that the Gra's soul had a spark of Mashiach ben Yosef (*Mosad HaYesod*, pp. 15, 59). See also *Chazon Tzyon*, p. 31, about a dream which the Gra had on his journey. The *gematria* of בשעריך ירושלם is equal to his name אליהו בן שלמה זלמן בן ישכר.
5. *Kol HaTor*, chs. 1, 4. The Hebrew expressions for the three main themes are: (1.) קִבּוּץ גָלִיּוֹת (2.) מִצְוַת הַרְחָבָה (3.) כִּי מִצִּיּוֹן תֵּצֵא תוֹרָה וּדְבַר ה' מִירוּשָׁלָםִ.
6. *Sanhedrin* 98a. See also *Kol HaTor*, ch. 1; *Mosad HaYesod*, pp. 19–20.
7. *Makkos* 10a; *Chazon Tzyon*, p. 39.
8. See Rav Yisrael's detailed autobiographical account in the preface to *Pe'as HaShulchan*.
9. *Berachos* 47b.
10. Some say he came in 1811.
11. See stories about him, *Toldos Chachmei Yerushalayim*, vol. 3, p. 182.
12. See *HaChalukah* by Rav Lunz; *Toldos Chachmei Yerushalayim*, pp. 148–149.
13. *Chazon Tzyon*, p. 66.
14. The numerical value of שערי צדק is the same as פרושים וחסידים.
15. *HaMaggid Doresh Tzyon*, p. 39.
16. *Chazon Tzyon,* p. 72.
17. *Tevuos HaAretz*, pp. 450–451.
18. *Toldos Chachmei Yerushalayim*, p. 205.
19. Ibid., p. 160.
20. Intro. to *Shaar HaTzimtzum*.
21. *Chazon Tzyon*, p. 78.
22. *Mosad HaYesod*, pp. 124–125.
23. *Teshuvos Mabit*, nos. 45, 196.
24. *Chazon Tzyon*, pp. 81–90.
25. *Tevuos HaAretz*, p. 472.
26. In letter by Rav Yosef Schwartz, *Meginzai Yerushalayim*, vol. 18, p. 11.
27. *Toldos Chachmei Yerushalayim*, vol. 3, p. 297.
28. *Shaarei Yerushalayim*, p. 18.
29. *Luach Eretz Yisrael*, vol. 2, pp. 235–236.
30. *Toras Moshe, parashas Emor.*
31. *Mosad HaYesod*, p. 149.
32. See *Safed: The Mystical City*, chs. 9, 10.
33. *Chazon Tzyon*, p. 130.
34. *Tuv Yerushalayim*, p. 109.
35. *Chibas Yerushalayim*, p. 242.
36. Some say the two parties were Perushim from Safed and Jerusalem.
37. *Kol HaTor*, end of ch. 4.
38. *Aliyos Eliyahu*, pp. 130–139.

The Hidden Light

THE PERUSHIM regularly sent emissaries to the Diaspora. However, not just anyone could become a representative for the members of the *yishuv*. The potential *shaliach* had to prepare well and stand before the leader to be tested before being accepted for a mission. Rav Moshe Maggid, who led the Perushim in the 1840s, even made the candidates memorize several *drashos* with which to impress their audiences in Europe.

In the first years of the settlement in Jerusalem, around 1820, a young scholar stood before the revered leader of the *yishuv*, Rav Menachem Mendel of Shklov, to be tested. At the conclusion of the meeting, the young man asked the Perushim leader, "How is it possible that someone of your greatness can bear to live in such poor conditions? It is so dark and stuffy in here!"

Ignoring the question, Rav Menachem Mendel dismissed the scholar, telling him only that "Tomorrow I will decided if you should go on *shelichus*."

The next morning, Rav Menachem Mendel informed the scholar that he was unfit for the mission. The bewildered young man sent a friend to ask why he had been turned down.

Rav Menachem Mendel replied, "A person who is perplexed over why anyone would want to live in Jerusalem in miserable conditions is not fit for the job of arousing Jews of the Diaspora to give charity. To me, this is a sign that he has not seen the hidden light of Jerusalem."

* * *

IN THE 1840s (5600), a similar comment was made to Rav Moshe Maggid about his residence in the Holy City. He answered by quoting a verse in *Psalms* (118:5): "From the straits I called unto God, He answered me with expansiveness."

He explained himself: "In *chutz laAretz* my physical being was in a state of expansiveness, but my soul was in straits. Now, here in Jerusalem, my body is in straits, but, *Baruch Hashem,* my soul is in a state of expansiveness!"

(*Chazon Tzyon*, pp. 61, 120)

The Immovable Stone

JUST AS today, there were a number of Greek-Orthodox Christians living in Jerusalem during the 1800s. Sometime during the first quarter of the century, an unsavory band of these Greeks planned a master theft. In those days, the cheapest way for the non-Jewish residents of the city to get cut stones for their houses was simply to climb up the Mount of Olives at night and carry away Jewish grave-markers. Indeed, the Moslems had been saving time and money for many years by doing just that. In those days, Jewish gravestones were cut thin and were comparatively light to carry.

However, this brazen group conspired to take one dating from much earlier times — the massive headstone from the grave of Kalba Savua, father-in-law of the talmudic sage Rabbi Akiva, which was located in the Tomb of the Kings. They intended to place it in one of their houses of worship.

One night they descended into the gigantic cave in which the tomb was located and lifted the mighty stone slab from its resting place. They then proceeded to hoist it up over the top of the cave. The task of lifting the heavy slab was grueling. When they finished, they decided to leave it there and go to their homes and rest. At dawn, they would return and take it with them.

When they returned, they were bewildered to discover that the stone had disappeared. They searched the area in the early morning light, but to no avail. Finally one of them suggested that they go down to the cave. Though it was physically impossible for the heavy slab to move by itself, maybe it had somehow fallen back down there.

The others discredited the idea, but the one who suggested it stubbornly entered the cave anyway. Soon he called out in surprise, "I found it!"

The rest of the group clambered into the cave. To their astonishment, the stone was resting on the tzaddik's grave just where they had found it the previous night!

Undaunted by this strange turn of events, the band returned that night and tried to remove the slab again. After two more attempts, and two more miraculous returns by the stone to its original place, they raised their hands on high and acknowledged the message being sent to them from Heaven: this slab must remain where it is.

(*Chibas Yerushalayim*, p. 243)

The Courageous Decision

A BEDOUIN armed with a sword strapped to his belt handed a note to the head of the Ashkenazic community. Rav Menachem Mendel read the hastily written message: "Please help us and save us as soon as you can! We are a group of Perushim who recently disembarked at Jaffa port. Shortly after starting the journey to Jerusalem, we were taken captive by Bedouin bandits. We fear for our lives, and every minute feels like an eternity. Please take action and save us!" It was signed: Yosef Luria and Zalman Leib Zeitlin.

Rav Menachem Mendel glanced up at the Bedouin and then back at the note. He recognized the signatures. They were the emissaries of the Jerusalem community sent to greet the newcomers at Jaffa port and escort them to the Holy City. The Bedouin aggressively demanded 1,000 gold coins ransom money.

At an emergency meeting of the Perushim, the true gravity of the situation became clear. The settlers had been placed in a terrible dilemma. True, they could redeem their brethren, but this would encourage the Bedouins to make this kind of kidnapping a standard procedure. (And where could they, so poor in material wealth, hope to constantly come up with such vast sums of money?) On the other hand, if they refused outright, surely the merciless Arabs would not spare the captives' lives.

Time was of the essence. Someone suggested they perform *goral haGra*, a method of opening the Tanach to receive an answer to an important question. They solemnly opened the Tanach at random and counted seven pages, seven verses, seven lines, seven words, seven letters. The eighth letter was the key. Next they searched for the first verse which began with that letter. The verse which appeared said, "The redeemed of the Lord shall return, they will come with singing to Zion" (*Isaiah* 51:11).

Quickly, while some members hurried to collect the ransom money, others prepared to take action. With the money tightly bound in a leather pouch, two members of the community went with the Bedouin down the mountain towards Jaffa. What the Bedouin did not

New immigrants landing at Jaffa. Steamers and seafaring ships had to anchor a kilometer off shore since there was no harbor for large vessels. Passengers and their cargo were ferried to Jaffa in small Arab boats. This was only the beginning of their struggles to reach the Holy City.

A Bedouin Camp

know was that a group of armed Perushim, called *anshei gevardiah* (men of valor), were secretly trailing behind him.

When they reached a spot not far from present-day Bnei Brak, the Bedouin told the two Jews to wait until he returned. Within a half an hour he returned with three members of his gang.

"Raise up your hands!" ordered one of the bandits.

They raised their hands.

"The money!" he thundered. "Did you bring the money?"

"Yes. But we want to be sure that you will free our brethren first."

The leader looked at his companions and grinned. "All right. Follow us."

They walked across a field until they came to a stone wall. Inside was the Bedouin camp. The Jewish captives were pinned inside a makeshift prison cell in a corner of the encampment. The leader called to the prison guards to release the captives, and the Perushim gave him the bag of money.

As the Bedouins gathered around their leader to divide the money up, the two Jews told the captives to quickly run away, without even taking any of their belongings.

As soon as they were all outside, the *anshei gevardiah* leapt out of hiding and, screaming fiercely, attacked the startled bandits. Within minutes, seven Bedouins were killed, two injured, and the rest had fled for their lives. All of the money was retrieved.

The *anshei gevardiah* escorted the caravan of newcomers to Jerusalem. Amidst joyful singing, they entered the Holy City, with the verse from *Isaiah* on their lips.

(*Chazon Tzyon*, pp. 187–188)

Passover Miracle

CHOL HAMOED Passover, 1824. The clear spring air seemed to magnify the stillness of the Jerusalem night. Suddenly, the echo of harsh banging on Rav Menachem Mendel's door broke the pristine silence. Before the leader of the Perushim could get up and answer the insistent knocking, Arab soldiers broke the door open and barged in. With no word of explanation, the Arabs roughly bound the revered tzaddik and led him off to the city's dungeon. His son, Rav Nasan Nata, met with a similar fate.

When the Jews of Jerusalem woke up to the news that their beloved leader had been taken captive, a wave of fear and anger washed over them. However, no explanation was necessary. Obviously, some high-ranking Moslem was in need of money, and there was no easier and more effective way to raise quick cash than to imprison a celebrated Jew and demand that his brethren redeem him or else... Experience had painfully taught that the threats of torture and flogging that accompanied these demands were no bluff.

They soon learned the details behind their misfortune. It seemed that a pasha from a distant land was passing through Jerusalem on his pilgrimage to Mecca. Such a religious experience demanded a bountiful reward, and the poor Jews of Jerusalem would be made to pay for it. The pasha decided that the Sephardim should add 81,000 *grushim* to his coffers, and the Ashkenazim another 75,000. It remained irrelevant to him that the total number of Ashkenazic families in the Holy City amounted to a few hundred people, while the Sephardim numbered well over a thousand.

In addition to taking Rav Menachem Mendel hostage, the greedy pasha combed the city for other regal citizens whose captivity would spur the Jews to abide by his decree. Several other important members of the Jewish community were also chained and imprisoned, including a ninety-year-old Sephardic sage. The cruel pasha did not discriminate against old people.

Rav Menachem Mendel was soon transferred to a detention cell outside the city. His health quickly deteriorated, and soon his very life was endangered.

In the meantime, one of Rav Menachem Mendel's disciples, Rav Shlomo Zalman Shapiro, was at his wits' end. Every minute was crucial, yet there was nothing he could do to save his mentor's life. He walked aimlessly near the ruins of the Churvah Synagogue, hoping that some idea would come to him. From out of nowhere, an Arab suddenly approached and told him that the pasha's translator was passing nearby.

Rav Shapiro introduced himself to the translator, and explained the danger hovering over Rav Menachem Mendel and the turmoil his death would bring upon the entire Jewish *yishuv*. This translator had been hired to accompany the pasha only as far as Damascus. However, a close friendship had developed between the two of them, and he had continued on with him to Jerusalem. He quietly listened to Rav Shapiro.

When Rav Shlomo Zalman finished his moving plea, the translator answered, "I am willing to help you free your leader. I am from Aram Zovah where I am friends with a certain wealthy Jewish family by the name of Pizato. I feel indebted to them and will therefore do what I can for you."

He then set off to rejoin the pasha's entourage, which was encamped outside the city wall. In the meantime, Rav Moshe Sozin, the Rishon l'Tzyon and a close companion of Rav Menachem Mendel, spoke before the Sephardic community. He explained that all of one's valuables should be contributed to redeeming a captive, especially one as great as the Perushim's leader.

Miraculously, a few hours later Rav Menachem Mendel and his son were released. Rav Menachem Mendel raised his feeble hands in thanks, and announced that that day, the last day of Passover, would be remembered always as a day of personal redemption. In the time of Moses, the Red Sea miraculously split for the Chosen People. Now, he too felt the miraculous hand of God who saved him at the very last minute.

(*Toldos Chachmei Yerushalayim*, vol. 3, pp. 162–163)

Montefiore's Dream

SIR MOSES Montefiore embodied a unique blend of noble English sensitivity with an insatiable thirst to aid his fellow Jew. He lived in a generation when most Jews concentrated their energies on making a living and caring about communal and national affairs. Sir Moses, however, cared about helping his impoverished brethren wherever they might be. With the nascent industrial revolution widening man's view into a semi-global perspective, Moses Montefiore's heart was focused on the needs of the Jews in Eretz Yisrael.

What awakened this guardian of Jerusalem and Eretz Yisrael to his Divine mission? In 1877 (5637), when Sir Moses was ninety-three years old, one of his relatives, Leonard Montefiore, visited him at his mansion in Ramsgate. During their conversation, Leonard broached the subject.

"It is interesting that you should ask me," answered the revered tzaddik. "You are the first person who ever has. Although I've never divulged to anyone how I initially became interested in this cause, I feel that now is the right time."

Sir Moses sat up at the edge of his chair and stretched out his hand. "Do you see this ring?" he said as he removed it from his finger. "Take a good look at it," he added as he handed it to Leonard.

Engraved on the ring were two Hebrew words: קוֹנֵה הַכֹּל (Possessor of everything).

"I have worn this signet for many years as a reminder of the first wondrous expe-

Sir Moses Montefiore's private carriage

rience which led me to travel to Eretz Yisrael."

Looking warmly at the young man, Sir Moses said, "You are from the younger generation and are apt to view this type of behavior as silly, but really it is only because you never experienced this type of awakening."

Sir Moses Montefiore (1784–1885), dressed in a uniform when traveling

Reclining in his chair, he gazed out the window. "It all started from a dream I had one night." Responding to Leonard's raised eyebrow, he continued, "Yes, a whole lifetime's mission began from a simple dream!

"One *motzei Shabbos*, while my dear Judith and I were singing 'Eliyahu Ha-Navi,' we both felt elated, and discussed the idea of visiting the Holy Land and climbing Mount Carmel — as well as other holy sites. Right then and there, I promised her that we would go there someday.

"That night I dreamt that I saw a venerated old man. He showed me a picture of Eliyahu the Prophet with one hand while pointing in the direction of Eretz Yisrael with the other. He then whispered in my ear, קוֹנֵה הַכֹּל, 'possessor of everything.'

"I woke up and went back to sleep. Again, I dreamt the same dream and woke with the words קוֹנֵה הַכֹּל resounding in my ears. Unbelievably, I went back to sleep and a third time I had the same dream!"

Leonard was speechless, hardly believing what he was hearing.

Sir Moses continued, "This dream made such a deep impression on me, that I felt compelled to act on the promise I had just made Judith much sooner than I had thought to. In fact, I immediately let all my other commitments fall to the side and prepared for the journey with my wife without delay. We wanted to see how our fellow Jews were faring in the Holy Land."

Sir Moses looked at Leonard piercingly with a twinkle in his eye. "Whether or not you feel that the dream was ridiculous, you cannot deny that there is a lot for you and me to do for Eretz Yisrael!"

(*Chazon Tzyon*, pp. 77–78)

The Poisoned Cup

The following story took place shortly before the Egyptian takeover of Eretz Yisrael in 1831 (5591). At that time, as always, Jerusalem's Moslems reveled in expressing a sense of superiority over their Jewish neighbors. Indeed, they would often stoop to harassing hapless individuals in order to prove their point, especially if they could profit from it.

ONCE, A new immigrant from Istanbul caught some Arabs' attention. His noble dress and refined mannerisms identified him as a well-to-do Jew. They spied on his lodgings and his daily schedule, and finally they contrived a scheme to relieve him of some of his riches.

One afternoon, a tall, personable Arab approached the Jew from Istanbul.

"Good afternoon," he said with a friendly smile.

"Good afternoon," the Jew replied in Arabic.

"Winter is approaching, you know," the Arab said in a more serious tone. "Everyone is storing up charcoal for the cold months ahead. Look over there," he pointed to the corner of the open square. "Those Bedouins have their camels loaded with charcoal. Not only is their price good, but they will deliver it right to your door."

The immigrant was no fool. He glanced at the camels and remained silent. "This might be a ploy to steal some of my money," he thought to himself.

"Thank you very much, but I already have a large supply of charcoal," he answered politely but curtly.

"I understand, my dear friend. I only wanted to save you the time and energy of going to the *shuk* yourself. You have nothing to be afraid of, certainly not from me."

The Arab seemed sincere and, what's more, he spoke very convincingly, offering a seemingly good deal. He said, "All right, let us do this: the Bedouins will bring the charcoal to your house now, and you can pay whatever price you feel is reasonable."

"While they are unloading," he added, "we'll sit in your house and drink some coffee and smoke some nargileh [oriental tobacco pipe]."

Despite his initial misgivings, the Jew acquiesced.

While the Bedouins began to unload the sacks of charcoal, the two of them sat down to drink coffee. They were joined by the chief Bedouin. The mundane conversation helped pass the time as the smoke from the nargileh slowly filled the air.

As the Bedouin sipped his coffee, he suddenly uttered a grunt and keeled over backwards. He laid motionless on the floor.

"Murderer!" cried the Arab as he jumped up from his seat. "What have you done? You've placed poison in the coffee!"

The Jew tried to explain that it was impossible. He himself had drunk from the same pitcher of Turkish coffee.

The Arab paid no attention to him. "You have plotted to murder us because you hate us Moslems. Not only will you pay with your life, but all your Jewish brethren will pay for this with their blood!"

The dumbstruck Jew began to panic. "No, no! Please don't do such a terrible thing," he pleaded.

"All right." The Arab spoke more calmly. "I'll take pity on you and your fellow Jews. But there is only one way to save you all. Lock your courtyard gate so that nobody may enter. Then, in another hour, when it is dark, I'll send two men to remove the corpse and secretly bury him."

"I'm doing all of this," he added with sincerity, "because you are a dear friend of mine. Still, it will be necessary for you to pay a large sum of money so that I can make all the arrangements."

The Jew stared at the body of the Bedouin and eagerly agreed to pay whatever amount would save him and his fellow Jews from a pogrom led by a frenzied mob. He quickly went to a room and returned with a small fortune, relieved that he had averted a tragedy.

After dark, two men came with a large burlap sack. They placed the dead body inside and slung it over their shoulders, and awkwardly made their way out of the courtyard and into the street. There, they placed the sack on the ground. In plain view of the Sephardic Jew, the "dead" Bedouin jumped out of it and smiled broadly. The three quickly disappeared in the night, leaving the hapless Jew gaping after them. He had just had a firsthand lesson in the sly cunning of his Moslem neighbors.

(*Tevuos HaAretz*, p. 495)

In Search of the Lost Tribes

Rabbi Yehudah bar Simon said: The Ten Tribes and the Tribes of Yehudah and Binyamin were not exiled to the same place. The Ten Tribes were exiled to a place beyond the Sambatiyon River, while the Tribes of Yehudah and Binyamin were scattered around the world.

Midrash Rabbah 73:6

In the future, the people of Yehudah and Binyamin will go to them [the Ten Tribes], and bring them to Eretz Yisrael.

Midrash

THE PERUSHIM wanted with all of their hearts for the Mashiach to come. Their enthusiasm in moving to Eretz Yisrael was but one manifestation of this desire. They also felt that bringing the Ten Tribes back from exile would speed up the redemption. Over the course of several years, they made numerous attempts to generate enthusiasm about the subject by writing and publicizing letters.

In 1815, Arabian nomads came to Jerusalem with news of a "tribe of Jews" in Yemen. The excitement this news caused among the tiny Perushim community was immeasurable. The *yishuv* decided to send two of its members to investigate the fantastic report. They set out across the desert with two Arab escorts. A year later they reached the capital of Yemen and interviewed the Jewish leaders there. To their dismay, they learned that while the Ten Tribes were rumored to live somewhere in the wilderness of Yemen, no one knew of their exact whereabouts. After the two Perushim returned to Jerusalem and gave their report, the matter was laid to rest for several years.

In 1830, Rav Yisrael of Shklov, head of the Perushim in Safed, decided to take action. He sent Rav Baruch of Pinsk to Yemen with three letters for the king of the Tribes.

The main letter, opening with words of greeting, described the development of the Oral Law down to the time of the Vilna Gaon. After dramatizing the trials and tribulations of Jews throughout the ages, Rav Yisrael related the story of the Perushim's immigration to Eretz Yisrael, and their hope that they — the Perushim — would be the first wave of the ingathering of the Jewish people to their homeland. He concluded by requesting four things: that the Lost Tribes pray for Jews the world over; that they send ordained rabbis to Eretz Yisrael empowered to ordain other rabbis so that the Sanhedrin might be revived; that they send money for the *yishuv*; and that they answer the specific halachic questions asked in a second letter. With these in hand, Rav Baruch left Safed in Cheshvan, 1830.

As soon as Rav Baruch departed, Rav Yisrael sent another letter to his dear friend and patron, Tzvi Hirsch Lehren of Amsterdam, enclosing copies of what he had written to the Lost Tribes. Rav Lehren read the letters excitedly, and translated his enthusiasm into action by publishing them and sending them to the heads of Jewish congregations throughout Europe. He saw in this endeavor the fulfillment of the words of the *Zohar* which said that at the beginning of the messianic times, the Ten Tribes would be revealed. The success of such a mission would surely lead Jews everywhere to repent, and repentance was the key to having the Mashiach reveal himself and fulfill his lofty task in the world.

When Rav Baruch arrived in San'a, the leader of the Jewish community, Rav Yosef Elkara, received him with great honor and promised to help him find the Tribes. He told Rav Baruch that a sect of Adenian Jews were reported to stem from the Lost Tribes. Rav Baruch, already two years on the road, was bolstered by the news and set out by camel across the endless desert on the journey to Aden.

At one point he met a shepherd boy who on first glance looked more like a Bedouin than a Jew. Rav Baruch questioned him and discovered that he had *tzitzis* and tefillin with him, and that he claimed to be from the Lost Tribes. Excitedly, Rav Baruch asked permission to meet the king of the Tribes, but was flatly refused. At best, the shepherd agreed to take the letters to the king and return with a reply. In the meantime, Rav Baruch continued on to Aden and waited.

Months passed without any response. In the meantime, Rav Baruch became the Yemenite monarch's personal physician, and over the course of time his original mission receded to the back of his mind. He eventually wrote to the Perushim of Safed, telling them the details of his journey. Shortly thereafter, he was murdered.

With his passing, the search for the Lost Tribes ended. Yet everyone knew that they lived somewhere beyond the Sambatiyon River. It seemed that the time for them to come out of exile had not arrived. Someday, however, Hashem will open the gates and allow them to come back to Eretz Yisrael. Then, as a united people, the Jews will enter the era of the Mashiach.

(*Aliyos Eliyahu*, pp. 63–69; *Chazon Tzyon*, pp. 67–69)

The Granddaddy of Mussar

IF RAV Yisrael Salanter was the father of the *mussar* movement, then Rav Zundel of Salant was the grandfather. Time and time again, Rav Yisrael acknowledged that his mentor was none other than Rav Zundel, the foremost disciple of Rav Chaim of Volozhin.

When the Holy City merited to have the tzaddik live inside its walls (in 1838), her residents far underestimated him. This is not to say that they didn't recognize that he was a *gadol b'Torah*. On the contrary, they eagerly requested him to sit as *rav* of the community, and he humbly acquiesced — but only on condition that he not be reimbursed for his time. Yet, even so, his greatness had been only partially tapped.

Once his son-in-law, Rav Shmuel Salant, immigrated in 1840, Rav Zundel quickly relinquished the title to him and spent his days immersed in learning in the Menachem Tzyon Synagogue. Still, people came to him with their halachic queries. In his typical manner, he "studied" the *Shulchan Aruch* along with the questioner until the other told him the correct halachah.

Rav Zundel placed the honor of his fellowman above nearly everything else. Once, a fellow Jew took Rav Zundel's *shtender* from its place and moved it to another side of the synagogue. When he left, he neglected to return it to its proper place. This continued to happen many times, causing the elderly

Rav Zundel to keep dragging it back himself. Adding to the inconvenience was the fact that the *shtender* had a built-in compartment that was laden with books, which made it quite heavy.

At an opportune moment, Rav Zundel approached the man and gently told him that he, Rav Zundel, gave him full permission to use the *shtender*, but could he please return it when finished.

The man stiffened and a disrespectful expression crossed his face, yet he held his tongue. As Rav Zundel returned to his place, he chastised himself for insulting the man's feelings and immediately returned to seek his forgiveness. The man, however, refused to accept his apology.

Without the slightest sign of embarrassment, Rav Zundel climbed up on the *bimah* and called out to everyone in the Churvah Shul, "*Rabbosai!* I have erred in the honor of my fellow Jew and unwittingly caused him pain. Therefore, before everyone present I beg him to forgive me." Then he burst into tears.

The man, obviously shaken, quickly and wholeheartedly forgave him.

(*MiGedolai Yerushalayim*, pp. 48–49)

19th Century

From Napoleon to Beyond the Walls

Part II

Bound Within the Walls: 1840-1870

כָּל הַמִּתְפַּלֵּל בְּמָקוֹם הַזֶּה בִּירוּשָׁלַיִם
כְּאִלּוּ הִתְפַּלֵּל לִפְנֵי כִּסֵּא הַכָּבוֹד,
שֶׁשַּׁעַר הַשָּׁמַיִם שָׁם הוּא וּפֶתַח פָּתוּחַ לִשְׁמוֹעַ תְּפִלָּה,
שֶׁנֶּאֱמַר, וְזֶה שַׁעַר הַשָּׁמַיִם.

פרקי דרבי אליעזר, פ׳ ל״ה

Anyone who prays in Jerusalem is thought to be praying before the Heavenly Throne.
There the Gate of Heaven is surely open and (God) is receptive to hear these prayers,
as it says (Genesis 28:17), "This is the Gate of Heaven."

Pirkei d'Rabbi Eliezer 35

The Turning Point

In 1840 (5600), Turkey reasserted its control over the Holy Land. The return of Ottoman ascendancy in Eretz Yisrael would usher in dramatic changes for the Jewish community of the Holy City. The Sultan realized that in order for him to maintain his newly regained control, fundamental governmental reforms had to be instituted in the Empire. This turning point in the history of the Empire in general and the Holy City in particular welded together Jerusalem's Ashkenazic and Sephardic kehillos. Together, they would face the uncertainties of the new era.

Return to Ottoman Rule[1]

Sultan Mohammed died in 1840 and his son Abdul Majid reigned in his place. Majid successfully drove out the Egyptian army from Eretz Yisrael and reaffirmed Ottoman sovereignty over the Middle East. His attitude towards the Jews appeared unaltered from that of his father. Apparently, the insult which the Jews committed against the Empire by soliciting the goodwill of the Egyptian insurgents, and thereby obtaining special rights and privileges, was forgiven. The Sultan earned a reputation as a beneficent monarch and tried to improve the conditions of his subjects in Syria and Eretz Yisrael.

Sultan Abdul Majid (1840–1861)

In the second year of his reign, the Sultan put a stop to the hatred caused by false blood libels. Next he welcomed the establishment of foreign consulates in Jerusalem. By 1844, six countries had opened consulates in the Holy City, including Austria, England, France, and Russia. The presence of these foreign embassies was of mutual interest to Turkey and to the countries they represented. First, there was an increase in commerce due to the influx of pilgrims and new residents. Second, the consuls protected their native citizens against unlawful acts and discrimination.

Furthermore, the Sultan elevated the status of Jerusalem from a small provincial town to a major city, called a *sanjak*, and likewise granted its mayor a title of distinction.

Though Abdul Majid generally looked kindly upon his Jewish subjects, there were exceptions. In 1845 (5605), the Sultan was swayed by gossip against the Jews of the Holy City when they endeavored to purchase land outside the city walls. Imaginary fears of some kind of Jewish autonomous colony — like a Yehudiah — convinced him to deny their request. A new law was promulgated whereby foreign residents were forbidden to buy land. Thus, for the next seventeen years, no construction was permitted outside the walls — a situation which only intensified the already overcrowded conditions inside the city.[2]

The Arab opposition to expanding outside the walls stemmed from an illusory fear that their Jewish tenants would abandon them in a whirlwind exodus to the newly built suburbs. They were willing to prevent expansion at any cost in order to retain their income — even if it meant that they themselves would suffer from congested living conditions.

The Maggid Speaks

During this period, the Perushim community was at a low ebb, barely able to hold its own under the crushing conditions. In addition to the onerous yoke of poverty they bore, the world that they, and the other Jews of Jerusalem, found around them was unrelentingly hostile. Although the Jews comprised seventy percent of the city's population, they were discriminated against at every turn by the governing Moslem minority. The Jews lacked equal rights, police protection, justice in the civil courts, and freedom of expression.

In these discouraging times, a ray of light suddenly burst into their lives. With the news that Rav Hillel Rivlin's son, Rav Moshe the *maggid*, was on his way from Russia, expectations soared in the frail community. Aside from being the son of their beloved leader, the *maggid*'s dynamic speeches throughout Europe on behalf of the *yishuv* elevated him even more in their eyes. As much as they needed physical respite, they thirsted for spiritual elevation as well.

Rav Moshe Rivlin had been foretold of his mission in life at a very young age. When he was fifteen years old, his father took him to Vilna to visit the Gra. The lad impressed the Gaon with his power of speech.

"This gift," remarked the Gaon, "has been Heaven-sent to you to so that you might be the spokesman for Zion. When Chazal say, 'This is Zion for whom no one seeks' (*Jeremiah* 30:17) — meaning that it needs to be sought after — it applies to you." The Gra added that דּוֹרֵשׁ צִיּוֹן ("seeker of Zion") has the same numerical value as "Moshe ben Hillel ben Binyamin."[3] And indeed, Rav Moshe had answered his Divine call and become one of the most famous *maggidim* of Europe.

Rav Moshe left Shklov for Jerusalem in Tamuz, 1840 (5600), with trunks full of clothing for the needy, medical supplies, and cash. Arriving in Constantinople, he was forced to wait three months until the Turkish-Egyptian war ended. He took advantage of the delay by meeting with Jewish leaders there. At the time, a number of world-famous Jews were also in the Turkish capital. Sir Moses Montefiore had come on a special mission to save the Jews of Damascus, where both a blood libel had endangered the community, and the Rav of the city, Rav Yaakov Entebbe, had been imprisoned and tortured for six months. Through the personal efforts of Montefiore, Rav Entebbe and several other members of the community who had been imprisoned were freed in Elul. Rav Tzvi Lehren, the controller of the Amsterdam funds for the *yishuv* and a close friend of Rav Yisrael of Shklov, was also in the capital, as well as Rav Shemarya Luria.

In addition to these influential Jews, a young prodigy on his way to Eretz Yisrael was there as well. Twenty-five-year-old Rav Shmuel Salant (a friend of Rav Yisrael Salanter) had spent the last three years as a lecturer in the Volozhin yeshivah. When he became ill, the doctor ordered him to move to a warmer climate. He interpreted this injunction as a call to follow his father-in-law, Rav Yosef Zundel of Salant, to Eretz Yisrael.

While in Constantinople, Rav Rivlin had several meetings with Sir Moses Montefiore concerning the state of the *yishuv*. Rav Moshe had exchanges with all the other personages mentioned as well. The *maggid* spoke before all of them and received pledges of financial aid for the *yishuv*. He repeated what his father had told Sir Moses, that the philanthropist's name, Moshe ben Yosef Eliyahu, equaled the numerical value of בְּטוּב יְרוּשָׁלָם ("for the good of Jerusalem").[4]

An early steamship

In Kislev, 1840 (5601), the seas were opened to travel, and Rav Moshe Rivlin and Rav Shmuel Salant sailed on the first steamship to carry Jewish passengers to Eretz Yisrael.

Uplifting the Yishuv

The fifty-nine-year-old *maggid* poured all his energies into the needs of the community. After an immediate dispensing of money and clothes for the needy, he sought to quell the inner strife between the leaders of the Perushim. First he spoke before the community concerning *shalom*. He then met with the leaders of the Shklov faction and begged them to forgo their so-called first-come benefits for the sake of peace. The times demanded unity, especially if their mission to built a cohesive community was to be a prelude to the coming of the Mashiach. His pleas were accepted, and the road to peace was paved.

The *maggid* alternated the location of his sermons, one time speaking in the Menachem Tzyon Synagogue and another in Sukkas Shalom. In this way, he welded together the opposing sides. Rav Nasan Nata, Rav of the Menachem Tzyon Shul, came to listen at the Sukkas Shalom Synagogue, and Rav Yeshaya Bardaky, Rav of Sukkas Shalom, reciprocated by going to the Menachem Tyzon Shul.

Furthermore, Rav Rivlin instituted a *moatzah ha'gedolah* (council of leaders) comprising the following rabbis: Rav Yosef Zundel of Salant, Rav Yeshaya Bardaky, Rav Nasan Nata, and Rav Asher Lemil. All communal issues of the *yishuv* fell under their jurisdiction. Its membership would change four times over the next several decades, but its tasks would remain essentially the same.[5]

In the same way, he reshuffled the *beis din*. The previous Chief Rabbi, his brother, Rav Eliyahu Rivlin, stepped aside for Rav Shmuel Salant, as did Rav Zundel of Salant. Rav Salant would remain in this post for the next seventy years. Rav Eliyahu went on to become the head of the Perushim Kollel.

The *maggid's* charisma had an impact on the Sephardim as well, and they, too, came to hear him speak. As a result of his unique rapport with all groups of the Jewish community, he succeeded in establishing a *vaad ha'achdus* (Committee for Unity), comprising Ashkenazim and Sephardim. Slowly, the friction between the two major *kehillos* of the city subsided.

Rav Rivlin utilized his position as emissary of peace to convince the Sephardim to reduce the debts owed them by their Ashkenazic neighbors by a third. Generally speaking, the Sephardim were in a higher income bracket, due to their well-organized system of *shelichus,* which extended throughout the Mediterranean basin. The *maggid's* genuine love of his fellowman won the hearts of everyone, particularly the Rishon l'Tzyon, Rav Avraham Gagin, and Rav Yaakov Entebbe.

On Lag b'Omer, 1842 (5602), the Perushim's Talmud Torah, originally in the *chatzer* of Rav Hillel Rivlin, moved to larger quarters in the Churvah complex. In the special dedication ceremony, the *maggid*, a gifted composer and musician, played the fiddle and led the joyous Perushim with one of his inspiring compositions.

In the last chapter, we saw that one source of friction between the Ashkenazic and Sephardic communities was that the Sephardim had a monopoly on religious services in the city. This was because only the Sephardic community had official sanction in the eyes of the Sultan. However, due to the change in climate in the empire, this was no longer the case. Rav Rivlin, hoping to solidify a firm and independent community, took advantage of the Sultan's willingness to reform and invested his energies in establishing separate religious institutions for the Ashkenazim. One of his successes in this endeavor was to create a *chevrah kaddishah*, a burial society, independent of the Sephardim. Land was purchased on the Mount of Olives with a donation from Mrs. Devorah Falk of Kenigsberg that was specifically given for this purpose. It was permitted for a foreigner to purchase land for a cemetery since it was essential for the Jewish community at large. Initially, the Sephardim opposed the move, but over the next few years they came to terms with the new reality.

An Added Dimension

The biggest hurdle facing Rav Moshe was the housing problem. Two avenues of action were undertaken, one concerning the area within the city walls and the other concerning the area outside them. Inside the walls there were deserted Jewish houses that had been confiscated by crafty Moslems. They cleverly scraped away the name of the Jewish landowner on the document of sale and filled in their own name in its place. The authorities, handsomely bribed, were accomplices to the crime. Rav Rivlin worked so aggressively to redeem these houses that his life was threatened. Once, while he was walking outside, Arab kidnappers approached Rav Moshe from behind. They covered his head with a burlap sack and started to whisk him away. Just then, a group of *anshei gevardiah*, the Jewish patrol, came into sight. They immediately attacked the kidnappers and beat them up. Fear of Moslem reprisals kept tensions high in the wake of this incident, until the *anshei gevardiah* kidnapped a member of a leading Moslem family.[6]

The second tactic focused on expanding outside the city's walls. As we mentioned previously, in 1845 the Perushim leaders charted a plan of expansion outside the city walls. With money from a special fund, land was purchased near the English consulate, and a wall was erected as a first step to building houses. However, shortly after this, the Sultan issued his prohibition against all land purchases by foreign citizens outside the city walls. The decree would only be repealed seventeen years later.

The *maggid*'s efforts on behalf of the community helped them survive an era of weakness and disjointedness.* However, he was taken from his people only a few short years after his arrival in the Holy City. On the last Shabbos of the year 5607 (1847), he addressed the community. In the course of his speech, he quoted the verse: "Behold, your time has come to die" (*Deuteronomy* 31:14). He then went on to beseech his fellow Jews to continue with the building of Jerusalem and to remain united. Later that day, in his house, he passed away.

* See story, "Jerusalem Blood Libel," in *Bygone Days: 1840–1870*.

The 1840s

In the wake of the Damascus blood libel of 1840, the Sultan gave more attention to his Jewish subjects. An influential Jew from Constantinople, Count Avraham de Kamundo, played an instrumental part in procuring a firman from the Sultan which bestowed the status of Chacham Bashi ("Leading Wise Man") on the Rishon l'Tzyon. The firman was written in gold letters on a huge folio measuring one meter long by half a meter wide, its borders decorated with silk tapestry. The emissary who delivered the firman remained in Jerusalem to ensure that the citizens of the city accorded the Chacham Bashi the honor due him.[7]

Chacham Bashi

The Sultan's *firman* did not merely confer a change in title. The status of the Chacham Bashi affected the Rishon l'Tzyon personally and the entire Jewish community of Jerusalem as well.

For generations, the Sephardim elected a religious leader, called the Rishon l'Tzyon, whose tasks equaled that of the Chief Rabbi of the Ashkenazim. A lifetime appointee, he acted as the spiritual guide for the Jewish community.

The Chacham Bashi's power now extended beyond the courtroom of the *beis din*. His decisions could not be overturned by Turkish civil courts; they were final and absolute. His power to excommunicate and punish any wayward Jew was supreme, and he could only be brought to court in the Ottoman capital. He was responsible for seeing that the Jews paid their annual head tax to the Turkish government. In times of need, he could turn directly to the High Gate of the Sultan's court, thereby saving precious time in an emergency.

Wherever he walked, a Turkish sentry preceded him with an ivory-tipped staff. His attire projected nobility: his black robe was embroidered with gold thread over the chest, and his turban was also decorated with gold thread. In front of his house stood two sentries, and another ten Turkish soldiers patrolled the Jewish Quarter around the clock to make sure the area was safe for him. This inaugurated a new state of peace between the ethnic groups of the city, and for the first time in generations, the Jews felt more relaxed in their own city.

The Chacham Bashi with Turkish guard

Foreign consuls respected the Chacham Bashi, and they brought any matter dealing with the Jewish people to his attention. Additionally, once every month, all the scholars of the city met with him. Finally, at the conclusion of the Day of Atonement, he was escorted home by the scholars as a sign of respect.

The combination of foreign consuls protecting their citizenry and the Rishon l'Tzyon's accreditation as Chacham Bashi created a new status quo in the Holy City. The author of *Shaarei Yerushalayim* wrote: "Now there is greater freedom for the Jews than ever before. If a Moslem even utters a disgraceful word to a Jew, he can be reprimanded for it. The Sultan has decreed a law of equality throughout the empire. Today one may be imprisoned for cursing a Jew."[8]

Though graft, crime, and violence could not be entirely erased, the Ottoman Empire was taking major steps to curb them — especially when they were aimed at the Jewish minority.

Throughout the remainder of Turkish rule over Eretz Yisrael, seven sages held the position of Chacham Bashi. They were: Rav Avraham Gagin (1842–1848), Rav Yitzchak Kobo (1848–1854), Rav Chaim Nisim Abulafia (1854–1861), Rav David Chazan (1861–1869), Rav Avraham Ashkenazi (1869–1880), Rav Meir Panijel (1880–1892), and Rav Yaakov Shaul Elyashar (1892–1906).

Rav Avraham Gagin

Born into a rabbinical family of Constantinople in 1787 (5547), Rav Gagin was an acknowledged master in both Halachah and Kabbalah. He grew up in Jerusalem, studying in Toldos Yitzchak Yeshivah. He later sat on the *beis din* of Rav Yehudah Navon and wrote a book of responsa entitled *Chukei Chaim*. After his first wife passed away, he married the daughter of Rav Avraham Sharabi, the head of Beis El Yeshivah. When Rav Sharabi died in 1827, he became the head of Beis El and was known as Rabban Chassidim. In keeping with the hundred-year-old tradition, he moved into the apartment in the Beis El building in which Rav Shalom Sharabi had lived. Through his wife, he inherited the vast library of the Sharabi family. It contained thousands of volumes, including seventy hand-written manuscripts by Rav Shalom Sharabi himself.

Rav Avraham Gagin (1787–1848)

Rav Yaakov Entebbe, who suffered tremendously at the hands of his persecutors during the Damascus blood libel of 1840, chose to spend his last years in the Holy City. Arriving before Passover, 1841, he spent the holiday as the guest of Rav Gagin. He wrote: "Just last year I was in the deepest misery. Every night during the festival of Passover I was in their clutches, under cross-examination in an attempt to make me a denier of the faith... Now, the Lord, praised be He, has saved me from Egypt [the place of bondage], and brought me to Jerusalem, the city of God, to rejoice in the festival with rabbis of the city. The Seder night I joined Rav Gagin, and together with his sons, I felt the fullness of the Festival of Redemption."[9]

These two men were very supportive of the Ashkenazic community and did everything they could to help relieve their European brethren's difficult plight. Indeed, Rav Entebbe became so close to the Perushim that he engaged his daughter to one of them — an occurrence that, while not unheard of, was all too rare. Rav Gagin worked together with Rav Moshe Rivlin to bridge the gap between the two *kehillos*. When a heated disagreement between the Sephardim of Hebron and the Chabad Chassidim of that city was brought to the Chacham Bashi for a compromise, Rav Gagin successfully negotiated a bilateral settlement satisfactory to both parties.

The Rishon l'Tzyon inaugurated a special fund for women called *Kupas Kiryas Chana*. Chana referred to the three most important mitzvos that women fulfill (חנ"ה = חלה, נדה, הדלקה), separating challah from the dough, fulfilling the laws of family purity, and lighting the Shabbos candles. Whenever a women fulfilled one of these three mitzvos, she would place a coin in a box. Periodically, the boxes would be collected and the money used for charitable needs of the community.

In 1845 (5605), the Chacham Bashi married his son, Rav Shlomo Moshe Chai, to the daughter of the Rav of Tiberias, Rav Chaim Nisim Abulafia. The wedding, held in the Holy City, was a gala event. Afterward, due to various considerations, Rav Abulafia decided to remain permanently in Jerusalem. In 1854, he became the Chacham Bashi.

The Beck Publishing House[10]

Rav Gagin recognized the need for a Jewish publishing house, which until then was non-existent in Eretz Yisrael. Rav Yisrael Beck had attempted to open a printing shop in Safed during the 1830s, but the venture ended in failure when his wooden press was destroyed by Druse rioting against Ibrahim Pasha. When Rav Beck moved to Jerusalem, Rav Gagin encouraged him to open a publishing house in the Holy City. Rav Beck turned to Sir Moses Montefiore for help in 1839. Sir Moses promised to send a new press from England, which arrived in 1841. It was a Clymers and Dixon (London) offset press, the newest model of the day.

In those days, it was necessary to procure a *firman* from the Sultan in order to operate a printing press anywhere in the Ottoman Empire. The Chacham Bashi used his influence to expedite the process, and very shortly, permission was granted. Furthermore, Rav Gagin strengthened the Beck press by officially prohibiting the establishment of any other Jewish print shops in the Holy City for a period of twenty years. Also, as a form of copyright protection for the author and publisher, Rav Gagin forbade any other printer in the world from reprinting the new books for a period of ten years. This latter measure was a common procedure in those times.

Model of the Beck printing press

Known as the Beck Press, Rav Beck's shop was officially called Masa'as Moshe and Yehudis ("The Gift of Moses and Judith") after the generous patrons who donated the printing press. With renewed enthusiasm, the fledgling publisher printed the Chida's *Avodas HaKodesh*, followed by other classical and modern works. Lady Judith Montefiore asked Rav Beck to print a set of festival *machzorim* for her. In 1844 he sent her the leather-bound copies, which she prayed from until her passing some twenty years later.

Around this time, there was a surge of manuscripts written about the holiness of Eretz Yisrael. In 1844, Rav Beck published *Chibas Yerushalayim* by Rav Chaim Horowitz of Jerusalem, with approbations by Rav Gagin and Rav Entebbe. The following year, he published Rav Yosef Schwartz's *Tevuos HaAretz*, and in 1852, *Tuv Jerusalem*, authored by a member of Rav Gagin's *beis din*, Rav Yitzchak Parchi.

Sir Moses' Humility

Sir Moses Montefiore had met with Rav Gagin in 1839, on his second trip to Eretz Yisrael. After Rav Gagin became Chacham Bashi, the two were in close contact concerning communal issues in the Holy City. A certain incident concerning one of these issues reflected Sir Moses' God-fearing attitude.

Unfortunately, the problem of Christian missionaries seducing innocent Jews in Jerusalem was an old scourge — even in the ostensibly benign surroundings of a Christian hospital — and was countered by various activists. However, at this time, a relatively new danger began to rear its head, as secular Jews from overseas began marshaling efforts to open various institutions in the Holy City. As this was a relatively new phenomenon, these sly tricksters had many opportunities to convince unsuspecting people of goodwill to support their endeavors.

In 1844 (5604), a group of European secularists planned to open a hospital in Jerusalem. For such a noble project, they naturally tried to enlist the aid of Sir Moses Montefiore, the benefactor of the Jewish people. Sir Moses, having firsthand knowledge of the health problems in Jerusalem, innocently agreed to support them.

The reaction from Jerusalem came in the form of a personal letter from the Chacham Bashi to Montefiore. Even something as beneficial as a hospital posed a grave danger as long as secular Jews controlled and operated it. All the *rabbanim* of the Holy City stood united in their opposition to it. Realizing his mistake, Sir Moses retracted his pledge and wrote an apology to Rav Gagin.

Dated 21 Tamuz, 5604, Sir Montefiore's letter read (in part):

...From the moment I read [your] letter [of the Rishon l'Tzyon] and saw your warning that they [the secularists] may try to mislead those who come to Jerusalem to go astray from the right path, I became panic-stricken. Therefore, I relinquished my hold from either doing good or bad for their hospital project.

You dwell in the heart of our Holy City, and certainly see the pros and cons of the situation and how it might affect our Jewish brethren better than me.

I have mentioned before that my sole purpose is to raise the banner of Torah on high. My prayer is that He will plant His fear in our hearts, guarding us from straying after dangerous persuasions.

Furthermore, I want to make it clear that I have no intention of backing any school in Jerusalem where both the students and the teachers are not fully controlled by the sages of Jerusalem, as they feel fit. I know that the leaders of the city are capable of guiding our sons and daughters in the right way....[11]

Amending the Chalukah System[12]

In 1849 (5609), the Ashkenazim revamped their *chalukah* system. As we have mentioned before, the *chalukah* was the backbone of the Jewish *yishuv* in Eretz Yisrael. Due to the financial support that was provided by Jews throughout the world, the Jews in Eretz Yisrael managed to survive.

With the ever-growing needs of the expanding population, a proposal was adopted to subdivide the Ashkenazim into various *kollelim*. Each of these groups represented an area in Europe and Russia where the individuals of that *kollel* emigrated from. The assumption behind the new arrangement was that the Jews of a given geographical area would probably be more enthusiastic about supporting immigrants who came from their area rather than simply giving to the *yishuv* as a whole.

The Perushim subdivided into seven such *kollelim*: Reisen, Minsk, Vilna, Poland, Pinsk Horodna, and Holland; and the Chassidim subdivided into four: Chabad, Poland, Volhynia, and Hungary. The idea worked well, and a marked increase of funds flowed into the *yishuv*. In time, other *kollelim* were created, such as Kollel Warsaw and Kollel America.

Over the decades to come, other amendments were made in the structure of the *chalukah* system, with varying degrees of success. This subdivision, however, continues to be an integral part of how the *chalukah* system functions in its modern-day form.

The Austrian Post Office, located inside the Jaffa Gate, was the principal means by which the chalukah reached the Yishuv

The Right of Self-Identity

Jerusalem in the mid-nineteenth century had one of the fastest-growing Jewish populations in the world. This population was far from homogenous; with its mixture of Jews from various cultural backgrounds, Jerusalem was truly the crossroads of the world. At that time, the Perushim outnumbered every other group by three to one. However, the Sephardim, whose uninterrupted roots went back much further, and who, until recently, had comprised the pre-eminent segment of the Jewish population — both numerically and otherwise — regarded their ancient hold on the city with aristocratic pride. Finally, there were the Moroccans and the Chassidim.

Although they were Sephardic and Ashkenazic respectively in their ethnic origins, both of them nevertheless formed distinct sub-groups in the populace. Until this time both of these communities lived in the shadows of their parent cultures. Now, however, they would become independent congregations unto themselves.

The Moroccan Congregation[13]

Sephardic Jewry is generally classified as those Jews living along the Mediterranean basin, from Spain, France, Italy, and Greece on the northern shores of the Mediterranean, to Morocco, Egypt, Eretz Yisrael, and Lebanon on the southern shores. Eretz Yisrael, standing at the hub of the spiritual world, attracted Jews of all backgrounds. One group, called Morishkas, claimed a foothold in the Holy Land since the time of the destruction of the Second Temple. This indigenous group, small in number, had all but disappeared by the nineteenth century. They had completely integrated into the general Sephardic community.

As a rule, whenever a Jew came from the Mediterranean basin, he automatically integrated into the existing Sephardic community. However, there were several exceptions to this, notably the Moroccans, the Jews of Constantinople, and the Yemenites. The Jews of Constantinople, generally well-to-do, built their own synagogue and retained the flavor of their original home community. The Moroccans, on the other hand, were poor and leaderless, and had to submit to the powerful Sephardic *kehil-*

lah, which had a vested self-interest in remaining as homogenous as possible. Yet, the Moroccans persisted in keeping to themselves, and desired to retain their native customs and express them in an open manner.

The Moroccan community had a long, rich history, especially in the wake of the Spanish Expulsion, when such great scholars as Rav Yaakov Berav and the Radvaz sojourned in the country. Morocco produced several *gedolim* of note, such as Rav Chaim Attar, and such noble families as the Azulai (the Chida), the Toledano and Abuchatzera (the Babba Sali), to name but a few.

By 1840 (5600), the Moroccan Jewish population in the Holy City numbered in the hundreds. Mostly in the lowest income bracket, they lived in overcrowded, shabby conditions. Some of the aged Moroccans spent their time at the Kosel, hoping a visitor would give them a coin.

As they were officially part of the Sephardic ethnic grouping, they received funding from the Sephardic *chalukah*. However, they felt an urgent need to set up their own *chalukah* system, in order that funding could be channeled directly to them from Morocco. This would both give them the autonomy they desired and increase the support they so desperately needed — in a manner similar to that of the Ashkenazic subdivision. The Sephardim flatly opposed the suggestion, fearing a loss of funding and authority.

As their numbers grew, the Moroccans' need to express their self-identity correspondingly kept apace and demanded an outlet. In 1848, their quasi-leader, Rav Moshe Turjeman, together with his son Rav Yaakov, clandestinely sent a *shaliach* to Morocco to collect for their *kehillah*. From one angle, the mission was a huge success, as the *shaliach* returned with some substantial donations. However, there were serious repercussions as well. When word of what the Turjemans had done eventually got out, the ensuing negative backlash from the Sephardic establishment nearly toppled over the weak *kehillah*.

The Moroccan Tzaddik

About five years later, in 1854 (5614), a twenty-eight-year-old tzaddik emigrated from Morocco to the Holy City. Rav David Ben-Shimon, a *talmid chacham* of distinction, stunned his students and colleagues when he announced his plans to move to Jerusalem. His love of Eretz Yisrael burned inside him day and night, and as soon as he set foot in Jerusalem, he delved into the laws and customs of the Land. The outcome of his studies came in the form of several books, the most famous one of which was entitled *Shaar HaChatzer*, "Gate of the Courtyard."

Rav David lived in the Moroccan Quarter. His fervent desire was to remain obscure and anonymous, so that he could dedicate his life to Torah study. However, his wish was not destined to be fulfilled. The first one to reveal his greatness was Rav Yehudah Pappo, whose father authored *Pelei Yoetz*. Once, while Rav Yehudah lay seriously ill in bed, the *chachmei Yerushalayim* came to visit him and offer words of encouragement. Due to his weakness, Rav Yehudah was unable to rise for any of them. However,

נכבדות מדובר בך עיר האלהים סלה : יפה נוף משוש כל הארץהר ציון ירכתי צפון קרית מלך רב

אחת שאלתי מאת ה' אותה אבקש שבתי בבית ה' כל ימי חיי לחזות בנועם ה' ולבקר בהיכלו

ספר

שערי צדק

ומישם יפרד והיה לארבעה ראשים : שער החצר :
שער המטרה : שער הקרים : שער המפקד :
הן הן הדברים : על ארני היראה והמוסר מחוברים :

שער החצר

כשמו כן הוא בס"ר במדב"ר נבא רב הקדמות מרז"ל מהמפרסים הם המדברים · מתעלות אדמת הקדש לנו לעינים וראשי מיברים · בו ימלאו טפש לנפשם המסתופפים בחגרות ה' ימירו כמאורי · אתיא תוך תוך מעלות במספר תרי"ג פקודי ה' ישרים · ומגב אסיפ"א מה שחנן ה' את עבדו קול מרים · קרי חדא ופרי תלת · מדלג על ההרים · לא לחכמים לחם המה הגבורים · כי אם להילדים אשר כגילי להם לבדם נתנה האר"ם ויתר הדברים · הרימותי ידי ל ה' בעלתו ינחני יוריני מדרכיו הטובים והישרים · ילילני מלעג השאננים קנאים פוגעים אך סוררים · יחזירם למיטב לעבדו שכם אחד יישר העוברים · ובא לציון גואל בן ישי חי במליל ובשירים :

נדפס ע"י הרב השיש וכו' מוהר"ר ישראל ב"ק ס"ט
על מכבש הדפוס תפארת משה ויהודית ס"ט
תחת ממשלת אדונינו החסיד סולטן עבד איל עזיז יר"ה

פה עה"ק ירושלים תובב"א

שנת ברכת ה' היא תעשיר לפ"ק

Title page of the first edition of Shaar HaChatzer *(1862)*

as soon as he gazed on the Moroccan tzaddik, he immediately jumped out of bed and stood upright before him. Everyone present gaped in puzzlement and waited for Rav Yehudah to unravel the mystery for them.

After Rav Ben-Shimon left, Rav Pappo explained, “Please don’t be offended, my dear companions, that I didn’t rise up for you. As you can see, I am suffering tremendously and I’m very weak. However, as soon as this young Moroccan *rav* crossed the threshold, I received a Heavenly message that he was a tzaddik, and I should make every effort to stand before him. Therefore, I girded myself with every ounce of strength left in me and stood up.”[14]

Rav Ben-Shimon could no long cloister himself, and day by day, more and more people came to his house for advice and halachic rulings. Unable to refuse them, he empathized, aided, and gave his halachic decision to everyone who sought him out. Soon the Moroccan tzaddik took up the cause of his Moroccan brethren and became the leader they so desperately needed.

The incident which awakened Rav Ben-Shimon to his mission was not directly related to the myriad problems facing the community. He was initially galvanized into action by the slight given to a Rav's honor at his funeral. Rav Yosef Elimelech, a native Moroccan, had spent his last years in Jerusalem, after decades of service as Rav of Mogador, Morocco. In addition to his rabbinic duties, Rav Yosef Elimelech had amassed a fortune through international trading. At his funeral, the Sephardic *chevrah kaddishah*, thinking he had left a substantial amount for his heirs, demanded a much larger sum than required by taxation before agreeing to proceed with the service. In truth, he had lost most of his wealth before immigrating, and his sons were unable to pay the fee.

When Rav Ben-Shimon heard of the dilemma, he saw it as a severe insult to the honor of the deceased. It was forbidden to forestall the burial over the issue of payment. Likewise, he interpreted it as a threat to the Moroccan drive for self-esteem and independence.

Without hesitation, he forcefully led the funeral possession to the Mount of Olives. He withstood a confrontation there and buried the Rav of Mogador with all the honor due him.[15]

A Leader of His People

By 1860 (5620), Rav David Ben-Shimon (known by the acronym, Rav HaDevash) had succeeded in firmly establishing a Moroccan *kehillah*. He single-handedly oversaw every aspect of the development and growth of the community. They had their own synagogue, *mikve*, *talmud Torah*, yeshivah, and various other institutions. Furthermore, a compromise with the Sephardim allowed them to send emissaries to Morocco on a permanent basis.

Sensitive to the needs of the poor, Rav Ben-Shimon opened a butcher shop which catered exclusively to them. Meat was prohibitively expensive for most Moroccans, and at best they could only afford the bones. Now, they were able to purchase the loin cut. Though it was not considered a choice cut, it provided the protein that people so desperately needed.

He selected Rav Elazar Tuvo as Rosh Yeshivah. When Rav Ben-Shimon passed away, Rav Tuvo would become the Rav of the Moroccans. At the same time, Rav David's son, Rav Raphael Aharon Ben-Shimon, the future Chief Rabbi of Cairo, would replace Rav Tuvo as Rosh Yeshivah.

By 1866 (5626), the Moroccan network of projects and institutions had expanded to such an extent that Rav Ben-Shimon created a committee of seven *rabbanim* to supervise the community's affairs along with him. This freed him for other tasks, such as traveling to various cities where he spoke and aided immigrant families.*

During Sir Moses Montefiore's sixth visit in 1866, Rav Ben-Shimon met with the renowned philanthropist to discuss the Moroccan cause. At that meeting, Sir Montefiore requested a report of all the community's institutions and welfare societies. Based on the report, Sir Moses would be able to assess their needs and respond accordingly.

* See story, "Saving a Soul," in *Bygone Days: 1840–1870*.

Beyond the financial aid engendered for the community, this meeting had other important consequences as well. Several years earlier, Sir Moses had funded the first attempted Jewish settlement in Eretz Yisrael. Located near Jaffa, it was called Beira (now known as Gan Montefiore). It had initially failed due to overwhelming hardships and dangers faced by the settlers. Now, Sir Moses foresaw a chance of beginning it anew. Aware of the ruggedness of the Moroccan Jews and their fluency in Arabic, he discussed with Rav Ben-Shimon the possibility of having Moroccans man the settlement. Rav David responded positively to the idea, and shortly thereafter, five families moved to Beira filled with the enthusiastic ideal to become self-supportive through working the land.[16]

Rav Raphael Ben-Shimon (1847–1929)

A decade later, when Montefiore made his final trip to Eretz Yisrael, he landed at the Jaffa port and was very eager to see his new settlement. In the interim, unconfirmed reports had reached London that this second attempt had also failed. His heart was filled with joy and relief when he saw that the Moroccans had succeeded, and that the orchards were under good care.[17]*

Rav Ben-Shimon was held in high esteem by all factions of the Jewish community. He discussed communal and halachic matters with the Rishon l'Tzyon and with the leaders of the Ashkenazim, Rav Shmuel Salant and Rav Meir Auerbach. In 1874, a controversy erupted around these two great Ashkenazic leaders concerning their uncompromising stance for the purity of the *yishuv,* which was being threatened by a malicious report from England. Rav HaDevash came out in their defense, as did the Rishon l'Tzyon.

On 18 Kislev, 1879 (5640), Rav Ben-Shimon passed away, at the age of fifty–four. Jerusalemites were shocked by the news of such a vibrant, loving leader being snatched from them in his prime. The funeral procession was the largest in many years, reflecting his reputation as a peacemaker who had few enemies.

* See story, "By the Work of Your Hands," in *Bygone Days: 1870–1900*.

Entrance to the Tzuf Devash Synagogue (in the Moslem Quarter)

In the quarter of a century (1854–1879) in which he gave himself over to helping his Moroccan brethren, Rav Ben-Shimon dramatically helped to shape them into a vibrant community, capable of retaining their unique heritage. From the foundation stones which he laid, they would be able to thrive and expand in the future. Later, the community's main synagogue was renamed Tzuf Devash, after the tzaddik who built up the congregation as a labor of love.

The First Chassidic Dynasty[18]

During the 1700s, Chassidim, more than any other Ashkenazic group, had immigrated to Eretz Yisrael in large numbers. They settled in Safed and Tiberias, but not in Jerusalem, for fear of punishment by militant Moslems who considered all Ashkenazim as their debtors since the time of Rav Yehudah HaChassid and his followers.

Even with the great influx of three hundred Chassidim led by Rebbe Menachem Mendel of Vitebsk in 1777, Chassidim visited the Holy City only rarely. Rav Gershon Kitover, who disguised himself as a Sephardi and actually lived in the Holy City, was an outstanding exception.

In the first half of the nineteenth century, until after the earthquake of 1837, only a handful of Chassidim lived in the city — even though the debt had been erased and Ashkenazim could legally live there. The most famous of these was the author of *Chibas Yerushalayim*, Rav Chaim Horowitz. Rav Aharon Moshe of Brody, the first unofficial leader of the Chassidim in Jerusalem, was a disciple of the Seer of Lublin. In his will, he expressed his love of Jerusalem and warned all those who wished to settle there to be exceedingly careful in their conduct.*

With the passing of Rav Aharon Moshe, Rav Yisrael Beck and his son Rav Nisan Beck acted as the focal point of the Chassidic community. Their labors were directed at enriching Jerusalem with a more Chassidic atmosphere. They were men of action and responsibility who wished to sit in the shade of the Chassidic masters, but who were forced by circumstances to assume a leadership role. With their efforts, the small foothold Chassidus had in the Holy City was strengthened.

The Lelov dynasty had the distinction of becoming the first Chassidic dynasty to flower in Jerusalem. The aged Lelover

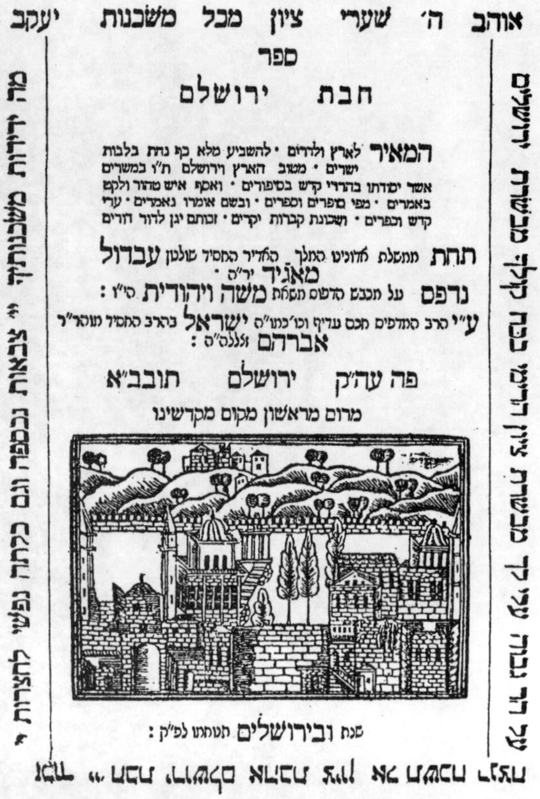
אוהב ה׳ שערי ציון מכל משכנות יעקב

ספר

חבת ירושלם

המאיר לארץ ולדרים · להשביע מלא כף נחת בלבות ישרים · מטוב הארץ וירושלם ת״ו במשרים אשר יסדתו בהררי קדש בסיפורים · ואסף איש טהור ולקט באמרים · מפי סופרים וספרים · ובשם אומרו נאמרים · ערי קדש וכפרים · ושכונת קברות יקרים · זכותם יגן לדור הורים

תחת ממשלת אדונינו המלך האדיר החסיד שולטן עבדול מאגיד יר״ה ·

נדפס על מכבש הדפוס מעלת משה ויהודית ס״ו :

ע״י הרב המדפיס מכס עדיף וכו׳ כמו״ה ישראל בהרב החסיד מוהר״ר אברהם זללה״ה :

פה עה״ק ירושלם תובב״א

מרום מראשון מקום מקדשינו

Title page of Chibas Yerushalayim, *printed in Jerusalem by Rav Beck in 1844*

Rebbe, Rebbe Moshe Biderman, had yearned to travel to Jerusalem for thirteen years. He dreamt of standing before the Wailing Wall and blowing the shofar, as if to usher in a new era in world history. Before leaving Russia in 1850, he traveled with his entourage from city to city to collect funds. In some cities, thousands came to greet the venerated tzaddik.

The Ruzhiner Rebbe, famous for his deep love of Eretz Yisrael, presented Rebbe Moshe with a silver plate for a *sefer Torah*.[19] When they parted, the Ruzhiner Rebbe blessed him with these words: "Both Rebbe Menachem Mendel of Vitebsk and Rebbe Avraham of Kalisk

* See story, "The 2,500-Year-Old Apology," in *Bygone Days: 1840–1870*.

went to Eretz Yisrael, but did not build a dynasty that continued after them. My blessing to you is that you will build a dynasty in Eretz Yisrael, and that it will continue until the Mashiach."[20]

The Lelover Dynasty

After Sukkos, 1850 (5611), Rebbe Moshe Biderman reached Jerusalem with his two sons, Rav Elazer Mendel and Rav Yitzchak David, and his six-year-old grandson, David. The elderly Rebbe Moshe, frail and sick, urged his sons to take him to the Western Wall without delay. Supporting him on their shoulders, they wound their way down to the Wall, hoping to utter praises to the Almighty there. Suddenly, some Moslem ruffians threw stones at them, forcing them to retreat. That same day, 13 Teves, Rebbe Moshe passed away.

For decades to come, Rebbe Moshe's *yartzeit* held a certain importance in the life of Jerusalemite Jews. Until his death, whenever it seemed that a drought was threatening, a communal fast was automatically proclaimed, as soon as possible. However, Rav Shmuel Salant would not declare a fast until after 13 Teves, since the rebbe had promised on his deathbed to intercede on behalf of the Jewish community in such a case — and hopefully the tzaddik's soul would awaken a merciful response in Heaven.[21]

Rebbe Moshe's son, Rebbe Elazar Mendel Biderman, followed in his father's footsteps for thirty-two years, until he passed away on the day after Shushan Purim, 1883. The new Lelover rebbe brought a fresh concept of undiluted Chassidus to Jerusalem, both in prayer and in daily activities. His long hours in supplication, especially on Rosh HaShanah, captivated Jerusalemites. Every evening he walked to the Western Wall to pray the Minchah and Maariv services. He usually finished Maariv an hour or two after everyone else had gone home. Sometimes Arabs heckled him or threw things at him, but he was oblivious to their presence.

When the Shiniver Rebbe visited Eretz Yisrael in 1870 (5630), his sojourn in Jerusalem proved to be the meeting ground where a lasting friendship developed between him and the Lelover Rebbe.[22]

Rav Elazar Mendel's sudden death at the age of fifty-four shocked and saddened the community. As Rav Akiva Shlesinger, a disciple of Rav Diskin, said, "That *motzei Shabbos* our joy vanished at the unexpected news of Rebbe Elazar Mendel's passing. He was unequaled in his manner of worship."[23]

Rebbe Elazar Mendel's son, Rav David Biderman, had been imbued with the teachings of Chassidus by his father and became the leader of the next generation. In the late 1860s, after his marriage, he traveled to Russia, where his goal was to penetrate more deeply into the world of Chassidus. In truth, when he first asked permission, his father answered, "When I have a question I go to the Kosel and come back with an answer." "True," answered Rav David. "But I need a rebbe who will answer my questions." Rav Elazar Mendel looked at his son and replied, "For someone who is worthy, the Kosel answers him. Believe me, when I say '*Gut Shabbos*' to the Kosel, I am answered!"[24]

While in Europe, Rav David met with many Admorim. However, the Karliner Rebbe, Rebbe Aharon, particularly enchanted the young tzaddik, and a close relationship formed between the two of them. Rav David Biderman's thirty-five-year reign (1883–1918) brought him into contact with all the *rabbanim* of Jerusalem, who held him in great esteem. Likewise, he had great influence on Chassidim of every type.

After his passing in 1918, his son, Rebbe Shimon Nata Nasan, became the Lelover Rebbe for the next twelve years. With his death in 1930, Rebbe Moshe Mordechai Biderman became the next link in the Lelover chain. Although he moved to Tel Aviv in 1943 to be closer to the fugitives of World War Two — and from there to Bnei Brak — he always maintained a *shetibel* in Jerusalem.

Thus, the blessing of the Ruzhiner Rebbe was fulfilled, and the Lelover dynasty still endures today.

The Chassidic Community

During the 1850s, the Chassidim formed three separate *kollelim*: Volhynia (headed by Rav Beck), Galicia (headed by Rav Moshe Shmekel Horowitz), and Chabad. A fourth one was formed later. Together, they numbered about three hundred families. In 1858, Chabad opened a shul called Beis Menachem, after Rebbe Menachem Mendel of Lubavitch. Their leader, Rav Eliyahu Yosef Rivlin (no relation to Rav Hillel and Rav Moshe Rivlin), a disciple of the Baal HaTanya, led them until he passed away in 1868. A number of Chassidei Kotzk moved to Jerusalem after their rebbe passed away in 1859. The Shiniver Rebbe, Rebbe Yechezkel Halberstam (son of the Sanzer Rebbe), visited around 1870. He came to Eretz Yisrael twice, primarily to oversee the building of the Sanz shul and *mikve* in Safed, but felt that his visit would be incomplete without touching the stones of the Holy City. His brother-in-law, Rav Naftali Chaim Horowitz, came in the late 1860s. A brilliant, eclectic, and eccentric individual with a reputation as an outstanding scholar and tzaddik, he earned the affectionate appellation of *ish pelei* — the "wonder-man" among his fellow Jerusalemites. In his intense desire to dwell near the Divine Presence, he chose to live as close to the Western Wall as possible. Concerned that ritually impure people might inadvertently defile the Temple Mount, he hung a large chain at the spot beyond which a Jew should not cross, basing his calculations on the Radvaz's measurements of the Temple Mount. This chain hung near the Shaar HaShalsheles (the Gate of Chains) in today's Moslem Quarter.

In 1869, Rav Hillel Moshe Gelbstein, a disciple of Rav Mendel of Kotzk, immigrated to Jerusalem. A tzaddik and kabbalist, he deeply felt the sanctity of the holy sites. Immediately he was inspired to study the laws of *kodashim* (Temple sacrifices), and urged others to learn these laws as well. He organized groups to study at the Wailing Wall, the tomb of Shimon HaTzaddik, and the tomb of Rachel. Rav Gelbstein led a minyan at the Wall for years, daily bringing benches and tables there, and even a *sefer Torah* when necessary. More

At the turn of the twentieth century, benches were used for the elderly at the Western Wall. Later, during the Mandate period, their use became controversial.

than this, he formulated a plan whereby he would purchase some Moslem courtyards facing the Wall and convert them into three shuls, one for the Sephardim, one for the Chassidim, and one for the Perushim. Unfortunately, his plan failed to materialize.

Later, in the 1870s, Kollel Warsaw built their own *shetibel*, called Ohel Moshe, and Chassidei Karlin followed suit around 1874. However, the place where Chassidim centered their religious activities was in the Tiferes Yisrael Synagogue. Finished in 1871, it was nearly as large as the Churvah Synagogue, and served their communal needs in the same way as the Churvah did for the Perushim.

Initially, the Chassidim had relied on the existing communal institutions of the Sephardim and Perushim for their needs. However, in the course of time they established their own institutions of learning, particularly Chayei Olam Yeshivah. In 1892, they also established their own rabbinic court.

The rancor which existed between the Chassidim and the Misnagdim in Europe was much more muted, even nonexistent, in Jerusalem. In the Holy City, the common goals of building a united Jewish community took precedence over most other considerations.

Pillars for the Future

As we noted in the last chapter, the influx of Ashkenazim — both Chassidim and Perushim — resulted in an historic upheaval within the ancient city. Jews now outnumbered Moslems, and Ashkenazim outnumbered Sephardim. It would take the city's residents — both Jewish and non-Jewish — some time to adjust to this new ethnological balance.

With Heaven's help, the reassertion of Turkish suzerainty heralded a more enlightened attitude towards the Jews by their gentile rulers and neighbors. One thing that had not measurably changed was the primitive living conditions in the Holy City. Modernization had not yet come to the Middle East, facing an implacable foe in the nightmarish maze of Ottoman bureaucracy. However, the Jews felt stronger and safer than ever before. Now, they turned their full attention on building the pillars of the future.

Light from Zion

The concept of an Ashkenazic rabbinical court became a reality in the 1840s. In the first years of the Perushim *yishuv*, they were not independent of the Sephardim, nor did they have the numbers to warrant having their own *beis din*. However, with the constant influx of immigrants, the latter situation soon changed. When Rav Zundel of Salant immigrated in 1837, an informal *beis din* with him at the head satisfied the community's need on a temporary basis. However, with the arrival of Rav Shmuel Salant, a twenty-five-year-old prodigy and the son-in-law of Rav Zundel, the scope and dimension of the *beis din* changed.

The timing of Rav Salant's move to Jerusalem was clearly Heaven-sent, benefiting both him and the city. As we noted earlier, his doctor in Volozhin had advised him to move to a warmer climate in the aftermath of a dangerous illness. Knowing that his father-in-law, Rav Zundel, would like to have him close by, he decided to come to Jerusalem. He couldn't have come at a more auspicious time, for the *yishuv* itself needed a halachic giant to stand at the head of the rabbinic court.

Living in a small, two-room flat in the Churvah complex, Rav Salant opened the *beis din* in a nearby room in 1841. Sitting with him on the rabbinic court were Rav Uri Shabbetai and Rav

Rav Shmuel Salant (1816–1909)

Binyamin David of Vilna. Rav Salant would serve as the Chief Ashkenazic Rabbi of Jerusalem for nearly seventy years.

The success of the *beis din* was a triumph for the *yishuv*. Both the Chacham Bashi and the major Jewish centers in Europe respected the *gaon* of Jerusalem and turned to him for advice.

On one of his extended trips abroad, in 1860, Rav Salant asked Rav Meir Auerbach, the Rav of Kalish, to replace him as Chief Rabbi. Rav Auerbach, who had just moved to Jerusalem, accepted. He was an outstanding scholar and author (*Imrei Binah*, responsa in halachah), and was considered one of the leading sages of the time. Upon Rav Salant's return, Rav Auerbach wanted to step down. However, Rav Salant implored him to remain in the position, claiming that his own time and energy were needed in other areas of the *yishuv*. Rav Meir Auerbach acquiesced. He subsequently relocated the *beis din* to another site in the Jewish Quarter, in the courtyard where he resided. With Rav Auerbach's passing in 1878, the post returned to Rav Shmuel Salant. This time he held the post until his death in 1909.

Etz Chaim Yeshivah[25]

Education has always taken strong precedence in every Jewish community, serving to link the generations in an unbroken chain winding back to the time of Moses at Mount Sinai. Until relatively recent times, free education was unknown, and the burden of support fell on the parents and the community.

In the 1840s and 1850s, the Perushim galvanized themselves to overcome the hurdles they faced in setting up an official educational system. A lack of physical space and funding were the foremost obstacles. They began by setting up classes in the women's gallery of the Menachem Tzyon Synagogue. They then proceeded to send urgent letters to Vilna concerning the needs of the *yishuv*. The response was positive, and a new fund was created whereby parents were subsidized according to their income bracket. Orphans received full scholarships. Soon another classroom opened, but due to lack of space in the Churvah complex, the organizers were forced to rent space outside the premises.

ספר
אמרי בינה
חלק ראשון
חידושים ליורה דעה
ובסופו קונטרס
מאות שאלות ותשובות
נדפס
פעה"ק ירושלם תובב"א

Title page of Imrei Bimah *(Jerusalem, 1871)*

In 1850, Rav Shmuel Salant traveled to Vilna to raise funds for the *yishuv*. At that time, there was a committee in the Lithuanian city that oversaw the assignment of funds to be directed to the Holy Land. Rav Salant presented a plan for setting up a *beis ulpana* for higher education (what we would call a yeshivah today) to the board of directors. The plan met with their approval and, moreover, they nominated Rav Salant as Rosh Yeshivah.

Upon his return to Jerusalem, Rav Salant quickly organized the yeshivah, selecting the more serious students in the community, and began delivering regular Gemara lectures in the Menachem Tzyon Synagogue.

The success of these endeavors brought more students, and, of course, a bigger drain on economic resources. By 1854, the situation had reached the breaking point. A reappraisal of the education system brought a new idea to light. It was decided to create a *mosad*, an official institution, to which money could be funneled directly. By enlisting donors and patrons, a solid foundation for the future would be ensured.

On 18 Sivan, 1855, the institution called Etz Chaim was born. Rav Yeshaya Bardaky and Rav Shmuel Salant jointly headed it. There was a *mashgiach* to personally supervise each student's progress, and rebbes to teach each class. According to a communal by-law, schooling was mandatory until the age of bar mitzvah, at which time the boy was examined. If his abilities pointed to areas other than learning, he was no longer subsidized. Instead, the yeshivah sent him to be apprenticed in a profession and made sure that he still maintained a schedule of study in the afternoon. On the other hand, if a boy showed promise in his studies, he entered the yeshivah.

In the first attempt to centralize the yeshivah, Rav Salant moved it to the newly built Shaarei Tzyon Synagogue across the way from the Churvah.

In 1856 (5616), Rav Moshe Yehudah Leib of Kotna, author of *Zayis Ra'anan*, settled in Jerusalem. He displayed a more than cursory interest in the yeshivah, throwing all his energies into strengthening it. He was soon giving a daily lecture in the afternoon, while Rav Salant continued to give his lecture in the morning. One of Rav Yehudah Leib's closest disciples was a young genius from Hebron, Rav Tzvi Michel Shapiro. The Rav and his prodigal student spent long hours together delving into Torah topics. Rav Shapiro later became a close comrade with Rav Yosef Chaim Zonnenfeld.

The following year another *gaon*, Rav Shimon Zarchi, moved to the Holy City. He lived with Rav Shmuel Salant for several months while searching for an apartment near the Churvah. Rav Zarchi's involvement in and commitment to the educational system was total, from joining the board of directors to personally shouldering some of the economic burden. He discovered the weak spots in the structure: classrooms were scattered throughout the Jewish Quarter, and there was a need for better organization in the *yeshivah ketanah*. Rav Zarchi devised a plan to centralize the entire institution by obtaining houses in the Churvah complex.

Rav Zarchi's plan was successful. The newly organized institution was named Etz Chaim Yeshivah. Included in the staff was Rav Eliezer Dan Ralbag, a native Jerusalemite who quickly rose under the tutelage of Rav Salant to become a dynamic *rav* in the yeshivah.

By the time Rav Zarchi passed away in 1860, the yeshivah was a flourishing institution, with philanthropists like Rav David Reiss donating money to build an extension. Rav Zarchi, who died while studying in the yeshivah on 9 Elul, was eulogized as "one who dies in the tent [of Torah]."

From 1867 to 1886, Rav Moshe Nechemiah Kahanov stood at the helm of the yeshivah. Author of a number of halachic works, he gave lectures and supervised every aspect of the yeshivah. Though he praised sharp students and those who knew whole tractates, he was also concerned with the more average students. He placed special emphasis on *hasmadah* (constant, uninterrupted study) as the real key to success, regardless of one's innate capabilities. He would walk around the *beis midrash* and repeat, *yegatah u'matzatah*, "the one who toils will find." Through his inspiration, the level of all the students' learning excelled.*

With his passing in 1887, Rav Ralbag led the yeshivah, with Rav Salant acting as *nasi*.

A Brilliant Idea

In 1889 (5649), a visitor to the Holy City presented a simple, but brilliant idea to the directors of the yeshivah. Rav Mordechai Yaffe spent some months in the suburb called Mizkeres Moshe. (As we shall see shortly, this was at the time after the Sultan had finally allowed building outside the city walls.) Every morning he noticed groups of boys heading off to the Old City to study at the Etz Chaim Yeshivah and returning home in the evening. Some of the boys

* See story, "Yoma d'Pagra," in *Bygone Days: 1840–1870*.

wore torn and tattered shoes, and others could not keep pace with their fast-walking peers. Seeking out Rav Shmuel Salant, he broached the idea of having the yeshivah open branches in various locations in the new neighborhoods. Rav Salant agreed in principle.

That same day, a philanthropist by the name of Yehudah of Minsk, living in Mizkeres Moshe, offered to built the branch in his neighborhood.

Over the coming years, branches of Etz Chaim were established in many suburbs. They helped alleviate the pressure on the main institution in the Old City and created a better atmosphere for the students.

By the turn of the twentieth century, when Rav Eliyahu David Rabinowitch became Rosh Yeshivah, the *talmud Torah* numbered over seven hundred students, and the yeshivah had one hundred and fifty pupils who received monthly stipends. The remarkable success of the yeshivah was really the success of Jerusalem in producing a new generation of scholars and tzaddikim to forge the future and guide the populace in the ways of our forefathers.

The Lemel School[26]

In 1854 (5614), Jerusalem was confronted with a policy-making decision that would affect the type of Jewish education presented to their children. Two different approaches would square off against each other, and the results would have repercussions that continue to reverberate in present times.

In that year, a forty-five-year-old Jew from Vienna, Ludwig Frankel, came on a special mission to the Holy City. A widow from his hometown, Mrs. Hertz-Lemel, had sent him to Jerusalem to open a school for the poorer Jews as a memorial for her late father. Called the Lemel School, the institution's curriculum would include classes in foreign languages, science, and vocational skills, in addition to Torah studies. The school was to be completely free of charge. Furthermore, the children would receive food and clothing according to their needs. To ensure the success of his mission, Frankel first rallied the Emperor of Austria and the Sultan in Constantinople to his cause. What he did not anticipate, however, was that Rav Yitzchak Deutsch of Vienna, aware of Frankel's secular views, sent an advance warning to the leaders of the Jerusalem community before his arrival.

When Frankel reached Jerusalem and presented his proposal to the leaders of the community, it met with a mixed reaction. Generally, the Ashkenazim and Sephardim were split down the middle over the issue, with the Sephardim for it and the Ashkenazim against it. The Ashkenazim, headed by Rav Bardaky, presented their opposition in a mass meeting of the leaders of both communities held at the home of the Chacham Bashi.

Frankel began: "Why is it so difficult to envision the type of school I have in mind? Is it against the Law?"

The revered Rav Bardaky, with his long, white beard and *peyos*, spoke with flashing eyes. "If I understand you correctly, this 'school,' as you term it, will be a place to study something other than just Torah. Although in essence this is not something forbidden by the Torah, nevertheless, it has nearly always been a cause for suspicion within our midst. This is because when both Torah and secular subjects are taught under the same roof, the students tend to view them on an equal footing. Once the supremacy of the Torah is called into question, the path to assimilation is opened up. Haven't we already seen the terrible results of this in Europe, in the wake the emancipation and the enlightenment?"

Undeterred, Frankel replied, "My aim is to follow the orders I received in Austria and to not depart from them. Also, Mrs. Lemel is not setting up anything which could endanger children. Therefore, if you accept her proposal, I am here to finalize it."

At the end of the meeting, it was decided to take a vote. Ten of the twelve Ashkenazim opposed, and nine of ten Sephardim voted in favor. Rav Yedidiah Abulafia, head of Beis El Yeshivah, joined the Ashkenazim in their opposition.

Throughout Frankel's stay in Jerusalem, the matter was discussed and debated; the pros and cons were weighed, and the principles and repercussions were measured. In the end, the Ashkenazim rejected the school, placing a *cherem* (ban of excommunication) on it in a special ceremony conducted at the Churvah Synagogue on 9 Sivan, 1856 (5626). A *sefer Torah* was placed on the *bimah*, black candles were lit, and the *cherem* was read before a full congregation.

The Sephardim, on the other hand, accepted the school, provided that they retained complete supervision over it. Their acceptance of Frankel's offer stemmed from the fact that the Sephardic communities were generally spared the scourge of the enlightenment that had swept throughout Ashkenazic communities in Europe in the previous generation. For them, it merely represented a positive, non-threatening step to gain knowledge and better prospects for the future.[27]

Alternative Education

The Lemel School opened its doors in Tamuz, 1856. Only a few Sephardic children enrolled, while not a single Ashkenazic child attended. No long afterwards, the student body would be supplemented with gentile children. Frankel returned to Vienna flushed with triumph. However, the victory rung somewhat hollow to Mrs. Hertz-Lemel, who was disappointed that no Ashkenazic children studied there.

In the meantime, word of the impassioned dispute between Frankel and the Ashkenazim reached the Austrian consulate. The consul, Mr. Yozef Pezemano, asked the Austrian representative of Ashkenazic Jews in Eretz Yisrael, Rav Bardaky, if the Lemel School represented a divergence from Jewish tradition. Rav Bardaky's response in defense of the Ashkenazim's decision was eloquent and persuasive, and became a model for future rebuttals.

In the same year, a girls' school opened. Named the Eveline Rothschild Girls' School, its program included French, geography, and sewing. In 1864, Baron Lionel Rothschild of London enlarged and expanded the school so that it could accommodate one hundred girls. The Ashkenazim did not object to sending their daughters to this institution, since the main opposition to "schools" centered on the education of their sons.[28]

In 1866 (5626), a Frenchman by the name of Yosef Blumenthal opened a school called Doresh Tzyon under the leadership of Rav Yitzchak Prague. A disciple of the Chasam Sofer, Rav Prague grew up in Jerusalem and married a Sephardic woman. He tried in vain to convince Ashkenazic families to send their sons to his school, which incorporated Arabic into the curriculum. The level of Torah study, however, surpassed that of most others of this sort in Jerusalem.

Integrating a strong Torah study program with Arabic, Doresh Tzyon grew into the central yeshivah for the Sephardim. In 1877, Sir Montefiore sent money for Arabic language study, half to Etz Chaim and half to Doresh Tzyon. The Ashkenazim returned the money, explaining that the ban of 1856 was still in effect. Forty years later, in 1906, Rav Zonnenfeld wrote a letter of recommendation for Doresh Tzyon, recalling the good deeds of Rav Prague and his son. Some years later, however, the quality of study dropped, and of the various yeshivos of this type, Rav Zonnenfeld favored a new institution called Bnei Tzyon Yeshivah.

In the coming decades, the issue over education, in its widest sense, would surface again and again, once over the establishment of a library, and another time regarding an orphanage, as we will discuss later. Each time, the Jews of Jerusalem would review the matter and carefully weigh the effects it might have, and then voice their opinions.

The Lemel School moved in 1904 to this location, and today is a talmud Torah

The Great Churvah Synagogue[29]

In the center of the Churvah complex stood a large, empty plot, where the shul of Rabbi Yehudah HaChassid had stood. The Perushim had envisioned this site as the sacred ground upon which they would one day build a gigantic synagogue. As we have mentioned previously, their ability to transform this dream into a reality was hampered by forces beyond their control. The most difficult obstacle lay in obtaining the necessary permits from Constantinople, without which it was impossible to begin groundbreaking.

On the seventh day of Sukkos, 1854, the English ambassador to the Turkish capital, Lord Napery, visited the Jewish Quarter in the Holy City, escorted by the British consul of Jerusalem. A number of Jews living in Jerusalem had British citizenship — due to the labors of Sir Moses Montefiore on behalf of the *yishuv*. On his tour, he asked why the lot was empty, and the answer provoked him to offer his services.

He told the Ashkenazi leaders to put the request for a building permit in writing, and he would do his best to present it to the proper authorities when he returned to Constantinople.

A half a year later, Lord Napery obtained the necessary permit and quickly notified the *yishuv* in Jerusalem. On that day — 8 Av, 1855 — the sensational news spread throughout the city, raising the spirits of the entire community. The actual *firman* was hand-delivered by Sir Moses Montefiore on his fourth visit in 1857.

Fortunately, half the money to build the synagogue had already been pledged a decade earlier by a wealthy Syrian Jew by the name of Yechezkel Reuven Sasson. Although he had passed away in the interim, his sons fulfilled their father's wishes and forwarded the money without delay.

At the same time the *firman* arrived from the Turkish capital, the Sultan's architect had come to Jerusalem to oversee renovations on the Temple Mount. Taking advantage of this opportunity, the Perushim leaders presented him with sketches of what they envisioned for the synagogue. The architect promptly converted the sketches into a detailed blueprint for a magnificent edifice. Together with an engineer, he oversaw the first stages of construction.

The groundbreaking ceremony commenced on the last day of Chanukah, 1855. On 17 Nisan, 1856 (5616), the cornerstone was laid. The honor of laying the first stone was accorded to Baron Alphonse Rothschild, the son of Yaakov Rothschild, who happened to be in Jerusalem at that time.

The actual construction was spread out over a period of eight and a half years. Throughout that period, work had to be halted time and again, usually due to lack of funds. One attempt to raise money involved painting the names of contributors on the windows of the synagogue. Rav Shmuel Salant, on his trip to Europe and England in 1860, obtained handsome donations, especially from Sir Moses.

Wherever possible, Jews were hired to work on the synagogue. All the woodwork and metalwork was done by Jews. Stones were brought from the quarries of Bethlehem, and long wood beams were transported from Jaffa.

The Churvah Synagogue

In 1862 (5622), the vaulted ceiling was completed. Finishing the dome demanded extra helping hands. Hundreds of Perushim pitched in. Rav Yeshaya Bardaky, the venerable leader of the community, received the honor of ascending the huge scaffolds and ladders, and fitting in the final stone of the vaulted ceiling. Cheers of joy broke out, along with dancing. Rav Bardaky delivered a short, vibrant speech,[30] followed by the first prayer service (Minchah) in the shul.

It would take another two years to finish the walls, floors, and furnishings. In the meantime, Jews prayed there on an irregular basis.

The inauguration of the Beis Yaakov Synagogue, named after Baron James (Yaakov) Rothschild, took place on 25 Elul, 1864 (5624). This milestone ceremony was really the culmination of decades of work and superhuman efforts by many behind-the-scenes Jews. The Perushim referred to it as the Churvah Synagogue. The building was the monumental pride of the *yishuv*. At forty-five meters in height, it was the tallest edifice in the Holy City.

For generations to come, the Churvah served as the focal point of the community. Men prayed and studied Torah there around the clock. *Gedolim* spoke before packed audiences, and Jews who

The interior of the Churvah Synagogue, which served the Yishuv from 1864 until 1948. The Holy Ark's intricate wood carvings dates back to the synagogue's formative years, while the magnificent mural designs on the walls was a later addition.

had been circumcised there were eulogized decades later in the same place.

Eighty-four years later, in 1948, Arabs destroyed the synagogue, leaving only parts of its walls and floor intact. Until 1999 it remained in ruins, allowing visitors no more than a glimpse of its former grandeur. Today, it is being rebuilt, bringing back to life the synagogue which had once ranked preeminent in the Holy City.

The First Jewish Hospital[31]

Of all the many charitable people who left their imprint on Eretz Yisrael and Jerusalem, perhaps the Rothschild family of Paris is the most well known. Baron James Rothschild, his son Alphonse, and his grandson Edmond (among others of this famous philanthropic family), each took part in building up the Jewish presence in the Holy Land.

In 1854 (5614), James Rothschild sent his personal representative, Dr. Albert Cohen, to set up a hospital in Jerusalem. The entire Jewish community eagerly awaited his arrival, realizing it was an important harbinger of the modernization and improvement of their health standards. Moreover, a Jewish hospital would reduce the dangers presented by the Christian hospitals, which were notorious hives for missionary activity.

Dr. Cohen purchased a building complex near the Zion Gate belonging to the Sephardim and converted it into the Meir Rothschild Hospital, named after James' father. The hospital was stocked with the latest medical equipment and textbooks, sent from Paris. Its green-painted rooms could accommodate up to eighteen patients at a time, half the space for men and half for women. There was also a small shul on the premises.

The Meir Rothschild Hospital accepted patients without charge, and medications were distributed for free. House calls, too, were usually without payment. In a normal year, over four hundred patients were hospitalized, and thousands of outpatients received medical advice and attention.

Dr. Cohen, after inaugurating the hospital, went on to implement other projects for the Rothschilds. He appointed Dr. Neiman, who had already been practicing medicine in Jerusalem for seven years, as hospital director.

When Alphonse Rothschild visited in 1856, he had only good news to report back to his father. There was already a visible improvement in the health standards of the populace and a reduction in the mortality rate. Upon hearing these tidings, James created a perpetual fund to ensure the continuation of the hospital.

In 1858 (5618), the Bikur Cholim Hospital opened to serve the Jewish inhabitants of the city. Smaller than the Rothschild Hospital, it started with twelve beds.

Fortunately, as we have noted, Jerusalem boasted a very large Jewish population at this time. However, these two modest hospitals were unable to care for all the ill among them. With no other option, many Jews were forced to go to a third hospital, this one run by British missionaries. In this institution, patients staying over for Shabbos were given missionary literature and openly proselytized. Over the coming decades,

Birkur Cholim Hospital, built in 1858, was located in the Jewish Quarter

both Jewish hospitals would markedly expand, all in an attempt to prevent innocent Jews from going to the British hospital.

Dr. Neiman retired in 1855 and was succeeded by Dr. Rotsigel. He died in the plague of 1865, and was replaced by Dr. London (1866–1875), and then by Dr. Schwartz (1875–1888), who in turn was followed by many others. Dr. Schwartz advised Baron Rothschild to build another hospital in the new city, which by then was growing at an astounding rate. Situated between the Russian compound and the complex called Beis David, the hospital opened its doors in 1888, offering medical attention to those in need. The Rothschild Hospital in the Old City was renamed Misgav Ledach Hospital and was run by a Sephardic group. Around the turn of the century, one more Jewish hospital was built in Jerusalem. As we shall see in a later chapter, Shaarei Zedek, founded by Dr. Moshe Wallach, would play a major role in the lives of Jerusalemites.

In the 1850s, the Rothschilds opened a fund to assist pregnant women and to aid those with newly born children during the first months after birth. Two midwives offered their services to poor families for free. Dr. Cohen, whose deep love of the Jews of Jerusalem kept him coming back to Eretz Yisrael and devising ways of helping them, initiated a free challos-for-Shabbos fund for needy families. Every week six hundred loaves of bread were distributed.

The words of the Sages (*Avos* 1:2), "The world stands on three pillars: Torah, *avodah* (prayer), and charity," achieved a tangible reality in the 1850s. These three things supported the Jews of Jerusalem in ways which rescued the present and secured the future.

Archeological Finds

Archeological expeditions to the Middle East picked up momentum in the middle of the nineteenth century. French, English, and American teams set up tents at various sites in and around Jerusalem, hired Arab laborers, and began digging under the earth's crust. Their goal was to explore the biblical past and reveal an accurate picture of ancient times.

The Tomb of the Kings

A prime target of these enthusiastic archeologists were those ancient caves which tradition regards as the burial sites of various Jewish heroes. One was the gigantic cave called the Tomb of the Kings, which lay north of the city on the way to another site — the cave of Shimon HaTzaddik. The many catacombs in the Tomb of the Kings, mostly inaccessible due to fallen rocks and debris, contained rich scientific finds. Edward Robinson, investigating the site in 1838, believed that Queen Helena (mentioned in Talmudic sources) was buried there.

The French archeologist, DeSaulcy, dug there in 1850–1851, and again in 1863. On his initial dig, credited as being the first archeological excavation in Eretz Yisrael, DeSaulcy unearthed several carved sarcophagi, one of which was inscribed with the words *malchah shada*, Queen Shada. Inside the sarcophagus were human bones, which were simply spilled onto the ground as they cleaned out the historic find before sending it to the Louvre museum in Paris.

When the Jerusalemites heard about this, they were shocked and infuriated at the blatant desecration of a Jewish grave. According to tradition, the site was the tomb of Kalba Savua, the wealthy patron of the poor during Talmudic times. *HaLevanon*, a Torah-oriented periodical, reported: "A French excavator came to Jerusalem and began to take out all the bones he came across, claiming that he was looking for the grave of Queen Helena. Later, he happily claimed that he found her bones in one of the chambers in a stone sarcophagus."[32]

In *Shaarei Yerushalayim*, written in 1867, the author graphically depicts the reaction in the Holy City: "Due to our many sins, Frenchmen came a few years ago and excavated the cave. Casting the dust and dry bones out of the coffin, they took it away, claiming they had

Tomb of the Kings

permission from the Sultan. Upon hearing this, the Jews mourned profusely, deeply pained over this terrible deed."[33]

That same day, a fast was declared and eulogies made, and the bones were reinterred near the tomb of Shimon HaTzaddik.

Until this time, the Tomb of the Kings had belonged to Arabs. In 1874, a Jewish woman from France by the name of Madame Bratrand sent 30,000 francs via the Austrian consulate in Jerusalem to buy the site from the Moslem owners, so that it would become the inheritance of the Jewish people. Her intention, as testified by the Rav of France, was to protect the site from further desecration.

After Madame Bratrand passed away, the brothers Pereire inherited the site. They in turn in turn passed it on to their heirs, who gave it as a gift to the French government. This obvious usurpation of the original gift caused a stir in Jerusalem and abroad. Unfortunately, there was no legal means of redress to correct the situation.[34]

Zedekiah's Cave

In 1854 (5614), the site known as Zedekiah's Cave was accidentally discovered by American diplomat, J. J. Barclay. The inconspicuous entrance lay fifty meters east of the Damascus Gate. Once inside, one gaped at the tremendous expanse of the underground cave that opened before him. Extending four hundred meters in the direction of the Temple, the gigantic cave vaulted two stories high in places.

Tradition claims that during the

Babylonian invasion, King Zedekiah fled the city on horseback via this cave. He was headed towards an underground exit far to the east, in the direction of Jericho. It so happened, however, that at the time, some Babylonian soldiers were chasing after a deer in the same direction, and were right on the spot when the king emerged. He was apprehended and exiled to Babylon.

Believed to be one of the main stone quarries for the ancient city, the pitch-black cave was cluttered with debris. The explorers entered with torches and lanterns, and found visible signs of masonry work.

When the Jews heard of Barclay's discovery, they too wanted to see what was inside. Rav Eliezer Shub entered with a group of about ten companions. The explorers were prepared for the worst. Besides torches for light, they took weapons with them in case they had to kill wild creatures, snakes, or scorpions. They also took a fifty-meter-long rope as a measuring tool.

With torches in hand, the group gingerly entered and climbed up and down the hills and valleys within the cave, amazed at the vast expanse. After walking as deep as the rope extended, they continued on a little further. Suddenly they heard the sound of rushing water and found themselves stepping into a cold stream. Panic-stricken, they clambered back out of the cave as fast as they could.

Once outside, the group was apprehended by the Turkish guard stationed at the Damascus Gate for possessing arms and on suspicion of fomenting an insurrection against the government. At

Cave of Zedekiah

the time, the Ottoman Empire was engaged in the Crimean War against Russia, and many Jews of the *yishuv* had Russian citizenship. The Chacham Bashi was informed of the arrest and turned to the Austrian consul, since all the prisoners were Austrian citizens. He chided them for carrying weapons at a critical time like that, warning them that they could receive the death penalty for such an action. After half a day's imprisonment, they were released on condition that they never repeat their behavior.[35] Eventually, the Turkish authorities installed an iron gate at the entrance of the cave. Today the cavern is lit up and pathways lead down its entire length, giving it the feeling of a underground city.

After the Crimean War ended in 1856, the Turkish government permitted non-Moslems to enter the Temple Mount complex. At a time when international relations were gaining importance in the world, the Turks sought to promote tourism from Europe. However, access to one site was still forbidden — the tomb of King David remained off limits until the British Mandate period.

Other signs of the new spirit of internationalism were also evident. Foreign governments were permitted to build schools, hospitals, hotels, and churches. During the 1880s alone, no less than seventeen churches and hospices appeared, the majority in East Jerusalem and on the Mount of Olives.

First Excavations Around the Temple Mount[36]

The science of archeology came of age in the Holy City during the 1850s and 1860s. It was during this period that full-blown expeditions, backed by funding from foreign societies became the norm. Previously, the field was the province of individual explorers, like Edward Robinson in the 1830s and Mr. Tobler in the 1840s and 1850s. These men primarily focused on accurately pinpointing historical sites. However, with the expeditions of DeSaulcy in the 1850s and Wilson-Warren in the 1860s, volumes of findings were published, filled with exquisite drawings.

One place, however, was forbidden territory for these zealous savants: the Temple Mount. Although the restriction

The first logotype of the Palestine Exploration Fund. The fund, founded in London in 1865, was a major archeological society whose work continued into the 20th century. The Society adopted three principles: 1. that its projects be carried out on scientific principles; 2. that the Fund, as a body, abstain from controversy; 3. not to conduct its affairs as a religious body.

Robinson's Arch, bulging out from the Western Wall on the right. On the left, workers are searching for remains of the other side of the arch. Today, the ground level has been lowered by over ten meters, and the area is part of the Southern Wall excavations.

against entry onto the Temple Mount by foreigners was eased after 1856, archeological explorations were still strictly forbidden. Thus, the most sacred spot on the earth was saved from defilement. The ban was subsequently reinforced by the Sultan in 1869, and, for whatever reason, neither the British mandatory nor the Israeli governments ever abrogated it.

Though the Turks did not allow excavations on the Temple Mount proper, they did permit digging *around* it. Two of the most famous sites there — Robinson's arch and Wilson's arch — were named for the explorers who discovered them. Robinson's arch was an arch-shaped protrusion along the Western Wall, south of the Barclay Gate (Gate of the Prophet). It was thought to have been part of an ancient bridge. Its 15.5-meter length indicated that the bridge must have been quite wide. In 1865, Charles Wilson searched for the support columns on the other side away from the Temple wall, without success. A few years later, Charles Warren continued to excavate deeper at the spot where Wilson had dug and revealed the columns, verifying the bridge theory. A cistern and passageway were also discovered nearby.

Wilson's arch, at the extreme northern end of the Western Wall, had actually been discovered earlier, by Tobler. It was believed to have been an ancient archway through which people walked when going to and from the Damascus Gate and the Dung Gate, dating back to the Temple times. Above the arch lay direct access to the Temple Mount via the Gate of the Chain. There was no histori-

Wilson's Arch

cal connection between the two arches.

In 1867, underground tunnels were discovered along the southern wall of the Temple Mount. Over thirty meters long, they started at the southeast side under the Single Gate. Other tunnels were also discovered along that wall, some leading to cisterns under the Temple Mount. In the middle of the excavation, the pasha ordered that the digging cease.

Sir Charles Warren made a number of significant digs between 1867 and 1870, mainly along the slope leading down to the Shiloach springs to the south of the city. His most important find was named the Warren Shaft, a maze of underground tunnels leading to a natural water spring. Apparently dug during the First Temple period, the shaft was a means for the inhabitants of the city to obtain water during an enemy siege.

Other digs were conducted on the eastern and northern sides of the Temple Mount, and more finds and theories were presented and discussed in journals such as those published by the Palestine Exploration Fund of London.

A hundred and fifty years later, modern excavations still continue to reveal more and more vestiges of the past. New archeological books analyze the findings, and theories are proposed to explain them. Yet, the whole truth will lay hidden from the realm of man's finite vision until the time when God will once again reveal His treasure house to us.

The Silence before the Storm

In the period before the Jews received permission from the Sultan to build suburbs outside the walls, they lived under cramped and stifling conditions. Sometime in the mid-1840s, the mayor of the city demanded that the Jews pay nearly the entire sum necessary to repair the road around the Jaffa Gate. When the Rishon l'Tzyon and the Perushim leader, Rav Moshe Rivlin, met with him, the pasha explained himself: "The sum I am asking is not excessive," he said. "I calculated it on the basis of a census of the city's populace. According to my estimate, the Jews live in two-thirds of the houses of the city, and number seventy percent of the inhabitants. Therefore, they should pay the most."[37]

The Jewish Predicament

The need for the Jews of Jerusalem to become self-supportive became a major issue in the mid-nineteenth century. Unfortunately, forces beyond their control denied them the right to use their talents in productive ways. James Finn, the British consul between 1845 and 1863, described the Jewish predicament in these words:

Worst of all, they had no employment whereby they might have received, if only bare bread and water. They had never any employment. There was none for them to have. And yet many of them were artisans, carpenters, tinsmiths, glaziers, dyers, tailors, etc. We knew this, because we had always found that it was in the Jewish Quarter we could find people able to do for us Europeans such work as the Oriental mechanics did not understand, and we knew by experience that the Jews were not only able to work, but that they were thankful and eager to be employed.

But there was no work for them. Oriental Christians have so great a prejudice and superstitious hatred of Jews, that they would not on any account have dealings with them. The Moslems had artisans of their own, and even when they needed and employed the superior skill or knowledge of some Jewish workman, it was long before the poor Jew could get the money due to him for his work, and in but too many cases, he was too timid to press for payment, and thus never got it at all.[38]

Jewish upholsterer with his utensils

Montefiore's Plan

On Sir Moses Montefiore's second visit to the Holy Land, in 1839 (5599), a plan to better the lot of his brethren in Eretz Yisrael crystallized in his mind. A man of vision, he perceived the bottleneck that was preventing them from becoming a strong, independent group. Their poverty stemmed from forces around them, and not from their own refusal to try and better themselves. On the contrary, they were strong-willed and eager to stand on their own two feet.

There were two main obstacles, besides those mentioned by Finn, that stood in their way. One was simply a language barrier. Barely a single Ashkenazic Jew knew Arabic, the language of the land, and even a significant proportion of the Sephardim knew only Ladino and Hebrew. Without Arabic, commerce and bilateral relationships could never become a reality. Secondly, vast stretches of arable land lay untouched and unproductive throughout the country. If Jewish farmers could bring out the potential wealth which lay dormant in the fertile soil, they would become self-sufficient and increase the amount of sorely needed produce for the city dwellers.

Montefiore was no mere dreamer. He began translating his plan into reality and prepared to financially back pioneers who shared his visionary spirit. Wherever he went he spoke about his idea and sought men of action to come forward and take up his call to return to the land.

The greatest hindrance facing his plan was the threat of thievery and physical attacks on the settlers by Arabs. In order to counter this threat, Montefiore planned to take Arabs partners into the settlement. The presence of these Arabs would hopefully keep their belligerent neighbors at a distance.

Sir Moses was unsuccessful in his attempt to interest Arabs in his plan. However, he remained undeterred, and in 1840 (5600), he chose to buy an orchard near Jaffa as his pilot project. Called Beira, this first Jewish farm had great potential for success. Unfortunately, epidemics and raids by neighboring Arabs forced it to close down. Montefiore temporarily laid aside his ambitious plans to encourage independent Jewish farming. However, as we saw previously, he would try again on a later trip in the mid-1860s, with a group of Moroccan Jews from Jerusalem. This time the plan met with success.

Sir Moses was not the only one to dream and plan. The same year he had his idea, Rav Mordechai Zoref of Jerusalem approached him with the proposition for a farm that would be manned by a minyan of Ashkenazic Jews working on a monthly rotation system. He himself had done joint farming near Jerusalem with Sephardic and Arab companions. Management would be supervised by Jews fluent in Arabic.

Similarly, he proposed diverting a certain river and creating a fish pond. His proposed farm, called Kefar Moshe, would have stables, sheep, cattle, vineyards, and even beehives. Since the following year, 1840, was a *shemitah* year, Rav Mordechai listed those projects which would be permissible according to Halachah.

Though this proposal by Rav Mordechai Zoref was shelved, a subsequent one he conceived was not. A few years later, he presented Sir Moses with a plan to open a weaving factory in Jerusalem. Rav Zoref traveled to England in 1845 to learn the trade. In 1854, Montefiore opened the factory with Jewish employees trained for the job. Unfortunately, the time was not ripe and the project failed.[39]

In 1848 (5608), dozens of aspiring Jewish fishermen teamed together and formed a consortium called *Chevras Shulei Dagim*. Comprising both Sephardim and Ashkenazim, they camped by the Jordan River and set to work. Though hampered by local Arabs, they succeeded for three years, until they were forced to abandon the enterprise due to Bedouin attacks.[40]

Avraham's Vineyard

Avraham's Vineyard[41]

The British consul, James Finn, reacted to the Jewish plight by opening a farm outside the Holy City. Avraham's Vineyard, as it was called, engaged more than a hundred Jewish workers. It was located on a knoll which tradition traced back to a prophecy of Jeremiah: "Behold, the days are coming, says the Lord, when the city shall be built to Hashem...and the measuring line shall go out further straight to the hill of Garev" (*Jeremiah* 31:37–38). The farm was located on the present-day site of Jerusalem's Geula neighborhood, on Ovadiah Street and the surroundings blocks.[42]

Devout Christians, Mr. and Mrs. Finn felt that the onset of the redemption was at hand, and that the Jews would be the princes of the world. In anticipation of this, they purchased the land and began what they called an industrial plantation. First, gigantic cisterns were dug, in expectation of the influx of Jewish exiles returning to the Holy City. A verse was engraved on each covering. One read: "Gather the people, and I shall give them water" (*Numbers* 21:16); another read: "The poor and needy seek water, and there is none, and their tongue is parched for thirst; I the Lord will answer them, I the God of Israel will not forsake them" (*Isaiah* 41:17).

Founded in 1852 (5612), the plantation became fully operational in 1854. Truly an altruistic project, there was no ulterior motive behind it to missionize innocent Jews. Mr. Finn wrote: "Strange to say, some of the Missionaries of the London Society were angered at the same time because we refused leave for them to come upon the ground expressly for religious controversy...The

James Finn

come Christians, but were, like the others, eligible for employment as being Jews in distress."[44] In the long run, however, Avraham's Vineyard proved to be a positive vehicle for Jewish employment.

The plantation produced vegetables, grapes, and almonds, as well as collecting precious water. The foreman was a Polish Jew, and all the workers were Jewish. None of these people actually lived on the plantation; they came there daily from the walled city. As the entire area between the Jaffa Gate and the vineyard lay barren and open to Bedouin attack, Mr. Finn hired a patrol unit to escort them to and from work. Fridays they worked only to midday, in order to give them time to prepare for Shabbos.

object of the institution was to relieve distress by means of honest industry. But at the same time, the perfect freedom and religious liberty of the work people were respected."[43]

In spite of this, the rabbis denounced the farm, fearing that naive Jews might be missionized. Mr. Finn admitted that "now and then it happened that one or two who applied for admission [of whom only Jews were accepted], and joined the others in the field had be-

Later, Mrs. Finn opened a soap factory on the premises. This project was also successful, and some of the soap was even exported to England. The plantation functioned until the beginning of the twentieth century, with Ashkenazic, Sephardic, Moroccan, and Yemenite workers, some of whom worked there for decades. When the enterprise shut down, Mrs. Finn donated the land for a Jewish orphanage, sometime around 1910.

Battei Machse[45]

In 1837, as refugees from the earthquake in Safed swarmed into Jerusalem, recommendations were given for alleviating the overcrowded conditions that prevailed in the city. In 1845, plans to build suburbs outside the wall were put into deep freeze when the Sultan decreed against any construction outside the walls. Instead, a more moderate step was taken, which consisted of purchasing a tract of land inside the wall and developing it.

At the fringe of the Jewish Quarter, between Rabban Yochanan ben Zakkai Synagogue and the southern side of the city wall, lay a barren piece of land. The

Battei Machse

Perushim bought it with money collected in Amsterdam, Volozhin, and from the Rothschild family. Tremendous care was taken to ensure that the Arabs who claimed possession over the land were indeed the legitimate owners, and that the purchase constituted a legally valid sale. In short, everything possible was done to leave no doubt as to who the new owners were.

In 1858 (5618), construction of Battei Machse ("The Sheltered Lodgings") began. Rav Tzvi Berlin, who had immigrated only a few years before, poured all his energies into the project. Four years later, the first eight lodgings were finished. When the final phase of construction was over at the turn of the century, there were a total of one hundred two-room apartments. The project was one of the largest and most spacious housing projects in the city.

The communal council decided not to sell the apartments outright. Instead, they retained control, and held a lottery to decide which families would live there. Furthermore, it was stipulated that every three years occupancy would rotate and new tenants would move in. There were a few exceptions to this rule against ownership. One of them was Rav Yaakov Ettlinger, author of *Aruch LaNer*. He never lived in the Holy City and eventually gave his apartment to Rav Avraham Shag when he moved to Jerusalem in 1873. After Rav Shag passed away a few years later, it was given to Rav Yosef Chaim Zonnenfeld, who lived there for over fifty years.

Another similar project began on the northern side of the city, near the Damascus Gate. A group of Moslem courtyards were purchased with the aim of demolishing them and replacing them with one huge neighborhood of new houses. The sale of *bab chatah,* as the Moslems called it, went smoothly, but due to threats from local Arabs, the second stage of actually tearing down the old houses had to be permanently shelved. The courtyards, however, remained under Jewish ownership and were occupied by Jews until the pogroms of 1922. They had their own synagogue and cheder, under the auspices of the Etz Chaim Yeshivah.

Two Lights of the Yishuv

The Rav of Kalish, Rav Meir Auerbach, moved to the Holy City in 1860, filled with the grandeur of Torah and the fieriness of the *chareidi* spirit. At a time when secular influences were making themselves felt in the lives of Jerusalem's residents, Rav Auerbach unhesitatingly took up the call of battle.*

As we saw earlier, Rav Shmuel Salant set off to Europe for the *yishuv* shortly after Rav Auerbach's arrival. He appointed Rav Auerbach as Rav of Jerusalem in his stead, and after his return he refused to take back the title. Thus, Rav Auerbach remained Rav of Jerusalem until his passing in 1878. (The famous Auerbach family of today are distant relatives of Rav Meir Auerbach.)

One of the members of Rav Auerbach's *beis din* was Rav Avraham Eisenstein. Rav Avraham had sat on the Perushim *beis din* in Safed before the earthquake of 1837. After that tragedy, which took the lives of his wife and children, he moved to Jerusalem, where, in addition to his duties as a *dayan,* he directed the Central Committee of the Ashkenazic community. His whole life centered on helping the *yishuv.***

The Rav of Kalish, independently wealthy, bought a courtyard near the Churvah which included a shul and extra living quarters. He allocated these to the poor to live in, on a rotation system. Later, when the suburbs outside the wall began developing, he gave handsomely to them get started. Together with Rav Salant, he formed the Central Committee, which harnessed all the Ashkenazic efforts under one roof. Living during dramatic times, Rav Auerbach eagerly supervised developments in the affairs of the *yishuv* and encouraged his fellow Jew to respond to the call of the day.

Another great light of Torah was Rav Yeshaya Bardaky. He had led the Perushim for thirty years, survived some of the trying periods of life in Eretz Yisrael, and had witnessed some of the greatest achievements of the *yishuv.*

Rav Bardaky came to Eretz Yisrael as a widower with two small children in the early 1820s, and the Almighty tested him even before he touched the holy ground. As his sailboat approached the coast, the mast broke and the boat capsized, tossing all the passengers into the Mediterranean Sea. Fortunately, Rav Yeshaya was a superb swimmer and made his way ashore with his two children on his shoulders.

He joined the Perushim of Safed, married the daughter of Rav Yisrael of Shklov in 1823, and became a member of the communal board of directors. Rav Yeshaya moved to Jerusalem in the

* See story, "Gunpoint," in *Bygone Days: 1840–1870.*

** See story, "The Fiery Torah," in *Bygone Days: 1840–1870.*

early 1830s and quickly attracted a number of followers who prayed and studied at his Sukkos Shalom Synagogue, known as the *chatzer* of Rav Yeshaya.

A Torah giant whose eyes glowed with knowledge and wisdom, he was an unrelenting warrior against all signs of secular influence.

Rav Bardaky's son, Rav Shlomo, married the daughter of Rav Shmuel Salant. He served as the chief *chazan* at the Churvah Synagogue throughout his life.

On 18 Cheshvan, 1862, Rav Yeshaya passed away. The funeral procession that night was followed by numerous Jerusalemites, who came to pay their last respects to the beloved tzaddik. The gates of the city, locked each night at sunset, were opened for the honor of the dead.

The first speaker to eulogize Rav Bardaky was the Rav of Kotna. He was followed by the Rav of Kalish. Suddenly, Rav Auerbach's eulogy was interrupted by the Rav of Kotna, who stood up again and emotionally continued to speak. Later, he explained his strange behavior. He had witnessed a pillar of fire before the coffin, a sign of the unique greatness of Rav Bardaky, which stirred him to lament the passing of this righteous man even more.[46]

The Plague of 1865

No one in Jerusalem would have guessed what lay in store for them in 1865. In the summer of that year, a cholera epidemic swooped down on the unsuspecting populace and raged fiercely for months on end. Neither the wise nor the rich, the young nor the old were spared. At its height, thirty Jews a day passed away.

Later, when the community could look back and put what had happened into perspective, they noticed that two great luminaries of the *yishuv* had passed away shortly before the plague's onset. The Rav of Kotna, Rav Moshe Yehudah Leib, died on 3 Shevat, and a week later Rav Yosef Schwartz passed away. The former spent his whole day cloaked in tallis and tefillin, teaching Torah at the Etz Chaim Yeshivah with no thought of recompense. Even in his house, he sat with the best students and taught them. Among them were Rav Yoel Moshe Salomon and Rav Michel Cohen, who together would later publish the periodical *HaLevanon*.

Rav Schwartz had been a man of all trades, knowledgeable in everything, influential in many areas, and a communal leader of distinction.*

Almost immediately after their passing, the country was hit by a devastating locust attack, which destroyed much of the crop and caused food prices to soar. It was a famine of crisis proportions for all but the very rich.

Right on its heels came the epidemic. It started in Transjordan, and hundreds of Arab fugitives brought it to Jerusalem. The Turkish authorities ordered a general quarantine over the city, forbidding Arab fugitives further entry. Unfortunately, it proved to be a futile measure — the deadly plague already had a firm foothold.

* See story, "Rav Schwartz Meets the Archduke," in Bygone Days: *1840–1870*.

Rav Yosef Schwartz (1804–1865)

The death toll was staggering. Nearly every home was affected by the tragedy. Orphans and widows roamed the streets, numbed by their loss. Rav Salant's father-in-law, Rav Zundel, succumbed to the illness. One of the famous Levi brothers, Rav Nachum of Shadik, died in the plague. He was the father of the Baharan family of Jerusalem, who built up Meah Shearim. Rav Naftali Hirsch Porush, a descendant of the Maharal of Prague, also died in the plague. After living the life of a Torah recluse for fourteen years in Mir, Poland, he had moved to Jerusalem where he spent his last eight years teaching Torah. The famous Porush family of Jerusalem descends from him. Rav Yosef Yoel Rivlin, the director of the Perushim office in Jerusalem passed away in Cheshvan. He was only forty-five years old and had been a sterling example of a pious Torah scholar.

Jews the world over offered assistance to the beleaguered community. Sir Moses Montefiore, for instance, sent medical supplies, plus four hundred pounds sterling to aid the needy. The noble Dr. Rotsigel, the director of the Rothschild Hospital, stopped at nothing to try and save precious lives. He printed health instructions to be used during the emergency and founded a group called *Ozrim l'Cholim* (Aiders of the Sick), by which trained volunteers gave medical aid to afflicted patients. Working around the clock, he made house calls under circumstances which endangered his health. Finally, the inevitable befell him and he caught the illness. Some weeks later, at the end of Elul, when he started to recover, he began making plans to extend the scope of *Ozrim l'Cholim*'s activities. Alas, to the sorrow of all Jerusalem, he fell into a relapse. His entire family became afflicted as well, and all of them passed away.[47]

In all, over a thousand Jews passed away during the four months in which the plague ravaged the Holy City. Stagnant water had aggravated the epidemic, and overcrowding had contributed to the terrible death toll. An abortive attempt was made to correct the situation by funneling water into the city from the Pools of Solomon, many kilometers away to the south. Montefiore donated three hundred pounds sterling on condition that water would be piped through the Jewish Quarter. Yet, these good intentions were thwarted when selfish water carriers secretly damaged the pipeline.

There was no way to bring the dead back to life. However, more than ever, there was an urgent need to break through the walls of the city and expand into the wilderness outside. That was the inevitable next step, and fortunately the Heavenly court agreed with it, as we shall see in the next chapter.

Tiferes Yisrael Synagogue

A few months after the plague had run its course, in 1866, a sign of spiritual revival boosted the *yishuv*. The Chassidim publicized a groundbreaking ceremony for their first synagogue on Chassidim Street. Named after the Admor of Ruzhin, Rebbe Yisrael Friedman, the Tiferes Yisrael Synagogue would become the life-center of the Chassidim of Jerusalem.

The Rebbe of Ruzhin, as *nasi* of Eretz Yisrael for Kollel Volhynia, poured his energies into helping the *yishuv*. He often repeated that the redemption would come about through earthly endeavors whereby Jews would naturally migrate to the Holy Land and build it up. This would be the long-awaited "ingathering of the exile." Every new immigrant was a sign of great things to come, and every new stone used to build a Jewish house in Eretz Yisrael was a step towards the ultimate goal.[48]

Until then, the Chassidim prayed in small, private locations, like Rav Yisrael Beck's house. The Tiferes Yisrael Shul was patterned after the Churvah Synagogue and was nearly as big. Its vaulted roof towered high over the city's skyline.

The land had been bought long before in a dramatic step to save it from falling into gentile hands. The Rebbe of Ruzhin, hearing that Czar Nicholas the First planned to buy the plot, sent a message to Rav Nisan Beck in Jerusalem to finalize the deal at soon as possible, regardless of the cost. When the Czar heard that the Jews had bought the site, he was reported as saying "I know about this Jew [Rebbe Yisrael of Ruzhin]. He is the one from the city of Ruzhin I once locked up who escaped from me." The Rebbe commented on the success of the purchase: "Our Sages say that when Jerusalem is built up, Cayzari is in ruins, and vice versa. Cayzari and Czar are similar in spelling, hinting that although Czarist Russia may be one of the great powers of the world now, as we start to build up Jerusalem — spiritually and physically — this Cayzari will begin to fall into ruins."[49]

After the Rebbe passed away in 1851, his son, Rebbe Avraham Yaakov of Sadiger, kept his father's dream of a central Chassidic synagogue alive. He was instrumental in collecting money for the building.

Built over a period of six years (1866–1871), the synagogue marked another crown for the Jews of Jerusalem. The Chassidim's foothold in the Holy City, fragile until then, suddenly had a firm foundation.

The central figure in seeing Tiferes Yisrael reach completion was Rav Nisan Beck. With his dynamic personality and vision, he withstood the turbulent waves of interference that threatened the project in the years before 1866. In 1869, when lack of money halted construction, Rav Nisan's chance meeting with Emperor Franz Joseph of Austria-Hungary ended in the monarch donating a handsome sum for the synagogue.*

* See story, "The Emperor's Gift," in *Bygone Days: 1840–1870*.

Tiferes Yisrael Synagogue, the main Chassidic shul in the Old City

On 15 Av, 1872 (5632), amidst a joyful and tearful crowd, the Tiferes Yisrael Synagogue was inaugurated. The event, participated by all facets of the Jewish community, was hailed as a turning point for Jerusalem. The Chassidim had achieved stature as an independent group, able to express their devotion to God in their unique manner of prayer. Rav Nisan Beck, who continued to play a prominent role in the synagogue until his death in 1889, received the honor of having the shul colloquially called after him.

The Tiferes Yisrael Synagogue and the Churvah Synagogue would be the heart of the *yishuv*. All communal activities and speeches, as well as many other functions, took place inside their walls. Built to last for many generations, they both suffered the same ignoble fate in 1948, when the Arabs blew them up and desecrated them.

At the same time the Tiferes Yisrael Synagogue was inaugurated, the first suburb outside the walls had sufficiently rooted itself to signal other parties to follow suit. Thus, concurrent with the success of the new synagogue inside the city, more and more Jews prepared to take the next giant step and resettle outside the walls.

The Emperor's Visit

At the end of 1869, a highly touted plan to link the Mediterranean Sea with the Red Sea was completed. After a ten-year period of construction, the Suez Canal project stood as one of the greatest engineering feats of the times. In terms of world commerce, the canal linked Europe with the Far East and ushered in a new era of world trade. Kings and aristocrats the world over descended upon the Middle East to attend the grand opening ceremony.

The Austro-Hungarian Emperor, Franz Joseph, expressed his wish to visit Jerusalem on his return trip home. The news electrified the city's populace. The Turkish government cleaned up the provincial capital, especially the Jaffa Gate area. The road from Jaffa to Jerusalem, until then impassable by coach, was improved and repaired. Even the simple folk tried to tidy up and present a good image to the royal visitor.

On the day of his arrival, all the dignitaries of the city stood inside the Jaffa Gate at specific spots, each with a makeshift decorative archway designed by that group. The Moslem *kadi* and Mufti, the patriarchs of the different churches, and the *rabbanim* of the Jewish community all lined up to greet the Emperor. Women and children eagerly awaited the royal entourage.

During his visit, the Emperor showed a particular fondness for the Jewish community. As we mentioned previously, he gave a generous donation for the Tiferes Yisrael Synagogue, a gesture no gentile had yet done for the *yishuv* in Jerusalem.

His visit signaled an upheaval of sorts within Jerusalem. No longer could the City of Cities remain backward and undeveloped. The era of the industrial revolution had transformed Europe into a modern, healthier place to live. However, except for the introduction of the telegraph (and this was decades after it

Emperor Franz Joseph (1830–1916)

was in common use in America and Europe), Eretz Yisrael lingered as a third-world nation, her residents languishing in primitive living conditions. The construction of the Suez Canal in Egypt marked a turning point in the way the nations of the world viewed the Middle East. The new "cause celebre" amongst governments and individuals was how to improve the lot of the masses in this area of the world.

Inauguration ceremony of the Suez Canal at Port Said, Egypt, 1869

At that time, some ten thousand Jews lived in cramped quarters inside the city's walls. There was literally almost no room to breathe. Yet, there was nowhere to go. Even Moslem residents of the city feared for their lives should they venture alone by day outside the safety of the walls. Merciless Bedouin tribes controlled the wilderness, and lawlessness ruled right up to the very gates of the city. The Turkish police were all but powerless to deal with the situation. As we shall see, the problem was acute, and the solution inevitable.

Notes

1. See *Tevuos HaAretz*, pp. 451, 490.
2. *Mosad HaYesod*, pp. 151–152.
3. *Chazon Tzyon*, p. 105.
4. Ibid., pp. 110–111.
5. *Mosad HaYesod*, pp. 26–27.
6. *HaMaggid Doresh Tzyon*, p. 45.
7. *Yehudi HaMizrach b'Eretz Yisrael*, vol. 2, p. 179.
8. *Shaarei Yerushalayim*, Gate 4, *Yishuv HaAretz.*
9. *Chachmei HaSephardim b'Eretz Yisrael*, p. 217.
10. See also *Beis HaDefus HaIvri HaRishon b'Yerushalayim.*
11. *Ma'asaf "Tzyon"* I (תרפ"ו), p. 88.
12. *Mosad HaYesod*, p. 10.
13. *Chachmei HaMaarav*, pp. 40–52.
14. Ibid., p. 39.
15. Ibid., pp. 43–44.
16. Ibid., pp. 78–79.
17. *Moshe v'Yerushalayim*, pp. 31–33.
18. *HaYishuv HaChassidi b'Yerushalayim*, pp. 70–81.
19. The Seer of Lublin gave him a silver kiddush cup. The Lelover Rebbe also took with him an ornate

royal cloak which Napoleon gave his father. He first immersed it in a *mikve* and eventually used it as a cover for the Holy Ark. (*Shosheles Boston*, pp. 113–114).

20. *Olam HaChassidus*, vol. 64.
21. *Dimuyos Hod*, vol. 1, p. 122.
22. *Shosheles Boston*, p. 150.
23. *HaYishuv HaChassidi b'Yerushalayim*.
24. *Shosheles Boston*, pp. 229–230.
25. Based on an article by Rav Yechiel Michel Tukachinsky, חצר רבנו יהודה החסיד, *Luach Eretz Yisrael*, vol. 9, pp. 119–167.
26. Lemel: *Mara d'Arah Yisrael*, pp. 238–250; *Yerushalayima*, especially pp. 158–168; Rothschild: see *Luach Eretz Yisrael*, vol. 10, pp. 194–199.
27. See *Yerushalayima*, pp. 201–210; *Luach Eretz Yisrael*, vol. 14, p. 27.
28. *Luach Eretz Yisrael*, vol. 10, pp. 194–198; cf. *Mara d'Arah Yisrael*, vol. 1, p. 245, who says the Ashkenazim placed a *cherem* on the school in 1865, including a punishment to parents who sent their children there.
29. Ibid., vol. 15, pp. 146–160; *Chazon Tzyon*, pp. 147–159.
30. He quoted the verse in *Ezra* 3:12–13, "Many of the priests and levites, and the chiefs of the fathers' houses, old men who had seen the First Temple, when the foundation of this Temple was laid before their eyes, wept with a loud voice; but many shouted aloud for joy: so that the people could not distinguish the sound of the shout of joy from the sound of the weeping of the people."
31. *Luach Eretz Yisrael*, vol. 10, pp. 169–190.
32. *HaLevanon*, vol. 14, no. 41, pp. 324–325.
33. *Shaarei Yerushalayim*, p. 36.
34. *Sefer HaYishuv*, pp. 39–42.
35. *Shaarei Yerushalayim*, p. 49.
36. See *Har HaBayis*, pp. 69–126.
37. *Mosad HaYesod*, p. 128 (n 37).
38. *Stirring Times*, vol. 2, pp. 62–63.
39. *Tzyon*, vol. 1, pp. 72–74.
40. *Mosad HaYesod*, p. 39.
41. *Sefer HaYishuv*, pp. 83–87.
42. Mrs. Finn writes: "According to Turkish law I was the legal purchaser and holder, although Europeans were not allowed to buy land in Turkey till several years later; but being only a woman and therefore 'nobody,' I was considered as a lawful purchaser." (*Reminiscences of Mrs. Finn*, p. 174).
43. *Stirring Times*, vol. 2, p. 73.
44. Ibid., p. 74.
45. *Sefer HaYishuv*, pp. 128–130.
46. *L'Chovavim HaRishonim*, vol. 1, pp. 4–6.
47. *Luach Eretz Yisrael*, vol. 9, pp. 180–183; *Tevuos HaAretz*, pp. 491–492.
48. *The Golden Dynasty*, p. 12.
49. *Toldos HaChassidus b'Eretz Yisrael*, vol. 1, pp. 73–74.

Jerusalem Blood Libel

RAV MOSHE Rivlin's sleep was broken twice in the same night. Each time he'd had the same dream: the offices of the *beis ha'vaad* had been broken into. Pushing away sleepiness, he dressed and called his *shamesh* to accompany him.

Silently the two men walked to the nearby *beis ha'vaad*, which was located in the Churvah compound. The lock had been bent and forced open. Gingerly, they entered the office and lit a lantern. On the benches and floor was blood. The two glanced at each other anxiously, understanding the imminent danger facing the Jews of Jerusalem. Taking rags, they wiped up the blood and cleaned the room of any trace of stains.

Sure enough, the next morning the Turkish authorities demanded entry into the *beis ha'vaad* office, in search of a gentile child lost the day before. Rumors led them to believe that the boy was murdered by Jewish leaders, and the *beis ha'vaad* was the number one place under suspicion.

Although nothing was found, the whole city was up in arms over the apparent crime. A British subject, Rav Rivlin immediately went to the English consul for advice and help. Together they devised a plan.

The consul requested an emergency meeting with the pasha's minister. He also demanded that the authorities bring the boy's father for interrogation. The father arrived several hours later and was cross-examined by the authorities. More and more questions, more and more contradictions, and finally the gentile broke down and admitted that his son was alive and staying with relatives in Bethlehem.

"But it was not my idea," he cried, pleading for leniency.

"Whose idea was it?" demanded the Turkish general.

"It was a priest from the Armenian monastery in Jerusalem by the name of so-and-so. He offered me a large sum of money if I would do everything he said, and promised me more afterwards."

The priest was summoned. The pasha's minister ordered that he be flogged until he admitted his guilt. Breaking down quickly, the priest explained his scheme in detail. Together with the beadle of the monastery, he broke the lock to the *beis ha'vaad* and slaughtered a goat inside. They timed it to coincide with the boy's early-morning disappearance. Their goal was to see the Jews persecuted — if not by the authorities, then by an angry mob whipped up to carry out a pogrom.

The Turkish court later convicted the officer and beadle of inciting a libel and sentenced them to life imprisonment.

(*HaMaggid Doresh Tzyon*, pp. 47–48)

The 2,500-Year-Old Apology

THE MONOLITHIC tomb of the Prophet Zechariah stands at the bottom of the Mount of Olives. Carved out of huge slabs of stone, its steep roof comes to a narrow point. A prophet and priest, Zechariah was killed for reproving the people (II *Chronicles* 24:20) in the time of King Joash.

In the 1840s, a Chassid named Rav Aharon Moshe of Brody, a disciple of Rav Yitzchak Yaakov of Lublin and Rav Uri of Starelsik, moved to Jerusalem. Known for his piety and righteousness, Rav Aharon Moshe regularly mourned over the destruction of the Temple and the ever-lengthening *galus*.

Zechariah's tomb is an inspiring sight, and it prompted Rav Aharon Moshe to study the story of the prophet's death. After thoroughly scrutinizing the episode, Rav Aharon Moshe strongly felt that the nation's sin in murdering him was a prime cause of the present *galus*. They had flatly refused Zechariah's admonishment to repent their idolatrous ways, and the king had ordered him stoned. Shortly after the prophet's assassination, the king's officers who had committed the murder were themselves killed by a small Aramean force. Thus, they had never repented for their ruthless act.

Rav Aharon Moshe devised a plan which he hoped would rectify their sin and thereby play a part in ending the painful *galus*. First, he penned a poetic letter addressed to the Prophet Zechariah, pleading with him to forgive the sinners. It ended with an entreaty for the prophet to pray for the redemption. Next, he commissioned Rav Mordechai Shnitzer to climb up the tomb and engrave his petition in the stone roof.

In addition to being a scholar, Rav Mordechai was a master craftsman. Having

Tomb of Zechariah as it appeared in the 19th century. In the foreground are the graves of numerous tzaddikim who especially requested to be buried near the tomb. Unfortunately, the graves were desecrated in 1948 by the Arabs and archeologists in search of wealth and artifacts hidden inside the tomb. Nothing, however, was discovered, yet the graves were never restored.

worked on tall buildings with ease and skill, he accepted the job without hesitation. One morning he set off to the Valley of Kidron with a chisel, long ladder, and ropes. Accompanied by Rav Aharon Moshe and an aide, Rav Mordechai placed the letter in the inner pocket of his coat for safekeeping.

At the tomb, he succeeded in climbing to the bottom ledge of the roof. As he began to scale up the steep incline, he lost his grip and slipped down. With nothing to grasp onto, Rav Mordechai tumbled head over heels off the tomb, landing on his head.

Rav Mordechai would eventually recover from the fall, though his condition remained serious for some months. Slowly he regained his health and lived twenty more years. He was instrumental in establishing Bikur Cholim Hospital.

Rav Aharon Moshe realized that the auspicious time for the redemption had not yet come. His job, as before, was to mourn over the past and present *galus.* The rest he left in God's hands.

(*Toldos Chachmei Yerushalayim*, vol. 3, p. 223)

Saving a Soul

IT WAS a warm, early afternoon in Haifa, and all the children were in school. Twelve-year-old Chaim Moshe, however, was wandering around from store to store. He innocently entered one shop, and after a time, marched on to another one. Most of the storekeepers knew the Moroccan lad and made small talk with him. His uncle's shop was his favorite, and there he learned to write and make calculations. His friendliness and alertness made his visits a welcome treat wherever he went.

One day, in the early 1860s, Chaim Moshe was hanging around one of the stores when a very special person entered. A distinguished-looking rabbi, dressed in Moroccan robes and turban, entered the shop. As soon as he noticed the boy, he stopped and stared at him a long time.

"Why aren't you in school, my dear boy?" he asked gently.

"There aren't any religious schools here, yet. I had a private rebbe, but my father could not afford to keep him. So, he teaches me a little every night."

"You must take me to your father!" replied the stranger.

The lad escorted the Rav to his house. Mr. Ben-Naim, surprised by the esteemed guest, sensed the stranger's sincerity and genuine concern for his son's welfare. The guest introduced himself as Rav David Ben-Shimon of Jerusalem, whose name was familiar to Mr. Ben-Naim.

Rav Ben-Shimon took out a small book from his pocket and began to quiz Chaim Moshe. Seeing that the boy had a sharp mind and a thirst for Torah, he turned to Mr. Ben-Naim.

"Let me take Chaim Moshe back with me to Jerusalem," Rav Ben-Shimon urged. "We have a cheder there where he will learn with other Moroccan children and, *be'ezras Hashem*, he will be able to fulfill his potential. As for his physical needs, he can live in my house, and I will take care of him as one of my own children. One of my sons is about his age, and I'm sure the two of them will get along nicely together."

Mr. Ben-Naim welcomed the suggestion. The enthusiasm of Rav David proved to be the decisive factor, especially when he added that Chaim Moshe would visit his parents regularly.

In those days it was at least a two-day journey from Jerusalem to Haifa. Mrs. Ben-Naim, overhearing the whole conversation from the kitchen, asked to speak.

"We so much want our son to learn Torah. But I don't know if I can bear to have him so far away."

Rav Ben-Shimon, understanding her feelings, tried to persuade her to let the boy go. However, upon seeing that Chaim Moshe's mother was adamant, he immediately recommended they send the boy to Tiberias. It was much closer, and the level of education there was also good. Mrs. Ben-Naim happily agreed to this.

Four years later, Chaim Moshe Ben-Naim visited Jerusalem. Rav Ben-Shimon welcomed him with open arms and gave him a copy of his book, *Shaar HaChatzer*. They spoke in learning, and the Rav saw a fine young man before him, developing into a true Torah scholar.

Chaim Moshe returned home with the book and a treasury of memories about the Moroccan tzaddik. As the years passed, Rav Chaim Moshe Ben-Naim matured into a *talmid chacham*, and eventually became the Rav of Gibraltar, a position he filled for many years.

Haifa in the mid-nineteenth century

Years later, Rav Ben-Naim wrote: "I have written about this childhood incident so that everyone will learn a lesson from it. From my story one can see how a great sage, just passing by a storefront, took interest in a boy loitering around, a boy about whom he knew nothing. As it turned out, Rav Ben-Shimon was under great pressure that day, with meetings set up and a timetable to keep. He was, after all, the *dayan* and leader of the Moroccan community in Jerusalem.

"Yet he pushed aside other commitments in order to fend for that boy. He also put himself on the line by lovingly offering to make him part of his own family, accepting all the responsibilities and burdens which this entailed.

"May the merit of his good deeds and thoughts stand before Him always."

(*Chachmei HaMaarav*, pp. 63–64)

A Proud People

Following is an excerpt from the memoirs of Mr. James Finn, the British Consul to Jerusalem between 1845 and 1866. As discussed in the history section, he was a genuine supporter of the Jews of Jerusalem.

BEFORE CONCLUDING this sketch of Jewish affairs, we may take notice of two curious peculiarities of Jerusalem — both founded on the idea of the place being still their [i.e., the Jews'] own — an idea which, although but a shadow at present in relation to other people, is not without weight among themselves. The customs are, of course, limited to the Sephardim, or Israelites of the country.

One is the coining of money, or rather of an equivalent to that special prerogative of royalty. The articles are small squares of brass foil, stamped with the Hebrew words בקור חולים, i.e., "Visiting the Sick." The practice seems to have originated in adopting a fictitious currency, on temporary occasions, as a mean of almsgiving, in anticipation of real money coming to hand. In the Jewish bazaar these pieces are current for all purposes of trade, and are sometimes accepted and passed among other inhabitants of the city as *paras*, though inferior in value to even that small coin. The Turks disapprove of the practice, and now and then take the trouble to prohibit it. The Jews, however, are proud of their show of independent royalty, and even if willing to discontinue it, would find it difficult to call in these tokens, so long as their heavy debt remains, for they do actually represent a certain amount of metallic value.

The other custom is that of getting possession of the great keys of the city gates on the decease of each Sultan of Constantinople, and after a religious service of prayer, and anointing them with a mysterious preparation of oil and spices, allowing them to be returned to the civic authorities on behalf of the new monarch. For the exercise of this traditional custom they make heavy presents to the local governors, who allow this harmless practice that has prescription to show on its behalf. It is a matter of "*bakhsheesh*" to them, and there is always a class of superstitious people to be found in Palestine who think that the benediction of the ancient "children of Israel" is worth having; the Jewish feelings are gratified, for their expectation of the future is refreshed, and the Jerusalem rabbis are enabled to boast all the world over among their people that they suffer the Sultan of Turkey to keep possession of the Holy City.

The Moslems imagine the ceremonial to be the benediction of the incoming reign, but for my part I should like to know what words are used in this consecration of the keys with the "anointed oil," and how many of these words have kabbalistic or "*roshei tevos*" interpretations and double meanings, for it would be vain to expect to find the formula in any printed books. I am told that in the Sephardic Synagogue are preserved small phials of the "anointing oil," remaining from over these ceremonials of many past Sultans; but at the time we are now considering (1853), the Jews had not for some years performed the ceremony, having had no opportunity of doing so, [not since Abdul Majid became Sultan in 1840].

(*Stirring Times*, vol. 1, pp. 116–119)

The Wonder-Worker

THOUGH HE lived a life of grinding poverty, the tzaddik, Rav Shalom Bachbot, never complained about his lot. Instead, he accepted his situation like Rabbi Chanina ben Dosa, knowing that the Almighty was setting aside his true portion for the World to Come.

As the festival of Passover approached, his wife discussed the family's holiday needs with him.

"We don't even have a single coin to buy the multitude of things necessary for the holiday," she sighed.

"My dear," he said, "let's make a list of everything we need."

As she mentioned each item, like wine or matzah, Rav Shalom jotted it down on a piece of paper. Beside each item, he wrote how much money they needed to purchase it. At the end, he drew a line and added up all the prices, with the total written in large numbers.

Rav Shalom, a teacher in the Moroccan yeshivah, called one of his students to his side.

"Take this piece of paper," he told the boy as he folded the paper over and over again, "and go to the Western Wall. When you get there, place it in one of the cracks of the Kosel stones."

The boy dutifully fulfilled the tzaddik's wish. On his way back from the Wall, a Bucharian Jew stopped him to ask for directions to Rav Bachbot's house. The boy guided him to the front door.

As soon as the stranger sat before Rav Shalom, he poured out his heart to the tzaddik.

"My daughter, my only child, is very, very ill," he cried out. "The doctors don't know what to do. Would the Rav please pray for her recovery?"

Rav Shalom agreed. Leaving a bag of coins on the table, the Bucharian Jew left, feeling that the tzaddik's prayers would influence the Heavenly judgment in favor of his daughter.

Rav Shalom handed the bag to one of his children. "Give this money to mother."

His wife opened the bag and counted the money. The amount came to exactly the sum Rav Shalom had written on the piece of paper. Not a penny more, nor a penny less.

* * *

JERUSALEMITES made a point of visiting Rav Shalom Bachbot after the Passover holidays. They came to get a blessing from him, and a date which he personally handed to each one. The tzaddik gave the date as a symbol for success and growth, like the tall date tree. His dates were especially sought after by those in need of better health, children, and the like. So powerful was the tzaddik's blessing, that people would send some of these dates to relatives overseas.

One year, a wealthy Moghrabi Jew received a date and asked that Rav Shalom bless his son with success. His son was studying medicine in Cairo, and a major exam was coming up. His father sent the date, leaving instructions for him to eat it just before taking the exam. The son laughed at the idea and threw away the date. On the day of the exam, he suddenly drew a mental blank and failed miserably.

The following year, the Moghrabi Jew again appeared before the tzaddik for a blessing for his son. This time his son carefully watched over the date until the day of the final exam. The results of the test amazed the young man and his professors. He had the top marks in the class.

When he returned to Jerusalem for vacation, the father took his son to the tzaddik for a blessing, warning him not to reveal what had happened to the first date he sent him a year ago.

When they entered Rav Shalom's house, the son bent down to kiss the tzaddik's hand, as was customary. Rav Shalom extended his hand with only two fingers outstretched.

"Since you showed disrespect to one of my dates, you may only kiss part of my hand!"

(*Chachmei HaMaarav*, pp. 241–242)

Wheat from Heaven

ONE WINTER in the mid-nineteenth century portended a year of drought in the Holy City. With the coming of spring, the crisis quickly grew to critical proportions for the entire populace. Not only was water measured by the spoonful, but wheat, vegetables, and other basic necessities were hardly attainable. From day to day the situation grew bleaker, and even a state of emergency declared by the authorities could not rescue the hungry children.

The Jews turned to prayer. One night, Rav Yeshaya Bardaky, the noble leader of the Perushim, organized a midnight vigil by the Western Wall. Men and women wailed and beseeched their Heavenly Father to have mercy on them, and shower them with sustenance.

At the conclusion of their prayers, they started to return homeward. They were quite surprised to find the narrow lanes crowded with mules laden with sacks of wheat, extending all the way to the *chatzer* of Rav Bardaky. Eagerly, they asked how much the precious grain cost.

The leader of the Arab caravan disregarded their questions.

"Where is Bardaky?" he asked.

On meeting the Perushim leader, the Arab offered to sell the whole train of wheat which he had brought from far away.

"I am willing," Rav Bardaky announced. "But I don't have cash to pay for it."

The Arab answered, "I am willing to accept a note from the Chacham, who is known to be trustworthy."

Unhesitatingly, Rav Bardaky wrote an IOU for the entire sum. Then he invited the Arab leader and his companions to dine with him and spend the night in his *chatzer*.

"Thank you, but we must be off at once."

Within minutes, the mules were unloaded, and they disappeared in the dark corridors of the city.

Days and weeks passed, yet the Arab never returned to claim payment for the wheat. Rav Bardaky inquired in every sector of the city, but without success. The gatekeepers confirmed his suspicions that the gates of the city were duly bolted as required by law, and that no caravan of mules had entered that day.

In gratitude to the Almighty, Rav Bardaky gave part of the wheat to the Moslem and Christian citizens of the city. In that way, he spread the greatness of the Lord's Name in the world.

(*L'Chovavim HaRishonim*, no. 2, pp. 23–24)

Rav Schwartz Meets the Archduke

RAV YOSEF Schwartz, who had arrived in Jerusalem in the early 1830s, was a man of many talents. As a communal activist, he stood prepared to help his people in any way he could. As a scholar, he translated his love of Eretz Yisrael into becoming the first modern topographer of the Land. The outcome of his research, *Tevuos HaAretz*, was published in the mid-1840s by the Beck Publishing House. A masterpiece, his book ranked among the most authoritative works concerning the sites and boundaries of Eretz Yisrael. Over the next decade, he had it reprinted in German and even in English.

When Archduke Maximilian visited Jerusalem in 1856 (5616), Rav Schwartz arranged to meet with him. The Archduke was the brother of the Austro-Hungarian Emperor, Franz Joseph, and his visit preceded the Emperor's by several years. Speaking flawless German, Rav Schwartz made a sterling impression on the Archduke. At the meeting, Rav Schwartz presented the noble visitor with a copy of the German edition of his book as a gift. This edition included original maps by the author.

Later, when Archduke Maximilian returned home and had ample time to review the book, he was very impressed by it. So much so, in fact, that he took the extraordinary and unprecedented step of having the book included in the mandatory reading list for Jewish students of higher education!

(*Toldos Chachmei Yerushalayim*, vol. 3, pp. 234–235)

Birth of a Tzaddik

ON THE seventh night of Passover, 1867 (5617), Rav Avraham Coyanca's aging wife gave birth to a son. The tidings spread quickly through the Sephardic neighborhood of Jerusalem — welcome news that gladdened the hearts of everyone.

Mrs. Coyanca was overjoyed to hold her first son in her arms. In her forty years of marriage, she had already borne one daughter and suffered six miscarriages. However, though others might have been surprised, she was not at all worried about this birth. Months ago she knew that she was destined to bear a son with a lofty soul, one who was destined to become a great tzaddik. How many tears she shed to be worthy to have this son!

Nearly a year before, she and her husband had attended the *yartzeit* commemoration of Shmuel HaNavi in Rama, a few hours' trek north of Jerusalem. Amidst the festivities, she poured out her heart to the Almighty. "If You will grant me a son, O Lord, I shall name him after the prophet Samuel." Soon afterwards she became pregnant.

A few months into her pregnancy, her deceased brother-in-law, Rav Vidal Coyanca, a kabbalist in Jerusalem who passed away three years earlier, came

Rav Benzion Coyanca (1867–1937)

to her in a dream. His broad smile lightened the room, and his voice chimed in her ears.

"I've come to tell you," he said, "that I'm going to be an important guest in your house."

She awoke and immediately interpreted the dream. Rav Vidal would, in some way, influence the child in her womb and guide him in the ways of righteousness. She joyfully kept her secret: she would bear a healthy son!

Now, with her newborn son in her arms, her dream of dreams had come true.

At the bris ceremony, the child was named Benzion Shmuel Vidal: Shmuel, after the prophet, Vidal, after the child's Heavenly mentor, and Benzion as an added tribute to God for giving them a son in Jerusalem.

* * *

BENZION'S REMARKABLE love of Torah could be measured by his phenomenal progress in learning. At the age of seven he knew most of the Tanach by heart and eagerly took up Mishnah and Gemara. At nine years, he expounded on a complex Torah subject before the *chachamim*, and, as a result, acquired the reputation of a young genius. Before his bar mitzvah, Benzion had begun writing Torah novellas.

Benzion's father, wanting his son only to study Torah, provided for his needs even after he reached adulthood. When his father passed away in 1892, Rav Benzion lost the family business. Several times he sat on the Sephardic rabbinical court, but he preferred being independent rather than living in the public domain. He therefore began publishing a bi-annual *maasef* (anthology) booklet of *chiddushei Torah* from Torah scholars. It was an instant success.

In 1900 he visited Baghdad, where the Ben Ish Chai tried to convince him to remain and become the Chacham Bashi. But again, Rav Coyanca felt his mission lay elsewhere.

In the end, he joined the Sephardic rabbinate in 1921. There he worked with other members of the rabbinate, such as Rav Kook and Rav Yaakov Meir, to strengthen Jewish knowledge in Jerusalem and Eretz Yisrael.

(*L'Chovavim HaRishonim*, vol. 10)

Gunpoint

THE KALISHER Rav, Rav Meir Auerbach, lived in a large courtyard at the beginning of Yehudim Street in the Jewish Quarter. In the courtyard was a *beis midrash* where he prayed, and where scholars studied Torah throughout the day under his patronage. His *beis din* convened in the women's gallery at regular times each day.

One evening, when he was alone in the *beis midrash*, someone told him of a certain Jew who had the audacity to lead other God-fearing Jews astray. Rav Auerbach could barely believe what he heard. Immediately, he sent for the man, who came into the *beis midrash* with an air of arrogance about him.

Without any regard for the venerable Rav's honor, the man spewed forth venomous remarks that conveyed both his hatred of his heritage and his entirely unfounded disrespect for the Rav of Kalish.

Rav Auerbach, as Rav of Jerusalem, slapped him on the face and scolded him for making such statements.

The man's eyes flashed with anger. Suddenly he reached inside his coat, pulled out a gun, and aimed it at the Rav of Jerusalem. In another second his enemy would be dead on the floor in a pool of blood.

Undaunted, Rav Auerbach pulled open his coat, revealing his heart, and addressed his assailant. "Shoot!"

A long moment passed in utter silence.

"I am absolutely sure," continued the Rav of Jerusalem, "that no bullet can kill me, since all of my actions throughout my lifetime have been for the sake of Heaven alone. I have never sought honor for myself or for my forefathers."

Rav Auerbach's stare penetrated straight into the man's eyes and he shook with fear. Without uttering a word, he turned and fled, never to be seen again in Jerusalem.

* * *

A SIMILAR story is told of Rav Yosef Chaim Zonnenfeld. One Shabbos afternoon in the 1920s, while he was learning with one of his grandchildren, two Zionist ruffians barged in and pointed a gun at him. Rav Zonnenfeld stood up and bared his heart. "Shoot!" he called out. The shocked young men quickly disappeared.

(*Betuv Yerushalayim*, p. 354)

Yoma d'Pagra

THE ROSH Yeshivah could hardly believe what he heard. "The *bachurim* are planning an outing — a day-long trip — called *yoma d'pagra*." Rav Moshe Nechemiah Kahanov, twenty years Rosh Yeshivah of Etz Chaim Yeshivah, wondered what had gotten into the boys' heads. Hadn't he stressed the importance of spending long and thoughtful hours studying Gemara, Rishonim, and *Shulchan Aruch*? What pained him the most was that the names of the *bachurim* planning the outing were among the top ones in the yeshivah.

He confronted the group with the question: "What is the *yoma d'pagra* that you are planning?"

One of the younger *bachurim*, Arie Leib, spoke up. "It was my idea," he confessed. "I planned the whole itinerary."

He boldly continued, "Really, we have no intention, *chas v'shalom*, of curtailing our *seder* of learning. On the contrary, we plan to review the gemara *Chullin* by heart as we walk!"

Rav Kahanov's expression lightened.

"Wonderful!" he exclaimed. "In that case, I'll come along with you!"

At the appointed time, the group set out for an outing in the Judean hills. With a backdrop of sun and view of mountainsides, the excursion thrilled everyone. The *bachurim* reviewed the gemara, including Rashi and Tosefos, and extending to the Rif and the *Shulchan Aruch*. Everyone was lively and shining with excitement. For the Rosh Yeshivah, it was a joyful sign of accomplishment — both to hear his students learning, and to realize that they were indeed true soldiers in the army of the Lord.

(*Luach Eretz Yisrael*, vol. 9, p. 152)

The Fiery Torah

RAV AVRAHAM Eisenstein was busy from morning to night, both sitting on the rabbinical court of Rav Auerbach and running the Central Committee office of the Perushim. Rav Yosef Rivlin said of him: "He was the first to come in the morning and the last to leave at night." The myriad problems facing Jerusalemites at the time demanded men of distinction to dedicate their lives for the cause. Rav Eisenstein, the paragon of leadership, did not shrink from his responsibility in the least.

Late at night, although exhausted from the day's exertions, Rav Avraham studied Torah with a renewed spirit. Once, he was fortunate to obtain a handwritten copy of the *Shitah Mekubetzes* on *Kodashim*. Realizing that it might be one of the few copies in existence, he ardently studied it.

One night, while examining the handwritten *sefer*, he dosed off and unwittingly nudged the candlestick next to him. It fell onto the corner of the manuscript, and within seconds the *sefer* caught on fire.

Startled, Rav Eisenstein jerked awake and extinguished the small blaze. The margin of the book and a good part of the text itself lay in ashes. He bemoaned the accident, and decided to rewrite the missing words and sentences through analyzing each topic in depth.

After untold nights of work, he completed the job and sent it off to be published. To his surprise, he learned of a second scholar who had recently discovered another handwritten copy of the same *Shitah* on *Kodashim*, and had already sent it to be published.

Instead of feeling letdown that his efforts were in vain, Rav Eisenstein rejoiced to see that all the work he had done fit in exactly with the original handwritten *sefer*.

(*Mi'Gedolei Yerushalayim*, p. 69)

The Emperor's Gift

EMPEROR FRANZ Joseph's visit to the Holy City was full of pageantry. Wherever he went he was literally given the royal treatment. So much so, in fact, that the Turkish government repaired the Jaffa-Jerusalem road so that his horse-drawn carriage could travel on it. Until then, from time immemorial, the only means of ascending to Jerusalem was by horse, mule, camel, or by foot.

The Kaiser used his time wisely, based on a prearranged itinerary. He attended meetings and programs, and went on tours of the various sites of the city as well. Included in his agenda was a tour of the Jewish synagogues — partially out of deference to the pluralistic views of the times, and partially out of concern for the large number of Jews who held Austrian citizenship. The Jewish population of 1869 equaled those of the Moslem and Christian inhabitants together. The total populace of the city consisted of about twenty thousand souls.

Thursday, 14 November, was a clear day. Escorted by an entourage of Austrian and Turkish nobility, the Emperor entered the Jewish Quarter and proceeded straight to the Rabban Yochanan ben Zakkai Synagogue. A large gathering of Jews awaited the monarch, among them the Rishon l'Tzyon, Rav David Chazan, and other leading rabbis.

When the Rishon l'Tzyon greeted the Emperor, Rav Nisan Beck stepped forward to translate from German to Hebrew and back to German.

Looking at the ancient synagogue, the Emperor asked Rav Beck, "Tell me the truth, is this synagogue really from the time of Rabban Yochanan ben Zakkai?"

"We do not know how old the actual synagogue which you are looking at is," admitted Rav Beck, "But deep down, where the foundation stones are, it is surely that old."

After a short exchange with the Rishon l'Tzyon and other rabbis, the Emperor continued on his walk, with Rav Beck as his guide. When his entourage approached the Tiferes Yisrael Synagogue, Franz Joseph stopped and stared at it, holding onto his hat as he bent backwards to look up the high walls of the building. Standing several stories high, the building lacked a roof and was no more than a skeleton.

"Who designed this synagogue?" the Emperor asked curiously.

feres Yisrael Synagogue, completed in 1872, was the main Chassidic shul in the Old Yishuv until it was destroyed by the Arabs 1948. It was popularly known as the Nisan Beck Shul after the man who was the guiding force behind its establishment and ontinuance.

"I did, Your Highness," replied Rav Nisan.

"Who taught Mr. Beck this occupation?"

"I did!" answered Rav Beck. "His Royal Highness should know that I taught myself in my own house."

The Emperor smiled and looked again at the impressive structure. Then he turned the discussion over to the economic side of building such a large synagogue.

"I assume that you collect the necessary funds by donations from fellow Jews?"

"Yes, Your Highness. But the recent famines and suffering of the Jews in Austria and Hungary have prevented me from asking them to help our cause. Consequently, the construction has stopped due to lack of funds."

Thinking quickly, Rav Beck attempted to take advantage of the hour and open the doorway to the monarch's help. He continued smoothly, "Now, however, through the honor of having the Emperor come here and enter this holy site, we hope that the roof will be completed soon."

Turning to move on, the Emperor beckoned Rav Beck to continue with him. All too happy, the venerated Rav escorted the Franz Joseph through the Jewish Quarter. After visiting the Rothschild Hospital, they proceeded to the Western Wall. The Emperor then turned to go up on the Temple Mount.

"If Your Highness will permit me," said Rav Beck politely, "I will take my leave here, since it is forbidden for a Jew to enter the Temple Mount."

The Emperor would not take "no" for an answer, and urged his esteemed friend to join him. Again, Rav Nisan repeated the halachic ruling. The Emperor, however, interpreted it as a Turkish prohibition or a fear of Moslem reprisals.

"You do not have to be afraid, Mr. Beck, since you are with me."

"No, no," Rav Beck politely corrected him. "It has nothing to do with our Moslem neighbors. Our Jewish Law forbids us."

"In that case," the Kaiser smiled, "I thank you, and bid you farewell."

After shaking the emperor's hand, Rav Nisan said good-bye and departed.

Within a short time, the meeting bore fruit. The Emperor sent a gift of a thousand golden napoleons to pay for the construction of the domed roof of the Tiferes Yisrael Synagogue, a synagogue which would soon echo with the fervent prayers of Chassidic Jews in the heart of the Holy City.

(*L'Chovavim HaRishonim*, vol. 1, pp. 15–16)

19th Century

From Napoleon to Beyond the Walls

Part III

Beyond the Walls: 1870-1900

פְּרָזוֹת תֵּשֵׁב יְרוּשָׁלַםִ מֵרֹב אָדָם וּבְהֵמָה בְּתוֹכָהּ.
וַאֲנִי אֶהְיֶה לָּהּ נְאֻם יְהוָה חוֹמַת אֵשׁ סָבִיב
וּלְכָבוֹד אֶהְיֶה בְתוֹכָהּ.

זכריה ב: ח-ט

Jerusalem shall be inhabited
like unwalled towns
because of the multitude of men and cattle that shall be in it;
for I, says the Lord,
shall be to her a wall of fire round about,
and will be the glory in the midst of her.

Zechariah 2: 8-9

Mapping the Future

According to everyone's calculation, the time had come to breach the walls and expand the city limits. Between 1840 and 1870, the Jewish community of Jerusalem had increased multifold, growing from 2,000 to 10,000 souls. Severe overcrowding did not just mean an inconvenient lack of privacy — it was actually life-threatening. The city's primitive infrastructure was ill-equipped to handle the strain placed on it. As a result of the poor sanitary conditions, the stifling odor of effluvium filled the air. Even worse, such conditions encouraged the outbreak of uncontrollable epidemics.

The Moslem community showed no signs of making the big leap outside the walls. On the contrary, they were even partially responsible for some of the attacks on the new suburbs. They preferred the status quo since it was economically to their advantage. In their eyes, being rich slumlords outweighed any desire to proceed with the next natural step in the city's march to the future. Aggravating things even more, the municipality had no rent-control system, and the Arabs had no compunction about inflating rental prices to levels that crushed their Jewish tenants. One Arab landlord arrogantly dismissed the pleas of his Jewish tenant not to jack up the rent: "Even if all you Jews were as thin as wood slivers, there still would not be enough room for all of you to live in the Churvah section [i.e., the Jewish Quarter]. You would still have to pay us whatever we demand!"[1] However, this downtrodden but indomitable people would become the pioneers of the future, boldly facing the dangers before them and setting a precedent for all to follow.

In order to truly appreciate and understand these first settlers' motives, we must realize that it was not only practical reasons that spurred them on — a spiritual calling beckoned them as well. This calling was rooted in the prophetic words of the Vilna Gaon, who had so often encouraged his disciples to build up Jerusalem in order to hasten the messianic redemption.

Givat Yerushalayim

The vast tract of land stretching from the walls of Jerusalem to Lifta (across from Givat Shaul), a distance of over three kilometers, was called Givat Yerushalayim, the Hill of Jerusalem.[2] The Jaffa Road cut through the middle of this expanse. It was here that most of the first suburbs of Jerusalem would be built. The settlements would eventually be referred to as the New City, in relation to the ancient city inside the walls, which would become known as the Old City.

If one were to peer beyond the walls of Jerusalem in 1850, he would behold almost utter barrenness on every side, stretching as far as the eye could see. Silwan (Shiloach) to the south had a small, semi-nomadic Arab population numbering a couple of hundred. Way off to the west was the village of Ein Kerem, with a monastery standing in its midst. Other than that, the rest of the view from the city walls showed a few small parcels of land farmed by local Arabs, producing grapes and olives and the like. Besides a few trees, the entire landscape was nothing but stones, thorns, and thistles.

Rav Yosef Rivlin is generally credited as having built the first suburb, called Nachalas Shiva, in 1869. In truth, however, there were two other efforts which preceded Nachalas Shiva, both of which had a lasting effect on the process of expansion.

Mishkenos Sha'ananim[3]

The story of Mishkenos Sha'ananim ("Serene Dwellings"), founded in 1855, began with the last will and testament of Judah Touro of New Orleans. In his will, he designated sixty thousand dollars for a needy project in Jerusalem.

Mr. Touro, originally from Boston, had migrated to New Orleans. There he amassed a fortune, partially in a shipping business along the Mississippi River. As his wealth grew, so did his generosity. He built synagogues in both Providence, Rhode Island, and in New Orleans, and gave handsomely to Jewish organizations. As a leading Jewish philanthropist, Judah Touro became a member of the Amsterdam committee for the needs of Eretz Yisrael.

It once happened that an urgent message reached the Jewish community of Jerusalem. The Amsterdam committee requested the Jews to pray by the Western Wall for two of their members, Judah Touro and a Mr. Yisrael, who, due to false accusations against them, found themselves in a tight bind. The request was fulfilled and a reply was sent to the committee ending with the following words: "As requested, may Yehudah and Yisrael be saved."

Sometime later, during a drought year, a shipment loaded with sacks of flour and other essential foodstuffs unexpectedly arrived in the Holy City. When the sacks were opened, each contained a piece of paper with the following words: "You have saved Yehudah and Yisrael."

When Judah Touro died in 1854, he left half a million dollars to various charities. Sixty thousand dollars were earmarked for Jerusalem, without designating a specific purpose for the money. The controllers of the will contacted Sir Moses Montefiore, asking him to distribute the funds according to his discretion for the benefit of the Jewish community in Jerusalem.

Together with Mr. Gershon Corset, Montefiore planned to build a hospital outside the walls. However, it became increasingly obvious to them that they would have to go to Eretz Yisrael and personally supervise the undertaking.

The greatest obstacle facing the project was obtaining a permit to build outside the walls. Even before setting off from England, Sir Moses met with Lord Clarendon to discuss the matter. Lord Clarendon, familiar with all the issues involved, presented a gloomy picture. As proof for his pessimistic view, he pointed to the British Consul in Constantinople, Lord Stratford of Radcliff, whose unsuccessful attempts on behalf of British subjects in Eretz Yisrael had reached a dead-end.

Sir Moses Montefiore, an optimistic believer in his mission for the Jewish people, forged ahead with his plan. In Sivan, 1855, he left London for Constantinople, arriving in the Turkish capital a month later. In an audience with the Sultan he achieved his objective, and Sir Moses left the palace with an official *firman* in hand.

In Av, 1855 (5615), Montefiore's party reached Jerusalem. Within a short time, a large tract of land comprising 38,000 square meters was purchased opposite Mount Zion for a thousand pounds sterling. The sale went smoothly, partly due to the owner's previous relationship with Sir Moses Montefiore. Dr. Loewe, Montefiore's personal secretary, recorded what transpired:

Achmad Aga Dijar, the previous mayor of Jerusalem, had met Sir Moses

Mishkenos Sha'ananim

in 1839 and a personal friendship developed between them. As it turned out, he was the owner of the tract of land that we sought.

When Sir Moses offered to buy the plot, he answered, "My dear, beloved friend. I received this land as an inheritance from my forefathers, and in no way am I willing to part with it for any sum of money. But for you, I shall give it as a present."

Every day when Sir Moses asked to buy it, he returned the same answer. Finally, the discussion of the matter lasted a good part of the day. Just when I, as translator, was simply running out of words in Arabic to reiterate Sir Moses' stand to him, he said, "My loyal friend, I swear by the hair on my head, that if Sir Moses will give me a thousand pounds sterling as a gift, I am prepared to go with him now to the kadi."

When I translated this to Sir Moses, he unhesitatingly counted out a thousand pounds sterling, and, together with Dijar and his party, we went to the British consulate and wrote a contract. Next we all went to the municipal Moslem court to register the sale. The judge asked both the owner and the buyer a number of questions, and had the agreement read aloud and signed by witnesses before him.

Mishkenos Sha'ananim became the first tract of land outside the walls to be legally owned by a Jew. Montefiore ordered a stone wall to be built around the entire area. Forty Jews worked for two weeks on the retaining wall. At that time, Jerusalemites called the land "Moshe and Yehudis' vineyard."

On Sunday, 5 Elul, Sir Moses laid the cornerstone for the first two buildings. At the ceremony, Sir Moses first put a copy of the contract in the hole, and Mr. Corset placed Mr. Touro's ring there. Then Sir Moses put the cornerstone in place.

Although the original plan called for a hospital to be built, this idea was soon abandoned. First, Baron Rothschild had just opened the first Jewish hospital inside the city walls, reducing the immediate need for medical assistance. Furthermore, sick people were afraid to stay so far away from the city. Though today we would consider the five-minute walk no more than a stone's throw away from the city, at that time, wild animals lurked everywhere and Bedouins terrorized the area. Limited by the specifications of the *firman*, and in any event lacking a clear idea for an alternative, plans to develop the property were temporarily laid aside.

Battei Yehudah Touro

The land lay unused until Sir Montefiore returned in 1857. At that time, a new plan was drawn up to build housing for the poor. It was called Battei Yehudah Touro, although it would be referred to by its original name of Mishkenos Sha'ananim as well. The new neighborhood would have two long rows of houses, two synagogues, cisterns, a *mikve*, a public oven, and a windmill. The windmill, which Montefiore sent from London, was envisioned to serve a dual purpose. First, tenants of Battei Yehudah Touro would be able to grind their own wheat nearby, obviating the need for them to take it into the Old City. Furthermore, the Jews living inside the Old City would also profit. Until this

The Windmill

time, the Moslems had a monopoly on wheat grinding; the new and cheaper facilities would allow the Jews to circumvent the Moslems' exclusive hold in this area.

The windmill, unfortunately, had a short lifespan. Even though it was built on top of a hill to catch the wind, it quickly became evident that the fluctuating breeze was not steady enough to operate it efficiently. The best place for a windmill was near the seashore, where a steady wind blew. Jealous Moslems also tried to interfere, and even tried to cast an evil spell on the project. Despite its failure, the windmill remained in place, and in future generations it would become a monument to the Jews' nascent efforts to create their own future.

Another innovation was more successful. A metal hand pump was installed to bring water up from the underground cisterns. It was such a novelty that people used to walk over to the suburb just to see it.

Montefiore sent an architect from

London to design the new housing project. In 1860, after a series of delays — due both to the city council's reticence and the architect's ignorance of how things proceed (or don't) in the Middle East — the houses were completed.

Each home was comprised of two rooms, plus a kitchen and pantry — a layout that would become the standard format of all new housing during the initial period of expansion. The front door of each house was reinforced with metal bars, and the windows had metal grating specially imported from England. Well built and with ample room outside for a garden, Battei Yehudah Touro stood ready to house its first tenants.

However, there was one small problem that impeded further progress — people did not want to move in! Montefiore added incentives, such as free rent and free seeds for the vegetable gardens. Finally, some twenty families ventured to the new location. Their resolve did not last long. Afraid to be in the wilderness all by themselves, they soon returned to the city.

Undaunted, Sir Moses offered even more incentives, including a yearly stipend and complete ownership of the houses (his plan had initially called for a rotation system whereby every few years another family would replace the preceding one). Even this was only partially successful. The settlers spent the day in Mishkenos Sha'ananim, and at nightfall returned to the safety of the walled city.

Mishkenos Sha'ananim, located between the Sultan's Pools (foreground) and the Windmill, as it appears today

The settlers had a valid basis for their fears. Wild animals threatened them at night, and there was the ever-present Bedouin threat. A Jewish tradesman, Rav Zalman Basan, built traps which caught foxes every night for some time. Two residents were murdered in Bedouin attacks, one as he walked home from the city at dusk, and the other as he chased after the attackers.

On the other hand, during the cholera epidemic of 1865 that raged inside the walls, no one in Battei Yehudah Touro became sick.

On Montefiore's sixth visit in 1866, he personally toured the new neighborhood and spoke with many of the residents. In a highly optimistic entry in his diary he wrote: "I very much desired to see it, and to meet the worthy people living there.... These secure houses are highly regarded among the citizens of the city. Many wish to stay there for a spell and recover their health.... How clearly do we see the benefits of building more housing projects for the poor outside the walled city."

In a meeting with the leaders of the *yishuv*, Sir Moses posed the question: "In what way can I best be of help?" Unanimously, they resounded, "By offering housing and farming opportunities!"

On 25 Nisan, 1866 (5616), another cornerstone was laid in Battei Yehudah Touro for an additional four houses in a ceremony which included leaders of the Jewish and Moslem Quarters. The construction, however, was not completed until 1871, and even then the houses remained empty until Montefiore's last visit in 1875.

A contemporary author captured the spirit of the times in these words:

Yehudah Touro, how fortunate is your lot,

Between high mountains you built a splendid name,

As an eternal memorial of blessing, your name is your inheritance,

Therefore, your brethren shall praise you, you are compared to us [as if you actually lived in Jerusalem yourself].[4]

Machane Yisrael

A second small Jewish "colony" — as they were called in those days — was established by the Moroccan community near the Mamilla pools, in what is today a downtown district of the New City. Founded in 1868 by the Moroccan leader, Rav David Ben-Shimon, it was the first colony actually funded by the Jews of Jerusalem themselves.

The neighborhood was tiny and the houses poorly built. However, the residents were a courageous and spirited lot. The Tzuf Devash Synagogue, named after the founding *rav*, remained lit throughout the night. Men studied in different *mishmeros*, providing a double benefit: the Torah that was learned served as a spiritual shield against the dangers of the night, and the men studying were attentive to possible surprise attacks by Bedouins.

Known as both Shechunas HaMaaravim and Shechunas Mamilla, this particular suburb was destined to stand outside the limelight of historical perspective. On the other hand, a strong new impetus to break through the walls was gaining more and more momentum in other quarters. Young, fiery Ashkenazim were about to purchase a tract of land along the Jaffa Road and boldly raise the flag of a Jewish colony. Their efforts would change the face of Jerusalem forever.

Nachalas Shiva

The story of Nachalas Shiva, preserved and well documented, deserves close attention. Based on its success, a slow but steady exodus from the walled city gradually made the New City a reality. In the wake of Nachalas Shiva's founding, some of its founders would move on to spearhead the formation of many other colonies as well. What began as a simple conversation between close friends, eventually developed into the New City of Jerusalem.

Rav Yosef Rivlin and Rav Yoel Moshe Salomon, both in their twenties, are credited with having proposed the new colony. After the plague of 1865, when the Moslem landlords terrorized their Jewish tenants with fourfold hikes in rent, activists tried to arouse their Jewish brethren to the urgency of building colonies outside the walls. At the time, Mishkenos Sha'ananim was no more than a pilot project with mixed success, and Shechunas HaMaaravim was not yet in existence.

Bonei Yerushalayim

According to one version of the events, Rav Salomon, whose parents died in the plague, fervently tried to arouse his friends to act. One day he walked with some friends to the future site of Nachalas Shiva, part of which was a pea and lentil farm at the time. The Arab farmers asked what he wanted there, and to their surprise he offered to buy the land at half a *grush* per square meter. "What for?" they asked. "To grow peas and lentils like you," was the reply. The simple farmers were dazzled by the idea of becoming "wealthy" overnight. That night, Yoel Moshe shared the news with his close friend Yosef Rivlin.[5] Thus, it was a spontaneous act by Rav Salomon that set the stage for everything which followed. However, the genius responsible for actually creating the new colony — the person who organized it, fund-raised for it, saw the sale of the land through, and traversed all the bureaucratic hurdles — was Rav Yosef Rivlin.[6]

As early as 1857 (5617), Yosef Rivlin created an organization by the name of Bonei Yerushalayim (Builders of Jerusalem).[7] This organization was the outgrowth of a discussion between Rav Rivlin and Sir Moses Montefiore in 1855. Montefiore saw in the enthusiastic young man the image of his grandfather, the *maggid*, Rav Moshe Rivlin, whom he had known personally. Montefiore offered Rav Yosef a post in London on the board of directors controlling funding for Eretz Yisrael. At the time, someone had also suggested to Sir Moses that he remain in Jerusalem. Thus it was that Rav Yosef answered Montefiore's suggestion: "The optimum way of progressing the plan of expansion is when you [Sir Moses Montefiore] will be in London, and I shall be here in Jerusalem."[8]

In 1859 (5619), Rav Yosef, together with Rav Salomon and Rav Michel Cohen, traveled to Russia and Europe to arouse interest in his organization and enlist members. The three men succeeded in collecting eight hundred rubles over the course of their journey, which was later used to help purchase Nachalas Shiva.

A breakthrough in the seventeen-year deadlock over building outside the walls came in 1861. The *firman* which Montefiore secured in 1855 from the Sultan applied only to the plot of land called Mishkenos Sha'ananim. Perhaps, the *rabbanim* reasoned, the Sultan might be convinced to view this small step as the precedent for a much larger one. Therefore, they decided to send a two-man delegation to Constantinople to seek an all-encompassing *firman*. Rav Yosef Rivlin and Rav Benzion Lyon arrived in the Turkish capital with certificates and letters. There they met with the Sultan's secretary. At first they discussed only general issues, such as improving sanitary conditions in the Holy City. Finally, they broached the subject of buying land and building on it. Responding in the name of the Sultan, the secretary gave his unqualified approval. The official annulment of the prohibition reached Jerusalem in Teves, 1862.[9] In practical terms, the right of foreigners to purchase land materialized only after 1867.

Land Acquisition

In the following years, the members of Bonei Yerushalayim concentrated on convincing their brethren in the Holy City to join their cause. In the late 1860s, the momentum of the movement picked up, and after an unsuccessful land deal fell through, the site on which Nachalas Shiva was built was finally bought in 1869.

The problems encountered in purchasing land comprised the most difficult and aggravating stages in building the colony. Arab fellaheen came to the Vaad office with offers to sell their land. Proof of ownership was sometimes no more than a piece of paper signed by the village sheik that the land belonged to so-and-so. Another problem was clearly identifying the boundaries of a private plot — no easy task in the days before surveyors. Nachalas Shiva, for example, was a combination of several plots and was registered with these boundaries: Jaffa Road to the north, the Moslem cemetery to the south, a group of trees with a pile of rocks to the east, and a stone wall to the west.

Registration of Nachalas Shiva in the Turkish land office had to be handled with finesse, lest the Arabs suspect them of wanting to move outside the walls. Though the Sultan had given his approval, resistance at the local level by disgruntled Arabs could still derail the entire proceedings. Throughout the process of bargaining over the land, the pioneers claimed that they wanted it to grow wheat for Passover and to build water cisterns. When a price agreement was finally reached, they themselves did not go to the land office. Instead, they sent Ester Lumzar, the wife of one of the original settlers, disguised in Arabian dress. She was chosen because she was a Turkish subject who spoke fluent Arabic, and could hopefully acquire the *kushan* (the certificate of registration) without raising undue suspicion. The ploy worked and Nachalas Shiva came into existence.

However, even with a sale legally consummated, the settlers' ownership was contested. Inevitably, Arabs who had not been party to the sale would claim that the land was really theirs and had been sold illegally. The results of this unexpected backlash were exorbitant monetary compensations — both over and under the table. In the end, the cost of these compensations equaled the cost of the land itself.

The down payment for Nachalas Shiva came from the funds that Bonei Yerushalayim had collected in Europe. Still short of the necessary amount, the settlers turned to Rav Meir Auerbach and Binyamin Beinish Salant, the son of Rav Shmuel, who loaned them the remainder. Over the years, these loans became a gift to the new Jerusalem.

The Seven

Nachalas Shiva ("Inheritance of the Seven") was named after the seven partners who agreed to build houses on the site. From the hindsight of over a hundred years, it is difficult to imagine how daring their plan was. Some Jerusalemites thought that the group's leader, Rav Yosef Rivlin, was possessed by a *dybuk* (a dead spirit) that goaded him into a suicidal plot. His cohorts, respected members of the Ashkenazic community, were also considered extremists. At one point, some people even brought Rav Rivlin to *beis din*, arguing that it was an offense to endanger his own life. "People thought we were crazy," recalled Rav Salomon, "and cruel hearted."[10] However, Rav Shmuel Salant and Rav Meir Auerbach were both in favor of expansion, and remained silent.

Rav Yosef Rivlin grew up with the ideals of the Vilna Gaon's dream in his heart. His grandfather, Rav Moshe the *maggid*, had actively pursued the dream and had done much to bring it into tangible reality. Rav Yosef would help form the vanguard that actually achieved it. As early as 1855, during his engagement party, he had clearly expressed his wish to eventually live outside the walls. His father-in-law-to-be, seeking to protect his daughter from such a dangerous lifestyle, wanted to break the *shidduch*. However, his daughter voiced her opinion, "I am in favor of his plan, and wherever he goes I shall follow him."[11]

Rav Yosef had developed an excellent reputation as a student in the Etz Chaim Yeshivah. When his uncle passed away in the plague of 1865, Rav Rivlin was asked to replace him as director of the Central Committee. There were those among the community who opposed his nomination, feeling that at twenty-eight years of age, he was too young for the position. However, Rav Salant insisted on the appointment. Rav Rivlin did not fall short of Rav Salant's expectations and admirably filled the post until his death in 1896.

History recalls him as the "father of the suburbs" because of his fearlessness in building the New City. Over a dozen colonies owed their existence to him.

Rav Yoel Moshe Salomon, a descendant of Rav Shlomo Zalman Zoref, was a disciple of the Rav of Kotna and Rav Auerbach. With the encouragement of his father-in-law, Rav Yisrael Beck, he utilized his writing skills, and over the years he published the periodicals *HaLevanon* and *Yehudah v'Yerushalayim*. He, too, worked courageously to build up the *yishuv*, and was the backbone of Petach Tikva. Of the seven original settlers, he alone remained in Nachalas Shiva and passed his house on to his children after him.

Nachalas Shiva

Rav Leib Lumzar and Rav Yehoshua Yellin grew up in the same house. Orphaned suddenly at the age of three months, Rav Leib was adopted by the Yellin family, where he grew up with Yehoshua, four years his junior.

Rav Chaim HaLevi, known as Rav Chaim Kobner, had played an important role in the building of the Churvah Synagogue a decade earlier, and was eager to help the *yishuv* expand.

Rav Shmuel Salant's son, Rav Binyamin Beinish, was also a member of Nachalas Shiva. He, too, would go on to found other suburbs in the years to come.

The last of the seven was Rav Michel Cohen. A *talmid chacham* and writer, he wrote for *HaLevanon,* as well as for another journal called *Chavatzeles*. He also published another periodical, entitled *HaAriel*.

Together, these men set down a code of rules — both economic and social — as well as a time schedule that called for building two new houses a year. Nachalas Shiva was the first neighborhood in the New City bought by Jewish settlers under a long-term repayment plan. The Bonei Yerushalayim organization laid out the money, and via a non-interest mortgage system, home ownership was made possible for families who otherwise would have been unable to build their own houses.

These avant-garde men put their lives on the line for the sake of Jerusalem. After they had laid the groundwork, hundreds more signed up as interested members in 1866. However, this large group claimed that for security reasons, it was unsafe to move until at least fifty families lived there, protected by a stone wall. Nevertheless, the original seven proceeded with their plans. In the beginning of Iyar, 1869 (5629), a drawing was held among them to determine who would be the first two settlers to begin building. Rav Yoel Moshe Salomon and Rav Michel Cohen won, but when the former begged for more time, Rav Yosef offered to begin immediately, and Rav Salomon passed the winning ballot to him.

Stone Houses and the Lone Pioneer

The cornerstone ceremony took place on Lag b'Omer, 18 Iyar, 1869 (5629). A large crowd gathered at the site, with all the *rabbanim* of the city present. Speeches were delivered, and everyone present felt that a new sense of destiny reigned over them. During the ceremony, Rav Yosef placed an earthen jug in the ground before cementing the cornerstone over it. Inside the bottle was a handwritten letter from the Vilna Gaon to his great-grandfather, Rav Hillel Rivlin.[12]

Work proceeded rapidly, and by the beginning of Tamuz the first two houses were completed. As in Battei Yehudah Touro, each house was comprised of two rooms, a kitchen, and a pantry. A month and a half later, on 27 Av, Rav Yosef Rivlin moved into his flat on the corner of Jaffa Road closest to the walled city.

Everyone was apprehensive about the move. By Turkish law, the gates of Jerusalem were closed and locked at nightfall, and reopened at sunrise the next morning. This law remained in force until the turn of the twentieth century. Thus, once Rav Yosef chose to remain outside after dark, there was no way for him to re-enter, no matter what the reason. Due to safety considerations, Rav Yosef would not allow his wife to move with him; instead, he took a fellow Jew by the name of Nisim Shemesh as a companion. In the morning, friends would wait anxiously by the Jaffa Gate to see if the two men were coming. No one knew what might have befallen them during the long, dark night. Naturally, they were relieved to see them alive the next morning.

Once, while Rav Rivlin was meeting with friends at his brother's house in the Old City, they purposely locked the door, announcing to him that it was dangerous for him, and that that night he should remain in the city. He forcefully burst through the door, saying, "If I stop living there for even one night, *chas v'shalom*, the entire new *yishuv* will end!"

In time, more houses went up, yet only this one Jewish owner actually lived and slept in the settlement, a post which he manned faithfully. Cistern water was used for washing and laundry, while drinking water was brought by fellaheen in waterskins. On Shabbos, Rav Yosef returned to his wife inside the walls.

Rav Yosef's trust in God was coupled with basic self-preservation techniques. First, he built a high wall around the two houses. Then he paid a Turkish soldier, whose job was to patrol outside the walls, to pay special attention to his area. Later, he hired an Arab to stand guard throughout the night. As a spiritual defense, he wrote a *sefer Torah* in his house.

Rav Yosef even opened a coffee shop on his rooftop. Run by Gavriel Zukerman, its aim was to lure his fellow Jews out of the walled city so that they might feel free to move about without fear. He also hoped to quiet the dissatisfaction of Moslem landlords with this, as if to say that here was nothing but a coffee shop, not a new suburb.[13]

Only two and a half years later, in the spring of 1872, did more settlers move in. At that time, Rav Yosef finally felt confident enough to bring his wife to the new neighborhood. Within twelve months she gave birth to their first child, a daughter whom they named Nechamah. After fifteen years of marriage, the couple saw the birth as a sign of Heavenly approval for their move. Rav Yosef opened a minyan in his house, supplemented by men from the city, and taught a daily *shiur*. The first synagogue was consecrated in Sivan, 1874 (5634).

More and more, Nachalas Shiva made its mark on the map. Young and old walked over to visit the site and

View of Jerusalem around 1870. The Jewish Quarter, inside the walls of the Old City, is on the right. Further along the wall is Zion Gate leading to the Mount of Zion. Across the valley is Mishkenos Sha'ananim and the windmill, built a few years earlier. On the other side of the city (out of view) is the Russian Compound, a hospice for Russian pilgrims, and the first houses of Nachalas Shiva.

marvel at the progress of the tiny settlement. The fields had disappeared under foundation stones for new houses. In 1873, ten milk cows arrived from Amsterdam, and the growing colony added a dairy as one of its endeavors. In the summer of that year, Nachalas Shiva acquired its own carriage service from the Jaffa Gate to the colony and back again, run by Feivel Treber. The new service made transporting the daily supplies of food and produce from the Old City a pleasure, as well as boosting the number of excursions by Jews outside the walls. In the course of time, as more and more suburbs developed, the carriage service catered to their needs as well.

When Sir Moses Montefiore came on his seventh and last trip in 1875, after an absence of nine years, he marveled at the new suburb. "How overjoyed was Sir Moses when he approached Givat Yerushalayim and lifted up his eyes and saw the new Jerusalem built up outside the walls of the city," wrote his personal secretary, Dr. Loewe. "Just a few years ago there was not a single family living outside the walls. Now, there are a large number of houses belonging to Jews, in a settlement called Nachalas Shiva, comprising some fifty families."[14]

Price Tag

The settlement's first years were not all bright. There were Bedouin attacks, thievery, and even murders. One of the saddest episodes during this period was the death of Rav Yosef's wife. One day in the summer of 1873, when Rav Yosef was in the Old City, an Arab intruder attacked her. She wrestled with him, and managing to extricate the dagger from his hand, stabbed him to death. However, she fell into a state of shock from the traumatic experience, suffered a heart attack, and died soon afterwards. Shortly thereafter, Rav Rivlin's only daughter died. A year later, Rav Yosef remarried. With his new wife, he would father several more children.

In Adar, 1875 (5635), a gang of Arabs infiltrated late at night into the house of Rav Moshe Leib Tefer and seriously wounded him. Members of the colony rushed him to the Old City for medical assistance, only to be refused entry by the gatekeeper. Finally, they bribed him to open the small doorway and quickly continued to the hospital, only to find that it was too late.

The Turkish authorities repeatedly claimed that they could not provide protection to anyone outside of the city's walls. More than once it was proven that the instigators of the Bedouin attacks were none other than jealous Moslem landlords. To counter these attacks, the *anshei gevardiah* took their own initiative. Several times they chased after the attackers and, in daring lightning charges, killed them.*

In Nachalas Shiva, members volunteered to patrol every night. On one of the rooftops, a bell was set up to alert everyone of an attack. Despite all these efforts, the enemy was not deterred. When other suburbs were established, they too became prey for enemy attacks, and more Jewish blood was spilt.

Jewish lives were a high price to pay, and everything was done to prevent tragedy — short of disbanding the colonies. However, the decision to build and

* See story, "The Ram's Horn," in *Bygone Days: 1870–1900*.

remain was not made solely by the handful of brave, young settlers. The *gedolim*, particularly Rav Shmuel Salant and Rav Meir Auerbach, rallied to the cause and gave their blessing and aid. Thus, the momentum continued to gather, and more and more colonies became beacons on the map of Jerusalem.

Beis David

On Rosh HaShanah, 1872 (5633), a new member of Nachalas Shiva received an aliyah to the Torah. Inspired by Rav Rivlin's sermon, he asked that a *mi'-sheberach* be given to all Jews who contributed towards the expansion of the colonies. In a gesture of gratitude and praise to the Almighty, Rav David Reiss vowed to build a new colony of ten houses from his own pocket which would be available as housing for poor Jews. Immediately after Rosh HaShanah, he fulfilled his vow. The new colony would be built on the opposite side of Jaffa Road from Nachalas Shiva, on land previously purchased by the Central Committee.

Who was this generous man, and why did he take on the role of builder of Jerusalem?

Rav David Reiss immigrated to Jerusalem in 1866 from Russia, where he had amassed a fortune. Childless, he and his wife decided to use their wealth to build and strengthen the physical and spiritual body of the *yishuv*. Towards this end, they dedicated a *chatzer* in the Jewish Quarter. This *chatzer* consisted of several houses and two shuls. The houses were given to the poor on a rotation system, and the two synagogues — one for the Perushim and the other for the Chassidim — were consecrated as an eternal inheritance to the Jews of Jerusalem.

The ten houses of Beis David were

Beis David. The first entrance, built in the 1920s, leads to Rav Kook's house. Further along the lane is the entrance to the courtyard of Beis David.

built in the form of a square, in order to facilitate self-defense. As with the *chatzer* in the Old City, these houses were dedicated for the poor Ashkenazim on a three-year occupancy plan. They were finished in 1877, along with a synagogue.

Later, in the twentieth century, the Central Committee (Vaad HaKlali) built their offices on the second-story wing. Rav Kook, after becoming Chief Rabbi, built his house on the second story of the opposite wing in 1923.

The chatzer and beis midrash presumed to be that of Rav Meir Auerbach, located in the Jewish Quarter. As the Rav of Jerusalem from 1860 to 1878, he used his influence to forge the expansion of the New City. Independently wealthy, he loaned and gave outright grants to see the new settlements get established. Although he aided many colonies, Rav Auerbach took a special interest in Meah Shearim, the subject of the next chapter.

Meah Shearim

Beis David was a welcome addition to the "colonial movement." However, the real measure after Nachalas Shiva was Meah Shearim. The second major colony outside the walls, its conception and birth would become a model for all future expansions.

The Hundred Signers

The success of Nachalas Shiva inspired others within the Old City to picture themselves as living courageously in the wilderness around Jerusalem. At the end of Cheshvan, 1873 (5634), over a hundred interested parties convened a mass meeting to organize a new colony. For three consecutive days the conference reverberated with discussions concerning the practical ramifications of the plan and the hopes and fears of the members. Both Rav Salant and Rav Auerbach participated in the meetings. Rav Salant, speaking in the name of his father-in-law, Rav Zundel, repeated what he heard in the name of the Vilna Gaon: The mitzvah of expanding the *yishuv* in Eretz Yisrael is one of the pivotal points in sanctifying the Name of God.

There were several distinct differences between the new colony and its predecessor. First, its envisioned size would dwarf that of Nachalas Shiva. A hundred or more families living together would fortify themselves against any enemy, as well as provide for all their own needs, like a self-sustained village. Also, the process of buying the land and the houses was based on a different system, which allowed all incoming money to be reinvested in new housing.

Officially, Meah Shearim came into existence on Rosh Chodesh Kislev, 1873 (5634).[15] At the beginning of Kislev, between Thursday and *motzei Shabbos* of *parshas Toldos*, one hundred and seventeen men signed up. *Parshas Toldos* hinted at two appropriate names for the new colony. One verse stated: "Yitzchak sowed in the land, and that year it produced a hundredfold (*meah shearim*), for God blessed him" (*Genesis* 26:12). The other verse read: "He dug another well, which was uncontested, and he called its name Rechovos, saying, 'Now the Lord has widened for us and we shall be fruitful in the land'" (*ibid.* 26:22). Both names were used: the colony was named Rechovos and the organization — to which around a hundred people had signed — would be called Meah Shearim. Soon, the number of members reached one hundred and forty. In the course of time, the name

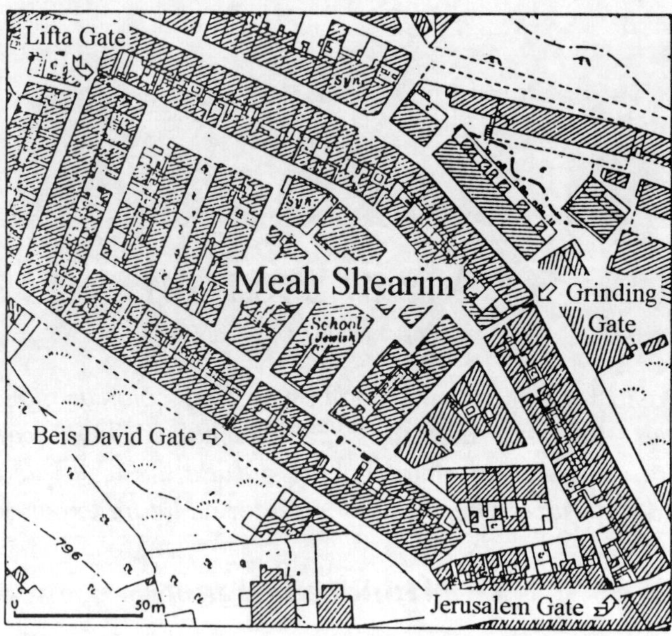

Meah Shearim

Rechovos was forgotten, and the colony itself would be known as Meah Shearim.

These names were pinned on the new colony by Rav Yosef Rivlin, who was one of the founding fathers of the new suburb. Proverbially known as the *shteitel-macher* (the village maker), Rav Yosef founded over a dozen new colonies. The names he chose were steeped in mystical connotations. Meah Shearim (מאה שערים), for instance, had the same numerical value as עתה יגדל נא כח אדנ״י ("Now, I pray, let the power of my Lord be great" — *Numbers* 14:17), each adding up to 666. According to the Vilna Gaon's commentary to the *Zohar*, this number is imbued with esoteric significance.[16]

Everyone had to contribute a down payment to the organization. Those who did not have the wherewithal to cover this expense sold their wives' jewelry or gave a portion of their monthly *chalukah* income.

Rav Meir Auerbach supported Meah Shearim in every way possible.* Besides sitting in on committee meetings, he gave money to buy part of the land, and bought five houses, although he never lived in any of them. He donated most of the houses to people who could not afford to buy otherwise. In his will, he passed the remaining ones on to his descendants, stipulating that if one of them left Eretz Yisrael, he would forfeit his portion of the inheritance.

Vineyard of Cadcod

The land upon which Meah Shearim was built had been called by the Arabs Kerem Cadcod, the vineyard of Cadcod. Though there was no direct connection between the Arabic name and the Hebrew word *cadcod*, still the visionaries found an allusion to it in the verse, "I will make your windows of rubies

* See story, "The Cosigner," in *Bygone Days: 1870–1900*.

(*cadcod*), and your gates of beryl, and all your borders of precious stones" (*Isaiah* 54:12). The selection of a site was one of the paramount decisions facing the committee members. Their choice of this one was dictated by several reasons, among them the price of the land. Sites along Jaffa Road were markedly more expensive due to their prime location — along the main thoroughfare between Jerusalem and the Jaffa port. Kerem Cadcod stood to the north of the city, completely isolated, and with the same amount of capital they could purchase a much more sizable tract of land.*

The location had an emotional pull as well. According to some authorities, the vineyard of Cadcod was within the ancient walls of Jerusalem. The Gemara in *Bava Basra* 75b says: "Rabba said that an old man told him that he had seen Jerusalem standing with a diameter of three *parsah*." The organizers of the colony made a simple calculation: Jerusalem could not extend to the east because of the Mount of Olives and the Valley of Kidron, nor to the south. That left most of the three *parsah* extending to the west and north, which included Kerem Cadcod. This opinion provided for practical ramifications as well. In its original conception, the plan for Meah Shearim had called for a park and orchard. However, since these were forbidden inside the Jerusalem of antiquity, the committee excluded them from the plan.[17]

A few weeks later the land was bought for the price of 49,000 Turkish liros. It was comprised of three parcels, for a total of thirty-two dunams (a dunam being approximately the size of an acre). It was registered in the name of Rav Benzion Lyon, a British citizen and founder of the colony, who would be able to access the services of the British consulate for the advantage of the whole community.

Building a Fortress

In the beginning of Iyar, 1874 (5634), the cornerstone of Meah Shearim was laid amidst a jubilant gathering, by what would be the middle gate on Meah Shearim Street. A jug was placed under the cornerstone, which contained the names of the committee members and the first settlers written on parchment. The first cluster of ten houses was finished eight months later, around Chanukah. However, the move into these houses was delayed until Adar to allow rainwater to fill the cisterns.

Aware of the official moving date of 8 Adar, 1875, some Moslems planned a shocking attack the night before on Nachalas Shiva. The morning of the eighth witnessed the excited new settlers leaving the Jaffa Gate with cartloads of possessions. However, they were suddenly sobered at the sight of fugitives from Nachalas Shiva hastening into the city for safety. First reports indicated a massacre, but a few hours later the *rabbanim* officially stated that "only" one Jew was killed. The purpose of the attack, which had largely been thwarted by militant Jewish fighters, was to annihilate the Jewish colony and halt all further expansion. Though it failed, it did cause the move into Meah Shearim to be postponed by a few months.[18]

* See story, "The Saving Hand," in *Bygone Days: 1870–1900*.

The Meah Shearim Talmud Torah complex, built after the turn of the twentieth century, comprises a talmud Torah, yeshivah, and kollel. The beis midrash was one of the largest in Jerusalem.

In Iyar, 1875 (5635), the first homesteaders moved into Meah Shearim, including Rav Yosef Rivlin and Rav Avraham Furst. The following summer, a second cluster of ten houses was finished, along with a communal oven to bake bread, and a *mikve*. Over the next two years, another twenty-nine houses rose, and by 1880, a hundred houses were completed, built in such a way as to close off Meah Shearim on all sides, creating a fortress-style colony with metal bars on each of its four gates. The gate to the south was called the Jerusalem Gate, the one to the north, Lifta Gate, to the east, Grinding Gate, and to the west, Beis David Gate. The gates were locked every night until 1911, when the Turkish authorities requested that they remain open.

The central *beis midrash*, Yeshuos Yaakov, was built in the center of the colony. The ground-breaking ceremony took place amidst a huge gathering, on 9 Kislev, 1874. Rav Meir Auerbach was given the honor of laying the cornerstone. The other main synagogue, called Yeshurun Yaakov, was completed in 1877. The women's gallery was built as a donation by the patron of Meah Shearim, Rav Meir Auerbach.

By 1881 (5641), after seven years of construction, the houses were officially registered with the Turkish housing authority. At that time, the population of Meah Shearim comprised over a hundred families, and the infrastructure included a *talmud Torah*, a hospice for guests, a *mikve*, synagogue, and *beis midrash*. It was a thriving community, with carriage service to the Jaffa Gate, and a vegetable *shuk* stocked by Arab villagers.

Behind this successful backdrop lay unforgettable stories of leadership, struggle, menacing enemies, and survival. The success of Meah Shearim, the second and largest colony outside the walls of Jerusalem, ensured that the process of expansion was irreversible.

Founding Fathers

Rav Zalman Baharan was to Meah Shearim what Rav Yosef Rivlin was to Nachalas Shiva. As the life-force of the community, he stood at the crossroads of every decision made and every action taken. Nothing took place in the new neighborhood without his knowledge and consent.

As a child, Rav Zalman told his parents, "When I grow up, I shall build up a desolate place here in Jerusalem." A scholar and peer of Rav Yosef Rivlin, he breathed life into Meah Shearim, giving classes and lectures, acting as treasurer, supervising construction, dealing with absorption problems, and the like. Yet, his lot was so destitute that he himself could not afford to buy a house in the new neighborhood. He remained in Battei Machse throughout his life, selling *esrogim* for a living and teaching Torah to hundreds of boys, always feeling that his mission lay in strengthening this new colony. Later, he organized other suburbs with the same altruistic motives.*

תקנות

חברת מאה שערים ת"ו, הנוסדה
שנת תרל"ד.

ועתה נתקנו תקנות נחוצות ומועילות עפ"י
אסיפה כללית מכל חברי החברה, בחדש
תמוז שנת תרפ"ה.

— ירושלם תרפ"ה —

דפוס „תחדש"—בתי ורשה ירושלים.

The takanos (bylaws) of the Meah Shearim society, which stressed unity in religious, social, and community affairs, became the guidelines for the bylaws of later building societies.

Every day he walked out to Meah Shearim to supervise the construction. Wherever he went, Rav Zalman always carried a pocket Gemara with him. Once, while learning with his students, he was called away to an important meeting with the Moslem mayor concerning the colony. Just then, he and his students were stumped by a difficult Tosefos. As he stood up to leave, he turned to his students and said, "While you argue and discuss this Tosefos, I will argue and discuss matters with the pasha." When he arrived at the mayor's office, he had to wait for some time. Opening his pocket Gemara, Rav Zalman analyzed the entire topic with new eyes, and before long unraveled the Tosefos in a manner that stunned everyone with its clarity and originality.[19]

Once, the Vaad of Meah Shearim offered him a free house as a gesture of gratitude for his selfless deeds on behalf of the community. However, he ada-

* See story, "The Wealthiest Jew in the City," in *Bygone Days: 1870–1900*.

mantly refused the generous offer. Indeed, he became so distraught over the idea of reaping reward for his selfless acts in this world that people feared for his health.

Rav Avraham Furst was known as the "father" of the colony. One of his primary concerns was to make sure that peace reigned between all the residents of the new neighborhood. He provided medical aid to members of the community and led the nightly security patrol. A *talmid chacham*, Rav Furst gave the leading lecture in Gemara, and was known as a man of distinction.

In the early years of Meah Shearim, a man named Rav Yehoshua Berman bought a small plot of land near the neighborhood and built himself a house and small bakery. He called it the Berman Bakery, and within no time he saw his handiwork blessed. Later, he bought larger equipment and expanded the bakery, which would remain next to Meah Shearim for many years before moving to its present-day location in Givat Shaul. Today, it is the second-largest bakery in Jerusalem.

Polluted Marshland

The pioneers of Meah Shearim faced many of the same type of homesteading problems which confronted the settlers of Nachalas Shiva. Snakes and foxes were commonly seen. In fact, some foxes cunningly lurked outside the doorways of the houses after nightfall, waiting for an opportunity to go in and wreak havoc. When the man of the house would open the door to go and pray, the fox would dash inside, frightening and endangering the lives of everyone there. This problem was so bad that, for a period of time, the men had to pray alone in their own homes. Foxes were not the only animals the pioneers faced. One night, when a settler went outside, he was confronted by a small lion in his path and breathlessly dashed back inside his house as the roaring beast ran after him.[20]

Unfortunately, Meah Shearim was not insulated from Bedouin attack either. In one attack, a settler was killed, his valuables stolen, and his wife's earrings torn off her ears. The assailants escaped in the cover of night. The wife, an American citizen, sought justice through the American consul, but although there was an investigation, no arrests were made. In another attack in Nisan, 1880 (5640), when construction of the community was nearly concluded, a large gang of Bedouins attacked. Vigilant settlers, headed by Rav Benzion Lyon and Zundel Pach, repulsed them. However, a thirty-eight-year-old man by the name of Rav Yisrael Chaim Sheinbaum died from wounds sustained during the attack, leaving a bereaved wife and family. Increased protection by a stalwart night patrol, and the locking of the gates once the last houses were built, curtailed further attacks on the community.

Apart from Arab attacks and wild animals, the fledgling colony faced another problem — this one entirely unforeseen — which nearly caused it to fold shortly after the first residents had moved in — yellow fever and malaria. The source of the diseases was quickly identified as a swamp in a valley to the east of the new neighborhood, in what would later become Beis Yisrael. The marshy area was locked in by hills on all sides except for the eastern one, which had a low ridge of earth preventing the water from draining. The stagnant water festered with disease-carrying mosquitoes. The odor emanating from the swamp was so putrid that birds did not even fly over it.

It was imperative that a solution be found. Women and children, always the first to be affected, refused to live in Meah Shearim. Every day the situation worsened. At that time, of course, there were no pumping machines to drain the swamp. The crisis would have to be solved by ingenuity alone.

The Rivlin Plan[21]

Yosef Rivlin came to the rescue in what he called "the pipe, rope and dog rescue operation." Due to the danger of human beings approaching within fifty meters of the swamp lest they become contaminated, Rav Yosef devised the following plan: A seventy-meter-long pipe was brought to Meah Shearim and placed on the western side of the swamp. Attached to one end of the pipe was thick rope, fifty meters long. This rope was tied to a dog and a very long leash put around the animal's neck. The idea was to send the dog directly down to the swamp's edge, while the person holding the leash would stand back in safety and guide it around the swamp to the other side. The dog was led around the swamp pulling the lax rope with him. When he reached the eastern side, by the ridge, the rope was untied from him. A group of settlers then pulled on the rope and dragged one end of the pipe into the heart of the swamp, while leaving the other end on the hill by Meah Shearim.

Next, hundreds of waterskins of fresh water were quickly emptied into the pipe at the upper end. As the fresh water splashed into the swamp, courageous men with shovels dug through the mound in several places as quickly as possible. Rav Rivlin was among them, working in the face of the deathly disease. As furrows were carved into the ridge, the water escaped and flowed further down the valley. More and more fresh water was shot down the pipe to dilute and wash away as much of the stagnant swamp water as possible. As a result of this operation, the swamp was entirely drained.

Rav Rivlin and his team waited a few days until the swamp dried completely. Then, in order to test the dangerous area, they set birds loose to see if they would fly over the swamp. To their delight, the birds flew overhead, and some of them even landed on the ground, proving that the swamp was completely decontaminated. The deadly mosquitoes had disappeared, and life could resume as normal.

Settlers of a Different Brand

The settlers of Meah Shearim reflected a different image than those of Nachalas Shiva. First, they were all Ashkenazim by descent, while Nachalas Shiva was mixed, seventy percent Ashkenazim, thirty percent Sephardim. More than that, many of those who settled in Meah Shearim adhered to the most *chareidi* philosophy, while those in Nachalas Shiva portrayed a more classical Orthodox view.

For these Ashkenazim, the move out of the Old City was steeped in spiritual dangers with long-range repercussions. Secularism had already reached the shores of Eretz Yisrael and lured innocent Jews into its net. The Torah bastion of the Old City was invulnerable as of yet, but an enclave in the wilderness was potentially a prime victim. Therefore, the members of Meah Shearim clung to the ideals of Judaism with an intensity rarely seen before. They built Meah Shearim into a fortress of purity and Torah commitment that would rally against any invasion of secularism into its midst.

The residents' piety and righteousness was manifest in every aspect of their lives. Rav Shlomo Houminer, one of the settlers of Meah Shearim, was once walking to the Western Wall to pray when he was accosted by Arab thugs. Instead of wrestling with them, he stood his ground and said, "Don't you know I'm on my way to pray? And do you think I'm only going to pray for myself? I'm also praying for you!" Looking right in their eyes, he added, "Don't we all have the same Father?" The Arabs were taken aback, seeing in him a pious person who harbored them no ill will, and quickly dispersed.

Suburbs of the 1870s

Nachalas Shiva and Meah Shearim proved that areas outside the Old City's walls could be successfully settled. In their wake, other groups formed and joined in the expansion of greater Jerusalem. In the remainder of the decade, another three colonies would come to dot the city map, each in a different area. Battei Nisan Beck lay to the north, between the Damascus Gate and Meah Shearim; in the west lay Even Yisrael, past Nachalas Shiva on Jaffa Road; finally there was Beis Yaakov, the most remote suburb built during the century, which lay between what would eventually be Machane Yehudah *shuk* and Shaarei Zedek hospital.

Each of these first suburbs was built far away from one another, as if without any program of expansion. Usually strength came from building close together, especially around Jerusalem where the settlements were prey to Bedouin attacks. However, the expansion was not as haphazard as it appeared. The founding fathers had proceeded according to a rough plan, based on two considerations. Purchasing land was a complex stage in building a colony. It was almost impossible to legally acquire one gigantic stretch of land — from Nachalas Shiva to Shaarei Zedek Hospital, for example. Furthermore, in fulfillment of the imperative to expand the *yishuv*, it was deemed praiseworthy to homestead in locations that were removed from one another.[22]

The Chassidim purchased land outside of the Damascus Gate in 1879, and soon thirty houses stood ready for occupancy. Officially called Kiryas Ne'emanah ("The Village of Faith"), colloquially it became known as Battei Nisan Beck, after its founder. Originally planned for twice that number of houses, the second half was built up by Persian Jews, whose homes lacked the high quality standards of the other housing projects.

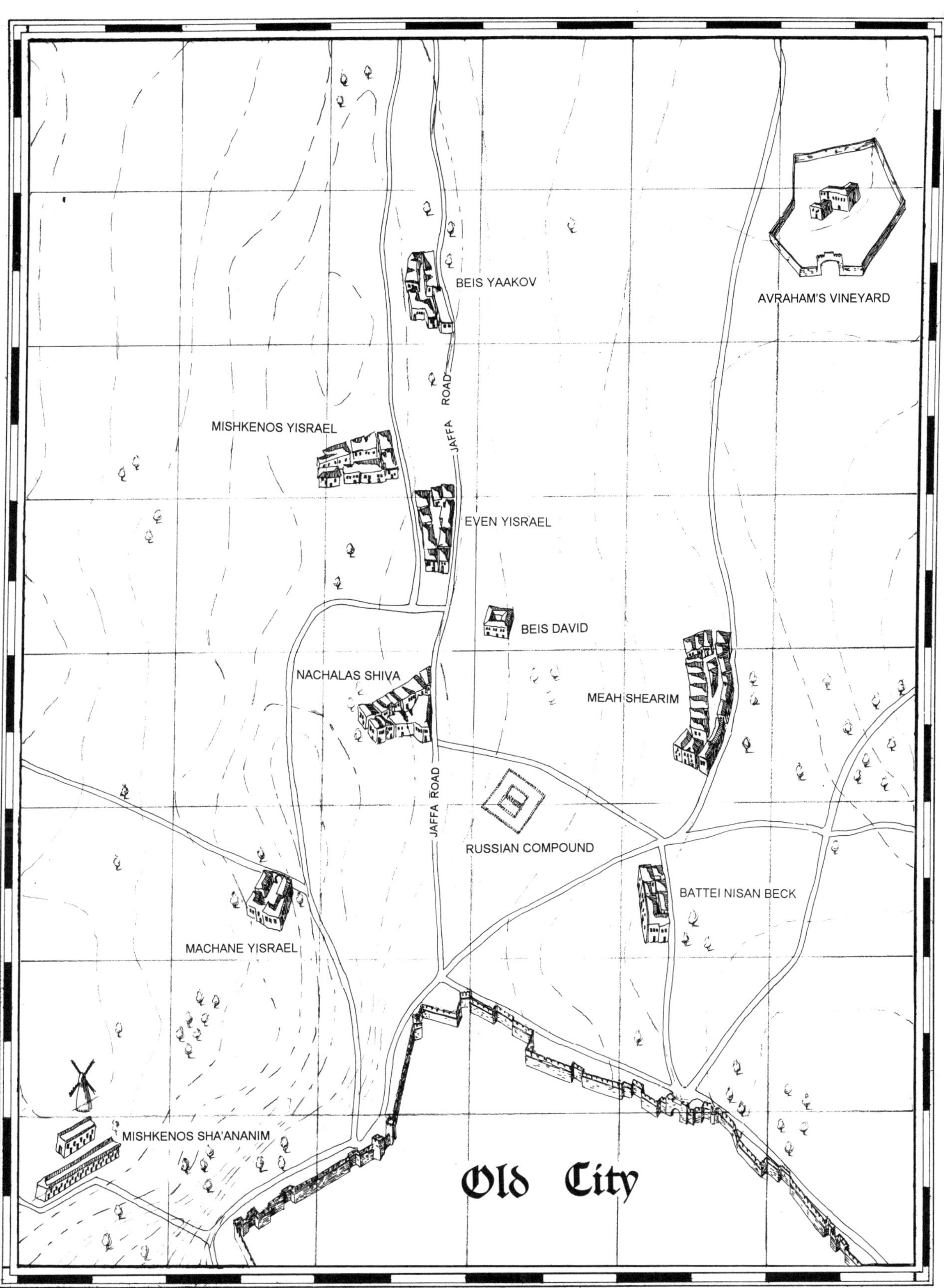

Map of first neigborhoods outside the Old City, built between 1854 and 1880

Rav Nisan Beck lived there until he was forced to sell his house to cover his debts. He moved back into a rented flat in the Old City, where he died in 1890 at the age of seventy seven.

During the riots of 1929, Battei Nisan Beck suffered the most from the Moslems' fury. Arabs plundered, murdered, and vandalized the three synagogues, and then set them on fire. Afterwards, only a few Jews returned, and the rest of the neighborhood was occupied by Moslems and Christians. After 1948, the last of the Jewish residents escaped before East Jerusalem and the Old City were taken by the Arab forces.

In Iyar, 1875 (5635), at the same time that settlers were first moving into Meah Shearim, the suburb of Even Yisrael ("Stone of Israel") was founded. Patterned after Meah Shearim, lots were cast in 1878 to decided who would be among the first to move into the new neighborhood. As a member of the group that organized the new settlement, Rav Shmuel Salant was included in the lottery, and his name was picked. A staunch advocate of the expansion process, he nevertheless declined the opportunity — not out of reluctance or fear for his safety, but because of his deep-seated love for the Old City. Indeed, after he emigrated from Europe, he never spent a single night away from there. Once, after the wedding of Rav Salant's granddaughter in 1895, the venerable sage returned home late to find that thieves had stolen everything of value. Luckily, the police caught the culprits and returned all the stolen property to its rightful owner.

In Elul, 1875, the Beis Yaakov suburb was formally founded, although the actual building would not get underway for another two years. The colony was founded by Rav Moshe Graf. In addition, the elderly Rav Yehudah Aryeh Loytas pledged 11,000 *grushim* for the central synagogue. Already eighty-seven years old, Rav Loytas lived to see the dedication of his Beis Yehudah Synagogue. This neighborhood's beginning was even more precarious than the others. The colony stood on the outermost fringe of greater Jerusalem, and when the first houses were ready for occupancy, no one wanted to move in. Eventually, residents did settle there, but soon the suburb stood on the verge of bankruptcy and collapse. However, though things appeared very bleak, salvation was literally right around the corner.

In the midst of Beis Yaakov's struggles, a tract of land right next to the colony became the major marketplace of the city. At first called Shuk Beis Yaakov, fellaheen brought their produce there to sell. Stalls, tents and pavilions were erected, and the area soon became the market center outside the walled city. Butchers and merchants opened shops. Both small and large animals were bartered there. Much later, around 1929, the market was rebuilt with permanent shops and officially renamed Shuk Machane Yehudah.

The *shuk*'s establishment had a dramatic impact on Beis Yaakov. The previously struggling neighborhood was suddenly on much surer footing, and more and more people opted to live there. Additionally, Fievel Treber put the neighborhood on his carriage route, making Beis Yaakov the last local stop. Soon the colony turned into the central "bus" station for those going to and fro the Jaffa port. In those days, nine car-

This photograph, taken around 1900, shows the carriages lined up outside the Jaffa Gate. This was the main terminal from where the carriages bused people to the various neighborhoods.

riages made the run, leaving Jerusalem in the early afternoon and arriving at the Jaffa port the following afternoon. This was the only means of transportation until the introduction of the railroad in 1892.[23]

The last major colony to be started during this decade was called Mishkenos Yisrael ("Dwelling Places of Israel"), built near the present-day center of town on what is now Agrippas Road. With a membership of a hundred and forty, this suburb was viewed with great anticipation. Unfortunately, its very size contributed to its downfall, and with soaring debts on the members' shoulders, construction had to be halted.

The man to pull them out of debt, Yechiel Pines, was the comptroller of the newly established Montefiore Fund. The story of this fund's creation, and the storm it caused in Eretz Yisrael and abroad, is of vital importance in understanding the subsequent development of the *yishuv*.

Montefiore's Final Mission

Near the end of 1874 (5634), the ninety-year-old champion of the Jewish people, Sir Moses Montefiore, felt that the time had come for him to retire from public life. Of his myriad activities, the most dear to him had been his directorship of the Amsterdam Fund, which was responsible for funneling money to Eretz Yisrael from around the world. The committee members, too, looked upon his involvement as almost indispensable, and couldn't imagine how things would operate without his wise guiding hand. However, the elderly knight of the Jewish people was insistent, and the members resigned themselves to adhere to his wishes. In recognition of his thirty-three years of leadership, they decided to dedicate a charity fund in his name, to be called the Montefiore Testimonial Fund. Money was collected from throughout the Jewish world, with great success. When asked what the fund should be used for, Sir Moses pointed to Eretz Yisrael and Jerusalem. Building houses and farms, and setting up businesses in the Holy Land had priority in his eyes.

The Two-Man Commission[24]

The twenty-man committee handling the fund was presided over by Lord Meir. Though the money was earmarked for Eretz Yisrael, a disagreement broke out between the members over how to best channel the funds there. It was decided that an on-the-spot evaluation of the needs of the Jewish community would offer the best guide. Consequently, a two-man commission left for Eretz Yisrael in the winter of 1875.

The two men were members of the committee. Sir Shmuel Montague, a banker, was a leader of the liberal movement, and a member of parliament. Dr. Asher Asher, besides his communal activities, acted as secretary of the committee for the metropolitan synagogues of London.

They arrived in Eretz Yisrael in Adar II, 1875 (5635), and spent a total of fifteen days in Jaffa, Jerusalem, and Jericho. During their stay in Jerusalem, they resided in a hotel run by a Jewish apostate. While in the city, they met with foreign consuls, and visited some Jewish schools and homes. It rained and snowed during most of their visit, limiting their activities. Apparently, they abstained from meeting with the *rabbanim* of the city.

Upon their return home, they presented their findings. Their shocking report gave a scathing picture of the *yishuv* which utterly stunned the members of the committee. According to their portrayal, a substantial number of Ashkenazic Jews were defectors from the Russian army, and most of the poor were categorized as lazy vagabonds who came to collect free handouts via the *chalukah* system. Others, who lent money at interest to Arabs, hungrily waited for their monthly stipend. The ten percent who did work, they claimed, barely scraped out a living because they did not try harder.

Wherever they looked, they saw only the negative side of things. The Jews were unconcerned about personal hygiene, their houses were in shambles, and their children poorly educated. They showed no interest in building, working, farming, or in taking any initiative to improve their future. Even the Rothschild Hospital did not escape their vindictive eyes, and it was characterized as primitive and dirty. In contrast, they had nothing but praise for the missionary hospital, which they claimed was the epitome of what a hospital should be — despite the fact that they handed out Hebrew copies of the New Testament to patients. They even ridiculed the ban which the rabbis of Jerusalem had placed on Jews going there.

Their report failed to mention a word about the new suburbs that were burgeoning outside the city walls, all of which were organized independent of international funding. The only positive finding which the commission voiced was the cleanliness of the Jewish homes. However, even this so-called "praise" was poisoned by their caveat — that the sole reason for the tidiness was to project a misleading image to the visitors from England.

Their conclusions were grim: "The *chalukah* is the source of all of these problems. Those who control the *chalukah* are selfish, and their high-handed rule is focused primarily on furthering their own self-benefit." Their twofold recommendation included: 1) Revamping the *chalukah* system by sending two European agents to supervise the allocation of money. In addition, these agents' actions would be monitored by the Vaad in London. 2) The establishment of a loan foundation that would be directed solely to businesses and building enterprises.

The Disputation[25]

The Montague-Asher report, meant to be confidential, soon became public knowledge and caused a furious reaction in many circles. Jerusalemites were shocked and angry. The report threatened the whole *yishuv*, and most directly the continuation of the expansion program. Even those "enlightened" Jews of Jerusalem who disapproved of the *chalukah* openly voiced their resentment at the report's oversimplification and blatant misrepresentation of the truth.

The report also caused a stormy reaction in the Diaspora, especially by those Jews who had personally visited the *yishuv* and understood the true situation. They vehemently objected to the report, adding that the two-man commission had knowingly distorted things out of some personal interest.

The *yishuv* sent Sir Moses Montefiore a detailed refutation of each accusation against the *yishuv*, signed by Rav Auerbach and Rav Salant. They called the report a exaggerated defamation of the *yishuv* of the worst order. One by one, they quoted each paragraph of the report and refuted it. For example, the education system was one of the best in the world. Similarly, the health of the children was equal to their counterparts in Europe. The benefits of the *chalukah* system were shared equally by the giver and the receiver. Supporting the *yishuv* in Eretz Yisrael was an unparalleled mitzvah, giving the Jews in the Diaspora a portion in Eretz Yisrael. So, too, the *chalukah* was administered properly by men of repute. Poor people living on handouts existed in every city of the world. Jerusalem, with its disproportionate number of elderly and widows, might have appeared to be more needy on the surface. Yet, the city had a number of soup kitchens and *chesed* groups supporting them. All in all, there was no foundation to any of the report's findings.

Montefiore's Last Visit

The valiant benefactor of the *yishuv*, Sir Moses Montefiore, was equally shocked by the scathing portrayal. Could it be that since his last visit nine years earlier, the *yishuv* had degenerated so much? Impossible!

Together with his personal secretary, Dr. Eliezer Loewe, he set out on his seventh trip to Eretz Yisrael. On each of his trips he had been on a mission to befriend the *yishuv* — to aid it and watch it come into its own. Hadn't he tried to set up a Jewish farm in 1839, started a weaving factory, imported the first printing press, began a settlement near Jaffa called Gan Montefiore,* built Mishkenos Sha'ananim, and guided funds into the *yishuv* at every opportunity? Now, however, the Montague-Asher report had blackened his whole life's work. The ninety-year-old warrior of the *yishuv* decided to trek over land and by sea, climb the mountain of God, and spend weeks in the Holy City to personally evaluate and discern the truth. His sixty-five-page diary of the trip was a testament of valor and sincerity, of loyalty and hope.

On the day of his arrival at the Jaffa port in Tamuz, 1875 (5635), he hurt his leg. As a result, most of his trip would be spent in a chair. But the invincible monarch could not be thwarted by his personal handicap. When he was unable to walk about, he sent either Dr. Loewe or his personal physician to investigate a school or a new suburb. *Gedolei Yisrael* sought his council, and gentile dignitaries came to welcome him. Day and night, emissaries from Safed, Tiberias, Hebron, and, of course, leaders of institutions in Jerusalem, waited to have an audience with him. He met with groups of women, as well. Wherever he went in the city, crowds filled the streets to greet him. Sir Moses was universally loved by all segments of the Holy City's populace.

This trip was charged with his final mission — to save the *yishuv*. Several times he met with the leaders of the

* See story, "By the Work of Your Hands," in *Bygone Days: 1879–1900*.

Ashkenazic and Sephardic communities to discuss communal issues. When Rav Kahanov, Rosh Yeshivah Etz Chaim, presented the classes for inspection, Sir Moshe was delighted to hear them also sing before him. The same thing occurred at the Doresh Tzyon School.

The Wonder of Jerusalem

Sir Moses was enraptured with Jerusalem. His curiosity about people, institutions, and the progress in building and services was insatiable. He found healthy, well-educated children, industrious people clinging to the Torah and mitzvos, and signs of progress everywhere. A group of craftsmen showed him their works, including a watchmaker who repaired his pocket watch, a lithographer, an engraver, and a goldsmith. All of them were on par with their European counterparts. Montefiore commissioned Rav Chaselvitzer to write a *sefer Torah* for him, he himself penning the first word, *Bereishis*. He commented, "When I left London, I had just finished writing a *sefer Torah*. Now, before leaving Jeru-

Sir Moses Montefiore (1784–1885)

salem, bless the Lord, I still feel well, and I have begun writing another one."

The new colonies were the fulfillment of his vision. Since his last visit, progress in this area had been dramatic. Four new suburbs stood where before there was nothing but barren land, and more were being planned. During the course of his stay, he was invited to lay the cornerstone for a new row of houses in Meah Shearim. However, due to health reasons, he was forced to decline the honor. Instead, he sent Dr. Loewe to represent him.

He was forced to admit that hazardous sanitary conditions in the city posed serious dangers to the general health of the populace. This, of course, had been a problem of long standing in the Holy City. However, it was not the residents' fault, nor was there anything they could do to improve the situation. After noting this in his diary, Sir Moses added: "All the physicians in Jerusalem assured me that once the sanitary conditions improve (and that depends mainly on the Turkish authorities), then this city will become one of the healthiest places in the world."

At the end of his trip, Montefiore went to the Western Wall before bidding farewell to his beloved city. He reminisced: "When I came in 1866, I endeavored to have a roof constructed to protect Jewish worshippers from the sun and rain, but at the last minute the plan fell through. Recently, I heard that a Jew volunteered to install stone benches for visitors to sit on, but he was prevented. Later, he petitioned for a permit to place some large marble slabs for sitting there, which was granted. Soon afterwards, however, they were all stolen.

"While standing at this holy place which has remained with us as a remnant of the Temple, we did not forget to pray for our loved ones and dear relatives. I hope that our prayers were accepted in Heaven."

Sir Moses left before sunrise on 15 Av. Among the few to bid him farewell was Rav Shmuel Salant. Sir Moses' last words to them were, "Everything will be well."

The Feud

Upon returning to London, Montefiore expressed his opinions concerning his expedition: "If you ask me if it is reasonable to aid them, I shall answer you positively. From every point of view they are fitting to receive aid. Are they willing and capable of working? Without any doubt! Are they physically and mentally prepared for this? They surely are! Are we obligated as Jews to support them? We are clearly enjoined to do so from our Holy Writings. However, if this is not enough of an answer, then learn from the gentiles and how they honor and support men like these who sanctify their lives to serve God.... We, to whom God revealed Himself on Mount Sinai, certainly have a far greater obligation to support our brethren, to save them in times of distress, and to endeavor to better their lot."

Montefiore reiterated his opinion: the funding should be used to buy land around Jerusalem and build housing. When? Immediately.

Thoroughly contradicted by the venerated philanthropist's words, Montague attempted to backpedal and reduce the gap between his point of view and that of Sir Moses. The committee, caught in between, remained divided over the issue. Friction flared between Montefiore and the members of the Vaad. In the end, the committee adopted a policy close to the one Montefiore advocated, with one major exception: they nominated a communal leader from Russia, Rav Yechiel Pines, to represent them in Eretz Yisrael, and to channel the funding as he saw fit. His appointment was viewed as a direct insult to the *rabbanim* of Jerusalem, and as unquestionably going against the wishes of Sir Moses Montefiore.

The Montefiore Testimonial Fund

The Montefiore Testimonial Fund, originally named as a tribute to the man who spent half a century fostering the *yishuv*'s development, had become a profound source of dissatisfaction to Sir Moses. In the course of time, however, the Fund functioned in ways that would make him feel very proud, despite the involvement of the new comptroller.

Pines moved to Jerusalem and eagerly began investing moneys into various enterprises, all of which failed. He soon concluded that the optimum outlet for the moneys lay in housing projects. Besides expanding the *yishuv* beyond the walls of the Old City, many job opportunities would become available to Jewish workers — both as laborers in the construction and as shopkeepers in the new neighborhoods.

He came to his decision just at the time when Mishkenos Yisrael was on the brink of bankruptcy. Forty-four houses were completed (out of the one hundred and forty planned), yet most of the members had stopped their monthly payments, and there was a mountain of unpaid bills. Pines made an agreement with the organization that another eighty houses would be built on a portion of the land. This would be backed by the Fund and repaid in small installments over a long period of time. The new buildings would be called Mizkeres Moshe, after Sir Moses Montefiore, and would include a number of public buildings such as a synagogue and *mikve*.

Thus, the Fund began a long history of aiding the expansion of Jerusalem. With the new infusion of funding, Mishkenos Yisrael was saved, and Mizkeres Moshe came into existence.

Sir Moses' Legacy

Throughout his long life, Sir Moses Montefiore had conducted himself as he felt a messenger of Hashem truly should. Dr. Eliezer Loewe, his personal secretary, wrote of his last days: "Sir Moses often repeated, 'I always tried to do the most according to my ability. I'm sure that I made many mistakes, but I trust God that He shall forgive those who cleave to Him humbly. Death is compared to a short rest, after which one awakes full of spiritual rejuvenation. Every time I pass the tomb of my wife, Judith, I recite the verse which is written there in Hebrew: "In Your hand I shall deposit my spirit...at the time of sleep, and I shall awake with my spirit inside my body; Hashem is mine and I shall not fear."'"

Sir Moses died on 16 Av, 1885

The tomb of the Montefiores in Ramsgate, England

(5645), at the age of one hundred. Lucid until the very end, he kept asking Dr. Loewe, "Is there something else I need to do? If so, tell me and I shall do it. Perhaps my signature is needed on some charitable document. Give it to me and I shall sign it." When Dr. Loewe assured him that everything was in order, Sir Moses lifted his hands to Heaven and said, "*Baruch Hashem*, the Lord has given me the means to do all of this."

He commanded that his tomb be built to resemble the structure he had constructed over the grave of the matriarch Rachel. He also requested that a sack of soil from the Tomb of Rachel be added to his grave. During his last visit to Eretz Yisrael, he had ordered a headstone engraved with the verse: "For Your servants have cherished her stones, and favor her dust" (*Psalms* 102:15), and this stone was erected over his grave.

Jews throughout the world mourned his passing. He had stood at the crossroads of time, marshaling his considerable influence for the betterment of the Jewish people. He stood before princes and kings, and achieved miraculous breakthroughs through barriers that seemed impenetrable. He freed Rav Meir Leibush, the Malbim, from jail, put an end to the Damascus blood libel, and obtained the *firman* from the Sultan's hand that permitted building outside the walls of Jerusalem. Most of all, he was enamored with Eretz Yisrael and its sages. They were engraved on his heart day and night. He had earned the title of father of the *yishuv*, and his efforts on their behalf lived long after him.

A month after his passing, two stone plaques were erected in his memory at the entrance ways to Mishkenos Moshe and Ohel Moshe, both of which were built with moneys from the Montefiore Testimonial Fund.

Jerusalem Faces the Future

In the last quarter of the nineteenth century, the Jews of Jerusalem would establish a model of existence that would set the scene for generations to come. The yishuv was no longer a tiny enclave merely searching for stability and better living conditions. The population had exploded, jumping from 10,000 Jews in 1870 to twice that figure by the turn of the century. Furthermore, there was a tremendous diversity of people, ranging from the most pious to the most derelict. A flock of that dimension and variety could not be controlled by a single leader or group. Therefore, a new awareness of the realities of life became necessary, and a search for new guidelines became the city's next testing ground.

The two main flashpoints were the new wave of periodicals that reached Jerusalem's street corners, and the arena of traditional education versus progressive "schools."

The Jewish Press[26]

The power of the printed word both strengthened and threatened Judaism throughout the world. With the advent of the industrial revolution, printing presses became more accessible, dependable, and cheaper to operate. As a result, a flood of periodicals, magazines, and newspapers reached the public, some presenting a forum for Torah debates, and others concerned with political and social reform. The newly created Reform movement made optimum use of the printed word to spread its menacing philosophy to innocent Jews. In Europe, this was countered by the efforts of *gedolim* such as Rav Yaakov Ettlinger, the author of *Aruch L'Ner*, among others. Jerusalem, too, would face this problem, but there the battle would be carried out in a different manner.

In 1862, Jerusalem's first periodical appeared. Entitled *Toras Tzyon*, it contained a selection of essays by *rabbanim* on traditional Torah topics. Published by two young men from Etz Chaim Yeshivah, Rav Leibel Lomzer and Rav Yoel Moshe Salomon, only one issue made it to press.

The following year, another group of young Jerusalemites published the periodical *HaLevanon*. Rav Yoel Moshe Salomon had recently returned from Kenningberg, Russia, with a printing

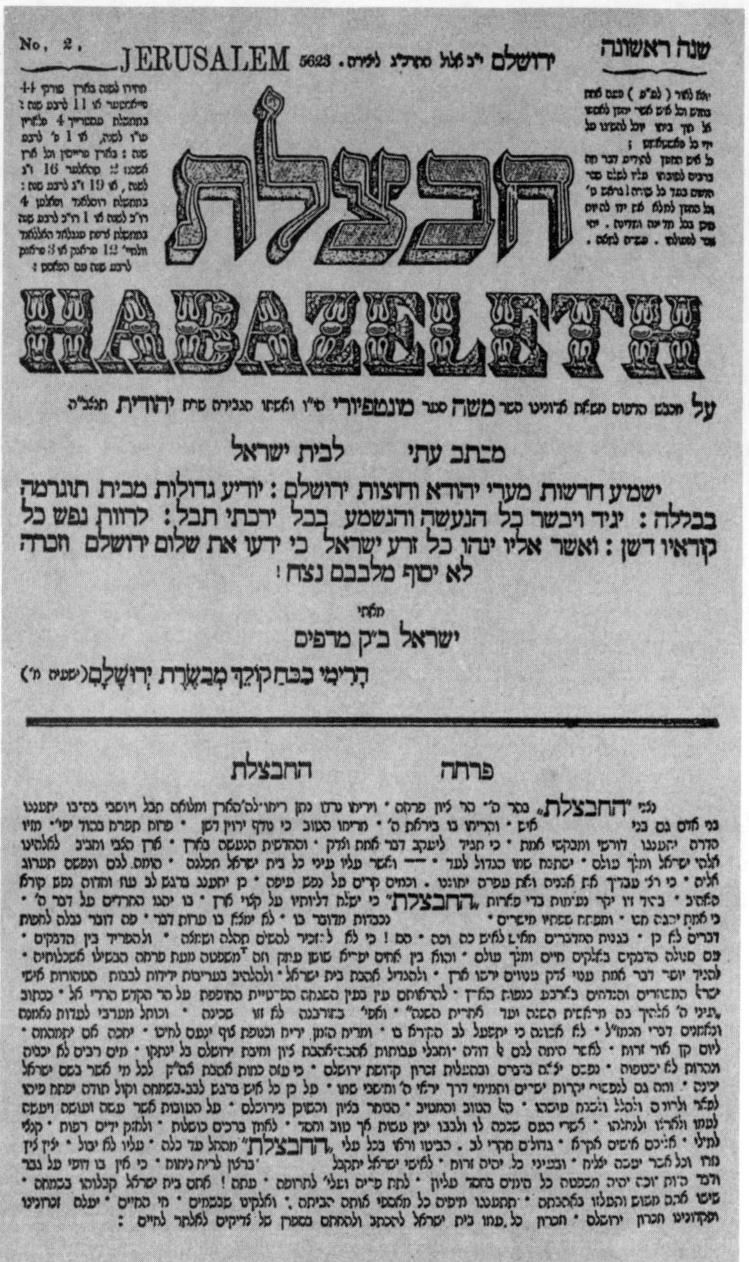

שנה ראשונה

No. 2. JERUSALEM

חבצלת

HABAZELETH

מכתב עתי לבית ישראל

ישמיע חדשות מערי יהודא וחוצות ירושלם : יודיע גדולות מבית תוגרמה בבלה : יגיד ויבשר כל הנעשה והנשמע בבל ירכתי תבל : לרוות נפש כל קוראיו דשן : ואשר אליו ינהו כל זרע ישראל כי ידעו את שלום ירושלם חכרה לא יסוף מלבבם נצח !

ישראל ב"ק מדפים

פרחה החבצלת

Chavatzeles, like other periodicals of the day, was book-size, running from 8 to 32 pages

press. While in the Russian city, he had apprenticed himself and learned the art of lithography. A close friend, Rav Michel Cohen, was a talented writer, and the third partner, Rav Yechiel Beril, was the organizational genius behind the whole endeavor. A monthly, it survived for one year before being forced to close due to both a lack of funds and not having a legal permit. In the wake of the closure, Rav Yechiel Beril traveled to Constantinople to obtain a license; however, he was unsuccessful. He then continued on to Paris, where he published *HaLevanon* as a bi-weekly.

The journals of that period were

Three of the early publishers (left to right): Rav Yoel Moshe Salomon, Rav Yisrael Dov Frumkin, and Rav Michel Cohen

about the size of a standard book, running anywhere from eight to thirty-two pages; newspaper-size periodicals and dailies would not arrive on the scene until the twentieth century. Their circulation was not limited to Jerusalem. Indeed, as mail service improved, much of their success depended on a strong list of subscribers from the Diaspora. Whenever a war broke out, like the Turkish-Russian war, most of the journals folded for lack of funds.

Another crucial factor for new publications was obtaining a license from the Turkish authorities. This, too, was a major deterrent, since the Turkish government frowned on issuing permits — an attitude that would persist until 1908. Beril was only the first victim.

Between 1862 and the outbreak of the First World War, sixty-two periodicals appeared in Jerusalem. Some only had one issue, and others survived for a quarter of a century and more.

HaLevanon, published in Paris for five years before moving to London, was a very popular and successful journal. Throughout its run, it maintained its original theme of presenting articles on Jerusalem. Writers such as Rav Meir Auerbach, Rav Shmuel Salant, and Rav Avraham Ashkenazi filled its pages.

In 1863, Rav Yisrael Beck, the grandfather of the Jerusalem printing world, published a bi-monthly called *Chavatzeles*. It, too, folded after six months.

For the next seven years, no journals were published in the Holy City. In 1870, *Chavatzeles* reappeared, under the joint editorial direction of Rav Yisrael Dov Frumkin and Rav Michel Cohen. In addition to Torah articles, the periodical covered a variety of news events in the city, topical issues like "Discovery of water," and "*Shalom* Jerusalem."

Rav Frumkin, the son-in-law of Rav Yisrael Beck, was a bright, enthusiastic young man, with very independent ideas. A Chabad Chassid, he began his publishing career at the age of nineteen. Though he opposed secularism, he allowed several writers of dubious character to publish their articles in his paper, and for this reason he was chastised by the *rabbanim*. In 1883, the Turks imprisoned him for six weeks for writing derogatory statements about the American ambassador to Turkey, who was visiting Jerusalem at the time. Although it had a rocky history, incurring the wrath of the *gedolim* more than once, *Chavatzeles* survived longer than any other periodical, for a total of forty-one years.

Rav Michel Cohen, an outstanding student from Etz Chaim Yeshivah, broke off from Frumkin in 1873 and opened his own journal called *Ariel*. It lasted for three years, until it was forced to close due to financial problems. Later, Rav Cohen wrote for a variety of periodicals.

In 1877, Rav Yoel Moshe Salomon returned to the publishing world with *Yehudah v'Yerushalayim*, a bi-monthly periodical. The purpose, he wrote, was "To awaken love of Yehudah and Jerusalem in the hearts of Jews all over the world; to strengthen the banner of Torah, *yiras shamayim*, wisdom, and knowledge; to strengthen the *yishuv* and the expansion of colonies, and to emphasize the importance of the Holy Land as a place suitable for Jewish settlement." The journal lasted only two years.

Rav Salomon personally labored to reach the goals he so ardently espoused. A graduate of Etz Chaim Yeshivah, he understood the needs of the times, especially the need to expand outside the walls of Jerusalem. In addition to helping with the establishment of the new suburbs around Jerusalem, he was one of the founders of Petach Tikva.

The Salomon Press did not close with the failure of its first periodical. Indeed, it would survive for a hundred and thirty years. Until 1939, it was located in Jaffa Road near Nachalas Shiva. It then moved to Rav Kook Street, not far away. Throughout its long history, the Salomon Press stayed in the family. Four generations of fathers and sons manned the press and provided quality literature to the Jewish people.

Danger Signs

The remaining sixty-odd publications ranged from Torah journals to secularist papers. One of the earliest papers with secularist leanings appeared in 1884. Called *HaTzvi*, it was published by Eliezer Ben-Yehudah, the so-called "father of modern Hebrew," who had immigrated to Eretz Yisrael the year before. The paper's message quickly became quite obvious, and within a year, the rabbinic court placed a *cherem* on it. The paper lasted into the twentieth century, though its founder got into trouble several times with the Turkish authorities.

In 1895 (5645), a provocative article in *HaTzvi* about the Maccabees nearly backfired on the publisher, and threatened the entire *yishuv* as well. The article seemed aimed to awaken nationalistic sentiments similar to those that inspired the valorous acts of the Maccabees. It was interpreted by the Turkish authorities as a call to all Jews to band together and rebel against the Ottoman Empire. Ben-Yehudah and his father-in-law, the article's author, were arrested on charges of sedition.

However, Ben-Yehudah's irresponsible act had not only endangered himself and his father-in-law; it threatened the entire *yishuv*. Rebellion against the Sultan by a minority faction in the empire could bring swift and merciless repercussions. When news of the article reached Constantinople, a major cabinet meeting was held with the Sultan Abdul Hamid. A blown-up report was presented, painting the Jews of Jerusalem as revolutionaries preparing to join forces with international Jewry in order to conquer Eretz Yisrael and rebuild the Temple. Fortunately, the Sultan, going against his ministers' recommendations, decided to hear the testimony of the Jews themselves before choosing a course of action.

The Jerusalemites were well aware of the threat facing them, and tensions had been running high since the article's publication. Rav Salant called for an emergency meeting to discuss a plan of action. He first reviewed the ongoing uneasiness between the *yishuv* and the Turkish government. Out of unfounded suspicions, the Turkish government had banned further Jewish immigration on several occasions, as in 1884, and limited visas to a maximum of thirty days. For a short time, they even reinstituted an old law forbidding foreigners from purchasing land. Rav Salant had labored to convince the mayor that the propaganda from the European press was not the view of Jews of the *yishuv*. However, this new article originated in Jerusalem itself, and carried much more damaging weight.

Rav Yosef Chaim Zonnenfeld, one of the leading rabbis of the *yishuv*, suggested presenting a united front with the Sephardic Rishon l'Tzyon, Rav Yaakov Shaul Elyashar. The Sephardim were innocent of any collaboration, since only the Ashkenazic world press portrayed the mass influx of Jews to Eretz Yisrael as the next stage in the messianic process. A joint communique was issued condemning the article, reiterating that it was solely the opinion of its author.

When the Sultan's request for clarification of the matter reached Jerusalem via the Chacham Bashi of Turkey, a joint reply signed by the Rishon l'Tzyon and Rav Shmuel Salant was quickly dispatched to the capital. In their reply, they quoted the three oaths which God bid the Jewish people to abide by: not to conquer Eretz Yisrael, not to rebel against the nations in the Diaspora, and not to attempt to force the messianic redemption. Moreover, Jews were commanded to pray for the welfare of the nation in which they lived. The Sultan, pleased with their answer, dismissed the idea of any punitive action against the Jews of Eretz Yisrael.[27]

Herut was another progressive newspaper, which included world news, science, literature, and specifically Turkish affairs. Begun in 1909, it was published three times a week. In 1902, the Sephardim published a similar paper in Ladino.

A much longer-running periodical was a quarterly entitled *Torah MiTzyon*, which had a twenty-year history (1887–1907). Published by Rav Shmuel Zukerman, it included articles by the *rabbanim* who were living in Jerusalem. Scholars like Rav Yaakov Shaul Elyashar (Rishon l'Tzyon) and Rav Yaakov Orenstein illuminated its pages.

The Zukerman press gained a reputation as one of the best printing shops in the city. Rav Zukerman apprenticed himself to Rav Yisrael Beck in 1872. Later he traveled to London, where he headed the Hebrew press in one of the largest printing firms in the country. When he returned to Jerusalem, he bought the original Beck press and opened his own shop. He was also one of the founders of the Beis Yisrael and Zichron Tuvia neighborhoods.

Rav Yosef Chaim Zonnenfeld's son, Rav Avraham Aharon Zonnenfeld, published *Ohr Torah* between 1897 and 1900, which included articles by leaders of the Jerusalem community.

Between 1896 and 1914, Rav Benzion Coyanca published another Torah journal, called *Ma'asef*. One of his patrons was Baron Wolf Rothschild of Frankfurt. This periodical ended with the outbreak of the First World War, as did a number of others. Rav Coyanca later became the first Sephardic Chief Rabbi of Jerusalem in 1921.

Three types of periodicals existed in Jerusalem: There were the purely Torah-oriented (*Ma'asef, Torah MiTzyon*, etc.), Torah with topical issues (*HaLevanon, Chavatzeles*, etc.), and the secularist papers (*HaTzvi*). Many gullible readers did not sense the insidious danger posed by the latter type of paper. There willingness to read them led to growing problems concerning the education of the next generation.

The Rav of Brisk[28]

Few Jerusalemites realized how great an impact a certain new immigrant from the European town of Brisk would have on the Holy City. However, when sixty-year-old Rav Yehoshua Leib Diskin arrived in Tamuz, 1877, the welcoming committee consisted of the cream of Jerusalem's Torah leadership. Though asked to take a leading role in communal affairs, the Brisker Rav shied away and remained aloof.

While Rav Diskin successfully managed to avoid playing an obvious role in communal activities, he could not prevent eager students from drawing to his side. Among those who became his disciples were Rav Yosef Chaim Zonnenfeld, Rav Yaakov Orenstein, Rav Tzvi Michel Shapiro, and Rav Naftali Hertz HaLevi, who later became the Rav of Jaffa.

Rav Diskin was a master scholar, who could study fifty pages of Gemara a day with the same involvement as he studied one page in fifty days. He chose to learn the Tractate *Bava Basra* with his small-knit group of students, and after forty days they had only finished one page. During that whole period, Rav Diskin neither entered into a discussion based on *pilpul* (hair-splitting analysis of a topic based on making inferences from

Rav Yehoshua Leib Diskin (1818–1898)

the text and building an intricate logical structure), nor utilized his vast command of sources to aid in his understanding, nor referred to any Later Authorities. He simply penetrated into the depths of each Rashi and Tosefos on the page. When he noticed that his students were confident in their grasp of the gemara, he commented, "It is a mistake to think that we have fully understood this gemara. We have only scratched the surface, like children in cheder, with whatever mental abilities we possess. Still, it is not proper to remain on this page any longer. Yet, we should never forget that we are far from understanding the simple meaning of the text. We should pray for the Almighty to open our eyes and reveal His Torah to us."

Every *motzei Shabbos*, Rav Diskin gave a lecture on the weekly Torah reading in his house. Besides his disciples, other men came to hear the Brisker Rav speak. One of them was a hardworking elderly Jew. This man enjoyed asking questions, sometimes one after the other. Though the scholars were annoyed by his behavior, Rav Diskin always stopped and succinctly answered his queries. One Saturday night, when the lecture continued late into the night, the man quietly left to go home. The Brisker Rav interrupted his lecture and escorted the old man downstairs and through the courtyard to the gate. When he returned, he commented, "One should never allow an elderly man to walk downstairs in the pitch dark."

At one of these *motzei Shabbos* talks, his awe-inspiring concern for his fellowman's honor was revealed, stunning all those present. The class was considered informal, and the participants were accustomed to drinking tea during the course of the lecture. Due to his poor health, Rav Diskin needed extra sugar in his diet, and his tea was always strongly sweetened. Once, the server unwittingly placed three heaping teaspoons of salt into his glass. As the Rav sipped the tea, his expression remained unchanged, and he quickly proceeded to finish the glass. Just then, his wife noticed that the server had confused the salt with the sugar, and made quite a fuss about it. When asked why he had endangered his health by drinking such bitter water, he answered, "What would you have me do — embarrass a Jew in public?"

Though Rav Diskin had originally moved to the Old City, he eventually left there due to health reasons. First he lived in a suburb called Kerem, located in what is now Geula, and later in Battei Ungarin, next to Ohel Moshe Yeshivah in Meah Shearim.

Despite his refusal to take an official role in communal activities, his concern for his fellow Jews prompted him to take action whenever he felt it was necessary. During the famine of 1879, two men died of starvation, collapsing in the women's gallery of the Churvah Synagogue. When Rav Diskin heard of the tragedy, he immediately ordered that a soup kitchen be established to ensure that every Jew would have something to eat.

His house became the address of all those seeking advice for their personal problems. Once, the father of a rowdy, uncontrollable boy came to discuss the matter with the Brisker Rav. Things had reached a point where the boy was influencing other children to revolt against their parents. The child had such a wicked streak that even close relatives agreed that drastic steps were in order.

The father asked if he should send the boy to a secular school, and divorce himself from his son completely. "No," replied Rav Diskin. "Let things remain as they are. Even if he does not learn a thing in the cheder, at least the air will be full of Torah and perhaps he will breathe some of it. Also, be sure to pray for him, and *be'ezras Hashem*, you will see results." Sure enough, over the course of time the boy grew up to be a respectable, Orthodox Jew.

Once, a certain scholar was insulted publicly and felt very hurt. He went to Rav Shmuel Salant and demanded, "Since I am a *talmid chacham*, the other party should be reprimanded and forced to make an official apology to me."

"A *talmid chacham*," mused Rav Salant thoughtfully. "You know, I never even considered myself as a *talmid chacham*. The only person I know who fits that category is Rav Yehoshua Leib Diskin."

Only the most difficult halachic questions were brought to Rav Diskin. He was, as one of his disciples described him, a rabbi's rabbi. It seemed that his mission in Jerusalem was to stand at the city's gate and protect it from the new "spirit of the times" that was sweeping Jewish communities across the globe. The secularists were now mounting an assault on the fortress of the spiritual world, and only a man of vision and courage could keep them at bay.

A Historical Perspective

The battle which Rav Diskin waged against the secularists and Zionists towards the end of the nineteenth century seems light-years removed from the realities of the modern world. In order for us to somewhat fathom the war, it is imperative to understand the historical context in which he, and those who followed after him, stood. The secularists of those times were of a different breed than their counterparts today. They were not second- or third-generation assimilated Jews, unthinking and unknowing of where they stood and why. The "emancipators" of yore had to wrestle with the awesome notion that they were renegades bent on severing their bond with the Almighty. Their ideological stance forced them to take an extreme stand. Indeed, this was the only way they could quell their fear and guilt and live with the magnitude of their deeds. However, this was not all; their nominally religious upbringing gave them an intimate knowledge of their enemy from within. Many of them still had beards and professed to be Orthodox, and cunningly peppered their speeches with Torah cliches. All of these battle tactics lulled many into falling for their agenda.

Jerusalem, the citadel of purity, was the ultimate prize craved by these masters of deception. She was fertile ground for their machinations, for most of her residents had not had firsthand experience with the "enlightenment" that had wreaked so much havoc in Europe. The first confrontation came in the 1850s with the Lemel School. The proposition for this institution provoked a dramatic response by the Ashkenazim, which shocked the school's representative. The *cherem* they declared against the school would be invoked time and again in the following decades. Indeed, the reaction to this first major skirmish set the guide-

Rav Avraham Shag (1801–1876). He was the mentor of Rav Yosef Chaim Zonnenfeld.

lines for Rav Diskin and others when faced with similar battles in the future. In 1872, when Heinrich Graetz and G. Levy came on the seemingly innocuous mission of setting up an orphanage for Jewish children, they were aghast at the reception they received on Shabbos at the Churvah Synagogue. Before the entire congregation, Rav Yisachar Ber Zwebner, the son of Rav Avraham Shag, extended the *cherem* in the name of the *gedolim*.

It was precisely at this incipient stage that drastic offensive steps were needed in order to vanquish secularism and prevent it from gaining a foothold in the Holy City. Otherwise, like a small brushfire left unsmothered, it would quickly blaze out of control through the entire *yishuv*, with disastrous results.

It was for this reason that Rav Diskin often reacted with the full brunt of his authority to snuff out the early flames of what could later pose a grave danger to Judaism — even though others might consider his response extreme. One small incident will serve to illustrate this point. Once, when a respected Torah scholar living in the *yishuv* came to speak with the Brisker Rav, he spoke in Hebrew rather than in Yiddish. This man was known as a true fighter for the *yishuv*, as well as a lover of the Holy tongue. Yet, Rav Diskin refused to listen to him, replying that so long as Ashkenazic Jews were in *galus*, Yiddish was their sole language. Obviously, he did not fear that a solid pillar of the *yishuv* like this scholar would succumb to the progressive influences of an Eliezer Ben-Yehudah. As a visionary, however, the Brisker Rav foresaw the grave danger of using Hebrew as a platform for progressive, secular, and Zionistic ends — which is precisely what happened over the course of time.

Incidentally, in later years, Rav Yosef Chaim Zonnenfeld lamented the fact that the *chareidim* had allowed the Zionists to make Hebrew their war cry. Had the first Ashkenazim (the Perushim of the first half of the nineteenth century) spoken Hebrew in Jerusalem, as had the Sephardim, the Zionists might not have been able to avail themselves of this powerful symbolic weapon.[29]

Language was not the only thing the secularists had going for them. At the turn of the century, events unraveled on the world's stage which played a prominent role in tipping the scales against the Torah-observant camp. At this stage in history, the world was in a tremendous state of flux. Vast empires like Russia and Turkey were crumbling. Countries were devastated by war, unending pogroms brought terror and death to European Jewry, and uncounted ideological movements caused major social upheaval. Worst of all, perhaps, the global economy tumbled into an abyss during the First World War. Jerusalem bore the brunt of it all, and grinding poverty was the rule of the day. The Zionists, with vast financial resources at their command, manipulated people's affiliations during this period and made a permanent incursion into the citadel.

Education — in the widest sense — was the pivot upon which the future of Judaism depended. The slightest crack in this edifice could wreak havoc on the generations to come. Consequently, when Dr. Herzberg came to open his orphanage in 1881, the Brisker Rav responded with a full frontal attack. In a move that surprised some members of the community, Rav Yehoshua Leib announced his decision to found his own orphanage. He asked Rav Zonnenfeld to lead the Diskin Orphanage, along with Rav Yaakov Blumenthal. As we shall see, the new institution grew at a remarkable rate, thus offsetting the Reform version and its philosophy of total abandonment of Jewish tradition.

With the perspective of hindsight, our debt to leaders like Rav Diskin and Rav Zonnenfeld is clearly apparent. These men stood at the crossroads of time, and battled against any hint of progressiveness within the ranks of Judaism. Responding to the challenge of the moment, they exchanged the quiet, peaceful visage of the scholar for that of the warrior facing mortal combat. In the life-and-death struggle in which they were engaged, there was no room for compromises, truces, or wishy-washy stalemates. They girded themselves with the words of King David: "It's a time to act for God, [otherwise] they will undermine Your Torah" (*Psalms* 119:126). Some say that without their courageous efforts, there would not be a shred of Orthodox Judaism left in the Holy City today.

The Battle Cry[30]

Six months after the Brisker Rav's arrival in 1878, he reinstated the *cherem* against any changes in the educational system. Issued by one of the greatest sages of the generation, his *cherem* carried tremendous weight, especially after 284 *rabbanim* from all sectors of the city signed it. The *cherem* was a significant departure from the previous ones, in that its scope was much broader. It stipulated that it was forbidden to study any "off-limit" subjects — even from a teacher whose motivations were known not to be suspect, and for no matter how short a time — even if only a day or two. Furthermore, it applied equally to both male and female, young and old.

That same year, a dangerous new enemy appeared in Jerusalem, one who initially seemed to be sympathetic to the *chareidi* cause. Posing as one of their own, he would insinuate himself within their unsuspecting midst, only to cause tremendous damage later.

Michel Pines, the controller of the Montefiore Testimonial Fund, befriended the entire leadership of the *yishuv* (except for Rav Diskin). He projected an image of sincerity, dedication to Torah scholarship, and interest in communal leadership. In 1880, two years after his arrival, the naive community could scarcely believe their eyes when he opened a school in Even Yisrael, the neighborhood in which he resided. Though cloaked in the guise of a vocational school intended merely to train young men in a trade, its real purpose was nothing less than to introduce progressive studies and undermine the existing system of education. The unsuspecting *yishuv* did not react immediately to the school. After all, Pines had a two-year record of excellence.

In Teves, 1881 (5642), the Brisker Rav bemoaned the danger, crying out, "Our Torah is in danger! One by the name of Michel Pines has opened a place for prayer and study — yet he is a heretic!" He lost no time in declaring a *cherem* on the school, forbidding anyone to send their children to study there.

Rav Diskin's dramatic assault against this seemingly minor step away from tradition had a strong effect, especially on Pines. To be singled out as a heretic while garbed in Torah tradition and holding an impressive post in the *yishuv* was a bitter pill to swallow. Rav Diskin based his claim on a book which Pines had written in *chutz laAretz*, called *Yaldi Ruchi*. Reviewed by Rav Yosef Chaim Zonnenfeld, it was denounced as a heretical work.

Michel Pines decided to meet with the Brisker Rav and try to ameliorate the tension between them. The Rav agreed to the meeting, but only on condition that a third party be present. During the course of their discussion, Rav Diskin clarified his position: "If you have come to Jerusalem to ease the burden of the poor, then you are welcome. But if your intention is to construct a new wing in our educational edifice, then I testify that every house and courtyard chimes with words of Torah, and there is nothing for you to add."

Pines left the meeting with a frown, and quickly committed his sentiments into writing in a pamphlet entitled "Hear, O Mountains, My Complaint." He then sent copies of it to Torah leaders throughout the Diaspora. His goal was to rally support for his views, claiming that he had been an innocent victim in the dispute with the Brisker Rav. *Gedolei Yisrael*, however, could not be fooled. Leaders in the Diaspora, like the Netziv and Rav David Friedman of Karlin (Pines' brother-in-law), spoke out against the author of the pamphlet. Thus, Pines' attempt to arouse world sympathy failed.

Michel Pines spent the rest of his life in Eretz Yisrael, becoming more and more aligned to the progressive movement and eventually dropping his facade entirely. Those who before had only rebuffed him now openly castigated him. For example, in 1894, his brother-in-law, Rav Friedman, took offense at Pines' allegiance with those who profaned the *shemitah* year: "I am very distressed to see how the poisonous waters you drank in your youth, when you read many non-religious books, have reached your innards and corrupted you."

In 1882, shortly after the Brisker Rav's censure of Pines, another progressive front tried to make headway in the citadel of Jerusalem. Nisim Becher, the founder of the Alliance Israelite Universelle institutions (Kyach), came with a group to open a school in the Holy City. This was actually the second attempt by Kyach to establish a beachhead in Jerusalem. Some fifteen years earlier, in 1868, the influential Yosef Kreiger opened the first Alliance School, but it closed shortly thereafter.

Becher's organizers arranged for him to attend the celebrated Churvah Synagogue for his first Shabbos service in Jerusalem. Pompously, he seated himself along the eastern wall, where the notables of the community are traditionally assigned. A group of his followers were stationed outside, keeping an eye open for possible troublemakers.

Rav Yehoshua Leib Diskin was outraged at this affront to the *yishuv*'s dignity. He called Rav Zonnenfeld to go with two other *rabbanim*, Rav Yaakov Orenstein and Rav Yitzchak Shlomo Blau, and reiterate the *cherem* before the entire congregation. The ruffians blocked the trio's entry, and in the ensuing scuffle, only Rav Zonnenfeld succeeded in slipping in. He immediately climbed the *bimah* and emphatically screamed out the *cherem*. Within seconds he was pounced upon and beaten up, and only escaped by a miracle. He later commented about the bruises, "These are my badges of honor!" Unfortunately, this episode was only one example of a new tactic used by secularists to achieve their ends — force. Later, in a similar encounter, they nearly killed two *chareidim*.

The new *cherem* was signed by seventeen Sephardic rabbis, who in turn issued their own *cherem* against the Alliance School. The ban had a great impact on the *yishuv*. For years not a single Ashkenazi sent his son to this or any other progressive school, and only a handful of Sephardim sent their children. To supplement the student body, the schools accepted gentile youths whose parents served in foreign consulates.

The ban included a punishment for those who transgressed it, namely, termination of their *chalukah* stipend — the main source of a family's support. This harsh measure gave some physical bite to the already serious spiritual consequences of defying the *cherem*. As a result, it helped ensure almost universal compliance by parents who otherwise might not have been so concerned about the matter. An exception was Mr. Yehoshua Yellin, who, though upset at losing the precious income, nevertheless sent his son David to the progressive school. Yellin's action proved a dire warning to the entire community. David Yellin became a secular writer and staunch Zionist.

The First Library

In Jerusalem of the late nineteenth century, the idea of a lending library was a completely foreign concept. Today, even when every Torah family has a sizable collection of books in their house, lending libraries still exist in most communities. However, in those days — despite the increasing number of books reaching the public — very few people had the resources to acquire their own private collections. Under such circumstances, a library might appear to be a positive vehicle to quell the public's thirst for knowledge. In response to this need, Rav Frumkin opened a library called Tiferes Yerushalayim in 1875, under the supposed patronage of Sir Moses Montefiore. However, the institution immediately aroused a storm of protest, as it was alleged to have heretical books on its shelves. Frumkin denied the accusation. When Rav Michel Cohen, a previous associate of Frumkin, testified that the library did indeed contain such literature, the *rabbanim* issued a ban, entitled *Gachalei Aish* (Coals of Fire). Rav Salant, Rav Auerbach, Rav Shag, and Rav Kahanov were among the signatories. Montefiore, for his part, knew nothing of the matter.

Frumkin offered to make a compromise, promising that from that time onward, the library would contain only sacred books. The *rabbanim*, however, flatly refused, and the library was forced to close its doors. For the next fifty-two years, until 1927, there was only one library in the city, set up by Ben-Yehudah and Pines in 1887.

One institution that was lucky enough to have its own library was Etz Chaim Yeshivah. Rav Chaim Berlin, after he passed away in 1913, bequeathed his vast collection of thousands of *sefarim* to the yeshivah.

The Diskin Orphanage

With the ban against the Alliance School and the closure of Rav Frumkin's library, the blatant dangers of secular penetration seemed to have been successfully repulsed. But like a crafty fox lurking in the background, the secularists soon returned in a new guise. Their next targets were defenseless orphans and wayward Jewish children. Jerusalem, unfortunately, had more than its share of orphans, due in large part to the periodic epidemics which swept through the city, and bereaved families of their loved ones. In a noble, humanitarian gesture, a Reform group from Berlin decided to open the German Orphanage in the Holy City. In 1872, Heinrich Graetz came to Jerusalem to found the institution he hoped would become an instrument of secular education, openly stating that among its studies would be "essential sciences."

As we noted previously, Graetz's hopes for an enthusiastic reception were shattered by Rav Yisachar Dov Zwebner's invocation of the *cherem*. The secularists immediately denounced his action as that of a private party. However, Rav Meir Auerbach stepped forward and forcefully countered that Rav Zwebner was speaking for all the leaders of the *yishuv*.

Though the community was united in its stance against the orphanage, Graetz had a powerful ally in Rav Ezriel Hildescheimer, the Rav of Berlin. It seemed that Rav Hildescheimer did not see the danger in the same way as did the leaders of the *yishuv*. Unfortunately, this served to somewhat weaken the religious camp's opposition. However, when word of Rav Hildescheimer's approval became known in Europe, a great outcry resulted, and he retracted his support.

Eventually, a ban signed by three hundred rabbis, including Rav Heller of Safed and Rav Eliyahu Mani of Hebron, was issued. The vigorous opposition had the desired effect, and for the time being, the Berlin Home for Children was prevented from opening its doors.

In 1881 (5641), the reformers finally succeeded in opening their orphanage in the city, under the direction of Dr. Herzberg. Called the Berlin Institute, it attracted some Sephardic children and gentile youths. Jewish leaders compared it to the missionary schools, especially after learning that one of its teachers was a bona fide missionary. Later, one of the heretofore respectable members of the *yishuv*, Chaim Hirshenson, joined the teaching staff, and eventually became the home's director. Sadly, instead of having a salutary effect on the outlook of the institute, the reverse was true, and Hirshenson alienated himself from the community.

The Diskin Courtyard, where the orphanage began, is located in the Moslem Quarter of the Old City

As soon as the Berlin Institute opened its doors, the *cherem* was broadcast in every synagogue. Rav Leib Chefetz, one of Rav Diskin's prominent disciples, was attacked by thugs. He was seriously hurt and then arrested on false charges. Only through the combined efforts of Rav Diskin and Rav Salant, did the authorities release Rav Chefetz the following day.

Rav Yehoshua Leib Diskin realized that the only means available to neutralize the enemy was for the *yishuv* to open its own home. Without the financial resources of the wealthy Reform movement, he applied all his energies to thwart the enemy's offensive. For the premises of the new orphanage, Rav Diskin purchased a courtyard in the middle of the Moslem Quarter. He chose the upper-floor apartment as his home.

The complex cost more money than he had available. He signed a contract which gave him a deadline to pay the remaining amount of a thousand napoleons, and dispatched letters to friends in Europe requesting aid. According to Turkish law, if he failed to pay on time he was liable to serve a jail sentence. As the deadline approached, and his requests went unanswered, he turned to Rav Moshe Wittenberg, a wealthy Jew who had immigrated from Russia. Rav Wittenberg agreed to donate the entire sum on condition that the courtyard would be registered in his name. He, in turn, would consecrate the courtyard as a Jewish orphanage. The other rooms would be rented to Jews, with part of the rent money being funneled back into the orphanage, and the rest going to other charities Rav Wittenberg supported. The Brisker Rav was more than delighted with this arrangement.[31] That same year, the Diskin Orphanage opened its doors with Rav Zonnenfeld as its director. When the Brisker Rav's son, Rav Yitzchak Yerucham Diskin, immigrated in 1908, he headed the orphanage. After his passing, Rav Zonnenfeld again took up the reins.

Fifteen years after it opened, the Diskin Orphanage outgrew the courtyard and moved to larger premises outside the walls of the city, eventually relocating to its final home in Givat Shaul. As for the original premises, families moved in and remained there until the riots of 1929.

The Berlin Orphanage was successfully neutralized, barely drawing anyone through its doors. The Brisker Rav's fortitude had played a decisive role in withstanding the secularists every advance. For the meantime, the city's sanctity was preserved. However, in the early twentieth century, its ability to withstand the "spirit of the times" would be called very much into question.

Sacred Places

Just as Jerusalem is surrounded by mountains, so she merits to have holy shrines, tombs, and graves in and around her walls. They, too, have become part of the Holy City's mystique. Few Jews come to Jerusalem without touching the Western Wall, entering the Tomb of King David, or traveling to the Tomb of Rachel. These sites are an indigenous part of the city and add a fuller dimension to one's Jerusalem experience.

The Western Wall

The Jews cherished the closeness to God they could feel when praying at the Wailing Wall. The little strip of the site accessible to them, twenty-five meters long by four meters wide, was difficult to reach due to the Moslem section called Moghrabi. Only by following a labyrinth of corridors could they make their way there, often to find that the small area was already crowded with other Jewish pilgrims.

Near the end of the century, Baron Edmond Rothschild visited Jerusalem and was appalled at the situation. He decided to buy the whole Moghrabi section and demolish the houses in order to clear a gigantic plaza where Jews could easily and comfortably gather at this holy place. The Moghrabi section was occupied by low-class Arabs from North Africa whose houses were of the cheapest quality in the Old City. The results of his discussion with the Moslem authorities were positive. They conditioned the sale on building better housing for Moghrabi's residents at another location. He immediately agreed. Though the cost was high, he wished to do so as "a merit

Baron Edmond Rothschild (1845–1934)

View of the Moghrabi section, where today stands the plaza, which left only a four-meter-wide area for the Jews to pray at the Kosel

and honor to the Jewish people."

Concerning the proposed plaza, the Moslems insisted that no construction of any type could take place there, including a retaining wall or fence, or any permanent structures of stone or wood. Only trees could be planted to beautify the area. Furthermore, mule-trains and gentiles would not be kept from using the plaza, thereby disturbing the Jews praying there. These prerequisites made the proposition very unattractive, and in the end, the plan was shelved. Only in 1967 was the Moghrabi section demolished and a plaza with a retaining wall built.[32]

In 1871 (5631), Rav Hillel Moshe Gelbstein took upon himself to lead a minyan every day at the Western Wall for Minchah and Maariv. Over the next forty years he faithfully led the minyan, bequeathing the responsibility to his son on his passing. Before Shabbos would set in, he would bring a table and lantern to aid his fellow worshippers, and a Moghrabi Arab would carry them back to his house at the conclusion of the services. The Gelbstein minyan stopped meeting just prior to the First World War.[33]

The Tomb of King David

In I *Kings* 2:10, it says, "So David slept with his fathers and was buried in the City of David." He passed away on the festival of Shavuos, 6 Sivan, 836 B.C.E. (2924). Since it was Shabbos afternoon, he was buried the following day.

Though modern savants conjecture as to the exact location of the cave, there is a definitive opinion of the Ari Zal which removes all doubt for religious Jews. He affirmed the traditional site on Mount Zion as the area below which lies the cave in which the kings of Israel are buried. In addition to King David and King Solomon, eight other kings of Israel are mentioned in Scripture as being buried there. They are: King Rehoboam, King Abia, King Asa, King Jehoshaphat, King Jotham, King Josiah, King Amaziah, King Hezekiah, and Jehoiada the Priest.

According to Joshephus, King Solomon placed a large treasure in the tomb from which, some eight hundred years later, Hyrkanus removed three hundred silver bars to give to Antiochus. Later, Herod sought to do the same thing, but when he sent two boys there in the middle of the night, he watched as flames of fire lashed out of the cave and killed them. He sealed the entrance and built a beautiful monument over it.*

Throughout medieval times, the Tomb of David remained inaccessible to Jews. When Suleiman the Magnificent built the wall around the Old City in the 1530s, he was outraged to learn that Mount Zion was not included. The engineer responsible for the oversight was put to death and buried inside the Jaffa Gate.

Both the Christians and Moslems revered the site and built places of worship there. The Moslems, as the rulers of the land, prohibited both Jews and Christians from entering the chamber where a tombstone marked the spot over which King David was buried.

In the mid-nineteenth century, the author of *Shaarei Yerushalayim* wrote: "Whenever we seek to go and pray there, we have to pay twenty piasters bribe money per person. However, they never permit us to go all the way to the tomb. Instead, we are forced to go to another spot close by, called in Arabic *zamiah*, and pray from there. Yet, before we can finish even ten psalms we are ordered to leave."

Today, the hall above the Tomb of David is open daily to everyone.

The Place of the Deshen

Until the First World War, a huge mound of ashes lay near the cave of Shimon HaTzaddik. Archeologists disputed if these ashes were the remains of burnt sacrifices on the Altar of the Temple, or if they were nothing more than the waste products from a soap factory. In the medieval book, *Kaftor v'Ferach*, the author writes: "There is a tradition that the place where the ashes (*deshen*) were spilled was north of Jerusalem, a short distance by horseback." This, too, was the conclusion in the Gemara (*Zevachim* 106a).

British Consul James Finn wrote about the ashes in a London journal in 1857, reporting that the mound was closer to the Tomb of the Kings. Ash specimens were examined by Dr. Rotah of Germany, who reported conclusively that the ashes were from animals and not byproducts of a factory.[34]

Another opinion maintains that the *deshen* is closer to Shmuel HaNavi Street, near the Dushinsky Yeshivah.[35]

* See story, "David HaMelech, May He Live Forever," in *Bygone Days: 12th–16th Centuries.*

The Cave of the Prophets

Tradition places the graves of the last three prophets, Haggai, Zachariah, and Malachi, in a huge cave near the top of the Mount of Olives. Rav Ovadiah Bartenora wrote that it was the cave of the Prophet Haggai, without mentioning the other two prophets. In any case, its long, winding tunnel, full of catacombs, was the undisputed property of the Jewish people.

In 1883 (5643), news leaked out that fellaheen from the Arab village of Tur were preparing to sell the cave to the Russian archbishop. The *Chavatzeles* paper ran a feature article on the sale, demanding immediate action to annul it. The city's Jewish inhabitants, shocked by the news, turned to the Rishon l'Tzyon to intervene. Rav Yaakov Shaul Elyashar sent a telegram to Constantinople, and the Sultan's court replied with a "stop order" to the mayor of Jerusalem. The telegram, besides curtailing the sale, added that the cave was a holy site for the Jews and was not a salable piece of property.

Meanwhile, the archbishop disregarded the order and appealed to the Russian consulate in Constantinople to do everything in their power to finalize the sale. When Rav Frumkin, the publisher of *Chavatzeles*, got wind of this, he contacted Mr. Avraham HaLevi of London, secretary of the Agudas Achim Commit-

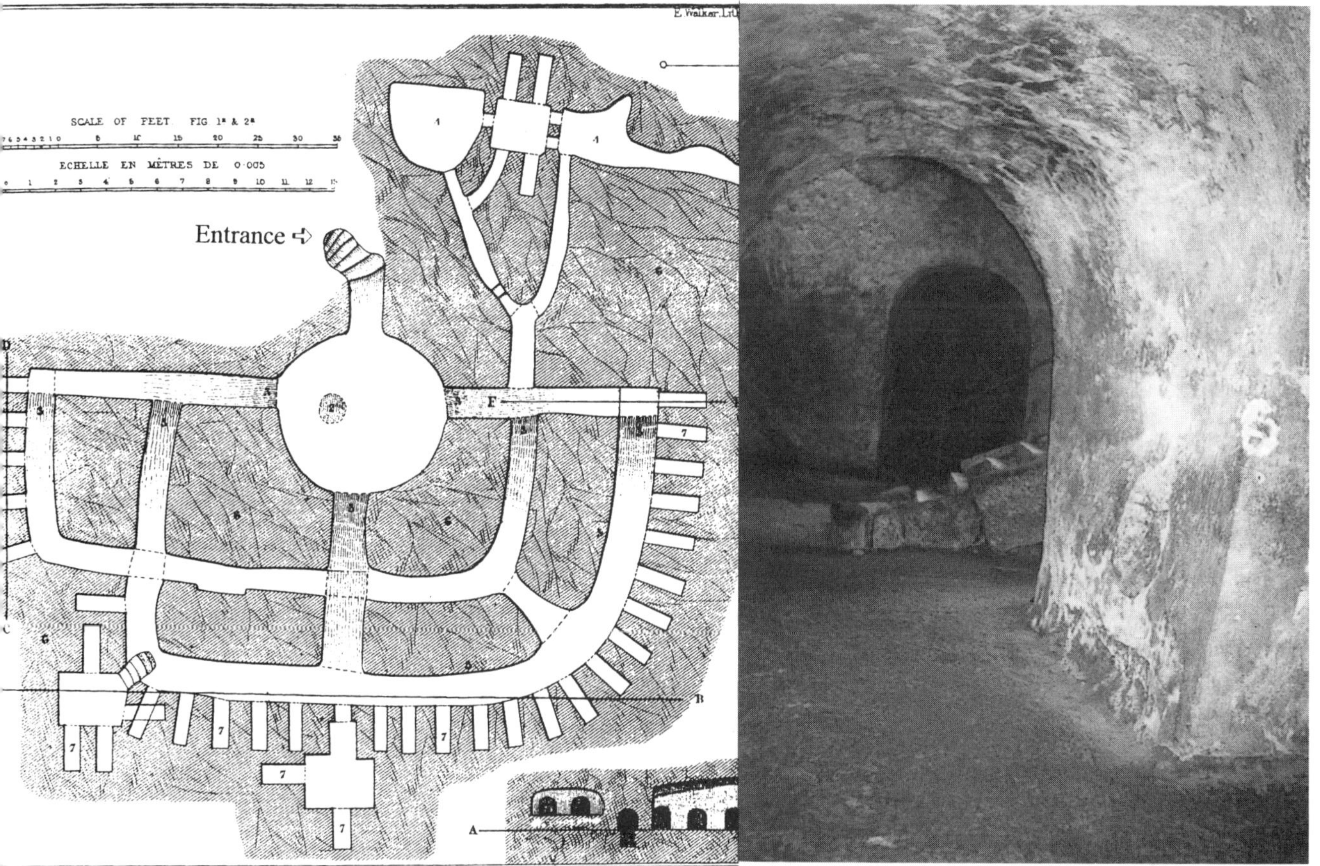

A sketch of the Tomb of the Prophets. On the right is a view inside the cave.

tee, to intercede in the Sultan's court.

The archbishop claimed that his purpose in buying the cave was solely for scientific reasons. He would not build a church over the site or even place a cross there. Relentless pressure was applied by the Russian consul in Constantinople, until the Sultan's court agreed to allow the sale. Like the Cave of the Kings, which fell into French hands, the Cave of the Prophets fell into Russian possession. Though no construction was carried out there, the area was cordoned off. Today, an Arab family living nearby opens it daily for tourists.[36]

The Cave of Shimon HaTzaddik

Shimon HaTzaddik lived in the time of the Second Temple. He served as High Priest for forty years, and led communal affairs in the period after the Great Assembly. He died on 29 Tishre, about 310 B.C.E. (3450), and was buried in a cave north of Jerusalem. Throughout the ages, Jews have come to his cave to pray in his merit.*

The site gained importance after 1730 when the Arabs temporarily closed the Tomb of Shmuel HaNavi. From then onwards, marriages were performed there, and the festivities on Lag b'Omer were an annual event at the cave.

In 1876 (5636), the mayor of Jerusalem offered to sell the land surrounding the Cave of Shimon HaTzaddik to the Jews. The underground cavern had long been a holy place for Jews, but in recent years the Arab who controlled the area made life very difficult for visitors, even demanding a fee to enter.

The mayor's offer was interpreted by the leaders of the community as a Heaven-sent opportunity to acquire control of the site. Money was collected by both the Sephardic and Ashkenazic communities, and a contract was signed that year. Rav Avraham Ashkenazi, the Chacham Bashi, and Rav Meir Auerbach represented their respective communities. For 15,000 francs, the cave and the surrounding orchard of eighty olive trees became the inheritance of the Jewish people.[37]

Later, in 1891, a Sephardic community established a settlement, Nalachas Shimon, near the cave. The driving force behind this community had been Rav Avraham Ashkenazi, who had passed away in 1880. The group was forced to abandon the neighborhood after the riots of 1929.

The Cave of Shmuel HaNavi

Shmuel HaNavi is buried in his hometown of Rama, eight kilometers north of Jerusalem. He had the distinction of anointing the first two kings of Israel, Shaul and David. Of all the sacred sites in Eretz Yisrael, the cave of Shmuel HaNavi was among the two or three most celebrated sites on the Jewish pilgrim's itinerary.

As we discussed earlier, the prophet's *yartzeit* on 28 Iyar was a landmark occasion. Thousands of Jews came from places as far away as Egypt and the Euphrates Valley to pray at his tomb and

* See story, "The Day of Rain," in *Bygone Days: 17th Century*.

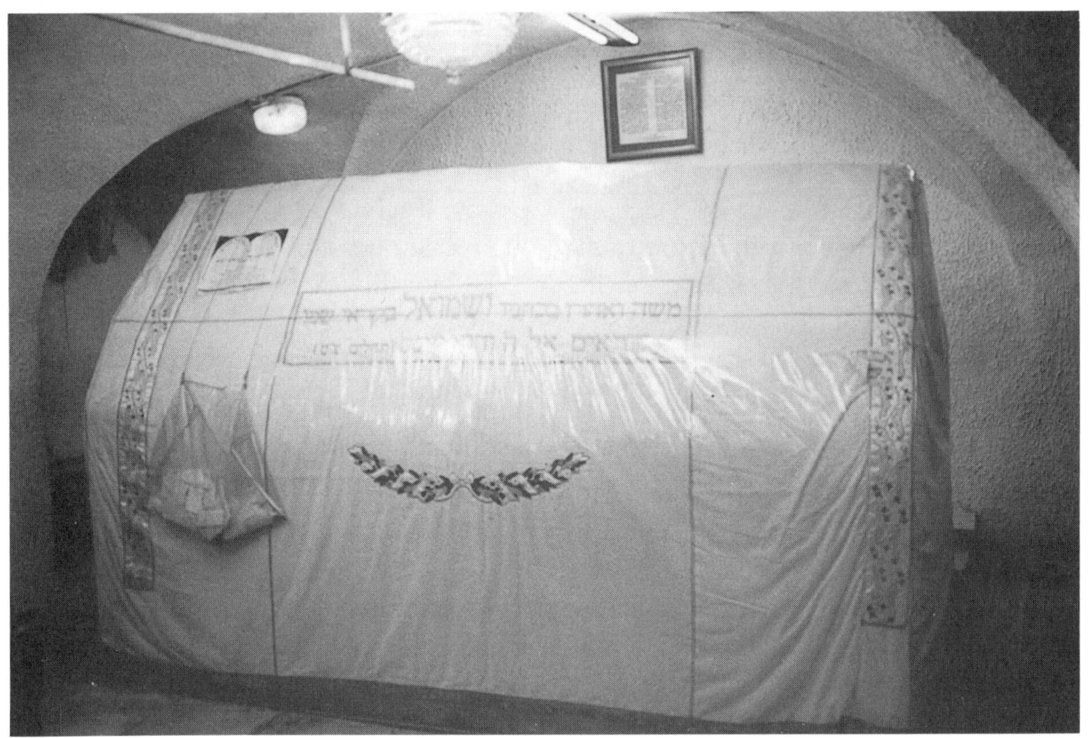

The Tomb of Shmuel HaNavi lies underground, with a mosque over it

participate in the festivities called the *zei'ara*. Many stayed for a week or more. Some first stopped at Meron in the Galilee to join the festivities by the grave of Rabbi Shimon bar Yochai, whose *yartzeit* was on 18 Iyar, before coming to Jerusalem.

The Radvaz mentions that a synagogue stood there in the sixteenth century.[38] In 1555 (5315) there was an unsuccessful attempt by the Moslems to evict the Jews. The Turks imposed an annual tax on the Jewish pilgrims, and without legal permission the festivities could not be held. The latter generally resulted in bribery to assure the safety of the *zei'ara*. Sometime in the 1730s the Jews lost their hold on the site. A hundred years later the Arabs built a mosque over the cave.

In 1885 (5645), the mayor of Jerusalem announced that he forbade festivities by the Jews at the cave on the *zei'ara*. When the Chacham Bashi, Rav Yaakov Shaul Elyashar, heard of the decree he immediately arranged a meeting with the mayor.

"You have to understand," the mayor explained. "I have reports that in the past years Jewish pilgrims have written their names on the walls and generally not acted in a manner befitting this holy place. Therefore, I have no recourse other than to lock the mosque."

The Chacham Bashi reassured him that the Jews would act properly, and recommended that he place guards there.* The mayor agreed, and the *zei'ara* took place as scheduled.[39]

Several attempts were made to start a Jewish settlement near the cave. In the late 1880s, a group headed by Rav Yitzchak Rivlin bought a large tract of land which contained three wells and

* See story, "The Telegram," in *Bygone Days: 1900–1918*.

fruit trees, and established a settlement called Nachalas Yisrael. From the outset, forces beyond the settlers' control caused this colony to fold. In 1895 (5655), a group of thirteen Yemenite families farmed the land of Nachalas Yisrael. After a few years they, too, were forced to return to the safety of the city.[40]

In the 1930s, the Bostoner Rebbe bought land near Rama, where Shmuel HaNavi is buried, with the hopes of building a settlement called Givat Pinchas. Others placed their lots with him, and plans for the new settlement were drawn up. However, the times were not auspicious and he had to forfeit his down payment when he was unable to amass the money needed.

Today, the site is visited daily, and on 28 Iyar, thousands come to pray there. Recently, too, archeologists have excavated the surroundings and have revealed giant slabs of stone.

The Tomb of Rachel[41]

Since ancient times Jerusalemites have been accustomed to going to the Tomb of Rachel to pray. Only a few hours' walk to the south, the Tomb of Rachel was (and still is today) a source of comfort to the downtrodden.

Over the generations, the edifice above Rachel's grave has changed numerous times. At some unknown time, an open-walled, canopy-type shelter was erected of stone and mortar. At other times the monument consisted of twelve stones, representing the twelve tribes.

In 1841, Sir Moses Montefiore gained permission from the Turkish authorities to restore the tomb. He built the large, two-room building that we know today.

The Tomb of Rachel, built by Sir Moses Montefiore in 1841,as it appeared in 1900

The Tomb of Rachel as it appears today. The dome, built by Montefiore in 1841, is no longer visible from the street. The renovations, completed in 1997, were made for security reasons.

A month before he died, in Tamuz, 1885, Sir Montefiore pledged to have it renovated. It was his final gift to Eretz Yisrael.

Into the twentieth century, the tomb was locked around the clock. However, anyone who wished to go and pray there could get the key from the beadle of the Churvah Synagogue, who would escort him to the tomb and open it.

The tomb's lock was extraordinary. Tooled by Reb Zalman of Jerusalem, it had a brass key that was fifteen centimeters long. The beadle kept it with him at all times. It was not uncommon that someone would knock at his door in the middle of the night.

"Please," would come the voice of a Jew, "so-and-so is having strong labor pains. We need the key right away."

As soon as he received the key, the person would dash to the bedside of the expectant mother and place the it under her pillow. Immediately the pains would subside and the delivery would take place uneventfully.

A native Jerusalemite by the name of Rav Shimon Munzon had the distinction of being the first beadle of the Churvah Synagogue. He inherited the coveted position from his father, Rav Avraham Munzon, who had been active in that capacity first in the Menachem Tzyon Shul and later in the Churvah Synagogue when it opened in 1864. Rav Shimon *Shamesh*, as he was called, also had the keys to the Tomb of Rachel and was responsible for its upkeep. He fulfilled his duties faithfully until his death in 1906.[42]

There is an ancient tradition — a *segulah* — to tie a scarlet thread around one's neck or wrist as a protection against all kinds of dangers, especially for pregnant women. Before the thread may be used, it must first be wound around the Tomb of Rachel. This transforms the simple thread into a special *segulah* whose validity has been proven over and over again.* Even today, one can find women circling the tomb with a long scarlet thread in their hands.

Rooftop view of the Old City. In the left foreground is one of the main east-west thoroughfares. On the upper right is the Tiferes Yisrael Synagogue.

* See story, "The Wallach Hospital," in *Bygone Days: 1918–1948*.

Greater Jerusalem

No less than forty new suburbs were founded around Jerusalem between 1880 and 1900. A new impulse to build came after 1889, when a large influx of immigrants that would be known as the First Wave arrived from pogrom-torn Russia. Some of the neighborhoods were small, some large, some survived and others vanished over the course of time. Yet each had a core of men dedicated to building that particular suburb. In this section, we will describe a handful of these new colonies, as well as new areas of residence in the Old City itself.

A Survey

By the turn of the century, some fifteen thousand Jews lived outside the walled city, in approximately fifty neighborhoods. These ranged in size from as small as six houses (Shevat Achim) to as big as three hundred (Meah Shearim). At least as many Jews lived within the Old City, making the total population around thirty-two thousand. In all, some 3,000 homes were built during the thirty-year period from 1870 to 1900.[43] This surge of expansion and development did much to alleviate the pressure inside the Old City. Yet, the steadily growing influx of Jews to Eretz Yisrael, known as the First Wave, kept the population growth far higher than the housing projects could handle.

New Suburbs*

Beis Yisrael

The Beis Yisrael suburb was built in 1886 on land stretching below Meah Shearim that had once been a swamp. Drained a decade earlier through the ingenious plan of Yosef Rivlin, the hilly area was bought by a sincere group of settlers and turned into a thriving neighborhood. Rav Yosef Chaim Zonnenfeld and Rav Zalman Baharan were its spiritual leaders; Rav Aryeh Leib Dayan (Hershler) and Rav Shimshon Aharon Polansky its *rabbanim*; and Rav Shmuel Zukerman and Rav Yechezkiah Mandelbaum its communal leaders.

Originally, a huge outdoor pool was used to collect rainwater, but after a few years, public buildings were erected over this site, and it was replaced by underground cisterns.

The hub of activity in this mixed Ash-

* See map, p. 387

kenazic-Sephardic neighborhood was the Beis Yaakov Synagogue.* It stood on the main street, which was later named Zonnenfeld Street. Years later, the owners of the private houses underneath the shul dedicated them for sacred purposes, and the *shetiblach* of Beis Yisrael came into existence.

In the twentieth century, the Ashkenazi kabbalist, Rav Asher Zelig Margolios, lived and taught in Beis Yisrael, as well as Rav Gershon Lapidos. After the Second World War, the Mir Yeshivah relocated in the neighborhood. Today, Chassidic shuls such as Zweille, Karlin-Pinsk, and Chabad stand there, as well as a number of Sephardic shuls.

Yemin Moshe[44]

In 1886 (5646), Jerusalemites heard that Montefiore's nephew, Mr. Yosef Sebag Montefiore, was preparing to sell the windmill and the surrounding land to the Alliance Israelite Universelle institutions (Kyach), who hoped to build a progressive school there. Yosef Sebag, his uncle's personally appointed executor, thought they were Sir Moses' private property.

In reality, however, the land had been purchased with money from the estate of Judah Touro. In 1856, Mishkenos Sha'ananim was built on one third of the property. Later, Sir Moses built the windmill, while the rest of the land remained undeveloped. *Rabbanim* in Jerusalem had proof that the entire tract had been bought and consecrated for housing for the poor citizens of Jerusalem. A series of letters went back and forth between Jerusalem and London, and the younger Montefiore withdrew his plan.

Shortly before the century's end, the neighborhood of

Yemin Moshe

Yemin Moshe began to rise. Comprising a hundred and fifty houses, half-settled by Sephardim and half by Ashkenazim, it became the fifth suburb to be named after the grand patron of the *yishuv*, Sir Moses Montefiore.

Battei Warsaw[45]

Starting at Kikar Shabbos and extending to Meah Shearim as one long complex of houses, Battei Warsaw was built in the mid-1890s under highly unique circumstances.

Yaakov Tennvarzal, a wealthy, elderly Jew from Warsaw, saw that his children were drifting away from traditional Judaism. He therefore decided to give his money to worthy causes rather than let them squander it after his death. Without revealing his real intent, he liquidated his entire estate for the considerable sum of 130,000 rubles and traveled to Eretz Yisrael with the money.

In Jerusalem, he surveyed the needs of the *yishuv* and felt that the housing shortage had priority over other causes. Meeting with Rebbe David Biderman, the Lelover Rebbe, he handed him 52,000 rubles in cash to buy the land for Battei Warsaw. The two men then proceeded over to the Russian consulate, and in the presence of the consul, Tennvarzal signed a will directing that the entire sum of 130,000 rubles be allocated for the building project. The following day he died.

When Tennvarzal's children heard of the will's contents, they sought to contest it, claiming that their father had been mentally incompetent. The consul testified that he personally supervised the writing of the will, and that the deceased was completely sane at the time. The court ordered that the 52,000 rubles belonged to the Battei Warsaw corporation, while the remaining money had to be returned to the children.

After the first twenty-four houses were occupied, the *Chavatzeles* paper wrote: "How great a feat of kindness did the deceased patron [of Battei Warsaw] perform, earning an eternal blessing for himself when he cunningly enabled poor scholars to live in such wonderful quarters."

Two synagogues were built, one for the Perushim, called Ohel Yitzchak, and the other for the Chassidim, called Ohel Shmuel.

Bucharim Neighborhood

Jews from Bucharia, Tashkent, and Samarkand (in southeastern Russian near the Afghanistan-China border) began to immigrate to Eretz Yisrael as early as 1872. Sephardim by descent, most of these immigrants were men of means, coming from villa-type homes in Russia. As their numbers grew in the 1800s, they desired to build spacious houses for themselves.

In 1891 (5651), the community, headed by Rav Yaakov Meir, broke ground on a new neighborhood. Although it faced some initial problems, the suburb became one of the most beautiful neighborhoods in greater Jerusalem. Shlomo Musayoff was the first to build, and over the years, Chatzer Musayoff became the center of the quarter, containing a synagogue, *mikve*, and yeshivah. The Bucharim Quarter, flush with Beis Yisrael and extending on

The Mashiach's house, built in 1905

both sides of Yechezkel Street, stood out from afar. Once, when Jamil Pasha passed by the neighborhood, he commented, "How beautiful and opulent, an honor and a glory!"

After the First World War, impoverished Bucharian refugees from the Russian Revolution inundated the neighborhood. Spacious living quarters were divided to provide housing for the influx of people. The overcrowding and poverty eventually lead to the deterioration of the once-prestigious neighborhood.

On 19 Ezra Street, Elisha Yehodioff built a house for the Mashiach and his guests in 1905. The impressive Beis Yehodioff, a two-story mansion, measured 55 meters long by 20 meters wide. Built in the fashionable Italian Renaissance style, it was the largest private house standing in Eretz Yisrael at that time.

During the First World War it was used as a Turkish command base, and later, under British rule, Jewish soldiers in the British army made their Passover Seder there. Today, it houses two religious girls schools, Beis Chana and Beis Yaakov.

Battei Milner[46]

In 1892, a man by the name of Shlomo Milner built a small neighborhood next to Battei Ungarin, comprising thirty-five flats. In the course of time, it became incorporated as part of Battei Ungarin itself.

A wealthy industrialist from Romania, Milner sought to benefit Jerusalemites with the wonders of the industrial revolution. He chose as his pilot project a large steam mill near Battei Wittenberg, a neighborhood we shall review shortly.

He proudly proclaimed, "Within ten years people will forget that mills were once run on horsepower!" Milner was avant-garde for his time, and a man who sought to better the lot of his brethren in the Holy City.

Knesses Yisrael[47]

In 1888 (5648), the Central Committee of Knesses Yisrael, the oldest established body uniting the *yishuv*, sought to purchase land between Agrippas and Bezelal Streets. The purchase itself turned into one of the most dramatic episodes in the expansion beyond the walls.

It was during this period that construction began on the Jaffa-Jerusalem railroad, and the future Knesses Yisrael was the site proposed for the Jerusalem station. Christian societies from Germany, Greece, and Armenia rushed to buy all the surrounding land, which bordered on Mishkenos Yisrael and Mizkeres Moshe. As a result, the property values became quite high. The Central Committee could not outbid the wealthy Christian factions, and a gloomy picture of the future loomed before them. The threat of a Christian neighborhood next to Jewish ones was twofold: expansion in that direction would be stopped, and worse, the proximity of Christian elements could easily result in missionary activity.

As a last-ditch effort, the committee members attempted to prolong the legal procedures in the Turkish municipality, hoping that the societies would become fed up and abandon their plans. Even this attempt seemed doomed to failure. During this entire time, special prayers

Jewish laborers building one of the new neighborhoods at the beginning of the 20th century

were conducted, both in synagogues and by graves of the tzaddikim in Jerusalem, Hebron, Safed, and Tiberias. Fast days were declared as well.

After months of uncertainty, in Sivan, 1888 (5648), news arrived that the French railroad company had decided to build the station further outside the city limits to the south, where it is located today. Naturally, the Christian parties rushed to purchase land there, in what is today the German Colony. This freed the original site and allowed the Central Committee to build a new suburb, Knesses Yisrael, there.

There was, however, one German by the name of Gibler, who had put a down payment on part of the land and would not relinquish his hold. He openly announced his intention of going through with the purchase just to infuriate the Jews, whom he held in contempt. After building a stone wall around the area, he proceeded to the municipality office to formally register his purchase. Suddenly he was stricken with apoplexy and collapsed dead.

With the last stumbling block removed, the committee purchased the land. Construction began in 1891, with five houses being built. Knesses Yisrael would ultimately grow into a flourishing neighborhood of over one hundred and seventy homes.

Jewish Presence in the Old City

The great advances in building outside the walls could not offset the steady influx of new immigrants to Jerusalem, and the Old City remained overcrowded well into the twentieth century. Out of necessity, Jews moved out of the Jewish Quarter into the other sections of the city, especially the Moslem Quarter. Ashkenazim, Sephardim, and Moroccans built synagogues and yeshivos throughout the area. The *maggid* of Jerusalem, Rav Benzion Yadler, grew up in the Moslem Quarter and recalled that twenty-two synagogues and two large yeshivos, Toras Chaim and Chayei Olam, existed there before the end of the nineteenth century.

Until the riots of 1929, one of the main thoroughfares was the Street of Chains (Rechov HaShalsheles). For the Jews, it led down from the Jewish Quarter and Hebron Street to the Kosel, and for the Moslems, it led straight up to the Temple Mount. During this period, Jews walked alone without fear of their Arab neighbors.

Midrash Ha'Agunah[48]

In 1863 (5623), a young, well-to-do couple moved to Jerusalem. Shortly after their arrival, they bought a courtyard in the Moslem Quarter off Hebron Street. Alter and Chaya Shadlizer set themselves up in their new house, grateful for the opportunity to serve the Almighty in the Holy City.

One day Alter did not return home. Chaya was at her wits' end with worry over her husband's mysterious disappearance. She told her neighbors, who in turn notified *rabbanim*. Soon the Turkish police initiated a search. All their efforts were in vain; he had vanished without a trace. Some suspected that he had been kidnapped and murdered. In those days, one could be attacked and slain for a few coins, especially if caught walking alone outside the walled city.

The lonely woman became an *agunah*, a woman whose husband's death could not be conclusively substantiated and was forbidden to remarry. Chaya accepted her unfortunate circumstances with dignity. She decided to consecrate the upper story of the courtyard as a *beis midrash* for scholars to study Torah.

Kollel Warsaw became the heirs of the courtyard, and the Zortkov Chassidim prayed there. Later, in the twentieth century, Chassidei Breslov prayed there. During the earthquake of 1927, the northern wall was damaged, and Rav Shmuel Anshin collected funds to repair it. In 1936, the Chassidim were forced to abandon the courtyard due to the infamous Arab riots of that year.

Shomrei HaChomos[49]

The Hungarian *kollel* called Shomrei HaChomos was established by disciples of the Chasam Sofer in 1862. A *beis midrash* was not built until the 1870s, outside what is today the tunnel leading from the Western Wall to the Damascus Gate. Later, when the *kollel* built a new housing project near Meah Shearim called Battei Ungarin in 1892, the Shomrei HaChomos yeshivah in the Old City continued to thrive. In 1904 they built a second story, one floor for the Chassidim and one for the Perushim.

In the middle of the construction, the Turks voiced opposition to the additional floor, claiming its roof would then be higher than the Dome of the Rock on the Temple Mount. Before the Turks could obtain an injunction, all the members of the *kollel* labored throughout the

The Shomrei HaChomos shul, now in ruins, was one of the religious hubs of the community located in the Moslem Quarter

night to finish the roof. According to Turkish law, once the roof of a building was erected, the building could no longer be demolished.

Upstairs were the two shuls, and downstairs was a *beis midrash* called *mishmorim*, where scholars studied twenty-four hours a day on a rotation system (*mishmeros*). There was also a *mikve*.

Even after the riots of 1929, Jews still studied there. However, fears of further violence caused them to transfer one of the Holy Arks to a synagogue in Meah Shearim called Khal Yerei'im. They were forced to vacate the building during the riots of 1936. Not long afterwards, Arabs destroyed it.

Rand Courtyard

In 1900 (5660), Rav Mendel Rand, a Sanzer Chassid, immigrated to Jerusalem. His mission was to transform his wealth into enduring acts of kindness for the more unfortunate Jews of the city.

At that time, the closest building to the Temple Mount in which Jews lived stood in the cotton market shopping area. The eastern end of this building reached within a meter or two of the Wall, and from its upper rooftop one had a clear view of the Temple Mount. At quiet times, one heard Jews praying at the Wall. Among the famous *rabbanim* who lived there were Rav Naftali Chaim Horowitz, the son-in-law of the Sanzer Rebbe, and Rav Shneur Zalman of Lublin, author of *Toras Chaim*. The previous owner of the building had put it up for sale due to his critical financial situation, and Christian buyers sought to purchase it. Rav Rand, realizing the true value of the property, convinced the owner to keep it in Jewish hands, and bought it himself.

Rav Mendel had a personal reason for securing that particular building. He explained, "When the Mashiach will come, a flood of Kohanim and Levi'im will congregate at the Western Wall in order to ascend the Temple Mount. Surely it will be crowded, and being a Kohen, I will be pushed in the crowd. Instead, I shall buy a courtyard near the Temple Mount and will be able to ascend without delay."

The three-story building contained thirty rooms, several courtyards, cisterns, four shop fronts, and numerous storerooms. Dozens of families lived there free of charge.

In 1909, Rav Mendel built Battei Rand behind Machane Yehudah in the New City as free housing for the poor. Rav Mendel lived in his Old City courtyard for twenty years before moving out to Battei Rand.

After the 1929 riots, Arabs usurped the premises.

Courtyard of the Brisker Rav[50]

As we mentioned previously, Rav Yehoshua Leib Diskin purchased a courtyard in the middle of the Moslem Quarter in 1881 as the premises for his new orphanage. He chose the upper-floor apartment as his home since its windows faced the Temple Mount.

Until he moved outside the city walls a few years later for health reasons, Rav Diskin's disciples studied with him there. They were dedicated scholars and future leaders of the *yishuv*.

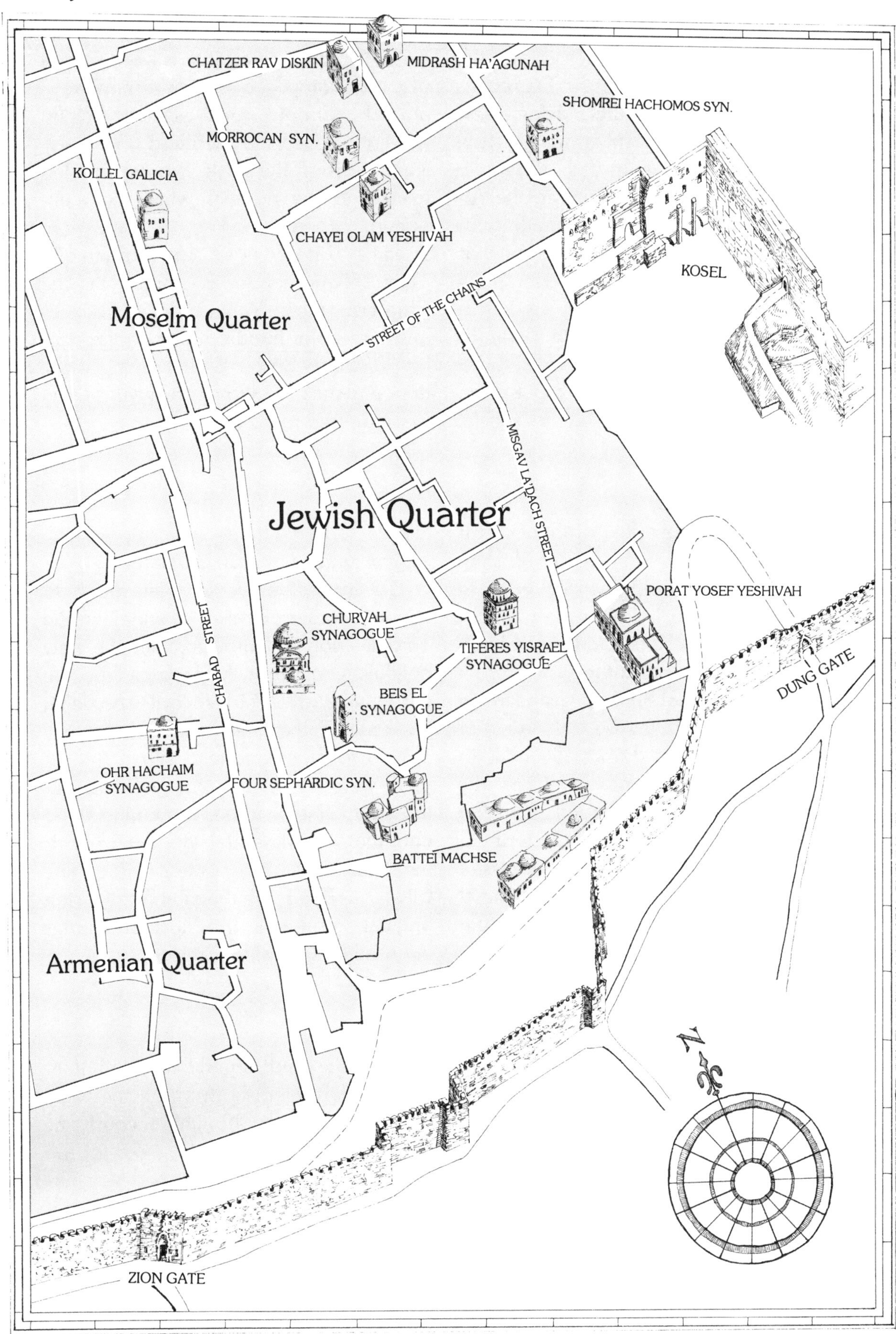
CHATZER RAV DISKIN
MIDRASH HA'AGUNAH
SHOMREI HACHOMOS SYN.
MORROCAN SYN.
KOLLEL GALICIA
CHAYEI OLAM YESHIVAH
KOSEL
Moselm Quarter
STREET OF THE CHAINS
MISGAV LA'DACH STREET
Jewish Quarter
PORAT YOSEF YESHIVAH
CHURVAH SYNAGOGUE
TIFERES YISRAEL SYNAGOGUE
CHABAD STREET
BEIS EL SYNAGOGUE
DUNG GATE
OHR HACHAIM SYNAGOGUE
FOUR SEPHARDIC SYN.
BATTEI MACHSE
Armenian Quarter
N
ZION GATE

Every day around sunset he would walk with a few students through the Moslem *shuk* and go out the Damascus Gate. He would stroll around for a few minutes, enjoying the pleasant air, and then return to his courtyard. Wherever he went in the Moslem Quarter, the Arabs regarded him with awe, standing for him and taking care that his way was unobstructed. As he walked along the crowded corridors, he would bend over now and then to pick up little slivers of wood, saying they could be used for heating pots of food in the orphanage. His wife eventually sewed a special pocket for them.

On one of his walks outside the city walls, he commented that a nearby flock of sheep comprised a certain number of animals. Curious, one of his disciples went and asked the shepherd how many sheep were in the flock. It corresponded exactly to the number which he mentioned. When asked to explain, Rav Diskin said it was not a superhuman gift. "This phenomenon is found in the Chumash, when Yaakov 'lifted his eyes and saw four hundred men approaching' (*Genesis* 33:1). With nothing more than a glance, Yaakov perceived exactly four hundred men."

Chayai Olam Yeshivah

Chayai Olam consisted of three courtyards on Hebron Street in the Moslem Quarter. The institution was founded in 1886 by two rabbis visiting the country, Rav Yehoshua of Kotna and Rav Chaim Elazar Waxs. The philanthropist who accepted the financial burden was a simple but extraordinary Jew by the name of Pinchas Neminosky. Principally built to cater to the needs of the Chassidic community, it was headed by the Lelover Rebbe, Rav David Biderman. Chayai Olam Yeshivah was successful from the outset, and ran the fastest-growing cheder in Jerusalem. By the turn of the century there were four hundred children studying there. Besides the *talmud Torah*, there was a *yeshivah ketanah* and a *yeshivah gedolah*.

The institution would later move to new and larger premises overlooking the Temple Mount. Unfortunately, the new building was seriously damaged by the earthquake of 1927. While it was being renovated, the yeshivah temporarily moved to other quarters. When the repairs were completed, the yeshivah returned to the building, remaining there until the Arab riots of 1936. After the riots, Chayai Olam relocated in the New City, at Kikar Shabbos. Today, the original premises in the Moslem Quarter are used by Chassidei Breslov.

Battei Wittenberg

We previously saw that Rav Moshe Wittenberg was the first major benefactor of the Diskin Orphanage. However, this was by no means the limit of his charitable activities. Rav Wittenberg emigrated from Vitebst, Russia, in 1881. A Chabad Chassid, he brought with him a vast fortune and eagerly invested it in building Jerusalem both inside the walls and out. He soon bought a courtyard near the Damascus Gate next to the Austrian Hospital, and opened a synagogue called Tefillah l'Moshe. As many as thirty guests would join him at his dinner table.

Buying the three-story building required extraordinary planning and diligence, and at one point it looked like his effort had totally failed. Just when he was about to conclude the deal with the Arab-Christian owner, a Catholic monastery bought it from under him. He spent a year bargaining with the monastery to buy the courtyard, and in the end, he paid them a thousand napoleons over and above the initial cost.

Among the people who lived there was Rav Moshe Blau, who later played an important role in the *yishuv*.

Rav Moshe, childless, gave a thousand napoleons to the Diskin Orphanage that same year. In 1885, he built Battei Wittenberg near Meah Shearim. Comprised of forty houses, it included a synagogue and was commonly called Shaarei Moshe.

The Yemenite Community

Yemenites began settling in Jerusalem in the 1880s, bringing with them their distinctive traditions. Their first settlements were in Shaar HaPinah, near Meah Shearim, in 1888, and in Shiloach the following year. Shaar HaPinah initially comprised forty houses and gradually expanded as the years went by.

Shiloach, on the other hand, grew at a different pace. A Yemenite leader named Rav Boaz HaBavli joined forces with the Ezras Nidachim Society, headed by Rav Yisrael Dov Frumkin, to build a formidable Yemenite community. By the turn of the century, there were over a hundred and twenty families living there. Unfortunately, they were forced to abandon the site in the 1930s due to security reasons.

Shaar HaPinah neighborhood

Rav Zaddok standing at the head of his class of Yemenite children

In 1891, Rav Avraham Elindaf immigrated and tried to organize a *talmud Torah* according to the Yemenite tradition. He first lived in Mishkenos and then in Nachalas Tzvi, both Yemenite areas. The latter neighborhood was located near Meah Shearim, and named after its patron, Baron Moshe Hirsch (Tzvi). From an original thirty houses, it expanded to over seventy. Rav Elindaf printed the Yemenite Bible called *Tag*, comprising the Chumash, the *Targum*, and the commentary of Rav Sa'adiah Gaon, and the Yemenite *machzor* called *Tachliel* with the commentary of Rav Yechiel Zalach.[51]

Another Yemenite, Rav Zaddok by name, integrated into the Ashkenazic community of Meah Shearim. Orphaned at a young age, he grew up under the guidance of the Diskin Orphanage's directors. From there he gained an affinity for the Ashkenazim, which led him to live in Meah Shearim, where he worked repairing sewing machines. When he saw the influx of Yemenites and the need to strengthen their educational level, he opened a cheder for Yemenite children.

In 1910 (5670), the Yemenite community purchased their own separate burial grounds on the Mount of Olives, with the generous aid of Baron Edmond Rothschild.

Known for their assiduousness and good nature, the Yemenites created a good name for themselves among all of Jerusalem's residents. Rav Shalom Yitzchak HaLevi was their Chief Rabbi until his death in 1973.

The Close of the Century

During the last years of the decade, signposts for the future were already in sight. Physically, the city was slowly modernizing. In 1892, the first locomotive made its inaugural climb up the mountainous route from Jaffa to Jerusalem. There had been several futile attempts at building a railroad line in the past, beginning with Sir Moses Montefiore in the 1850s. At that time, the British philanthropist commissioned Mr. Galloway, the engineer who built the Alexandria-Cairo railroad, to plan the Jaffa-Jerusalem line. Opposition arose from European powers, and in the end the plan was abandoned. In the 1860s, a German engineer by the name of Zimpel presented a proposed route, and in 1872, a Frenchman, Forbes, was granted a *firman* to build the line on condition that he finish within one and a half years. Forbes, however, was unable to raise the necessary funding. Finally, in 1892, a Jew, Yosef Navon, built a single, narrow-gauge rail. While the train puffed up the steep mountains towards Jerusalem, agile passengers would hop off, pick some flowers, and climb back on the moving train.

The introduction of the railroad brought a dramatic transition in the Middle Eastern country. Until then, the road from Jaffa to Jerusalem was full of caravans of camels — as many as a hundred a day — carrying food and merchandise on their backs. With the widening of the road in 1869 for the visit of Kaiser Franz Joseph, horse-drawn carriages began to traverse the route, over a two-day trek. The train, in addition to being more efficient and reliable, also offered protection from Bedouin attacks. As a result, the caravans quickly dwindled away. The carriage service, however, remained into the twentieth century.

Unfortunately, the progress on the physical front was not matched by a change in the Arabs' attitude towards their Jewish neighbors. In 1892, a vicious booklet published in Egypt was circulated in Jaffa and Jerusalem. Its aim was to prove that the Jews traditionally slaughtered a Christian child before Passover as a cultist blood rite. Written in Arabic and French, it quickly reached the hands of many Moslem government officers. The revered Rishon l'Tzyon, Rav Meir Panijel, sent an urgent message to the mayor of Jerusalem, imploring him to ban the pamphlets. The mayor agreed and ordered them to be confiscated and burnt. Just then, a Christian child disappeared in Jaffa, causing tensions to run very high. Fortu-

Yosef Navon

nately, the child was found the next day alive and well.[52]

On the other hand, a new high point was reached in the Jewish community with the arrival of the Lubliner Rav, Rav Shneur Zalman, in 1892. A Lubavitcher Chassid from birth, he was eagerly sought by the Chassidim of Jerusalem to head their *beis din*. Yielding to their request, he soon became the community's spiritual leader. Still, he refrained from formally involving himself in communal affairs, claiming it stifled his clarity in learning Torah. His brilliant analytical mind, coupled with a photographic memory, amazed the *chachamim*. Every Friday morning, Rav Shmuel Salant and the Rishon l'Tzyon came to his house to share Torah ideas with him. Their discussions would often last for hours.

Rav Shneur Zalman passed away on Shabbos night, 5 Nisan, 1902. All Friday, the weather had been hotter than usual. At sunset, a sudden torrential downpour swept through the city, accompanied by thunder and lightning. Rav Salant, who was sitting with a group of *rabbanim*, ordered one of them to go quickly to the Lubliner Rav's house and see if he was still alive. He explained his sudden behavior: "I just saw a pillar of fire — a sign of the passing of a great tzaddik — and I'm sure it must be in honor of Rav Shneur Zalman. Such a pillar of fire only comes down to accompany the greatest of souls, perhaps one in a generation, to their eternal abode."[53]

The year 1898 (5658) was a crucial year for Jerusalemites. On 29 Teves, the Brisker Rav passed away. During his twenty years of leadership, he had marshaled superhuman powers to withstand the progressive elements from all sides. Now, a vacuum set in. The frail and venerable Rav of Jerusalem, Rav Shmuel Salant, was not in a position to fight the way Rav Diskin had, and the younger, fifty-year-old Rav Zonnenfeld did not feel himself suited for the task. Thus, an ominous period set in for the *yishuv*.

The Centennial Crossroads[54]

Two more events occurred later in 1898, both on the same day, which would harbor ill for the city. Dr. Theodore Herzl arrived in Jerusalem, as did Kaiser Wilhelm II, the King of Germany.

The preparations for the Emperor's visit were unprecedented. Five months before his arrival date, the city began to prepare itself. A huge cleanup and repair program highlighted the physical charm of the Holy City, and numerous streets and roads were paved. These preparations were so massive in scope that workers were brought in from Egypt to help complete the job. Additionally, the walls of the city were deliberately breached, for the first time in nearly four hundred years. This was done to allow the Kaiser to ride into the Old City on horseback. Turkish law normally reserved this privilege for citizens of the empire. However, when the Emperor insisted, a compromise was reached whereby a gap was made in the wall next to Jaffa Gate. It was a low wall bridging the deep moat which surrounded Midgal David. The moat outside the Old City was filled in. As a result, the Emperor would not technically be entering through one of the city's gates. With the passage of the High Holidays, an air of excited anticipation grew for the imminent royal visit.

The Jews established a special committee of ten men — half Sephardim and half Ashkenazim — to plan the community's reception for the Kaiser. Money had been sent from the Diaspora specifically for his visit, with a letter urging the *rabbanim* of Jerusalem to make every effort to honor the German monarch in a befitting manner.

Breaching the Jaffa Gate in preparation for the Kaiser's visit

Each faith designed a festive "gate" through which the Emperor would pass as he approached the walled city. Above the flower-bedecked arch erected by the Jewish community were the words (in Hebrew and German): "Welcome in the name of the Lord, may you be blessed by the house of the Lord!" Silver ornaments from *sifrei Torah* decorated the gate, and long embroidered curtains from the Holy Arks hung on both sides. On both ends of the arch stood platforms, one for the two Chief Rabbis, and one for *rabbanim* and communal leaders.

The Kaiser was scheduled to arrive in Jerusalem on Shabbos, 13 Cheshvan, 1898 (5659). He and his entourage landed at Jaffa port on Friday. Amidst fanfare and international media coverage, he met with Jewish leaders at Mikve Yisrael, just outside of Jaffa. Herzl was among the people there. He greeted the Emperor and requested in the name of world Jewry that he intercede before the Sultan on their behalf. The Jewish people, he explained, needed a homeland of their own, and by birthright Palestine was best suited for them. The idea had been initially raised at the first Zionist Congress in Basel, Switzerland, a year earlier, but to date the Ottoman Empire had expressed no interest in the proposal. The Kaiser promised to raise the topic with the Sultan.

That same day, Friday, Herzl eagerly sought to reach Jerusalem in order to attend the ceremonial parade organized for the following morning. Herzl chose to travel by train, even though this entailed traveling on Shabbos. From the train station, he hurried to join the prayer services in the Old City. However, when he entered the Churvah Synagogue on Shabbos night, he did not anticipate the

The archway built by the Jewish community in honor of Kaiser Wilhelm II (seen riding on the white horse)

yishuv's reaction to his arrival. The entire community was shocked and outraged over his wanton transgression of the Shabbos.

At that time, the *yishuv* numbered over 30,000 souls, and few Jews openly transgressed the Shabbos. Even those who sent their children to progressive schools were all Orthodox. The gravest backsliding that occurred was on Friday afternoon, when some shops closed later than the *rabbanim* decreed. Herzl's precedent shocked and appalled Jews of every stripe and color.

The Rav of Jerusalem, Rav Shmuel Salant, placed a *cherem* on Dr. Herzl, forbidding anyone from approaching him, talking with him, or having anything to do with him. Except for a few well-wishers, the *cherem* was honored by everyone.

The ceremonial welcome to the Kaiser began around eleven o'clock the next morning. Most Jews prayed with the first minyanim and came out in full force to greet the Emperor. The Kaiser spent his nights in elaborate pavilions set up in an open lot near Nevi'im Street (Street of the Prophets). These were his lodgings throughout his visit. Proceeding from his encampment towards the Jaffa Gate, he passed tall banners with German and Turkish flags on them. A round of cannon shots announced the beginning of the parade.

The Kaiser first passed through the arch belonging to the Jews. Children stood grouped according to their *talmud Torah*, each boy wearing a colorful ribbon symbolizing the Turkish-German flags. As Wilhelm approached the children, they began singing an original song in Hebrew and German in his honor. When he approached the platforms, the *rabbanim* recited the blessing: "Who gives from His glory to flesh and blood," and the Jews answered "Amen."

The Rishon l'Tzyon, Rav Yaakov Shaul Elyashar, stepped forward, bowed, and spoke words of praise in Hebrew. Rav Salant then followed suit and presented the Emperor with an ornate scroll from the community. Kaiser Wilhelm was touched, mentioning how Kaiser Franz Joseph had visited Jerusalem thirty years earlier and received a similarly impressive welcome by the Jewish community.

Everyone from the *yishuv* participated in the ceremony, from adults to toddlers. One man, however, refused to join. Rav Yosef Chaim Zonnenfeld stayed home that Shabbos. When asked to explain his strange behavior, he answered, "The Vilna Gaon said the German people are from the seed of Amalek. When our Sages commanded us to run and see a king, even a gentile one, and recite a blessing, they were not speaking about a king such as this."[55]

This sobering statement from the future Rav of Jerusalem reflected the inner drama that was unfolding at the gates of the Holy City. On the holiest day of the week, a man of such lineage pompously entered Jerusalem riding on horseback. His visit, as highly touted as it was, did not go down in history as a turning point for the Jews or as a crowning point for the Kaiser. The Jews of Jerusalem were left in their same predicament, and the Emperor's good word for Herzl's proposal made no impression on the Sultan in Constantinople.

Furthermore, Sultan Abdul Hamid presented a highly attractive piece of land on Mount Zion to the Emperor as a gift, which Wilhelm immediately consecrated for the Catholic Church. A few years later, the mammoth Dormition Abbey was built on the site, another heartbreaking sign of the *galus*.

Herzl, for his part, ignored the ban placed on him by Rav Salant and proceeded to the Western Wall, where he disparaged the religious Jews he found praying there. Next, he proudly entered the Temple Mount, a sin of grave proportions. The *Chavatzeles* paper reported the entire incident, writing that half of Herzl's intention in coming to Jerusalem was to meet with the Kaiser again and the other half was to wantonly transgress the prohibition, punishable by Divine excommunication (*kares*), of walking on the Temple Mount.

From the Temple Mount, Herzl climbed the Mount of Olives and gazed at the magnificent view of the Holy City. Surrounded by thousands of graves of tzaddikim, he commented, "This land [the Mount of Olives] will make a good site for new houses!"

Some of the city's Jews did befriend him. Among them were Eliezer Ben-Yehudah and David Yellin, both secularists of the first order. Several times Herzl tried to meet with Rav Zonnenfeld, but Rav Yosef Chaim flatly refused.

Rav Akiva Yosef Shlesinger, a disciple of the Kesav Sofer and one of the founders of Petach Tikva, was a strong opponent of any form of secularism and Zionism. He wrote: "Zionism is worse than Amalek or Haman. The latter sought to destroy the Jewish people physically. Zionism, however, seeks to build us up physically, but its motives are not pure. Its goal is to increase heretics who are full of secularism and debauchery...."[56]

The citadel of Jerusalem suffered debasement from two world leaders. The breach they made in the physical and spiritual walls of the city could not be easily repaired. The physical violation was most tangibly evident in the change it caused in the *eruv* (the halachic enclosure of a public area enabling one to carry on Shabbos and festivals). Until then, the very wall of the Old City constituted the *eruv*, permitting Jews to carry freely inside the walls on Shabbos. However, with the opening for the Kaiser, the *eruv* was invalidated and had to be halachically repaired with a wire spanning it on top of the wall.

Thus, Jerusalem was left precariously open to the onslaught of formidable enemies. It would courageously attempt to battle them with whatever armaments it could muster.

Scanning the 19th Century

Scanning the annals of nineteenth-century Jerusalem, one cannot help but regard the members of the *yishuv* with a sense of awe and admiration. That such an insignificant group, who faced hostility wherever they turned, could rally to build a place of Torah in the Holy City is truly wondrous. Fighting cruel Moslem neighbors and indifferent government officials, they emerged victorious. From a minuscule minority to a vibrant majority, the Jews led the way to the reality of a greater Jerusalem. Confronting all the threats of the nineteenth century, especially that of secularism, they retained their ancient tradition in its pristine form.

Now, at the close of the century, a few *rabbanim* perceived the early warning signs of a grave danger, the likes of which they could barely imagine — Zionism. How to assess the threat and, better yet, how to plan a united strategy against this new enemy, was the task which lay before them in the twentieth century.

The Jaffa Gate, viewed from inside the Old City, as it appeared for hundreds of years. To the left is the continuation of the moat around the Citadel of David and part of the low level outer wall of the city which was breached for Kaiser Wilhelm II.

Notes

1. *Shechunos b'Yerushalayim,* p. 34.
2. *Mosad HaYesod*, p. 151.
3. *Shechunos b'Yerushalayim,* p. 23–24.
4. Rav Yaakov Sapin, *Kochvei Boker*.
5. *Esara Doros b'Eretz Yisrael*, vol. 2, p. 77.
6. *Shechunos b'Yerushalayim*, p. 34.
7. Based on the verse (*Psalms* 147:2), "Builder of Jerusalem, O Lord, the outcasts of Israel shall enter."

8. *Reshis HaYishuv Chutz l'Chomos Yerushalayim*, p. 12.
9. *Mosad HaYesod*, p. 152, n. 89.
10. *Esara Doros b'Eretz Yisrael*, vol. 2, p. 78.
11. *Reshis HaYishuv Chutz l'Chomos Yerushalayim,* p. 13.
12. *Chazon Tzyon*, p. 101.
13. Ibid., p. 31.
14. *Shechunos b'Yerushalayim*, p. 45.
15. The *gematria* of חדש כסלו is the same as אבן שלמה, hinting at the influence of the Vilna Gaon, whose name also has the numerical value of אבן שלמה (*Sefer Meah Shearim*, p. 11).
16. *Mosad HaYesod*, pp. 204–205.
17. *Shechunos b'Yerushalayim*, p. 53.
18. *Mosad HaYesod*, p. 212.
19. *L'Chovavim HaRishonim*, vol. 2., p. 13.
20. *Shechunos b'Yerushalayim*, p. 62.
21. *Mosad HaYesod*, pp. 232–235; another source claims that the idea originated with Rav Zonnenfeld (*Kach Nifrazu HaChomos*, pp. 186–190).
22. Ibid., p. 224, n. 11.
23. *Shechunos b'Yerushalayim*, p. 71; *Mosad HaYesod*, p. 231.
24. The report is quoted at the end of *Moshe v'Yerushalayim*, pp. 83–96, together with the refutation of the *rabbanim* of Jerusalem. Also, *Shechunos b'Yerushalayim*, pp. 76–78.
25. Ibid.
26. Culled from *Kovetz Maamarim (L'Divrei Yemei HaItonos b'Eretz Yisrael),* vol. 2, and *Luach Eretz Yisrael,* vol. 15, pp. 107–136.
27. *Guardians of Jerusalem*, pp. 193–197.
28. *Amud Aish*.
29. See also *Al Chomosiach Yerushalayim*, pp. 114–116.
30. *Mara d'Arah Yisrael*, vol. 1, pp. 249–277; *Amud Aish*, ch. 8; *Guardian of Jerusalem*, pp. 294–310.
31. *Battim u'Mosdos Yehudahiyim*, pp. 42–43.
32. *L'Chovavim HaRishonim,* vol. 4, pp. 42–43.
33. Ibid., p. 44.
34. *Zachor l'Avraham*, pp. 98–99.
35. *Yerushalayim, Ir HaNetzach*, p. 96.
36. *Meginzei Yerushalayim*, vol. 4, pp. 5–6.
37. *Sefer HaYishuv*, pp. 35–36.
38. *Responsa*, vol. 1, n. 513.
39. *L'Chovavim HaRishonim*, vol. 9, pp. 25–26.
40. Ibid.
41. See *Yesod L'Kra — Ohel Rachel Imeinu*.
42. *L'Chovavim HaRishonim,* vol. 18.
43. *Luach Eretz Yisrael*, vol. 5, pp. 59–71.
44. See *Shechunos b'Yerushalayim*, pp. 131–136, for more details.
45. Ibid., pp. 124–125.
46. *Sefer HaYishuv*, pp. 47–48.
47. *Mosad HaYesod*, pp. 259–263.
48. *Battim u'Mosdos Yehudahiyim*, pp. 47–48.
49. Ibid., pp. 18–19.
50. *Amud Aish*.
51. *Zachor l'Avraham*, pp. 27–29.
52. *Nasi'im b'Yisrael*, pp. 51–53.
53. *M'Gedolei Yerushalayim*, p. 115.
54. *Mara d'Arah Yisrael*, vol. 2, pp. 44–46; *Nasi'im b'Yisrael*, pp. 173–177.
55. Ibid., vol. 1, p. 200.
56. Ibid., vol. 2, p. 46, n. 53.

Needs of the Hour

The priority which the rabbanim gave to building the first neighborhoods outside the walls of the Old City is epitomized by the following two stories.

RAV SHMUEL Salant's only son, Rav Binyamin Beinish, had a reputation for delivering one of the finest Gemara lectures in the *yishuv*. His class met regularly every afternoon in the Menachem Tzyon Shul. Recently, however, he had started coming late and sometimes did not even appear at all.

One of the group decided to voice his disappointment to Rav Shmuel, who lived in a small house next to the Churvah Synagogue. The man knocked on the door and was welcomed by the Rav.

"With the Rav's permission," the man began respectfully, "I would like to take this opportunity to praise the Rav's son's *shiur* which I attend every day. His understanding of the Gemara is sharp and his presentation is clear. He delves into the hardest parts with ease, and makes us all feel — rightfully so — that we are in the presence of a *gadol b'Torah.*"

"*Baruch Hashem*," answered Rav Salant humbly.

"Recently," continued the man, "ever since Rav Binyamin Beinish started to work with Nachalas Shiva, both as partner and as secretary, he excuses himself more and more. Often he arrives late, and a number of times he has not shown up at all."

After a pause the man nervously continued, "We would like to ask the Rav to insist that his son keep his Torah commitment and return on a steady basis every afternoon."

Rav Salant refused, saying, "I am sure you will find another qualified lecturer. Rav Binyamin Beinish, you should know, contributes to the building of the new *yishuv* in ways that cannot be replaced by anyone else. Jerusalem cannot forgo him!"

* * *

IN THE fall of 1872 (5633), when the last of the fifty houses of Nachalas Shiva were nearing completion, it became imperative to finish the roofs before the first rains fell.

One day the director of the Etz Chaim Talmud Torah, Rav Zalman Rivlin, received a message to please send fifty boys to help finish the roofs. He vacillated, recalling the words of the Sages, "School children should not be interrupted while learning, even to build the Temple."

When he asked Rav Shmuel Salant what to do, the venerated sage unhesitatingly replied, "This is an exception!"

(*Shechunos b'Yerushalayim*, p. 39 and p. 44)

The Biographer

IN 1871 (5631), a young scholar from Kelm visited Jerusalem. Twenty-three-year-old Aryeh Leib Frumkin walked around with pen and paper in hand, interviewing scholars and laymen alike. His mission was to collect biographical sketches of the *gedolim* of Jerusalem throughout the generations. This naturally led him to the leading rabbis of the city: Rav Auerbach, Rav Salant, and the Rishon l'Tzyon, Rav Avraham Ashkenazi.

Rav Aryeh Leib's father had spent his last years in Jerusalem (passing away in 1867), where he set aside time to discuss Torah thoughts with the *rabbanim* of the city. Father and son (Aryeh Leib was an only child) corresponded frequently during that period. One of Aryeh Leib's letters included his Torah insights, which his father proudly showed to Rav Shmuel Salant.

"If these are your son's Torah insights," said Rav Salant, "then he might become one of the leaders of the next generation if he continues in this way...."

At one point early in his visit, Rav Aryeh Leib climbed the Mount of Olives to pray by his father's grave. As he looked around, he noticed that many of the gravestones had fallen over and were neglected. He decided to repair part of the cemetery, and labored at this project for months, spending hard-earned money on the task. Naturally, he recorded every grave site and the inscription written on the headstone.

When the Rishon l'Tzyon noticed how organized the young scholar's notes were, he encouraged him to compile them in book form. Rav Auerbach seconded the motion. This was the beginning of a lifetime's work, called *Toldos Chachmei Yerushalayim*.

Returning to the Mount of Olives, Rav Frumkin recorded over a thousand graves within a few months' time. His mission turned out to be Heaven-sent, for soon afterwards, the Turks began building a road across the mountainside and destroyed every grave in their path.

Inside the city, Rav Aryeh Leib took advantage of the personal libraries of *gedolim* like Rav Auerbach and scrutinized the array of responsa in their pos-

Rav Aryeh Leib Frumkin (1848–1916)

session. Even more important, he interviewed the old-timers who still remembered the early Perushim, such as Rav Menachem Mendel and Rav Yisrael of Shklov, and events such as the coronation of Rav Yosef Chazan as Rishon l'Tzyon in 1818. There were some who still recalled Napoleon's campaign and the Jerusalemite reaction to it in 1799. The one who befriended him the most in this endeavor was Rav Yitzchak Prague. A *talmid chacham* in his own right, Rav Prague was a disciple of the Chasam Sofer and had lived in Jerusalem for over thirty years.

After nearly a year's toil, the first volume of Rav Frumkin's work was in the final stages of preparation. However, at that time the young scholar was unexpectedly called back home to his wife and children in Russia. A couple of years later, he had the manuscript published in Vilna. The success of *Toldos Chachmei Yerushalayim* propelled him to continue with a second and third volume. They were eventually published posthumously by Rav Eliezer Rivlin in 1928.

Rav Aryeh Leib Frumkin returned several times to Eretz Yisrael, living in Jerusalem and Petach Tikva, where he passed away in 1916 at the age of sixty eight.

(Culled from the Preface to *Toldos Chachmei Yerushalayim*, vol. 4, pp. 11– 22)

Blast of the Ram's Horn

LATE ONE night in Nachalas Shiva, the stillness was suddenly shattered by startling noises. Waking abruptly, Yosef Rivlin sat up in bed and bent his head towards the window. The spring air rippled across his face. Listening carefully, he realized that he was hearing the sound of men and animals jostling around. Fully alert now, he carefully peered outside. In the darkness he discerned a large number of silhouetted figures approaching Nachalas Shiva with a herd of horses or mules.

His mind reeled when he heard one of the leaders call out, "Remember! Slaughter them all, and then take the storehouse of lumber!"

Rav Rivlin was not the only one who had heard the commotion outside. "Yosef! Yosef!" called one of his neighbors as he burst into Rav Rivlin's house, "What should we do?"

Within seconds another several neighbors stood breathlessly at his door.

Yosef Rivlin, the founder of Nachalas Shiva, stood transfixed for a moment. "We have no choice," he whispered in a calm but serious voice. "The danger is so great and imminent, I must take advantage of every possible weapon — both physical and spiritual."

Everyone knew that Rav Yosef had received special kabbalistic formulas from his grandfather, Rav Moshe Rivlin, who had in turn received them from his father, Rav Hillel Rivlin, who had gotten them directly from his mentor, the Vilna Gaon.

The enemy was only a minute away from the locked entrance to Nachalas Shiva. Dozens of Bedouins with clubs, daggers, and guns were on the warpath. The lives of close to fifty families, including women and children, were at stake.

Rav Rivlin reached for his gun and his shofar. He stood by the window and concentrated deeply for several long seconds. Then he took the ram's horn to his lips and sounded the shofar notes blown on Rosh HaShanah. As he took a second breathe, he fired a shot blindly in the dark and then blew again. T'ru t'ru t'ru...***crack!***...T'ru t'ru t'ru....

The Bedouins were terrified. "Run for your lives!" one shouted hysterically. "The Jews are killing us!" screamed another.

With the angel of death at their heels, they dashed away into the enveloping darkness.

Rav Yosef and some of the braver settlers went outside to investigate. Amazed, they found tens of mules and all types of weapons strewn on the ground. Not far away they heard the groans of an injured Bedouin. He had fallen down and been trampled, and lay gasping in pain with a broken leg.

They took the man prisoner and questioned him. He withheld nothing. "After killing everyone, we were going to steal all the lumber and carry it home on the mules."

"Who was behind the scheme?"

"Some landlords in the city promised us all the wood as a reward for killing everyone."

"This time," said Rav Rivlin to his comrades, "The Lord was with us. Let us pray that the fear which the Almighty put into them will keep them away from us forever."

(*Mosad HaYesod*, pp. 197–198)

The Miser's Roundabout Present

IN CHESHVAN, 1872 (5633), Rav Yosef Rivlin, one of the pillars of the *yishuv*, received an urgent request. An elderly, well-to-do Jew, lying sick in bed, had summoned him to come immediately to his side. A widower without any children, the man had no one to care for him.

Rav Rivlin left the office of the Central Committee and walked to the man's house. "Why would he ask me to come?" Rav Yosef pondered. "We have nothing in common. He's always hoarded his wealth, barely giving a penny to charity. He always rebuffed our pleas to join in building the *yishuv*, yet now, he's suddenly calling me to come see him."

The man lay on his deathbed, obviously near the end.

"I have an important request to ask of you, Yosef," he spoke in a frail voice. "I want to give you 370 gold napoleon coins."

Rav Yosef looked at him in amazement. This was a vast sum of money and could provide some much-needed relief for the oppressed community.

However, the old man was not done speaking. After a pause, he continued, "I want you to promise me that when I die you will take the money and place it under my head in the grave!"

Rav Rivlin could hardly believe his ears.

"You are to do it yourself," he commanded, "and in such a way that no one will know about it."

Rav Yosef tried his best to convince the man to change his mind and use the money to create a worthy legacy for himself. What an honor to man and God to bequeath the money to a good cause — in this case, the building of the new *yishuv*. However, the miser remained untouched and unconvinced. In the end, Rav Rivlin agreed to the strange request, promising to fulfill it to the letter.

A few days later the man died, and Rav Rivlin escorted the bier to the cemetery. Based on conversations with *rabbanim*, he set out to perform the miser's last wish — with a slight twist. After the body was placed in the grave, Rav Yosef duly placed the satchel of coins under the man's head. With a heavy heart, he asked forgiveness from the *niftar*, as was customary. Then, in a low voice he added, "Our Sages tell us that not silver nor gold escort a person to the next world. The only things he can bring there are Torah and good deeds. Therefore, it is a great merit for you that your money should be consecrated for the building of Jerusalem." With these words, Rav Yosef retrieved the satchel and dedicated it to the building of the *yishuv*.

Later that day, Rav Elazar Ralbag notified the *beis din* of a similar story. The old miser had summoned him the day before, and handed him 2,000 ruble notes together with a sack of Turkish coins, and ordered him to exchange them for gold napoleons. Rav Ralbag had done so, but the old man had died before Rav Elazar could return with the coins. When the old man had initially given the money to Rav Ralbag, he had explained that his motive was to hide it away. Had he received the coins, he probably would have asked Rav Elazar to perform a favor similar to the request he had made of Rav Rivlin. Thus he would literally have taken his entire fortune to the grave. The *beis din* decreed that this money should also be dedicated to the same noble cause. In this way, the old man would have some measure of merit when facing the court on High.

(*Mosad HaYesod*, p. 155)

The Saving Hand

SHORTLY AFTER Passover, 1873 (5633), the new colony of Meah Shearim began taking shape. Most of the land of Kerem Cadcod had already been purchased, and everything was progressing smoothly. No one could guess the surprise that lay in store for them.

One of the few remaining unsold plots in Kerem Cadcod belonged to an Arab from a nearby village. Unable to support himself solely from what his small holding produced, he worked in the vineyard of a German missionary in order to supplement his income. Naturally, the German tried to influence him to not sell his share in Kerem Cadcod to the Jews. In order to get relief from the German's constant badgering, the Arab pretended to acquiesce. In reality, though, he was not interested in losing out on what would be a handsome profit, and he secretly sold the land.

The missionary, unaware of what had transpired, still worried that the simple Arab would succumb to the lure of money. He was so upset at the prospect of the Jews buying the land, that he decided to murder the poor man just to prevent the sale! One day, when the Moslem was working in the German's vineyard, the missionary beckoned him over as if to speak with him. Catching the Arab by surprise, he pulled a knife and stabbed him to death. After burying the corpse, the German went to the Arab's village and cunningly told them that the dead man was the victim of a Jewish plot to murder him. The outraged villagers stormed into the pasha's office in Jerusalem and demanded revenge. If the authorities did not arrest and convict the guilty parties, they would take the law into their own hands.

Both the mayor and the villagers knew that Yosef Rivlin, as the leader of the Meah Shearim corporation, was the man to reckon with. The villagers were seething with anger. However, the mayor sensed something amiss in the story and sent Rav Rivlin a message to leave the city immediately. Rav Yosef, an English subject, also received a similar dispatch from the British consul. Indeed, this second message added that it might be in his best interests to leave the country until the storm blew over. Undaunted, Rav Yosef was not willing to go that far. However, he did agree to drop out of public sight in Jerusalem.

In truth, the entire governing board of Meah Shearim was in danger. However, Rav Rivlin suffered the most, especially when rumors flared that he had absconded with the down payments of the association's constituents.

Members of the Central Committee, including Rav Meir Auerbach stood by Rav Rivlin's side and encouraged him. Rav Yosef sensed the escalated tensions bombarding him from all sides and decided to enlist the aid of special kabbalistic prayers that were effective only in times of emergency. On the day that he performed the last in a series of *segulos,* news spread throughout the city that after a painstaking investigation, the mayor had arrested the German missionary on charges of murder.

As far as the Jews were concerned, this was just another example of the mighty hand of God rescuing them from their plight.

(*Mosad HaYesod*, p. 208–209)

The Report

TENSIONS WERE running high in Jerusalem during the summer of 1873. An Arab terrorist group called *jihart el-charabei* had been wreaking havoc on Jewish property, both within the walled city and outside. The Turkish police could not patrol everywhere all the time, which left the *anshei gevardiah*, armed with French and British weapons, to take up the slack.

At one point, the mayor's secretary told a Jewish friend that the pasha had reached a dead end in trying to bring peace to the city. Just that day, the secretary revealed, the mayor said that since the disturbances were rooted in Moslem landlords' resentment over the Jewish exodus from the city, he must write the Sultan about it. The letter would include a request that the Monarch forbid all construction outside the walled city.

The situation facing the Jews was grave indeed. One word from the Sultan could stymie the expansion of the *yishuv* for years to come, and all progress would be brought to a halt. Alarmed and shaken, the Jewish leaders sent a telegram to London begging Sir Moses Montefiore to intercede on their behalf. Sir Moses immediately cabled a telegram to the British consul in Jerusalem, imploring him to help. In turn, the consul told the Central Committee that they should send some leading rabbis to meet with the mayor, and he, for his part, would do everything he could.

Rav Shmuel Salant and the Rishon l'Tzyon requested an urgent meeting with the mayor. At the conference, they began to list the Jewish grievances — thefts, attacks, murders, and the latest news of the kidnapping of two Jewish children (who were miraculously returned safe and sound).

Rav Salant wept as his listed the tragedies. At the end, he requested from the mayor two things: more protection, and aid to speed up the development of the suburbs. He solemnly concluded that this was the only way that peace could be achieved.

"The mayor should take into account," added the Rishon l'Tzyon, "that Jews throughout the world feel indebted to the Ottoman Empire for their tolerance of the Jewish people, and its constant efforts on our behalf."

After listening to the rabbis, the mayor said, "The settlements outside the walls of the city are the direct cause for all the disturbances within the city walls by the Moslem landlords. The situation has become intolerable and must be dealt with."

The *rabbanim* quickly responded, "The leaders of our community are investigating different ideas which might mitigate the landlords' anger."

"I hope you succeed," he answered. "I will be much more relaxed once all this has blown over."

The mayor went on to tell the rabbis that the British consul had just spoken with him about the Jewish residents of the city, emphasizing the positives aspects of the community.

"I am surprised," he ended, "to find out that the British consul knew about a proposed report I was planning to send to Constantinople. And even more so, to find out that you, too, know of it."

Rav Yosef Rivlin answered the mayor. "A holy spirit hovers over the Jewish leaders, and from heaven comes an early warning sign of dangers to the community. Did not Joseph interpret the dreams of Pharaoh by such a holy spirit?"

The mayor smiled. "Yes."

When bidding farewell, the mayor promised to shelve the report and do everything in his power to aid the Jews.

(*Mosad HaYesod*, pp. 199–201)

The Cosigner

MEAH SHEARIM was in the thick of yet another economic deadline. The board of directors turned to a certain wealthy Jew and asked him to lend a large sum that would cover most of the debt. He agreed, on condition that an equally reliable person be a cosigner. Who? He mentioned the name of Rav Meir Auerbach, the Rav of Kalish, as a possible candidate.

When the members approached the Rav of Kalish, he asked them, "What will be my reward?"

Stunned by his question, they looked at him in surprise.

Before they could reply, he explained himself. "I mean to say: What is the reward which I should *pay* in order that you should give me such a wonderful mitzvah which has no loss at all!"

They all laughed. Seeing that the wealthy *rav* was in a receptive mood, one of the members jokingly asked him, "If so, perhaps the Rav would like to donate the sum of gold napoleons equal to the numerical value of his name [Meir, מאיר, equals 250] for purchasing land?"

"Yes!" Rav Auerbach responded joyously. "In fact, in addition to the sum of 250 napoleons for the land, I'll throw in another 250 napoleons for building expenses!"

This was only part of the generosity which the cosigner poured into Meah Shearim. Among his other gifts were the women's gallery of the Central Synagogue and several houses for the poor.

(*Shechunos b'Yerushalayim*, p. 52)

By the Work of Your Hands

WHEN SIR Moses Montefiore landed at Jaffa port in Tamuz, 1875, he was very eager to hear about developments in his first agricultural enterprise, the nearby Gan Montefiore. On his last trip in 1866, he had met with Rav David Ben-Shimon, and the two men had discussed the idea of sending Moroccans to farm the orchard. Before this time, the project had all but collapsed due to Bedouin attacks and a harsh epidemic. Rav Ben-Shimon assured Sir Moses that Moroccans, adept at working outdoors, were very capable of successfully manning the farm. In addition to their hardiness, they had another advantage over the first group of settlers — they were fluent in Arabic. Before Montefiore returned to England, several families were selected to go to Gan Montefiore. Now, nine years later, unreliable reports had reached him that the settlers had failed to keep their word, and the farm was desolate, perhaps due to the Moroccans' reluctance to work for their bread.

The leader of the plantation, Rav Yaakov Simol, met with Sir Moses in Jaffa, and drew a completely different picture of the farm. He assured Montefiore that he could be proud of the farm's success. Close to a thousand fruit trees were harvested yearly, producing a fair income for the settlers.

Rav Yaakov then went on to voice some needs of the farm, as well as those of the small Jewish enclave in Jaffa. Sir Moses referred to Rav Yaakov as "the father of the Jaffa's poor" due to the loving concern he had for his fellow Jews.

"Allow me to ask you a question," said Sir Moses. "Let me preface it by saying that there are some people in the Diaspora who believe that the Jews in Eretz Yisrael are loafers who prefer handouts to an opportunity for real work. Therefore, let me ask you, why don't these Jews in Jaffa that you mention go out and earn their bread?"

Rav Yaakov began to cry. "There is no truth to this slanderous accusation. The reason these people are so impoverished is that there are no job opportunities available to them."

"All right. I believe you," Montefiore reassured him. "But let us make a test. I'll offer one sterling to every needy person who will to go to Beira [Gan Montefiore] and fill the cistern with water. According to the calculations of my secretary, this should take about fifty-eight man-hours of work. Are there any people here who would be willing to do this?"

"Yes!" he answered. "I can get dozens in a minute."

"Then do so."

The conversation had taken place at midday. Rav Yaakov went to gather the men together, and within a short time he had close to thirty men ready to work. They all went out to Gan Montefiore, escorted by Sir Moses' private secretary Dr. Loewe and Dr. Eikin, his private physician.

The job entailed drawing water via an eight-man circular pump. It was exhausting labor, requiring a new shift of men every ten minutes. While one shift worked, the others sat and recited Psalms together. At the end of the day, the group prayed Minchah and Maariv together. That night, they all slept in the settlement in order to continue the job as soon as possible the next morning.

The next day was the fast of 17 Tamuz. They started early in order to finish before the heat of the day weakened them. By ten o'clock the pool started to overflow. Everyone was delighted to finish.

Sir Moses commented, "I, for my part, never doubted for a moment that our brethren want to work and are eager to make their own livelihood. My purpose in this test was simply to prove to certain parties the fallacy of their claim."

(*Moshe v'Yerushalayim*, pp. 36–37)

For the Sake of the Holy Shabbos

YOSEF KREIGER had an unusual job. An aide to the pasha of Jerusalem, he was one of a mere handful of Jews officially employed by the Turkish empire. Early one Friday morning in Cheshvan, 1882 (5643), Kreiger finished praying, ate a quick breakfast, and set off for the village of Motza, a few kilometers outside of Jerusalem on the road to Jaffa. In his official Turkish uniform and velvet hat, he cut a striking figure. The many badges of honor decorating his shirt testified to his devoted and loyal service to the empire. As the personal translator/emissary of the mayor of the city, one of Yosef's duties was to greet foreign dignities at Motza, a stopover on the journey from Jaffa, and escort them to the city.

The American ambassador to Turkey, General Wallace, had disembarked at Jaffa port the day before and was due to reach Motza at 9:00 A.M. Kreiger, in keeping with his efficient image, arrived shortly after eight. He checked to see that the visitor's lodge was tidy and then waited for the ambassador to arrive.

Hours passed and General Wallace still did not arrive. Obviously, something or someone had delayed him. As the sun stretched further to the west, Yosef's impatience turned into apprehension. Shabbos was approaching and he did not want to be stranded outside Jerusalem.

His nervousness dissipated when he saw the ambassador's carriage approaching. He gracefully welcomed the General in the name of the mayor and escorted him to the lodge. There a small group of Arab instrumentalists performed for the ambassador while he relaxed from the journey and sipped his coffee.

Meanwhile, Kreiger left instructions with his second-in-command, and, begging the ambassador's forgiveness, quickly departed. He galloped on his horse back to Jerusalem, and arrived right at candlelighting time. Before going to services, he met with the mayor and explained what had happened and the

Motza, the last rest stop for travelers from Jaffa to Jerusalem, is located in a valley seven kilometers outside the Holy City. From there travelers would make their final ascent to Jerusalem. Dignitaries were greeted there by emissaries of the city.

reason for his sudden return to the city. The mayor, familiar with Kreiger's religious obligations, nodded his approval.

When the ambassador arrived at his hotel an hour later, Yosef smilingly stood there to greet him, the mayor at his side.

General Wallace's faced burned with anger. "How dare you insult me," he snapped.

Before Yosef could utter a word, the ambassador demanded that the mayor fire him immediately. The pasha tried to soothe the excited ambassador and defend Yosef, but was unsuccessful on both accounts.

Soon Yosef and the mayor realized who was responsible for arousing the General's wrath against him. Missionaries had used the opportunity of Yosef's "slight" to take revenge against one of their great enemies. Kreiger was an activist, responsible for numerous rebuffs of their dangerous activities. Now, they had jumped at a chance to rid themselves of their hated adversary.

The mayor sent a telegram to Constantinople in defense of Kreiger. In the end, however, the ambassador's demand was acceded to, and Yosef was recalled to Constantinople. The victorious missionaries danced with joy at their success.

Yosef Kreiger accepted his fate with dignity. In the capital of the Ottoman Empire, he quickly ascended the ladder of success in the imperial court. Soon he was sent to Salonika, where he served as a high-ranking officer.

Wherever he went, Yosef Kreiger remained a loyal Jew first and a noble servant of the Sultan's court second. When he passed away in Elul, 1904, he was mourned by both the Jewish and gentile communities in which he faithfully served.

(*L'Chovavim HaRishonim*, vol. 7, pp. 8–12)

The Hidden Treasure

THE SUN was setting over Jerusalem the evening before Passover, as the men returned home from shul to begin the search for *chametz*.

Nasan Zamiro, the beadle of one of the Sephardic synagogues, headed home with a heavy heart. Tomorrow night would be the Passover Seder, and he had nothing for the festival. So destitute was his situation, that the extra sum he received for the holiday called *kimcha d'pischa* had all but evaporated in paying for other expenses. Worst of all, his Arab landlord had recently demanded the rent for the entire forthcoming year. Zamiro did not know where to turn. Struggling to maintain a sense of calm, he entered his shabby, two-room flat.

His wife smiled anxiously, but remained silent. Poor Nasan felt like crying. Instead, he mustered his courage and began the search for *chametz*. With a candle in one hand and a feather in the other, Nasan slowly searched for crumbs of bread, going from corner to corner. When he finished, he remembered that the cellar was part of his domain and needed to be checked as well.

Nasan descended the stairs and continued the search. The cellar was damp and unlivable, and had not been used in years. Nasan came to a niche in the wall, and to his surprise, the candlelight revealed an old pottery urn. Curious, he unlodged the urn from its place. It turned out to be surprisingly heavy. He opened it, and on pouring out its contents, Nasan took a deep breath — the floor was littered with gold coins and precious jewels!

Later that evening, after counting the treasure, he figured that it was worth a hundred and fifty Turkish liros, a fabulous sum of money.

Nasan, a simple God-fearing Jew, told his wife that he must go at once with the urn to the rabbis and ask what he should do. Its true owner might be alive and want to claim it.

The *rabbanim* investigated the matter and concluded that the mysterious urn was ownerless. They duly informed Nasan that the treasure was his.

Hardly believing his good fortune, Nasan ran home to share the news with his wife. In an instant, their lives were transformed from the depths of poverty to the heights of wealth.

Later, Nasan decided to invest part of the treasure in a new home outside the walls. At that time, 1875, the new suburb called Even Yisrael was in the building stage. On the first day of *chol hamoed Pesach*, Nasan went to the head of the suburb, Rav Yosef Rivlin, and handed him the amount of money necessary to purchase a house in the new neighborhood.

In this way, the Zamiro family became builders of the new city and transformed a handful of coins and jewels into stones for the future.

(*Sefer HaYishuv*, pp. 16–17)

Glimpses of Rav Salant

THE FACE of the Jerusalem *yishuv* was molded by the tzaddik, Rav Shmuel Salant. The epitome of humility, kindness, and Torah excellence, he faithfully guided his flock for nearly seventy years. His knowledge of Talmud and Jewish Law was astonishing, and he did everything in his power to strengthen the crown of Torah in the Holy City. Refusing to be called the Rav of Jerusalem, he preferred to be called Rav Shmuelke. Following are presented some brief glimpses into the life of this venerable tzaddik.

Once Rav Salant and his *beis din* had no choice other than to take action against a Jewish merchant who had refused to abide by the court's decision. Notices were posted informing the community that it was forbidden to shop at this man's store until he agreed to comply with the *beis din*.

Rav Shmuel's house, located in the Churvah compound, was always open. The outraged merchant lost no time in personally expressing his feelings to the Rav of Jerusalem.

"If you don't retract your prohibition against me," he yelled, with his hands waving in the air, "then I'll break all the windows in your house!"

In his typically humble manner, Rav Salant answered, "What do you think I'll do then — acquiesce to your demand? No, I'll send someone to the glazier and order new windows!"

* * *

MRS. YADLER, the mother of the *Yerushalmi maggid*, owned a grocery store in the Old City. Once she sold a large quantity of flour on

Rav Shmuel Salant (1816–1909)

credit to a matzah bakery, for the price of twenty napoleons. When the baker refused to pay, she had no recourse other than to take him to *beis din*. The court heard both sides of the case and concluded that the baker was obligated to pay for the flour. The tough old baker obstinately refused to comply, claiming that the court had misjudged the case.

Rav Salant sat at the head of the *beis din*. In a sharp voice, Rav Shmuel snapped, "Why don't you want to pay her the thirty napoleons for the flour?"

"I only owe her twenty," blurted out the merchant. "Why do you say 'thirty'?"

"At your own admission," replied the Rav, "I require you to pay the entire amount. You have until this time tomorrow."

The next day the man did not appear. Rav Salant sent him a message: "I want you to know that I've never started something in my life which I did not finish. If you do not pay immediately, I'll have notices put up throughout the city that it is forbidden to patronize your shop."

This time the baker changed his mind and paid the twenty napoleons.

* * *

A SHOEMAKER on Yehudim Street in the Old City began to take off his *kipa* while working. When Rav Salant heard about this, he sent his aide to order the man to wear it. The aide, however, returned with a negative reply from the shoemaker.

Rav Shmuel got up and put on his coat and marched down Yehudim Street to the shop in question.

"Put on your *kipa* right now!" the Rav said in a stern voice.

"But my head is covered — by the ceiling of the shop and...."

"My son," Rav Shmuel interrupted, "I didn't come here to argue with you. Put on your *kipa*, and don't be a cause for laxity in Halachah here in Jerusalem."

(*Betuv Yerushalayim*, pp. 374–375)

The Innocent Thief

A FEW WEEKS before Pesach, 1885 (5645), Jerusalemites were earnestly preparing for the festival. Every Jewish home was cleaned from top to bottom, as every crumb of *chametz* was meticulously sought out. Even though most families faced overcrowded and uncomfortable living conditions, everyone was uplifted with an undeniable sense of rejuvenation.

Yet, this year a certain anxiety could be felt in the air. Funds from *chutz laAretz* were overdue, and extra cash was essential for added expenses of the festival. Those Jerusalemites connected with Kollel Minsk turned to their *gabbai*, Rav Shlomo Zalman Porush. He reassured them that the funds would arrive any day, and that he would personally notify them and allocate the money as soon as it came.

Rav Shlomo Zalman was a remarkable man. Besides his work with Kollel Minsk, he supervised Chevras Shaarei Chesed, the city's free loan society. His reputation as one of the foremost *gabbai tzedakah* (charity collectors) in the city was impeccable, and his home in the new suburb of Zichron Tuvia was open day and night for the poor and downtrodden. Rav Porush had a keen interest in every communal project, large and small. A man of the times, he poured all of his energies into his people and into his city. As the days passed, he personally felt the distress of each member of the Kollel.

With no other choice, Rav Shlomo Zalman approached one of his neighbors, Reb Feivish Stoller, for a loan. Reb Feivish, a semi-retired carpenter, had saved his pennies over the years and had accumulated a substantial amount of money. He immediately agreed to lend the full 200 napoleons until the money arrived from Russia. Rav Shlomo Zalman wrote him an IOU, received the cash, and immediately divided it among the *kollel* members.

A few days later the long-awaited funds arrived, together with a note saying that only 110 napoleons were included in this dispatch and that the remainder would be forthcoming in a few weeks.

Rav Porush went to his neighbor and gave him the money he had received. He apologized that the other 90 napoleons would be a few more weeks in coming. Reb Feivish replied that that would be fine. To Rav Shlomo Zalman's later regret, he neglected to get a receipt for the amount he had just returned.

The rest of the money arrived after Pesach. Rav Shlomo Zalman knocked on his neighbor's door and presented it to him.

"What!" exclaimed Reb Feivish. "But where are the other 110 napoleons?"

"Don't you remember, my dear friend, that I returned that sum to you before Pesach?"

"No. In fact," Reb Feivish asserted, "I'm absolutely certain you never returned me any of the loan until today."

Rav Shlomo Zalman stared at his neighbor in total disbelief. He knew that Reb Feivish's memory was weak due to his age, yet 110 napoleons was a gigantic sum of money. Slowly, Rav Shlomo Zalman tried to help Reb Feivish to recall the transaction between them, but to no avail. The conversation ended with Reb Feivish demanding they resolve their disagreement in *beis din.*

Not long after, they stood before the *beis din* of Rav Shmuel Salant. Rav Shlomo Zalman admitted he received the loan of 200 napoleons, but claimed he returned 110 of them several weeks earlier, without getting a receipt from Reb Feivish. In turn, Reb Feivish claimed he never received the 110 napoleons and that the entire amount was still due him.

The *beis din* ruled that if Rav Shlomo Zalman took a Torah oath that he had indeed paid the 110 napoleons, he would only have to return the remaining 90. Otherwise, he would have to pay the full amount. Rav Shlomo Zalman

The Beis Yaakov Synagogue, located in the heart of Beis Yisrael

asked permission to consider what to do, and was granted three days.

Rav Porush was in a quandary. Never in his life had he uttered a Torah oath, and he was petrified just thinking about it. Yet everything he had said was true. He was not a thief, *chas v'shalom*. Finally, he made up his mind.

"I have made my choice," he said before the *beis din*. "I will pay the money and not swear. I only ask permission to repay it over a long period of time."

Reb Feivish consented, and the two parties turned to leave the court room.

Suddenly they heard Rav Shmuel Salant call out, "No! This case is not yet closed!"

The two men returned and stood before the court.

Looking at Rav Shlomo Zalman, Rav Salant said, "This case is not a personal case between two individuals. It is a communal case. Even though you claim your innocence, you will taint your image as the upright *gabbai tzedakah* of the city by paying the money. People will no longer view you as a true leader of the community. Therefore, I obligate you to swear before the court that you paid, and uphold your integrity."

Rav Shlomo Zalman felt his heart pounding. "Please give me some time to reconsider," he muttered.

The next few days were like Tisha b'Av for Rav Shlomo Zalman. He recited Psalms endlessly and mulled over the words of the Rosh Beis Din.

Finally he reappeared before the court and consented to take the oath.

When he returned home he announced to his family that he was putting his house up for sale.

"Why?" they asked.

"When I first agreed to pay the money, I planned to sell our house and buy a smaller one. I intended to take the difference and pay Reb Feivish. Though I have sworn and am free of paying the money, I don't think it is fair of me to derive any pleasure from it. Therefore I want to continue with my plan, but instead of giving it to Reb Feivish I will consecrate it for a noble cause."

Before he could sell his house, Reb Feivish appeared breathlessly at his door. In his hand was the lost money bound in its original satchel. He accidentally found it that morning in the back corner of his closet, having deposited it there and completely forgotten about it. He begged Rav Shlomo Zalman to forgive him for all the trouble he had caused. Overjoyed, Rav Porush forgave him wholeheartedly.

Reb Feivish announced that he did not want to keep the money for himself. Instead, he sought to consecrate it for a holy purpose. At that time, the new suburb of Beis Yisrael was planning to build a shul, but sorely lacked funds. Reb Feivish decided to donate the 110 napoleons for the construction of the Beis Yaakov Synagogue.

The new shul was dedicated in 1887 (5647), and an engraved stone was put on the northern wall. In compliance with Reb Feivish's wishes, there is no mention of his name. Instead, it reads: "This *beis midrash* was built by a generous man who prefers to remain anonymous. He donated 110 napoleons...."

[According to another version, Rav Shlomo Zalman sold his house and gave the money to Reb Feivish. Later, when Reb Feivish found the satchel, he returned the money to Rav Shlomo Zalman. Though the money was legally his, Rav Shlomo Zalman refused to accept it, preferring to consecrate it for a mitzvah. Consequently, he dedicated it to the Beis Yisrael Synagogue.]

(*Shechunos b'Yerushalayim*, pp. 96–97,
and *Shamu v'Tichi Nafshechem*, no. 135)

The Wealthiest Jew in the City

ONE DAY the mayor of Jerusalem conferred with his chief of municipal affairs. Together they reviewed the deeds of sale for properties in the greater Jerusalem area. To the mayor's surprise, he noticed that a disproportionate number of lots and buildings were owned by a Jew named Zalman Baharan.

"He is certainly the wealthiest Jew in the city!" the mayor said to his minister. "I should get to know him."

"Shall I send for him?" asked the minister.

"By all means," smiled the mayor.

The officers whose duty it was to fetch Rav Zalman misunderstood their orders. They thought the mayor wanted him arrested and imprisoned. Not finding him at home, they went to the main synagogue of the Old City. Finding him there, they demanded that he accompany them. Rav Zalman, draped with his tallis and tefillin, silently complied.

Several hours passed and the mayor wondered why Mr. Baharan had not come. "Where is this Baharan?" the mayor asked his personal secretary. "Why hasn't he come yet?"

The secretary looked at him in surprise. "He's been here over an hour. He was placed in jail as you ...."

"What?!" interrupted the mayor excitedly. "In jail?! This is a grave error. Bring him to me at once!"

Outside the mayor's office was a spacious waiting room. Within minutes Rav Zalman was sitting quietly on a chair, his tallis and tefillin wrapped in a satchel. He whispered mishnayos by heart, completely at ease.

Several times the mayor came out of his office to greet the wealthy man, but was disappointed to see only a poverty-stricken Jew sitting in the corner and staring at the floor. He angrily called his secretary.

"Twice I have been fooled today," he raged. "Where is the Jew Baharan?!"

"Didn't you see him in the waiting room?" asked the secretary. "He has been sitting there waiting for you nearly an hour."

The mayor returned to the waiting room and looked at Rav Zalman.

"Are you Zalman Baharan whose wealth sprawls throughout the city?" questioned the mayor dubiously.

"Yes," answered Rav Zalman.

"But how can it be?" continued the puzzled mayor. "From your dress I would never have thought you so wealthy."

"In this, too, you are correct," replied Rav Zalman, who was clothed in tattered garments. Explaining himself, he said, "It just so happens that I recently divided up all my wealth among the poor of the city."

In reality, Rav Zalman had told the mayor a white lie. A gentile might comprehend that an eccentric wealthy person would one day decide to relinquish his entire fortune. However, he would be unable to fathom how a poor person who had never tasted life's riches could control the vast holdings of others without seeking to become wealthy himself.

Rav Zalman had a reputation of impeccable honesty. Jews throughout Jerusalem regarded him as the one man who would guard their holdings as his own. He would never allow the Turkish officials to alter a single letter on a deed of sale, nor let an inch of property mistakenly slip into a neighbor's legal contract. These credentials had made the registrar's office full of property "legally" owned by Rav Zalman.

His poverty was as proverbial as his integrity. A scholar of the highest caliber, he had been asked to become Rosh Yeshivah of Etz Chaim Yeshivah after the death of Rav Moshe Nechemiah Kahanov in 1886. He refused, preferring to teach a group in his house for free. His class was regularly attended by twenty-five students. He supported his family on the meager earnings he received from exporting *esrogim*. Firmly committed to expanding the boundaries of Jerusalem, he occupied the center stage in the building of Meah Shearim — and that of many other new neighborhoods as well. All his activities were performed altruistically, and he refused to accept payment for his invaluable services.

The mayor of Jerusalem accepted Rav Zalman's explanation. He invited him into his office, and the two men sat and discussed various issues and topics. The mayor did not attempt to hide his appreciation of his guest's wisdom and knowledge of the world.

As a result of this meeting, a certain comradeship developed between the lordly mayor and the humble Jew. In the coming years, Rav Zalman would use this friendship to the advantage of his brethren, and his relationship stood the Jews of Jerusalem in good stead.

(*HaPoseach Shaar*, pp. 117–119)

The Book Dealer

EVER SINCE Rav Shneur Zalman, the Rav of Lublin, moved to Jerusalem in 1892, Shimon Moss the book dealer was in a quandary. For years Shimon employed a clever strategy to increase his sales. Whenever a new book appeared, he would take it to various *rabbanim* for appraisal, hoping they would in turn purchase it from him. And whenever a rare volume became available, he brought it to the *rav* he thought might be most interested in it.

The Lubliner Rav, however, was an enigma. On the one hand, he had one of the largest private libraries in the Holy City, containing thousands of books. This made him a perfect candidate for Shimon Moss's efforts. On the other hand, whenever Rav Shneur Zalman even glanced through a book, his brilliant mind instantly photographed every page, line, word, and letter. His memory was truly phenomenal. Poor Shimon was afraid to show him a book for fear that he would "steal" its contents with his eyes. Yet, he knew that Rav Shnuer Zalman was a genuine bibliophile and avidly collected books.

In time, Shimon Moss learned how the Lubliner Rav reckoned things. True, he photocopied the contents of a book in his mind. But if he felt that the book was one he would have bought anyway, he would purchase it. Otherwise, he simply returned it to Shimon with a polite "No thank you."

One time, Shimon showed Rav Shneur Zalman a rare, early printing of the Rambam's *Mishneh Torah*. Quickly leafing through the volume, the Lubliner Rav closed it and handed it back to Shimon. "I'm sorry, Shimon," he said, "but a page is missing in the chapter on *Pisulei Mukdashim*."

(*MiGedolei Yerushalayim*, p. 111)

The Maggid's Illness

RAV ZERACH Braverman, a close disciple of the Brisker Rav, sat next to the ailing *maggid* of Vilkamir. The *maggid* lay pale and weak in bed, and, deeply concerned for the elderly man's health, the Brisker Rav had sent Rav Zerach to his bedside.

"Tell your mentor," the *maggid* said, "that I'm not in need of his condolences. In fact, he is the cause of my illness!"

"What do you mean?"

"Just that!" snapped the *maggid*. "Until now I believed that there was still one righteous man left in the world — your rebbe; but now I've learned that this is not so. This has so pained me, that I've become sick from it."

Rav Zerach stared at him in disbelief. He fumbled for words, but the *maggid* of Vilkamir interrupted him.

"I command you to return to the Rav of Brisk and inform him of this."

Perplexed, Rav Zerach Braverman hurried back to Rav Diskin's house. When he told his mentor what happened, the Brisker Rav simply nodded, "It's true. He is ill because of me."

Seeing the baffled expression on his disciple's face, Rav Diskin explained. "This is what happened: Not long ago, a member of a prominent family here in Jerusalem committed a sin which usually is publicized by the *beis din*. Rav Shmuel Salant, however, decided not to embarrass him in public due to his distinguished family lineage. My opinion was sought on the matter, and I agreed with Rav Salant. When the *maggid* heard of this, he thought I had fallen into the trap of flattery."

Rav Zerach looked at his rebbe in suspense. The Brisker Rav motioned him to come over to his desk. In a drawer, there were a number of *mussar* books, such as *Chovos HaLevavos* and *Mesillas Yesharim*.

"See these," he said, pointing to the books. "I never say or do a single thing without first measuring my intended action on the scales of righteousness. Therefore, I want you to return to the *maggid* of Vilkamir and tell him in my name that there was no flattery on my part. I based my decision on a *Yerushalmi* which clearly states that if we know that the sinner will not continue in his evil ways, it is forbidden to embarrass him for what he did due to the honor of his family."

Rav Diskin looked at his disciple and said, "Now return to the *maggid* with the explanation I have given you."

When the *maggid* heard the explanation, his face lit up.

"Return this message to your rebbe: I feel better already. *Be'ezras Hashem*, in another few days I shall come visit him!"

(*Betuv Yerushalayim*, p. 326–327)

The Passing of a Gaon

THE BRISKER Rav, Rav Yehoshua Leib Diskin, had been sick in bed for two weeks. Diagnosed with pneumonia, the eighty-four-year-old *gaon* lay weak and feverish. On Wednesday, 25 Teves, 1898 (5658) the doctors gave up hope.

News of his critical condition spread through the city. The synagogues filled with men and women praying for his recovery. There was literally no room to move in the Churvah Synagogue, even late at night. The sound of the shofar filled the air, calling people to repent so that they might be worthy of having the tzaddik remain in their midst. Telegrams were dispatched to Jewish communities throughout the Diaspora informing them of Rav Diskin's condition and asking them to pray for his recovery.

Thursday night his condition worsened. Rav Shmuel Salant ordered messengers to call out in every lane and suburb that everyone — including children — should rise at midnight and gather in the synagogues to pray.

By midnight, all the synagogues in the city were filled with the echo of Psalms from thousands of mouths. In every shul, the Holy Ark was opened, *slichos* and the thirteen *midos* were recited in unison, and the blast of the shofar loudly resounded.

That Friday a number of people fasted, including the children from the Diskin Orphanage. Others went to the graves of tzaddikim to pray for Divine mercy.

Rav Yehoshua Leib Diskin remained in his room, wearing tallis and tefillin. In the late afternoon, an hour before the commencement of Shabbos, he took off his tefillin, looked at them, and put them back on. Again and again he repeated his actions, taking them off and putting them on.

Outside, the horn signifying the arrival of candlelighting time was sounded. Now Rav Diskin removed his tefillin for the last time.

Near the end of Shabbos, thousands of Jews flocked to Rav Diskin's yeshivah, Ohel Moshe, located next to his house in Battei Ungarin, to find out firsthand about his condition.

It did not take long for everyone there to find out. After Havdalah was concluded, they heard him call out *Shema Yisrael* as his soul left his body.

News spread quickly throughout the city. Rav Salant convened an emergency meeting of his *beis din* to decide how and when the funeral should take place. On the one hand, if they were to make the funeral that night, it could result in mourners trampling one another in the dark, narrow alleyways. Additionally, with the whole Jewish Quarter vacated, it would be an open invitation to Arab thievery. On the other hand, part of the mitzvah of honoring the dead was to bury the body as soon as possible. Moreover, in Jerusalem there was a special prohibition against having a body lie unburied overnight. In the end, it was decided to conduct the funeral the following day.

Rav Salant and the Rishon l'Tzyon, Rav Yaakov Shaul Elyashar, issued a

Ohel Moshe Yeshivah

joint statement demanding that all shops remain closed throughout the day. That day the yeshivos and chederim would remain empty. The entire Jewish community would participate in the Brisker Rav's funeral, even those individuals who personally disagreed with his principles.

After Shacharis, thousands of people surrounded the Rav's house. The new suburbs were desolate, protected by mounted Turkish police.

The eulogies were delivered outside the Ohel Moshe Yeshivah. The first one was delivered by Rav Diskin's closest disciple, Rav Yosef Chaim Zonnenfeld. He was followed by Rav Yaakov Shaul Elyashar and other *rabbanim*. After the eulogies, the funeral procession left from Meah Shearim, and proceeded to the Churvah Synagogue in the Jewish Quarter. Leading the cortege were youngsters from the Diskin Orphanage, and immediately after them walked the children from all the Ashkenazic and Sephardic chederim of the city.

The Rav's body was placed by the *bimah* in the Churvah Synagogue. Standing there were the Rav of Jerusalem and the Lubliner Rav, Rav Shneur Zalman. Rav Salant opened his eulogy with the verse in *Lamentations* 5:15: "The joy of our heart has ceased, our dance has turned into mourning. The crown of our head has fallen; woe to us that we have sinned!" Several times he had to pause, either because of the wailing in the audience or because he himself burst out crying.

Next the Rav of Lublin spoke, but could not finish due to his weakness. After he recited Kaddish, the procession headed for the Mount of Olives via the Zion Gate. At the gate, Rav Yitzchak Winegrad, Rosh Yeshivah Toras Chaim, gave a eulogy. As the funeral proceeded down the mountainside into the Valley of Kidron, one could see the magnitude of the procession. The entire 30,000 Jewish inhabitants of the city came to pay their last respects. In all the history of the *yishuv*, there had never been such a large funeral. When the bier reached the Avshalom monument, Rav Polansky spoke. Slowly, the procession reached the grave site, high up on the Mount of Olives. Before sunset on 29 Teves, 1898 (5658), Rav Yehoshua Leib Diskin was laid to rest.

For years afterwards, Rav Yosef Chaim Zonnenfeld walked to his rebbe's grave on his *yartzeit* and recited the whole book of Psalms.

(*Amud Aish*, pp. 220–225)

20th Century

Birth Pangs of the Ancient City

Part I

The Decline of Turkish Rule: 1900–1918

וַאֲנִי בַּה׳ אֲצַפֶּה
אוֹחִילָה לֵאלקֵי יִשְׁעִי יִשְׁמָעֵנִי אֱלקָ.
אַל תִּשְׂמְחִי אֹיַבְתִּי לִי
כִּי נָפַלְתִּי קָמְתִּי
כִּי אֵשֵׁב בַּחֹשֶׁךְ ה׳ אוֹר לִי.

מיכה ז׳׳ח

Therefore, I shall look to the Lord;
I shall wait for the God of my salvation: my God shall hear me.
Rejoice not against me, O my enemy.
When I fall, I shall arise;
when I sit in darkness, the Lord shall be a light to me.

Micah 7:8

Jerusalem Enters the 20th Century

The years between 1900 and 1917 marked the decline of Ottoman sovereignty over Eretz Yisrael. During the same period, there was a sharp rise in Zionist activities and immigration to the Holy Land. The Jerusalem yishuv, caught between these two elements, felt increasingly threatened. In spite of this, the community continued to expand and grow on all fronts, until the First World War changed the face of the entire world.

The Sultan's Half-Jubilee[1]

Throughout the length and breadth of the Ottoman Empire, the twentieth century opened with elaborate festivities in celebration of the Sultan's twenty-fifth year on the throne. Abdul Hamid had done much to upgrade the empire from its archaic past, though he was in some measure dependent on foreign enterprises to facilitate his plans for modernization. Telegraph and railroad lines, for instance, expanded in the empire through private concessions. It was true that Turkey could not compete with its European counterparts in the realms of scientific and industrial advancement; however it drew the world's interest for political and military reasons.

The residents of Jerusalem had much to be thankful for. Overall, the hundreds of years of Turkish sovereignty had given a sense of security to the city's inhabitants. In the last fifty years, things had improved even more. In that time, several consulates had come to the city. This gave the numerous foreign residents an address where they could air their grievances. Previously, they were afforded no rights or recognition by the government, and their complaints about injustice were often ignored. Now, the consulate protected them and represented their causes before the Turkish mayor of the city.

Though Sultan Abdul Hamid never visited Jerusalem during his long and stable rule, he had done much for the city and for every segment of its population. It was during his reign that the move to expand the *yishuv* fully came into its own — for which the Jews felt indebted to him. The Christians, too, benefited from his gracious leadership. In 1890, he agreed to the opening of another gate on the northwestern corner of the city walls. Officially called the Abdul Hamid Gate, but better known as the New Gate, it allowed Christian pilgrims easy passage to the new Notre

The Clock Tower erected over the Jaffa Gate in honor of the Sultan's 25th year of reign. The domed structure to the right was a public water fountain.

Dame hospice just outside the Old City. Thus, Jerusalemites joyfully celebrated the momentous occasion, and warmest regards were sent to the Turkish capital.

On the day of the actual anniversary celebration, the Jews wished the monarch a long and healthy reign and continued peace in the empire. In commemoration of the event, all segments of the population contributed to the building of a *sabil*, a stone clock tower rising high over the Jaffa Gate. Next to it stood a water fountain, from which anyone could come and drink. Monuments were built in other cities as well. In Jaffa, a clock tower was built, and in Shechem, a shrine was also built over the grave of Yosef HaTzaddik, the son of Yaakov. Later, in 1920, the British dismantled the *sabil* in Jerusalem, feeling it was aesthetically incongruent with the grandeur of the ancient city wall.

At the time, the relationship between the empire and the Holy Land seemed friendly and secure. However, this celebration would turn out to be the last pageantry the Ottoman Empire would enjoy from Eretz Yisrael before losing its grasp on the country in 1917.

New Neighborhoods

The period between 1900 and the outbreak of the First World War witnessed continued development of the Jerusalem suburbs. The Arab expansion outside the walls of the Old City, very small at the end of the last century, continued at a very slow rate. Their largest endeavor, privately financed and without a masterplan, was Sheikh Jarrah northeast of the city. Following is a review of some of the Jewish neighborhoods.

Battei Broide[2]

Rav Yaakov Yosef Broide of Warsaw was a prosperous Jew who chose Jerusalem as a recipient for his philanthropic endeavors. Being childless, he wanted to build homes and synagogues for the poor, in fulfillment of the verse (*Isaiah* 56:5): "I shall give them in My house and within My walls a memorial better than sons and daughters." Other childless men before him had shared this sentiment and built up neighborhoods — such as Rav David Reiss (Beis David), Rav Moshe Wittenberg (Shaarei Moshe), and Rav Menachem Neitin (Battei Neitin).

Through the efforts of Rav Naftali Tzvi Porush of Jerusalem, Rav Broide bought a large parcel of land next to the neighborhood of Knesses. The plot was originally called in Arabic *kerem musa amram*. It was so large that Rav Broide immediately sold half of it to the Central Committee, who later extended the Knesses suburb onto it.

Battei Broide. Facing is the large synagogue and to the left a section of the houses.

Rav Broide accepted only members of the Perushim community as tenants. He explained: "I am childless, and have therefore requested that the tenants will pray and study in my synagogue — where I would like to always have a minyan. However, such a thing can only come about if all the tenants pray the same *nusach* (order of prayers). I have no personal preference for one group over another, but as my forefathers were Perushim, I set the Ashkenazic *nusach* as the one to be used in my synagogue. Therefore, the members of the community should all be from the Perushim community."

Rav Broide did not stop at just buying the land; he also contributed towards the actual building expenses. At one point he sent seven large crates full of books for the shul, which included his private library.

The inauguration of the synagogue took place in 1903, with the whole affair paid for by the Central Committee. When Rav Broide found out about it, he protested, saying that he did not want to receive any favors at the expense of the poor, no matter how minor the cost. Rav Porush, however, recommended that he accept so as not to offend the members of the Committee. He would find a way to repay them at another time. He agreed, and later left in his will 400 pounds sterling, which the Central Committee used to purchase the land for Knesses 3.

Battei Neitin[3]

Shmuel Levy was one of a handful of Americans who immigrated to Jerusalem in those days. He soon became an accepted member of the *yishuv*, making a living as a tailor. Around the turn of the century, Reb Shmuel returned to America to collect for the community. There he met Rav Menachem Neitin, an immigrant from Russia who had amassed a fortune in Chicago. He convinced the childless Rav Neitin to come to Jerusalem and help build up the *yishuv*. In the Old City, Rav Neitin bought a courtyard near the Zion Gate, which he gave to the needy Jews from his native hometown in Russia. He also built a *beis midrash* called Menachem Zion, where his confidant, Rav Shmuel Shpitzer, gave lectures morning and night.

In 1901, he build a neighborhood next to Meah Shearim which was named after him, Battei Neitin. Eventually comprising sixty houses and a synagogue, Battei Neitin became known for the righteous men who lived there, such as Rav Shmuel Houminer and Rav Shalom Eisen.

Chatzer Strauss[4]

There were two unrelated men with the surname Strauss who helped strengthen the *yishuv* at the beginning of the twentieth century. The American philanthropist, Nathan Strauss, will be discussed later. Here we are concerned with Shmuel Strauss, a German banker who poured money into charitable causes in the Holy City. He identified himself with the *mussar* philosophy espoused by Rav Simcha Zissel of Kelm and gave handsomely to see that it would be propagated in Jerusalem.

Around the turn of the century, a

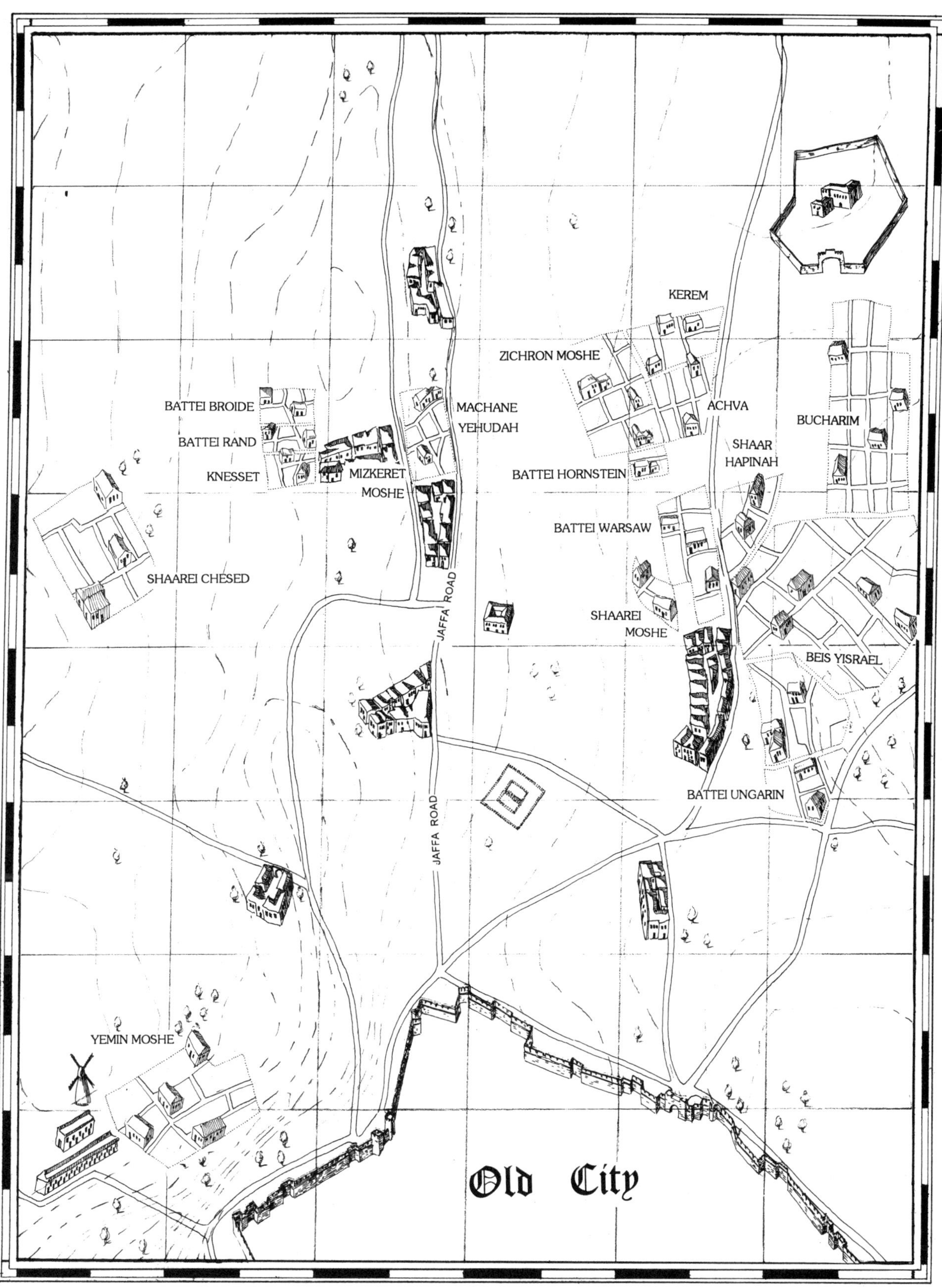

Map showing of some of the thirty-eight new neighborhoods built between 1880 and the First World War. Commercial areas, such as outside the Jaffa Gate and along Jaffa Road, are not shown. Unnamed neighborhoods were built prior to 1880 (See map, p. 305).

number of Rav Zissel's disciples immigrated to Eretz Yisrael and established the Beis HaMussar in the Old City. Rav Shmuel supported the group and influenced Baron Rothschild to follow suit. As their community grew, the members opened Ohr Chadash Yeshivah, which became very popular among the Ashkenazic residents of the *yishuv*. For a time, Rav Yosef Chaim Zonnenfeld was Rosh Yeshivah of Ohr Chadash.

Rav Simcha Zissel remained in close contact with his group of disciples. He wrote: "Residents of Jerusalem!... How fortunate you are to dwell there. If I had dove's wings to fly, I would travel and settle with you... Were I in better health, I would travel to Jerusalem and join you there."

At the turn of the century, Rav Strauss built the group a neighborhood in the Musrara suburb, off Shivtei Yisrael Street. Chatzer Strauss became the center of the *mussar* movement in Jerusalem, with luminaries such as Rav Leib Broide, Rav Yitzchak Blazar,* and Rav Naftali of Amsterdam living there.

Shaarei Chesed[5]

In 1908, a charity organization called Shaarei Chesed purchased a spacious tract of land to the southwest of the Old City. The plot had ample room to accommodate two hundred houses. Designed in long, parallel rows, the homes were connected to one another, leaving each one a front and back yard. At that time, Shaarei Chesed was the first neighborhood to build to the southwest of the city.

The needy residents were offered an extremely lenient payment plan, with modest installments and no interest or service charges. In this way, they were able to acquire their own houses over the course of time. Other building projects usually had a rotation system whereby every three years a new tenant would occupy the house rent-free. In Shaarei Chesed, the tenants paid a low mortgage and became the permanent owners.

The cornerstone ceremony took place in 1909 (5669), on Lag b'Omer. Thousands of Jews were present. Rav Shmuel

Shaarei Chesed as it appeared prior to World War One

* See "The Tailor and the Rav," and "The First One in Heaven," in *Bygone Days: 1900–1918*.

Salant was given the honor of laying the first stone. The ninety-two-year-old tzaddik, delighted to partake in the expansion of the Holy City, was too frail even to walk. Some of his disciples carried him in a chair from his house to a waiting carriage. Even the ride along the rough, unpaved road proved burdensome. The carriage pulled close to the construction site, with Rav Salant remaining seated inside. From his perch in the carriage, he handed a stone to one of the *gabbaim* of Shaarei Chesed to place in the ground for him. He blessed the project, as did Rav Chaim Berlin, president of the organization. This was Rav Salant's last public appearance. He passed away three months later on 29 Av.

In the first year, thirty houses and a shul were built, and by 1914 over sixty families lived in the neighborhood. Because they were so isolated, it was necessary to hire a night watchman to patrol the area. Human incursions were not the only threat facing the settlers. Foxes would sneak into the neighborhood at night and steal chickens.

The man who poured all of his energies into building Shaarei Chesed was Rav Naftali Tzvi Porush, who also played an prominent role in other suburbs. After the First World War, Rav Yaakov Moshe Charlap served as Rav of the suburb.

Zichron Moshe

Around the same time, the more "progressive" elements in the city built neighborhoods like Zichron Moshe, Achva, and Geula. They were the centers for the intellectual, free thinkers of the day. Zichron Moshe, for example, was funded by the Montefiore Testimonial Fund in London, through Yechiel Michel Pines. It was for this reason the neighborhood was named after Sir Moses Montefiore.

The streets and houses were carefully designed to allow abundant light and air. A magnificent synagogue called Ohel Yaakov was built in the middle of the neighborhood.

Shaarei Tzedek Hospital[6]

The burgeoning populace and expanding suburbs in the city were accompanied by growth in other areas as well. More people meant that more services and infrastructure were necessary, and new hospitals, orphanages, yeshivos, and other institutions sprang up to accommodate the need.

In 1902, the Central Committee (*Vaad HaKlali*), still the focal point of the *yishuv*, moved to the New City. It occupied the second floor in the Beis David courtyard, across the street from Nachalas Shiva, where it still stands.

The Rothschild and Bikur Cholim Hospitals also moved to the New City from their original settings inside the Jewish Quarter. The Rothschild Hospital moved in the late 1880s, and the Bikur Cholim Hospital relocated on Strauss Street in 1910, although it did not open its doors until the early 1920s. However, the first actual new hospital to be built outside the city walls was Shaarei Zedek. Situated on Jaffa Road, this hospital became the most important medical institution in Jerusalem, under the leadership of its dynamic director, Dr. Moshe Wallach.

Shaarei Zedek Hospital on Jaffa Road

Dr. Wallach was a young, Orthodox physician from Cologne, Germany, who agreed to go to Jerusalem and set up a clinic. On his arrival in the early 1890s, Dr. Wallach settled in the Jewish Quarter. There he opened a clinic and pharmacy. Within a short time he recognized the urgent need for a new hospital to serve the Jewish community. An attempt to buy land inside the Old City failed, partially due to Rav Yehoshua Leib Diskin's disapproval of the proposed site, near the Damascus Gate. When Rav Diskin heard of the organizing committee's plans, he commented, "May the Shechinah not rest with the work of your hands." Soon afterwards, the sale fell through, and the group ended by purchasing a large strip of land on the outskirts of the New City on Jaffa Road. Apparently, Rav Diskin sensed the anti-Semitic feelings of the Moslems who lived on that side of the Old City.

Construction got underway in 1896. Amazingly, the project foreman for this two-story model hospital was a complete novice to the building profession. Rav Yaakov Mann taught at Etz Chaim Yeshivah, where his reputation lay in delivering a high-level lecture in Gemara. He expressed an interest in the hospital's plans to a surprised Dr. Wallach, who subsequently introduced him to the hospital's architect and engineer, Theodore Sandel. As the two men pored over the blueprints together, Rav Mann astonished Sandel with his clarity and suggestions for revisions in the plan. Rav Mann's only "training" was his in-depth studies of Tractate *Eruvin*, which had attuned him to all the intricacies of architecture! Having secured the position,

Rav Yaakov soon supervised a crew of three hundred workers at the construction site. Even while on the job, he walked around with a small Gemara in hand, which he studied at every available moment. The dedication ceremony took place on 20 Shevat, 1902 (5662), in the presence of religious and lay leaders.[7]

As director of the new hospital, Dr. Wallach concerned himself with every facet of its operation. He brought all halachic matters to the attention of Rav Zonnenfeld, with whom he developed a very close relationship over the years. His role in the institution was so central, that in the course of time the hospital became known colloquially as "Wallach's Hospital."*

During the First World War, Shaarei Zedek was used as a Turkish military hospital. In 1917, the Turkish surrender to the British forces took place there, and it was there that General Allenby received the keys to the city from the Turkish mayor.

Much later, in 1979, Shaarei Zedek moved to its present location, near Bayit Vegan. By that time, the old facility had been unable to meet the needs of Jerusalem's booming population for many years. The new Shaarei Zedek Hospital, over ten stories high, is a fully equipped modern facility and continues to serve the Jerusalem community in the same caring spirit as its founder.

Beis Strauss

Besides the natural drive to expand, Jerusalem witnessed a series of efforts to reach out and help the more unfortunate residents of the city. A particularly noble endeavor along these lines was undertaken by the American philanthropist, Nathan Strauss, who founded the Macy's department stores. His visit to the Holy City in 1910 was a shocking experience for him. Deeply touched by the Jerusalemites, whom he regarded as guardians of the faith, he took it upon himself to better their physical lot in life. He was so concerned with his self-proclaimed mission that he passed up the opportunity to travel on the Titanic's maiden voyage in order to intensify his efforts on his brethren's behalf. Initially he was stymied, as he found that these dignified and noble people were not ordinary beggars. Their heritage wove them together into an intricate fabric of mutual help. Whenever he gave money to one person, the individual would turn right around and give it so someone else

Jews congregating in the courtyard of Beis Strauss. Rav Yosef Lavon, seated to the left, is handing out stipends.

* See story "The Homeopathic Cure," in *Bygone Days: 1900–1918*, and "The Wallach Hospital," in *Bygone Days: 1918–1948*.

whom he thought was needier! Eventually, Strauss had the idea of setting up a soup kitchen, located a hundred meters from the gate leading into the Temple Mount on HaShalshelet Street. Called Beis Strauss, the free soup kitchen for the poor of Jerusalem — regardless of faith — opened in 1912.

Yosef Navon directed the kitchen for twenty-two years, dishing out as many as fifteen hundred servings a day. Soon after the kitchen opened, Nathan Strauss entered to see firsthand how it was being operated. To his surprise and delight, Yosef Navon, thinking the stranger was in need of a free meal, offered him a place to sit and served him a plate of food. Immediately, Strauss made him director of the soup kitchen. Today, the premises of Beis Strauss are used by the Ministry of Education, as well as house a *kollel*.[8]

A Growing City

Two new orphanages also opened during this period. One was the Blumenthal Orphanage, established by Rav Avraham Yochanan Blumenthal. Built around 1900 near the Bucharim Quarter, it was home to eighty-five orphans by 1920. The other orphanage was founded by Rav Yaakov Meir, the future leader of the Sephardic community, and became known as the Sephardic Orphanage. It opened in 1908, and was supported by the Baruchoff brothers. The Diskin Orphanage moved to their enormous premises in Givat Shaul in 1922.

Rav Blumenthal, who headed the orphanage for over 50 years

The city also had old-age homes, an institute for the blind, and even a mental hospital called Ezras Nashim Hospital, which moved from the Old City to the New City at the turn of the century.

In 1908, the Etz Chaim Yeshivah purchased land next to Machane Yehudah, under the leadership of Rav Yechiel Michel Tuketzinsky. It was designed to be the largest yeshivah in Jerusalem and housed both the *talmud Torah* and yeshivah under one roof. The first wing opened in 1909, but the complex was not fully completed until 1936.

Of further historical interest is an edifice on Jaffa Road across the street from Machane Yehudah, still standing today. In 1906, the American immigrant Shmuel Levy bought a one-story house at the site. His intention was to add more stories and have the building serve as a hostel for new immigrants like himself. When the additions were completed, he consecrated the ground floor as a synagogue, called Zoharei Chamah (Sunrise) Synagogue, which still serves

Shmuel Levy's four-story building, which still stands today across the street from the Machane Yehudah shuk, included a synagogue on the ground floor and a hospice. The sundial was added later. In order to cover the costs of construction and upkeep, Levy sold lottery tickets like this one, each worth 20 francs. Two grand winners received 2,000 francs each.

the area. The upper floors were guest rooms, which Levy provided as a public service. In addition, he commissioned Rav Moshe Shapiro, whose natural engineering talents were honed by his Talmudic studies, to construct a mammoth sundial outside the fourth floor. Levy also added two smaller conventional clocks on each side of the sundial (one on European time and one on Arabic time), so that people could know the hour even on cloudy days. The dial can still be seen, accurately tracking the sun's progression as it has for decades.*

In 1910, a Jewish philanthropist by the name of Zalman Parsiz visited the city. In addition to generously donating money to various yeshivos and charitable organizations, he decided to enhance the area by the Western Wall by erecting two large street lamps. He was particularly concerned about Shabbos

* See story, "The Sundial," in *Bygone Days: 1900–1918*.

A photograph from the turn of the century. The pathway leads to the Kosel through a field of cactus bushes where today stands the Kosel plaza. The Jewish Quarter is to the left. In the 1920s, a two meter high wall was built along the corridor, which became the main artery by which Jews could reach the Kosel, and a desolate field replaced the cactus plants.

night, when throngs of people went to pray and receive the Shabbos there. He explained to the Turkish authorities that it was disrespectful to do so in the dark, and they agreed. Unfortunately, the most powerful sheik in the Old City opposed the idea, and even this small token of religious expression was denied the Jerusalemites.[9]

Shops and businesses sprouted everywhere — particularly on Jaffa Road, which became the business district, and the area around the Jaffa Gate. Until the First World War, Jerusalem's astonishing growth rate made it the Jewish capital of Palestine. In 1914, on the eve of the "Great War," close to 50,000 Jews lived in the city. The change in the city's demographic profile was awesome: the Jews outnumbered their Moslem neighbors five to one, a watershed ratio which would never be attained again. Furthermore, nearly all development outside the walls was initiated by Jewish organizations concerned with Jewish expansion. From this aspect, a wave of enthusiasm engulfed the Holy City.

However, there were other considerations that did dampen this optimistic view. Put simply, it was impossible to unite such a large populace under one banner. More and more people espoused a new diversity of values that clashed with the traditional Torah orientation that had previously shaped the city's character. This situation could be directly traced to the influx of immigrants that comprised the Second Wave.

Between 1904 and 1914, an average of a thousand new faces entered Jerusalem each year, with all the attendant absorption problems this implies. The vast majority of the Jewish population was strictly Orthodox, but for the first time, secular Jews began to publicly profane the Shabbos. This naturally engendered growing tensions. As of yet, however, the threat of Zionism had not reared its head; only after the First World War would this ideology become a major point of contention.

View of Jaffa Road towards the Jaffa Gate, with the Clock Tower and the domed water fountain visible at the end

Signs of Danger

There were numerous signposts that the future portended danger. The Russian-Japanese War of 1905 was one example, and the rising tensions between Austria-Hungary and Germany was another. The Turkish Empire, extending over a vast geographic area, could not remain a unified nation forever. The world was in flux and the different cultures under the Turkish flag yearned for self-expression.

Jerusalem was still the heart of the Jewish world in Eretz Yisrael. As its population spiraled higher and higher, a diversified atmosphere began to cloud the city. Leadership grappled in a fog for stability and strength. Some of the venerated rabbanim of the yishuv had passed away or were approaching the end of a long, successful life of Torah leadership. However, new rabbis of superlative qualifications were not stepping forward.

Though no one knew of the global war awaiting them, the premonition was in the back of some astute men's minds that something was amiss. As in the times of a threatening thunderstorm, people tried to do their best under the circumstances.

The Last Chacham Bashi[10]

The Rishon l'Tzyon had enjoyed the title of Chacham Bashi since 1842, when Rav Avraham Gagin was appointed to that august post. As the Turkish Empire declined sharply in the decade before the First World War, the illustrious position of Chacham Bashi lost much of its power and glory as well.

When Rav Shaul Elyashar passed away in 1906, the Sephardic leadership was split over who should replace him as Chacham Bashi. One of the candidates was Rav Yaakov Meir who, a few decades later, would become the first Chief Sephardic Rabbi in the Rabbinate. When it became increasingly clear that a compromise was impossible, the Chacham Bashi of Constantinople, Rav Moshe HaLevi, attempted to make peace between the opposing factions. He asked Rav Eliyahu Moshe Panijel, a Sephardic sage of Jerusalem who was visiting Constantinople at the time, to accept the honored position. The various factions in Jerusalem agreed to his nomination, and peace was restored.

Rav Panijel, whose uncle, Rav Meir Panijel, served as Chacham Bashi from 1880 to 1892, had been a leader in the Sephardic community for many years. An excellent speaker and composer of *piyutim*, he was beloved by his fellowman. He played an important role in founding the Misgav Ladach Hospital in 1879. On one of his frequent trips overseas as a *shaliach*, he met with Rav Moshe HaLevi in Constantinople. In Adar, 1907, Rav HaLevi procured the necessary *firman* from the Sultan which officially invested Rav Panijel as Chacham Bashi of Jerusalem.

When the new Chacham Bashi landed at the Jaffa port in Nisan a month later, he was welcomed by a committee of Sephardic rabbis. In Jerusalem, Rav Panijel was greeted by Turkish nobility and leading rabbis of the city. In keeping with the long-established tradition, his inauguration took place in the Rabban Yochanan ben Zachai Synagogue in the Old City.

Through his connections overseas, he quickly received funding to strengthen the existing Sephardic institutions and to open an old-age home.

However, the calm that had been restored by his appointment was not destined to last. When Sultan Abdul Hamid was overthrown in 1908, a new Chacham Bashi by the name of Rav Chaim Nachum came to power in Constantinople. In turn, this led to new elections for the honored post in Jerusalem. Rav Panijel, nearly sixty years old, chose to retire.

Rav Eliyahu Panijel (1850–1919)

During the last years of Turkish rule, Jerusalem would not enjoy an officially sanctioned Chacham Bashi whose power and authority were backed by the empire. Instead, the role reverted to the traditional post of Rishon l'Tzyon. From 1908–1918, three men filled the position. The last one was Rav Nisim Danon (1915–1918), a native Jerusalemite who had served as Rav of Beirut, Izmir, and Rhodes.

Not surprisingly, the Ashkenazim were also faced with a similar dilemma during this crucial junction in Jerusalem's history.

Shepherds of the Yishuv

At the turn of the twentieth century, the aging Rav of Jerusalem, Rav Shmuel Salant, desired that a younger man should share the burden of shepherding the massive flock with him. His first choice was Rav Yosef Chaim Zonnenfeld, an unsurpassed *talmid chacham* and communal leader. Rav Yosef Chaim humbly rebuffed the nomination, as he had when Rav Diskin tried to permanently install him as head of his *beis din* in 1880. At that time, Rav Zonnenfeld had temporarily taken the position, with the understanding that he would step down once a suitable replacement was found. In that instance, Rav Yaakov Levi accepted the post, after returning from a three-month journey overseas. Now, however, Rav Zonnenfeld flatly refused.

In 1898, a meeting of Jerusalem's religious and lay leaders resulted in a letter being sent to Rav Chaim Ozer Grodzensky of Vilna, requesting him to search for a suitable appointee. It so happened that just when the letter reached Rav Chaim Ozer, Rav Eliyahu David Rabinovitch-Te'umim was passing through Vilna. At the time, Rav Eliyahu David was the Rav of Mir, having previously served as the Rav of Ponevitch. Rav Chaim Ozer felt he was eminently suited to fill the position, and broached the idea with him. With Rav Rabinovitch's consent, Rav Chaim Ozer wrote the *rabbanim* of Jerusalem, proposing his nomination. Shortly thereafter, a response was received agreeing to the proposal.

Known by the acronym Aderes, Rav Eliyahu David arrived in Adar, 1901 (5661), and was ceremoniously honored at the Shaarei Zedek Hospital synagogue. Rav Salant immediately announced, "I now present the honorable *gaon* with the power of the rabbinate." In his humility, the Aderes refused to sit at the head of the table, selecting a seat to the side instead.

This title of Chief Rabbi of the Ashkenazim had never been officially given to any Ashkenazic *rav* before. Even the revered Rav Salant, who was universally recognized as filling the position, shunned the official title, preferring to be called Rav or Dayan instead. Rav Auerbach, too, had never been officially declared Rav of Jerusalem by all the *rabbanim* of his day. Thus, the Aderes was the first Ashkenazic Rav of Jerusalem with a formal, written declaration signed by all the *rabbanim* of the Holy City.

During the four years he lived in Jerusalem, the Aderes demonstrated his authority in a number of areas. He was the first *rav* to set up an *eruv* outside the walls of the Old City. Until then, two Jewish watchmen stood at the Jaffa Gate — the main thoroughfare to the New City — from Shabbos morning till sunset. They would ask everyone who was about to go to the New City if they were carrying something in their pockets. If so, the guards took the item and kept it until nightfall. Realizing that this procedure was outmoded, the Aderes instituted a number of *eruvim* around different neighborhoods.

He designed the *eruv* himself and defrayed the entire cost from his own pocket. When asked why, he explained: "Our Sages say that many people commit some type of thievery — even if unintentional, and without realizing who the victim was. This puts them in a terrible quandary, for when they later learn of their mistake, they do not know whom to return the money to. In such a situation, Halachah mandates that they donate the amount to public causes, whereby the wronged party may come to benefit from it. Since an *eruv* is one of the most universally used public services, the victim will surely end up using it. Thus, erecting an *eruv* serves as an

Rav Eliyahu David Rabinovitch (1843–1905)

excellent 'insurance premium.'" Therefore, Rav Eliyahu David explained, he preferred to pay the cost from his private savings.

Rav Rabinovitch was deeply concerned that the man in the street be treated fairly and honestly. When he discovered that the weights and balances used in shops could easily be manipulated to the owner's advantage, he demanded that every Jewish shop display a certificate that the *beis din* checked its scales regularly. The Rishon l'Tzyon was delighted with this decree and issued a similar ruling.

Concerning the commandments attached to Eretz Yisrael, particularly *terumah* and *maaser* of produce, the Aderes was among the first to set up an organization to ensure that the tithes were taken. Until this time, either the individual shopkeepers were responsible — with no one supervising their activities — or the purchasers did it for themselves. The *Yerushalmi maggid*, Rav Benzion Yadler, was appointed to oversee the task.

The threat to the educational system remained a constant problem. Rav Rabinovitch once wrote to the Rav of Hebron on *chol hamoed* (when we refrain from writing) pleading with him to curtail the activities of a new progressive school which had recently opened in that city.

The Untimely Death of the Aderes

Once, a few weeks before he passed away in Adar, 1905 (5665), he revealed to the *Yerushalmi maggid*, Rav Yadler, that he never imagined that the "fire" of secularism had spread so far in the Holy City. He felt strongly about shouldering the battle. Rav Yadler encouraged him, suggesting that he write a public letter calling the community to action, which he did. The Aderes commented, "Even though I don't have strength to hold a pen, I will muster every last strand of muscle power to write about this imperative topic." As he slowly wrote, he said, "Each word is being written with my blood! Yet I rejoice that I'm using my last energies to fortify traditional education from the threat of secular influences."

After the Aderes's untimely death at the age of sixty-two, a new replacement was sought for his position. Another *gaon* had recently arrived from Moscow, Rav Chaim Berlin. The son of the famous Rosh Yeshivah of Volohzin, the Netziv, Rav Chaim was perfectly suited for the post. Rav Berlin's original intention in moving to the Holy City was to retire from public life. However, with the needs of the hour impressed upon him, he yielded and joined with Rav Salant in communal leadership. After Rav Salant's death in 1909, Rav Chaim became the next Rav of Jerusalem, albeit unofficially, serving until his death in 1913.

Once, a truckload of almonds entered Jerusalem. The almonds were *tevel* — lacking all separation of *terumah* and *maaser*. The merchants asked permission to separate the tithes in the city, but Rav Berlin refused and ordered that the nuts be returned to their point of origin, and the separations performed there. He explained that though in essence the procedure could be performed in the New City, he was hesitant to be lenient and allow it even once. This was because he was afraid of setting a precedent for laxity concerning the performance of a Torah commandment. One mistake could result in Divine punishment for unsuspecting Jews who ate the food while still in a *tevel* state.

The Yerushalmi Maggid

Rav Benzion Yadler began his lifelong career as the *Yerushalmi maggid* at the beginning of the twentieth century. His father, Rav Yitzchak Zev Yadler, gave lectures every day in Gemara, Halachah and *mussar* in the Menachem Tzyon Synagogue. Rav Benzion's first twenty years were plagued with a mysterious blindness. For months at a time his vision evaporated and then returned. His condition caused him to study as much as possible by heart.

Rav Benzion's mentor, Rav Zerach Braverman, had been a close disciple of the Brisker Rav, enjoying the special privilege of studying with him privately. Before the end of the century, Rav Zerach began teaching at Degal Torah Yeshivah in the Old City. He later founded Meah Shearim Yeshivah. Rav Zerach exhibited a rare skill at pedagogy; however, there is no doubt that his effectiveness as a teacher was equally enhanced by the fatherly concern he had for his students.

Once, an orphan by the name of Michel Zlatnik was reluctantly sent by his mother to be apprenticed as a carpenter. As was often the case when the head of the household died, the child's learning was sacrificed in the scramble to put bread on the table. Rav Benzion's father knew the boy to have a sharp, inquisitive mind, and mentioned to Rav Braverman, "I found a diamond for you!"

Without delay, Rav Zerach spoke to the boy's distraught mother and convinced her to place her son under his tutelage. Within a matter of a few years,

Rav Zerach Braverman

Michel was among the top students in the yeshivah. When he became of marriageable age, Rav Braverman combed the city for a suitable match for his "diamond" and personally acted as father/*shadchan*. Rav Zlatnik went on to become one of the most outstanding lecturers at Etz Chaim Yeshivah.

Rav Benzion Yadler (1871–1962)

Rav Benzion first rose to prominence in 1902, when Rav Shmuel Salant invited him to speak at the Churvah Synagogue on Shabbos, *parshas Zachor*. This was a supreme honor for the young man, for this discourse was reserved for the most renowned speakers of the *yishuv*. Rav Benzion, relatively unknown in the community, had been nudged into speaking the previous year by one of his teachers. At first he had only addressed his fellow students in the yeshivah. It turned out that his teacher's hunch about his talents had been correct. Slowly, Benzion began speaking publicly, in the synagogues of Yemin Moshe, Meah Shearim, and Beis Yisrael. This, however, was to be his major debut, and it was an unqualified success. With his words of Torah and dramatic voice, he so enamored his audience that some remarked afterwards, "If we had not heard him speak with our own ears, we would not have believed that a native-born Jerusalemite could *darshan* so eloquently."

The *maggid* used his God-given talents to the utmost. A frequent speaker, Rav Yadler became a legend in his own time. He did not confine himself to Orthodox circles, but regularly traveled around the country to arouse young and old to keep the mitzvos, especially those concerning the Land of Israel.

On 20 Sivan, 1903 (5663), news reached Jerusalem about the devastating pogroms then taking place in Russia. In the hopes of arousing Divine mercy, a general fast was declared in the community. Everyone was directed to pray together at the Churvah Synagogue in order to heighten the effect of the fast. In the middle of the service, the Rav of Jerusalem asked the *Yerushalmi maggid* to speak.

Parallel Forces

The tremendous growth of Jerusalem's population in the early twentieth century resulted in numerous educational institutions opening their doors. These included both traditional yeshivos, and a new breed of secular schools that catered to the city's burgeoning irreligious element. Most of the first progressive schools before the turn of the century were staffed by Orthodox teachers. However, with the worldwide turn away from tradition that occurred in the early part of the century, completely irreligious schools got a foothold in Jerusalem.

We will now review a few of these institutions, starting with some of the new yeshivos whose light and holiness shone forth in the city. When a small yeshivah opened in the New City in 1909, few people realized the power of Torah which would emanate from it. Shoshanim l'David, a Sephardic yeshivah at the end of Beis Yisrael on Zonnenfeld Street, nurtured one of the great Sephardic rabbis of the time. Rav Yaakov Chaim Sofer of Baghdad came to Jerusalem in 1904 specifically to study Kabbalah at the Beis El Yeshivah in the Old City. When Shoshanim l'David opened in 1909, Rav Sofer studied there in a small upstairs room day and night. The outcome of his quiet endeavors was a halachic classic entitled *Kaf HaChaim*. The book was a commentary on all of the *Orach Chaim* section of the *Shulchan Aruch* and part of *Yoreh Deah*. It soon became a standard halachic work for both Sephardim and Ashkenazim, complementing the *Mishnah Berurah*. For several years, Rav Sofer delivered a sermon on Shabbos afternoon in the yeshivah. He passed away in 1939.

Rav Chaim Leib Auerbach (1883–1954)

The light of Torah was also brought into the world by another yeshivah at this time. In 1906, Yeshivas Shaar HaShamayim (the Gate of Heaven) opened under the leadership of Rav Chaim Leib Auerbach, the father of Rav Shlomo Zalman

Auerbach. The yeshivah propagated the study of the mystical Torah, something unique in the Ashkenazic world. In 1927, after the original building in the Old City suffered from the earthquake, it was decided to rebuild the yeshivah in the New City. In 1992 they moved to new, expanded premises on Rashi Street.

Paralleling these holy institutions, several secular schools also opened their doors to the public. The most famous was the Bezalel School of Art. Founded in 1906 by Professor Boris Shatz of Berlin, the main school was in Jerusalem, with a branch located in Lod. The school in Jerusalem grew quickly, eventually encompassing a student body of over 450 youths. As its name implies, the school's curriculum was centered on teaching the arts, from silver- and goldsmithing and jewelry making to engraving, painting, sculpture, silk-screening, and photography. Quality workmanship of the students was sold to support the school. Students regularly walked to the nearby neighborhood of Shaarei Chesed to draw and paint the houses and children of the new residential area. The observant Jews of Shaarei Chesed, who scoffed at the irreligious school, called the students *Bezalelnikim*.

During the First World War, the Bezalel School of Art, like most institutions in Jerusalem, nearly closed it doors for lack of funds. In 1929, a decade after the war, it closed completely, until a companion society in Berlin reopened it in 1935 under the direction of Yosef Bodko of Germany. The coed school, besides its emphasis on creative arts and crafts, espoused a philosophy of total abandonment of traditional Jewish values.

Reaching Out

In 1913, Rav Benzion Yadler organized a month-long trip by the *gedolim* to visit Jewish settlements throughout the Galilee and strengthen their Torah observance. Included in this historic event were Rav Yosef Chaim Zonnenfeld, Rav Avraham Yitzchak Kook, Rav Yonasan Horowitz, Rav Yaakov Moshe Charlap, and Rav Yadler. The group went to towns and settlements where there was no *mikve* for women to immerse, no tithing of produce, and very little Shabbos observance. There was, however, reform-style shuls, secular education, and the like. The task of engendering a revolutionary overnight turnabout necessitated the presence of the greatest rabbis of the Land. Rav Zonnenfeld felt the mission to be of such lofty importance that he agreed to go despite the fact that he had not spent a significant amount of time outside Jerusalem since his arrival forty years earlier.

Traveling by train, wagon, mule, and on foot, the entourage went from Jerusalem to Jaffa, and from there to Hadera and Zichron Yaakov, where they spent their first Shabbos. Finding the synagogue designed with the *bimah* at the front of the shul in Reform style, the *rabbanim* refused to enter until they received a promise that it would be corrected right after Shabbos. Some of the other settlements in the Galilee they visited included Afula, Merchaviah, Tel Adashim, Yabanel, Dagania, Tiberias, Safed, and Rosh Pina. At various stages in their journey they were joined by the Rav of Haifa, Rav Baruch Markus, and the Rav of Tiberias, Rav Moshe Kleyeras.

The trip received much advance public notice, and the communities were prepared to welcome and listen to the distinguished travelers. As soon as the group arrived at a settlement, trumpets were blown to announce a general assembly. Men sat in the synagogue and the women in the women's gallery. Different *rabbanim* spoke on keeping the Shabbos, Jewish education, the sanctity of marriage, and the importance of the commandments connected to the Land of Israel. At the end, the *Yerushalmi maggid* spoke.

During one of the speeches given by Rav Kook, someone in the audience shouted, "Here, on our settlement, we will never take tithes!" Rav Kook, angered by the outburst, retorted with strong words of rebuke. Rav Zonnenfeld assuaged Rav Kook, "Don't worry. This man will one day repent, and will himself perform all the necessary steps in separating the tithes correctly." True enough, the words of Rav Zonnenfeld were fulfilled.

The *rabbanim* succeeded in instituting reforms in nearly every place that they spoke. Rav Yadler wrote: "It is impossible to convey in words the impact which the *rabbanim* had on strengthening religious commitment in Eretz Yisrael. Wherever they went, the settlers rejoiced as if it was a festival day. They put aside their work and beckoned them to return on a yearly basis. Just seeing the faces of these *rabbanim* etched a permanent memory in their minds.... Happy were those who saw and met them!"[11]

Such an extended journey naturally brought Rav Zonnenfeld into close contact with Rav Kook for the first time. They set aside their ideological differences for the sake of uplifting the general level of religious observance in Eretz Yisrael. With the success of their mission, each returned to his home with a new respect for one another. Later, after the First World War, their ideological differences would surface in a struggle over the religious rulership of the Holy City — but the two men would always maintain a cordial personal relationship.

Eve of the First World War

Before the advent of the First World War, when the wheels of time would seem to grind to a halt, Jerusalemites continued about their affairs as normal.

The relationship between Jews and their Arab neighbors stood at an all-time high. Rav Benzion Yadler, depicting the mood at the turn of the twentieth century, described it as follows:

The hub of Jewish activity in the Moslem Quarter of the Old City is centered around Hebron Street (so named to always recall the merits of the Patriarchs, who are buried in that city), and northward towards the Damascus Gate... There were twenty-two synagogues in that area, both Ashkenazic and Sephardic, and two Ashkenazic yeshivos, Toras Chaim and Chayei Olam, as well as Sephardic ones....

The neighborhood was mixed with Arabs. Nevertheless, one was not afraid to walk alone through the alleyways, and there did not exist any animosity between Moslem and Jew. In fact, a spirit of benevolence existed there.... There was visible proof of the verse (Deut. 28:10), "All the peoples of the world will

Rav Chaim Berlin (left) and Rav Yitzchak Yerucham Diskin (right)

see that the Name of God is called upon you, and will be in awe of you."

....Fortunate is the one who saw all of this![12]

However, with the growing secular immigration between 1904–1914, known as the Second Wave, Jerusalem's visage changed expression. Not only did the secular/Zionist youth create a stir in the old established *yishuv*, but the status quo between Jew and Arab likewise altered. As Rav Yadler continues:

But due to our many transgressions, all this changed when lewdness usurped modesty, and long hair with clean-shaven faces replaced peyos and beards. Mixed company of boys and girls replaced night watches, men and women teachers replaced cheder rebbes, and secular books replaced traditional ones.

Thus, God implanted hatred inside the Moslems towards the Jews, [which later led] to many deaths...[13]

The problems caused by the Second Wave were augmented by a serious vacuum in the leadership of the *yishuv*. With the passing of Rav Shmuel Salant in 1909, Rav Chaim Berlin accepted the post. Originally intending to fill the position in a substitute capacity, Rav Chaim served until his death in 1913. With his passing, no one rose to guide the *yishuv* through the turbulent years that would follow. With Rav Zonnenfeld still adamant in his refusal to take the post, the best prospective nominee was Rav Yitzchak Yerucham Diskin, the son of Rav Yehoshua Leib Diskin, who had immigrated to Jerusalem in 1908. He declined, however, choosing to remain as the director of the Diskin Orphanage instead. The floundering of the community played into the hands of the Zionists, and together with other major factors it allowed them to gain a foothold in the Holy City.

The Crisis of the First World War

The First World War completely altered the face of Jerusalem. It was truly a living nightmare — both in the events that transpired during the actual course of the war, and in its far-flung repercussions, which would be greater than anyone could have imagined.

It all began on 29 October, 1914, when the Sultan entered the war on the side of the Germans. Soon, German soldiers were stationed in Jerusalem, and British forces were assaulting the city from afar. Buildings were confiscated, like the Sephardic Orphanage, which became offices for the German command and stables for their horses. The mobilization of the Turkish army brought in its wake the conscription of all able-bodied men throughout the Empire. For the religious Jews, such a call-up was a death warrant. Young men hid or fled from the city in order to evade the draft.*

There was one type of exemption — a permanent deferment granted to anyone legally recognized as a scholar. This included *roshei yeshivos*, *dayanim*, and rabbis.** However, students who were merely studying in the yeshivos were ineligible. Their plight became a major issue in the *yishuv*. A decision was made to send a personal representative to Constantinople and to present the case before the city's Chacham Bashi, Rav Chaim Nachum. It was hoped that through his influence, the necessary deferments would be obtained.

Rav Benzion Yadler was chosen as the spokesman for this important mission, in spite of objections raised by some people that his *chareidi* appearance might interfere with its successful conclusion. While Rav Benzion was in *chutz laAretz*, two Jews by the name of Rav Golomav and Rav Ber devised all sorts of ways to save the boys from the army. Rav Braverman, Rosh Yeshivah Meah Shearim, hid students in his house, feeding and taking care of all their needs. Unfortunately, some of these young men were caught and executed as deserters.

Rav Yadler wrote of his trip: *"Praise the Lord! He guided me to the right people [in Constantinople].... The next day I went to meet one of the wealthy, influential Jews of the city who had direct connections with the Sultan's court. When I learned that he was not home, I left him a message that, due to my limited time schedule, I had to continue on to the home of the Chacham Bashi. As it turned out, while I was engaged in a conversation with the Chacham Bashi, the phone rang. It was the wealthy Jew, who said that he was waiting for me to come to see him. This naturally impressed the Chacham Bashi very much, and he did everything possible to help me obtain the deferments. His success was no less than a miracle."*[14]

With the war raging on all sides, it was Heaven-sent that Rav Yadler found a neutral ship going to Eretz Yisrael. When he arrived back home, the news of his success brought joy and relief to many families in the Holy City.

Rav Avraham Kook, the Rav of Jaffa, had left Eretz Yisrael just before the outbreak of the war in order to attend an Agudas Yisrael Convention. When the war broke out a month later, in Av, he became stranded in Switzerland (the convention having been postponed). In 1915, he moved to England to accept the post of Rav of London. There he met with an array of lay leaders, including Dr. Chaim Weizmann and Nachum Sokolov. Together with these men, he tried to influence members of Parliament to grant autonomous national rights to the Jewish people in Eretz Yisrael — if and when Eretz Yisrael would fall into British hands.

* See story, "The Draft Dodger," in *Bygone Days: 1900–1918*.

** See story, "Jamil's Reign of Terror," in *Bygone Days: 1900–1918*.

With the onset of the war, all construction and development in Jerusalem was brought to a halt. Bikur Cholim Hospital on Strauss Street, for instance, languished half-built for several years before it was finally completed. Expansion of neighborhoods like Shaarei Chesed came to a similar standstill.

Psychologically, the war was horrifying. However, the physical impact was even more devastating. The influx of Turkish and German troops drained the country's economic resources. True, opposing armies never fired on the city and ravished it like communities in Europe, yet Jerusalem became isolated from the rest of the world. The *yishuv*, which had been supported from time immemorial by the *chalukah* system, braced itself for the worse. Due to the global war of unprecedented proportions, all sources of foreign revenue dried up. As a result, the *yishuv* was subjected to a prolonged period of hunger and starvation, from which very few were spared.

Schools and yeshivos closed their doors, and institutions were forced to limit their activities to the bare minimum. Soup kitchens tried to extend a helping hand, but the number of needy people far outnumbered the available resources. The Amsterdam Aid Fund, directed by Rav Moshe Auerbach, labored to help in every way possible, including paying monthly wages to yeshivah teachers, rabbis, and students. In those terrible times, a man of stature was needed to shoulder the difficult burden of leadership. Rav Zonnenfeld rose to the occasion, playing a crucial role in overseeing the multitude of decisions that needed to be made. Rav Auerbach wrote: "Nothing was done without Rav Chaim Zonnenfeld's advice and approval."

The Catastrophe

A critical point was reached when hundreds began dying of starvation. Unfortunately, there was no way to halt the catastrophe. People sold expensive jewelry for a loaf of bread, and their blankets for mere pennies. Out of necessity, some were compelled to sell their valuable sets of the Talmud to Arab peddlers, who used the pages to wrap their wares. Coupled with the lack of sustenance, typhus and cholera epidemics took their toll on feeble Jerusalemites.

Efforts to raise money in the Dias-

Rav Yosef Chaim Zonnenfeld (1851–1932)

pora, especially in America, were thwarted by a number of factors. A joint appeal to the American philanthropists Jacob Schiff and Nathan Strauss yielded a $50,000 donation for the *yishuv*. However, when the money arrived in September, 1914, on the American steamer North Carolina, it mysteriously disappeared. Six months later, the Joint (the American Jewish Relief Fund) sent a relief ship called the Vulcan carrying $100,000 worth of food supplies and $25,000 in cash for the needs of Jews in Eretz Yisrael. A committee was set up to oversee the relief effort, but when the *yishuv* was denied equal representation, it boycotted the meeting. As a result, most of the supplies and money went to Zionist institutions. Other relief ships were prevented from reaching the shores of Eretz Yisrael, which heightened the crisis even more.

To further the dilemma, Jamil Pasha, the mayor of Jerusalem, decreed that every foreign resident must either change his status and become a Turkish citizen or face exile. Since many Jews of the *yishuv* were legally British, Austrian, or Russian citizens, the decree was a direct assault on them.* The *yishuv* tumbled into confusion. Most refused to become Turkish citizens — which would lead to immediate recruitment into the Turkish army — and were forced to go into exile, mostly to Egypt and other surrounding countries.[15]

After three dark years, the British forces marched on the offensive up to Jerusalem. On the day before Chanukah, 24 Kislev, 1917, Jerusalem's mayor surrendered to General Allenby, commander of the British forces, at the Shaarei Zedek Hospital on Jaffa Road. Two days later the British forces entered the Old City via the Jaffa Gate. General Allenby chose to enter the Old City on foot as a sign of respect for the ancient city. The weak and famished populace cheered the liberating army.

The statistics were shocking: in a pe-

Poverty and starvation were evident on everyone's face

* See story, "The Hideaways," in *Bygone Days: 1900–1918*.

riod of three years, 11,000 Jews died of starvation and disease in Jerusalem, and another 7,000 were exiled. More than one-third of the Jewish population had disappeared, leaving behind orphans, widows, and a downtrodden people. The once-dynamic *yishuv* was a ghostly shell of its former self. The edifice of Torah Judaism that had sustained Jerusalem for nearly a hundred years had painfully crumbled. Worst of all, the Zionist threat that had been kept at bay before the war was now in control of most of the *yishuv*'s lifelines. Largely confined to Jaffa until now, where they reigned supreme, they eagerly sought to spread their net over the Holy City and conquer it.

A Fearful Premonition[16]

Several decades before the First World War, Rav Yehoshua Leib Diskin reflected upon the state of the *yishuv* and the *rabbanim* who led it. Four months before he passed away, in Elul, 1897, news of the First Zionist Congress in Basel, Switzerland, made headlines. Rav Diskin told his disciples, Rav Braverman and Rav Prankintal, to write to three of the leading *rabbanim* of Europe in his name. The letter concerned the vital importance of organizing a conference to discuss the Zionist threat. He added: "This is one of the greatest dangers to the Jewish people in all times. It can uproot large segments of our people."[17]

Rav Diskin's sober attitude stemmed from a deep conviction that a philosophy which publicly denied the Torah, openly claiming that it is possible to be a Jew without mitzvah observance, was a brazen form of heresy. There existed an imminent danger that innocent Jews would be swayed from the true path. Therefore, he felt it imperative that world Jewry act at once against this massive threat while it was still in the embryonic state. He felt that a world conference should declare a *cherem* against all Zionists, publicly excommunicating them from the Jewish people in the same way that the Sages excommunicated the Samaritans. In practical terms this meant not to eat of their bread, drink from their wine, nor to marry with them. He ended with these words: "I am sure that if we do not take such [drastic] action, in the end the Jewish people will feel great remorse."

Other leaders did not feel that such a radical stand was necessary. They were of the opinion that Orthodox Jews, firmly anchored in Torah and mitzvos, could not be lured away by blatant heretics. Thus Zionism would fail to attract the masses and would remain at most a fringe group with little power. Furthermore, since the Christians were wooing the Zionist leaders, a *cherem* could cause many Zionists to counter by outright mass apostasy.

It was this moderate opinion that held sway, and no convention took place. Only much later did world Jewry create a body — Agudas Yisrael — to counter the major threat that the Brisker Rav had predicted so many years earlier. By then, however, Zionism was a well-organized, hard-line movement, with tremendous resources and a sophisticated propaganda machine which the relatively small Orthodox resistance was hard pressed to counter.

The Brisker Rav lamented the fact that world Jewry did not follow his advice. "The time will come," he sighed, "when they will sadly be forced to agree that I was right."

Though his warning went unheeded in Europe, Rav Diskin charted a course for a future battle in the Holy City. Strength in numbers was insufficient in and of itself. It was vital to have leadership and unity as well. These sentiments were echoed a decade later by Rav Shmuel Salant before his death in 1909. He, too, saw the threat that sectarianism posed to the Ashkenazic bastion, and the danger of a ship floundering without a helmsman.

Both men also saw Rav Yosef Chaim Zonnenfeld as the man of the hour — a staunch leader who could unite the people and guide them through the turbulent storm ahead. But factionalism splintered the ship's hull, and Rav Zonnenfeld's profound humility kept him from rising to the occasion. Only years later, in 1920, did he accept the post of Rav of Jerusalem.

There was one factor which the Brisker Rav and Rav Salant did not foresee, and that was a world torn asunder. The First World War caused a worldwide upheaval that was unequaled in history. Millions of lives were lost, leaving entire peoples broken and a shattered world economy — and no one suffered more than the Jews. Nowhere was this more evident than in Eretz Yisrael. The war years played perfectly into the Zionists' hands, and they utilized every resource available to further their cause. Never had authentic Judaism stood at such a dangerous crossroads. The Zionists were eager to hoist their flag over Eretz Yisrael, and the battle for Jerusalem became the battle for a nation's soul.

Notes

1. *Tevuos HaAretz*, p. 494.
2. *Shechunos b'Yerushalayim*, pp. 126–130.
3. Ibid., p. 129.
4. Ibid.
5. Ibid., pp. 137–142.
6. Culled from *Betuv Yerushalayim*.
7. *Ish al HaChomah* (*Guardian of Jerusalem*), p. 267.
8. *Battim u'Mosdos Yehudayim b'Rova HaMuslami b'Yerushalayim HaAtika*, pp. 11–12.
9. *Masa'os Moshe*, p. 101.
10. See *Nasi'im b'Yisrael*, pp. 205–221.
11. *Betuv Yerushalayim*, pp. 180–186.
12. Ibid., pp. 60–61.
13. Ibid.
14. Ibid., pp. 154–156.
15. See also *Al Chomosiach Yerushalayim*.
16. *Mara d'Arah Yisrael*, vol. 2, pp. 42–44.
17. Ibid.

Bygone Days

The Sundial

ONE DAY in 1901 (5661), an important sheik by the name of Nimar summoned Rav Moshe Shapiro to his office. When Rav Shapiro appeared, the sheik extended his hand and warmly invited him to sit down. After the two men exchanged pleasantries, the sheik got down to business.

"I understand that you are an expert at designing and making sundials. Is that correct?"

"Yes," Rav Moshe answered, wondering where the conversation was leading to.

"I would like to offer you the job of making a sundial to be hung outside the Dome of the Rock. We Moslems, like you Jews, must pray at set times, and such a sundial will be of great benefit to us."

Rav Moshe's mind reeled. He thought to himself, "How can I go up on the Temple Mount and build a sundial at the place where our forefathers bought sacrifices to atone for sins!"

Sheik Nimar, one of the most powerful Moslem leaders in the city, leaned forward on the edge of his chair. "We, too, have a number of craftsmen who can perform the job. But your credentials are superb, and more than that, we feel that having a Jewish artisan do the job will improve Moslem-Jewish relations."

Rav Shapiro was indeed a topnotch sundial maker. He had already made a number of them on the outer walls of synagogues, such as on the Churvah Shul in the Old City. Because of his labors, his fellow Jews could now accurately know the times for Minchah, and candlelighting on *erev Shabbos*.

Seeing his nervousness, the sheik recommended that they continue the conversation in the privacy of his villa. There, the sheik treated his guest graciously, yet subtly applied pressure on him to accept the offer.

"If the sheik will permit me," Rav Moshe interrupted. "I think it is better if I had a couple of days to think the matter over carefully."

The sheik agreed and repeated his belief that Rav Moshe was the ideal man for the job.

From the sheik's villa, Rav Moshe went straight to Battei Machse and

One of the sundials built by Rav Moshe Shapiro still stands across the street from the Machane Yehudah shuk on Jaffa Road, and still shows the correct time.

knocked at the door of Rav Yosef Chaim Zonnenfeld.

Rav Yosef Chaim listened to the craftsman's story and advised him to return on the second day with a two-pronged strategy. Rav Moshe listened carefully, and with a sense of relief, agreed to implement Rav Yosef Chaim's plan.

At the appointed time, Rav Shapiro met with Sheik Nimar. "First and foremost," the artisan said, "the sheik should be aware that even if it is permissible for me to execute the proposal, the cost for such work is considerably high."

The sheik smiled, walked over to a safe, and withdrew a satchel. He placed it on the table, saying, "It is yours! Thirty thousand gold napoleons! And if that is not enough, I can easily double or triple that amount."

Rav Moshe realized that his first strategy — asking an exorbitant fee — did not deter the sheik in the least. Therefore, he quickly turned to the second ploy. "I previously mentioned my doubt over the permissibility of my executing the project," Rav Moshe began. "This is because I am not sure whether I am permitted by Jewish Law to work on the Temple Mount. Therefore, I suggest that this question be referred to a competent rabbi."

"Whom do you suggest?" asked the sheik.

Knowing that Rav Zonnenfeld's name commanded respect in the Moslem community, he suggested Rav Yosef Chaim. The sheik agreed at once.

Rav Shapiro met with Rav Zonnenfeld that day. Rav Yosef Chaim looked at the sundial maker and asked him whether the sum of thirty thousand gold napoleons sounded appealing.

"What do you mean?" asked Rav Moshe.

"If earning such a large sum of money is important to you," Rav Yosef Chaim continued, "then perhaps we could devise a way for you to ascend the

Temple Mount and build the sundial."

Rav Moshe was suddenly steeped in a personal dilemma. For years he had lived on the fringe of the economic security belt. Such an enormous amount of money could change his lot forever. Yet....

"I beg you to give me until tomorrow to answer you," replied Rav Moshe confusedly.

The following day, Rav Shapiro returned. "I will not build a sundial on the mosque for any price in the world!" His voice was confident and resolute.

Rav Yosef Chaim was moved to tears. Embracing the craftsman, he exclaimed, "Master of the Universe, who is like Your people, Israel!"

The sheik accepted Rav Zonnenfeld's judgment, but the Moslem masses were fiercely indignant over this seeming rebuff to their religion. Sheik Nimar counseled Rav Moshe Shapiro to leave Jerusalem until the incident would be forgotten, which he did.

Later, Rav Moshe built a sundial above the Zoharei Chamah Synagogue on Jaffa Road near Machane Yehudah, and another in Shaarei Chesed.

(*Ish al HaChomah, [Guardian of Jerusalem]*, pp. 147–150)

The Tailor and the Rav

TWO TYPES of Ashkenazic tailors lived in Jerusalem. One type produced men's suits in the European style. The other type, tailored by Rav Shmuel Shneider, made suits in the traditional Jerusalem style. Both types of tailors had ample work.

Rav Shmuel Shneider set aside every free minute to study Torah and over the years acquired a reputation as a very learned man. Though he sat in his shop and sewed the whole day, people regarded him with the respect due a *talmid chacham*.

One summer day in 1904, Rav Shmuel received a message from the Rav of Petersburg, Rav Yitzchak Blazar, requesting that he come and measure the *rav* for a suit. Rav Blazar, author of *Pri Yitzchak*, had recently arrived with his family in the Holy City and wished to dress in the style of the land.

Rav Shneider knocked on Rav Blazar's door and was welcomed into his home. When the Rav of Petersburg beheld Rav Shmuel's countenance, he rose in honor of the Torah, thinking that one of the dignities of the *yishuv* had come to greet him. Immediately he engaged the tailor in a discussion on themes of Torah and *mussar*. The two men spoke at length, sharing Torah insights with one another.

Finally, Rav Shneider stood up and said, "Forgive me, but I would like to take your measurements for a suit."

Rav Blazar's face shone. "Behold, this is the Yerushalmi tailor, and I did not know it! Oh, Jerusalem! How fortunate you are that a tailor like this lives in your midst!"

(*Betuv Yerushalayim*, p. 402)

The First One in Heaven

RAV YITZCHAK Blazar and Rav Chaim Berlin formed a close relationship while living together in Jerusalem. Both were getting on in years and felt the wear and tear on their bodies. In the year 1907, they entered into a pact with one another that very few people would imagine making. They agreed that whichever of the two died first would visit the other in a dream and tell him of his experience in the next world.

Rav Yitzchak Blazar (1837–1907)

In Av of that summer, Rav Blazar passed away, at the age of seventy. During the week of mourning, Rav Berlin concentrated on reviewing his dreams of the night before, but could not recall his beloved companion visiting him. However, a few days later, Rav Itzalleh (Blazar) appeared to him as clearly and vividly as if he were truly alive and standing before him.

"Well," asked Rav Chaim, "what is it really like there?"

"It is unbelievable!" replied his friend. "The profundity of the Divine judgment is immeasurable. The sins of the tongue are the worst of all before the Heavenly tribunal. Do not despair, though, my dear friend. Those who are humble and lowly, forbearing and forgiving, receive special consideration!"

(*A Tzaddik in Our Time*, p. 339)

The Telegram

THE VENERABLE Rishon l'Tzyon, Rav Yaakov Shaul Elyashar, received a telegram on 26 Tamuz, 1906 (5666). It read:

Warsaw, July 13, 1906
To the Esteemed
Rabbi Yaakov Shaul Elyashar, שליט"א

May peace be upon you,

I, the Rav of Noviminsk, make the following request in the name of the entire community, asking you to intercede on our behalf at a time of great distress.

A few months ago, a local government official by the name of Nasalink was murdered. In the presence of the court, the brothers Eliezer and Noach Horowitz — presently in Jerusalem — testified that they witnessed the crime and pointed to five gentiles as perpetrators of the murder. Based on their testimony, the five were found guilty and sentenced to death. Now, we expect our gentile neighbors to retaliate in force against us. Therefore, I request that the Rishon l'Tzyon speak to these two men and demand they confess that they only gave their testimony out of hatred for the accused. If they admit the truth, the convicted prisoners will be reprieved from the death penalty, and the Jewish community will be saved from a pogrom.

Please forward their testimony via the Russian consulate in Jerusalem, who will forward it by telegram to the Warsaw authorities.

Signed by
Rabbi Shmuel Yaakov Rabinovitch
Noviminsk, District of Warsaw

Rav Elyashar turned to his secretary, Rav Chaim Michel Michlin, and asked him to find the two brothers mentioned in the telegram. An hour later, Rav Michlin returned with the Horowitz brothers, who vehemently denied the accusation in the telegram. They were the sole witnesses to the crime, and everything they said in court was the absolute truth. Nothing could sway them to change their version of the events.

Puzzled by the contradiction between the telegram and the testimony of the brothers, the Rishon l'Tzyon called a special meeting at his house with some other *rabbanim*. If the telegram was authentic, then a threat to an entire Jewish community loomed in the air, and an immediate reply was called for.

Rav Michlin read the telegram out loud to the assembled rabbis and told them what the Horowitz brothers said to the Rishon l'Tzyon earlier that day. For the next two hours, the *rabbanim* discussed and debated what to do, and finally arrived at the wording of a return telegram.

Throughout the long evening hours of discussion, Rav Yaakov Shaul Elyashar remained silent. The venerated sage sat back in his chair and stared at the floor. Suddenly, he signaled that he wanted to speak.

"My dear companions," Rav Elyashar began in a low tone. "Before you send off this reply you have formulated, let me present you with my candid appraisal."

Everyone turned to the Rishon l'Tzyon and waited for him to continue.

"My personal opinion is that this telegram is a forgery! The authors of the telegram are none other than the relatives of the convicted murderers, who seek to save their loved ones from death. If the Horowitz brothers retract their testimony, then the whole case against them will fall through.

"But there is a grave danger here," continued the Rishon l'Tzyon. "Should we wire that the brothers spoke falsely, this might incite a pogrom against the Jews of the community.

Rav Yaakov Shaul Elyashar (1817–1906)

"Therefore, it is my opinion that we should either do nothing, or if you feel that some reply is in order, we should circumvent the issue by stating that it is forbidden for me, as Chacham Bashi, to interfere with the internal problems of a foreign country."

Silence hovered in the air. Finally one *rav* spoke. "Forgive me, please. But should the telegram not be a forgery, both possible suggestions which you propose could lead to a catastrophe for the Jewish community there."

After a few moments of thought, Rav Elyashar said, "In that case, I recommend that we ask the Rav of Jerusalem, Rav Shmuel Salant, his feelings on the matter. Whatever he says we will do."

Turning to his secretary, the Rishon l'Tzyon called, "Since this matter is of the utmost importance for the safety of hundreds of Jews, please go at once to the Rav of Jerusalem and ask him for his advice. Show him the telegram, but do not tell him my opinion."

Though the hour was after midnight, Rav Chaim Michel aroused the ninety-year-old Rav of Jerusalem and presented him with all the facts.

Rav Salant sat and contemplated the matter for a few minutes. "In my humble opinion, the telegram is a forgery. The Rav of Noviminsk never sent it. It is probably the work of cunning relatives who want to save their accused brethren from death."

"That is precisely what Rav Yaakov Shaul Elyashar said, too," interrupted Rav Chaim Michel excitedly. "But what should we do now?"

"One possibility would be not to answer anything. Another possibility would be to write that the Rishon l'Tzyon is a Turkish citizen and is forbidden by law to enter into matters such as this which pertain to other nations."

When Rav Michlin returned to the Rishon l'Tzyon's house, everyone was amazed to hear how the two Chief Rabbis of Jerusalem had independently arrived at the same conclusion.

The next morning, Friday, a short telegram was wired to the Rav of Noviminsk in which the Rishon l'Tzyon exempted himself from interfering.

The next day, Shabbos, 28 Tamuz, Rav Yaakov Shaul Elyashar passed away at the age of eighty-nine, and was mourned by the entire *yishuv*.

A few weeks later, it was reported that had the *rabbanim* of Jerusalem fallen into believing the telegram, the consequences would have been disastrous for the Jewish community of Noviminsk. Thus, the wisdom of the leading sages of Jerusalem had saved the lives of an untold number of Jews.

(*Nasi'im b'Yisrael*, pp. 177–180, and *Rav Shmuel Salant*, pp. 11–24)

A Jerusalem Archivist

DURING THE first two decades of the twentieth century, a soft-spoken Sephardic *rav* from Yemin Moshe made daily excursions to different areas of the city. Rav Yitzchak Badahav searched the *sheimos* closets (where old, torn, and worn-out books and writing are collected before being buried) in every shul and yeshivah looking for discarded books that he could catalogue. Indeed, his massive library consisted of little more than books and manuscripts he had found in such places.

Whenever Rav Yitzchak met someone, he broached the subject of his archives. Maybe this person had something that would add a new dimension to his life's work.

Rav Yitzchak did not limit himself to books. He saw the value of saving certain placards which were posted in the city. Some of them were important declarations and open letters to the Jews of the *yishuv* signed by the *rabbanim*. When brought together under his watchful eye, these documents portrayed a living history of the *yishuv*.

Rav Badahav worked day and night at gathering, organizing, and cataloguing everything he deemed worthy of saving. Sometimes he even bought rare books at the price of having food on his table. For him, having a new volume for his collection was more precious than a solid meal.

His labors were directed at organizing an updated version of the Chida's *Shem HaGedolim*, which would list all Jewish books that had come out since the Chida passed away a hundred years earlier, together with their authors. His catalogue, called *Kovetz Ginzei Tzyon v'Yerushalayim*, was first published in 1906. A second volume was published in 1910.

Rav Yitzchak's efforts were unique at the time. His mission was a true labor of love, executed without receiving any financial compensation for his time. In his own way, Rav Badahav was bringing out the hidden light of Torah which emanates from Jerusalem, the Holy City.

(*Kol Sinai*, no. 7, Sivan, 1962)

The Homeopathic Cure

ANOTHER LONG day was coming to a close. Dr. Moshe Wallach, director of Shaarei Zedek Hospital and tireless hero of modern medicine, stood by the front door of a humble home in the Jerusalem suburb of Shaarei Chesed. Inside the house, a six-year-old child lay half conscious, losing the battle against a severe case of diphtheria.

"I'm very sorry to tell you," Dr. Wallach said, carefully measuring his words to the boy's mother, "that I have done everything medically possible to save your son's life. At this point everything is in Heaven's hands." Encouragingly, he added, "If he passes the night all right, then I believe he will survive." With this, the doctor bid her farewell.

The child's mother stood at the door, her eyes following the doctor as he rode off on his donkey, followed by his aide. With her husband abroad at the time, she was alone with two smaller children to take care of. Fortunately, neighborhood friends lent her a helping hand.

Later that night she decided to implore the Rav of Shaarei Chesed, Rav Yaakov Moshe Charlap, to pray for her son. He listened quietly as she poured out her heart.

"I have an idea," he said. "Here in Shaarei Chesed lives Rav Shmuel, who moved from Safed with his wife and small children. He told me that while on *shelichus* in Europe he studied a new type of medicine from a Jewish doctor. He has already used it several times here with remarkable success, though people say it is not his little bottles that give the cure, but the Almighty Who blesses his handiwork. Would you consent to speak with him?"

"Anything that might save my precious child is worth a try!"

Rav Charlap took out his pocket watch. "It is very late now. I think it is best if I go and get him. In the meantime, you return home."

Soon Rav Shmuel was by the child's bedside. He carefully examined the boy, his breathing and the color of his tongue. Then he removed a dozen or so small vials from a leather bag, each one with a number written on it. They all seemed exactly alike, filled with a colorless liquid that looked like water. He opened one, put a drop on his finger and placed it in the child's mouth. After five minutes he repeated it with a drop from another vial. This procedure continued for several hours, late into the night.

At first there was no change in the boy's condition. Slowly, however, his breathing improved and his color returned to normal. By three o'clock in the morning, the boy was fully conscious, smiling and talking to his mother.

Rav Shmuel packed his precious vials up and headed for the front door. As soon as he stepped outside he saw two men approaching on donkeys. In the dark he could not make out who they were.

"Gershon," said one of the riders to the other. "You go inside and see if there is any reason for me to follow you."

Gershon Porush, Dr. Wallach's personal aide, approached Rav Shmuel and asked how the child was doing. A minute later, he returned to Dr. Wallach. "The child is playing with toys!"

Dr. Moshe Wallach entered and examined the child. "His spectacular recovery is no less than a miracle!" he declared.

Outside, in the silence of the night, Rav Shmuel stood at the threshold with a smile of satisfaction on his face.

(*Esara Doros b'Eretz Yisrael*, pp. 165–166)

A Chassidic Segulah

RAV YOSEF Chaim Zonnenfeld's married daughter, Leah Sheinker, lived next door to her parents, in Battei Machse. Her husband, Rav Shmuel Sheinker, came from Poland in 1892 and joined the budding *mussar* movement in the city. Later, he was responsible for bringing Rav Yitzchak Blazar and Rav Naftali Amsterdam, two of the great *mussar* luminaries, to Jerusalem. After his marriage, Rav Shmuel studied Kabbalah every Shabbos night with his father-in-law.

One day, Rav Yosef Chaim received word that his daughter was in labor. She had already borne several healthy children, and this pregnancy had also passed without incident. But now, in the last hours before childbirth, she was experiencing a very difficult time, and the midwife was quite fearful.

Rav Yosef Chaim stood by his daughter's bedside, next to his son-in-law. Leah's suffering was much greater than what normal labor pains should have caused. After a few moments in thought, he said, "At the present, this is neither a medical case nor a situation in which reciting Psalms will be sufficient."

Turning to Rav Shmuel, he added, "I suggest that you go right away to the Lelover Rebbe, Rebbe David Biderman, and ask him for a *segulah*."

The Lelover Rebbe heard Rav Shmuel Sheinker's story. "Listen to me," he said. "There is a shul right across the way from your house in Battei Machse. Take a long cord and tie one end of it to your wife's hand. Tie the other end to the door of the Holy Ark. Then have her pull the cord towards herself, thereby opening the door of the Holy Ark. As you surely know, opening the Holy Ark is an ancient *segulah* for an easy childbirth. May you soon be blessed with a healthy child and a happy mother."

Rav Shmuel returned to Battei Machse and had his wife perform the *segulah* suggested by the Rebbe. Sure enough, the pains subsided immediately and within an hour she gave birth to a baby boy.

The baby was named Yisrael. Rav Yisrael Sheinker grew up to be the head of Knesses Bnei HaGolah Yeshivah.

(*Sippurim Yerushalmim*, vol. 1, pp. 168–169)

The Tefillin Maker

EVER SINCE Moses came down from Mount Sinai, Jews have been wearing tefillin. Throughout the millennium, it has only been possible to fulfill this precept due to God-fearing men who labor to make them according to the Mosaic Tradition. Tefillin are made completely from animal hide — even the threads and parchment upon which the four *parshiyos* are written. Down through the ages, tefillin makers have devised numerous techniques to competently fulfill the many intricate laws regarding their craft.

Today, most tefillin are made from the thick skin around the neck of the cow, called *gassos* (thick) tefillin. Though they are markedly more difficult to make than the thinner-skinned *dakos* (thin) tefillin, they have much greater longevity. With the advent of electricity and accurate cutting machines, the process of creating *gassos* tefillin is much less laborious and more accurate.

There was one man who lived in Jerusalem at the turn of the twentieth century who single-handedly initiated the making of *gassos* tefillin. He used neither electricity nor elaborate machinery, yet the tefillin that came out of his small shop were perfect, like the best that are produced today. Collectors offer up to ten thousand dollars for a pair of these tefillin — a hundred years after they were made — if the owner can be persuaded to part with them.

This craftsman's name was Rav Nasanel (Sofer) Tefilinsky. He lived in the suburb called Kerem, where he developed an overriding love for this precious mitzvah. Rav Nasanel was, according to everyone's estimate, a perfectionist of the highest order. After mastering all the laws pertaining to tefillin, he turned to the practical side of flawlessly producing them. First, he went to the slaughterhouse, where he chose a cow that had been slaughtered properly and was not found to have any halachic problems (i.e., not *treif*). The thick hide was set aside for the *battim*, the medium for tefillin straps, and the thin for parchment to write the *parshiyos* which would be placed inside the *battim*.

He took the hide home, where he worked on it, removing the hair and soaking it in a tanning solution. Using specially designed metal blocks, he pressed the thick hide and molded it slowly into shape. It took him an entire year to finish one pair.

Rav Nasanel was not the first to make *gassos* tefillin, but none before were perfect like his. Even the ink with which he wrote the *parshiyos* was prepared by him alone. A hundred years later, the quality of his ink is still readily apparent, the Hebrew letters radiating as if they had just been written!

When the Chofetz Chaim published the first volume of the *Mishnah Berurah* (which included the laws of tefillin), Rav Nasanel Tefilinsky sent him a pair of his tefillin for appraisal. The Chofetz Chaim sent back this reply: "These tefillin are flawless according to all the halachic authorities. They are made with every possible consideration for perfection, to the point that words cannot describe."

Soon orders came from all over the world, many more than he could ever possibly keep up with. The Munkacher Rebbe, Rav Chaim Elazar Shapiro, wrote: "In Jerusalem there is an exceptional craftsman, a tefillin maker, whose wondrous work I have seen... Both my father and I ordered from him tefillin — the beauty and halachic perfection of which I have never before witnessed. But he works very slowly and refuses to give precedence to one buyer over another... At the outbreak of the [First] World War, my father died, and the communication and transportation breakdown left no way to get them here."

Rav Nasanel died a year after the First World War, at the relatively young age of fifty-two. His "disciples" continued to produce high quality *gassos* tefillin, and today there is a vast industry producing them. Yet, for some reason, no one has ever attained the pinnacle of perfection that he reached with his.

(*MiGedolei Yerushalayim*, pp. 195–199)

Hideaways

IN APRIL, 1917, when the war had stretched out nearly three endless years, the Americans entered on the side of the British and Russians against Germany and Turkey. The sudden American participation brought immediate and piercing repercussions to the Middle East. In Eretz Yisrael and throughout the Ottoman Empire, orders were given to arrest and imprison all American citizens.

Since the beginning of the war, the mayor of Jerusalem, Jamil Pasha, had wielded the full authority of his power in menacing and cruel ways against the Jews of the city. People were liable to be imprisoned or exiled for the slightest violations of the law. The lives of everyone in the city were balanced on a precarious tightrope. Now, Jamil set out to expedite this new order with a vengeance.

Rav Tzvi Pesach Frank (1873–1960), as he appeared in 1918

A number of Jews, although of European stock, had American passports or visas. These people were now faced with drastic alternatives, each worse than the other. Some fled to farms outside the city, where Turkish police would have a difficult time finding them. Others chose to go into hiding in the cellars and attics of Jerusalem homes in order to remain closer to their families.

Rav Tzvi Pesach Frank, the future Rav of Jerusalem, came to Eretz Yisrael from Poland in 1892 on an American visa. He lived in the Old City with his wife and children, and refused to take either option.

The situation grew more threatening day by day. However, Rav Frank staunchly disregarded his wife's pleas to go into hiding. He felt it was important to be close to his family.

One morning Rav Menachem Sacks, his son-in-law, begged him, "If they catch you they will surely throw you into jail and expel you to Damascus. There, Heaven forbid, they might hang you. Please!" The young man spoke frantically. "Come with me right now!"

Rav Frank gave in to the urgent pleas of his son-in-law, and allowed himself to be led out of the house. Winding through the Old City, Menachem led him through little used back alleys, so as not to be seen on any of the main thoroughfares.

Seconds after they left, the Turkish police burst into the Frank home. When their search proved fruitless, they took Mrs. Frank into custody, as the mayor had directed. The screaming children did not stop them from shoving her out the front door and taking her to the Moslem Quarter, where she was placed in detention with other Jewish women.

Jamil Pasha's cunning usually paid off. By locking up wives of American citizens, he knew that the men would come out of hiding and give themselves up rather than have their wives suffer in jail. Mrs. Gita Malka Frank, however, secretly sent a message to her husband not to surrender. Jerusalem needed him.

Rav Tzvi Pesach Frank, a *dayan* on the Perushim *beis din*, heeded his wife's words of encouragement. During his weeks in hiding, he took advantage of the "opportunity" to study the laws of the Temple service in detail. Precisely at this time of utter darkness, half starved and estranged from mankind, he chose to delve into the light of the messianic times when the Third Temple would be rebuilt.

In the Moslem jail, more and more women were released every day, as their husbands yielded to the psychological pressure of imagined punishments their wives might suffer in prison.

At the beginning of Kislev, 1917, the remaining prisoners were marched outside and led under guard to the Damascus Gate, from where they would be taken to Syria. As the group passed the entrance to the Wittenberg courtyard, about a hundred meters from the Damascus Gate, Gita Malka dashed inside and disappeared into a vacant cellar. Fortunately, her disappearance was only realized later, after she had had time to find a better refuge.

For weeks both she and her husband remained in hiding, each in a different location. On the eve of Chanukah, Jamil surrendered to General Allenby, commander of the British forces. The fluttering white flag also meant that the Jewish fugitives were free to return home.

(*Masua l'Dor*, pp. 43–46)

The Draft Dodger

"THE TURKS are here!" yelled a woman. "Quick, let everyone know!"

An army van drove into the Shaarei Chesed neighborhood and stopped next to one of the synagogues. A group of armed soldiers got out along with a captain. Everyone knew the reason for the surprise raid. They were searching for Jewish evaders from the Turkish army. It was the height of the First World War and manpower was in special demand. The rabbis, however, had a different perspective on the war. Every Jew who entered the Turkish army had almost no chance of survival. Therefore, they endorsed a policy of draft dodging and desertion. This led to hideaways in both the Holy City and

Jewish soldiers in the Turkish army. Their fate, especially as Jews, was unknown.

throughout the country. In Jerusalem, the Shaarei Chesed neighborhood became an enclave for the "renegades." Similarly, the small settlement of Petach Tikva in the center of Eretz Yisrael was a popular refuge.

Without asking directions, the soldiers marched straight to Tevil's house. She was known as a kind lady who harbored fugitives, and within minutes they had their first captive. Yaakov Schwartz, twenty-four years old, who studied in a yeshivah full-time. Together with his wife and two small children, he lived with Tevil. The captain seized Yaakov and ordered his men to pack a few of his clothes. His wife screamed and cried.

Tevil stepped forward and spoke to the group in fluent Arabic. With a calm demeanor, she attempted to bribe them with twenty golden coins. However, the captain was a loyal supporter of his nation and would not budge.

"Well, then," she said matter-of-factly, "I invite you to a farewell meal for this young man. He is about to bid good-bye to his family and march to his destiny with his valiant Turkish countrymen!"

Still, her smile and warmth could not soften the rugged captain's military facade. Quickly, Tevil picked up Yaakov's three-month-old baby and hugged him in front of the Turkish captain. "Who knows when he will see his little baby again. Please, join us in this last meal before parting." This time he acceded to her wishes.

Within minutes the table was set with all kinds of sweets and cakes. From Reb Lipa's grocery they brought extra-strong beer and wine. Soon the soldiers were drinking liberally. The captain, however, partook only of the food but not of the intoxicating beverages, since it was forbidden by his religious creed.

In the meantime, Tevil organized dozens of neighbors to be on hand for the grand farewell procession. With the soldiers dead drunk, she raised her voice with a smile, "Everyone come inside and bid farewell to a loyal citizen of the country." Dozens of men squeezed into the room, hugging Yaakov and acting in a boisterous manner.

"Yaakov," she called, "please take your little baby and return him to the bedroom." As soon as Yaakov entered the second room, one of the neighbors was waiting with Arab garb in his hands. Within seconds Yaakov climbed out the window dressed as an Arab and mounted a waiting donkey. As he scurried away, Tevil kept talking to the captain in Arabic about the latest news from the front.

Within twenty-four hours, Yaakov was in Petach Tikva, safely outside the grasp of the captain and his soldiers.

(*Esara Doros b'Eretz Yisrael*, pp. 155–156)

Jamil's Reign of Terror

THE TRAGIC circumstances that overwhelmed Jerusalem during the First World War were augmented by the vicious edicts of the city's mayor, Jamil Pasha. Anyone could be arrested and imprisoned without having charges leveled against him. He could be chained and flogged without reason. Jamil's whims were the law of the land.

One of his favorite pastimes was to devise and implement new ordinances whose sole intent was to oppress the city's residents. Once he demanded that everyone walk on the right side of the street. Trespassers of the law would be executed. It was not uncommon for groups of soldiers to enter a neighborhood and arrest as many as fifty to sixty people at a time, including the elderly and sick. After having a rope tied around their arms to prevent them from escaping, these unfortunate victims were marched to police headquarters for interrogation. Fortunately, most of them were allowed to go home. Whenever a dead horse or mule had to be removed, a Jew was ordered to drag the carcass outside the city. Prominent Jews over forty-five years old, the age at which one became exempt from serving in the army, were forced to become city street sweepers and garbage collectors.

According to Turkish war law, any deserter or draft dodger could receive the death penalty. Jamil, in an apparent show of amnesty, gave seven days for all army deserters to return without any punishment. If they refused, or if anyone was caught hiding a deserter or draft dodger, both would be executed. There was no doubt that the pasha meant business; one morning, Jerusalemites woke up to find five deserters hanging next to the Jaffa Gate — three of whom were Jewish.

On the seventh day, Rav Sender Freidus, a young office worker at Ohel Moshe Yeshivah, knocked on Rav Moshe Blau's door.

"Please hide me," he pleaded. "Please!"

Rav Blau thought to himself, "What would Rav Yosef Chaim Zonnenfeld do in such a case?"

He then answered unhesitatingly, "Yes, you may come in, Sender. May the Lord protect us both."

When the police came to search his house for deserters, Rav Moshe let them inside. After a few tension-filled minutes, the police left without discovering the hideaway. Both Rav Moshe and Rav Sender gave thanks to the Almighty for saving them.

Not long afterwards, Rav Blau was walking along Jaffa Road on his way home to the Old City. It was Friday afternoon and the streets were nearly empty. Suddenly, a soldier approached him. Rav Moshe knew it could mean trouble, but he was not afraid. He carried with him a certificate of deferment which all scholars received, called a *visiko*, which he handed to the soldier. The soldier looked at it, but was not satisfied. Rav Moshe, fluent in Arabic, politely explained that he was a Jewish scholar, but the soldier, who only spoke Turkish, did not understand him.

The soldier held him by the arm and started to march him to the police headquarters at the Russian Compound. Using sign language, Rav Moshe tried to assure his captor that he would not escape, and asked him to release his hold. In response, the soldier only tightened his fist harder around Rav Moshe's arm and forcefully pulled him along.

When Rav Moshe stood before the jail captain, he was sure that he would be freed. However, the captain summarily had him led to a dark cell and locked up. He was shocked to find over thirty Arab criminals living there in filth, with not even enough room for everyone to sit on the floor. He immediately staggered over to the single, small window for air and cried for help. His voice echoed in the dark. A sense of shock fell upon him, and horrifying pictures of a terrible fate flashed through his mind. There was no room to sit, and he felt like he would soon faint.

Rav Moshe Blau (1886–1946)

An hour later, the dungeon door opened and a package of pitos was thrown inside. Each inmate received one of the round, flat pieces of bread. Rav Moshe, not yet on the list of prisoners, received nothing at all. One of the Arabs tore his pita in half and gave it to Rav Moshe, who thanked him profusely.

Another hour passed.

"Moshe! Moshe! Are you here?" someone called through the window. Rav Moshe looked up and saw Rav Nasanel Cohen.

"Yes, here I am!" shouted Rav Moshe.

"I've come to tell you that we know what happened to you and are making every effort to free you. Be patient."

An hour later, the dungeon door opened and Rav Blau was called to follow the jailer outside. Without any explanation, he was set free.

Rav Nasanel told him how they discovered his whereabouts and managed to have him freed so quickly. When the soldier was pulling him along Jaffa Road, a young child saw what was happening. Recognizing who he was, and understanding what was happening, the boy quickly ran and told Rav Moshe's father what he had seen. The elder Rav Blau sent one person to search for his son, and another to the Austrian embassy to plead with the consul to help facilitate Rav Moshe's release.

Rav Moshe listened. "One can never reckon the ways of Heaven," he said. "Had the soldier understood me and let me walk unguarded to the Russian Compound, the lad would never have suspected that I was really in custody and about to be imprisoned. How much more would I have suffered! Blessed is the Lord, who watches over His people always."

(*Al Chomosaich Yerushalayim*, pp. 60–63)

The Father-Son Relationship

SHMUEL BINYAMIN lay deathly ill in his hospital bed. For weeks his condition had deteriorated and now, Friday morning, it took a turn for the worse. The thirty-five-year-old tzaddik was the apple of his father's eye, full of potential to become a great rabbi for the community.

Sitting by his bedside was his father, holding a book of Psalms in his hand. He rocked back and forth and whispered the melodious Psalms which he hoped would reach the firmaments and awaken Divine mercy. Every now and then he glanced at his son and lovingly grasped his hand.

Shmuel Binyamin was barely conscious. It seemed that the Heavenly Gates would not open, and both father and son realized they would soon depart from one another. As the afternoon sun lowered past the western hills of Jerusalem, Shmuel Binyamin stopped breathing. His father, having already buried a number of his children over the past forty years, controlled his emotions as he gently closed his son's eyes. In a solemn tone, he and all those present intoned the verse: "Hear O Israel, the Lord your God, the Lord is One."

It was 6 Iyar, 1917 (5677). The hour was late, and mothers were about to light their Shabbos candles. Since it was impossible to bury Shmuel Binyamin before Shabbos, his father quickly arranged to have people at the Bikur Cholim Hospital say Psalms in his son's room. He then briskly walked to his home in the Battei Machse section of the Jewish Quarter.

At home he quickly donned his Shabbos attire, and shrugged off the inquiries about Shmuel Binyamin, saying, "Hashem is merciful." At the synagogue, he sat in his regular seat and prayed with the same devotion as always. After Maariv, many congregants passed by, and to each one he smiled and wished a "Good Shabbos."

Even at home, he did not give the slightest hint that something was amiss. He sang with his resonant voice and discussed the weekly Torah portion with his family members.

At the end of Shabbos, immediately following the Maariv service, he could no longer restrain himself and fainted in the shul. Men rushed to his side. "*Rabbeinu!*" one called out. Another bent over and saw his color return. "Are you all right, Rav Zonnenfeld?" he asked. Rav Yosef Chaim Zonnenfeld sat in a chair for a few minutes and mournfully recounted what had happened.

As head of the burial society, Rav Yosef Chaim insisted on taking part in the ritual purification of his son's body. When cautioned that it might injure his health, he responded: "How can a man offer a sacrifice [in the Temple] without standing beside it?"

After the arduous funeral procession to the Mount of Olives, the mourners returned to the Old City. Along the way, a prominent secularist stepped out in front of them.

"*Shavuah Tov!*" he callously called out to the group. Turning to Rav Yosef Chaim, he let forth a biting comment, "Now, Rav Chaim, you must admit that you have been punished by Heaven for fighting against us so vehemently!"

The tasteless and arrogant words seemed to freeze in the air. Rav Zonnenfeld looked at his assailant and answered in a firm voice, "You are completely right! I have been punished from Heaven! But your reason is wrong. It is because I've not done more in the fight against you and your fellow secularists who have cut down the tree of Torah and profaned the commandments. Most of all, I've been punished for not taking up the fight earlier and with more zealousness."

Without another word, Rav Yosef Chaim Zonnenfeld proceeded homeward. In the darkness of night, Rav Yosef Chaim meditated on the fond memories of his dear son, may he rest in peace.

(*Mara d'Arah Yisrael*, vol. 3, pp. 27–29)

In Honor of the King

ON 21 SIVAN, 1917 (5677), when the Emperor Franz Joseph died, the Jewish world joined in the mourning. He had been a righteous king, a seeker of peace, and one who befriended the Jewish people. During his visit to Jerusalem in 1869, for instance, he donated a thousand gold napoleons towards the construction of the Tiferes Yisrael Synagogue.

In Jerusalem, Rav Yosef Chaim Zonnenfeld eulogized the Emperor. Following are some excerpts from his speech.

....With the departure of our Emperor and loving king, let us relate a small parable. Once there was a father who lovingly gave himself over to his children. He worked hard to amass wealth for his children throughout his lifetime. When his time came to leave this world and return to where he came from, he called his children to gather around him.

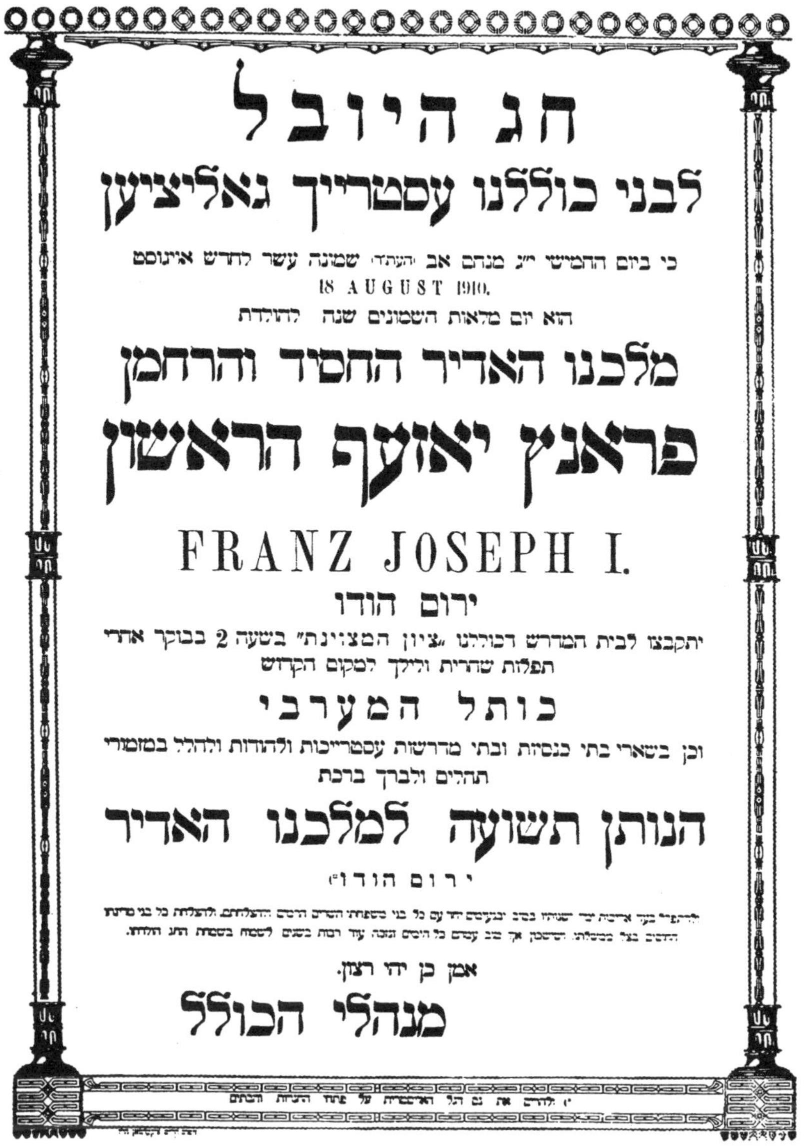

חג היובל

לבני כוללנו עסטרייך גאליציען

כי ביום החמישי י"ג מנחם אב העתדי שמונה עשר לחדש אויגוסט

18 AUGUST 1910.

הוא יום מלאות השמונים שנה להולדת

מלכנו האדיר החסיד והרחמן

פראנץ יאזעף הראשון

FRANZ JOSEPH I.

ירום הודו

יתקבצו לבית המדרש דכוללנו „ציון המצוינת" בשעה 2 בבוקר אחרי תפלות שחרית ולילך למקום הקדוש

כותל המערבי

וכן בשארי בתי כנסיות ובתי מדרשות עסטרייכות ולהודות ולהלל במזמורי תהלים ולברך ברכת

הנותן תשועה למלכנו האדיר

ירום הודו

אמן כן יהי רצון.

מנהלי הכולל

Announcement calling on members of the Austro-Galician Kollel to pray together at the Kosel on the 80th birthday of Emperor Franz Joseph (18 August, 1910 [5670]) for his continued longevity.

"I am about to leave you," he said to them. "My dearest children, everything that I possess I leave to you. Also, I have appointed a diligent man to replace me, who will honestly continue my work. He shall guide you for your betterment. One thing, though, you must always remember. Be honest with him, be eager to relate to him, and be responsible to him."

The children wholeheartedly swore to their father to abide by his wishes.

Soon thereafter, he went on to his reward. Although the children had drawn some encouragement and comfort from his parting words, they mourned and cried profusely, with tears streaming down their faces.

This is our situation today. With his passing, the father of our homeland has left everything to us. Even the garments that he wore he did not take with him — neither his clothes nor the body which garbed his soul; these he left with us. Yet the "I" has disappeared and is no more.

The children remain and weep, surrounding the garment. Still, they intensely feel devoted to his replacement...

There is another point I wish to recall about his Highness. Our Emperor constantly endeavored to withdraw himself as much as possible from conflicts in order to strengthen peace. He could not stand to see bloodshed....

Now the time has come, for us who are gathered here, to pray that his soul should rest in peace. We should recite the appropriate Psalms with feeling, tearfully, at this hour when his soul has left us and his body is being brought to its final resting place. Let our tears be considered as a last gesture of a gift-offering before the Almighty, as our Sages say that they are collected and stored away in a holy chest. Like precious stones, these tears glisten in the wreath of praise that is bound from the good deeds of the one who has left us to go to the world of truth....

May it be His will that He shall fulfill soon the prophecy that in the future God shall wipe away the tears from everyone's face, and with a united heart and mind, God shall transform everyone, and peace shall rule between all parties and nations. Amen.

(*Mara d'Arah Yisrael*, vol. 1, pp. 194–195)

20th Century
Birth Pangs of the Ancient City

Part II
The British Mandate Period: 1918-1948

The Jewish people asked God, "Jerusalem and Your people are in a state of disgrace to everyone around, won't You redeem us?"
"Yes," He replied.
"Swear to us," they said.
And this is the oath which He swore, "Just as He redeemed them from Egypt, so He will redeem them from Edom."

Midrash Rabbah (Exodus 15:18)

Post-World War I

In the wake of the World War, a series of socio-political upheavals were unleashed that would transform the entire globe. To give but one example, the Bolshevik Revolution segregated a vast segment of mankind behind the Iron Curtain. Locked inside were three million Jews, whose future identity as members of the Jewish faith was put in danger by the atheist banner of Communism.

In a wider sense, people around the world experienced a surge of awakening. Marxism developed into Communism, and Darwinism uprooted religious tradition and supplanted it with agnosticism. In the realm of the intellect, Freudian thought opened a Pandora's box that seemed to promise a total restructuring of interpersonal relationships, and would completely change how we view the world of the mind.

All of this multidimensional change took place against a backdrop of rapid technical transformation that stripped the world of its ignorance. The telephone, radio, movie camera, automobile, and airplane made the steamship and telegraph seem primitive in comparison. Mankind lived on a smaller planet, which created a need for coexistence that was greater than ever. Recognition of this fact paved the way for the League of Nations, which was the forerunner of the United Nations.

The Jewish World After World War I[1]

The Jew was thrust into turbulent times that buffeted him from all directions. On the one side, the scars of the war were a painful reminder of something the entire world hoped would never be repeated. The carnage and economic collapse was simply too heavy a price for what basically amounted to a large-scale territorial war. The search for peace and stability required an openness and willingness on everyone's part to adapt to a new, universal era. On the other side, Judaism had to address the issues of the times in order to withstand the temptations that this new world presented.

To complicate matters, a prewar Jewish movement devoid of Torah and mitzvos gained credence in the eyes of more and more Jews around the world.

Zionism hoisted its flag on the ideology of a national homeland for the "wandering Jews" scattered across the globe. At first, its proponents did not even necessarily envision such a homeland in the land of their birthright, Eretz Yisrael. Incredibly, at the sixth Zionist Congress in 1906, the African country of Uganda was proposed as a suitable location. However, the movement's young founders quickly readjusted their sights and proclaimed the land of their forefathers as their natural home.

The First World War was a crucial period for the formation of the Zionist movement. In England, Dr. Chaim Weizmann's scientific experiments in the field of ammunition led him into contact with British politicians. Together with other political and religious Zionists, such as Nachum Sokolov and Rav Kook, a united front lobbied for a national homeland in the name of the entire Jewish people.

The British foreign minister, Lord Arthur James Balfour, was among those influential politicians who rallied to the Jewish cause. On 2 November (17 Cheshvan), 1917, just weeks before the surrender of Turkish troops in Jerusalem, he issued the famous Balfour Declaration. It proclaimed the intent of the British government to help establish a homeland for the Jews in Palestine. However, it added the important caveat that such an establishment was only viable so long as it did not discriminate against the local non-Jewish population.

Jewish reaction to the Balfour Declaration was heavily one-sided in favor of the "voice of redemption." After centuries of persecutions and suffering, Jews rallied to the call and beamed with a new spirit of independence. Naturally, the Zionists, who were greatly responsible for this major breakthrough, deemed themselves the heirs to the Jewish homeland.* Their vision centered on the motto: One can be a good Jew without the limitations of a Heavenly Father Who commands him to keep six hundred and thirteen commandments. It was enough to join the effort to build the land of Palestine and create a country where Jews were free to act as an independent nation just like all the other nations of the world. Such a country would separate religion from state and pattern its constitution after the ones enjoyed by the enlightened countries of the Western world. The only real difference between this state and any other one on the planet was that here a Jew could live and build a society in cooperation with other Jews without the threat of anti-Semitism.

* In 1922, the famous Russian journalist, Hillel Zeitlin, interviewed Rav Zonnenfeld. He asked: "Maybe the *chareidim* have no right to the Jewish Agency, since the Balfour Declaration was accomplished through Zionist efforts?"

Rav Zonnenfeld answered with a parable: "Once a *shadchan* [matchmaker] succeeded in reuniting a couple who had been divorced for some time. After their remarriage, the *shadchan* knocked on their door and claimed as his service charge the right to live in their home. Was the *shadchan* right in his claim? No! So, too, in the case in hand: the Torah promised us the Land of Israel on condition they we fulfill all the commandments. When we sinned, we were exiled from the Land. Now that the Zionists played the role of a *shadchan* to encourage a world power to return Eretz Yisrael to the Jews, does that entitle them to sleep in the palace of the King?"

Foreign Office,
November 2nd, 1917.

Dear Lord Rothschild,

I have much pleasure in conveying to you, on behalf of His Majesty's Government, the following declaration of sympathy with Jewish Zionist aspirations which has been submitted to, and approved by, the Cabinet.

"His Majesty's Government view with favour the establishment in Palestine of a national home for the Jewish people, and will use their best endeavours to facilitate the achievement of this object, it being clearly understood that nothing shall be done which may prejudice the civil and religious rights of existing non-Jewish communities in Palestine, or the rights and political status enjoyed by Jews in any other country".

I should be grateful if you would bring this declaration to the knowledge of the Zionist Federation.

The Balfour Declaration

Most Orthodox leaders quickly perceived the dangers inherent in the Balfour Declaration. The formation of such a state would surely be controlled by the Zionists, who openly advocated the uprooting of traditional Judaism as the first step of nationhood. The Belzer Rebbe, Rav Issacher Dov Rokeach, said: "Woe unto the Jewish people for the Balfour Declaration!" This view was shared by many *rabbanim*. However, the Orthodox leadership stopped short of actually defaming the declaration, which would appear as being ungrateful to a world power that did not fully grasp the intricate religious implications involved.

Other leaders, like Rav Tzvi Pesach Frank, who headed the Perushim *beis din* in Jerusalem from 1918 to 1958, urged his students to study the laws of the Temple service. "Now that we see the signs of the redemption...it is certainly recommended for scholars to study these laws."[2]

Rav Zonnenfeld, on the other hand, expressed this view: "If we had the power, we would ordain a new day of mourning over Jerusalem and call for the public reading of *tikun chatzos* [prayers recited at midnight over the destruction of the Temple], in order to shed additional tears over this third destruction of Jerusalem and the Temple."

For some time after the British took control of the Holy City, the bell-chimes over the promise to create a Jewish homeland drowned out the cries of starving Jerusalemites. A popular parable of the day described a wonderful wedding in which the two fathers embraced and returned each and every guest's wishes of *mazal tov*. The bride and groom, however, were left without any food or drink in their private room after the long day fast, which brought them to tears. Only when they fainted did someone remember to bring them food. Thus, the Jewish world was overjoyed with the trumpeting of the Balfour Declaration as at a wedding. But in their merriment, they forgot the poor scholars and starving families of Jerusalem.[3]

The Era of British Rule

The British takeover of Jerusalem in 1917 (5678), and the rest of Eretz Yisrael in 1918, launched a thirty-year period of governorship in Palestine. Being the first Western power to control the Middle East, they naturally instituted many reforms in the physical and civil makeup of the country.

Jerusalem, the largest city under their rule, became the capital of the country during the Mandate period, a distinction it had not had since the Bar Kochba rebellion against the Romans in 130 C.E. From 1918 to 1920, the country was ruled exclusively by a military governor, Sir Ronald Storrs. From 1920 to 1948, in addition to the military governor, there were seven High Commissioners who served as the supreme representatives of the British government. The first, Sir Herbert Samuels, was a Jew who prayed at the Churvah Synagogue in the Old City during the festivals. He served from 1920 to 1925. The last, Sir Alan Cunningham, served from 1945 to 1948.

The first reform, to which the British

British Mandate currency

gave top priority, was to improve the water supply to the Holy City. Not long before the war, the Turkish government succeeded in piping in water from the south, around 150,000 liters (40,000 gallons) per day. Still, that quantity was not adequate to serve the robust population of seventy-five thousand souls.

In 1918, the British laid a pipeline from Solomon's Pools in the south to a reservoir in the Jerusalem suburb of Romema. With the use of an electric pump and purifying equipment, it provided seven times the amount of water the city previously had, and was the first substantial and uninterrupted water supply in two thousand years. During the 1930s more pumping stations were set up, and in 1936 a major source came from the Rosh Ha'ayin springs on the coast.

The same year, 1918, the British widened and re-laid the narrow-gauge railroad tracks, so as to update this vital means of transportation to and from the coast. The new railroad remained in used until the late 1990s, when parts of it were upgraded.

City planning began in stages. In the spring of 1918, Sir Ronald Storrs, the military governor, forbade the destruction of all ancient and historical sites. To safeguard the esthetic motif of the Old City, he forbade the use of iron in roofing within the walled city, thereby retaining the tradition of vaulted roofs. Building permits throughout the city were issued on condition that the outer wall of buildings be made of Jerusalem stone. This, too, was done to preserve the flavor of the Holy City.

In 1921, the British civil authorities established a commission to draft a zoning plan for the city. The British

Sir Winston Churchill (right) with the first High Commissioner, Sir Herbert Samuels, at a tree planting ceremony on Mount Scopus

Colonial Secretary, Sir Winston Churchill, made an official visit at that time. The following year the commission issued its proposal, which reserved the area surrounding the Old City as a park zone. This included wide areas to the south and east reaching to Mount Scopus, and north to Nachalas Shiva and the Russian Compound. Two major areas, one stretching along the last kilometer of the railroad line and the other between Jaffa Road and Malchei Yisrael

Street, were zoned for industry.

In keeping with their sensitivity to Mid-Eastern architecture, the British ordered changes in the walls around the Old City. The most significant one was the dismantling of the imposing clock tower above the Jaffa Gate. Originally built in 1905 in honor of the Sultan, it rose high over the ramparts of the city, and was believed to interrupt the "line" of the ancient wall. Outside the same gate they demolished the large water fountain that had been built concurrently with the clock tower.

In addition to an array of government and military buildings throughout the city, the British built the central post office on Jaffa Road and the Rockefeller Museum. In the early 1930s, the King David Hotel and the YMCA were built.

Immigration laws were established which set the stage for a new wave of both Jewish and Arab immigration. To give an example of the scope of this immigration, forty thousand Jews and twenty thousand Arabs settled in Jerusalem between 1931 and 1944. This influx came about despite a series of "white papers" which attempted to curtail Jewish immigration and forced illegal means of bringing new immigrants ashore.

The official census of 1921 and 1931 graphically depicts the surge in population.

1922	*Jews*	*Arabs*	*Christians*	*Total*
Jerusalem	34,000	13,500	14,500	**62,000**
Old City	5,500	9,500	7,000	**22,000**
1931				
Jerusalem	54,000	20,000	19,500	**93,500**
Old City	5,200	12,200	7,700	**25,100**

For the Sake of Jerusalem

Perhaps the most crucial period in Jerusalem's history since the destruction of the Temple took place during the formative years of the British Mandate. A tug-of-war between two Jewish camps, one the Zionists and the other the established Orthodox, was dividing the city. The ramifications of this struggle had a direct effect on Jewry at large.

*The Rise of Zionism in Eretz Yisrael**

In the beginning of 1918, three months after the British takeover, a delegation of Zionists came to Palestine. Their mission was to save Jewish institutions which had crumbled during the war. Led by Dr. Chaim Weizmann, the delegation included representatives from England, France, and America. They brought with them a letter of recommendation to General Allenby, as well as large sums of money earmarked for needy causes.

Their purpose was to take control of three pivotal areas of Jewish society: education, congregational life, and the Rabbinate. Using Jaffa (Tel Aviv) as their home base, they set out to conquer the stronghold of Jerusalem.

The Zionists devised a different strategy to besiege the citadel of education than had their predecessors. Whereas the proponents of the enlightenment sought to add a few seemingly innocuous topics like science and language to the curriculum, the Zionists' objective was to make Hebrew the language of the land.

The ancient tongue of the Jewish people became the banner of the Zionist cause in the early days of the movement. Their whole cultural edifice of body over spirit, imitation of gentile customs, and integrating men with women was welded together with the national language.

However, the Hebrew advocated by the Zionists was not the unadulterated Holy Tongue of Scripture, the Talmud, and rabbinic writing — commonly referred to as classical Hebrew. Rather, they infused many words with foreign sources, which resulted in the modern Hebrew spoken in Israel today. This influx of gentile words to bolster the an-

* It is beyond the scope of this work to present anything more than a sketch of *some* of the complex issues at stake. The English reader is referred to *Guardian of Jerusalem* for a more thorough scrutiny of the subject.

cient tongue severed it from its source and reduced it to an invented language. Rav Zonnenfeld lamented the fact that the earliest Perushim settlers, a hundred years before, had not adapted Hebrew as had the Sephardim, and instituted Hebrew as the language of Eretz Yisrael. The Zionists would then have been deprived of a powerful tool.

Rav Shmuel Salant compared the use of Hebrew to the use of wine. Wine, which is used to sanctify the Shabbos and Holidays, loses its kosher status when touched by a gentile or by a Jew who publicly profanes the Shabbos. Similarly, the Holy tongue, once used by the Zionists, was no longer the sacred Hebrew language.

When Weizmann came to Jerusalem, he saw the scars of war wherever he went. He personally met with directors of various yeshivos and educational institutions, and noted the grinding poverty under which they labored. His offer of conditional aid was quite tempting: the Zionists would completely finance the revitalization of the yeshivos if they would agree to come under the jurisdiction of a Zionist committee based in Eretz Yisrael. If they refused, he threatened to withhold all backing.

The haggard Jewish survivors of the war heard out Weizmann's proposal. It was true that the British conquest brought an air of relief and the hope of a promising future. However, in practical terms, the populace was still hovering between life and death, suffering from extreme economic privation. As a result, some were willing to consider his offer. The Institute for the Blind, under the auspices of secular directors, accepted without hesitation.

The yeshivos turned to Rav Zonnenfeld for guidance. His answer was an emphatic "No!" He explained that Jewish education was the key to the preservation of authentic Judaism and must not be compromised.

In the face of Rav Zonnenfeld's unwavering opposition, Weizmann called for an emergency meeting at the home of Rav Yitzchak Yerucham Diskin, where he retracted some of his demands. Attending the meeting were Rav Zonnenfeld, the members of the *beis din,* and the heads of the major institutions. Weizmann agreed that the money could flow into the institutions without Zionist control. However, he insisted that Hebrew be the language of instruction in every *talmud Torah*. If they still refused his offer, he warned them, the Zionist movement would blacken the name of the institutions throughout the world.

Rav Zonnenfeld was not to be intimidated. He firmly answered, "The Torah institutions are ours. No one in the world will force us to change against our will what we feel is the right system of education."[4]

Denied of his goal, Weizmann stormed away from the meeting and temporarily returned to Jaffa. However, he was not yet ready to admit defeat. On 2 Sivan, 1918, he called a meeting of all the city's school teachers (rebbes), to be held in the Etz Chaim Yeshivah. These teachers were from the most impoverished segment of the populace. Again, Weizmann eloquently reiterated his compromise: the money would be under the yeshivah's control, as well as the subjects to be taught. He only asked that they consent to one thing — that Hebrew be the spoken language. He left the hall so that they could discuss his plan privately.

In the middle of their discussion, the head rebbe of Talmud Torah Shomrei HaChomos, Rav Avraham Aharon Prague, interrupted them. "*Rabossi!* My comrades! I'm surprised that you are even debating the matter. Didn't we receive these children from Hashem and their parents as a deposit, in order to teach them? They don't want any change in the traditional educational system. Do we have the right to alter it just because of our economic suffering? Therefore, I recommend that we all say 'No.'"[5]

Rav Prague's emotional plea saved the yeshivos from succumbing to Weizmann's plan. For the time being, all of the Zionist leader's offensives had been rebuffed. After four months, he was forced to hand over the money to the Jerusalem institutions with no strings attached.

Over the coming generations, the burning issue of Hebrew as the national language slowly cooled down. In the 1950s, someone once brought up the subject with the Chazon Ish. He chided the questioner, saying that the war over Hebrew had been lost and was no longer an issue.

Weizmann versus Rav Zonnenfeld

Dr. Weizmann correctly perceived that the man who reigned over the Jerusalem *yishuv* was Rav Yosef Chaim Zonnenfeld. He personally met with Rav Zonnenfeld several times at his house in Battei Machse, where he engaged the Rav in lengthy debates. Though Rav Yosef Chaim was diametrically opposed to his opinions and beliefs, he never ordered Weizmann out of his house.

In the midst of one particularly stormy debate, Rav Yosef Chaim suddenly asked, "What is your profession?"

"I'm a chemist," Weizmann replied warily.

"Well, then," continued the sage, "as a scientist, could you please explain to me why man was created without hair on the palm of his hand?"

Weizmann reeled. With major questions concerning the fate of the entire Jewish people hinging on their conversation, the revered leader of the *yishuv* was posing a nonsensical question!

Rav Yosef Chaim filled the silence with an answer: "Perhaps this is to hint to us that a person should be careful about the cleanness of his hands!"[6]

At another meeting, Weizmann tried to convince Rav Yosef Chaim that the small innovations he sought in the educational system were harmless.

"You are a man of the world," Rav Zonnenfeld said. "Could you tell me why every nation keeps a standing army, at such expense, even though they rarely need to go out and fight?"

"Of course," replied Weizmann. "The whole time they are preparing themselves and building their courage for the eventuality of battle...."

"Precisely," interrupted Rav Yosef Chaim. "And the same holds true for our children in yeshivos. We are preparing them and instilling in them the courage to battle for the sanctify of Jerusalem — which you are trying to uproot."[7]

Dr. Weizmann wrote about his staunch enemy in these words: "He claims that Orthodox Jews came to Eretz Yisrael decades before us [the Zionists], sailing on small crafts after extended pe-

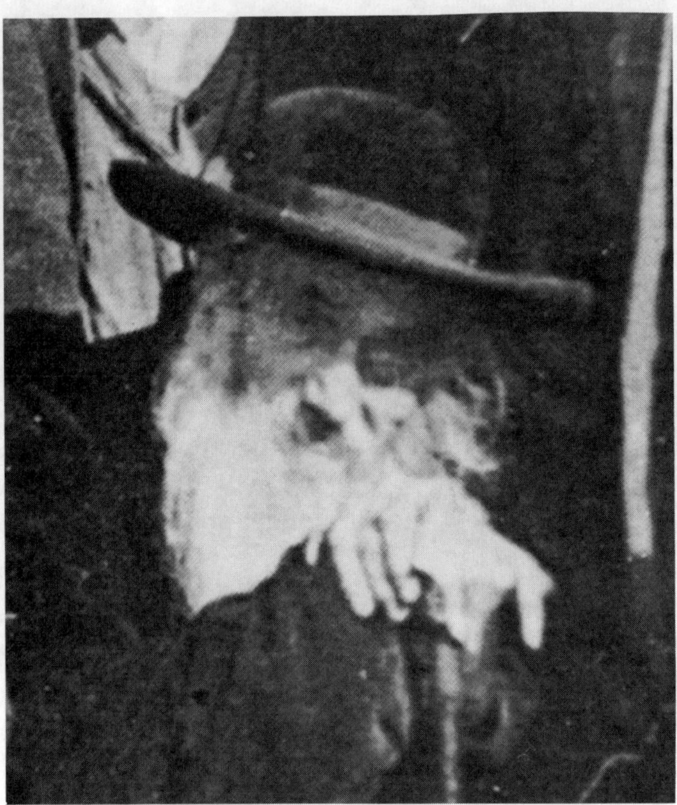

Rav Yosef Chaim Zonnenfeld (1851–1932)

riods of wandering. Then they had to ride for days on donkeys, camels, or by foot until they reached Jerusalem. In Jerusalem it sometimes took weeks until they found proper shelter. [Thus, from beginning to end,] their pathway to Eretz Yisrael was filled with suffering. But we [the Zionists] began to come only when travel became comfortable, by ship and rail. Thus, in his opinion, the spiritual leadership belongs to the *chareidi* camp."

In a telegram to London, Weizmann captured the essence of their duel with these words: "As long as Rav Zonnenfeld is alive, we have no possibility of controlling education in Jerusalem."

At the end of Tamuz, 1918 (5678), Dr. Weizmann returned to England with deep antireligious sentiments implanted in his heart.

Chief Rabbinate

Re-examining their objectives, Weizmann and his colleagues changed their strategy. Instead of concentrating on education, they aimed higher and moved the battlefront to the arena of the rabbinical leaders. If they could persuade some prominent religious leaders in Eretz Yisrael to side with them and establish a new rabbinate, then Jews everywhere would side with the newly united Zionist-religious front.

In December, 1918, Weizmann returned from London to implement the plan. His vision was grandiose — a Su-

The first Chief Rabbis, Rav Yaakov Meir (left) and Rav Avraham Kook (right)

preme Rabbinical Council that would eventually become the universal authority in Jewish law, similar to the Sanhedrin in the times of the Talmud. Its authority would include an appeals court for considering decisions made by other "lower" rabbinical courts.

The plan caused a storm among rabbis everywhere. Especially controversial was the concept of an appeals court, which, according to many opinions went against the Talmudic ruling (*Bava Basra* 138b) that one rabbinical court may not question the proceedings of another one.

In the end, Weizmann established a Rabbinate Office (*Misrad HaRabbanut*) which included such members as Rav Chaim Moshe Elyashar and Rav Eliyahu Panijal of the Sephardic *rabbanim*. Rav Tzvi Pesach Frank and Rav Yona Rom of the Perushim also joined, as well as Rav David Lippman Shuvaks and Rav Fishel Bernstein of the Chassidic *beis din*. The fact that such notable rabbinical figures were willing to join ranks with the Zionists, for whatever reasons, was a mark of success for Weizmann.[8] He immediately sought to capitalize on their participation by seeking official recognition from the British government as the sole religious body in the Holy City. However, the Orthodox City Council (*Vaad HaIr*), the representative body of *chareidi* Jewry in Jerusalem, defended its right to exist and successfully thwarted this aspect of Weizmann's plan.

After an abortive attempt to unite all *rabbanim* at a national convention in Iyar, 1919 (5679), the Rabbinate Office slowly dissolved. Eventually, in 1921, it was supplanted by the Chief Rabbinate.

At this point in time, the Orthodox community of Jerusalem was divided into moderate (Central Committee) and right wing (Orthodox City Council) factions. This division was not surprising when one considers how diverse the population had become by that time.

Still, everyone perceived the need for a Rav of Jerusalem to lead them. The Central Committee secretly offered the post to Rav Avraham Kook, who declined. When word of this attempt became public, the Orthodox City Council pleaded with Rav Yosef Chaim to accept the post, but he refused. Instead, on Sivan 23, 1919, he and Rav Diskin were made honorary presidents of the council. Soon the council became known as the *Eidah Chareidis,* a name it retains until today. They built their own *beis din*, and a strong independent communal and institutional structure.

A month later, Rav Kook wrote the Central Committee that he had decided to accept their offer to become Rav of Jerusalem. He left England at the end of Av and arrived in Jerusalem at the beginning of Elul, 1919.

Knowing that his appointment was controversial, he reiterated his stand that his move to the Holy City was in the capacity of a private individual, and not as a *rav*. Only four months later, on 8 Teves, did he officially accept the post of Rav of Jerusalem.

Four and a half months after Rav Kook's acceptance, in Iyar, 1920 (5680), in a dramatic scene at Rav Zonnenfeld's home in Battei Machse, Rav Diskin forced Rav Yosef Chaim to become Rav of Jerusalem.

A year later, in 1921, Rav Kook accepted the invitation of the Zionists to become the first Ashkenazic Chief Rabbi of Eretz Yisrael. Rav Yaakov Meir became the first Sephardic Chief Rabbi. The election convention saw an acrimonious battle between anti-religious Zionists and national religious members like Rav Kook. Only after many meetings and painful arguments did a Chief Rabbinate (*Rabbanut HaReshit*) come into existence. The background which led Orthodox rabbis like Rav Kook to join forces with radically anti-religious Jews — with deep repercussions for modern-day society — is a subject that demands scrutiny.

Torah and Eretz Yisrael

Throughout the centuries of *galus*, most Jews lived in the Diaspora. As discussed earlier, only a few large-scale (for those days) immigrations succeeded in forging their way to the Holy Land. They were the Baalei Tosefos in the twelfth century, Rav Yehudah HaChassid and his followers in 1699, and the Chassidic aliyah of 1777.

The influx of Ashkenazim at the turn of the nineteenth century marked a new era, both quantitatively and qualitatively. The driving force behind the Perushim was the vision of their master, the Gaon of Vilna, who perceived in their actions a significant step towards the messianic era. By the mid-nineteenth century, the Jewish presence in Jerusalem outnumbered that of the gentiles.

Later in the nineteenth century, Rav Tzvi Kalisher, a disciple of Rav Akiva Eiger who lived in Europe, renewed efforts to strengthen the *yishuv*. His initial attempt consisted of writing to famous Jewish philanthropists in order to enlist their aid. He was encouraged in this endeavor by such notable *rabbanim* as Rav David Friedman of Karlin, Rav Yaakov Ettlinger, Rav Yitzchak Elchanan Spector, and Rav Shimon Sofer of Cracow. In the

Rav Tzvi Kalisher (1795–1876)

course of time, Rav Kalisher developed and propagated an elaborate messianic scheme. In his book, *Drishas Tzyon*, he enumerated a threefold plan: a great influx of Jews to Eretz Yisrael, working the Land, and building an altar on the Temple Mount where sacrifices could be offered.

Rav Kalisher's novel, full-scale approach met with mixed reaction among the *rabbanim* of the time. Most of the above-mentioned leaders objected to his plan. Some feared that a massacre might result at the hands of the Turkish ruling power if they suspected the Jewish people of rebelling against them due to an increase in immigration. Others felt that there was no halachic basis for bringing sacrifices until the Mashiach came and rebuilt the Temple.

The *rabbanim* in Jerusalem also opposed his scheme. In 1863 (5623), Rav Meir Auerbach, the Rav of Jerusalem, wrote a lengthy letter which emphasized the first objection of potential reprisals from the Sultan against mass immigration. Later, other *rabbanim* voiced even stronger disapproval. Besides the rebuttals against increased immigration and offering sacrifices, farming the land of Eretz Yisrael also met with strong resistance. This was because working the land necessitated a knowledge of the laws associated with Eretz Yisrael — *terumah, maaser, shemitah*, etc. — which could easily be profaned by secular farmers.

During this same period, the secular organization Alliance Israelite Universelle (Kyach) of France was interested in establishing agricultural settlements in the Holy Land. Rav Kalisher worked with the group when they opened the Mikve Yisrael farm near Jaffa in 1870. A few years later they offered him the position of *rav* of the settlement, which he happily accepted. In 1876, while preparing for the journey to the Holy Land, Rav Kalisher passed away.

Lovers of Zion

At the same time, a new movement called Lovers of Zion (Chovavei Tzyon) initiated what was later called the First Wave of immigrants to Eretz Yisrael (1881–1903). Intended as a religious aliyah, it quickly became overrun with secular Jews. After the death of Rav Kalisher, Rav Naftali Tzvi Berlin headed the movement to prevent the Reform from taking control of it, but was unable to withstand a dominating secular influence.

1883 (5643) was a decisive year for the movement. Rav Shmuel Mohliver and Rav Yehudah Elkalai founded the Yishuv Eretz Yisrael Society, focused on religious settlement in the Holy Land. A rift between the Chovavei Tzyon movement, now completely secular, and the religious Zionists reached the breaking point when Nechemiah Natenson claimed that the religious wanted to control Eretz Yisrael. In 1887 an attempt was made to heal the rift, but rabbis like the Netziv and Rav Spector flatly refused.

Orthodox rabbis who agreed, at least in part, with Rav Kalisher's ideas, were eager to continue efforts to built up Eretz Yisrael. Since the Zionist movement could not be a vehicle for them due to its secular bent, they started their own organization in 1902, called the Mizrachi Movement. Their founder was Rav Yitzchak Reines, the Rav of Lida, Lithuania. The word Mizrachi was a fusion of two Hebrew words, *merkaz ha'ruchani*, the "central religious" movement. It provided expression for religious Jews who aspired to similar views as the Zionists regarding the settlement of Eretz Yisrael — with the major difference that it was based on fulfillment of the Torah and commandments.

Rav Avraham Yitzchak Kook was later viewed as the spiritual mentor of the Mizrachis. As a young genius at the Volohzin Yeshivah in the 1880s, Rav Avraham was seen as having the potential to be a great teacher of his people. At the yeshivah he befriended the more progressive students and began writing poetry in eloquent Hebrew. After his marriage to the daughter of the Rav of Ponevitch, the Aderes, he moved to Boisk, where he became very close with the *rav* of the city, Rav Mordechai Elishberg. Rav Elishberg was a prominent leader in the Chovavei Tzyon Movement. Following his death in 1900, Rav Kook replaced him as Rav of Boisk. Soon afterwards, his father-in-law moved to Jerusalem to assist Rav Salant as Rav of Jerusalem.

In 1904 (5664), Rav Kook accepted the post of Rav of Jaffa, which had become vacant the previous year with the death of Rav Naftali Hertz HaLevi. Rav Kook's charismatic personality captivated both religious and non-religious Jews. Jaffa was the center of Zionistic activities in Eretz Yisrael, and within no time he gained firsthand knowledge of the "new *yishuv*." The Second Wave of large-scale immigration, mostly irreligious Jews, was between 1904–1914. Rav Kook saw a tremendous paradox in the Jewish youth that comprised this influx: they came to sacrifice themselves to build the Holy Land without any religious inspiration whatsoever, combining a heretical philosophy with an unmatched idealism.

He strongly felt that the two types of Jews — religious and secular — were really two sides of the same coin and could each benefit from forming an alliance. During the years prior to the First World War, Rav Kook developed and expanded his philosophy of Torah and Eretz Yisrael. He wrote that building up and settling the Land atoned for all sins. His views met with opposition from a number of *rabbanim* in Eretz Yisrael and abroad, as did some of his halachic opinions — particularly concerning the observance of *shemitah*.

As we mentioned previously, in the

fall of 1913 Rav Kook traveled around the country with a group of Jerusalem *rabbanim* on a historic trip. Headed by Rav Zonnenfeld and Rav Benzion Yadler, the mission's intent was to foster a higher level of Torah commitment amongst the various settlements of the Holy Land. The next summer, a month before the outbreak of the First World War, he traveled to Europe to attend the Agudas Yisrael Convention and was unable to return to Eretz Yisrael until after the war. While in exile, he was appointed Rav of London, and from there he returned to the Holy Land in 1919, where he finally accepted the post of Rav of Jerusalem.

Rav Zonnenfeld commented about the Zionist Chief Rabbinate, so ardently supported by Rav Kook: "The first Chief Rabbi whom the Zionists will crown over them will be a *kohen* [Rav Kook was a *kohen*], the second will be a Levite, the third an ordinary *yisrael*, and the fourth a Reform Jew who will destroy the covenant."

Rav Kook and Rav Zonnenfeld

In the 1920s, Jerusalem became a seething cauldron of religious sentiments, with the Chief Rabbi, Rav Kook, on one side, and the Rav of Jerusalem, Rav Zonnenfeld, on the other. They differed on nearly every major issue confronting both the community in the Holy City and the Jewish world at large. The whole gamut of Jewish life — cultural, political, and religious — reached a boiling point during this period. Some of the issues which surfaced at the time included support for the Hebrew University, *shemitah*, female suffrage, *shechitah*, appeals courts, and the Rabbinate. Last but not least, there were the plans for a Maccabee sporting ground near the Bucharim Quarter, which would have inevitably lead to many evils in the eyes of observant Jerusalemites, including Shabbos dese-cration and immodest behavior.

Battei Machse quarter of the Old City. Rav Yosef Chaim Zonnenfeld lived there, and everyone who sought him made his way to his house.

There was also tension over the power to nominate trustees for institutions. The controversy peaked at the time of Rav Kook's election. Under Turkish rule, all religious institutions enjoyed the status of a *wakf*, a consecrated place, independent of government interference. When England gained hegemony over of the country after the First World War, the Zionists sought control of nominees to these institutions. The British responded by placing all organizations under the auspices of the secular City Council. The Orthodox community swiftly reacted with telegrams sent back and forth to London appealing the decision. In the meantime, Rav Kook, as Chief Rabbi, took the authority for himself. In the end, the British gave every institution the option to remain under the Turkish *wakf* or accept secular control. Naturally, Rav Zonnenfeld chose the former option.

On a personal level, each of the two antagonists respected the other as a superb Torah scholar. They could be found sitting and talking casually at social functions like bar mitzvos and weddings. Rav Yosef Chaim always referred to Rav Kook as the Rav of Jaffa, implying that the temperament of the mixed Jewish elements there was far more conducive to his ideology.

Assistance from Abroad

Rav Zonnenfeld did not stand alone in his battle against the secular and religious Zionists. First and foremost, he was backed by the worldwide Agudas Yisrael Movement. Since its inception in 1909 in Hamburg, Agudas Yisrael raised the banner of protection and guidance for religious Jews throughout the world. The issues at stake in Jerusalem were ones that affected all of Jewry, with ramifications that could influence Orthodoxy for generations to come.

The Gerrer Rebbe, Rav Avraham Mordechai Alter, came to Jerusalem three times as an Agudas Yisrael representative (1921, 1924, and 1927).* He marched into the battlefield to appraise the situation firsthand; to hear from the *rabbanim* and report back to the Diaspora. Furthermore, he tried to mediate between Rav Kook and Rav Zonnenfeld. On several occa-

Rav Avraham Mordechai Alter (1865–1948)

* See story, "The Gerrer Rebbe's Blessing," in *Bygone Days: 1918–1948*.

sions he unsuccessfully tried to convince Rav Kook to resign from the post of Chief Rabbi.

On his return voyage to Europe he wrote a lengthy letter about his impressions and accomplishments. Concerning Rav Kook, he explained how both various individuals and the European press had misrepresented him as a profiteer:

....Rav Avraham Kook is a treasure chest of Torah and a man of exemplary character. Also, many attest to his unimpeachable integrity. However, his love of Zion knows no limits, leading him to declare the "unclean" to be "clean".... This is the cause of the strange statements in his works. I argued with him for a long time that although his intent is laudable, his actions...aid the transgressors even as they persist in their rebellion and violate all that is holy. His reply was that he was merely following the ways of God, as it says: "You give a hand to the transgressors" [Yom Kippur prayers]. I replied that about this we say: "Because of the hand that was sent against Your Temple" [Musaf of Rosh Chodesh]...

There are many among the chareidim whose motives are sincere, and I have become personally very close to some of them, for their company is pleasant. However, as the Akedas Yitzchak in parshas Pinchas maintains, theirs was not the proper approach. If they would have initially met peacefully with Rav Kook, they could have prevailed upon him to retract [certain statements from his works] and would have thus avoided the vilification of a talmid chacham and the raging fire of dispute.

All agree that increased Orthodox immigration is imperative and that the unity of all God-fearing Jews is necessary in order to allow new immigrants to properly organize and keep Torah Judaism without having to mix with various other elements.[9]

On his second visit in 1924 (5684), when he came with the Sokolov Rebbe, Rav Yitzchak Zelig Morgenstern, and the Rav of Bendin, Rav Chanoch Henich, the antagonists were still at odds. In the words of the Sokolov Rebbe:

The main conflict stems from opposing doctrines. Rav Zonnenfeld...as a native of Hungary and a close disciple of the Ksav Sofer, follows the path of the Chasam Sofer, who demanded pure and uncompromising Judaism. Therefore, Rav Kook's concessions to, and compromises with, the irreligious deeply disturb him. However, Rav Zonnenfeld's primary opposition is to the concept of an official rabbinate in general, and to a government-appointed Chief Rabbi in particular...

Rav Kook, on the other hand, though a great talmid chacham who possesses great knowledge in many areas, as well as being a superb speaker, cannot be considered as following the approach of the tzaddikim of the earlier generations. Rav Kook is already tied to the spirit of the times and speaks enthusiastically about the "resurrection of our nation."[10]

On his third and last trip in 1927 on behalf of Agudas Yisrael, the Admor of Ger was accompanied by the distinguished Admorim of Slonim and Boyan, and Rav Menachem Mendel Landau of Strekov. The Gerrer Rebbe attempted to influence Rav Kook to resign his post, but to no avail.

These visits are indicative of Agudah's battlefront efforts to guide the important events taking place in Jerusalem. There was, however, another Heaven-sent messenger to help propagate the Orthodox cause to the world at large.

Dr. Yaakov DeHaan

As esteemed as Rav Yosef Chaim was in the eyes of Orthodox Jewry, he lacked a worldly activist who could represent the interests of the *yishuv* with foreign powers. Such an emissary for the community came in the person of Dr. Yaakov DeHaan.

Yaakov Yisrael DeHaan, born in a traditional home in Holland in 1881, was swept away by the waves of assimilation and entered into a political career. One of the most astute lawyers in Holland, his personal charisma quickly gained him entry into prestigious governmental circles. A gifted linguist, DeHaan's reputation matched those of his non-Jewish counterparts, and he soon became the toast of European society. Yet, he never forgot his roots, bravely crusading against injustices perpetrated against his brethren. While trying to save imprisoned Jews in Communist Russia, his religious consciousness was awakened, and he returned to the faith of his fathers.

He first joined the Dutch Mizrachi movement, but he soon yearned for a deeper expression of Judaism. He eventually decided to move to Jerusalem, "the heart of the Jewish nation," and bear the banner of his people. In recognition of his service to the state, the Queen of Holland had him depart the country in her special train-carriage.

DeHaan arrived in Eretz Yisrael in Sivan, 1920 (5680), a month after Rav Yosef Chaim became Rav of Jerusalem. He poured his energies into the Mizrachi political machine and was elected to their Education Committee. The raging battle in Jerusalem between the *yishuv* and the Zionists caught his attention and he wanted to understand the issues firsthand. He therefore arranged to meet with Rav Zonnenfeld and discuss matters with him.

Deeply moved by the Rav of Jerusalem's "poetic soul," Yaakov DeHaan underwent a soul change of the most profound sort, cleaving to Rav Yosef Chaim Zonnenfeld as a loving son to his father. His personal drive to champion the Orthodox cause soon led him to be nominated as political secretary of the Orthodox City Council, where his years of international diplomacy were utilized to the fullest.

Dr. Yaakov DeHaan (1881–1924)

The Zionists had a well-organized, highly effective lobbying system centered in London. They centralized all peripheral Jewish groups under one canopy in order to create a united organization. Through the powerful Jewish Agency, they initially succeeded in fooling the British into believing that the same single body also existed in Eretz Yisrael. The unsuspecting Orthodox leadership in the Holy Land did not realize how far they were misrepresented before the British, which only accentuated the strained relationships between them. Dr. DeHaan's, with his dexterity in international diplomacy, helped re-balance the scales.

The Zionists were disturbed by his alliance with the Jerusalem *yishuv*. However, as long as he maintained ties within the Zionist camp, where his charisma had put him on something of a pedestal, there was little they could do to isolate him. His life, however, was threatened, and in the course of time the Zionists succeeded in severing his source of income as the foreign correspondent for a Holland newspaper.

Dr. DeHaan firmly believed that the only path to peace in the Middle East was through directly negotiating with the Arabs and building relations with them. His endeavors in this arena were marked with great success. He first obtained signed commitments from Arab leaders that they were prepared to grant full rights to Jews, including the right of immigration, as long as they did not demand a political state. The Zionists, however, would not agree to adhere to such a policy and were outraged by his efforts.

When King Hussein, the highest authority in the Arab world at the time, visited Transjordan, the Zionists sent a delegation to welcome him. Dr. DeHaan created another storm when he prepared a welcoming committee of his own, comprising Rav Yosef Chaim Zonnenfeld, Rav Avraham Chaim Naeh, Rav Rueven Shlomo Yungreis, and himself. Their meeting on 19 Adar, 1924 (5684), put the *yishuv* and Agudas Yisrael on the map.

The importance of the delegation's meeting was heightened by the rumor that the British wished to grant King Hussein sovereignty over the Holy Land. Thus, the secularists reacted by painting the delegates as vile traitors. For years the Zionists had worked to persuade the world, especially the Arab world, that they were the sole representatives of the Jewish people. As such, they viewed this act by an independent Jewish movement as tantamount to treason.

Yaakov DeHaan's last mission was to present the Orthodox cause before the new Conservative Party in England. Only a few months before, the Labor Party had lost control of the country. As a result, a delegation headed by Dr. DeHaan planned to leave Eretz Yisrael at the beginning of Tamuz, 1924 (5684), to meet with the new government. The mission, kept secret for security reasons, leaked out to the press a few days prior to the expected departure. Dr. DeHaan refused to heed warnings that his life was in imminent danger and that he should go into hiding. The following evening, as he left the Shaarei Zedek Hospital Synagogue after the Maariv service, he was shot dead. The assassin escaped in the dark.

When Rav Zonnenfeld heard the tragic news the next morning, he rent his garments and mourned grievously for the devoted champion of Orthodoxy. Over twenty-thousand Jerusalemites escorted him to his final resting place.

Without a political leader to represent it, the *yishuv* was deflated and unable to proceed with a strong offensive against the Zionist camp's elaborate machinery. Another DeHaan never appeared to battle the community's cause in world politics. Had he been allowed to follow through with his ingenious ideas for the *yishuv*, it is impossible to say where things might have led to.

Jerusalem, as it appeared in 1918. The Jewish Quarter is in the center, with the prominent Churvah and Tiferes Yisrae Synagogues rising above the rest of the city. In the foreground are the terraced slopes of the Silwan (Shiloach) region, now heavily populated by Arabs. The Dung Gate is below the Jewish Quarter, and leads through a field to the Moghrab section where the Kosel is located. (Compare with the photo on page 394)

A City in Flux

In spite of all the confrontations on the religious front, Jerusalem's Jewish population swelled month by month. New neighborhoods came into existence and commerce thrived. Yet, this growing Jewish society became a catalyst for Arab terrorism, stemming mainly from a fear that the British overlords would give the Jews a homeland in Eretz Yisrael. For reasons which will be discussed, the British, pinned between the Jewish and Arab causes for self-identity and political freedom, sided with the Arabs. In the end, the Holy City was trapped in a state of flux, in a three-way struggle for power.

Growing by Leaps and Bounds

Jerusalem took on a new, urban look during the Mandate period. The steady influx of immigrants necessitated a wider economic base. The commercial district on Jaffa, King George, and Ben Yehudah Streets blossomed, especially after the riots of 1929, when many shops that had been destroyed in the Old City relocated there.

Naturally, more and more suburbs sprung up. To list just a few (see table at end of this book): Rechavia (1921), Talpiot (1922), Bayit Vegan (1922), Kiryat Moshe (1924), Geula (1925), Sanhedria (1926), Tel Azra (1931), and North Talpiot (1935). The expanse of land called Neve Sha'anan, where the Knesset would one day be built, was purchased from Arabs on the night of Shavuos by religious Jews. This sale took place around 1920, when Yosef Chagiz and Rav Naftali Porush seized the opportunity to finalize the deal. In order to circumnavigate the halachic problems involved with making such a purchase on a holiday, they used a child to carry the money.[11]

Jewish suburbs were predominately to the west and north of the Old City, while Arab suburbs were to the south and east. This natural separation was a blessing in disguise, creating a clear demarcation and barrier between the two major antagonists of the Holy City. The boundaries inside the Old City, however, were not so well defined during the early years of the Mandate period, and many Jews inhabited the Moslem Quarter. Unfortunately, this resulted in conflicts on many occasions.

Bayit Vegan as it appeared in 1928

Between 1922 and 1931, the city accommodated over thirty thousand new Jewish inhabitants. The capital boomed with enterprise, businesses, and a varied citizenry. The Jewish majority that had been achieved decades earlier had been maintained, and now held at over sixty percent. The British, however, gave precedence to the Arabs in such important areas as civil law. To give but one example, the Arabs were permitted to have their own courts which, in addition to the English courts of law, handed down justice in civil and property litigation.

In Tamuz, 1927 (5687), a violent earthquake shook Jerusalem. Miraculously, no human lives were lost, although a number of building were seriously damaged. Aside from numerous churches, several yeshivos were badly damaged, such as Beis El, Chayei Olam, and Shaar HaShamayim, to name but a few. In the Sephardic Talmud Torah, Rav Eliyahu Pardes was in the middle of delivering a lecture on the upper floor when the building swayed and cracked. Luckily, everyone escaped before the upper floor collapsed. Later, some of the buildings had to be razed due to their unsafe condition. The third story of the old Bikur Cholim Hospital (located in the Old City) had to be demolished in order to prevent it from collapsing.

Arab Unrest

There were three major Arab riots in Jerusalem during the pre-Second World War era. The Moslems were united in their opposition to the Balfour Declaration, which they viewed as a conspiracy by the Zionists and British to take over the country. Naturally, the Zionists tried to mitigate these accusations. Weizmann met with Emir Faisel, who agreed that America should step in to help pacify the growing unrest. However, nothing ever came of the idea.

In Adar, 1920 (5680), Arabs rioted in the Galilee, ravaging the area and killing seven Jews. A month later, on 16 Nisan, Arabs from Hebron rioted in Jerusalem, killing six Jews. One of the martyrs was Rebbe Mordechai of Rachmistrivka. World Jewry complained to the British over the lax security policy. Peace was restored, but tensions remained high.

In 1926, the Arabs rioted again, but miraculously no one was injured. They claimed the Zionists were about to force them out of Eretz Yisrael and plunder their property.

Problems next surfaced around the Western Wall. The Mufti of Jerusalem, Haj Amin, was a power-thirsty, vehement anti-Semite. At that time, some Arabs held a vague suspicion that the Jews were bent on conquering the Temple Mount. Using this fear as a pretext, Amin unleashed a barrage of hate-filled speeches. His provocative action led to stone throwing and escalated tensions.

In the summer of 1929 (5689), the Zionists founded the Jewish Agency, which acted as a central political organ to voice the Zionist cause to the world. The Arabs were up in arms over this new independent expression on the part of the Jews. The immediate result in Jerusalem was a heightened strain in the relations between the two sides, which would ultimately erupt in the infamous Arab riots of 1929. The stage for the upcoming drama was set a few months earlier, when Haj Amin moved his residence to a position where he could personally view the Western Wall from his window. In order to harass the Jews, he had an opening made in the Moghrabi section to allow Arab traffic to pass by the Western Wall area. Arab mules laden with produce marched along the four-meter-wide area to and fro, leaving droppings wherever they went and harrying the Jews who went to pray there. In Sivan, the Mufti found concrete proof of a Jewish plot to capture the Temple Mount. A picture used in a Jewish sukkah depicted Jerusalem with the Golden Dome in the center. For his purposes, this constituted conclusive evidence.

The Arabs then charged that the Western Wall belonged to them, and that the Jews had no more than a sentimental claim on the area. Rav Avraham Kook fought against this audacious declaration, ardently asserting the Jewish right to the Kosel. Should the Arabs interfere with Jews praying, he warned, there would be no peace. A committee to protect the Wall was set up. On 8 Av, the British requested that the Jewish youth guard disband, as well as the expected crowds of young Jews coming to Jerusalem for Tisha b'Av. Rav Kook, however, refused. On Wednesday night, 9 Av, irreligious youths from across the country marched to the Wall, boister-

A British sentry "guards" the Kosel

ously celebrated there, and proceeded to the Chief Rabbi's house in the New City. Surprisingly, there were no incidents.

A week later, on Friday afternoon, 17 Av, 1929 (5689), the Arabs unleashed a full-scale massacre. Marching down Jaffa Road in the direction of the Old City, Arab villagers attacked everyone and everything in sight. The hospitals filled with the injured, while in the synagogues men opened the Holy Ark and prayed fervently for Divine mercy. Able-bodied Jews went to counter the Arab mobs, trying to prevent more Jewish blood from being spilled. Miraculously, the Jews withstood a planned attack on Meah Shearim.

Shabbos night, shots came from the direction of Givat Shaul. The Diskin Orphanage, with three hundred children locked inside, was under siege. The staff members there blew a shofar to signal for help. Quickly, Jews raced to the English police and begged for their assistance. The British reluctantly agreed and sent a contingent of soldiers, who managed to restore order after a great deal of difficulty.

The next morning, reports circulated about the extent of the riots outside of Jerusalem. The most shocking news came when an Arab taxi drove in from Hebron with two Jewish refugees. Sent by the Rav of Hebron, Rav Yaakov Yosef, they told of the massacre at the Slobodke Yeshivah of Hebron. Over twenty students had been murdered, plus forty men, women, and children, some of whom had been burned alive. Furthermore, sixty Torah scrolls were set on fire. Communication had been severed when the British cut the telephone wires between Hebron and Jerusalem.

On *motzei Shabbos*, attempts were made to telegram the news to the Diaspora, but the British blocked the lines. When Rav Kook learned of the tragedy, he fell backwards and fainted. When he regained consciousness, he wept bitterly and tore his clothing in grief as he recited: "Blessed be the True Judge." Only the next morning did he succeed in getting a cable sent off to Beirut, and from

Toras Chaim Yeshivah, located in the Moslem Quarter, desecrated during the Arab riots

there news reached the Diaspora. An uproar was created throughout the world over the British's callous aloofness.

In Jerusalem, rescue operations went into action to save and protect Jewish lives. This was the only occasion that all political barriers dropped and a united rescue operation was mounted, involving the *chareidim*, the religious Zionists, and the irreligious.

In the aftermath of the tragedy, the Zionists sought to use the riots for political ends, and threatened to retaliate for them as well. The Orthodox camp spoke out against both these intentions.

Several months later, in Cheshvan, 1929 (5690), the British finally set up a commission to investigate the reasons behind the disturbance.

Some years later, in 1936, a third Arab riot blazed across the country. The Jewish resistance forces, like the Haganah and the Irgun, brutally attempted to counter the Arab savagery. This led to more and more arrests on the part of the British, and ever-spiraling tensions. The most daring counterattack by the Jews was the bombing of the King David Hotel, which resulted in the death of a number of innocent people.

The whole country became a hotbed

of growing unrest and heightened consternation. In hindsight, all of these bloody acts of murder and destruction were but more pangs in the inevitable series of birth throes that would awaken the Jewish people to their noble mission.

In the Halls of Torah

In the midst of the whirlwind years of the 1920s, the yeshivah world continued to flourish. Just as children had to eat, so they had to learn Torah. Additionally, many of them continued their studies into adulthood. We will now review the status of some of the many religious educational institutions that existed during this period.

Porat Yosef Yeshivah

Porat Yosef Yeshivah, the leading Sephardic yeshivah in Jerusalem, laid its cornerstone in 1914, but due to the war, construction was delayed until much later. A philanthropic Jew from Calcutta, India, by the name of Yosef Shalom paid for the building, which overlooked the Temple Mount. Interestingly, Shalom's first choice of how to better the lot of his brethren in the Holy City was to build a modern hospital. He wrote to the Ben Ish Chai in Baghdad for his opinion. The reply he received changed his mind. The Ben Ish Chai explained that even though the Jerusalemites had many physical requirements that needed to be taken care of, there were other philanthropists who would happily see to these. Spiritual needs, however, would not have the same eager patronage. Therefore, it was more important to build a yeshivah than a hospital.[12]

Inaugurated in 1923, Porat Yosef was soon filled with young, eager pupils. In addition to the huge *beis midrash* where the yeshivah students learned, there were two other smaller study halls for married men, plus fifty more rooms for dormitories, offices and a library. The first Rosh Yeshivah was Rav Shlomo Laniado. In 1948, the complex was destroyed, only to be rebuilt on the same location after the Six Day War.

Rav Ezra Atiyah served as Rosh Yeshivah from 1925 until his death in 1970. He was the focal point of the yeshivah, and many young Sephardim chose to study there due to his brilliant reputation. Among his most famous students were Rav Ovadiah Yosef, Rav Yehudah Tzadkah, and Rav Benzion Abba Shaul.

Rav Ezra Atiyah (1881–1970)

Porat Yosef Yeshivah stood between 1923 and 1948

The Chazon Ish, on his visit to Jerusalem in the 1930s, discussed Torah subjects with Rav Atiyah. Afterwards, the Chazon Ish commented, "His method of thinking through a gemara is like that of the Early Authorities!"[13]

Most of his writings were destroyed by the Arabs when they captured the Old City in 1948.

Etz Chaim Yeshivah

The Etz Chaim Yeshivah, the oldest educational institution in the Ashkenazic community, received a new injection of Torah leadership when Rav Issar Zalman Meltzer immigrated in 1925. He accepted the post of Rosh Yeshivah, a position at which he had excelled in the Russian city of Slutzk. When the Ridvaz, Rav Yaakov David Villavsky, resigned as Rav of Slutzk in 1903 to open a yeshivah in Safed, Rav Meltzer replaced him, and became Rav of the city as well. The Communist regime forced him to move in 1923, and eventually he settled in Eretz Yisrael.

Not only did Rav Meltzer bring a rich, thriving Torah outlook with him, he also radiated a genuine love for his students and fellowmen. In 1935, he published the first of his nine-volume commentary on the Rambam, entitled *Even HaEzel.** He requested Rav Tzvi Pesach Frank to review each edition before publication and added Rav Frank's glosses at the

* See story, "The Bar Mitzvah Drash," in *Bygone Days: 1948–1998.*

end of each volume.

Another outstanding member of the faculty was the *mashgiach*, Rav Yechiel Michel Tuketzinsky. Besides his dedication to the yeshivah, Rav Yechiel Michel produced a yearly calendar with the times of sunrise and sunset. It was printed on a large folio and included all the Ashkenazic customs connected to prayers on weekdays, Shabbos, and holidays. Today, it is updated every year by his son, Rav Nisan Tuketzinsky. Rav Yechiel Michel also wrote two classics, *Gesher HaChaim* (laws of mourning), and *Ir HaKodesh v'HaMikdash* (holiness of Jerusalem).

Diskin Orphanage

The Diskin Orphanage, founded in 1880 by Rav Yehoshua Leib Diskin, moved from one rented quarters to another as it expanded. The site for its permanent premises in Givat Shaul was purchased in 1894, during the lifetime of its founder. At that time, Givat Shaul was a remote hillside at the very outskirts to the west of the city.

The inauguration ceremony of the new building, one of the biggest in the city, took place on the first of Nisan, 1927 (5687), in the presence of religious and lay leaders alike. A procession marched to the new premises carrying Torah scrolls. The revered Rav of Jerusalem, Rav Yosef Chaim Zonnenfeld, walked with the procession, refusing the comfort of an automobile ride, saying, "Having merited to witness this great day and the celebration of this beautiful mitzvah, nothing seems too difficult for me." The venerated tzaddik had been one of the orphanage's directors since it was founded nearly fifty years earlier.

Diskin Orphanage in Givat Shaul

Hebron Yeshivah

After the massacre of twenty-three students at the Slobodke Yeshivah in Hebron, the institution moved to Jerusalem despite the entreaties of Rav Yitzchak Gerstenkorn to relocate the yeshivah in the new town of Bnei Brak. Rav Yechezkiel Sarna, who was in Jerusalem at the time of the massacre, opened the yeshivah a few weeks later in Elul, 1929, in the neighborhood of Geula. It soon became known as the Hebron Yeshivah. Though the backbone of the student body came from Europe and Russia, a number of Jerusalemite students studied there as well.

The institution's large *beis midrash*, built on Chagai Street a few years later, became the hub of the yeshivah world in the New City. Hebron produced numerous *roshei yeshivos* and *rabbanim*. The following yeshivos were founded by alumni from this hall of Torah: Heichal HaTalmud (Tel Aviv), Ohel Torah (Jerusalem), and Toras HaAretz (Petach Tikva).[14] Much later, Hebron Yeshivah moved to a new and larger campus in the Givat Mordechai neighborhood.

Merkaz HaRav Yeshivah

In 1923, Yeshivas Merkaz HaRav opened on the premises of the Chief Rabbi's house and private *beis midrash*. Rav Kook was Rosh Yeshivah, later followed by Rav Charlap. Still later in 1951, Rav Kook's son, Rav Tzvi Yehudah Kook, led the yeshivah.

The yeshivah moved to Kiryat Moshe in 1964. The major expansion of the campus came in the late 1970s when Mr. Morris Wohl donated the Yad Wohl *beis midrash*. There, young men study the normal yeshivah curriculum based on the unity of Torah, Eretz Yisrael, and *am Yisrael*. Their mentor is Rav Avraham Kook, and his writings are the foundations of the institution's philosophical outlook.

Shemesh Tzadakah Synagogue

The city saw many new synagogues constructed during this time as well. One of them was a Sephardic shul called Shemesh Tzadakah. Located near Hebron Yeshivah on Chagai Street, it was built in 1929 by Rav Zadkah Chuzin of Baghdad. Rav Chuzin, a *talmid chacham* and renowned *mohel*, would not permit a *chazan* to lead services until he felt confident in his ability to pronounce every word distinctly and with devotion. As Rav of the shul for over thirty years, Rav Chuzin filled it with a spirit of holiness that continued to radiate long after his departure. Rav Yaakov Muzafi, a great Sephardic halachic authority, became Rav when he immigrated to Eretz Yisrael in 1951, at first serving jointly with Rav Chuzin.[15]

The Sabba Kaddisha

In the spring of 1930 (5690), the Munkatsher Rebbe, Rav Chaim Elazar Shapiro of Hungary, visited Eretz Yisrael. A Chassidic Rebbe with thousands of followers, his two-week trip aroused hordes of well-wishers and *rabbanim* to

Rav Shlomo Eliezer Elfandari (1820–1930)

greet and meet with him. The purpose of his visit, besides visiting the holy sites of the country, was to meet the oldest living tzaddik of the generation, Rav Shlomo Eliezer Elfandari. Rav Elfandari, known as the Sabba Kaddisha (the "Holy Grandfather"), was reported to be nearly a hundred and twenty years old. His knowledge of Torah was phenomenal, and his teaching career dated back to 1845, when he became a Rosh Yeshivah in Constantinople. As mentor of the Sdei Chemed (Rav Chaim Chizkiyahu Medini) and the Kiryat Arba (Rav Yitzchak Akrish), he was a staunch defender of the truth, which earned him the title of a fiery zealot. The Munkatsher Rebbe, himself a child prodigy and scholar of the highest order, had maintained a personal correspondence with Rav Elfandari for some time, and wished to meet with him face to face.

In 1925, the Sabba Kaddisha had moved from Safed to Jerusalem for health reasons, and he was under the supervision of Dr. Wallach of Shaarei Zedek Hospital. Every Friday he studied together with Rav Velvel Minzburg, the Chassidic halachic authority of the city. He also befriended Rav Tzvi Pesach Frank, and the two would spend hours together delving into Torah topics.

On the day of Rav Shapiro's arrival, a neighbor informed the Sabba Kaddisha that the Munkatsher Rebbe's train had arrived at the Jerusalem station, where a huge crowd had welcomed him.

"*Ach*," sighed Rav Elfandari enigmatically, "if only his departure will be in the same spirit as his arrival."

A natural affinity bound the two men together as soon as they met. After taking leave of the venerated Sephardic sage, Rav Shapiro went to Battei Machse to visit the Rav of Jerusalem, Rav Yosef Chaim Zonnenfeld. Rav Yosef Chaim lay in bed weak with old age, but as soon as the Munkatsher rebbe entered, he stood up and greeted him warmly.

The Munkatsher's historic trip injected fresh energy and enthusiasm into the *yishuv*, especially the Chassidic community. On Tuesday morning, 22 Iyar, 1930 (5690), the day before the Rebbe's scheduled departure, the Sabba Kaddisha passed away. Rav Elfandari left the world fully conscious and aware until his last breath. The Rebbe fell on the floor and cried at the loss of the tzaddik. Later that afternoon, all Jerusalemites participated in the funeral. The Sabba Kaddisha's prophetic words had sadly come true.[16]

Rav Tzvi Pesach Frank

Rav Yosef Tzvi Dushinsky

A New Leadership

During the 1930s, the leaders of both the religious camps in the city passed away. Rav Yosef Chaim Zonnenfeld died on 19 Adar II, 1932 (5692), and Rav Avraham Yitzchak Kook departed from the world on 3 Elul, 1935 (5695). Their passing did not signal an end to religious/political confrontation in the Holy City. Their achievements provided guidelines for the future leaders of the *yishuv*, and their successors — great rabbis in their own right — continued to carry the banners which their predecessors had hoisted years before.

Rav Yitzchak Herzog replaced Rav Kook as Chief Rabbi of the country, and Rav Tzvi Pesach Frank became Chief Rabbi of Jerusalem. They maintained close contact with one another, often discussing communal issues together.

When Rav Tzvi Pesach came as a teenager to Jerusalem in 1892, he astonished the rabbis with his profound grasp of Gemara and Halachah. He was especially close with Rav Shmuel Salant and joined his *beis din* in 1908. Rav Shmuel groomed the young prodigy to become one of the great religious leaders of the next generation. In 1895, Rav Frank married the granddaughter of Rav Chaim Yaakov Shapiro, who headed Rav Salant's *beis din* in the early 1900s. Rav Salant's *beis din* was better known as the Perushim *beis din* in order to distinguish it from the Chassidic *beis din*. In 1918, Rav Frank became Rosh Beis Din of the Perushim, a position he retained for the next forty years. Now, in 1936, he was asked to fill the vacancy left by the death of Rav Kook.

Many were relieved by Rav Frank's willingness to become Chief Rabbi of Jerusalem, as the secularists had been eager to install a puppet candidate to that important position. As Chief Rabbi, Rav Frank quickly pushed forward his plan to establish a Religious Council (*Mo'aza Datit*) in every city to centralize the power of the rabbinate.

The previous year, in 1935, an institute called Midrash Bnei Tzyon opened. Its purpose was to propagate the study of the complicated laws pertaining to the Holy Land, such as *shemitah*, *orlah*, and *maaser*. Among the members were Rav Shlomo Zalman Auerbach (Rosh Yeshivah Kol Torah), Rav Eliezerov (Rav of Katamon), Rav Bukspan of Karlin Yeshivah, and Rav Yitzchak Rosenthal. Rav Frank, who headed the institute for the next twenty-five years, gave regular lectures and wrote articles which were published in the *Kerem Tzyon* journal.[17]

The importance of the institute could be measured by the constant stream of queries sent to it by kibbutzim and moshavim throughout the country.

During Rav Yosef Chaim Zonnenfeld's last weeks in Adar, 1932, the Rav of Hust, Rav Yosef Tzvi Dushinsky, was visiting Jerusalem. Rav Zonnenfeld beseeched the Rav of Hust to replace him as Rav of Jerusalem. At the funeral, Rav Dushinsky eulogized him. Shortly thereafter, he returned to Hungary after Passover without directly answering the sages of Jerusalem as to his intentions.

Not long afterwards, the *yishuv* sent Rav Moshe Blau to Hungary to influence him to accept. Rav Blau was the right-hand man of the *yishuv*, its spokesman to the world at large. Rav Dushinsky finally acceded, after Rav Chaim Ozer Grodzensky of Vilna and the Gerrer Rebbe agreed that he was the perfect choice for the position. He arrived with his family and twenty-five of his students in Elul, 1933, and immediately set to work to strengthen the *yishuv* and its institutions.*

As a prominent Hungarian Rosh Yeshivah for over thirty-five years, Rav Dushinsky also opened his own yeshivah on Shmuel HaNavi Street. Called Yeshivas Beis Yosef (later renamed Beis Yosef Tzvi), he gave three lectures a day in Gemara and Halachah.

These two replacements, one the official government *rav*, the other the de facto *rav*, were *gedolim* in their own right. They faithfully carried the banner of their predecessors and would reinforce Yiddishkeit during a very difficult and dangerous period.

The 1930s

The 1930s were characterized by growing unrest on all fronts. With demonic despots taking power in Europe during the Depression, the world was heading for a terrifying collision between opposing forces. In Jerusalem, as well, there was growing unrest, and the British overlords had little control over events. Increased Arab-Jewish incidents such as bombings and riots wreaked havoc, injuries, and death.

After the Arab riots of 1936, a commission arrived from London in Cheshvan, 1936 (5697), to investigate their cause and to propose steps to secure a lasting peace. Lord Earl Peel headed the commission, which heard testimony from both sides, including civil, military, and religious leaders. The conclusion of the commission was a proposal to divide the land of Palestine, with Jews living in the western half and the Arabs in the eastern half.

The Arabs unanimously rejected the Peel Plan, claiming that the Jews intended to take control of the country and force them out of the Land. On the other hand, Jewish reaction to the Peel

* See story, "The Rav and the High Commissioner," in *Bygone Days: 1918–1948*.

Proposal was mixed. The Zionists, Mizrachis, and Agudas Yisrael disagreed on a united stand, as did the *rabbanim*. For some it was a question of all or nothing, quoting the verse in *Deuteronomy* 7:2, "Do not give them [the seven Cananite nations] a resting place [in the Land]." According to them, the Land of Israel was not a dividable piece of property; it was the inheritance of the Jewish people.

Others, however, felt it was a necessary concession for the sake of peace and for the consolidation of an independent Jewish state. Rav Grodensky of Vilna and Rav Frank of Jerusalem were among those who believed in the latter view. Rav Dushinsky's reaction was, "Though the Torah binds the Jewish people to Eretz Yisrael, it is the same Torah which commands us not to conquer the country in a warlike manner (and expel the inhabitants), nor to aspire to control minority groups."[18] Thus, his opinion coincided with the view of Rav Chaim Ozer Grodzensky.

Ultimately, the proposal was shelved. However, after the Second World War, it became the blueprint for the famous United Nations Partition Plan, in which the nations of the world officially endorsed the existence of an independent Jewish state.

During the 1930s, the British expressed a strong determination to answer Arab grievances concerning a perceived preferential treatment for the Jewish residents of the country. Based on their 1922 Statement of Policy, the British tried to appease both sides, which in reality was impossible. In the end, the British took on the role of arbiter between the two antagonists. In theory, they were supposed to be impartial, but in fact they leaned overtly to the Arab side. The reason for this lopsided arbitration was due to several interlocking factors.[19] The weakness of the League of Nations in controlling the administration of the mandates allowed the British unrestrained decision-making power, and the English did not hesitate to use this power as they saw fit. This free license, combined with the British sense of fair play, compelled them to make several concessions to the Arabs at the Jews' expense, for the following reason: Since the British had acknowledged the right of the Jews to establish a homeland with the Balfour Declaration, they tried to re-balance the situation by siding with the Arabs during the Mandate period. This was demonstrated by the first High Commissioner, Sir Herbert Samuels, himself a Jew. He deliberately professed a policy of showing the world that a Jew could be fair to the Arabs. As is often the case when a Jew is appointed to a position of power, he bends over backwards to show that he is not unduly favoring his brethren. This attitude led Samuels to openly favor Arab causes, with the resultant repercussions visible from the onset of the Mandate.

The issue of immigration was of prime importance. The delicate balance of power between the Arabs and Jews was determined in part by the number of citizens each had in the country. At first, the British agreed to facilitate Jewish immigration in so far as it did not damage the economic position of the Arabs. However, in the 1930s, the British could no longer use that same measuring stick due to the constant disturbances and riots. Therefore, they designed a series of White Papers to redefine their policy on immigration.

One result of this was a severe curtailment of Jewish immigration. Unfortunately, this move could not have come at a more crucial juncture. It was merely a matter of time until the Nazis ignited a war that would precipitate the greatest genocide in human history. People throughout Europe sought to escape to safer territory. Jews, especially, sought visas to reach places like England, America, and Eretz Yisrael. Notwithstanding the difficulty and expense involved in obtaining such documents, the final result depended on the willingness of these nations to absorb them.

In May, 1939 (5699), the British issued a White Paper that restricted Jewish immigration to Eretz Yisrael to a total of 75,000 until 1945. This was the final in a series of six White Papers, and by far the most ominous. The document caused Jews in Palestine to demonstrate for the sake and safety of their defenseless brethren in Europe, who were faced with the grim specter of Nazism. In issuing the White Paper, the British succumbed to Arab pressure to allow a slim Arab majority in the country. Unfortunately, this came at the price of an untold number of Jewish lives.

PALESTINE

Statement of Policy

Presented by the Secretary of State for the Colonies to Parliament by Command of His Majesty
May, 1939

LONDON
PRINTED AND PUBLISHED BY HIS MAJESTY'S STATIONERY OFFICE
To be purchased directly from H.M. STATIONERY OFFICE at the following addresses:
York House, Kingsway, London, W.C.2; 120 George Street, Edinburgh 2;
26 York Street, Manchester 1; 1 St. Andrew's Crescent, Cardiff;
80 Chichester Street, Belfast;
or through any bookseller
1939
Price 2*d*. net

Cmd. 6019

The White Paper of 1939

Illegal immigration continued in spite of increased surveillance by the British army. Those caught by the British were imprisoned together with Arab and Jewish criminals, and political prisoners from the various Jewish underground groups. Prisons and detention camps in places like Jerusalem, Latrun, Ramla, Akko, and Bethlehem (for women) were filled to capacity.

As early as 1931 (5691), the British asked the Chief Rabbi to nominate a chaplain for the prisoners, who would periodically visit them in the same way as the Moslem Mufti came to visit Arab inmates. Rav Aryeh Levin, a close disciple of Rav Kook, accepted the position. For him, the weekly experience became a major life mission. He succeeded in initiating changes for the benefit of the Jewish prisoners. First, he demanded a separate ward for Jewish inmates, stemming from reports that Arabs sodomized

Jewish youngsters who had been arrested for illegal entry into the country. Initially meeting with stiff resistance, he persevered, and finally Ward 23 was assigned for Jewish prisoners.

Next, Rav Aryeh pushed for the installation of a kosher kitchen. At first Colonel Scott of the Criminal Investigation Department (CID) was puzzled by the chaplain's concern; however, he soon agreed and made arrangements for the proper accommodations.[20]

Rav Levin's Shabbos visits became proverbial. Inmates eagerly awaited his arrival and the warm affection which he showed them. He led the services and read from the *sefer Torah,* and instilled a Jewish spirit into their lives.*

The number of political prisoners increased daily, some facing life sentences for carrying weapons, and others facing the death sentence. It was hard to justify such severe punishments, and the result was only further unrest. It was a sad chapter in the British attitude towards its Jewish Palestinean subjects during the Mandate period.

Influx of Chassidic Rebbes[21]

In the late eighteenth century, masses of Chassidim came from Europe to settle in the Holy Land. Initially, they were forced to avoid Jerusalem because of the ban against all Ashkenazim which existed in those times. However, in the early mid-nineteenth century, individual Chassidim began settling in the Holy City. Distinguished by their own customs and dress, they preferred to retain their individuality by praying and interacting together. From time to time, a Chassid would travel to Russia or Poland to regenerate his spirit by visiting his Rebbe's court. The Chassidic movements, from their inception with the Baal Shem Tov, were exclusively rooted in Eastern Europe and Russia. By the turn of the twentieth century, the great courts of Lubavitch, Ger, Belz, Karlin, and Sanz — among others — boasted tens of thousands of followers. The Rebbe, as the focal point and life force, gave the Chassidus direction, and wisely guided his followers.

In Eretz Yisrael, large enclaves of Chassidim lived in Safed, Tiberias, and Hebron. In Jerusalem, a few small *shetibels* opened in the mid-nineteenth cen-

Rav Yisrael Shem Tov, founder of Chassidus

* See story, "Father of the Prisioners," in *Bygone Days: 1918–1948.*

tury. However, until shortly before the onset of the twentieth century, no Chassidic rebbes lived in the country. At that time, the Lelover Rebbe, Rebbe Elazar Mendel Biderman, and his son, Rebbe David, immigrated and became the sole *Admorim* in the Holy City. Rebbe David Biderman traveled several times to Russia to rekindle the inner sparks of Chassidus in his heart. The Tiferes Yisrael Synagogue, open since 1872, became the hub of Chassidic activities.

The Chassidim opened their own rabbinical court at the end of the century. The first *rosh beis din* was Rav Shneur Zalman of Lublin. In the decades that followed, other *roshei beis din* included Rav David Shuvaks and Rav Velvel Minzburg.

The second quarter of the twentieth century witnessed an influx of Chassidic Rebbes, some coming for a visit and others to plant permanent roots in the Holy City. Before the Second World War, over a dozen *Admorim* visited or settled in Jerusalem. Among those who visited were the Gerrer Rebbe (1921, 1924, 1927, 1934), the Sokolover Rebbe (1924), the Bostoner Rebbe (1925, 1929, 1934), the Boyaner Rebbe (1935), the Karliner Rebbe (1939), the Tolner Rebbe (1924), the Sochotshover Rebbe (1924, 1935), and the Slonimer Rebbe (1929).

Rachmistrivka

The first rebbe of the twentieth century to settle in Jerusalem was Rebbe Mordechai Twersky, the Rachmistrivker Rebbe. Arriving in 1906 (5666), Rebbe Mordechai wondered why people came to him for consultation. "I'm not one to stand long in prayer, neither do I sing nor say a Torah *drash*, so why do they come to me? The only thing I do is to start the day by saying that I want to fulfill the commandment to love my fellow Jew. Thus I can truly say that I love each and every Jew. Perhaps this is why people come, for they know they will find a receptive heart to listen to their sorrows."

During the riots of 1920, he was injured and died from his wounds.

In 1926, his brother, Rebbe Nachum Twersky, moved to Jerusalem with his sons and grandson. Although he came to live a private life of Torah study, he soon acquiesced to the call of Jerusalemite Chassidim and opened the Rachmistrivka court in the Musrara neighborhood. When he passed away in 1936, at the age of ninety-six, his son Rebbe Avraham Dov Twersky led the group through the war years. After he died in 1945, the banner of the dynasty

One of Rav Twersky's ornaments

was carried by his brother, Rebbe David Twersky until he passed away in 1949. From then until 1982, Rebbe Yochanan Twersky, who originally came with his grandfather in 1926, built up the court, opening a yeshivah called Meor Einayim in Geula in 1963. Today, the present Admor, Rebbe Yisrael Mordechai Twersky, has a large and faithful following.

Zweille

When the Zweiller (pronounced "Zviller") Rebbe, Rebbe Shlomo Goldman, arrived in 1925, he brought with him his grandson, Rav Mordechai. As they approached the shores of Eretz Yisrael, he told his grandson, "I am throwing my cloak of leadership of the dynasty into the sea [he left his son, Rebbe Gedaliah Moshe Goldman, as Rebbe in Zweille]...I demand that you do not reveal my identity to anyone."

For a time, Rebbe Shlomo managed to remain anonymous. After a quarter of a century as Rebbe of Zweille, he changed his lifestyle and lived as an ordinary Jew. For three years he resided in Beis Yisrael and studied in the Chayei Olam Yeshivah without attracting any attention. He traveled on buses and went to the market, and was known as the Zweiller Yid.

One day, a visiting Jew from Zweille entered the Chayei Olam Yeshivah. Gazing around, he noticed Rebbe Shlomo learning, and asked someone who the man was.

"The Zweiller Yid."

"Oh, Heavens!" he burst out. "This is none other than the *Admor* of Zweille, Rebbe Shlomo!"

From that day onwards, the Zweiller Rebbe emerged from anonymity and opened his doors to the needs of the individual and the community. Soon the Rebbe's humble abode in Beis Yisrael became an address that was much sought after.* People with all kinds of problems came to receive his advice and blessing.

The Zweiller Rebbe left a unique imprint on all who came in contact with him. Some experienced miraculous healing from his blessings, often given in a disinterested and nonchalant manner that made the recipient erroneously believe that the Rebbe was unconcerned with his problems. He instituted a dramatic change in the *kollel* system under his auspices, paying the scholars once a week rather than the traditional monthly stipend. The burden of daily needs on

Rebbe Shlomo Goldman (1869–1945)

* See story, "Forty Days Straight," in *Bygone Days: 1918–1948.*

the families was thereby greatly eased.

The Zweille dynasty remained in Beis Yisrael, building a large synagogue-yeshivah complex called Beis Mordechai in 1939. After Rebbe Shlomo passed away in 1945, his son Rebbe Gedaliah Goldman, who moved to Jerusalem in 1936, continued to lead the court. He guided his Chassidim with the low-profile attitude of his father until his death in 1949 at an early age. The dynasty remains vibrant today, with Rebbe Avraham Goldman continuing to widen the influence of Zweiller Chassidus.

Boston

Rebbe Pinchas David Horowitz, the Bostoner Rebbe, was the second native *Admor* born in Jerusalem (Rebbe Shimon Nata Nasan Biderman, the Lelover Rebbe from 1918–1928, was born a few years earlier). He was related to the Lelover Rebbe on his mother's side and to Rav Yeshaya Horowitz, author of the *Shelah*, who resided in Jerusalem in the 1600s, and Rebbe Shmelke of Nikelsberg on his father's side. Rebbe Pinchas David was very close to Rebbe David Biderman.

Rebbe Pinchas David Horowitz, the first Admor of Boston, with his youngest son, the present Bostoner Rebbe

Furthermore, when the Chassidic master Rav Shneur Zalman of Lublin came to Jerusalem in 1892, he studied with him. Later, after his marriage, he moved to the Galilee and became close to Rav Moshe Kleyers, the Rav of Tiberias. He returned to Jerusalem in 1912 when his father passed away, and headed Kollel Galicia. Before the outbreak of the First World War, Rebbe Pinchas David went to Europe to raise funds for the *kollel*, where he became stranded. In an attempt to return to Eretz Yisrael, Rav Yaakov Meir, Rav of Salonika, Greece, assisted him in obtaining a visa and passage on a ship bound for the Holy Land. However, the liner returned to port after two days at sea due to the presence of warships on the Mediterranean. In 1915, Rav Horowitz was forced to sail to America, where Providence brought him to Boston, Massachusetts. There he set up his court and built a dynasty.

Rebbe Pinchas David returned to Jerusalem three times (1925, 1929, 1934) with the hope of permanently settling there. In 1934 (5694), he moved with his family and brought the flavor of Boston Chassidus to the Holy City. He dreamt of buying an outlying area of Jerusalem where he could establish a

Bostoner settlement. Upon careful consideration, he decided on a site near the cave of Shmuel HaNavi as a suitable location. After acquiring the land with a downpayment, the next step was to interest people in developing and settling it. The Rebbe had planned to enlist the aid of American investors. Unfortunately, those were still the lean years of the Depression, and his valiant efforts yielded no fruit. Shortly after the purchase, his health declined, and in 1936 he and his family returned to America. He passed away in Kislev, 1941 (5702), and was reinterred on the Mount of Olives after the Second World War.

The Bostoner Rebbe's dream of establishing a court in Jerusalem lay dormant for nearly fifty years. However, in 1985, Rebbe Levi Yitzchak, the present Bostoner Rebbe, built a synagogue and complex in the western suburb of Har Nof, called Givat Pinchas.

Sochotshov

Rebbe Pinchas David Horowitz was not the first *Admor* to plan a large building complex in Jerusalem for his Chassidim. As early as 1891, the Sochotshover Rebbe, Rebbe Avraham Burnstein, sent his son and son-in-law to Jerusalem to purchase a site. Unfortunately, the Turkish government had reinstated a law prohibiting foreigners from buying land.

In 1924 (5684), his grandson, Rebbe David Burnstein, came with his brother, Rebbe Chanuch, seeking to buy land. He put a down-payment on a site south of Ramla and returned to Poland to collect the remainder. Harsh Polish decrees curtailed his efforts and he eventually lost the right to the land, along with the money he had already paid.

Rebbe Chanuch Burnstein remained in Jerusalem, first settling in the Bucharim neighborhood before moving to the new Bayit Vegan suburb in 1924. There, on Chida Street, he quietly lived and studied. His brother, Rebbe David, became Rebbe of Sochotshov in 1926 when their father, Rebbe Shmuel, passed away. When Rebbe Chanuch learned of his brother's death in the Warsaw ghetto in 1942, he was devastated. Later, he accepted the role of *Admor* of the dynasty.

After Rebbe Chanuch passed away in 1965, his son Rebbe Menachem Shlomo Burnstein continued the leadership of the dynasty. Alas, he died in a traffic accident four years later, leaving an eight year old son to fill in his place. The young Rebbe Shmuel Burnstein grew up and is today the Admor of Sochotshov.

The Sochotshov dynasty is still located in Bayit Vegan, where it maintains a large yeshivah called Avnei Nezer.

Amshinov

Another *Admor* to open his court in Bayit Vegan was Rebbe Yerachmiel Yehudah Meir Kalish, the Rebbe of Amshinov. In 1933 (5693), he came with his father, Rebbe Shimon Shalom Kalish, and remained for approximately one year. On his return to Poland, Rebbe Shimon Kalish urged his Chassidim to move to Eretz Yisrael and helped them obtain visas. He said, "*Chutz laAretz* is the hallway to Eretz Yisrael." During the war, he and his son managed to escape to Japan via Shanghai, and from there to America, where Rebbe Shimon passed away.

In 1946, Rebbe Yerachmiel Kalish settled in Tel Aviv, where he made ties with Rav David Wein of Holon and Rav Yosef Kahaneman of Ponevitch in Bnei Brak. Thereafter he moved to Bayit Vegan, where he established a yeshivah and quietly fostered a growing following. He passed away in 1976 and was succeeded by his grandson, Rebbe Yaakov Aryeh Yeshaya Milikovsky, the present Rebbe.

Rebbe Yerachmiel Kalish (1901–1976)

Alexander

The Alexander Rebbe, Rebbe Yehudah Moshe Danziger, moved to Jerusalem in 1933, where he joined the Chassidic *beis din*. Not yet an *Admor*, he lived in the Knesset neighborhood, spending his days and nights immersed in his studies. When the *beis din* was forced to close during the lean years, Rebbe Danziger worked in diamonds to support his family. In 1947, after the war, surviving Alexander Chassidim turned to him as the sole survivor of the Alexander dynasty and crowned him Rebbe.

As early as 1928, the Alexander Rebbe opened a *beis midrash* called Beis Chassidim in the neighborhood of Beis Yisrael. Not long afterwards, he opened a yeshivah called Yismach Yisrael.

In 1956, Rebbe Danziger moved his court to Bnei Brak.

Gerrer Dynasty

The last *Admor* to settle in Jerusalem prior to the Second World War was the Gerrer Rebbe. In 1934 (5694), Rebbe Avraham Mordechai Alter left his thousands of Chassidim and moved permanently to Eretz Yisrael, where he settled in Jerusalem. Author of *Imrei Emes*, a work of insights on the Torah, he was a genius who never forgot anything he learned.

A half a year after his arrival in the Holy Land, he went back to Poland for a short time, only to find himself unable to return so quickly. He was in Warsaw at the time when the Germans invaded Poland in 1939. During the bombardment, a shell landed in his courtyard, which killed his son-in-law and impaired his hearing. Only through miracles did he escape Warsaw and reach Eretz Yisrael in 1940.

Building his court in the Geula neighborhood, the Gerrer Rebbe became a focal point for Chassidim in Eretz Yisrael. Having personally suffered at the hands of the Nazis, he could empathize with the fugitives of the war who came to him with their heartbreaking stories. All left feeling strengthened.

With his passing in 1948, he left a thriving Chassidus. His son, Rebbe Yisrael Alter, continued to lead the Gerrer Chassidim. In part three, "Rebirth of a Nation," we will further discuss the Gerrer dynasty, along with other Chassidic dynasties who came during and after the Second World War.

The Second World War

With the German invasion of Poland on 1 September, 1939, the Jews of Jerusalem — like Jews throughout the rest of the world — feared for the safety of their brethren in Eastern Europe. The largest concentration of Jews worldwide lived in the area of Europe between France and Russia. The full depth of the tragedy, especially the Holocaust, only became revealed slowly during the course of the war.

When the German commander Erwin Rommel began his North African offensive against the British 8th Army in February, 1941, the Allied Powers seemed to have the advantage. However, the brilliant tactician quickly disavowed everyone of this notion, and Rommel was initially quite successful in his advances. Rommel landed at Tripoli, Libya, and moved eastward across the Western Desert towards Egypt. His first goal was the Suez Canal, and his second goal was Palestine. After a number of stunning victories, Rommel's advance was finally arrested at the Battle of el-Alamein in August, 1942, only sixty miles west of Alexandria. The British counter-offensive, under General Montgomery, began on 23 October, 1942, and by January, 1943, Rommel had retreated past Tripoli into Tunisia.

The inhabitants of Eretz Yisrael were very apprehensive during this entire time, and a general fear of the worst gripped most people. Though the populace was protected by British forces, Rommel's successes appeared to auger ultimate victory for the German forces.

In the summer of 1941, Jews gathered by the grave of the Ohr HaChaim on the Mount of Olives. It was his *yartzeit*, an auspicious time to ask the tzaddik to intercede on their behalf. Among those present was Rebbe Yisrael of Husyatin. He had set up his court in Tel Aviv in 1937 and had done everything possible to aid refugees. Now, at the height of Rommel's campaign, he prayed for the downfall of the German invasion. Suddenly, the Rebbe exclaimed excitedly, "The wicked will not come, they will not enter into Eretz Yisrael!" When people looked at him in wonder, he explained his outburst. "I have just seen the Divine Name of Hashem shining brightly. This is a Heavenly sign that the enemy will never enter the Land."[22]

When Rommel crossed into Egypt in the summer of 1942, the British command in Jerusalem ordered the Friedman factory to produce ammunition for the British army. When the factory failed to produce the needed quota, General Bruce met with Chief Rabbi Yitzchak Isaac Herzog one Thursday. He asked Rav Herzog that the three hundred Jewish employees, most of whom were religious, be permitted to work on Shabbos. The Chief Rabbi delayed his reply, and by default, the factory was closed that Shabbos. Later the following week, Rommel's army began to retreat at the Battle of el-Alamein, signaling a reduc-

The Gerrer Rebbe, Rebbe Avraham Mordechai Alter, speaking at the Churvah Synagogue during the Second World War

tion in the need for ammunition.[23]

At one point during the war, a young yeshivah student asked Rav Tzvi Frank if he should join the Palmach forces.

"No," replied Rav Frank. "The atmosphere prevailing in the Palmach is not conducive for a religious youth like you."

"But the Nazis are about to enter Eretz Yisrael!" the youth exclaimed.

"Don't worry," answered Rav Frank, "Jerusalem will be a refuge."[24]

Even after Rommel was repulsed, the remaining two and a half years of the Second World War draped the Holy Land in a heavy cloud. Little could be done to aid Jews in the European war zone. The greatest weapon the *yishuv* had at its disposal was prayer. Prayers at the Western Wall, although limited by the British, were a powerful resource that transcended time and place. Engaging in them was a duty in which everyone felt responsible to participate.

A mass assembly was arranged at the Churvah Synagogue at the height of the war. Hundreds of rabbis came to participate. One of the most moving speeches was given by the Gerrer Rebbe, Rebbe Avraham Mordechai Alter.

"We, the Jewish people," he proclaimed, "are in the depths of a mighty threat from which, God willing, we shall be saved."

Sometime in the middle of the war, a group of kabbalists from Jerusalem traveled to Tyre on the Mediterranean coast of Lebanon. There they prayed that the evil Axis powers would be defeated and their wickedness nullified. Perhaps their concentrated efforts played a part in stopping Rommel's army.[25]

End of the Mandate Period

When the Second World War ended in Europe in May, 1945, and later that summer in the Far East, mankind breathed a great sigh of relief. The price of war in terms of human lives was estimated between thirty-five and sixty million, including the six million Jews killed in the Holocaust. Never had mankind spilled so much blood nor inflicted so much suffering. The tragedy of this world war, in which nothing was gained and so much was lost, became a lesson for the future. One practical outcome was the establishment of the United Nations, a global body intended to act as an international early warning system to maintain world peace.

As one of its first orders of business, the United Nations focused its attention on the unrest in the Middle East. The British had proved powerless to arrest the growing tension and disorder brought on by the nationalist sentiments of the Arab and Jewish inhabitants of Palestine. Since the end of the Second World War, the Arabs threatened reprisals if more Jews were allowed into the country, and the Jews protested against the callous curtailment of immigration of displaced war refugees. Shiploads of Jews were turned away at Haifa port and sent to the island of Cyprus. Perhaps one of the saddest episodes in the chronicles of the Mandate period occurred in 1947, when the British forced the Exodus, a ship full of refugees, back to Europe. As punishment, it was not permitted to dock at Cyprus, and no country allowed it to anchor at its ports. Finally, it was forced to return to Germany.

The detention camps and prisons were packed with Jewish political prisoners. The "father of the prisoners," Rav Aryeh Levin, gave the dejected men new courage. He passed them secret messages and always sent back regards to their families. He did everything humanly possible to save those who awaited the gallows. The growing number of detainees was only a harbinger of the volcanic eruption which loomed ahead.

The British police force maintained a tenuous peace. At one point the ratio of British enforcement agents to Jews in the detention camps was one to six. Nevertheless, despite the British presence, bombings and lightning attacks from both Arabs and Jews escalated markedly. By the end of 1947, the United Nations Security Council had drawn up a Partition Plan that created two autonomous states, one Jewish and the other Arab, with Jerusalem becoming internationalized. In order to balance the populations in the Holy City, each side with around 100,000, the boundaries of greater Jerusalem were extended to include Bethlehem. Both sides deemed the proposal unacceptable.

President Truman, a true friend of the Jews, openly supported the Partition Plan, and later the formation of the State of Israel. Disregarding advice from his Secretary of State, George Marshall, Truman later commented, "I felt that Israel deserved to be recognized and I didn't give a damn whether the Arabs liked it or not."[26]

After thirty years of guardianship over Palestine, the British officially announced their intention to relinquish their duty as caretakers. The warring parties would have to resolve their dispute by peaceful means before the 14 May, 1948 deadline, or else face each other in a military struggle.

The months before the deadline were chaotic and life-threatening. Arab residents living in Jewish areas were told by their leaders to evacuate immediately. Some 200,000 Arabs fled the Galilee, from Haifa to Tiberias, under the assumption that a quick Arab victory would reinstate them and give them the choicest Jewish property as a trophy. Their motto was: "Drive the Jews into the sea." Yet, the Arab League suffered internal bickering which hampered its effectiveness, and its potential massive power was translated into a feeble guerrilla-type warfare. Their forces were commanded by Abdul Khader Husseini, a charismatic leader who began his offensive by destroying convoys of food trucks on their way to Jerusalem, near Latrun.

The British maintained their policy of one-sided indifference, which both strangled and fueled the Jewish cause at every turn.

In Jerusalem, Dov Joseph, a Canadian lawyer, became the Chief of Civil Affairs. His job entailed organizing the allotment of food, water, and fuel for the 100,000 Jewish residents of the city. Fearing an Arab cut-off of precious water at the main pumping station on the coast at Rosh el-Ayin, he immediately ordered every private cistern filled with water. His foresight saved the city, when, on 7 May, the Arabs succeeded in cutting off the water. The emergency reserves of water were sufficient to sustain the populace for at least three months. Water tanks made regular bi-weekly trips through every section of the city.

Food rationing began in April, 1948. Operation Nachshon succeeded in bringing three convoys of foodstuffs from Tel Aviv to Jerusalem before the Arabs set up roadblocks at Latrun. The situation looked grim: there was barely enough rationed food to last a month. Milk, eggs, and meat began to disappear. The Machane Yehudah marketplace became desolate.

On the military side there was a race to obtain arms from European outlets for the inevitable outbreak of war on 15 May, the day after the British withdrawal. The Haganah and Irgun acted as individual units. The Irgun's independent attack on the Arab village of Deir Yassin on the western outskirts of Jerusalem, was highly condemned at the time as a massacre. Yet decades later, evidence was uncovered which revealed that the Arabs distorted the incident for

Sir Alan Cunningham embarking from the Haifa port on 14 May, 1948

political reasons.[27] The attack was countered by an Arab massacre of over seventy doctors and nurses on their way to the Mount Scopus Hospital via the Arab neighborhood of Sheikh Jarrah. The British, with the manpower to save the convoy, persisted in their policy of indifference.[28]

As the last days of the countdown before the British withdrawal approached, a blanket of grave uncertainty lay over the city and throughout the country. Jerusalem was completely cut off from food and water supplies. The hundred-plus British stations, military bases and buildings in and around Jerusalem would be up for grabs on 14 May. A crucial factor in the upcoming duel would be how many of these fortifications each side could take over.

A state of alert existed side by side with a need for normalcy. Schools and shops remained open. The Shabbos table echoed with traditional songs.

As the Haganah prepared the physical war plans, the religious civil populace prepared the spiritual ones. Periodically, the synagogues filled with special prayer services beseeching Divine protection at this hour of need. The eyes and hearts of Jews throughout the world turned to Palestine and the Holy City as the British evacuated the last soldiers.

Sir Alan Cunningham, the last British Chief Commission of Palestine, set off on the morning of 14 May. On that day the angels of war took over and the besieged city of Jerusalem gripped itself for the inevitable.

Notes

1. This and all the following sections until "In the Halls of Torah" are culled from *Mara d'Arah Yisrael* and *Ish al HaChomah* (*Guardian of Jerusalem*).
2. *Har Tzvi*, Introduction.
3. *Masua l'Dor*, p. 51.
4. *Mara d'Arah Yisrael*, p. 86.
5. Ibid.
6. Ibid., vol., p. 90.
7. Ibid.
8. We will shortly discuss Rav Kook's ideological motivations for joining Weizmann's camp. However, it would seem that the allegiance of these four men was dictated by entirely different considerations than those of the future Chief Rabbi. Apparently, they hoped to secure whatever holding they could for the religious camp from within the establishment. They felt that by working under the canopy of the Zionist rabbinate, they could achieve more results than standing alongside the *chareidi* opposition.
9. *Mara d'Arah Yisrael*, vol. 2, pp. 223– 225.
10. Ibid.
11. Told by Rav Yehudah Palai.
12. *V'zos l'Yehudah*, p. 47.
13. *Oros m'Mizrach*, p. 226.
14. *Achar HeAsef*, p. 150.
15. *Dimuyos Hod*, vol. 1, ch. 12.
16. *Masaos Yerushalayim,* pp. 240–246, p. 315.
17. *Masua l'Dor*, p. 66.
18. *Mara d'Arah Yisrael*, vol. 3, p. 121.
19. Based on *Palestine: A Study of Jewish, Arab, and British Policies*, vol. 1, pp. 256–257. It is interesting to compare this attitude with an earlier British one. In 1839, the British opened the first foreign consul in Jerusalem. In April, 1841, Lord Palmerston circulated a message that "the British government felt an interest in the welfare of Jews in general, and was anxious that they should be protected from oppression" (*Stirring Times*, vol. 1, pp. 106–107). This, in fact, was precisely what the British consulate did, especially under the direction of Consul James Finn.
20.. *A Tzaddik in Our Time*, pp. 202–203.
21. *Toldos HaChassidus b'Eretz Yisrael.*
22. *The Golden Dynasty*, p. 239.
23. *Masua l'Dor*, p. 96.
24. Ibid.
25. *Toldos HaChassidus b'Eretz Yisrael*, p. 29.
26. *Yated Ne'eman,* 29, January, 1999. George Marshall opposed recognition of Israel not only based on strategic and geopolitical arguments, as publicly announced at the time, but also on personal hostility. "They have stolen the land, they don't deserve the land," Truman's adviser Clark Clifford recalled General Marshall saying.
27. *Yated Ne'eman*, 27 March, 1998, p. 4.
28 See *O Jerusalem* for details.

Bygone Days

The Abominable Movie House

JERUSALEMITES WOULD recall the blizzard of 1919 as the heaviest snowstorm they had ever experienced. Over the course of three straight days, more than a meter of snow fell, with drifts rising much higher. Few ventured outside, but being inside was not necessarily a guarantee of shelter, as many roofs caved in from the unaccustomed weight of the snow.

On the third day of the storm, the indefatigable Rav Yosef Chaim Zonnenfeld headed out of Battei Machse in the direction of the New City, a small satchel in his hand. The black silhouette of the lone tzaddik against the awesome white sea of snow was the only figure moving across the pristine landscape. The reason for his journey was quite simple: several days earlier, he had been asked to perform the circumcision of a newborn child in Meah Shearim. Rav Yosef Chaim marched slowly across the field, his face shining in anticipation of participating in the mitzvah of bris milah. When he arrived at his destination, he was happily greeted by everyone present, who had naturally assumed that the blizzard would prevent him from coming.

Inside the synagogue, the venerated tzaddik rested for a few minutes before proceeding with the ceremony. Among the guests in the shul was a Jewish renegade who built the first movie house in Jerusalem, in partnership with an Arab investor. This Jew had obstinately rebuffed numerous pleas by Rav Zonnenfeld and his *beis din* to halt construction. When he opened the theater in defiance of the *rabbanim*, tensions in the community quickly escalated.

Rav Yosef Chaim turned to him and quoted the verse (*Isaiah* 1:18): "Though your sins be like scarlet, they shall be washed white as snow."

"Yes," continued Rav Yosef Chaim, "though your offense is terrible, for you are leading many to transgress, on this day of snow your sin will be washed away, for with the help of God, it will end completely."

Turning to everyone else present, he called out in a loud voice, "Is the movie house still standing?"

"Yes, I believe it is," someone replied.

"Well, the day is still young."

Not long afterwards, someone reported that the roof of the movie theater had collapsed under the burden of the snow.

A smile crossed the tzaddik's face. "Sometimes," he explained, "for the sake of a single field which needs water, God brings rains to the entire area; and sometimes, for the sake of a single building which must fall, an entire city has to suffer a heavy snowstorm!"

The Arab partner refused to see a Heavenly sign in the disaster and rebuilt the theater, going so far as to show movies on Shabbos. A few weeks after reopening, a fire broke out on Friday night which destroyed the whole movie house. Nothing was left but a heap of burnt rubble.

(*Ish Al HaChomah, Guardian of Jerusalem*, pp. 211–212)

The Gerrer Rebbe's Blessing

IT WAS a warm spring night in 1921. The Old City was quiet, and most of its residents were sleeping as the hour approached midnight. However, there was one house in the Jewish Quarter that was crowded with people. Jews of all stripes were on hand to get a blessing from the famous Gerrer Rebbe, Rebbe Avraham Mordechai Alter. This prince of Polish Jewry was visiting the Holy City for the first time, and his presence was the talk of the town.

Visitors were admitted to the Rebbe's room one at a time. As people entered, they immediately sensed the holiness that emanated from the tzaddik. The Rebbe said a few words to each person, listened to his requests, and blessed him.

When a ten-year-old Sephardic boy entered the room, the Rebbe looked fondly at him and asked him his name.

"Yehudah Zadkah," replied the boy as he kissed the Rebbe's hand.

"Why have you come, my dear child?" asked the Rebbe.

"I yearn to see the face of the great tzaddikim," he answered unpretentiously.

The Rebbe smiled.

"What are you studying in cheder?"

"Mishnah *Shabbos*."

"Do you know how many chapters there are in that mishnayos, Yehudah?"

"Twenty-four," he answered unhesitatingly.

"And do you know why Rabbi Yehudah HaNasi, who organized the mishnayos into six orders and each order into tractates and each tractate into chapters, decided to divide *Shabbos* into twenty-four chapters?"

Yehudah looked downward. "No," he answered. "But if the Rebbe will give me a few minutes I will go and ask one of my relatives and return."

The Rebbe nodded.

Yehudah quickly dashed off to the Shoshanim l'David Synagogue near the

Rav Yehudah Zadkah

Rav Yaakov Sofer

Bucharim Quarter in the New City. Though the hour was late, his uncle, Rav Yaakov Chaim Sofer, was sitting and studying. Breathlessly, the boy posed his question.

"Yes," answered Rav Sofer, author of *Kaf HaChaim*, "there are several reasons for this. I will tell you one of them. The twenty-four chapters correspond to the twenty-four books which comprise the Written Law, the Tanach. Therefore, everyone who keeps the Shabbos holy is considered as if he fulfills the entire Torah."

Without wasting a minute, Yehudah ran back to Rebbe Avraham Mordechai Alter's room. When the Gerrer Rebbe heard his reply, he blessed the boy with success in his Torah studies and growth in his fear of Heaven. Then he took a half-*grush* coin from the table and handed it to the boy. "This coin is a *segulah* for you, Yehudah. May the Lord watch over you and bring you success in life." Yehudah kissed the Rebbe's hand and returned home.

The next day Yehudah's mother knotted thread around the coin and told him to wear it as a necklace under his shirt. When he went to cheder, his teachers were surprised at his newfound clarity in Torah studies. Yehudah, however, knew the secret behind his success.

Years later, when Rav Yehudah Zadkah was Rosh Yeshivah of Porat Yosef, he would fondly recall the coin the Gerrer Rebbe gave him that night. He testified to its hidden power and deeply regretted that over the course of time it was lost.

(*V'zos l'Yehudah*, pp. 46–47)

Not for All the Gold in the World

A WEALTHY Jew from Europe came to Eretz Yisrael in the early 1920s to visit the Holy Land and to allocate some of his fortune to needy causes. A strong supporter of Zionist and secular concerns, he nevertheless felt obliged to seek out the leaders of the religious movements. His visit with Rav Kook, the Chief Rabbi of Eretz Yisrael, ended with a gift of 5,000 pounds sterling for the institutions under the Rav's supervision.

Upon the conclusion of his visit to the Chief Rabbi, he proceeded to Battei Machse, where Rav Zonnenfeld, the Rav of Jerusalem, lived. Rav Yosef Chaim welcomed him and together they sat down to discuss communal issues. The guest was quickly taken by Rav Chaim Yosef's dynamic personality. In the middle of their conversation, the philanthropist took out a certificate worth 25,000 pounds sterling, a truly enormous sum of money, and told Rav Zonnenfeld that the money was for the institutions under his guidance.

The note lay on the table as their conversation continued from the *yishuv* to Eretz Yisrael at large. Finally, the topic of Zionism was broached. Rav Zonnenfeld explained the *chareidi* point of view with his typical clarity and unswerving commitment to Torah principles.

"Is it not obvious," interrupted the guest, "that Herzl was a prophet of the times?"

The guest was immediately frozen to his seat as the revered Rav of Jerusalem shook from head to foot with rage. A second later, Rav Zonnenfeld stood up, and with the intensity of a lion yelled, "In my very house words of heresy have been uttered!" Next, he tore the certificate to shreds.

Shocked, the man left the Rav's house. Standing in the courtyard outside, he struggled to regain his composure. What disturbed him most was Rav Zonnenfeld's refusal to accept his gift.

Later, he returned and spoke with a member of Rav Zonnenfeld's family, beseeching him to convince the Rav to accept his original gift, along with an additional 25,000 pounds sterling. However, Rav Chaim Yosef refused to budge. Money tinged by one with Zionistic leanings could never be funneled into the *chareidi yishuv*.

(*Mara d'Arah Yisrael*, vol. 1, pp. 170–171)

Funeral of a Righteous Woman

ON WEDNESDAY morning, the first of Adar I, 1924 (5684), an unusual funeral took place in the Holy City. In a remarkable move, Rav Yosef Chaim Zonnenfeld, the revered Rav of Jerusalem, ordered all the Jewish shops in the city to remain closed during the burial ceremony. Such a decision was normally reserved for the death of a well-known tzaddik or *rosh yeshivah*. However, this funeral was an exception. A Sephardic woman had passed away that morning, and Rav Zonnenfeld felt that her burial deserved the same respect as those of great tzaddikim.

This woman was the daughter of the late Moroccan Rav of Jerusalem, Rav David Ben-Shimon. Her name was Delisia. In 1875 she married an Ashkenazic scholar by the name of Rav Yosef Krosz, the secretary of Kollel Ungarin. Delisia had inherited her father's noble qualities and had turned her versatile talents to furthering various communal causes. She founded and led a charity organization called Ezras Nashim. Each Friday afternoon poor families received food and money. Before the festival of Sukkos, the needy received new clothes free of charge, and on the eve of Pesach, a sum of money was issued to poor families from a special fund. The Ezras Nashim organization did not differentiate between Sephardim and Ashkenazim, or Yemenites and Moroccans; it worked to benefit all congregations equally.

Her name had become synonymous with charity, and her integrity was a model for all to emulate. Wealthy Jews happily sent her donations, knowing that every penny would be wisely put to use. Several times she traveled to Cairo, where her brother, Rav Aharon Ben-Shimon, was Chief Rabbi, and collected for the needy of Jerusalem. Delisia helped marry off numerous orphans, outfitting them for the occasion, securing a dowry, and covering all the other expenses as well. She treated each one as her own child and truly rejoiced at their weddings. She also kept an eye on the impoverished people who sat at the Western Wall. Since most of them were physically handicapped, she felt a special urge to aid and uplift them however and whenever she could.

Though she never bore any children of her own, she was the mother of hundreds of orphans and needy children. When she married Rav Krosz, he was a widower with five small children. She instinctively mothered them as if they were hers, giving them the same love and care that their real mother would have provided them.

For nearly fifty years, the poor of Jerusalem had found in her the encouragement and warmth they sought in their hour of need. Her days and nights were dedicated to carrying out her self-imposed mission of assisting the Holy City's downtrodden residents. Now that her time had come to leave the world, Rav Zonnenfeld felt that the inhabitants of the city owed her this show of respect. *Rabbanim* and dignitaries from every congregation in the city took part in the procession. The poor and impoverished wept, calling her the "mother of the unfortunate," an epithet which only partially described her greatness.

(*Chachmei HaMaarav*, pp. 104–105)

Nothing in Order

THE RESIDENTS of Battei Ungarin went all out to greet their special guest from Srik, Austria. General Gkoslevki, president of the Austro-Hungarian Empire, was familiar with the Jewish citizens of his country — both those living in Jerusalem and in Austria. Funds often flowed via official government channels to Eretz Yisrael.

Rav Yosef Chaim Zonnenfeld, as the leader of Kollel Ungarin, personally showed the distinguished visitor around the bustling neighborhood. As the two men strolled about, they discussed sundry topics. The Austrian president was impressed by everything he saw and heard. The neighborhood was clean and orderly, with a fresh and vibrant spirit about it. At one point during the tour, Gkoslevki asked to visit the development office.

In the office, the secretary of the *kollel* rummaged through piles of letters and forms, pulling out one here and one there. He then showed them to General Gkoslevki, commenting on how benevolent the president had always been towards Austrian citizens residing in Jerusalem.

"Not long ago," said the general, "I recall that we played a part in transferring a large sum of money to the *kollel*. If you do not mind, I would like to see the pertinent documents."

The secretary nodded and began looking for them. From one pile of letters to another, he quickly glanced for the documents the general had referred to. Other members of the office staff joined in the search, but in the end they were unable to discover the whereabouts of the missing papers.

General Gkoslevki dropped his smile. He turned to Rav Zonnenfeld and commented, "I am really shocked to see how unorganized this office is! If I am not mistaken, the name Jew is synonymous with orderliness. Don't you have one night a year in which you set forth a plan [Seder night]!"

Pointing to the mess on the table, he said, "If so, why can you not find the document?"

Without waiting for a reply, he turned back to Rav Zonnenfeld. "Ask of me any letter, receipt, or document, and I'll be able to get it for you in an instant. Even if it was dated a long time ago, within a minute or two you will have it in your hands."

Rav Yosef Chaim smiled at his guest. With his classical, candid approach, he addressed the indignant official.

"As you see, we are not organized here at the *kollel*. Yet when a philanthropist comes to give us a donation, we receive him without an appointment and with genuine friendliness. Thus he merits to receive abundant blessings from Heaven.

"On the other hand," continued Rav Yosef Chaim, "when someone arrives with a need we can help fulfill, we also assist him whenever he comes, without set hours. Thus, without any order, we equally accept givers and receivers whenever they enter our *kollel.*"

President General Gkoslevki was quite impressed with Rav Zonnenfeld's answer. In fact, as a result of this encounter, he became a loyal friend of Rav Chaim Yosef, corresponding with him and sending generous donations to Kollel Ungarin.

(*Mara d'Arah Yisrael*, pp. 159–161)

The Wallach Hospital

The Shaarei Zedek Hospital, colloquially known as the Wallach Hospital, after its founder and director, Dr. Moshe Wallach, opened its doors in 1902 (5662). Operating under primitive conditions, without running water or electricity, the forty-bed hospital earned a sterling reputation for quality care. All this was due to the fiery personality of its director and his demand for excellence on the part of the entire staff.

Following are a few excerpts from the "Recollections" of Dr. Wallach's head nurse, Schwester (sister) Selma. This remarkable woman served in the hospital for over half a century. Her dedication to both her profession and her director won the hearts of thousands who crossed her path.

[DOCTOR WALLACH] could look back with pride on a life of self-sacrifice. How great were his achievements! Friends who knew him from the beginning of his career in Jerusalem compared him with Dr. Albert Schweitzer in Lambarone. Even if things were not quite as uncivilized here as in Africa, they were primitive enough.

In spite of his great severity and austere way of life, Dr. Wallach had a sense of humor. Since he was so demanding of himself, one forgave him a great deal. He was a stern leader, and everybody knew how he could scream. Nevertheless, he often said nothing, even when he well knew that matters were not being handled according to his wishes.

Once a woman was standing outside the locked gate after hours when Dr. Wallach was just about to leave for the day.

Oh, please, let me in for five minutes," she said. "I want to see my husband, who was operated on yesterday. Quickly, before that crazy man Wallach comes, let me through."

Dr. Wallach replied: "I'll let you in, but really, only five minutes. I'll wait for you at the door."

After five minutes he called her out. At the gate she thanked him many times over and asked, "What is your name? You are such a kind person."

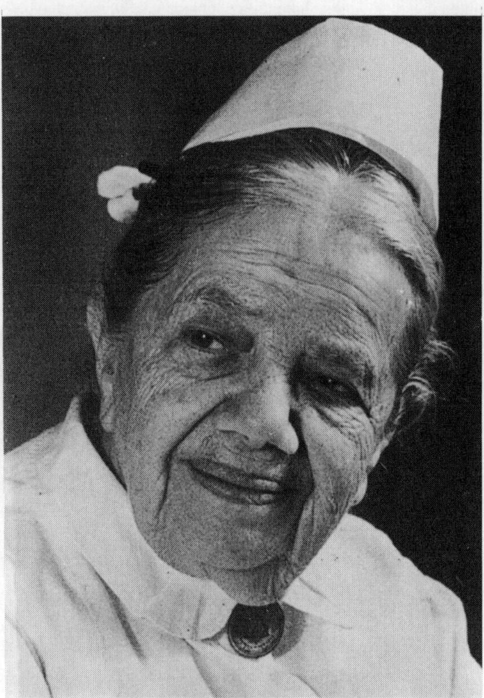

Dr. Moshe Wallach (left) and his head nurse, Schwester Selma (right)

"I am the crazy man Wallach!" he answered.

From 1920 until 1930, I [Schwester Selma] was responsible for everything from heaven to earth. One of my duties was to oversee the kashrus in the tea kitchens. This task was not easy for me, as Dr. Wallach was quite demanding in matters of religious observance in the hospital.

Dr. Wallach was the only doctor in the establishment. He often went to meetings of the Agudas Israel, and at those times I was left exclusively in charge. Often I had to take the initiative medically, in matters far beyond what my position would have normally dictated. There was, of course, no telephone yet that would have enabled me to call Dr. Wallach. With God's help, I always managed to do the right thing.

[A few weeks after I arrived in December, 1916], there were two epidemics. We were the only Jewish hospital in the New City. The old Bikur Cholim Hospital had also started building its new hospital in the New City; however, construction had been halted due to the [First World] War. People with typhoid, typhus, and meningococcal meningitis, all very severe cases, were hospitalized with us. Thousands of typhoid cases passed through our hospital, probably caused by dirt; there was hardly any water during that dreadful time. Additionally, the people suffered terribly from hunger, for there was hardly anything to eat. Meat and bread were especially scarce.

In order to protect the nursing assistants in some measure against infection, I put them into overalls such as laborers wear today, and had them pull hoods over their heads. I might also mention that I had only untrained personnel to

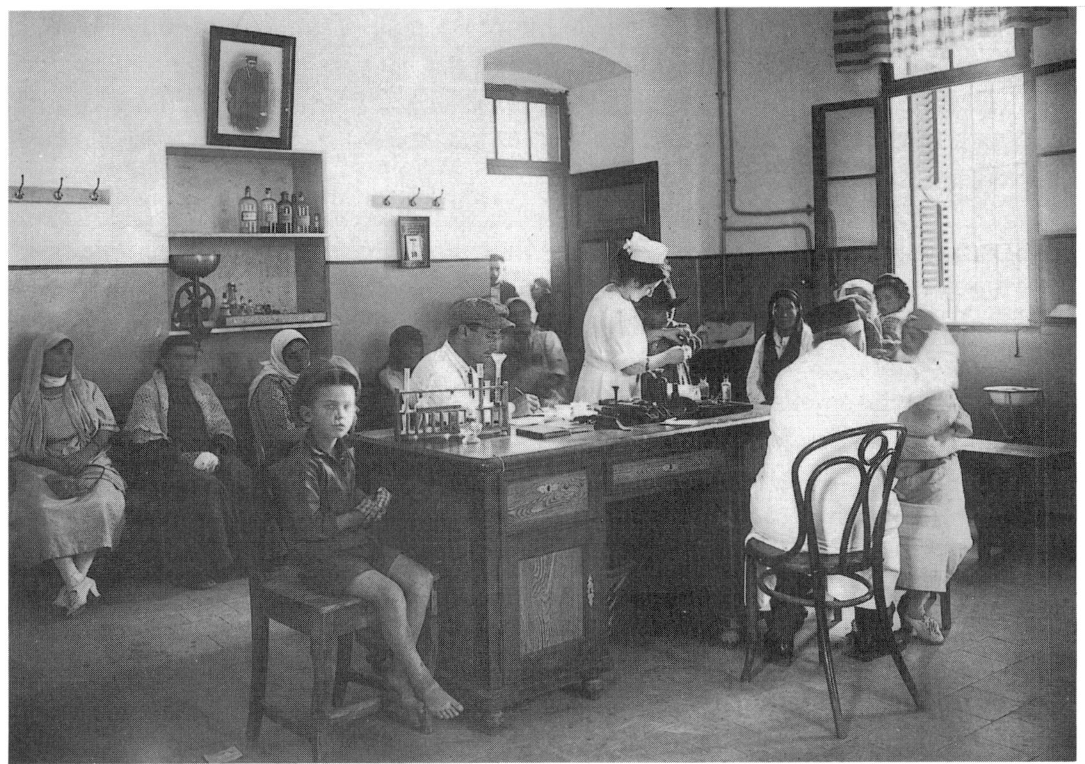

Dr. Wallach receiving patients

help me. Patients stood waiting for admission in a line that stretched from the hospital all the way to Machane Yehudah. Somehow, 150 beds were placed on the premises, which normally held only 43. However, even this was insufficient. The nurses quarters were also taken, and all the girls had to move to the basement. It took more than a year for the epidemics to cease.

During my career as midwife, I had the following experience several times: if a cesarean section had to be made on a very religious woman, the family first went to a rabbi for advice; there was no question that one had to receive permission to carry out such a procedure. If the rabbi gave his consent, the relatives then went to Rachel's tomb in Bethlehem, a long distance from Jerusalem in those days. Before going to the tomb, one of the family members would come to the hospital and measure the distance from the woman's bed to the Holy Ark (in the hospital synagogue on the first floor). They would then acquire a red thread that measured this same length, take it with them to the grave, and wrap it around the tomb. They would then return to the hospital, and tie the thread to the foot of the woman's bed and lay it along the corridor, down the stairs to the Holy Ark. While this was being done, a prayer was recited. Finally, after this entire ceremony was concluded, the operation could be started. One was often afraid that the babies would not wait that long!

Dr. Wallach had a Persian Jew trained as a male nurse and he was quite skillful. However, he always smelled very strongly of garlic. One day Dr. Wallach told him that he would have to leave the hospital if he continued to smell so much. Later on he was also trained as an anesthesiologist. He had an expert touch and administered the anesthesia at least as well as is done nowadays with the most modern apparatus.

The problem of the nursing staff was, of course, extremely difficult. Young girls with no previous experience whatsoever received practical, hands-on training at the hospital. The first trained nurse we had was a Dutch nurse, who returned to Holland after a short while because of the extremely primitive circumstances in the hospital.

With the combination of difficult conditions at the hospital and the strict demands of Dr. Wallach, it was obviously very hard to get suitable people on the staff, much less ones who would consent to stay for an extended period of time. When the occasional person came who was both qualified and willing to stay, it was like winning a lottery. Over the course of time, work slowly became more normal, although some things remained difficult.

In the early days, there was no modern transportation. Therefore, getting the patients to the hospital was complicated indeed. If somebody had to be brought in, it had to be done by stretcher. We did not have enough personnel to send along and therefore the relatives had to help or hire porters.

Tracheotomies, which usually had to be done quickly, were performed by Dr. Wallach himself. He was a pioneer in this operation in Palestine.

Dr. Wallach would not let a baby cry without coming running: "Nurse, have a look what is going on! Maybe the baby is sore or thirsty, or it has a stomach ache."

Dr. Wallach and Dr. Shabbetai [who joined the staff later] used to go around constantly painting everybody's throat, no matter what they complained about. Loads of people used to come after sundown on Saturday night to have their throats painted.

There was a sign on the wall of the clinic's waiting room telling men and women to sit separately. Nevertheless, Dr. Wallach used to walk into the room several times during the morning to make sure that this rule was observed.

Dr. Wallach worked until the age of eighty. On his seventy-fifth birthday, a big celebration was arranged in his honor at the Malachi Hotel, in the presence of the Englishman in charge of the Health Department. Many speeches were given, and his colleagues assembled a quartet to entertain the guests. Dr. Wallach then addressed the crowd himself, speaking in German. The first speaker mentioned all the accomplishments of Dr. Wallach and what he had achieved. At the end, Dr. Wallach said, "The speaker could not have referred to the Dr. Wallach who is sitting here; he probably meant my predecessor."

[Concerning the choice of a successor, Dr. Wallach] always used to reply, "I wish I could be my own successor, but this cannot be, of course."

Dr. Wallach passed away in his ninetieth year. There was a tremendous turnout for his funeral; half the town was there and many people came from all over the country. It was his last wish to be interred on the hospital grounds, next to Rav Dushinsky.

For many years to come the hospital was called the "Wallach Hospital," and even today there are still people who call it by that name.

(Culled from *My Life and Experiences at Shaarei Zedek*)

Donkeys and Bicycles

During the Mandate period, the British appointed a Jewish layman as leader of each area. The leader, or muchtar, of Meah Shearim publicized this notice in 1928.

Mea Shearim Quarter. Jerusalem, March 1[illegible]th 1928.

District Police Headquarters,

J e r u s a l e m.

Sir,

Subject:- Donkeys & Bicicles.

Reference:- Your 168/A/ID of 15th Ult.

With reference to the above quoted subject, my intention was not to prohibit transport through Mea Shearim Quarter, but I should like to orde all riders to descend from their bycicles or donkeys before entering the gates of Mea Shearim and to be guided by hands. By this means all accid will be avoided.

I hope that my request will be complied with, I am thanking you in a ticipation,

Yours Respectfully.

Muchtar.

בקשה למשטרת המנדט ממוכתר מאה שערים שלא יסעו על החמורים והאופניים [illegible]

בתוך שכונת מאה שערים' רק יסיעו אותם בידים. מתוך [illegible]

The Hundred-Year-Old Message

RAV SHIMSHON Aharon Polansky, the Rav of Teiplik, sat in his small house in the Beis Yisrael neighborhood of Jerusalem, staring off unseeingly in the distance.

"What am I to do now?" he thought. "This is the second time these *rabbanim* have come to me with this proposal. I already said no to them the first time, so why do they return with the same offer?"

Rav Shimshon Aharon mulled over the circumstances he found himself in, his mind in a turmoil. Only recently he and his family had fled from Poland with nothing more than the clothes on their backs. The year was 1925, and he had arrived penniless in Eretz Yisrael. He quickly made his way to the Holy City and found the house of Rav Yosef Chaim Zonnenfeld. The Rav of Jerusalem immediately took care of all his physical needs. He arranged for him to live in this humble abode in Beis Yisrael, furnished it, and made sure that the Rav of Teiplik received a monthly stipend. In a short time, Rav Polansky had become the unofficial Rav of Beis Yisrael.

Now delegates from the Zionist Rabbinate had come to offer him the prestigious position of *dayan* on their *beis din*. The new post included a spacious apartment, a bigger income, and other fringe benefits. The first time they made the offer, Rav Polansky refused without any difficulty. This time, however, he felt confused and disturbed.

It was late in the afternoon, and he decided to walk to the Old City to pray Minchah with Rav Zonnenfeld in the Battei Machse Synagogue. After Minchah he told the Rav of Jerusalem what was bothering him.

"How do you want to reply to them?" asked Rav Yosef Chaim.

"Obviously, in the negative. But they keep coming back and putting pressure on me, so perhaps I should acquiesce to their wishes."

The Rav of Jerusalem thought for a minute.

"Didn't you once tell me about a short inheritance note you received from your grandfather?"

"Yes," Rav Polansky answered. "I showed you the note which my grandfather, may he rest in peace, left for me. I was hoping you might be able to help me decipher the message he addressed to me a hundred years ago — before I was even born. He said that his grandson would one day go to Eretz Yisrael and would then be in need of his advice. When I fled Poland, that piece of paper was the only thing I took with me."

"Let me see it a minute," beckoned Rav Yosef Chaim.

"It's in my house in Beis Yisrael. Right after the Maariv service, I'll go and fetch it."

"Heaven forbid!" smiled the Rav of Jerusalem. "After Maariv we will both go together to Beis Yisrael. I have a neighborhood committee meeting there.

Perhaps this time I'll be able to unravel the cryptic message."

Later, they both sat in Rav Shimshon Aharon's home and studied the writing on the slip of paper. Rav Yosef Chaim held it in his hands and sat deep in thought. After a short time had passed, he addressed Rav Polansky.

"Your grandfather already saw with clarity that one day the Zionist delegates would come knocking on your door. A hundred years ago he perceived the conflict you would be in and guided you to the right decision. That is why he said that his grandson, once in Eretz Yisrael, would need his message, and that by following his words, he would be carrying out the will of the Almighty."

Rav Shimshon Aharon fingered his beard in nervous expectation.

"The message reads: ות״ל עיין ברע״ב והגר״א. Let us analyze it piece by piece.

"ות״ל is an abbreviation for the words in the Mishnah *Avos* (I:10): 'Do not seek to become intimate with the ruling authorities' (ואל תתודע לרשות).

"The rest of the message comes to explain the meaning of the Mishnah to you. עיין ברע״ב והגר״א is clearly understood: study the commentaries of Rav Ovadiah Bartenora and the Vilna Gaon on this Mishnah. They say that the reason one should not become intimate with the authorities is in order to not accept the position of Rav from them."

Rav Polansky's eyes stared in awe at the Rav of Jerusalem. Ever since his childhood, he had sought to unravel the mysterious message. Now, that very night, Rav Zonnenfeld had been Heaven-sent to divulge the secret to him.

"Surely, this is the true meaning of the message!" exclaimed Rav Shimshon Aharon excitedly.

The cloud of doubt which had enveloped Rav Polansky disappeared. His answer to the delegates would be crystal clear, echoing the call which his grandfather pronounced a hundred years before.

(*Kach Nifrazu HaChomos*, pp. 213–222)

The Security Deposit

IN THE 1930s, one of the upcoming tzaddikim of Jerusalem was Rav Asher Zelig Margolios. Still a relatively young man, Rav Asher Zelig sought out all the famous *rabbanim* of the time. He was especially close to the kabbalists, like Rav Chaim Shaul Deweik and Rav Shlomo Eliezer Elfandari, and later in life he would become the greatest Ashkenazic kabbalist of his generation.

In 1933 he heard that Rav Yeshaya Karelitz, known by the acronym Chazon Ish, had moved to Eretz Yisrael and settled in Bnei Brak. Rav Asher Zelig decided to travel to Bnei Brak and pose a question to the halachic giant. Over the past year he had headed a free loan society in the Beis Yisrael neighborhood, where he lived. In the course of time, a number of borrowers had left security deposits with him as guarantees of repayment. Sometimes, the due date passed and they did not come forward to pay back the loan. Should he sell the items they deposited or not?

The meeting with the Chazon Ish made a deep impression on the young tzaddik. However, he was entirely baffled by the answer he received to his query.

"Never sell the security deposit," cautioned the Chazon Ish, "since it could lead to *pikuach nefesh*, a life-threatening situation."

"What," asked Rav Asher Zelig to himself, "does selling the deposits have to do with *pikuach nefesh*?"

Rav Asher Zelig Margolios

No sooner had the question flashed through his mind when the Chazon Ish explained himself. "Indeed, once the jewelry of Reuven's wife is sold, Shimon will buy it for his wife. Therefore, hold on to the deposits until such time when the owner can redeem them."

The answer still left the young sage bewildered, and he asked Rav Karelitz what the connection was between Reuven and Shimon and a life-threatening situation. However, the Chazon Ish remained silent.

"Surely there is another level in his answer that I am unable to grasp," thought Rav Margolios. "I shall follow his advice and wait."

Months passed and the festival of Passover approached. On the eve of Passover, in mid-afternoon, someone knocked at his door.

"I'm sorry to interrupt you at this time," said one of the residents of Beis Yisrael. "But I have come to repay the loan I took and get back the jewelry I left as a deposit."

Rav Asher Zelig returned the jewelry and wished the man a happy and kosher Passover. Once he left, Rav Margolios stood by the door, deep in thought.

His wife, standing in the kitchen, noticed the perplexed look on her husband's face.

"Don't you understand," she said smilingly. "On the festival it is customary for young couples to visit their parents. When a young married woman visits her mother-in-law she has to wear her best jewelry. How can she present herself when her jewelry is lying in the free loan society's safety box?"

Rav Asher Zelig lit up with understanding. "Yes, now I understand the words of the Chazon Ish. Since jewelry has such importance in the eyes of women, what would be the outcome if I had sold Reuven's jewelry and Shimon bought it from the shopkeeper? How would Reuven's wife feel without her jewelry on the festival, and how would she have reacted when she saw them being worn by Shimon's wife? Yes, indeed, I now see the wisdom in the Chazon Ish's words!"

(*Kach Nifrazu HaChomos*, pp. 223–226)

Rebbe Shlomo of Zweille

RAV EPHRAIM Zalman Halprin could not hide his anxiety. Earlier that Friday morning, sometime in the early 1940s, he had received an urgent telegram from his family in Canada. His grandson was in serious condition in the hospital after a car accident. He was asked to gather a minyan and recite Psalms for the boy's recovery. Although he had fulfilled the request, he still paced nervously back and forth.

"What's the matter, Rav Zalman?" Rav Yitzchak David Burnstein inquired of his friend.

As he listened to Rav Halprin's story, Rav Yitzchak David shook his head slowly back and forth.

"I recommend that you go to the Zweiller Rebbe and ask that he give your grandson a blessing," Rav Burnstein said. "He is known to have tremendous power to intercede on behalf of the ill."

Rav Ephraim Zalman agreed, and the two men set out to the Rebbe's house in Beis Yisrael. When they arrived, they were told that the Rebbe had left for the nearby *mikve* at noontime, and they could see him there if it was urgent.

Soon they were inside the Beis Yisrael *mikve*. The Rebbe was already in the immersion pool with a serene look on his face. Rav Yitzchak David approached the pool and bent over to tell the Rebbe about the boy's condition. He then handed the Rebbe the telegram.

Rebbe Shlomo immersed with the telegram in his hand. After he lifted his head out of the water, he began to read the telegram out loud. When he came to the words "he is in serious condition," he said "he is well," and when he came to the words "the doctors fear for the worst," he said "the doctors say he is fine."

Rav Yitzchak David turned to Rav Halprin. "Do you hear what the Rebbe is saying!"

'Doesn't the Rebbe see what is written in the telegram?" asked Rav Halprin in surprise.

Unperturbed, Rebbe Shlomo of Zweille reread the contents of the telegram, looking at the print very closely. Again his mouth uttered the same auspicious words as before.

"If the Zweiller Rebbe reads the telegram as we now hear it," Rav Burnstein said to Rav Halprin, "there is nothing to worry about. You can relax and feel confident that everything is all right with your grandson."

Rav Zalman Halprin

Rav Halprin left feeling much better. After the conclusion of Shabbos, he waited until it was nightfall in Canada before calling his family. They told him the boy had made a sudden, marked recovery.

"When did you first notice the change in his condition?" he asked.

"Very early Friday morning, about twelve noon your time in Eretz Yisrael."

"Yes," thought Rav Halprin, "that is just when the Zweiller Rebbe read the telegram with a good interpretation!"

The meeting with Rebbe Shlomo of Zweille had a magnetic impact on Rav Ephraim Zalman Halprin. Soon afterwards he began to visit the tzaddik on a regular basis, and in the course of time became a loyal and devoted follower of his. Rav Halprin spent the rest of his life founding a network of *taharas hamishpachah* (family purity) organizations in Jerusalem.

(*Tzaddik Yesod Olam*, pp. 90–91)

Father of the Prisoners

AS EARLY as 1927, Rav Aryeh Levin began visiting Jewish prisoners who had been found guilty of political crimes like possessing a weapon or smuggling contraband into the country. The British overseers of Palestine stiffened their grip on the necks of the Jews in direct proportion to the Arabs' penchant for stirring up violent riots. In response, the Jewish underground, comprising groups like the Haganah, the Palmach, and the Irgun increased their activities, which led to many of their members being jailed.

In 1931 the British authorities requested that the Chief Rabbi appoint a prison chaplain who would visit the captives on Shabbos. Rav Kook turned to Rav Aryeh Levin, who worked as the supervisor in the Etz Chaim Talmud Torah, and asked him to take the position. Rav Aryeh accepted, on the condition that he would not receive any compensation for his time. Every Shabbos morning Rav Levin walked from his house in Mishkenos to the Russian Compound, where the main Jerusalem prison was located. He prayed together with the prisoners, sat and talked with each one, acted as an emissary between them

The central prison where Rav Aryeh visited every Shabbos. Today it is a museum.

and their families, and generally filled the vacuum in their lives. He never tried to force his religious values on them; at most he gave them a Book of Psalms to read. The inmates were captivated by his genuine warmth and sincerity, and the honor and respect with which he treated them. At one point, the Arab inmates even became jealous of their Jewish cell mates, for their Mufti's visits were guarded and aloof.

Rav Aryeh would take each inmate's hand and cup it inside his own. Slowly he would rub and squeeze the prisoner's hand as he sat and talked with him. His eyes radiated love and warmth, and he spoke soft and soothing words of encouragement. Even the most stubborn prisoners succumbed to the simple, untainted love he had for his fellow Jew.

The most heartbreaking situation he encountered was the predicament of the prisoners who were condemned to death. Rav Aryeh made every effort to appeal the sentences and reduce the punishment. Once he even threw himself in front of the High Commissioner's moving limousine in order to present his petition to him. Concerning those he could not save, like Dov Groner, Moshe Barzani, and Meir Feinstein, Rav Levin said: "None of us has any idea how high is the spiritual rank of these martyrs."

The prisoners themselves spoke of his influence on them. Following are some of the comments they made about him:

"We counted our days in prison according to Rav Aryeh's visits."

"I still thank the God of Israel that as the door of Cell 48 opened to lead me into an unknown future behind bars, He sent me this merciful angel of His."

"If you never saw a camp of prisoners receive Rav Aryeh and give him welcome, you cannot know the power of love and faith."

"About this Jew there was always a wondrous aura."

"Whoever didn't experience his unique handshake cannot understand its essence. One hand shook yours in greeting; and the other patted it in affection, as he spoke with you in his calm and reassuring manner."

"His eyes illuminated the darkness of our cells... For us he was a bridge to the past generations, a link of prayer with the Almighty."

Mattityahu Shmuelevitz, whose death sentence was commuted to life imprisonment, wrote in a letter: "Yet there is one person in particular to whom I remain grateful first and foremost; a dear, precious Jew... who stormed heaven and earth for me; and more important — it was he who brought me closer to my Maker in those fateful days... He made closeness... to God... clear and obvious... I thank that precious man for being a pillar of support."

In 1965 (5725), Rav Levin was honored at a ceremony assembled by the veteran underground resistance fighters from the Mandate period. Timed to take place on his eightieth birthday, it was held in the courtyard of the old central prison in the Russian Compound.

Rav Aryeh stood up to speak. "The importance of this assembly is that it has brought friends together. Moreover, *this* meeting is taking place on the *other* side of the prison bars... It particularly gladdens my heart to see the families of the prisoners, especially the little children, since I have always loved small children."

Then he added, "I do not know if I shall be privileged to be with you again like this. All I ask of you is this: Tell your children: *There was an old Jew in Jerusalem who loved us very much!*"

With that he burst into tears, and among the thousands of people there, not a dry eye was to be found.

(Culled from *A Tzaddik in Our Time*)

Paralysis and the Pledge

SHABBOS IN Jerusalem's central prison was just as one would have expected. There was happy anticipation in the air as the prisoners waited for the arrival of Rav Aryeh Levin, who would bring some light and hope into their otherwise drab existence. Rav Levin arrived on time for his regular weekly visit. As usual, he had the prisoners join in the morning prayer service; and as usual, when the time came, he began reading the weekly portion from the Torah scroll.

As he was in the middle of the Torah reading, one of the Arab guards approached and asked him to come outside, as there were people who wanted to speak with him. Rav Aryeh, however, had no wish to interrupt the reading and motioned to the guard to be so kind as to wait until he was finished.

A few minutes passed by and once again the guard appeared with the same request. Once more, though, the rabbi motioned to him to wait until he finished reading from the *sefer Torah*. Soon, however, the captain of the guard himself came, and asked Rav Levin to accompany him. There could be no further doubt: something quite serious must be afoot. Rav Aryeh asked one of the inmates to continue the reading, and he left the cell with the captain of the guard.

Once outside, he saw his son-in-law waiting for him at the prison entrance. In his heart he knew at once that some accident had occurred. However, he did not utter a word, and they silently set off for the Shaarei Chesed neighborhood, where his married daughter lived. As they reached his daughter's home, Rav Aryeh saw members of the family and medical doctors gathered there. It was then that he learned the news: his daughter had been stricken by paralysis. The only comfort the doctors could give him was that in their opinion, her total incapacitation would likely give way to partial paralysis over the course of time, and perhaps in a number of years she would recover completely. After an emotional meeting with his daughter, he reminded members of the family that "the rescuing help of the Lord can come in the twinkling of an eye."

Rav Aryeh Levin

That night, when Shabbos was over, the Arab guard from the prison knocked at his door. Burning with curiosity, the inmates at the jail had bribed him to go to Rav Levin's home and find out the reason for his sudden departure. Rav Aryeh explained what had happened and sent them a message not to worry.

The next Shabbos the prisoners flocked around him and asked how his daughter was. "As well as can be expected," he said emotionally.

During the Torah reading, an unusual thing occurred during the *Misheberach* prayer recited after each of the seven *aliyos*, in which one asks the Lord to bless and protect the man just called to the Torah. It is customary that the man called to the Torah pledges a sum to charity.

As Rav Aryeh duly recited the *Misheberach* for the first prisoner called to the Torah, he was surprised to hear the man announce that he was pledging a day of his life for the recovery of the good rabbi's daughter. When the time came for the *Misheberach* of the second man called, he announced that he forfeited a week of his life for the sake of the sick woman. The third man called pledged a month of his lifespan; and so it went. At last it was the turn of the seventh man, Dov Tamari, who later became a professor at the Technion in Haifa.

"What is our life in prison worth," he cried, "compared to our rabbi's anguish? I pledge all the remaining days of my life to the complete recovery of our rabbi's daughter!"

Rav Aryeh looked at the young man and burst into tears. He was moved beyond words to see how devoted these men were to him and how much affection they bore for him. Unable to continue with the prayer service, he shook hands warmly with every single one of the inmates and went straight home.

That evening, after Shabbos, members of his family came to tell him that his daughter was beginning to show signs of recovery: she had started to move some limbs. A few days went by, and her health returned completely, in utter contradiction to the medical prognosis, which predicted a long period of illness and convalescence.

(*A Tzaddik in Our Time*, pp. 248–252)

Two Halves Make a Whole

RAV DAVID Batelman (1911–1943) lived twenty-seven of his thirty-two years of life in the Holy City. In every aspect of his life, he was the quintessential Meah Shearim Jew. He studied in Etz Chaim Yeshivah, where he grew in his Torah studies and matured in the fear of Heaven. These two qualifications made Rav David a suitable match for the daughter of a respectable Jerusalemite family. With the marriage dowry, the young couple decided to open a grocery store in Meah Shearim. However, though he dedicated all of his energies to running the business, he found that the Lord's blessing was not with him. Thus it was that after a few years, he sold the store and tore up all the IOU notes that customers had given him, saying, "Let this be an atonement for my sins."

After a number of odd jobs, Rav Batelman finally found his place as a teacher in a *talmud Torah*. Yet, even this stable job did not provide enough income to support his growing family. The lean years of the 1930s and the outbreak of the Second World War left many people destitute, the Batelmans among them.

One Friday morning in 1942 (5702), Rav David returned from the *talmud*

Torah to his home in Meah Shearim. With seven small children in the house, things were naturally hectic, and Shabbos preparations were going quite slowly. Normally, he would have pitched in to help right away. On this particular Friday, however, he told his wife that the funeral procession of a family acquaintance was scheduled to begin shortly, and he felt he should participate in the *levayah*. She agreed, nevertheless reminding him to hurry home as soon as possible, as it was *erev Shabbos* and she really needed his help.

On his way home from the funeral, he saw a large pile of *sheimos* — old, torn holy books that need burial — laying on the corner of a side street. Some of them were burnt. Rav David's mind reeled at the sight. How disgraceful it was to the leave the holy "word of God" neglected and abandoned like that! He immediately went to search for some burlap sacks. Then he returned and filled three large bags with *sheimos*.

The hour was late when Rav David finally arrived home, one of the sacks in hand. His wife was at her wits' end. He calmed her down and explained what happened. "We'll share the mitzvah for eternity," he added. Quickly he brought the other two sacks into the house and then assisted his wife with the final Shabbos preparations.

A few months later, Rav Batelman learned that he was dying of a terminal disease. He concealed the news as best he could from his wife. He wanted to make sure that his family would have only good memories of his last few months together with them.

One day he came home with some nylons for his young daughters. Mrs. Batelman looked at them. "But don't we need bread for the children more than these?" she asked.

"Yes and no," he replied. "Yes, because of course we need bread to survive. But isn't the Lord the provider of bread? Leave it in His hands to determine how much livelihood we shall have. Haven't we seen wealthy people becoming poor and poor becoming rich?

"But what *is* in our hands to do," he raised his voice, "is to guide our children in modesty and fear of Heaven. This we must do wholeheartedly, and that is why I chose to buy the girls nylons rather than bread."

Mrs. Batelman remained silent, accepting his words.

A few months later, on 2 Sivan, 1943 (5703), Rav David Batelman passed away. He was thirty-two years old.

His widow, now left with seven orphans to raise, recalled the episode with the burlap sacks and his promise to share with her all the mitzvos he had done, in the World to Come. Now she could better appreciate his greatness. She commented to those around her, "Although he offered to share with me everything he did, I want to give him my half, too."

(Told by Rav Moshe Batelman)

Forty Days Straight

During the last quarter of the twentieth century, Jews have been coming to pray at the Western Wall in ever-increasing numbers. In recent times, a custom of unknown origin has arisen to pray there for forty consecutive days, and countless stories testify to the efficacy of this practice. Numerous people, some searching for their intended, others to have a child, and still others seeking recovery from an illness and the like, have gone to the Kosel for forty days in a row and had their prayers answered.

It's distinctly possible that the following incident might be the source for this custom.

ONE DAY in the early 1940s, Mrs. Shalom Schwadron stood by the entrance to the children's room in her house and gazed at her five-year-old daughter. Chayale lay in bed looking at a picture book. The doctor had just left, after reiterating his gloomy prognosis. "She will never walk, Mrs. Schwadron," he said in a sober, clinical manner. "There is some blockage in her spine which prevents her legs from receiving the messages being sent to them by her brain. No therapy can help, either. Just as hair cannot grow on the palm of the hand, so your daughter has no hope of ever walking."

Chayale's mother looked lovingly at her daughter and wanted to cry. "But Hashem can do anything," she whispered to herself. "If He sent little Chayale to us, surely He will send us some means for her to walk."

She turned to her husband. "Shalom, I want to go to the Zweiller Rebbe and ask him for a blessing that our precious Chayale will walk."

Rav Shalom mutely nodded his consent.

That same morning, Mrs. Schwadron walked from her house in Shaarei Chesed to Beis Yisrael. There she found Rebbe Shlomo of Zweille in his house and poured her woes to him.

"What can I do?" he spoke quietly.

"Please," Mrs. Schwadron entreated. "surely there must be something?!"

Rebbe Shlomo remained silent a long time. Finally he spoke. "Wait here while I go to the *mikve*. When I return, we'll see what can be done."

The Zweiller Rebbe shortly returned with an idea. "You should go to the Kosel forty days straight and pray for your daughter's recovery."

Mrs. Schwadron was taken aback. In those days it was dangerous for a woman to go alone to the Kosel, even in the middle of the day. Tensions with the Arabs were high, especially with those Arabs who lived in the Old City. As soon as she voiced her reservations, Rebbe Shlomo said, "I will go for you."

So it was. Every day Rebbe Shlomo of Zweille, who went regularly to the Kosel, added a special prayer for Chayale's recovery.

On the fortieth day, Mrs. Schwadron reminded her husband that it was forty days since the Zweiller Rebbe had begun praying for Chayale at the Kosel. Rav Shalom took his change purse and walked to the entrance of the children's room. On the other side of the room Chayale lay in bed.

"Chayale," called her father. "Chayale, do you see this purse that I'm holding in my hand? Well, all the money in it is yours, if you can come over here and take it from my hand."

Chayale looked at her parents and sat up on the edge of her bed. She had never walked in her life, and now with a nervous smile on her face she put her feet on the floor and slowly stood up. Her feet were shaking.

"Come on, Chayale," repeated her father. "Come here."

Slowly she took her first step, then another and another. Soon she was running into the arms of her father.

"I did it!" she yelled with joy, an innocent smile on her face.

Mrs. Schwadron took Chayale in her arms and hugged her with tears of joy flowing down her cheeks. "Yes, you did!" she cried.

Soon, the news spread throughout Shaarei Chesed and later throughout the city. From that day onwards, Chayale walked liked all her friends.

Mrs. Schwadron's indebtedness to the prayers of the Zweiller Rebbe was matched by her deeds for the Zweille institutions. She regularly collected donations for Zweille and helped in any way she could. In fact, both she and her husband, Rav Shalom Schwadron, bought plots on the Mount of Olives next to the grave of Rebbe Shlomo. When their times came to pass away from this world, they chose to remain close to the Zweiller Rebbe, all because of the forty days he prayed for their daughter at the Kosel.

(Told by Rav Yitzchak Schwadron)

From the Depths

THE HOLOCAUST was a living nightmare that defies description. The death camps were an unbelievable horror story, the crucible in which the Lord's children were put through the ultimate test. Nobody who managed to survive came out unscathed.

In Elul, 1943 (5703), a young Chassidic Rebbe from Galicia committed the unspeakable crime of possessing a *machzor*, the prayer book for the High Holy Days. It was the week before Rosh HaShanah, and Rebbe Yisrael Chaim Hirsch, the Rav of Badishel, had borrowed it to jot down key words and phrases to help him in his prayers on the holiest of days.

Unexpectedly, a Nazi guard passed by and saw him. Cursing, the infuriated guard grabbed the *machzor* out of his hand and threw it to the floor. The Nazi then proceeded to beat the Badisheler Rebbe mercilessly with a club until he

Rebbe Hirsch built this beis midrash, which he called Rabban Yochanan ben Zakkai Shul after his father. It is located near Shmuel HaNavi Street and has a community mikve.

collapsed unconscious on the floor. Miraculously, the young rebbe survived, but the blows had taken their toll — he would remain forever deaf.

In the midst of his beating, Rebbe Hirsch prayed to the Almighty, "O Lord, please save me from the hands of this Nazi. Save me for Your sake, so that I may serve You. If You will let me live, I promise to build a shul with a *mikve* in Jerusalem, Your Holy City; Jerusalem, Your Holy City, Jerusalem...."

Years passed, and the Rebbe started a new life in *chutz laAretz*. After three decades, circumstances finally permitted him to immigrate to Eretz Yisrael. Now his dream could become a reality, and he could fulfill his vow, which had become, in many ways, his reason for being. On a quiet knoll not far from the walls of the Old City, he built a shul and *mikve* — in Jerusalem, the Holy City, Jerusalem....

(Told by Rebbetzin Hirsch)

The K'vitel

AFTER WORLD War Two, the Satmar Rebbe, Rav Yoel Teitelbaum, came to Jerusalem, where he remained for close to a year before leaving for the shores of America. Prior to his departure, one of his Chassidim, Rav Asher Zelig Margolios, timidly approached him with a question.

"Rebbe," Rav Asher Zelig asked apprehensively, "it is an established custom that Chassidim give their Rebbe a *k'vitel* when they come to him with a request for a blessing. But now that the Rebbe is leaving us, to whom should we give our *k'vitlach*?"

The Satmar Rebbe looking lovingly at his chassid. "It is very simple," he answered. "Go to the *shetibel* in Meah Shearim and look for a bar mitzvah boy. When he rolls up his sleeve to put on tefillin, see if his arm is tattooed with a number from the concentration camps."

The Rebbe stopped for a few seconds. Obviously, it was painful for him to think of the horrible pictures of the camps he had formed by listening to innumerable eyewitness accounts. (The Rebbe himself had been in Hungary, and towards the war's end had miraculously escaped the fate of most of his fellow Jews there.)

"If you find such a boy, know that he has probably lost his father and mother, his brothers and sisters. The whole world he knew as a child shattered before his eyes, and the daily confrontation with the angel of death made his innocent mind and heart reel and cry out. Yet, if he succeeded in coming to Jerusalem and in putting on tefillin and praying before the Creator of the universe, then you may certainly trust that any *k'vitel* you have will be received by the Heavenly court from the lips of this loving son of God."

(Told by Rav Shlomo Eliezer Margolios)

The Rav and the High Commissioner

ONE FRIDAY afternoon, Rav Dushinsky, Rav of the Eidah Chareidis, received an urgent phone call at his home on Shmuel HaNavi Street. A leading official from the Jewish Agency described a dilemma to him which the Agency was unable to resolve.

"Two Jewish families were caught by the British trying to enter Palestine from Lebanon," he told Rav Dushinsky. "If we don't do something right away, the British will send them back to either Syria or Lebanon. And you know what that means...."

"Yes," the sober voice of the Rav replied. "They will be sentenced to death as traitors."

"We at the Jewish Agency have done everything in our power to save them. Yet, all our efforts have failed."

After a momentary silence, the caller continued, "We are asking you to intercede on behalf of these poor, innocent people, to save them from death. Every minute is precious and there is no time to lose."

Rav Yosef Tzvi Dushinsky sat for a moment contemplating a plan of action and then rose to call his personal aide, Rav Alter Yebrov. It turned out that

Rav Alter was in the *mikve*, making his final preparations for Shabbos. He immediately dressed and hurried to the Rav's house. When he arrived, he was informed that an urgent meeting between Rav Dushinsky and the High Commissioner had been arranged, to take place half an hour later. Rav Alter would act as translator.

Arriving on time, the two rabbis entered the High Commissioner's office.

Sir Alan Cunningham beckoned them to be seated. The issue at hand was no secret.

"As Chief Rabbi of the Jews," spoke the High Commissioner resolutely, "I would like to put forth one question to you: As you know, there is a law forbidding Jewish immigration into the land. Should I permit someone to transgress this law? In fact, how would you deal with transgressors of Jewish law?"

Rav Dushinsky's answer was on the tip of his tongue. "I have heard that the High Commissioner is familiar with the Bible. Certainly, you will recall the verse in *Psalms* (125:3): 'The rod of wickedness shall not rest upon the lot of the righteous, so that the righteous shall not stretch their hands into iniquity.' This verse needs clarification. What causes the righteous to stretch out their hands into iniquity — which obviously implies transgressing the law? Is it not the 'rod of wickedness' — in other words, the laws fabricated by the wicked which are untenable to the righteous?"

Looking directly into the eyes of the High Commissioner, Rav Dushinsky concluded by saying, "We pray that the law against Jewish immigration will be repealed so that more Jews shall not be arrested for breaking the law."

A smile crossed the lips of Sir Cunningham. The Jewish rabbi had clearly softened his heart —in this instance at least. With Rav Dushinsky sitting in his office, he telephoned his decision to immediately accept the two families into the country.

Although Rav Dushinsky and his aide breathlessly returned home mere minutes before sunset, they could truly relax and enjoy that Shabbos knowing that the lives of two families had been saved.

(*Sippurim Yerushalmim*, vol. 2, pp. 234–235)

20th Century
Birth Pangs of the Ancient City

Part III
Rebirth of a Nation: 1948-1998

לְמַעַן צִיּוֹן לֹא אֶחֱשֶׁה
וּלְמַעַן יְרוּשָׁלַם לֹא אֶשְׁקוֹט
עַד יֵצֵא כַנֹּגַהּ צִדְקָהּ וִישׁוּעָתָהּ כְּלַפִּיד יִבְעָר.

ישעיה ס״ב א׳

For the sake of Zion I shall not hold My peace,
nor for the sake of Jerusalem I shall not be still,
until her righteousness goes forth with radiance,
and her salvation like a burning torch.

Isaiah 62:1

Birth Pangs of an Ancient City

As the end of the British Mandate loomed closer, the entire country tensed for war. Even before the final withdrawal of English troops on 14 May 1948, the major Galilean cities of Haifa, Tiberias, and Safed had already fallen into Jewish hands. However, the Jewish forces were not always victorious. On 12 May, Kfar Etzion, a settlement on the road to Hebron, fell to the Arab Legion in one of saddest episodes of the war.

In the months prior to the Israeli declaration of independence, the Arab forces prepared to bolster their manpower by enlisting regular armies of several Middle Eastern kingdoms. The first country to declare war against the beleaguered Jews was Egypt. Just before the deadline for the British pullout, King Farouk ordered his troops to move up the Sinai coast towards Tel Aviv. His army reached to within twenty-five miles of the city before it was rebuffed. With the successful defense of Tel Aviv, Jerusalem was left as the only major battlefield. The Holy City, isolated in every direction, would have to fight its own battle for survival.

The Siege

On 11 June, the United Nations succeeded in introducing a month-long truce between the warring factions. However, the three-week period preceding the truce was the most difficult time faced by Jewish Jerusalem in the modern era. The birth pangs of the new Jewish nation brought the 100,000 Jewish residents of the Holy City to the brink of the unthinkable abyss — total annihilation at the hands of their Arab enemies. It was during that time that the Old City was lost. Also, there were three unsuccessful attempts mounted to capture the Latrun stronghold and free the road to Jerusalem. The ruined vehicles from the armed convoys can still be seen today alongside the highway to Jerusalem.

As the siege continued, the Jews cut off the electricity to the Arab sectors of the city, since the power station was in their hands. On the other hand, the Jews had no running water and a rapidly dwindling supply of food reserves. Rationing had been in effect for some time, but soon there would be no foodstuffs left to parcel out. By 4 June, the

Chief of Civilian Affairs reckoned that there was barely enough bread and beans to last five more days.

An American by the name of David Marcus conceived a simple yet brilliant scheme to break the blockade on the Jerusalem highway. His plan was to bypass the Latrun crossing at the end of the Valley of Ayalon with a makeshift road via the gorge of Bab el Wad that followed shepherd pathways. The proposed road was still within shelling distance of Latrun, but it was hoped that the Arabs would not recognize the significance of what the Jews were attempting to do. At first, Marcus was not taken seriously. However, with no other options available, the army finally decided to implement his daring plan. He and a team of volunteers were provided with two bulldozers to work with. Laboring around the clock, they finished the "Burma Road" within nineteen days. Miraculously, the Arabs at Latrun chose to save their last shells for better targets, and on 19 June, convoys of vital supplies began to trickle into Jerusalem. The first convoy via the Burma Road carried 140 tons of precious food, and within the first week over 2,000 tons of provisions — enough for a four-month rationed diet — filled the city's storerooms. Running water became a reality when a 150-man team finished laying a sixteen-mile pipeline within less than three weeks. With the physical welfare of Jewish Jerusalem thus guaranteed, a new wave of optimism swept over the besieged residents, and the Arab stranglehold — both physical and spiritual — was broken.

During the height of the siege, a strange phenomenon occurred which indicated to the residents that Heavenly

The Burma Road

grace was with them. Just before the British evacuation, an out-of-season, three-day rainstorm struck Jerusalem. This downpour served as the catalyst for a new and unexpected crop of a wild herb called *khubeiza*. The spinach-like herb was healthy, filling, and nutritious. With water in their cisterns and this unexpected source of food, they had renewed vigor to face the onslaught of the war.[1]

At the war's outbreak, both sides threw all of their manpower into the confrontation. In truth, however, the adversaries found themselves woefully unprepared for the battles that would take place in the coming days and weeks. The Arab front had been severely weakened when their venerated leader, Abdul Khader Husseini, died on 6 April while leading a counter-assault to retake the strategically located Arab village of Kastel. His replacement was incapable of uniting the various factions that comprised the Arab forces. Transjordan's King Abdullah entered the fray on 18 May, sending a thirty-year-old major, Abdullah Tell, to lead the Arab army.

As for the Jewish side, although the various groups had not managed to put aside all of their differences and present a completely united front, they were not quite as riven by dissent as their opponents. Instead, they were hampered by a severe lack of arms. However, what they lacked in weaponry, they made up for in cunning, strategy, and bravery. The commander of the Haganah forces in Jerusalem was a tactician named David Shaltiel. When more than a hundred strategic British outposts and buildings went up for grabs, Shaltiel quickly took over the Central Post Office on Jaffa Road and the large Schneller military base in Geula. The Jews were thus consolidated in several strategic locations. In early May, the wealthy Arab section of Katamon had fallen into Jewish hands, and it became the new residence of the 1,700 fugitives from the Jewish Quarter of the Old City (whose downfall we shall discuss shortly) later that month. Throughout the second half of May and the beginning of June, fierce fighting took place, with extensive damage to buildings and property.

Due to intensive shelling from the Arab side of the city, Jewish shops were closed and streets deserted. Most people slept in cellars or hallways, keeping well away from glass windows. Jewish morale was not broken, yet the daily shelling and lack of basic necessities was a heavy burden for the city's residents to bear.

The factor which tipped the scales in favor of the Jews was the United Nations' thirty-day truce, which went into effect at the beginning of June. U.N. mediator Count Folke Bernadotte of Sweden succeeded in calling for a cease-fire, along with a theoretical freeze on all military activities beginning ten o'clock Friday morning, 11 June. During the thirty-day lull, the Jews broke the food and water embargo and secretly smuggled arms into the city. The Arabs, however, failed to capitalize on this grace period, and with the resumption of fighting on 9 July, the Haganah forces were clearly in a much better position to conquer the entire city. The United Nations quickly moved to introduce a total cessation of all hostilities, beginning on 19 July, except in Jerusalem, where the deadline was set for forty-eight hours earlier.

Hours before a final cease-fire took

effect on 17 July, Shaltiel made a last-ditch attempt to recapture the Old City. Entitled Operation Kedem, the offensive depended on a specially designed bomb nicknamed Conus that would hopefully blast a huge hole in the Old City wall near Mount Zion. In order to distract the Arab forces so that the 350-pound bomb could be put in position, artillery shells were hurled into the Moslem Quarter, and a minor attack was launched at the New Gate. This phase of the plan successfully carried out, the bomb was set off. To the chagrin of Shaltiel and his forces, the tremendous blast did little more than blacken a spot on the 400-year-old wall. However, there was no more time to plan a new attack — the clock had run out, and the seven o'clock in the morning cease-fire took effect.

With this second truce came the birth of the Jewish nation. Unfortunately, the Old City, the home of the Jews of Jerusalem for generations, was now off-limits. This was more than a mere physical loss. The Western Wall, the central point to which Jews the world over turned, was in alien hands. The entire Jewish people were shocked beyond words: not since the Crusaders had banned them from the Old City nearly nine hundred years before had they faced such a grim reality. Nineteen long years would pass before the Jews would be reunited with the place that was the desire of their hearts.

However, this loss of precious territory was not the only price paid for the birth of the new nation. Even more terrible was the six thousand civilian and military casualties. This may not seem to be an overly exorbitant number. However, when taking the relatively small size of the total populace into account, it was proportionally equal to 2,000,000 Americans.

The Jewish Quarter Falls

Psychologically speaking, the Jewish hold on the Old City was the focal point of the battle for Jerusalem. From time immemorial, the city had been contained almost exclusively within the walls. The reality of a New City sprawling well beyond the confines of the ancient walls was a relatively new phenomenon, boasting a history of less than eighty years.

In 1948, the Old City was predominately Moslem. The Jewish population had been steadily declining since the riots of 1929, and in the months prior to the outbreak of war, no more than five thousand Jews remained. In comparison, the Arab populace was three times as large. As the British departure from Eretz Yisrael drew closer, more and more people left to resettle in areas of the New City that had a greater Jewish population density.

This exodus was not in order to find safer ground on the other side of the wall. All of Jewish, or western, Jerusalem was equally vulnerable to being conquered by the Arab forces. Rather, there were two other important reasons: First, the proximity factor: In the Old City, Jews literally lived a stone's throw away from their Arab neighbors — too close for comfort in such tense and harrowing times. In 1937, the British had erected concrete walls at strategic locations, intended to serve as a buffer between the two antagonists. Now, the Arabs tore some sections of these walls down, even before the 14 May deadline. In contrast, people living in the New City had a natural barrier: the Jews controlled the west and part of the south sides of the city, and the Arabs the north and east, with an imaginary no-man's land in between.

Secondly, freedom of movement in and out of the walled City ceased some time before the deadline, leaving the British in control of all convoys between Old and New Jerusalem. The English decreed that entry of military supplies and armed forces into the walled city was strictly forbidden; however, in practice this law was only enforced against the Jews. As a result, at the war's outbreak on 15 May, the Haganah was represented by barely two hundred men, a mere shadow of the vastly superior Arab forces. By this time the Jewish population in the Old City had dwindled to under two thousand — all observant Jews, and mostly women and children.

The British High Commissioner, Sir Alan Cunningham, tried to persuade the Chief Rabbi, Rav Yitzchak Herzog, to order his fellow Jews to abandon the Old City for the sake of their lives. "No!" replied Rav Herzog. "These Jews who choose to remain are the trustees guarding the heritage of all past generations of Jews."[2]

Shortly after the Partition Plan was ratified by the United Nations on 29 November, 1947, the Jewish Quarter became an island under siege. Food and medicine reached the beleaguered residents via British convoys. Arab neighbors who were previously friendly suddenly turned cold, and all interchange between Arab and Jew ceased. British soldiers searched houses for weapons and arrested suspects daily.

During the months leading up to the British evacuation, the British presence in the Old City was a double-edged sword. On the one hand, their presence maintained a sense of order between the two antagonists, and provided a lifeline for the residents of the Jewish Quarter who were cut off from the New City. On the other hand, their confiscation of Jewish weaponry, coupled with numerous unwarranted arrests, sharply hampered the ability of the Jews to prepare for their defense once open warfare would break out.

"But the Arabs walk around openly with weapons!" yelled a Jew as he was being arrested.

"The Moslem Quarter is not under our jurisdiction," replied a British officer in a monotone.

Within the first few days of the outbreak of the war, Arab gangs attacked the Jewish Quarter and nearly overtook it. Only a united stand by soldiers and residents miraculously repelled them.

There were a few rabbis who galvanized the weary members of the tiny enclave, injecting trust and faith in their hearts. One of them was Rav Yitzchak Orenstein, officially the Rav of the Kosel since 1940. Rav Orenstein was a man dedicated to helping out those who were less fortunate than himself. For years, his three-story home was known as a welfare station for the needy. His house was on the edge of the Jewish Quarter and commanded a panoramic view of the Temple Mount, Mount Scopus, and the Moabite mountains in the distance. After the U.N. voted for the partition plan, the Haganah planned to use Rav Yitzchak's residence as a major outpost and blockade against the Arab forces. Unfortu-

Jordanian bombardment of the Jewish Quarter

nately, on 25 January, 1948, Moslem infiltrators succeeded in setting off a bomb in the basement. The three-story building collapsed, leaving only part of the southern wall standing. Four Jews died and many others were injured. Today, it has been rebuilt and renamed Beis HaKeshatos.

From the time of this bombing onward, the major concentration of Jews was in Battei Machse. There, Rav Orenstein continued to give support, advice, and encouragement to the embattled residents, until he was killed by flying pieces of shrapnel in the last days of the war.

Another leader of the community was Rav Mordechai Weingarten. He lived in the courtyard of the Ohr HaChaim Synagogue, across from Battei Machse on the way to the Armenian Quarter. As the last official *muchtar*, district head of the Old City, he acted as the British liaison with the Jews who lived there. On the day the British evacuated the Walled City, a British officer knocked on his door and presented him with the key to Zion Gate. The old, rusty, foot-long key was England's present to the Jewish people.

During the first day or two of the war, Rav Weingarten, Rav Minzburg, head of the Chassidic *beis din*, and Rav Chazan, head of Porat Yosef Yeshivah, pleaded with Moshe Russnak, the head of the Jewish forces in the Old City, to surrender. Too much Jewish blood had been spilled, and the imminent threat of a massacre of the entire *yishuv* by fanatic Arab soldiers loomed over the remaining residents. When a peace deal fell through, the Arab Legion arrived with cannons and an organized army headed by Abdullah Tell. On 19 May the Arab Legion began shelling the Quarter from the Mount of Olives. For ten consecutive days the Quarter was bombed into submission.

The continuous bombing of the Jewish Quarter terrorized the residents. The Arabs' main goal was to take control of the strategic Nisan Beck Synagogue, officially called the Tiferes Yisrael Synagogue. The famous Chassidic *shetibel*, built in 1870, was one of the Old City's most notable landmarks. Standing at the top of the staircase leading from the Kosel, the shul stood at the gateway into the Jewish Quarter. On 20 May, the Arabs began barraging it, and within a couple of days Arab soldiers controlled the synagogue and the adjacent lanes. They raised their flag from its domed roof and began firing in the direction of Battei Machse.

Late in the afternoon, Jewish soldiers stormed the synagogue, and a bloody duel ensued. Bullets whizzed in all directions, and the air was thick with exploding grenades. Both sides suffered heavy losses; however, it was the Jews who emerged victorious. Unfortunately, they were not allowed to savor their triumph. The shul was shelled throughout the night, and the next morning the Jewish defenders fled when a new wave of Arab soldiers attacked in overpowering numbers.

After the decisive victory over Tiferes Yisrael, Major Tell aimed his weaponry at the Churvah Synagogue. On Thursday, 27 May, the day of Lag b'Omer, the Arab Legionnaires bombed and stormed it. With the loss of the Churvah, nothing stood between the Jews and total annihilation. Miraculously, the victorious troops contented themselves with pillaging and looting the ruins, saving their bloodlust for another day. However, it was only a matter of time before the Arab Legion would conquer the entire Quarter, and at that time, a dismal fate surely awaited the survivors. It was imperative for the Jews to surrender.

Surrender of the Old City[3]

Friday morning, 28 May, Rav Benzion Chazan and Rav Velvel Minzburg, the two senior rabbis of the Old City, walked outside with a white flag and surrendered.

Rav Minzburg later wrote the following account:

[The week before the surrender] we continued our Torah studies in the yeshivah of the Kalisher Rav, in spite of the

grave danger. That was the week in which the enemy bombed and destroyed the Nisan Beck shul, where I had prayed all my life. On that day we buried nineteen Jews in a communal grave across the way from Shaar HaShamayim Yeshivah.

On Tuesday I spoke with the commander of the Jewish forces and asked him, "What will be the end?" "They are sending reinforcements," he answered. But they never arrived.

On Thursday, 18 Iyar, there was a general meeting at my house [Beis Rothschild] which included all senior rabbis — both Sephardim and Ashkenazim — as well as the commander of the Jewish forces [Moshe Russnak]. After the meeting, a shell exploded near me which demolished the staircase to my house. I miraculously survived; however, my hearing was impaired due to the intensity of the explosion and its close proximity.

The following morning [Friday, 19 Iyar], the commander of the Haganah informed us that we should surrender. Rav Benzion Chazan agreed to accompany me into the Arab area. I didn't pay any attention to my family's pleas not to endanger myself. I gave eighteen grushim charity to a needy person standing next to me as I said, "I am prepared to sacrifice my life for the sake of the Jewish people."

We stepped outside waving a white flag, yet the firing did not stop. Rav Benzion was injured lightly. He called to them in Arabic until the firing died down.

Two Legionnaires came over to us

Rav Velvel Minzburg (1873–1962)

Rav Benzion Chazan (1885–1951)

and escorted us to the headquarters of the Arab commander. He sent Rav Benzion Chazan back to fetch the commander of the Haganah while I remained there. He offered me cigarettes, coffee, and pickles, yet out of anguish I didn't touch anything.

Abdullah Tell was very impressed by his captive — how he sat patiently among the Legionnaire troops without any sign of fear. Finally, through an interpreter, Tell asked the rabbi for a blessing.

"I cannot bless you with success in this military campaign," answered the venerated sage. "Such a thing would be a curse for our people."

After a short silence, Rav Minzburg continued. "Nevertheless, I am prepared to bless you that you excel at your command and rise ever higher — on one condition: you must promise me that you will not harm any Jew of the city, neither you nor your soldiers."

Major Tell agreed (and kept his word). Then the Haganah leaders entered and an agreement of surrender was signed in the presence of Red Cross and United Nations observers. All able-bodied men would be sent to a prison camp in Transjordan. Women, children, and the elderly would be sent to the New City, while the wounded would be dispatched to one or the other depending on the extent of their injuries.

Friday, 28 May (19 Iyar), was an infamous day on the Jewish calendar. The 1,300 remaining refugees packed a handful of personal belongings and prepared to march out of the Jewish Quarter through the Zion Gate to the New City. The last two weeks had been a traumatic experience — a direct confrontation with death. Their happiness over surviving the harrowing ordeal was mingled with an inconsolable sense of loss — the closeness to God which Jews feel by the Western Wall that they would be leaving behind. It seemed to signify a palpable separation between man and God. In disbelief, Rav Velvel Minzburg exclaimed, "I could not fathom how it came about that they succeeded in exiling us from the Old City!"[4]

As the sun set and Shabbos candles were lit throughout the city, the last Jews squeezed through the Zion Gate. Some three hundred men were placed in detention until they could be transferred to Transjordan. It would be nine long months before they were freed. Although the survivors would eventually rebuild their shattered lives, they would always harbor a longing for their ancestral homes in the Old City.

The iron gates of Zion Gate were locked and bolted. Not a single Jew would walk through the alleyways and lanes of the Old City. No Jew would kiss the Wailing Wall or shed tears there. Rav Weingarten took the key to the Zion Gate with him and carefully guarded it as a special treasure. At that bleak time no one had any idea when the Zion Gate would again be opened to the Jewish people.

A Divided City

The official cease-fire agreement between the Jewish and Arab forces was signed on 30 November, 1948. Using a map that was scaled to 1:20.000, lines were drawn to demarcate the new boundaries. Using colored markers, each

The Musrara neighborhood remained desolate for three years until a compromise was reached.

side first delineated the furthest point under their control. Any open area between the two lines (red lines for Israel and green for Jordan) became no-man's land. In a number of cases, the two lines converged, leading to a delicate problem concerning the exact demarcation between the two sides. This dilemma was augmented by the fact that the thickness of the marker lines equaled seventy meters of land. Even with the U.N. arbitrator, it was almost impossible for the two sides to reach a compromise. For example, part of the neighborhood of Musrara, located between Meah Shearim and the Damascus Gate, remained deadlocked until an agreement was reached in July, 1951.

The first showdown over the "thick line" territory occurred in the beginning of 1950. At that time, an Israeli soldier was shot dead near the Mandelbaum Gate, in an area which the Israelis claimed belonged to them.

The Hebrew University stood on Mount Scopus, which was unequivocally within the Jordanian boundaries. According to a bilateral agreement, the university and the Hadassah Hospital remained in Jewish hands, with a convey permitted to travel there twice a week.

As time passed, both sides consolidated their positions, and built walls and fences for security reasons. The Jordanians had thirty-six military posts around the city, compared to nineteen for the Israelis. Two of the Israeli posts also functioned as gathering places, for both locals and tourists: Mount Zion and the

Notre Dame hospice. Mount Zion, located outside the Old City near the Zion Gate, remained in Jewish hands. Near the Tomb of King David is a winding staircase that leads to a watchtower, which has a superb view of the Old City, the Temple Mount, and a sliver of the Western Wall. In those days, the only means of reaching Mount Zion was from a steep staircase leading up from the Valley of Hinnom. People flocked to the watchtower in order to get a glimpse of the heritage that had been so painfully torn from their hands.

The Notre Dame hospice, located on Shivtei Yisrael Street, was just a stone's throw from the New Gate of the Old City. Its roof provided another vantage point onto the Walled City, from which one could see the Damascus Gate, the Dome of the Rock, and the top of the Mount of Olives.

Inside the New City, the life of Jewish Jerusalem resumed a stable course. The drama of the past six months that culminated in the War of Independence could best be likened to the pangs of a woman in birth travail. Suddenly, with the relief of the cease-fire, the birth of the Jewish state came about. Israel was young and full of self-confidence. As the young country prepared itself for the difficult task of running a nation, Jews the world over were awe-struck at the significance of the events that had taken place.

The Jewish Capital

For the first time in two millennia, Jews were in command of the political affairs of the country. This newfound freedom had several ramifications. Jews were now able to walk freely in the streets of the Holy City for the first time since the Second Temple era. They were no longer humiliated as second-class citizens, suspected of and incriminated in imaginary crimes at every turn. Especially after the recent genocide in Eastern Europe, the independent Jewish state gave expression to a newfound religious freedom. Moreover, its establishment signified the world's acceptance of a faith that was numerically almost insignificant.

This new freedom was interpreted in different ways. The Zionists prided themselves on having freed the country from the yoke of Arab and British supremacy. The religious saw the Hand of God granting His people asylum in their ancient homeland. It was an undeserved gift which would require a new allegiance to the Torah and commandments.

In 1949, Jerusalem became the capital of the new nation, which helped make it the focal point of the country. The Knesset became the political channel of democracy. The economy slowly developed, and socialized medicine and farming became hallmarks of the new social structure. Stamps and coins bearing Jewish motifs flooded the country, and Hebrew officially became the national language.

One of the first major issues facing the country centered on the authority of Torah Law in a government run by Jews — albeit, irreligious ones. Concerning "personal status" — marriage and divorce — there was a common consent that religious law should prevail, thereby maintaining the inherent Jewishness of the people. Shabbos was declared the day of rest, and on that day, government institutions were closed and public transportation was forbidden to operate. Thus the country had a definite tinge of Jewish identity.

The question of religious groups participating in an irreligious government was the cause of much soul-searching among the religious sectors of the country. The general position of Agudas Yisrael became the accepted opinion of many.[5] Agudah held that on a superficial level such a partnership was forbidden by the Torah. Yet, upon a deeper analysis, the present-day situation had precedents in ancient times, when Torah leaders associated with corrupt kings — both Jewish and Gentile — as well as with wicked Jews in powerful positions. Their participation was compelled by circumstances of the times, and if they had not consented to work with these people, the consequences would have been detrimental to religious Jewry.

Therefore, under the circumstances prevailing in modern-day Israel, a Torah voice in the government would act as a double-edged sword for the religious cause. First, it would rally support for religious goals, such as kashrus laws and funding for institutions. Secondly, it would oppose laws which countered religious ends, like induction of religious girls into the army.

It was clear, however, that all relationships with irreligious parties had to be conducted without any desire for personal gain. Even praise and honor for their leaders had to be curtailed and measured sparingly. This was because an open-armed relationship might be interpreted by innocent, unknowledgable Jews as condoning these groups' antireligious policies. Without any doubt, the sole purpose of forming religious parties and joining the Knesset was to protect the interests of the Torah camp. In no way did it represent a means of aiding the secular parties or consenting to their ideologies.

Over the coming decades, new religious parties formed to advocate a policy either more stringent than this middle-of-the-road one, or to represent an ethnic group such as the Sephardim.

Other religious factions, like the Eidah Chareidis and Neturei Carta, strongly vetoed any interaction whatsoever with the irreligious. However, the overwhelming majority favored participation in the government.

In the years since the formation of the state, no one party has ever managed to win a majority vote that would have allowed them to form a government by themselves. As a result, the larger parties always found it necessary to enter into coalition agreements with the smaller ones, including the religious factions. This allowed the religious parties to have an active role in the government, and occasionally to wield power in the Knesset that was far out of proportion to their size.

Thus, within the framework of a modern state, religious Jews concentrated on strengthening Torah in the Holy City and the entire country. In the final analysis, the Torah parties were able to accomplish much good through their participation in the government. However, their association was a far cry from the dream of making Jerusalem and Israel a light unto the world.

The Maturing Years

The period between 1948 and 1967 may be called one of growing up. On the one side, mankind as a whole was recovering from the Second World War. Advances in technology would bring humanity to the brink of outer space. On the other side, Eretz Yisrael, a small island surrounded by Arab countries, searched for self-identity and freedom. Nothing happened overnight. Building a new society on ancient ground necessitated tremendous perseverance. Yet, it was precisely during this period that the foundation stones of the country would solidify, with repercussions for future generations.

Blossoming of Yeshivos

The vacuum caused by the annihilation of European Jewry resulted in the flowering of Torah institutions in Israel and the United States. Refugees from the Second World War transformed the American continent into a wellspring of Torah. In the coming years, Rav Aharon Kotler built the Lakewood Yeshivah, and Rav Shraga Feival Mendelowitch built Torah v'Daas. Rav Yaakov Kaminetsky and the Admorim of Satmar and Bubov strengthen *yiddishkeit* in the New York area. Earlier fugitives from the 1930s, especially Rav Moshe Feinstein and the Lubavitcher Rebbe, were to become beacons of Torah in America.

In Eretz Yisrael, too, the Almighty planted a few roses that had been plucked from the European garden before it was trampled to death. In Bnei Brak, Rav Yosef Kahanneman built Ponevitch Yeshivah. In Jerusalem, Rav Yitzchak Zev Soloveitchik built the Brisk Yeshivah, Rav Eliezer Yehudah Finkel built the Mir Yeshivah, and the Belzer Rebbe rekindled his illustrious dynasty. The Satmar Rebbe, Rebbe Yoel Teitelbaum, emigrated from Switzerland in 1946 and spent a year in Jerusalem before deciding to settle permanently in America.*

Like the newborn nation, the yeshivah movement was in its infancy. The world was slowly recuperating from the exhaustive global war, and a new generation of youth desired to study Torah. Unfortunately, the influence of assimilation — even if not overt — pulled many young men with sharp minds into colleges, where their attention was turned

* See story, "The K'vitel," in *Bygone Days: 1948–1998*.

to ensuring a secure financial future for themselves. Yet, men of vision, survivors of the Holocaust, astutely perceived the importance of a strong Torah education. Following is a brief review of the three most influential yeshivos that were established in the Holy City in the wake of the Second World War: Mir, Brisk, and Kol Torah.

Mir Yeshivah

The Mir Yeshivah was established by Rav Eliezer Yehudah Finkel in the Beis Yisrael neighborhood. Rav Finkel had organized a student body as early as 1944, well before construction of the Yeshiva's own *beis midrash* got underway. Among his first students were Rav Yudel Shapiro (later Rosh Kollel of Kollel Chazon Ish), Rav Chaim Greinerman, and Rav Chaim Brim. Built between 1947 and 1953, the Mir Yeshivah officially opened its doors in 1949, when the first story was completed.

Rav Finkel's building, like Ponevitch in Bnei Brak, could sit hundreds of students. Yet, in the early days, there was nowhere near this number of students. Rav Finkel only smiled and said, "A time will come, God willing, when there won't be room to sit in this *beis midrash* due to overcrowdedness." When he passed away in 1965, there were over two hundred students in the yeshivah. After the Six-Day War, American students started to come to the Mir. The student body spiraled from five hundred in 1970 to nearly two thousand by the end of the century.

Among the other charismatic leaders of the Mir Yeshivah were Rav Chaim

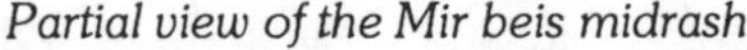

Partial view of the Mir beis midrash

Shmulevitz and Rav Beinush Finkel. Rav Chaim, a *gaon* in Torah, implanted a spirit of pure Torah study in the students' hearts. His Sunday night *shmuessen* (lectures) became proverbial, with the *beis midrash* full of people who came to hear him develop basic themes in human interactions based on the words of the Sages. Rav Beinush Finkel, son of Rav Yehudah Finkel, endeavored to initiate a new program of studies whereby the students would complete an entire tractate each semester. Until that time, most students focused their entire studies on several dozen pages of Gemara during a winter or summer session. "The holiness of a *mesechtah* [tractate]!" he exclaimed. "If only people would realize the holiness of a *mesechtah* that is completed...from cover to cover!"*

Brisk Yeshivah

The Brisker Rav, Rav Yitzchak Zev Soloveitchik, arrived in Eretz Yisrael in 1941. The son of Rav Chaim Soloveitchik and the grandson of Rav Yosef Dov Soloveitchik, Rav Yitzchak Zev became Rav of Brisk in 1918. One of the *gedolei ha'dor*, Rav Soloveitchik brought with him to Eretz Yisrael the Brisker method of Torah study. Over the coming years he taught a group of students in his house on Press Street. He also was responsible for opening an orphanage and refugee home for children, called Sanhedria.

When he passed away in the fall of 1959, his oldest son, Rav Yosef Dov Ber, continued to give the class.

Rav Yitzchak Zev Soloveitchik (1886–1959)

The yeshivah's expansion, like that of Mir Yeshivah, was due to the influx of young American *bachurim* in the late 1960s and early 1970s. Other sons of Rav Yitzchak Zev, including Rav David and Rav Meir, also opened Brisk yeshivos in the Geula neighborhood. They continued to imbue their students with the sharp, analytical method known as the *Brisker derech*.

When Rav Yosef Dov Ber passed away in 1981, his son Rav Avraham Yehoshua became Rosh Yeshivah. In the following years, he expanded the premises on Press Street and built a large *beis midrash*.

Today, the Brisk yeshivah's student body numbers in the hundreds. More than that, they are a strong force in the Torah world.

Kol Torah Yeshivah

Kol Torah Yeshivah was founded in 1939 by Rav Yechiel Shlesinger and Rav Baruch Kunshtat. Most of the first students came from Germany and other

* See story, "The Legendary Finkels," in *Bygone Days: 1948–1998*.

Rav Shlomo Zalman Auerbach delivering a gemara shiur at Kol Torah Yeshivah

European countries. During its formative years, the yeshivah did not cater to boys who wanted to remain involved in Torah studies for an indefinite period of time. Rather, the goal was to give young men a strong grounding in Torah before they married and entered the world of earning a livelihood.

During this period, the yeshivah was located in Rechavia. Only in 1957 (5717) did it move to its present location in Bayit Vegan. In its early days, the yeshivah faced an ideological battle with the "establishment." At that time, all major Ashkenazic yeshivos studied in Yiddish. Kol Torah was the first yeshivah to branch away from this enshrined practice and teach in modern Hebrew. This departure from the norm initially caused a fury throughout the yeshivah world. It finally subsided after the Chazon Ish publicly voiced his approval permitting Hebrew as the language used in Kol Torah.

The results of using Hebrew were unquestionably positive. Firstly, until this time, Sephardic boys had no opportunity of studying in an Ashkenazic yeshivah. Now, some chose to study in Kol Torah and avail themselves of Rav Shlomo Zalman Auerbach's lectures. Additionally, in the coming decades, more and more Ashkenazic yeshivos switched to Hebrew to accommodate a new generation which was not fluent in Yiddish. Thus, Kol Torah led the way in this very important change in the makeup of the yeshivah world.

The prize of the yeshivah was Rav Shlomo Zalman Auerbach. A Jerusalemite whose wide-brimmed Yerushalmi hat seemed out of place in a Litvishe yeshivah, Rav Shlomo Zalman won the admiration of his students and colleagues. His career in the yeshivah spanned over forty years, and he instructed thousands of students in his method of learning and analyzing the Oral Law.*

Besides his daily *shiur*, Rav Shlomo Zalman tested his pupils every month and also interviewed prospective students for the coming year. Deeply concerned about each student's progress, he would occasionally ask some of the boys to write down his lecture. He would then read over what they had written and mark down where a student misunderstood or skipped something. In this way, the young man became more astute at comprehending the *shiur*.

Rav Auerbach's power as a halachic authority first reached the wider Jewish public through the book *Shemiras Shabbos k'Hilchasah*. Written by Rav Yehoshua Neuwirth in 1965 (5725), this classic work concerning the practical laws of Shabbos was largely based on the halachic decisions of Rav Shlomo Zalman. In the course of time, more and more people came to his house in Shaarei Chesed to ask him halachic questions. Rav Auerbach primarily addressed modern-day concerns, ranging from questions involving electricity to organ transplants.

Today, Kol Torah Yeshivah ranks as one of the outstanding yeshivos in Jerusalem.

Rav Ovadiah Hadaya (1890–1969)

Beis El Yeshivah

One of the oldest yeshivos in Jerusalem, dating back to the 1740s, was Beis El Yeshivah. When the Old City fell into Jordanian hands in 1948, the *chachamim* of the yeshivah began to disband for lack of a place to continue their studies together. Rav Ovadiah Hadaya, a prominent *dayan* in the Rabbinate, offered the roof of his house on Rashi Street as a spot to rebuild Beis El. The Kabbalah yeshivah reopened in the

* See story, "To Be or Not to Be," in *Bygone Days: 1948–1998*.

1950s under the leadership of Rav Hadaya, a brilliant kabbalist.

After the Six-Day War, Beis El reopened at its original location in the Old City, while maintaining their new premises on Rashi Street.

Porat Yosef Yeshivah went through a similar transition. During the nineteen years (1948–1967) when the Old City was in Jordanian hands, the yeshivah built new quarters in Geula. Afterwards, they kept both sites.

There were other yeshivos which opened their doors during this period, such as Navardok Yeshivah. The older ones, like Hebron and Etz Chaim Yeshivos, had already produced leaders for the new generation. Now, the new ones joined them in guiding young men in the ways of their forefathers.

Vaad HaYeshivos

The network of yeshivos throughout Eretz Yisrael needed a representative body to assist them in their relations with the government, as well as support them in their time of need. In 1941 (5702), Rav Zalman Sorotzkin founded Vaad HaYeshivos to answer this need.

Rav Sorotzkin's initiative was not original. Vaad HaYeshivos existed in Europe until the Second World War.

Rav Zalman Sorotzkin (right) with Rav Chaim Leib Auerbach (left)

Originally founded by the Chofetz Chaim and Rav Chaim Ozer Grodzensky before the First World War, the institution succeeded in establishing vital links between the yeshivos and strengthening yiddishkeit in general.

Rav Zalman Sorotzkin was the perfect man to reestablish Vaad HaYeshivos in Eretz Yisrael. As Rav of Lutzk, he had been an Agudas Yisrael activist, and right-hand man of the Chofetz Chaim. His fundamental principle in creating Vaad HaYeshivos was to be non-discriminatory. Every yeshivah, be it Ashkenazic or Sephardic, Litvishe or Chassidic, was accepted by the *vaad*. The goal was to uplift the crown of Torah in Eretz Yisrael.

Rav Zalman was indefatigable, a paragon of leadership and humility. Besides his efforts to strengthen the yeshivos, he established the Chinuch Atzmai school system, which offered families with traditional backgrounds the possibility to send their children to religious schools rather than secular ones. He also wrote *HaDe'ah v'HaDibur* (*drash*) and *Aznaim l'Torah*, a commentary on the Torah.

Vaad HaYeshivos played a vital role during the formative years of the rebuilding of yeshivos in the post-World War Two era. Financial aid directed to the yeshivos saved some of them from closing. Free clothes to students and an interest-free loan society gave more stability to those in need. All military deferments went through Vaad HaYeshivos, as they do today.

Their publishing house of gemaros, *chumashim*, and other basic Torah literature gave yeshivah students throughout the country access to these works during a period when such books were relatively rare. In 1963 (5723), for example, more than 100,000 were distributed at reduced rates.

Today, too, Vaad HaYeshivos continues to serve the Torah community.

The Chassidic World

The Chassidic dynasties grew and expanded to such an extent in the post-World War II era that it is impossible to touch on all of the them. Herein we will review some of the numerically more significant ones, including Ger, Belz, Boyan, Karlin-Stolin, Breslov, and Toldos Aharon. Other dynasties with rebbes living in Jerusalem — like Sefinka, Biala, Komarno, Tolner, Slonim and Matersdorf — also made an imprint on the city. As well, there are many groups who maintain communities in Jerusalem, but whose courts are centered elsewhere, including Vishnitz, Satmar, Sanz, Bubov, and Nadvorna, to name but a few.

Gerrer Dynasty

When Rebbe Avraham Mordechai Alter passed away in 1948, he left three sons. The eldest, Rebbe Yisrael Alter, led the dynasty for twenty-eight years, until his passing in 1976. He was followed by his brother, Rebbe Simcha Bunim Alter (1976–1992), who was in turn followed by his brother, Rebbe Pinchas Menachem Alter (1992–1996). Today, Rebbe Yaakov Aryeh, the son of Simcha Bunim, leads the Gerrer Chassidim.

Under the reign of Rebbe Yisrael Alter, the dynasty grew into the largest Chassidic court in Eretz Yisrael. Though centered in Jerusalem, the Rebbe built Gerrer *shetibels* in major cities throughout the country, from Arad in the Negev to Chatzor in the upper Galilee. His influence went beyond the courtyards of his Chassidim into the arena of Agudas Yisrael, where he took a major role in shaping the goals of world Jewry. Known as the Beis Yisrael, after his book by the same name, Rebbe Alter labored to address the needs of the time and was highly respected by all of the Torah leaders of his generation.

His brothers successfully carried the banner of Ger Chassidus in the next generation. A central characteristic of Ger Chassidus is its strong emphasis on Torah study. The books of the great Gerrer Rebbes — the *Sefas Emes*, the *Imrei Emes*, and the *Beis Yisrael* — guide the movement's followers towards a deep appreciation of the Chassidic path which they follow. There is a vibrancy in Ger which even non-Chassidic Jews respect and admire.

Belz Dynasty

Another large European dynasty which suffered near-annihilation at the hands of the Nazis was the court of Belz. Rebbe Aharon Rokeach and his brother miraculously escaped the Germans' clutches and reached Eretz Yisrael in 1944. Thousands greeted them when they entered the Holy City, and loyal Chassidim beseeched the Rebbe to build his court in Jerusalem. Rebbe Aharon, however, felt his place was in Tel Aviv, where he could better assist refugees, and shortly afterwards he moved there.

In 1950 (5710), the Belzer Rebbe moved his court to Jerusalem. First he lived in Katamon, where he opened a yeshivah; however, plans were soon made to build a large *beis midrash*, yeshivah, and home for the Rebbe on Agrippas Street. The cornerstone ceremony took place in 1954, and on 15 Tamuz, 1957, the complex stood ready to be occupied. Unfortunately, a month later, on 21 Av, the Rebbe passed away.

The dynasty was left orphaned. Rebbe Aharon's brother had passed away in 1950, leaving a two-year-old son, Yisachar Dov Rokeach. That boy, the present Belzer Rebbe, was brought up by his uncle, and after his marriage to the daughter of the Vishnitz Rebbe in 1965, he remained in Bnei Brak to be close to the Vishnitz Rebbe. A year later, at the age of eighteen, he became Rebbe and moved to Jerusalem to take over his court.

Belzer Chassidim had a marked impact on the Holy City. In 1985, the Rebbe moved from Agrippas Street to a new neighborhood called Kiryat Belz near the Unsdorf-Matersdorf section of the city. Today it is one of the biggest Chassidic groups in Jerusalem, with numerous institutions throughout the city. The Rebbe plays an active and important role in matters concerning the Jewish community, both local and worldwide.

Boyan Dynasty

At the end of Malchei Yisrael Street stands the impressive Tiferes Yisrael Yeshivah. It was built by Rebbe Mordechai Shlomo Friedman of Boyan in the 1960s. A descendant of the first Ruzhiner Rebbe, Rebbe Yisrael Friedman, the Boyaner Rebbe lived in New York City since 1925. During his four visits to Eretz Yisrael after the Second World War, Rebbe Mordechai Shlomo built the dynasty for the future generation. The yeshivah opened in 1967, four years before the Rebbe passed away.

With the Rebbe's death, his grandson, Rebbe Nachum Dov Broyer, the present Rebbe, continued the dynasty from Jerusalem. Under his direction, Boyan Chassidim has earned a reputation for sincerity and excellence. They built two *shetibels* in Beitar, in order to provide inexpensive housing for young couples close to Jerusalem.

Karlin-Stolin Dynasty

The above-mentioned dynasties are all located on the northern side of Jerusalem. Further south, at the edge of Meah Shearim on Yoel Street, is the Karlin-Stolin *beis midrash*. The presence of Karlin Chassidim in Jerusalem dates back to the 1870s, when they built a *shetibel* in the Old City. Rebbes Elimelech and Moshe Perlow, who visited the Holy Land in the 1930s, were the only Karlin Rebbes to visit Eretz Yisrael before the Holocaust. (At that time, five of the sons of Rebbe Yisrael Perlow were Admorim in various cities in Poland.) The only one to survive the war (except Rebbe Yaakov, who lived in New York and passed away in 1946) was Rebbe Yochanan, the Karlin Rebbe of Lutzk, who miraculously succeeded in fleeing deep into Russia with his wife and daughter.

Rebbe Yochanan Perlow came to Eretz Yisrael in 1946, where he set up his court in Haifa. He traveled between New York and Eretz Yisrael, and strengthened Karlin Chassidus in both places. He bought the land upon which the *beis midrash* is built today. When he died in 1957, his daughter's son (the Rebbe had no male offspring), the present Rebbe, was one year old.

Karlin-Stolin Synagogue in Beis Yisrael

Rebbe Baruch Shochet, the present Rebbe, was raised in New York. In his youth, he was imbued with stories of the dynasty which he would one day lead. In 1962 (5722) at the age of seven, he officially became Rebbe. A major event in the Chassidic world was the bar mitzvah celebration of this youthful Rebbe, which took place in Jerusalem. For many years he lived in New York City, visiting Eretz Yisrael frequently, until he permanently settled in the Holy City in 1991.

Karlin-Stolin Chassidus is one of the oldest Chassidic dynasties extant today. It began over two hundred years ago with Rebbe Aharon the Great, a disciple of the Maggid of Mezeritch, and each rebbe has been a direct descendant of this exceptional man — something virtually no other group can claim over such a long span of time. Karlin is proverbial for its hospitality; a place where every Jew feels welcome. The style of prayer is unique — vibrant, loud, and enthusiastic. With its many institutions and varied communal activities, the dynasty is an important addition to the Holy City.

Breslov Chassidus

Further south, at the far end of Meah Shearim, we find several other Chassidic groups who have made a strong impact on the Jewish world. First is Breslov Chassidim. When Rebbe Nachman of Breslov died nearly two hundred years ago, no heir or disciple reigned in his stead. Yet his followers, though small in number, burned with enthusiasm to spread the teachings of their master. Most of the discourses, collected in two volumes entitled *Likutei Maharan* and *Likutei Halachos*, were penned by his chief disciple, Rav Nasan Sternhartz. Before he died, Rebbe Nachman recorded ten tales, each one steeped in esoteric meaning. These stories have been translated into dozens of languages, and express the yearning and trials that are part of the Jewish experience.

It is truly amazing that such a small Chassidic dynasty could survive so many generations without a Rebbe and, against all odds, grow into a large, vibrant Chassidus known the world over. The phenomenal growth had its roots in Jerusalem after the Second World War. One of the central figures at that time was Rav Avraham Sternhartz, a great-grandson of Rav Nasan. He arrived in Jerusalem from Uman in the Ukraine in 1936. At seventy-four years of age, he was a treasure trove of Halachah, Kabbalah, and Chassidus. A group of men studied regularly with him, some of whom became committed Breslov Chassidim. This assembly included such figures as Rav Asher Freund, Rav Gedaliah Koenig, and Rav Shmuel Shapiro. In 1940 (5701), Rav Avraham began what he called a *kibutz* in Meron, where Breslov Chassidim would pray together on Rosh HaShanah. The yearly pilgrimage to Meron stood in place of going to the Rebbe for the High Holidays. Decades later, with the opening up of Eastern Europe, a new generation of Breslov Chassidim chose to go to Uman on Rosh HaShanah, where they prayed at the grave of Rebbe Nachman. Today, as many as 5,000 loyal Chassidim and friends from around the world gather there for the High Holidays.[6]

Rav Avraham Sternhartz (1862–1955)

By the time of Rav Sternhartz's passing, in Elul, 1955, Breslov was firmly anchored in Jerusalem, with several hundred faithful Chassidim. In the 1960s they built a large *beis midrash* in Meah Shearim, and over the years their numbers grew steadily. The attraction to Breslov was partially based on the movement's emphasis on a unique expression of joy, which appealed to many young Jews. Also, Rebbe Nachman's teachings found a receptive ear in the searching minds of the new generation. There was a direct relationship between their growth and the *baal teshuvah* movement of the 1970s and 1980s.

Toldos Aharon Dynasty

Toldos Aharon, often associated with the appellation "ultra-orthodox," was conceived as an elite group of Jews who clung wholeheartedly to the ancient tradition of purity in Jewish life. These Chassidim dressed in long striped coats, once the standard garb of the Sephardic Jews of Eretz Yisrael. They opposed the establishment of the State of Israel, preferring instead to relate to the Holy Land as a place where one may achieve self-perfection through prayer and *avodah*.

The first Rebbe was Rebbe Aharon Rot, who immigrated to Eretz Yisrael in 1925. During the four years he lived in Jerusalem, a number of dedicated young men followed him and strove to emulate his exemplary model of Divine service. It was at this time that he opened a *beis midrash*, called Ohel Elimelech. However, in 1929, due to health reasons, he was forced to return to Europe. Ten years later, in the summer of 1939, he succeeded in returning with his family and son-in-law, Rav Avraham Yitzchak Kahn. When he passed away in 1947, his Chassidic group, renamed Shomrei Emunim, was small but resolutely dedicated to its path.

At that time, the Rebbe's son, Rebbe Avraham Chaim Rot, continued to lead Shomrei Emunim, while nine months later, Rebbe Avraham Yitzchak Kahn opened Toldos Aharon (at the insistence of the Belzer Rebbe). The latter group grew quickly, and in the course of the next fifty years the Rebbe succeeded in guiding his followers in the ways of righteousness. Their fervent style of prayer vividly expressed their devotion to the Almighty.

Rebbe Avraham Yitzchak Kahn (1914–1996)

In 1996 (5757), Rebbe Avraham Yitzchak passed away after a prolonged illness, and again the dynasty split into two, when two of his sons each started a court to express their individual brands of Chassidus.

The Six-Day War

In the spring of 1967 (5727), Eretz Yisrael stood on the threshold of a major conflict with Egypt. President Gamal Nasser called for the annihilation of the Jewish State and proceeded to amass the Egyptian army on the Sinai border. Simultaneously, he cajoled his Arab neighbors into joining him. In May, he ordered the U.N. peace-keeping forces to evacuate the Sinai. At the order of U.N. Secretary General U-Thant, the U.N. forces bowed to Nasser's demand, leaving an unobstructed path for the Egyptian forces. Finally, Egypt closed the Straits of Tiran, forcibly cutting off shipping to the port of Eilat, a move which was interpreted as an unofficial declaration of war against Israel.

When Nasser officially declared war on Monday, 5 June, he quickly announced that he had bombed Tel Aviv and Haifa, and that his army was moving swiftly up the Sinai coast. This led King Hussein of Jordan to also declare war, at 11:30 A.M. on the same day. Syria, too, entered, and within hours, the war was at a peak, like a wild brushfire on a windy day.

However, the enthusiastic Arabs had not properly measured the opposition. The Israeli forces were well prepared, and the morale of the soldiers stood at an all-time high. The Israeli success was amazing: over four hundred Egyptian planes were destroyed, while Israeli losses amounted to nineteen planes. On the ground, too, the Egyptians were inexorably driven back across the Sinai desert. Later in the campaign, Samaria, Hebron, and the Golan Heights would fall into Israeli hands.

In the weeks preceding the war, a rumor spread across the country concerning the contents of a will left by a simple shoemaker from Ramat Gan. Though he died several months earlier, he requested that his will be read and publicized on Lag b'Omer, which fell on 28 May. He foresaw three weeks of terrible tensions, followed by three days of tense battle with a victorious outcome unlike any enjoyed by the Jewish people in thousands of years. Indeed, his words came true.

History showed that not only did Nasser act rashly and deceitfully, but that King Hussein made a major blunder by entering the war. The territorial boundaries of Israel burst forth in every direction (except the western side which borders the Mediterranean Sea). The Sinai desert to the south, Samaria, Hebron, and Jericho in the center, and the Golan Heights in the north were all taken by Israel. The diamond of all the new territories, though, was the Old City of Jerusalem.

The Three-Day War[7]

The Battle for Jerusalem took barely three days. It began on Monday morning, 5 June, at the Government House, located on the southern side of the city. This building had served as the U.N. headquarters since 1948, and the Norwegian General Odd Bull of the U.N. Truce Supervision Organization tried to play a last-minute hand at maintaining peace. He sent a communique to King

Hussein at 10:30 A.M., which reiterated Israel's position: as long as Jordan remained out of the war, Israel would honor the peace treaty between the two countries; however, should they enter the war, they would face unequivocal retaliation. An hour later, Jordanian Legionnaires disdainfully took over the Government House, and the war with Jordan was on.

This Battle of Jerusalem differed markedly from the war of 1948. First, Jewish Jerusalem was not cut off and under siege as it had been in 1948. The Jerusalem Corridor prior to the 1967 war tapered from twenty kilometers wide on the coast to one kilometer wide at Jerusalem, yet there was more than one road to the Holy City in this narrow area.[8] Settlements along the corridor numbered over fifty, compared to four in 1948. Secondly, food was plentiful, with sufficient stockpiles for half a year. Thirdly, water was piped from two main stations via the National Water Carrier, instead of from a single pipe originating at the coast. Moreover, underground water was accidentally discovered in 1949 while drilling for a small dam at Ein Kerem, which could supply most of the city's water needs by itself. The Jewish/Arab population balance had also changed radically in the nineteen-year interim: the Jewish population had increased by 90% (100,000 to 190,000) while the Arab population increased by only 40% (65,000 to 90,000).

Within an hour of the outbreak of fighting, Jordanian shells landed a direct hit on one of the two water pipelines. Later that night the second pipeline also ceased to function when the electric power was cut off in the corridor. Fortunately, the damaged pipeline was repaired the next day.

The fighting quickly spread along the entire seven-mile border between East and West Jerusalem. Outdated Sherman tanks on the Israeli side faced modern Patton tanks on the Jordanian one. Major battles were fought at Ammunition Hill in the north and Ramat Rachel in the south. In every confrontation, the Jordanians were repulsed.

Causalities filled all the hospitals of the city. Nine hundred wounded were brought to Hadassah Hospital in the first fifty-six hours of fighting, many flown in by helicopter. Shaarei Zedek Hospital was hit by a Jordanian shell. It broke through the outer wall of the building and halted its flight next to an interior one, but fortunately it did not explode. On the other side of the interior wall was a corridor with eighteen newborn infants lying in carriages. The babies were all unharmed.*

The attack on the Old City began with the capture of the Rockefeller Museum, strategically located a stone's throw from the northeastern corner of the ancient Turkish wall. Jewish paratroopers stormed the museum at 6:00 A.M. and easily took control of it. On the night of 7 June, a major technical blunder occurred, wherein Israeli tanks turned the wrong way in an ill-fated attack on the Augusta Victoria hospices. Nevertheless, the following morning saw the assault on the Old City go ahead as scheduled.

The attack began and ended at the Lion's Gate. After breaking open the huge iron doors, the Israeli troops were surprised to discover that all the Legion-

* See story, "A Day in the Life of a Mohel," in *Bygone Days: 1948–1998*.

naires had evacuated the Old City during the night. The Arab troops had received an order to do so after the Israeli Air Force destroyed a convoy of reinforcements on their way from Jericho. Thus, the Old City fell without a major battle.

The exhilaration of a united Jerusalem peaked at the Western Wall, untouched by Jewish hands for nineteen years. Dazed Jews began to wander up to it, and to connect to it with a special rapport. There would a lot of cleaning up to do in and around the newly united city, but it was a small price to pay for the stunning victory. Unfortunately, the Israelis did not escape entirely unscathed; many Jews fell in battle and

A moment of awe, as soldiers view the Kosel for the first time in nineteen years

others were wounded in action. All in all, there were 700 dead and over 1,500 wounded.

The new borders of the country and the inclusion of the Old City into Jewish Jerusalem dramatically altered the face of the nation. National security, always a subject of great priority, never seemed so assured. Psychologically, too, the feeling of an enemy at one's doorstep was removed. Physical evidence of the city's previous division were quickly removed, and freedom of movement within the Old City bolstered the already high morale.

The Jewish Quarter had lain razed and desolate during the entire nineteen years of occupation, and the scars of the 1948 war were everywhere. The vandalized homes stood empty, and the wrecked synagogues were a shocking reminder of the past war. In a remarkably short time, the Jewish Quarter would once again ring with the sound of Jewish children playing outside, and the footsteps of men walking to shul with tallis and tefillin bags under their arms.

Most of all, the Kosel was back in the hands of its rightful owners, after nearly two thousand years. The Moghrabi neighborhood was demolished at the command of Uri Narkiss and replaced by a wide plaza. The ground level of the plaza was lowered by nearly two meters — thus revealing more of the Kosel — in order to allow easy access into Wilson's Arch. Jews came from all over the globe to the Western Wall to offer words of thanksgiving to their Creator. Truly, the eyes of world Jewry were focused on Jerusalem, the Holy City.

The United City

The expansion of the Holy City accelerated in the last quarter of the twentieth century more than ever before. New suburbs sprawled across tracts of land that had been inaccessible before the Six-Day War. Especially to the north, new neighborhoods such as Ramat Eshkol, Sanhedria HaMurchevet, French Hill, and Ramot housed thousands of families. One reason for this northern expansion was to connect the Mount Scopus complex with the rest of Jewish Jerusalem. Uninhabited areas in the other directions of the compass were also developed into housing projects for the burgeoning population. To the east were built Neve Yaakov, Pisgat Zev, Givat HaMivtar, and Maalot Dafna; to the south Givat Mordechai, Gonen, and Gilo; to the west Kiryat HaYovel, Kiryat Menachem, and Har Nof.

Teddy Kollek, who had a long tenure as mayor of Jerusalem, made decisions which had a permanent imprint on the landscape of the city. A colorful and highly controversial figure, Mr. Kollek authorized the construction of many public buildings, a soccer stadium, and many parks and playgrounds.

The hospitals, too, grew and modernized in order to accommodate the expanding population. Hadassah Hospital on Mount Scopus, built during the Mandate period, lay partially off-limits from 1948 to 1967. In the 1950s, city planners saw the great need for a large, modern hospital. At the time, the thrust for new housing projects was directed towards the west of the city. Therefore, in 1957 it was decided to build the new

Hadassah Hospital, one of the finest in the country, far west of the center of town, in Ein Kerem. What the planners did not foresee were the consequences of the Six-Day War, which opened up vast tracts to the north, east, and south. Nevertheless, Hadassah Hospital is still renowned as one of the best hospitals in the world.

Shaarei Zedek Hospital, built by Dr. Wallach at the beginning of the century, was unable to meet the needs of the fast-growing city. The hospital's board of directors therefore decided to build a new, completely modernized hospital, near Bayit Vegan. The third hospital, Bikur Cholim, remains at its original site on Strauss Street in downtown Jerusalem. Yet they, too, are planning a new hospital, the first of the twenty-first century.

The post-World War Two population boom, common throughout many places in the world, was likewise felt in the Holy City. The Jewish population rose from 100,000 in 1948 to 198,000 in 1967, to 306,000 in 1983, to 406,000 in 1993, to 422,000 in 1996 (see Table in Overview). As a percentage, the Jewish population went from 60% in 1948 to 74% in 1967, to 71% in 1983, to 70.5% in 1995. Thus, the number of Jews in Jerusalem at the end of 1996 (422,000), together with 181,000 Arabs and Christians, brought the total population to 603,000.

In education, the statistics speak for themselves. Of the 132,300 Jewish children in the Jerusalem school system in 1996–1997, 51.7% study in state schools and 48.3% study in *chareidi* schools. Just three years earlier, in the 1993–1994 school year, the percentages were quite different: 60% in state schools compared to 40% in the *chareidi chadarim*.[9] Thus, in the short span of three years there has been a phenomenal increase of close to 10% in the religious schools.

Metamorphosis in the Holy City

The post Six-Day War period brought with it, among other things, a new yearning for Eretz Yisrael. As the economy grew, a new security and freedom reigned. In the religious circles this was translated into strengthening the yeshivos and expanding the kollelim. More and more chutznikim (Jews living in the Diaspora) came to work and study, many eventually settling permanently in the Holy Land. Moreover, a growing awareness of essential Jewish values in such areas as shemitah, heksherim, and child education acted as a catalyst to give the religious front fuller expression. Though on one level the various religious groups seemed to be at odds, they were striving for a common goal on another one: The long awaited arrival of the Mashiach.

The Yeshivah World

We previously discussed the establishment of yeshivos in the aftermath of World War II. The yeshivah world experienced another burst of growth after the Six-Day War. The Mir and Brisk Yeshivos, discussed earlier, expanded beyond the wildest expectations of their leaders. Other yeshivos likewise expanded to fill the needs of a quickly growing population. For example, Kamenitz Yeshivah, established in the 1960s — including its Talmud Torah — had a couple of hundred students around the period of the Six-Day War. By the end of the century, it had grown fivefold. Hebron Yeshivah, built in the New City after the 1929 riots, could no longer remain in a *beis midrash* designed to hold 200 students, and a large campus was built in Givat Mordechai. Beis HaTalmud Yeshivah also moved from Beis Yisrael to bigger quarters in Sanhedria HaMurchevet.

Dozens, if not hundreds, of yeshivos and *chadarim* came into existence to cater to the needs of the younger generation. Among the major ones were Torah Ohr Yeshivah in the Matersdorf neighborhood, opened by Rav Chaim Pinchas Scheinberg; Ohr Elchanan Yeshivah, founded by Rav Simcha Wasserman; Itri Yeshivah, opened by Rav Elephant; and Iyun HaTalmud, founded by Rav Abba Berman.

The Sephardim likewise opened new houses of learning. Porat Yosef Yeshivah, the backbone of Sephardic yeshivos, opened a new *beis midrash* in

Geula after the creation of the State. After the Six-Day War, they rebuilt a magnificent structure on the site of the original building destroyed in 1948. Today, there are two Porat Yosef yeshivos. Over the course of time, other institutions opened as well, such as Ohr Baruch Yeshivah, Kol Yaakov Yeshivah, and Nachalat Moshe Yeshivah.

Once again Jerusalem resounded with the sound of Torah. Indeed, the Holy City now ranked as the Torah capital of the world in the eyes of Jews everywhere.

The Teshuvah Movement

The 1970s marked a turning point for Torah developments in Jerusalem. In the wake of the city's reunification in 1967 came a renewed enthusiasm amongst world Jewry concerning Eretz Yisrael. This interest was expressed practically through an increase in tourism and immigration. Furthermore, it was reflected in an upswing in enrollment by American students in yeshivos such as the Mir and Brisk. These students, all reared in religious homes, were expanding their horizons by studying Torah in Eretz Yisrael.

At the same time, a new phenomenon was beginning to take root in the Holy City. Assimilated Jews, generally from America and mostly college age, were being drawn to the practices of their ancestors. Their return to the Orthodoxy of their fathers was partially the result of the "anything goes" attitude of the 1960s. As attractive as this philosophy may sound in theory, in actuality people need to live within bounds, whether man-made or Divine. The freedom condoned by the hippy generation had two markedly contrasting results: either one lost his hold on reality or embarked on an inner search for what was really meaningful in life.

These first *baalei teshuvah* — referring to those who accept the yoke of Heaven upon themselves and begin fulfilling the 613 mitzvos of the Torah — were looked upon as outsiders by the religious community. Jerusalemites looked warily at these newcomers who, on the one hand, were mature adults, and yet on the other hand were ignorant of the most basic concepts and principles of Judaism that every religious child knew.

Despite the community's general mistrust, a number of rabbis came forward to guide these young men and women. Among the early leaders in the *baal teshuvah* movement were Rav Noach Weinberg (Shema Yisrael and Aish HaTorah Yeshivos), Rav Baruch Horowitz (Dvar Yerushalayim), Rav Nata Schiller and Mendel Weinbach (Ohr Someyach), Rav Mordechai Goldstein (Diaspora Yeshivah), and Rav Chaim Brovender (Shapells Yeshivah). Seminaries for women included Neve Yerushalayim, founded by Rav David Refson, and Eyat, headed by Rebbetzin Dina Weinberg. By the mid-1970s more yeshivos opened to cater to the needs of the growing body of students, which numbered in the hundreds. The success in Jerusalem branched out to nearly every major Jewish community in the Diaspora.

Concurrent with the opening of these yeshivos were outreach programs designed to shepherd in wandering young people. Helping individuals find the right place to discover their roots is a crucial stage in the process of return, and several rabbis took it upon themselves to tackle this very sensitive job. They included Rav Meir Shuster, who started in 1972, and Jeff Seidel, who came on the scene a few years later. Their vitality and *heimish* approach served to bridge the gap expressed by their formal attire, which contrasted sharply with the casual dress of the potential *baal teshuvah*. No matter what his appearance, every Jew was a diamond, a Jewish soul who inwardly craved to cleave to his Creator. These rabbis centered their activities at the Western Wall and in the Old City, but sometimes they could be found at other locations around Jerusalem.

Rav Meir Shuster (right) in action

In 1984 (5744), Rav Shuster opened the Heritage House in the Jewish Quarter, where travelers could stay for free. From there he would guide some of them to the yeshivah which best suited their individual needs. Averaging between 100 to 150 new *baalei teshuvah* annually, Rav Shuster's record over a quarter of a century is remarkable, to say the least.

The success of the American *baal teshuvah* movement was soon felt by assimilated Israelis who likewise sought their roots. New yeshivos opened to uplift these Jewish returnees, most of whom were Sephardim. Among the early places were Ohr HaChaim Yeshivah and Machane Yisrael Yeshivah. In the late 1980s, former Russian refusniks opened yeshivos for searching Jews of Russian descent, such as Shevut Ami (Return My People) and Machanayim.

The impact of the *baal teshuvah* movement cannot be underestimated. Thousands of young men and women have changed their lives midstream, settling down to a serious life of Torah study and observance, and commitment to marriage and family. The choice they made then will have ramifications for generations to come.

A City of Many Colors

Jerusalem after the Six-Day War became a truly cosmopolitan city, with a multilayered strata of cultural, political, and religious elements. In spite of the dominant nonreligious power that held sway in many areas of the municipality, the city retained its traditional flavor. Building ordinances, for example, reaffirmed the Mandate law that all buildings had to be faced with Jerusalem stone. The thrice-a-year pilgrimage — on Pesach, Shavuos, and Sukkos — to the Western Wall witnessed a major influx of Jews from around the country and the world. Tens of thousands would come to the Kosel for *birkas Kohanim*, to be blessed by hundreds of *kohanim*.

During these years, numerous organizations dedicated to aiding the public in various ways sprang into existence.

Yad Ezra

Yad Ezra is a non-profit organization dedicated to helping the needy and forlorn of the city. Conceived in 1952 by Rav Asher Freund, the initially modest help-your-neighbor project expanded to incorporate various communal services. Besides helping the needy, a strong emphasis is placed on offering training programs for mentally handicapped youths. A number of jobs involving light skills help these young men and women achieve a sense of accomplishment in life. Included among the programs are printing, bookbinding, carpentry, and a sewing workshop.

Pe'ilim–Lev l'Achim

Another group, called Pe'ilim, aimed at a completely different segment of the Jewish community. Created in 1950 by Rav Eliyahu Dessler, its purpose was to reach out and strengthen *yiddishkeit* among secular Israelis. The two Jerusalemite *maggidim*, Rav Shalom Schwadron and Rav Shabbetai Yudelevitch, traveled throughout the country under the organization's auspices. Later, Pe'ilim was renamed Yad l'Achim, and more recently (1993), a twin organization called Lev L'Achim added a much greater dimension to the outreach program. Rav Uri Zohar, the famous Israeli (ex-)entertainer whose odyssey back to observant Judaism shocked the public, is a devoted leader of the latter group.

Yad Sarah

In 1976 (5736), Rav Uri Lapoliansky founded an organization to help needy people in the field of health and welfare. From its humble beginnings as a neighborhood aid project,* Yad Sarah quickly expanded to fill an important vacuum in the city. Medical equipment, such as crutches, wheelchairs, hospital beds and expensive life-saving aids, were loaned to anyone in need. Besides aiding the sick, the organization saved many individuals from being hospitalized, thus saving the national health care system millions of dollars a year.

* See story, "From a Knock at the Door," in *Bygone Days: 1948–1998*.

Over the years, Yad Sarah has grown phenomenally, and today there are over eighty branches throughout the country staffed by over 5,000 volunteers.

Orphanages

The Diskin Orphanage, so famous in its time, closed its doors during this period. After the Second World War, orphans from Europe still lived in the institution. However, they were the last to use the facilities in their original context. As these men grew up and built their own homes, no new children replaced them. Times had changed, especially with the introduction of pubic welfare. Most orphans were kept within the family unit, living with relatives rather than being placed in a home. The Blumenthal Orphanage and Kiryat HaYeled remained opened for those orphans who needed a home. However, the gigantic premises of the Diskin Orphanage became the home of a number of yeshivos.

The girls' counterpart to the Diskin Orphanage, Beis Lapletos, was built in Meah Shearim to house refugees from war-torn Europe after the Second World War. The Toldos Aharon Rebbe was the moving force behind the organization. After the Six-Day War, a large campus called Girls Town was built in Kiryat Sanz. Today, these twin institutions serve a wide spectrum of girls, who are suitably prepared to build their future home in the Holy City.

Boys Town

Rav Alexander Linchner, the son-in-law of Rav Shraga Feivel Mendelowitz, founded Boys Town in 1949 (5709) with fourteen Yemenite boys. Construction of the campus in Bayit Vegan began in 1951, but did not officially open until 1954. Rav Linchner believed in a philosophy of Torah with *derech eretz*, a combination of studying Torah while gaining a basic vocational training.

By the outbreak of the Six-Day War there were six hundred students in Boys Town. Within the next ten years, the school expanded manifold. New buildings stood on the 17-acre campus which housed a variety of new programs, such as courses in applied engineering and computers.

Rav Alexander Linchner (1908–1997)

Rav Linchner became a legendary figure in his lifetime. His boundless energy, compassion, and love of the young generation, especially those who came from limited backgrounds, left a permanent imprint on everyone who met him. Today, his son, Rav Moshe Linchner, is the guiding force of Boys Town.

Besides those mentioned, there are dozens of other organizations and institutions which shoulder the vital responsibility of helping the more unfortunate residents of Jerusalem. Great strides have been made in medical, social, and educational fields, together with the primary assistance of food and clothing. These services strengthen the populace from within and better equip the needy to become fully active members of the community.

The Sephardic Influence

The Sephardic community as a whole went through a tremendous metamorphosis during the 1900s. By the turn of the twentieth century, the great influx of Ashkenazim into Jerusalem had already caused the Sephardim to lose their majority status. With the decline of the Turkish Empire and the subsequent transfer of power to the British at the end of the First World War, the Sephardic influence further declined. Under the British Mandate, they assumed a much less prominent role than they had previously.

The Mandate period ostensibly gave equal rights to both the Sephardim and Ashkenazim. Each had a Chief Rabbi to deal with the particular needs of their respective communities. Yet the overwhelming role played by the Ashkenazic community, both politically and religiously, overshadows the Sephardic influence during that period.

Only in the last half of the twentieth century did Sephardic Jewry again manifest itself as a strong, independent ethnic group. New rabbis stepped forward equipped to guide the young generation.

Rav Benzion Uziel (left) and Rav Yitzchak Nisim (right)

The Chief Sephardic Rabbis during this period were Rav Benzion Uziel (1939–1953), Rav Yitzchak Nisim (1953–1973), Rav Ovadiah Yosef (1973–1983), Rav Mordechai Eliyahu (1983–1993), and Rav Bakshi Doron (1993–).

Of particular significance was the influence of Rav Ovadiah Yosef. Born in Baghdad, he came to Israel as a child in 1924, where he studied in such Sephardic yeshivos as Bnei Tzyon and Porat Yosef. A prodigy, he published his first book, *Yebiah Omer*, when he was eighteen years old. At the age of twenty-five, Rav Ovadiah sat on the Sephardic *beis din*. He spent some years as Chief Rabbi in Egypt and Jaffa, later returning to Jerusalem. As Chief Rabbi and Rishon l'Tzyon, he enamored Sephardim throughout the country with his magnetic personality and total command of Torah Law. Due to his influence, the Sephardim set up their own religious political party.

Rabbis from the Last Generation

In the last half of the twentieth century, Jerusalemites have been blessed to have in their midst some *rabbanim* who may be ranked with the *gedolim* of earlier generations. Such was Rav Shlomo Zalman Auerbach. Born, raised, and died in the Holy City, Rav Shlomo Zalman came from an illustrious family. His father, Rav Chaim Leib Auerbach, headed Shaar HaShamayim Yeshivah, which specialized in the study of Kabbalah.

Rav Shlomo Zalman became Rosh Yeshivah of Kol Torah Yeshivah in Bayit Vegan, where he commanded the respect and honor of all his students. Furthermore, over a span of nearly fifty years, he answered tens of thousands of halachic queries. Shunning any involvement with politics and factionalism, Rav Shlomo Zalman's love of his fellowman was proverbial — he regarded Sephardi, Ashkenazi, Chassid, and Mizrachi equally. When he passed away on 20 Adar I, 1995 (5755), over 250,000 people escorted him to his final resting place, a tribute to his endearment by all Jewry.

The only other funeral of this size was that of Rav Moshe Feinstein. Though he lived most of his life in America, only visiting Eretz Yisrael for Agudas Yisrael conventions, Rav Moshe chose to be buried in the Holy City. His funeral, which took place on Shushan Purim, 1986, was attended by nearly as many Jews.

As the foremost halachic authorities of their generation, Rav Feinstein and Rav Auerbach had several things in common. Both were *gedolim* whose halachic decisions were widely accepted by the entire religious world, both were Roshei Yeshivos, and both were beloved by all segments of the population. Interestingly, the two men also shared a unique reputation: they were both known by their first names, something found very rarely in rabbinic circles.

Rav Shlomo Zalman's brother-in-law, Rav Shalom Schwadron, was another person who seemed to come from an earlier generation. Known as the Yerushalmi Maggid, Rav Schwadron captivated his audiences with meaningful messages that were delivered with spice and flavor. Orphaned at the age of seven, he grew up at the Diskin Orphan-

Rav Shalom Schwadrom (1914-1997)

age, later studying under Rav Leib Chasman at Hebron Yeshivah. He studied for years together with Rav Yosef Shalom Elyashiv and Rav Shmuel Wosner. Rav Shalom's long career of teaching and reaching out to his fellowman began at Ohalei Shem Yeshivah. Later, he served as *mashgiach* of Tiferes Tzvi and Beis HaTalmud Yeshivos. He also traveled throughout the country and overseas to speak and strengthen *Yiddishkeit.**

Soon his casual yet dynamic style of speaking led him to his ultimate life's mission — being a *maggid*. For more than fifty years he spoke to audiences that ranged from uneducated and uncommitted Jews to renowned Roshei Yeshivos and Admorim. All felt touched by his words, for he lived the very essence of his message. Every Shabbos night, for decades, he walked from his humble house in Shaarei Chesed to Zichron Moshe, where he spoke.

The *maggid*'s repertoire was full of recollections and parables. Some were recorded and published, like *She'al Avicha* (Hebrew) and *The Maggid Speaks* (English). He passed away on 22 Kislev, 1997 (5758), at the age of eighty-five.

Rav Yosef Shalom Elyashiv, *shlita*, is perhaps the last of the *gedolim* who may be reckoned amongst those who hearken back to an earlier generation. He is the greatest halachic authority alive today. The grandson of the kabbalist, Rav Shlomo Elyashiv (who lived in Jerusalem from 1922 to 1926, and whose prolific writings are known as the *Leshem*), he has lived most of his life in Meah Shearim. Every important issue facing modern-day Jewish life is brought to him for his appraisal, and his proclamations carry weight throughout the world.

For the Sake of Jerusalem[10]

Until 1948 and the creation of the State, the expression "demographic balance" always referred to the proportion of Jews to Arabs. Later, the term would generally refer to the percentage of religious versus secular Jews in the country and the conflict between them. Though the confrontation was not confined solely to Jerusalem, much of the battle for the sanctity of Jewish values took place in the Holy City.

1949–1950 (5709–5710) marked the opening of a new battlefront for the sanctity of Shabbos and the honor of the Torah. The new State had proclaimed as law that Shabbos was the official "day of rest." It was forbidden to open most shops, and all public transportation

* See story, "Forty Days Straight," in *Bygone Days: 1918–1948*.

was closed. The movie houses, however, were eager to sell tickets before sunset on Shabbos in order to screen the Saturday night film at a convenient time. One Shabbos day in the spring of 1949, a rally was held at the Zichron Moshe Synagogue to protest the movie houses' policies. One of the attendees was the Sephardic Chief Rabbi, Rav Benzion Uziel. After the rally, the participants walked to the nearby Edison movie house to engage in a peaceful demonstration. The police reacted with force, and many people were injured. Soon afterwards, on Shavuos, the Khal Yerei'im Shul (located in Meah Shearim, across the street from Shreiber's bookstore) became the target of an attack by soldiers riding through the neighborhood in a jeep. The rampage continued into Beis Yisrael and Battei Ungarin, leaving several religious Jews injured. Every Shabbos afterwards, police cars roamed through religious neighborhoods in order to intimidate the residents. One Shabbos in Tamuz, a bomb was thrown from an army van, which exploded in front of the Khal Yerei'im Shul. Miraculously, no one was injured. Tensions, however, were at a pitch.

A few months later, on Simchas Torah, a large stone was hurled through the window of Khal Yerei'im, fatally injuring Rav Nasanel Chaim Turnheim. He had studied in his youth at Toras Chaim Yeshivah in the Old City, and had been close with the Chazon Ish. His death brought a sudden quiet upon the city.

Throughout the years, the battle over the sanctity of Shabbos continued to erupt periodically. In the 1990s, there was a highly publicized conflict over the closure of Bar Ilan Street, a main thoroughfare that bisects exclusively *chareidi* neighborhoods.

Another stormy issue was sparked in 1958 (5718) when plans to build a mixed swimming pool without separate hours for men and women, in Emek Refaim were publicized. Not surprisingly, the Torah-observant residents of the city viewed this as a desecration of the sanctity of Jerusalem. When the Brisker Rav, Rav Velvel Soloveitchik, heard that the religious segment of the populace were deemed "a negligible minority," he called upon all Jews to rally together and demonstrate in force. On 16 Sivan, the largest demonstration of Jews until that time took place, with a crowd estimated at 40,000. All segments of the community joined the protest, including *rabbanim*, Admorim, Roshei Yeshivos, and all of their followers. Despite the impressive demonstration, the swimming pool was built and opened, a blatant assault on the holy atmosphere of the Heavenly City.

In 1979 (5739), Mayor Teddy Kollek decided to built a soccer stadium in northern Jerusalem. The proposed site was in Shuafat, situated near several densely populated religious areas. When Kollek announced his plans, his office was inundated with a barrage of protest. In order to reach the stadium, people would have to drive through Orthodox neighborhoods, and the whole image of Jerusalem would be defaced. Tensions in the city escalated until the mayor offered a compromise, whereby a new municipal law forbidding soccer games on Shabbos would be enacted. Rav Menachem Porush of Agudas Yisrael asked Rav Yosef Elyashiv how he should respond to the offer. "Although the mayor's suggestion is a step forward," answered Rav Elyashiv, "a law can always be changed; however, once a stadium is built, it cannot be moved. Nevertheless, I want you to consult with Rav Shlomo Zalman Auerbach." To Rav Porush's surprise, Rav Auerbach gave an identical appraisal of the situation.

After a mass demonstration in Jerusalem and unrelenting pressure from world Jewry, Kollek put a halt to the construction. Several years later, he finally succeeded in building his stadium, located in the south of the city. Interestingly, the religious neighborhood of Ramat Shlomo (named after Rav Shlomo Zalman Auerbach and home to thousands of Orthodox families) was established on Kollek's original site in Shuafat.

On 28 Shevat, 1999 (5759), the largest demonstration in modern times took place at the entrance to Jerusalem. Over a quarter of a million religious Jews rallied to protest against ongoing affronts by the government concerning issues that cut to the very core of our faith. Instead of fiery political speeches and provocative sermons, the calm and peaceful crowd engaged in the recitation of psalms and prayer, punctuated by heart-rending blasts from the shofar. The intention of the gathering was to call world attention (and that of the Heavenly court) to the painful conflicts and threats facing Torah true Judaism today.

The battle concerning the overall purity of Jerusalem as the Holy City is, regrettably, an ongoing tug-of-war. Much of the outcome is dependent on the demographic balance between the two sides. A study made for the Flussheimer Institute in 1996 showed that as many as 60% of the secular Jews would leave the city due to several factors, including secular-religious tensions, and a groundless fear of a religious takeover of the city.

Current statistics also bear out this trend. For example, the Jerusalem Institute published a projected demographic breakdown of the secular/orthodox community between 1990–2010. It is shown in the following chart.

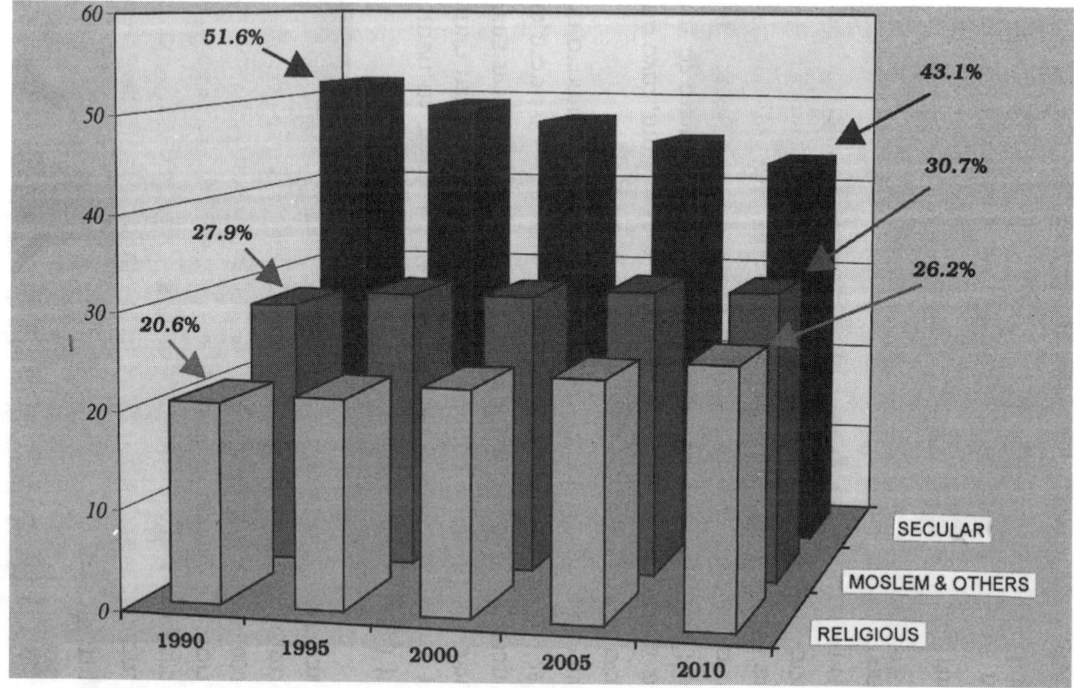

Courtesy of the Jerusalem Institute

This chart, covering the years 1990 to 2010, shows a rise of nearly 6% in the chareidi population of Jerusalem and an 8.5% drop in the secular population. The projected Arab increase is 3%.

On the one hand, these statistics and predictions might be regarded as a harbinger of defeat for the nonreligious populace. In truth, however, the real goal is to unite the Jewish people, and then go on to build the foundations for the future together.

Jews have labored and suffered to maintain an undiluted presence in the Holy City for generations. The battles taking place within her boundaries are but one more sign of the confusion our Sages predicted would take place prior to the advent of the Mashiach.

Our Arab Neighbors

With the Israeli victory in the War of Independence, the balance of power in the Middle East shifted radically. For centuries, both the Arab inhabitants of the Holy Land and the surrounding Moslem countries were in close collusion with the ruling foreign overlords — first the Turks, and then the Western imperial powers. Then, literally overnight, the Arab monopoly was broken, and they were forced to come to an accommodation with their Jewish neighbors. With the creation of the State in 1948, the antagonists were separated by a geopolitical border. On one side were the Moslem states and so-called Palestinian Arabs, nominally under Jordanian control. On the other side was Israel, wherein the indigenous Moslem and Christian populations submitted to Jewish rule. For decades, an uneasy peace existed between Israel and her enemies — both the Palestinians and the neighboring Arab states. That peace was broken four times during the second half of the twentieth century: the Sinai War (1956), the Six-Day War (1967), the Yom Kippur War (1973), and the Gulf War (1992). However, only one, the Six-Day War, saw fighting in Jerusalem.

The aftermath of each of these wars brought the Jews a new sense of freedom and security.[11] However, these victories could not ensure a complete cessation of the terrorist attacks that were carried out by such groups as Fatah and the PLO. In 1987 (5748), Arab terror gave rise to a new popular movement known as the *intifadah*, which many disaffected Palestinians openly supported or joined outright. Small, loosely organized cells carried out numerous, indiscriminate hit-and-run attacks on innocent civilians, including women and buses full of schoolchildren. After the Oslo Agreement, when the Palestinians signed a peace accord with Israel in September, 1993, a number of suicide bombings shocked the country. A disproportionate number of these tragedies struck Jerusalem. During the four-year period from January, 1994–January, 1998, 170 Jews were killed and 800 hundred were wounded by no less than eighteen bombs. Half of these victims were attacked in Jerusalem. Walking in the Moslem Quarter became life-threatening, as testified by the number of people who were slain there merely because they were Jewish.

Recent Archeological Finds

Due to the vast number of archeological diggings in and around Jerusalem during the last half of the twentieth century, only the most major finds will be discussed here.

The southern wall of the Temple Mount was first opened to archeologists after the Six-Day War. This area was a choice spot for the archeologists — it is close to the Temple and on level terrain, and was a thriving part of Jerusalem of yore. After a compromise with the Moslem Wakf, which left a large area untouched in order to accommodate Moslem gatherings, the digs began. Thirty years later, the archeologists completed their work and the area was opened to the public.

This site graphically displays the problem of unscrambling the layers of past civilizations who lived there. Every conquering people destroyed the structures they found and rebuilt their own on top of the ruins. In surveying the area, the finds may be divided up according to the following periods, which encompass the last two thousand years:

Herodian Period	70 B.C.E. – 70 C.E.
Roman Period	70 C.E. – 326 C.E.
Byzantine Period	326 – 638
Arab Period	638 – 1099
Crusader Period	1099 – 1290
Mamluk Period	1290 – 1517
Turkish Period	1517 – 1917

The southern wall excavations (1967–1998)

This site was occupied in earlier periods as well, such as during the First Temple era, and has been tentatively identified as the location of the biblical Ophel. However, the digs only went down as far as the Herodian period, where a wide thoroughfare was discovered on the Tyropean Way along the southwestern wall. All that remains from this time are a few storefronts made from huge, perfectly cut stone slabs, together with parts of an underground sewage system. Before the excavations, scars from the destruction of the Second Temple were scattered everywhere. Many of the giant Herodian stones were reused during the Roman and Byzantine periods for buildings, which complicates the dating of many stone slabs and columns. One such column has inscriptions in Greek, naming Caesar and other imperial Roman leaders.

Further along the southern side of the Temple Mount, large cisterns and *mikveos* were found. One *mikve* had stairs leading down into it from all four sides and might have been used by pilgrims before ascending into the Temple Mount complex. Byzantine houses were discovered with tiled floors and intricate patterns pressed into the plastered walls.

These relics of the past reflect the irony of Jewish Jerusalem. There is a tendency to hold them in high esteem merely because of their great age. In reality, however, they should serve to reveal our anguish upon seeing how foreign powers trampled on our sacred soil and despoiled it. Yet, there is another lesson in them as well. These artifacts are a testimony to the Jews' will to survive, something which none of these mighty kingdoms were able to do. They and their kingdoms have vanished, leaving nothing but stone relics for prosperity. The Jewish people, bearers of the covenant with Hashem, survive and proceed to fulfill the Divine mission they were charged with eons ago.

In the Footsteps of the Ancient One

It is hard to image what life will be like in the Messianic era. One thing, however, is clear: Jerusalem will be transformed beyond recognition. Divine worship will recommence in the Third Temple, and the Holy City will become the capital of the world, as all the world's nations pledge allegiance to the Mashiach. Furthermore, all of Jerusalem will be suffused with the radiance of the Shechinah.

We do not know precisely when or how these changes will come about. Yet by peering down the corridors of history, it is possible to discern the direction in which we are going. Throughout the nine-hundred-year period discussed in this book, a path unfolds before us whereby people and events progressively encouraged a spiritual revival of the Jewish nation. Graphically, a chart would show dips that approached the zero mark, with no significant highs until the middle of the nineteenth century — and even then, the ruling powers of the land generally prevented their Jewish subjects from attaining their goals. Similarly, in the early twentieth century, the *yishuv* seemed poised for a decisive victory over the seductive threat of Zionism. However, with the catastrophe of the two world wars and the regency of the British overlords, the opportunity was lost.

After the Second World War, world civilization reoriented itself to a nobler goal than simple domination over one's neighbors. It was precisely at that time that Eretz Yisrael burst onto the world's stage, with the creation of the Jewish State. In the fifty years since its inception, dramatic events have transpired — both in Israel and the world at large. Who didn't thrill at the victory of the Six-Day War, or celebrate the collapse of communism, to name but two examples.

In the midst of it all, the core of the Holy City has remained essentially un-

touched. Throughout the ages, Jerusalem has been a place where the wisdom of Torah has been propagated and the mitzvos could be fulfilled to their utmost, and this remains true today. The upsurge of Torah observance over the last few decades reaffirms that the line on the chart is moving ever higher and higher. This is essential for the unfolding of the dramatic events foreseen by the prophets.

As we march ahead in time, may we be worthy to go in the footsteps of the Ancient One.

Notes

1. *O Jerusalem!*, p. 345.
2. Ibid., p. 346.
3. *Dimuyos Hod*, vol. 1, pp. 227–228; *O Jerusalem!*, p. 445.
4. Ibid., p. 228.
5. See *Biyos HaZeman*, pp. 53–71.
6. See *Sippurim Yerushalmim*, vol. 2, pp. 95–110.
7. Based on *The Battle for Jerusalem*.
8. Before the Six-Day War, the large area between Tel Aviv and Jerusalem, including Samaria to the north and Hebron to the south, was almost entirely in Jordanian hands. Except for the Jerusalem corridor, the Holy City was isolated and surrounded by Arabs on all sides. The corridor came into existence with the truce signed between Jordan and Israel at the end of the War of Independence. This truce provided for an Israeli land corridor that would directly connect the two cities. In the wake of the 1967 war, the entire area on both sides of the corridor, from Mt. Herman to Eilat, became Israeli territory.
9. Jerusalem Institute for Israel Studies, *Statistical Yearbook,* no. 14, 1996, p. 266.
10. *Yated Ne'eman* (English), "Struggles in Jerusalem," issues 19 Adar II, 26 Adar II, and 4 Nisan, 1997.
11. Even the Yom Kippur War, which caused a tremendous amount of soul-searching among the Israelis after having been caught totally off guard by the Syrian attack, still resulted in a greater sense of security.

A Heavenly Sign

MOSHE AHARON was a very perceptive young man who strove to emulate the Torah personalities with whom he came in contact. An American boy like him could only stand in awe of the great sages he found in the Holy City. Likewise, some of the *gedolim* noted his refined character. The Brisker Rav, Rav Yitzchak Zev Soloveitchik, perceived the depth of his soul and asked him to join his special minyan on the High Holy Days.

Moshe Aharon, who came to study at Kamenitz Yeshivah, had one relative in the city, his grandfather. Rav Yaakov Yosef Herman, whose story has been recorded elsewhere, lived in the Geula neighborhood. Together they would spend hours discussing Torah and *mussar*.

Since Moshe Aharon Stern's parents lived in America, Rav Herman became his parent in every sense of the word. As the year 1947 (5607) began to unfold, Rav Yaakov Yosef discussed the idea of marriage and settling permanently in Jerusalem with his grandson. Moshe Aharon felt that in the short time he had lived in Eretz Yisrael he truly belonged there. For him the Land was spiritually alive, and it had become a vehicle for him to ascend in his search for perfection in Torah studies and character development.

Soon a match was proposed which Rav Herman thought might be suited for Moshe Aharon. The young woman had all the traits which the Sages praise a woman for, and the Kroizer family was well respected. The boy and girl met.

After the meeting, Moshe Aharon expressed his feelings to his grandfather. Of course, a decision of this magnitude could not be decided on the spur of the moment. Rav Herman listened and offered advice. After a second meeting, they spoke again at length.

"I suggest," Rav Herman said, "that we go together to the Kosel."

"Sure," Moshe Aharon agreed. "Do you have a specific reason?"

"Yes. There, at the Kosel, Hashem hovers and will be able to help us to come to the right decision. You know, Moshe Aharon, that choosing the right mate is one of the most important decisions in a man's life?"

"Yes," answered Moshe Aharon thoughtfully.

When they arrived at the Kosel they decided to say *Tehillim* before praying with a minyan. It was a brisk, windy afternoon, and the narrow lane open to Jews at the Kosel was nearly empty. As they stood by the Wall, a tightly wrapped piece of paper was dislodged by the wind from the cracks in the stones and fell at their feet.

"Look at this," Rav Herman interrupted his grandson. He pointed to the note on the ground. "Maybe Hashem is sending us an answer."

Rav Herman bent down and picked up the note. Slowly he unfolded it until it was completely open in his hands. Moshe Aharon looked at his grandfather.

A smile crossed Rav Herman's face. "Indeed! Moshe Aharon. Hashem has sent us a direct communication. Look for yourself what is written in this note."

Moshe Aharon took the note in his hands. Written on the paper was a verse which men say every day after donning tefillin. "I shall betroth you to Myself forever; I shall betroth you to Myself in righteousness and in justice, in kindness and in mercy. I shall betroth you to Myself in faithfulness; and you shall know the Lord."

Moshe Aharon Stern could barely believe what he read. The words from the prophet Hosea chimed in his ears.

Rav Herman asked, "Don't you think the message is absolutely clear?"

"Yes," Moshe Aharon replied. "Hashem has sent us a Heavenly sign that we cannot deny."

* * *

DURING RAV Moshe Aharon Stern's first year of marriage an incident occurred which foretold of his mission in life. It took place during the War of Independence.

The war which raged in Jerusalem during Iyar and Sivan, 1948 (5708), was the most direct assault on the whole Jewish community since the Crusaders pillaged the city eight hundred years earlier. Water and food were rationed. Bombs exploded without warning throughout the city. And the greatest fear for most of the citizens was the potential military advance of enemy troops stampeding through the city and massacring them and their families.

Rav Moshe Aharon devoted much time to strengthening his and his young wife's faith in God. On the surface, the war seemed to interfere with the Torah's commandment to rejoice with his wife during the first year of marriage. But with deeper introspection, Moshe Aharon understood that the danger of living through this war was really an educational tool on how to cleave to Hashem wholeheartedly as one cleaves to his spouse. His wife, too, was uplifted by this idea.

One day he was walking in the Zichron Moshe area of town. Carrying a large, thick *sefer* called *Oneg Yom Tov* in his left hand, he headed out of the synagogue and made his way homeward. Suddenly an eerie sound like a whistling trumpet foreboding danger passed over his head. It was a bomb about to crash and explode nearby. There was nothing that Moshe Aharon could do to protect himself, nowhere to run. He clutched the *sefer* tightly over his chest and froze as the bomb exploded. Shrapnel flew in all directions as the ground shook under the impact of the shell. A piece of shrapnel zoomed at him like a warrior's knife aimed for his heart. It tore through three-quarters of the *sefer* he was holding before it stopped.

Rav Moshe Aharon could hardly believe what happened. Were it not for the *sefer* which he instinctively held over his heart, he would no longer be among the living. Shaking from shock, yet totally immersed in praise of God, Moshe Aharon continued homeward.

Now, his mission in life was clear. Hashem had spared him in order to disseminate Torah to one and all. Over the next fifty years of his life, Rav Moshe Aharon Stern succeeded in fulfilling his mission. One of the great *baalei Mussar*, his name became a signpost in the Torah world.

(Based on an interview with Rav Yechiel Michel Stern)

A Letter Home

WHEN TWENTY-two-year-old Esther Cailingold was allowed to serve in the Haganah in the Old City, it was a dream come true. Disguised as a nurse, she entered the Jewish Quarter on a British convoy after Passover, 1948.

Her childhood experiences in England were instrumental in causing her to choose her course of action. Born in London and raised in an Orthodox home, she had volunteered to work with her father in a fire brigade during the Nazi air raids of the London Blitz. After the Second World War, she was deeply moved by the stories she heard of concentration camp victims, and felt compelled to offer her services to the Jewish people. In 1946 she came to Eretz Yisrael and began teaching. Soon, however, she became involved with the Haganah, helping their activities in any and every way she could.

The intensity of the combat during the bombardment of the Jewish Quarter was enough to cause even the bravest of people to tremble in fear. With Esther, however, it served only to bring out her sterling qualities. She used every minute for the enclave's defense, dashing back and forth with messages, food, and a good word for both soldiers and civilians.

On one of her outings, a shell exploded nearby and seriously injured her back. She was carried to Misgav Ladach Hospital, where she received the best treatment possible, given the pressing circumstances. Unfortunately, this did not prove to be very much, as conditions were truly primitive. There was no anesthetic left and very little blood plasma. Without electricity, operations were performed by flashlight. The overcrowded hospital was full of injured men and women, some groaning, others staring silently at the ceiling.

Friday, 28 May, when the refugees were leaving the Old City, the seriously injured were transferred to the Armenian monastery. Esther lay with a raging fever, her body wracked with pain. There was not even any morphine available to alleviate her suffering.

That Shabbos, one of the orderlies offered her the only sedative he could find — a cigarette.

"No," she said in a faint voice. "Shabbos!"

These were Esther's last words before lapsing into a coma from which she never recovered. Under her pillow, the staff found her final legacy — a letter she had written to her parents five days earlier.

Dear Mummy and Daddy,

I am writing to beg you that whatever may have happened to me, you will make the effort to take it in the spirit I want. We had a difficult fight here. I have tasted hell, but it has been worthwhile because I am convinced the end will see a Jewish state and the fulfillment of all our longings. I have lived my life fully, and it has been very sweet to be here in our land...

I hope one day soon you will all come and enjoy the fruits of what we are fighting for. Be happy and remember me only in joy.

Shalom,

Esther

(*O Jerusalem!* pp. 523–524)

The Mandelbaum Gate

The Mandelbaum Gate on Shmuel HaNavi Street served as the only crossing point between Jewish Jerusalem and East Jerusalem for nineteen years, from 1948 until 1967. The crossing derived its name due to a house that had stood near the site of the gate. Built by Rav Simcha Mandelbaum between 1925 and 1929, the two-story mansion provided ample living space for him and four of his married children. The house jutted out into the eastern side of Shmuel HaNavi Street — which after 1948 would become part of no-man's-land. Due to its strategic location during the War of Independence, the Arab forces succeeded in destroying most of the building.

The story behind Simcha Mandelbaum's acquisition of that precise plot of land and building his house there is a tale worth telling.

RAV SIMCHA Mandelbaum, a Karliner Chassid, lived in the Jewish Quarter during the first quarter of the twentieth century. He was a merchant by trade. When his wife, the daughter of the Kobiner Rebbe, came from Russia, she brought fifty hand-weaving machines with her. In Jerusalem, she hired Jewish women to weave stockings in their homes, which she then sold in a small shop in the Old City. Over the years, the couple was blessed with material success, and eventually, Rav Simcha felt the time had come to move to one of the new suburbs.

When a real estate agent suggested various houses in the upper-class areas like Rechavia, he laughed.

"Anyone can buy a house there! I'm looking to build a house with my own hands!"

The agent then proceeded to show him different plots in well-established neighborhoods.

"No, thanks," Rav Simcha replied. "If I'm already going to build, then I might as well do it in the biggest way possible."

"What do you mean by that?" asked the perplexed agent.

"What do you think of the idea of building in a place where my new house would extend the boundaries of Jerusalem by just a little bit more? Wouldn't that be something worthwhile?"

"Like 'two birds with one stone'!" smiled the agent.

"Yes!"

It was not long before his agent found the spot on Shmuel HaNavi Street. Mandelbaum surveyed the area with a critical eye. Across the street, further along in the direction of the Damascus Gate, stood Arab houses. Nearby was an Italian hospital and a church.

Pointing to the church and hospital, he said, "The gentiles who built those buildings are surely anxious to purchase this piece of land, as well as the adjacent plots. If myself and other people buy them, it will be a thorn in their

Rav Simcha Mandelbaum's house under construction

sides." With a sparkle in his eyes, Rav Simcha added, "Furthermore, I'll be extending the northern boundary of the Holy City!"

Thus the matter was settled. Rav Mandelbaum placed a down payment, and in due time the legal procedures were completed. Architectural plans were drawn up and construction got under way.

Rav Simcha wanted to take part in every phase of the building, and he frequented the site daily.

While digging the foundations, he discovered a few ancient coins dating back to the time of Bar Kochba. Engraved on them were the words, "Freedom of Jerusalem" and "Freedom of Israel."

Rav Simcha proudly showed the coins to all his friends. "This is a proof that the third wall around the Old City extended to this area."

Being a well-to-do merchant, Rav Mandelbaum wanted his new house to signify the splendor of Jerusalem. Therefore, its many rooms were decorated in a style befitting the regal status of the Holy City.

During the War of Independence, the Mandelbaum house became a strategic military stronghold. The Arabs attacked it in the first stage of an attempt to penetrate into the Jewish neighborhood of Meah Shearim. When the Jewish forces evacuated the building, the Arabs succeeded in setting off a bomb which partially destroyed it.

After the cease-fire, a border crossing between Jewish Jerusalem and the Arab side was erected only a few feet from the destroyed house. Naturally, it was named after the owner whose aim in building it was altruistic, a statement of the Jewish people's freedom to forge ahead with the expansion of the Holy City.

(*Esara Doros b'Eretz Yisrael*, p. 200)

A Parable for All Times

SHORTLY AFTER the Six-Day War, when the euphoria of the victory was still at its height, Rav Chezkel Sarna, Rosh Yeshivah Hebron in Jerusalem, had an informal meeting with David Ben-Gurion. At that time, the two senior citizens were at the height of their dazzling, albeit diametrically opposed, careers. The fiery Ben-Gurion posed a question to the Rosh Yeshivah which had been bothering him for quite a while — almost twenty years in fact.

"When the state came into being in 1948," he commented, "your yeshivah participated in the joyous Independence Day celebrations by raising a flag and reciting *Hallel* without a blessing. However, that only continued for a year or two. After that, you began reciting *Tachanun* and prayers of repentance on the very same day. What happened? Did the Torah change?"

"Let me answer you with a parable," smiled Rav Sarna. "It once happened that there was a barren couple who prayed and waited year after year for a child. After many years, they were finally blessed with a son. Just think how incredible their joy was at the time! Yet, shortly afterwards, they discovered that the boy was mentally retarded. What do you think they said to themselves? For this we waited, for this we yearned? Though they accepted their lot, all joyousness left their hearts.

"This is precisely what happened with the State of Israel. At the beginning of the state, we thought that the newborn nation would grow in the ways of our holy Torah. Therefore we participated in the Independence Day celebrations. But once we saw how the government specifically veered away from the Torah and sought to mold society according to atheistic values, we returned to saying *Tachanun* at the yeshivah."

Ben-Gurion argued with the Rosh Yeshivah, pointing to the government's many positive achievements. Whether in agriculture, industry, education, defense, and the like, the State of Israel had reached heights no one had ever dreamed of. Furthermore, who went out to fight? The secular Jews! Were it not for the irreligious, Ben-Gurion contended, the Arabs would have pushed the Jews into the sea.

"That is what you say," replied Rav Chezkel. "But we believe differently. Were it not for our prayers and supplications before the Heavenly court, you would not have been successful on the battlefield. Also, we studied extra hours every day so that in the merit of our Torah studies the Almighty would have mercy on us and save us."

Before departing, Rav Sarna presented the first Prime Minister with a gift — a book written by his brother-in-law, Rav Aharon Cohen, on the weekly Torah portion.

"Why are you giving me this book?" asked Ben-Gurion in surprise. "Surely you know I don't read such things."

"I chose this book not based on what *you* think you ought to read, but rather on what *I* think a Jew should want to read!"

(Told by Rav Yehudah Palai)

The Bar Mitzvah Drash

IT WAS Sukkos, 1949 (5710). Rav Shalom Schwadron walked with his son Yitzchak from their home in Shaarei Chesed to the Zichron Yosef neighborhood. There they would visit Rav Issar Zalman Meltzer, Rosh Yeshivah of Etz Chaim and author of the renowned halachic work *Even HaEzel*.

"We'll be at Rav Issar Zalman's house in just another minute," Rav Shalom told his son. "Since your birthday is on Simchas Torah, we won't be able to fulfill the ancient custom of visiting all the *gedolim* on that day. However, I think it's to your benefit that we visit at least some of them before your bar mitzvah."

Arriving at Rav Meltzer's home, they knocked on the door and were led to the Rosh Yeshiva's sukkah. Yitzchak's father and Rav Meltzer greeted each

Rav Issar Zalman Meltzer (1870–1953)

other warmly. The eighty-year-old Rosh Yeshivah extended his hands and clasped the bar mitzvah boy's hand in his.

"So this is your *pri hadar* [beautiful fruit]!" he smiled to Rav Schwadron. "*Mazal tov!*" he added to the lad.

"Thank you," Yitzchak replied shyly.

As the conversation progressed, Rav Meltzer asked the bar mitzvah boy to say his *drash*. Yitzchak stood up and proudly begin to relate the *drash* his father had written for him. It was built on a halachic contradiction and was quite intricate.

Suddenly the boy stopped in the middle and glanced at his father. Rav Shalom nodded at his son to continue, but Yitzchak continued to gaze at him doubtfully. Rav Issar Zalman looked on inquisitively, and quickly realized that the interplay between father and son had something to do with the content of the *drash* itself.

Rav Shalom pinched his son lightly on the arm. "Go on, Yitzchak, it's all right." He gave another pinch and smiled at his son.

Yitzchak took a deep breath and continued the *drash* at rapid-fire speed. "In the *Even HaEzel*... Yet, apparently the author of the *Even HaEzel* overlooked another Rambam in halachos...which contradicts his deductions..."

Yitzchak abruptly stopped, too shy to say this part of the *drash* directly in front of the illustrious author of *Even HaEzel* who was sitting before him. Rav Meltzer, however, waited patiently for the lad to finish the *drash*. After more prompting, Yitzchak continued.

"What a wonderful *drash*, Yitzchak," Rav Issar Zalman said after the boy finished. "I want you to know something. I am made of flesh and blood like you, and I am capable of making an error. Seeing that you asked a very difficult question on what I wrote in my book *Even HaEzel,* I admit that I apparently did not take that other Rambam into consideration, and therefore my conclusions were mistaken."

His words calmed the boy and left a very deep impression on him. After the two Schwadrons left Rav Meltzer's sukkah, one of the family members present asked Rav Issar Zalman, "Did you really overlook that Rambam?"

Leaning forward with a smile on his face, Rav Issar Zalman answered, "In truth, I actually did take that Rambam and the apparent contradiction it raised on my thesis into consideration. The boy's question was very profound, one which only a *talmid chacham* could have asked. However, the boy was correct in noting that I did not address it explicitly. Rather, I subtly wove the answer into my overall conclusions."

"So why didn't you say so?" the relative asked in surprise.

"If you must know, I wanted the bar mitzvah boy to feel good. Don't you think that that is more important than to prove he was wrong?"

(Based on an interview with Rav Yitzchak Schwadron)

To Be *or* Not To Be

RAV SHLOMO Zalman Auerbach, the dynamic Rosh Yeshivah of Kol Torah Yeshivah, stood at a major crossroads in his life. During the early 1950s, Rav Shlomo Zalman had gained a reputation for the clarity of his lectures. He tried to view the controversies and intricate case studies presented in the Gemara as real incidents, relating to them as if he witnessed them with his own eyes. Evaluating the proceedings under such a realistic light enabled the students to picture the Gemara better and thereby come to the proper understanding of it.

In addition to his talents as a teacher, Rav Auerbach was a foremost authority on practical halachic questions, especially those relating to electricity.

At one point, Rav Ezra Atiyah, the Rosh Yeshivah of Porat Yosef Yeshivah, asked Rav Shlomo Zalman to join his teaching staff. Rav Auerbach gave one lecture there, but after further consideration rejected the offer.

Now, however, he was faced with a greater decision — whether or not to leave teaching entirely. The Chief Rabbi of Israel, Rav Yitzchak Herzog, had eyed him as a prime candidate for the newly established Rabbinate. Rav Herzog, searching for *talmidei chachamim* of the highest caliber, had already convinced Rav Yosef Shalom Elyashiv to join.

Rav Shlomo Zalman pondered his options. In those years, the reputation and influence earned in such a post were far greater than that of a Rosh Yeshivah. Furthermore, there was the incentive of a more stable economic base. The more he weighed the Chief Rabbi's offer against his present circumstances, the more he was inclined to accept it.

While he mulled over the options, the heads of Kol Torah got wind of the offer. Naturally, they were very concerned and hoped he would stay with the yeshivah. They went to Bnei Brak to ask the Chazon Ish to intercede on their behalf. The Chazon Ish agreed.

When Rav Shlomo Zalman met with the Chazon Ish a few days later, he sat and listened quietly while Rav Karelitz stated his views.

"With the Rav's permission, perhaps I might explain my position," said Rav

Auerbach after the Chazon Ish finished speaking. "What can I do when my personal preference lies more towards halachos than in giving *shiurim* in the yeshivah?"

The Chazon Ish smiled. "Rav Shlomo Zalman," he said, "still and all, know one thing. If you will listen to my advice and remain Rosh Yeshivah, you will become both a great Rosh Yeshivah and a *posek*. But if you leave the yeshivah and go into the Rabbinate, you will only become a great *posek*."

What could Rav Shlomo Zalman answer back. Of course, the Chazon Ish was right!

(*Rabbeinu HaGadol*, pp. 36–37)

The Chida Lives On

One of the great Sephardic rabbanim of the last three hundred years was Rav Chaim Yosef David Azulai, better known by his acronym, Chida. Born in Jerusalem in 1724, he became a master of both the revealed and hidden aspects of the Torah. The latter half of his life he spent in Livorno, Italy, where he wrote nearly a hundred books. He passed away on 11 Adar, 1806, and was buried in the Jewish cemetery there. In 1960 his body was brought to Jerusalem and reinterred in the Har HaMenuchos Cemetery. The following story testifies to the greatness of the tzaddik.

IT WAS a warm spring day, Sunday, 20 Iyar, 1960 (5720), when three rabbis reached Lod airport. A dignitary of formidable repute was due to arrive that morning on a flight from Rome, and the rabbis had been sent by the Chief Sephardic Rabbi to greet him. However, they were only part of the formal committee that had been arranged to welcome the celebrated guest to Eretz Yisrael. A delegation of rabbinical and lay leaders were also on hand, as well as a representative from the Italian embassy.

The three rabbis were entrusted with an additional task. They were to take care of the entry visa and other sundry papers. They arrived early and received permission to enter through customs and go past the immigration officials in order to greet the visitor as soon as the plane landed.

"What a merit we have to escort the Chida to Jerusalem," one of them said.

"The man behind the scenes was Chief Rabbi Rav Yitzchak Nisim, you know," pointed out another. "He was the one who labored to get the Italian authorities to authorize the reinterment of the Chida's body in Eretz Yisrael."

"I understand that it wasn't easy, either," another *rav* added.

"You're right. If I'm not mistaken, the spot where his tomb was located was right in the center of town. The Livorno municipality decided to convert the area into a public park. When word reached here that they were going to reinter him in a new plot, Rav Nisim, as Chief Rabbi, began using his influence to have him brought here."

"Somehow," another *rav* said, "he was successful."

When the plane landed, the three rabbis were on hand to ensure that every detail of the last leg of the journey was handled properly. The casket was unloaded and brought into a special room, where it was placed on a table for inspection. The rabbis were aghast to learn that during the flight the coffin had fallen over and then been picked up and set upside down, and then had fallen down again and once more been turned upside down.

"We must open the coffin and rearrange the Chida's remains," said Rav Mordechai Eliyahu emotionally.

"*Chas v'shalom*!" another *rav* interrupted. "We can never do a thing like that."

"But it is not honorable to bury the Chida in such a state," insisted Rav Eliyahu. "What if the remains are in the wrong place?"

"I also disagree with you," said the third *rav*. "It is not within our jurisdiction to decide to open the coffin, much less rearrange what's inside."

After a few minutes of heated discussion, one of the rabbis left to finish arranging the necessary papers so that they could take the coffin with them from the airport.

Rav Mordechai persisted in his pleas to honor the dead and managed to convince his remaining companion. Then, in a spirit of trepidation mixed with great fortitude, he opened up the coffin along its length, just enough so that his hand could reach inside.

The funeral procession of the Chida

"I ask you, the Chida, forgiveness," Rav Eliyahu chanted with great emotion. "I am about to arrange your remains for your honor. Please have pity on me and forgive me if in any way I might not fulfill this mitzvah properly."

His right hand was inching its way inside the dark coffin as he spoke. "Dear tzaddik," he intoned, "please do this task yourself so that I shall not have to err in this mission. Please do it for..."

Suddenly, the coffin shook up and down on the table, and a rattling sound of the Chida's remains striking the walls of the coffin thundered throughout the room. Stunned, the two rabbis froze in their place. The *rav* standing next to Rav Mordechai fainted and collapsed on the floor.

Rav Mordechai had a split second to decide on a course of action. If he removed his hand to help his colleague, he knew he wouldn't have the courage to put his hand back inside. Instead, he waited for the coffin to rest again on the table and the sound to subside. He then slowly moved his hand from one end of the coffin to the other to be sure that everything was in the right place. It was.

As his friend regained consciousness and heard that everything was in perfect order, he kissed Rav Mordechai Eliyahu's hand. "Let me kiss the hand of the one who worked such miraculous wonders!"

When the third *rav* returned, he was amazed at the tale. However, there was no time for them to linger over the extraordinary event that had just occurred, due to the great crowd waiting outside.

Later that day, Jerusalem temporarily took on a new look. Tens of thousands of Jews lined the city's streets to follow the procession from the Yeshurun Synagogue on King George Street to Har HaMenuchos cemetery outside of Givat Shaul. The rabbis of the city had requested that shopkeepers close their businesses, both as a sign of respect and to enable everyone to participate in the cortege. Even the afternoon session of the Knesset was delayed in order to permit members to pay their last respects to the Chida.

In the 154 years since the passing of Rav Azulai, his renown has only become greater, and his name a legend in the annals of great Torah sages. In a sense, his reinterment in Jerusalem proved to some — at least the three in the luggage room of the airport — how the Chida lives on.

(Based on an interview with Rav Yosef Eliyahu)

The Legendary Finkels

The story of the Mir Yeshivah in the twentieth century is really the story of the renowned Finkel family. Each member of this extraordinary family was a giant in Torah, as well as an exemplary model of kindness and righteousness. After familiarizing ourselves with the family tree (only partially reconstructed here), we will weave a few threads of their deeds into a pattern portraying the lives of the legendary Finkels.

"HOW IS it possible to go to sleep if you haven't learned fourteen hours?" Rav Eliezer Yehudah Finkel asked one of his grandsons. "I don't understand how you could even think about it!" Rav Finkel himself lived by his own high standards of excellence. To give but one example of his remarkable diligence, he managed to review the entire Babylonian Talmud every year.

The Rosh Yeshivah, who single-handedly built the Mir in Jerusalem from scratch, acted like a father to all his students. His concern for their physical needs was surpassed only by his concern for their spiritual growth. He took advantage of any incentives which encouraged his students to greater accomplishments in Torah. Once, he even promised a bonus of fifty dollars (an enormous sum of money at the time) to any student who mastered an entire tractate by heart.

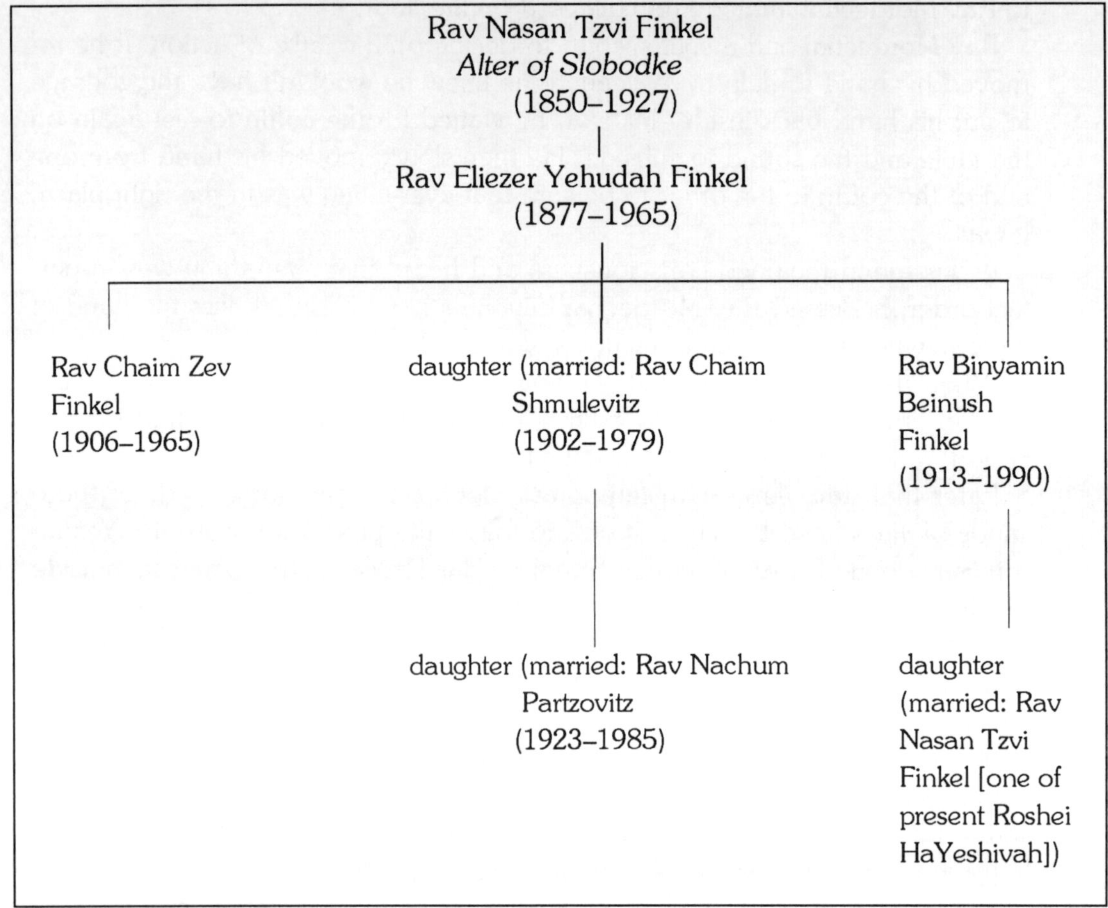

Rav Yehudah Finkel wore a famous two-pocketed vest. Both pockets contained money: one for charitable purposes and the other for students who said authentic Torah novella.

His son-in-law, Rav Chaim Shmulevitz, once remarked, "I envy my father-in-law for his ability to hear and read one hundred, and even two hundred, *chaburos* that all cover well-trodden ground, with the same thirst for the last as for the first!"

Rav Eliezer Finkel, seated to the right, listens to Rav Zalman Sorotzkin (standing) speak at the dedication of the Mir Yeshivah in 1949. Seated to the right of Rav Sorotzkin are Rav Chaim Shmulevitz and Rav Binyamin Beinush Finkel.

His son Rav Chaim Zev founded Heichal HaTorah Yeshivah in Tel Aviv in the 1930s. However, after the Mir was established in Jerusalem, he moved to the Holy City and became *mashgiach* at the yeshivah. Famed for his *mussar* talks, he was also at ease utilizing other methods of expression to induce love and faith in God in people's hearts, such as song and dance. Indeed, on the High Holy Holidays he served as *chazan* for the congregation, and his heartfelt supplications often brought others to tears along with him.

Rav Chaim Zev enjoyed mingling with Jews from all walks of life. At the wedding of a close relative, he preferred to sit at the beggars' table, conversing with those around him like old friends. With his respectful and friendly treatment of other people, he carried on the Finkel way of mixing Torah with love of one's fellowman.

His brother-in-law, Rav Chaim Shmulevitz, continued the tradition of humility and honor of Torah. "It's hard for me to understand the whole idea of *bein hazmanim* [semester break]," admitted Rav Chaim. "It's like having an interruption of life. Does one ever take a vacation from life?!"

Rav Chaim's statement illustrated his total immersion in Torah studies. In his earlier years he was known to study two days straight without breaking to eat or sleep. His crystal-clear memory and sharp analytical ability helped him become one of the great *roshei yeshivos* of his time. As one of his colleagues once remarked, "What can one say about a man who knows every [comment of the] Rosh in *Taharos* [sixth order of Mishnah] by heart!"

Rav Chaim's Sunday-night *shmuessen* attracted people from far and wide. In front of a full *beis midrash*, he would stand in silence by the *bimah* before starting. Rav Shlomo Wolbe explained his custom: "He did not need this time to prepare his words. He needed it to prepare himself for the *shmuess*. Only when he felt certain that his thoughts were from his heart, would he say them." The main theme of these talks, expressed with lucidity and simplicity, emphasized matters pertaining to interactions between man and his fellowman.

Rav Shmulevitz often said, "A leader of Israel must feel the joy and suffering of his fellow Jew as if they were his own." When visiting a friend who had lost his wife, Rav Chaim sat down and wept with bitter anguish over his friend's loss. After twenty minutes, he arose and said, "May God console you..." and left. The bereaved man later related that he took more comfort from Rav Chaim's visit than anyone else's, for he sensed that his friend had truly borne the agony of his loss with him.

A few months before he passed away in 1979 (5739), a young man came and asked him to pray for the recovery of a very sick person. After the young man left, Rav Chaim, himself ravaged by disease and wracked with pain, called his son to his bedside.

"Please dress me. I'm going to the Kosel."

"But father," his son protested, "you can hardly turn over in bed. How can you possibly go to the Kosel!"

"Dress me, please," Rav Chaim insisted. "I'm going to the Kosel."

Reluctantly, his son dressed him, and with the aid of another person carried him to a car which took him to the Kosel. At the Wall, Rav Chaim could barely stand, yet he entreated the Almighty for the well-being of another Jew. Then he returned to his sickbed.

Rav Chaim's son-in-law, Rav Nachum Partzovitz, became Rosh Yeshivah a short time after Rav Chaim passed away on 3 Teves, 1979. He had been groomed for the position by a lifetime of Torah studies in the Mir Yeshivah, where he had learned since 1938. His constant thirst for Torah was unquenchable. His peers described him as a *gaon* in explaining the meaning of the text of the Gemara, focusing his lectures solely on the commentaries of Rashi and Tosefos. "There is no imprecise word in Rashi," he would comment.

On a personal level, he accorded everyone — whether colleague, student, or unlearned person — the same respect. Once, a woman who regularly collected charity from Rav Nachum found him in the middle of a lecture at the Mir Yeshivah. She entered the classroom, walked over to him, and began to harangue him with her problems. The students were stunned to see how politely he listened to her. As she finished, he reached into his pocket and took out a sizable sum of money, and, with words of apology on his lips, gently handed it to her. Only then did the Rav continue his lecture.

Rav Beinush Finkel, the son of Yehudah Finkel, was a different type of Rosh Yeshivah than any of his predecessors. He hid his greatness behind a veil of silence. Though he completed Shas dozens of times and Mishnayos hundreds of times, he shied away from giving lectures and discussing Torah themes unless he absolutely had to. However, despite his attempts to disguise his greatness, Rav Beinish commanded the respect of the *gedolim*. His close friendship with the Brisker Rav, Rav Yitzchak Zev Soloveitchik, was well known — although Rav Soloveitchik was much older than him. Once, years before Rav Beinush became Rosh Yeshivah, the Brisker Rav called for him and handed him a bundle of his own handwritten notebooks. "I would like you to review these by such-and-such a time so that we can discuss them together," the Brisker Rav told him. At the appointed time, the Brisker Rav listened to Rav Beinush's critique on his Torah insights.

Rav Finkel treated the physical world around him in the same manner as the spiritual world. First and foremost, he believed that money was a threat to a person's self-perfection, which could warp and taint a person's formerly pure motives. Throughout his lifetime, Rav Beinush followed his philosophy to the utmost degree, even refusing to accept a salary (from his father, Rav Yehudah Finkel) for delivering lectures at the yeshivah. When he himself became Rosh Yeshivah, the physical burden of the yeshivah fell on him. His constant fear of the slightest possibility of paying interest on loans kept him in and out of the bank on a daily basis.

Yet Rav Beinush displayed his phenomenal humility and willingness to help others even in financial matters. Paupers who hesitated to enter banks and stores in order to exchange their handfuls of coins for bills would often turn to Rav Finkel to do it for them. This was a very embarrassing undertaking, for merchants and bank tellers looked askance at such people, pinpointing them as beggars. However, Rav Beinush happily took their change to the bank in order to protect their dignity — thereby incurring the clerk's scorn himself.

Rav Beinush was so concerned with other people's feelings that he never considered it below his dignity to help the unfortunate. Once he was found sitting on the floor, fixing the heater of the poor widow who lived below his flat.

After the Six-Day War, he began praying at the Kosel with a sunrise minyan (*vasikin*), a custom he maintained for the rest of his life. After his passing, an elderly woman knocked at the family's door.

"Please," she said, "you must tell me about the rabbi that passed away — was he tall, with a white beard? Did he pray *vasikin* every day at the Kosel?"

When answered in the affirmative, she broke down sobbing. She then explained that for years she had lived a wretched existence, standing in the heat and rain by the Kosel, collecting alms. What made her life bearable was the good-natured jokes that the tall *rav* traded with her every day. She simply could not imagine that such an unassuming man as that could be the Rosh Yeshivah of Mir.

(Culled from *Yeshivas Mir–Yerushalayim*)

Place Your Trust in God

Rav Shmuel Houminer (1913–1977)

RAV SHMUEL Houminer lived what he preached. From his youth onwards, he possessed only the simplest of worldly possessions. Born shortly before the outbreak of the First World War in Mizkeres Moshe, he understood what it meant to be frugal. The Jerusalemites of old honored the Talmudic dictums which placed spiritual wealth high above its physical counterpart.

A product of Etz Chaim Yeshivah, Rav Shmuel delighted in the Torah's profound words as another person would enjoy counting gold coins. Moreover, he sought to share his treasure chest of knowledge with his fellowman. At the age of twenty-six he published his first book, *Ikrei Dinim*, a digest of the laws of *lashon hara*, which went through dozens of printings. His mentor, Rav Issar Zalman Meltzer, praised it with these words, "It is worthy of being kept by all Jews in their tallis bags so that after davening they can study and gain from it."

As the years went by, Rav Houminer began publishing his masterpiece, a fifteen-volume work entitled *Eved HaMelech*, "Servant of the King." In it, he sought to pinpoint every place in the Torah where we find a Divine call to perfect our performance of one of the 613 commandments, or to excel at some human endeavor which elevates man out of the mundane world into a closeness to his Creator. Based on the Vilna Gaon's statement that the mitzvos are countless, he discovered thousands of mitzvos which a Jew must fulfill to be a true *eved Hashem*. Eventually published in over a dozen volumes and covering the entire Tanach, *Eved HaMelech* opened a doorway to a wider understand of man's relationship with God.

Yet the his most popular work was a pocket-sized book entitled *Mitzvas Bitachon*, guidelines to simple faith in the Almighty. No one is exempt from this all-encompassing commandment, and everyone must rely on it in his everyday life. Furthermore, at crucial junctions in life, trust in God supersedes everything else and anchors a person until calm times return.

Rav Shmuel believed that this was the ultimate mitzvah, for it embraced all the other ones. Therefore, it needed constant reinforcement. He realized that every person has several spare minutes throughout the day — such as during a short ride on the bus or while waiting in line at the bank. These times could be utilized as an opportunity to strengthen one's faith and trust in the Almighty. It was with this idea in mind that he wrote *Mitzvas Bitachon*.

One time he learned how one of the *gedolim* perceived this mitzvah. The Brisker Rav, Rav Velvel Soloveitchik, paid his married students on the last day of every month. When the appointed day arrived and he still did not have the necessary amount, he would borrow from here or there in order to pay on time. Once, on the appointed day, he was speaking with a friend. When Rav Soloveitchik mentioned that he still lacked the sum to pay his *avreichim*, the man said to him, "Wouldn't it be great if someone would appear and offer you a quarter of a million liros for your yeshivah. Then you would have no worries for several years."

"If someone handed me a quarter of a million liros," replied Rav Velvel earnestly, "I would not accept it."

"Why not?" asked his friend in surprise.

"I will not sell the mitzvah of trust in God for a quarter of a million liros!"

For Rav Shmuel, this story was worth millions.

He, too, lived what he preached. He humbly accepted whatever befell him, and cleaved faithfully to his Creator at all times. In 1976 (5736), at the age of sixty-two, he was diagnosed with incurable cancer. For three-quarters of a year he suffered unbelievably. Yet, whenever someone visited him, the only words he spoke were intended to strengthen his visitor's belief in the power of faith. If he was not better yet, that was not his business, it was Hashem's. His duty was simply to do the Almighty's bidding. Once, when seized by terrible pains, he prayed, "Master of the universe! Even if I am cut into pieces, under no circumstances will I give up on You. Therefore, I beseech You to give me courage and strength to fulfill the mitzvah of *bitachon*."

He said that at every second he was fulfilling three mitzvos: the mitzvah to accept suffering with love, the mitzvah of trusting God, and the mitzvah of prayer.

As he lived, so he died. He had been a legend in his own time. On 19 Sivan, 1977, he passed away, leaving a treasure trove of words and deeds for the coming generation. Indeed, his life was a model of modesty, diligence, compassion, and trust in God. Of him one could surely say, "He was an *eved HaMelech*."

(Moriah, Av, 5737)

A Day in the Life of a Mohel

SHAAREI ZEDEK Hospital was on round-the-clock shifts. The Battle of Jerusalem was at its peak, with bombs falling everywhere inside the Jewish part of the city. Civilians huddled in bomb shelters, with transistor radios tuned to the news. The army fought battles to the south at the Government House and northeast at Ammunition Hill. All the hospitals were filled with injured soldiers.

A bomb crashed through the wall of Shaarei Zedek Hospital during the Six-Day War. Fortunately it did not explode, nor were there any casualties.

Rav Yosef David (Yosele) Weissberg was a "recruiter" for a different sort of army. A *mohel* (ritual circumcision), his name would eventually become synonymous with dedication to the mitzvah of entering infant boys into Hashem's service on their eighth day of life. Despite the turmoil that had enveloped the entire city, Rav Yosele had come to Shaarei Zedek to perform a circumcision. Ignoring all the bustle around him, he marched upstairs to the maternity ward to examine the child. At least here, Rav Weissberg thought, among these innocent babes, I shall be protected from the wrath of the war.

Suddenly he froze, as a heavy whistling sound crackled through the air. Seconds later a bomb crashed into the building. It landed next to a wall in one of the corridors of the second floor, without exploding. On the other side of the wall, in the nursery, Yosele and the babies were utterly defenseless. In an instant, all his dreams of bringing another Jewish baby into the covenant in a peaceful ceremony were shattered. Pandemonium reigned everywhere. Some people pressed to get into the hospital's basement shelter. Others crowded into the hospital's synagogue where their voices rent the air in a plea for Divine mercy.

The greatest fear of most of the people, Yosele included, was that at any moment there might be another bomb. Thank the Lord, that was the only bomb to strike any hospital during the war, and, miraculously, no one was injured by it.

The bris took place an hour and a half later than scheduled. The *mazal tovs* were muted, due to the awareness of the awesome battle taking place in the city. However, one more soldier had entered the war, and maybe in his merit the scales would be tipped in favor of the Jews.

Rav Weissberg looked at the list of babies that awaited his services and decided to drive to Meah Shearim, where the next bris was scheduled to take place. After he finished there, he walked up to where his car was parked, on Baharan Road near Strauss Street. Suddenly he heard the eerie sound of a bomb about to land. He quickly scrambled a few meters to the entrance of a building, as the bomb exploded exactly where he had been standing a few seconds earlier. Had it not been for the safety of the entranceway, he would have died instantly.

Grateful for the miracle, Yosele nevertheless remained unfazed. Discarding the option of going to a nearby bomb shelter, he immediately set out to reach his car to get to the next bris. "What good would being in a shelter do?" he thought. "My wife and children are in a bunker on the other side of town. I cannot be of any assistance to them from here. But I can help to bring two more babies into the covenant on their eighth day."

After he finished these mitzvos, Yosele Weissberg returned to Shaarei Zedek Hospital. He wanted to help in any way he could. Injured soldiers lay in the hallways, and his fearlessness at the sight of blood made him well equipped to soothe and encourage the weak and wounded people around him.

By the end of the day, Rav Yosele returned home to his wife and family. They were safe and so was he. For Yosele, it seemed like nothing more than another day in the life of a *mohel*.

(Based on an interview with Rav Yosele Weissberg)

In Honor of Aharon HaKohen

ONE SUMMER day in 1970, Rav Mencham Mendel Gefner and Rav Shmuel Houminer ended their daily Torah study session. Both men were middle-aged *talmidei chachamim* from Meah Shearim.

Glancing speculatively out of the window, Rav Shmuel pondered, "You know, it's very interesting. The only *yartzeit* mentioned explicitly in the Torah is that of Aharon *HaKohen* (*BaMidbar* 33:38: "Aharon *HaKohen* went up Mount Hor at the command of God and died there… on the first day of the fifth month.") I wonder why this is so?"

Discussing the matter, the two men concluded that that day, the first of Av, was imbued with a special power of salvation due to Aharon's phenomenal merits. It might even be powerful enough to pull the Jewish people out of exile, if its potential was properly utilized.

At that point, they were struck with an idea: why not try and organize a group of 71 *Kohanim* to bless a large crowd on *Rosh Chodesh* Av! Seventy-one was the number of members that constituted the ancient *Sanhendrin*; thus, this number

Birchas Kohanim at the Western Wall

was certainly significant. Surely, a group of seventy-one *Kohanim* could invoke a powerful spiritual influence on behalf of the Jewish people! Rav Mendel Gefner, known as a man of action, immediately proceeded to try and implement the idea. Unfortunately, he fell ill and was bedridden the entire week before the appointed time, and the first attempt to conduct a public *Birchas Kohanim* never came to fruition.

A few months later, during the Ten Days of Repentance, something occurred that spurred Rav Mendel to renew his efforts. Rav Michel Houminer, son of Rav Shmuel, came to Rav Gefner with a newly discovered manuscript written by the Rokeach (Rav Elazer of Garmiza, who lived 700 years ago). Rav Michel eagerly pointed out a line that had captivated his attention: "If three hundred *kohanim* would stand on Mount of Olives and recite *Birchas Kohanim*, the *Mashiach* would come."

Rav Mendel felt goose pimples ripple across his body. "This is a clear sign from Heaven that I must act upon immediately!" he exclaimed.

During the following weeks, Rav Gefner sought the advice and blessing of some of the generation's leading sages, including the Rebbes of Vishnitz, Ger, and Slonim, the Brisker Rav, and the Stiepler *Gaon*. Each one encouraged Rav Mendel to act without delay on his holy mission.

He immediately discounted the idea of holding the event on Aharon HaKohen's *yartzeit*: the Rokeach had not mentioned any specific date, and the *yartzeit* was nine months away anyway. Instead, he chose a date that seemed particularly auspicious: Tuesday – the third day of Creation, the only day on which the word "good" is written twice. Specifically, the third of Kislev, which was just a few weeks hence, fell on a Tuesday, allowing him just enough time to organize everything.

Like a man on a Divine mission, Rav Gefner placed an announcement in the HaModiah newspaper and on the notice boards around the city, inviting *Kohaim* to assemble at the Western Wall for the *Shachris* service and bless their Jewish brethren.

The first two days of Kislev were wet and rainy, and the forecast for Tuesday was for more of the same. Nevertheless, *Birchas Kohaim* would take place as scheduled!

Early Tuesday morning, Rav Mendel set out for the Kosel, umbrella over his head. A sliver of doubt raced through his mind: How many Kohaim would brave the elements, and how many Jews would go out of their way to pray outside in such weather?

What a sight awaited him on his arrival! Hundreds of Kohaim and several thousand Jews were about to pray together. They had come from near and far to participate in the historic event.

Now the truth of something the Brisker Rav said became apparent to Rav Gefner: we see that people will travel great distances, even in inclement weather, in order to visit their Rebbe and receive his blessing. How much more would they be willing to go to the Kosel, where the blessing stems from the Almighty Himself!*

(Culled from Birchas Kohaim, Part II, pp. 11-36)

The Dream That Came True

This story spans nearly a century, from 1905 until 1987, and ties together two generations of the distinguished Auerbach family.

THAT NIGHT IN 1905 began like any other. Chaim Leib Auerbach, exhausted after a long day's studies, went to bed and quickly fell into a sweet slumber. Several hours later, he was startled awake by a particularly vivid and unusual dream. Nevertheless, he didn't ascribe any particular significance to it, and momentarily fell back asleep. However, his slumber was not destined to last, for he was soon reawakened by the dream's reoccurrence. This time, Chaim Leib sat up on the edge of his bed, pondering the import of his experience.

The newly married *avreich* realized that he had been granted a vision from Heaven. Awakening his wife to tell her he was stepping out for a while, Chaim Leib set out in the cool night air for the Battei Broide neighborhood. There, he hoped to discuss the import of his dream with Rav Shimon Horowitz, an outstanding Ashkenazi kabbalist at that time.

The streets were empty at that late hour. Yet as Chaim Leib approached Battei Broide, he heard footsteps approaching, and made out the faint silhouette of a Jewish man. As he drew closer, Chaim Leib was surprised to see that it was

* What followed this first successful *Birchas Kohaim* is history. Shortly thereafter, Rav Gefner established *chol hamoed* of Passover and Succos – times when Jews form all over the world visit Israel – as the date for this unique event at the Kosel. Today, this amazing event attracts 100s of kohanim and tens of thousands of Jews who stand in silent awe as the thunderous sounds of *Birchas Kohaim* echoes across the Kosel plaza.

Rav Chaim Leib Auerbach (1883-1954)

Rav Shimon Horowitz (1865-1947)

none other than Rav Horowitz!

"What are you doing out so late at night, young man?" Rav Horowitz asked his protege.

"I was on my way to see you," answered Chaim Leib. "You see, I had an amazing dream tonight and...."

"Very interesting!" interrupted the elderly tzaddik. "You see, I was on my way to see you, too, for I also had a fabulous dream tonight, and knew that you were somehow connected to it."

Within minutes, the stunned men realized that they had experienced the identical dream. In it, an august sage stood before them. His face shone with a brilliant radiance and his presence inspired them to utter humility. "Why is no one studying my Torah!?" the imposing figure thundered. "The power of my Torah will bring the Shechinah out of *galus*!" With that, the dream abruptly ended and the two men had woken up.

Rav Horowitz realized that the venerable sage was none other than the Arizal - Rav Yitzchak Luria. The Ari was bemoaning the fact that few men of high caliber were dedicating themselves to the study of *Kabbalah*. It was true that there was the venerated Beis El Yeshivah, which had produced such luminaries as Rav Shalom Sharabi, Rav Yedidia Abulafia, and most recently the author of *Shemen Sasson*. Additionally, a decade before, Rav Chaim Shaul Deweik had opened a new yeshivah, Rechovos HaNahar, also dedicated to studying the mystical aspects of the Torah. However, both these institutions catered to Sephardim; among the Ashkenazim, only a few individuals like Rav Shimon Horowitz chose to study *Kabbalah*.

Right then and there, the young Rav Chaim Leib and the elderly Rav Horowitz resolved to open a yeshivah for the study of the Arizal's *Kabbalah* amongst the Ashekenazim. It took an untold amount of effort and persistence, but within a year, Yeshivas Shaar HaShamayim had opened its doors in the Old City. Rav Horowitz was the Rosh Yeshivah, and Rav Auerbach was the director. It was literally a dream come true...

Over the years, the yeshivah grew and became the focal point where scholars of Ashkenazic descent could delve into the mysteries of the Torah. In 1948, however, the yeshivah suffered a severe blow when the Jordanians captured the Old City and demolished much of the Jewish Quarter.

Homeless, the yeshivah set up temporary quarters in various *battei midrashim* in the New City. Rav Chaim Leib Auerbach, who had become the institution's renowned Rosh Yeshivah upon Rav Horowitz's passing, continued to lead the yeshivah "in exile." Yet his dream was to see the yeshivah in its own building. In his last days, he requested his son, Rav Dovid Auerbach, to take it upon himself to fulfill that dream. Rav Dovid readily agreed to comply with his holy father's wishes.

The years passed. When Jerusalem was reunited in 1967 and the Old City once again came under Jewish control, the yeshivah tried in vain to reclaim its property (in fact, legal proceedings continue to the present day). In the meantime, Shaar HaShamayim had established itself semi-permanently in Mekor Baruch, on Rashbam Street. However, twenty years later, in 1987, the building was unable to accommodate the growing number of students, and a solution was urgently required.

At the time, one of the moving forces behind the institution was the director, Rav Chaim Malowicki. He found a building nearby on Rashi Street, but the Iraqi owner was suspicious of the Ashkenazi rabbis. Anxious to sell, she nevertheless suspected some kind of plot. As a result, negotiations were at a standstill.

Struck by inspiration, Rav Malowicki turned to Rav Yitzchak Hoffman, one of the scholars of the yeshivah, and asked him to speak to his son Pinchas, a successful businessman in New York. Pinchas Hoffman responded positively to his father's request, and asked his good friend and business partner, Reuven "Ruby" Schron, who was on his was to Israel, to negotiate a deal.

Once in Israel, Ruby met with Rav Shlomo Zalman Auerbach, Rav Chaim Leib's oldest son, and appealed to him to become Shaar HaShamayim's Rosh Yeshivah in the event that he succeeded in securing a permanent site. With his characteristic smile, Rav Shlomo Zalman told Ruby that his present commitments did not allow him to accept such a position – but that in any event, his brother, Rav Dovid, was perfectly suited for the job.

The following day, in a meeting that was short and to the point, Schron discussed the sale with the Iraqi woman. Dressed in his neat American attire, Ruby gave her an ultimatum: "Here is my lawyer's phone number. I am returning to the States tomorrow night. If you don't agree to consummate the deal by then, then everything is off and the yeshivah will look for another site!"

A few hours before Schron's departure, the woman agreed to the sale, and the papers were signed and sealed. Ruby returned home as one on the major contributors to the new building – together with Pinchas Hoffman and the Reichman brothers – and as the force that gave the eighty-year-old yeshivah a new breath of life.

A few months later, Schron returned to Eretz Yisrael, only to hear the sad news that Rav Dovid Auerbach had passed away. Meeting with Rav Shlomo Zalman, he was stunned by what he was told.

"I must share with you something," Rav Shlomo Zalman said warmly. "My brother died exactly thirty days after you bought the building – and they were the happiest days of his life! You see," he told the surprised businessman, "During all the years since our beloved father passed away, Dovid worried that he himself might die without fulfilling his promise. But after you came and helped push the deal through, he could rest easy, secure in the knowledge that he had kept his word. He rejoiced over this with his whole being."

What began as a dream of two scholars in the middle of the night in 1905, gained new dimension in 1987, when Rav Dovid Auerbach was able to join his father in *Gan Eden* with the full faith of a loving son keeping his promise.

(Retold by Ruby Schron and the Auerbach family)

Mountain View, Jerusalem

The Jerusalem suburb called Har Nof, on the western slopes of the Holy City, was designed in the mid-1970s to be a model neighborhood, equal to the best which Israel had to offer. Naturally, it was slated for the secular community. One man, however, by the name of Rav Yehudah Palai, ingeniously flipped the coin and succeeded in making it a model Orthodox community instead. The story, which reads like a comedy at times, is a saga of its own.

RAV YEHUDAH Palai, a disciple of Rav Eliyahu Lopian, knew all the right people in every segment of society, from the gedolim and political giants all the way down to the ordinary man in the street. His simple outward appearance and nonchalant, low-keyed manner veiled an astute mind and farsighted vision. He had proved himself a master in business and was particularly adept at forging lasting relationships with influential men throughout the country.

One day in 1978, he sat with Yona Mordechai, the head of the National Contractors' Union and owner of the Chevzibah Building Company. Yona was bemoaning his predicament. City planners, he explained, had finished designing one of the most prestigious neighborhoods in the country right on the outskirts of Jerusalem, temporarily called Givat Shaul Beis (later to be named Har Nof). Furthermore, the numerous plots in the suburb had been allocated to all the builders of the city through a lottery. To men like Mayor Teddy Kollek and Housing Minister David Levy, this development site heralded the most superbly designed urban area in Jerusalem. Yet, now that construction was under way, Yona was caught in a bind.

Yehudah listened and thought. Yona had braved the harsh winter elements and earned the honor of being the first builder to break ground in the new neighborhood, building a giant, forty-apartment building. He was writing checks to suppliers and employees and eagerly waiting for purchasers. Thus far, however, no one had signed on the dotted line. The general consensus of prospective buyers was that the area was too far removed from the center of town and did not warrant the exorbitant price tag. The situation had reached a critical impasse. Some builders called this new area the "Builders' Graveyard." Yona did not want his career to end on the mountainous slopes outside Jerusalem.

"I have the answer for you, Yona," Rav Palai smiled. "Let's offer the apartments to the Orthodox public at a bargain price. Don't you know that there is a tremendous lack of housing in Jerusalem for the religious community? It will save you and help them at the same time."

"But how can you be sure the religious will buy there?" Yona asked.

"That will be my job," answered Yehudah. "I personally guarantee that all forty flats will be sold."

With these words Yona Mordechai agreed. Eventually, he brought other builders to Rav Palai, who made the same arrangement with them. In all, seventeen buildings came under his jurisdiction, which guaranteed that some 400 families would serve as a religious vanguard in the new neighborhood. Although some buildings were sold to secularists, most of the apartments went to Orthodox buyers who were eager to take the leap into the forests around Jerusalem.

Initially, things were touch and go. Rav Yehudah began a propaganda program which encompassed various strategies. Newspaper advertisements announced that a new neighborhood for the observant community had opened in Givat Shaul Beis. The religious were enticed with assurances that every contract contained a provision stating that the buyer had to send his children to an Orthodox school. Some contracts even included a clause not to own a television set. In order to make the secularists believe that the area was truly set aside as a reli-

Har Nof

gious neighborhood, Palai advertised in the secular newspapers with ads such as: "Do not let the religious take over Har Nof!" Inside of Har Nof, he erected several large signs reading: "Keep the Shabbos Holy!" and "On this site will be built apartments for Toldos Aharon Institutions." Most secularists associated that name with the most radical Orthodox camp in Meah Shearim.

In June, 1980 (5740), a gathering was staged by the Contractors' Union in Har Nof to introduce the public to the new neighborhood. Such dignitaries as Mayor Kollek and Minister Levy were on hand, along with many of the builders. Before it was scheduled to start, Rav Yehudah went into Meah Shearim and asked a number of Orthodox men each to attend the gathering. He wanted their presence as a tool for his designs.

During the ceremony and tour of the site, a member of the union asked Rav Palai who these religious people were. "These are some of the buyers," he answered with a smile. And indeed some of them were.

At one point, Rav Palai's plan was threatened by another failure in the building industry. An oddly designed set of prefab apartments had been built in the secular community of Ramot, to the north of the city. When no buyers appeared, a religious group got control of the area (known as Ramot Polin) and offered the apartments at a discount. Yehudah Palai worked hard to induce potential buyers to opt for Har Nof. He even took a loss on some dwellings in order to make the neighborhood religious.

As the first families began to move in in the summer of 1984, all the public domains — once so carefully demarcated for secular kindergartens, schools, and cultural centers — became religious schools and synagogues. The small secular element, outsiders from the beginning, had no outlet within the neighborhood whatsoever.

After Rav Palai succeeded in placing most of the lower half of Har Nof under religious ownership, he influenced the Housing Department to divide the upper half of the neighborhood among religious institutions, thereby circumventing private contracting. This, plus the knowledge that half of Har Nof was already under religious hands even before an architect sharpened his first pencil, acted as a further deterrent to secular speculators and buyers. It is for this reason that today, one sees million-dollar synagogues and yeshivos in the upper half of Har Nof which are not found in other religious neighborhoods built in that period. Among them are Vishnitz, Imrei Shefer (Sanz), Yechavei Daas (Rav Ovadiah Yosef), Dvar Yerushalayim, Young Israel, and Ger.

Rav Palai's victory was not without a price. He was arrested under false charges and even brought to court by angry losers — but was never found guilty of any wrongdoing. Perhaps the biggest price in terms of personal danger to himself occurred during Chanukah, 1987 (5748), while he was inspecting one of his buildings in Har Nof on HaKablan Street. It was after work hours, and only he and his son were in the building. Minutes after they stepped outside, the towering structure suddenly caved in. Rav Yehudah and his son, standing in front of the building, managed to dash to safety. If they had they lingered inside a few minutes longer, they would have been trapped under tons of falling cement.

Today, over 2,500 religious families live in Har Nof. Few, if any, know the true story of how their neighborhood was once dedicated as a secular housing project. However, the man behind the scenes, Rav Yehudah Palai, who resides in the building which Yona Mordechai built, is completely satisfied with this extraordinary flip of the coin.

(Based on an interview with Rav Yehudah Palai)

From a Knock at the Door

THERE WAS a knock at the door. Uri looked at his watch. It was 11:30 P.M. Who could be knocking at this time? Uri asked himself as he walked over to the front door. Opening the door, he saw one of the neighbors standing there.

"I'm so sorry to disturb you," she said. "I know it's late, but my daughter is having a hard time breathing. Do you have a humidifier that I can use?"

It so happened that he had one and he quickly fetched it from the closet. "Here, take this," Uri said sympathetically as he handed it to her. "May your daughter feel better."

That incident on a winter's night in 1976 (5736) made a deep impression on Uri Lopiansky and his wife. As a young married couple who had recently moved to Jerusalem from Tel Aviv, they had settled in the Tel Arza neighborhood, near Bar Ilan Street. One of their first priorities was to meet their new neighbors and intergrate into the Jerusalem society. Uri grew up in Haifa and his wife in Tel Aviv. For them, Jerusalem was a completely new city with a heartbeat of it own. Within no time, the Lopianskys made their abode an address that all their neighbors could depend on for any on-the-spot needs. Sometimes a neighbor needed milk, bread, aspirin, or other commodities. The Lopianskys' door was always open for these acts of human brotherhood.

Now, when Uri closed the door, he pointed out to his wife that the need of a humidifier could be more life-threatening if not controlled early enough. Baruch Hashem, they had one which they were happy to lend. But maybe in other parts of the city no neighbor had one to give. What might start out as a very minor health problem could become very serious overnight.

In those days a humidifier was legally considered a cosmetic and heavily taxed by the government. Therefore, it didn't fit into everyone's pocketbook.

Uri and his wife started to put two and two together. They realized that there was a serious demand for medical equipment to be readily available to those who needed it. They started by buying a few basic items. Before long they borrowed money to purchase a wheelchair and other more expensive equipment. Next they received permission from the neighbors to use a basement as a storeroom.

The more they added to their service, the greater the demand became. Within a few months the free loaning of medical equipment coalesced, and the Yad Sarah Organization came into existence. Named after Rav Lopiansky's mother, this help-others organization was responsible for saving many people's lives by having equipment on the spot in the sick person's home.

It was very strange that until that night when a neighbor knocked on their door for a humidifier no one in the country had thought of such an idea. So simple and helpful, the Lopianskys' act of helping others has far exceeded their wildest dreams. Not only is it the biggest medical-help organization in the country, but other countries have come to copy it and intergrate it into their societies.

(Based on an interview with Rav Uri Lopiansky)

Embedded in the Kosel

ONE SUMMER DAY in 1980, Dr. Bob Friedman and his son Andrew buckled their seatbelts on an El Al flight to Israel. The excitement of a transcontinental flight showed on Andy's face. His father, a frequent international flyer, sat calmly reading the New York Times.

"Why aren't we moving?" asked thirteen-year-old Andy.

"The control tower hasn't given the okay yet," answered his dad.

Andy looked out the window. "This is the greatest gift I could ever have dreamt of for my bar mitzvah," he said.

"You deserve it, Andy." Bob Friedman turned to his son. "More than that, it's a present for me, too."

Bob Friedman had never been to Israel and had never put much thought into the little country with its long ancestry. Not even the Six-Day War or the Yom Kippur War stirred him into some kind of affiliation. Instead, he had excelled at climbing the ladder of American success. First was a medical degree from Jefferson Medical College in Philadelphia. Then, after working in various hospitals he settled down in Albany, New York, where he became director of a radiology department for twenty years. As a radiologist, Dr. Friedman attended conferences around the world, which gave him a cosmopolitan and universalistic view of mankind.

In Israel, the Friedmans' two-week guided tour was filled with a series of "hit-and-run" type views of all the sites from Dan to Beer Sheva. The July weather was excellent and the hotel service not bad. The two of them stayed with the bus load of fellow tourists, listening to their guide and absorbing everything he told them.

Andy was enthralled by all that he saw and heard. Bob, however, had been to a lot of the great historic sites on the globe, from the Great Wall of China to the pyramids in Egypt. Though he was pleased to see the ancient ruins at Caesarea and the fortifications at Masada and experienced pride in the country's accomplishments, Bob had not encountered anything which really moved him.

On the last day of the tour, after seeing the major sites of Jerusalem the previous day, they were led through the Old City. Like sheep of the flock, the Friedmans followed their shepherd from place to place. When they came to the Kosel plaza, their guide gave an historical digest of the Temple and the Wall. Afterwards, he told them that they were free to go up to the Kosel if they desired, but they should be careful to meet by the flagpoles in fifteen minutes.

Dr. Friedman and Andy strolled up to the Kosel. Aware of the significance of the place, they donned the kipos which they had brought for such occasions. One of Bob's sisters had asked him to stick a note into the Kosel, a request which he dutifully fulfilled. As he stood there facing the Kosel stones, Bob felt it appropriate to say a prayer, but nothing came to mind. Then he decided to rest his head against the Wall.

Suddenly Bob burst into tears. Spontaneously, without rhyme or reason, Dr. Friedman was sobbing like a baby. Andy, stunned by his father's behavior, looked around anxiously. It was completely unlike his father, the epitome of Western society, to breakdown into uncontrollable weeping. Bob pressed his head to the Wall and continued to cry, stopping to breathe, and then crying again.

During those intense minutes, thoughts raced through Bob's mind. He was both actor on a stage and spectator in the theater. The scene of the play was at the climax, and both performer and viewer were completely absorbed. He also saw his grandfather, the only Orthodox Jew he recalled from his childhood. Grandpa had died when he was four years old and left a nostalgic memory of the "old country" in the recesses of his mind.

Slowly, as he regained control of himself, Dr. Friedman wiped the tears from his bloodshot eyes and kissed the Wall. With his son by his side, he walked to the meeting place by the flagpoles. He tried to analyze what he had just experienced. At best he could only compare it to a comment his gentile friend had made when they were at the Great Wall of China. His companion called the experience an "intellectual communion." Bob called his experience at the Wall a "spiritual communion." Yet, so deep was the emotional wellspring within him, that for months he was unable to verbalize it distinctly.

He looked at the Kosel from afar and wondered what the God of his forefathers was asking of him. Slowly, after returning to Albany, he began reading about Judaism and attending Jewish study classes. In the course of time, a metamorphosis began to take place. Four years later he was shomer Shabbos, and in 1987 he was active in helping Soviet Jewry return to their roots.

Dr. Bob Friedman had reoriented his life goals and chose to make aliyah. His son Andy, beginning his path towards a medical career, joined him, eventually earning a medical degree from Hadasah, the Hebrew University's medical college. A fully observant Jew, Bob only wanted to live in the Old City close to the Kosel. For him, living within earshot of the Wall was fundamental for his Yiddishkeit. It was there, at the Kosel, that the ear of God listened to his wordless prayer and whispered the eternal sound which awakened his inner soul. Bob, in turn, wished to reciprocate by serving Him in the palace of the King of Kings.

(Based on an interview with Dr. Bob Friedman)

Model of the Temple with Jews ascending to the Temple Mount

Epilogue

The history of Jerusalem can be divided into two periods. The first was its period of grandeur — the First and Second Temples — and the destruction by wicked Babylonian and Roman despots. That period has not been touched upon in this work. The second period was the revival of a Jewish presence, called the yishuv, which began in Medieval times and continued until the present era. During this nine-hundred-year journey through the annals of Jerusalem, we saw the full spectrum of Jewish experience: striving and struggling, building and destruction, tasting freedom and being harshly oppressed.

However, there is one element which covers both periods. It is the unalterable, permanent core of the Holy City. In truth, an entire volume is needed in order to properly comprehend and appreciate the depths of this core. Yet, for the moment, a glimpse at the essence of the Eternal City upon which the Shechinah dwells will suffice. Even here, our approach is from a historical perspective.

Triumph of Time

Jerusalem, in its optimum status, is the city of three crowns: the crown of priesthood — for it is the location of the Temple, where the Divine service is performed; the crown of kingship — for it is the seat of the royal House of David, which holds the scepter of Jewish rulership; and the crown of Torah — for it is home to the Sanhedrin, the body of leading sages who give the nation direction in Torah Law.

Concerning the first two crowns, Jerusalem is the only city in the world to have the Temple built in its midst, and it alone is the residence of the royal House of David.[1] History testifies how the building of the First Temple during the reign of King David and his son Solomon ushered in a new era in the saga of the Jewish people. Likewise, at the end of time, the Mashiach, a scion of the House of David, will reestablish the Third Temple on its original site in the Holy City and bring about a glorious new chapter in the annals of the world. So it is, that for the duration of the long and heartbreaking exile, the Jews' aspiration for the messianic times has been intimately bound with the desire for Jerusalem to be rebuilt in all her former magnificence.

The Temple, the very heart of Jerusalem, may be likened to a pool into which cascaded a mighty waterfall. These waters — Divine influence — would then flow outward and nurture the entire world. When the Temple was destroyed, the waters dried up, and only a small trickle reaches us through the "cracks in the Wall." Thus, for thousands of years Jews have stood outside the Kosel HaMaaravi — the Western Wall — and pondered the Sanctuary's past splendor.

In a very real sense, Jerusalem plays a central role in the life of the Jew. First and foremost, we find that all prayer must be directed towards the Holy City.[2] Jews in Europe and America face east, in India they face west, in Beer Sheva north, and in Safed south. In Jerusalem, too, everyone turns to the Temple to pray. Thus, King Solomon entreated: "May you hearken to the prayer of Your servant, and of Your people Israel, when they pray towards this place" (I *Kings* 8:30).

The prayer book is replete with images of the Holy City. Every day, both on festivals and ordinary weekdays, we mention her in our prayers. Even the grace after meals, one of the first prayers learned by children, dedicates an entire blessing to its rebuilding. Thus, on whatever plane we find ourselves — physical (eating) or spiritual (praying) — we are exhorted to recall Jerusalem and the central role it played and will play again in the future.

Indeed, Jewish consciousness is permeated with the concept and reality of the ultimate Jerusalem. Thus, King David wrote: "If I forget you, O Jerusalem, let my right hand forget its skills" (*Psalms* 137:5). We can understand this in the following manner: to lose control of our body inhibits our potential from reaching fruition. Likewise, if we were to lose sight of Jerusalem, an essential aspect of our souls would wither up and deprive us of our full spiritual potential.

Our Sages aptly say that only those who truly feel the loss of the Temple and mourn over it will be worthy to witness its redemption.[3]

Mount Moriah

In addition to being home to the Temple and the Davidic dynasty, the City of God is also the source of all the world's Torah. This is expressed by the very name of the mountain upon which the Temple stands, as the verse states: "Solomon began to build the House of God in Jerusalem on Mount Moriah..." (II *Chronicles* 3:1). The name מוֹרִיָּה is derived from the root הוֹרָאָה, meaning to spread forth Torah Law to the world.[4] The prophet Isaiah captured this aspect of Jerusalem when he said: "From Zion shall go forth Torah, and the word of God from Jerusalem" (*Isaiah* 2:3).

It was on the Temple Mount where the Great Sanhedrin convened, in the Chamber of Hewn Stone. There, the sages would delve into every aspect of the Law. To qualify as a member of this body, one had to possess the most refined personality and character traits, as well as a phenomenal level of Torah knowledge.[5]

The Chamber of Hewn Stone was located on the northern side of the Temple Mount. Divided in half, the southern end encompassed the full holiness of the Temple area where only priests were allowed to be, and had a door leading out to the priestly area. The other half had a lower level of holiness — thus permitting seating, which was otherwise forbidden anywhere in the Temple courtyards — and a door which led to the outside of the Temple area. It was in this second half, in the form of a semi-circle, that the Sanhedrin of seventy-one judges convened.

The Smallest Letter

Phonetically, the word Yerushalayim is spelled with two *yudim*, one at the beginning and one near the end (ירושלים). Interestingly, however, of the 667 times the word Yerushalayim is found in Tanach,* it is only spelled with both *yudim* five times.** The question arises: why does the name of the Holy City begin with a *yud*, and why is the second *yud* so rarely found in Scripture?

Midrash Talpios (*anaf: Yerushalayim*) offers an answer to these questions: Jerusalem, the Jewish people, and the Lord are bonded together. Each one of these three begins their name with the letter *yud* (ירושלים ישראל, י-ה-ו-ה). This union is expressed in the verse: "You shall be My *segulah*" (*Exodus* 19:5), referring to the Jewish people and the Holy City as the most precious (*segulah*) parts of His creation. When the Temple was destroyed and the Jews were exiled from their city and their land, the names of all three were altered: Jerusalem lost its second *yud* and is now spelled ירושלם (why the second *yud* and not the first will be explained shortly). The Jewish people also deserved to lose a letter from their name Yisrael, but God in His mercy and abundant love of them chose instead to remove a letter from the holy Throne, as the verse in *Exodus* (17:16) says: "...for [the] hand is on the Throne of the Lord." The Hebrew word "Throne" is spelled כס instead of כסא, to show that as long as the Almighty's children are in exile, His Throne is incomplete. Also, in this same verse, the word "Lord," the Tetragrammaton, is spelled without the last two letters (ו-ה), alluding to the fact that with the destruction of the Temple, the Divine Presence could no longer descend into the world.

The reason why the second *yud* was removed instead of the first is tied up with the history of how the name Jerusalem came into being. Both Avraham and Malki Zeddek gave the Holy City a name. Avraham called it *Yerei* (*Genesis* 22:14), and Malki Zeddek called it *Shalem* (*ibid.* 14:18), and together they spell יר(ו)שלם, with only one *yud*. God chose to add a second

* Jerusalem is not mentioned in the *Chumash*. Instead, it is called "the place which God will choose" (mentioned 16 times in *parshas Re'eh*). The Rambam (*Moreh Nevuchim* 3:45) lists three reasons for this secrecy: (1) the nations would try to gain control of it through war and destruction, (2) the Canaanites, hearing how they would be ousted from Jerusalem, would do their utmost to destroy it, (3) the Tribes would contend with each other to have Jerusalem located in their territory. In fact, Jerusalem was not divided among the Tribes (*Yoma* 12a), so that every Jew would feel equally at home there.

** *Song of Songs* (1:5), *Ezra* (1:11), *Esther* (2:6), *Jeremiah* (26:18), II *Chronicles* (25:1).

yud in the name *shalem* (from שלם to שלים) to show that the priesthood was being transferred from Malki Zeddek to the descendants of Avraham. Malki Zeddek lost the priesthood due to an error he made by praising Avraham before praising the Lord. The honor of the king should have come before the honor of the servant. Thus God altered the name *shalem* by adding a *yud* from His Name, thereby blessing Jerusalem to make it the (future) city of the "priestly nation."

At the time of the destruction of the Temple, however, the Jewish people — the nation of priests — substituted the holy for the profane, from serving God to worshipping idols. Just like Malki Zeddek, they placed the servant (idols) before the king. Therefore, God removed the second *yud* which He had placed as a reward for their service to Him alone.

Thus, in coming generations when Jews would see the Holy City of Jerusalem spelled without the second *yud*, they would meditate on the reason why and try to distance themselves from transgression. In this way they would help rebuild the Holy City and bring about the redemption.

The Eye of the World

Jerusalem is the only city which has a Heavenly counterpart — the celestial Jerusalem that hovers high over the terrestrial one. The *Zohar* says that God swore not to enter His Heavenly City until the Jewish people would enter the earthly Jerusalem, as the verse in *Hoshea* (11:9) says: "...with holiness in your midst, and I shall not enter the city!"[6]

The Midrash offers us a parable to understand this idea: Once a king cast his wife out of the palace. The next day he went and asked her to return. "What?" exclaimed his wife. "Yesterday you kicked me out, and today you come to take me back?!" The king answered her with these words. "From the minute that you left the palace yesterday I also left and did not return. As proof of it, look at the dew that is still on my hair."[7]

Thus, God remains outside the Heavenly Jerusalem so long as we are scattered across the globe. When we return to the Holy City, our physical presence there will cause a parallel ingathering in its Heavenly counterpart.

This dual aspect of Jerusalem — existing on both a physical and spiritual plane — is reflected in the depiction of the Holy City as the eye of the world. More precisely, the planet is considered an eye and Jerusalem its pupil — the tunnel which connects the outer to the inner. The oceans which encompass the continents are the white of the eye which surrounds its working parts. The iris represents the land masses other than Eretz Yisrael. The thin band of color which joins the pupil to the iris is Eretz Yisrael. The pupil which acts as the lens of the eye is Jerusalem. Finally, the optic nerve, the essence of the eye, is the Holy of Holies and the pathway to higher worlds.[8]

This Divine channel runs two ways. What we do in the terrestrial Jerusalem is perceived in the Heavenly Jerusalem. Thus, we must be exceptionally careful what we do or say while in the Holy City. Likewise, the Divine influence which emanates from the Heavenly City first channels through the earthly Jerusalem, as its says: "God will bless you from Zion" (*Psalms* 128:5).

Like everything beyond our mundane perceptions of the world we live in, the ability to sense these Divine influences depends on preparing ourselves to become pure vessels to receive them. In the time of the Mashiach, when the veil of darkness shall be removed from us, this perception will be commonplace and complete.

Zion and Jerusalem

The name Zion has three distinct connotations. Sometimes Zion refers to Jerusalem, as in the verse: "God loves the gates of Zion more than all the dwellings of Jacob" (*Psalms* 87:2). For emphasis, both references to the Holy City are occasionally written in the same verse, as in: "Praise the Lord, O Jerusalem, praise your God, O Zion" (*ibid.* 147:12). Other times Zion refers to the Temple, as in the verse: "He will shake his hands against the mountain of the daughter [written: House] of Zion" (*Isaiah* 10:32). Most often, however, Zion is called *Har Tzyon*, Mount Zion, referring to the City of David.

Historically speaking, the city of Jerusalem and Mount Zion were originally twin cities.[9] Mount Zion included the Armenian Quarter and most of the Jewish Quarter, as well as what is today called Mount Zion. It also extended down the slopes to the south. Sometime at the beginning of the Second Temple era, the wall of Jerusalem was enlarged to included Mount Zion. Ezra and his *beis din* walked along the ramparts of the new wall in a ceremonial act to sanctify the new area. However, since the procession lacked the presence of a king and the *urim* and *tumim* as decreed by law, their act could not elevate Mount Zion to the high stature of holiness which the ancient city of Jerusalem possessed.[10]

Unfortunately, with the passage of time, the exact location of the boundary between the two areas was forgotten. As a result, certain stringencies were enacted concerning the entire walled city out of fear that one might make a mistaken calculation and transgress laws pertaining to the actual area sanctified by King Solomon.[11] Thus, for example, the manner of redeeming *maasar sheni* (the "second tithe" of produce which must be eaten within the walls of Jerusalem when we are ritually purified — a status no one can achieve until the time of the Mashiach — but which cannot be redeemed within the sanctified area), or shaking a *lulav* (according to the Rambam) have ramifications when done anywhere inside the Jewish Quarter.

Symbolically, Jerusalem and Zion are two inseparable parts of one whole. The *Zohar* describes them as two opposite traits, one of mercy (*rachamim*),

Zion, and the other of judgment (*din*), Jerusalem, making up a totality.[12] Today, there are individuals of lofty character who are capable of experiencing the unification of these two states. These people have succeeded in channeling and uniting Zion and Jerusalem on a personal level. Ultimately, the dream which we all harbor is that one day, in the not-too-distant future, these opposites will merge into a greater whole for all of humanity, and become manifest in the physical world as the messianic times.

The Untouchable Temple and the Indomitable People

With the destruction of the Temple, and the inability to become ritually purified, it is forbidden for Jews to ascend the Temple Mount. We may not set foot into the sphere of sanctity when our bodies are not properly prepared to do so.[13]

If so, is there anywhere that we, the remnant of Israel, can physically connect to the holiness which is our birthright? There is one place that remains to us — the Western Wall (also known as the Wailing Wall, or simply, the Kosel.) Though its full length is 490 meters, only 100 meters are easily approachable on a daily basis. The rest is covered by Moslem houses and shops. There is, however, a ten-meter stretch visible in the Arab Quarter called the Small Wall, where Jews used to pray. Recent excavations have made the entire northern section accessible, albeit, in an underground fashion. It is called the Tunnel, and was officially opened in 1996.

Exactly who built the Kosel is still a topic of debate. Most authorities believe that Herod built it as a retaining wall for the entire Temple Mount when he enlarged and beautified the Second Temple. As proof, they note the way in which the stones (called ashlar stones) of that period were chiseled with a smooth border around the edges. Others, however, claim that the Kosel was built by King Solomon on the foundation stones which his father, King David, laid for the Temple.[14] Timewise, the Herodian extensions to the Second Temple were build around 16 B.C.E. (3744), while the First Temple was completed in 823 B.C.E. (2937), a difference of more than 800 years.

Today, of course, the Kosel is the most revered shrine of our people. People approach it in many different ways. Some come and write personal requests on pieces of paper and squeeze them between the cracks in the stones. Others will not come right up to the Wall, refraining from even touching its stones with their hands. They claim that the holiness of the Temple Mount reaches between the cracks of the stones, and therefore touching the Kosel is like entering onto the Temple Mount itself. Most authorities, however,

The Small Wall, located in the Moslem Quarter next to the Iron Gate. Jews prayed here due to the fact that it is on ground level with the Temple Mount, and very close to the Holies and Holy of Holies.

permit us to touch the Kosel and to lay our heads against it. However, using it as a place to rest one's siddur is not in keeping with the holiness of the place.

The Kosel is a testimony of the Jewish people's indomitable faith. Though small and unprotected from the elements, the Kosel has nevertheless weathered the vicissitudes of time, as well as the wrath of man. Among the many large ashlar stones of the Wall, there is one which is the biggest cut stone in the world (14 x 4 x 3 meters), weighing nearly 400 tons!

The Temple (and Wall) has been belittled and ridiculed by most of mankind for thousands of years. Yet, God's beloved people have cherished it beyond human rationality. Throughout the millennia they cried over its destruction and yearned for its rebuilding. The Temple and the Kosel represent the ultimate resurrection of our people. May we, the living seed of all the past generations of yearning Jews, see it rebuilt in our time.

The Master Plan

Aside from the Almighty, nobody knows the master plan of the universe. How will the messianic age unfold? When, and under what circumstances? These are a part of the mystery of creation which God has not revealed. One thing, however, is certain. When the great events of the messianic times take place, they will center around Jerusalem.

Mankind has already witnessed several global upheavals and seems poised on the brink of even more. The unfolding of historic events on a biblical scale may be on the horizon. There are many ways in which we can prepare ourselves: study of Torah, fulfillment of mitzvos, prayer, and giving charity. In addition, we can study about the City of Cities, especially the Temple and the laws concerning it. This is our legacy.

Notes

1. *Berachos* 49a. Though not forced by law, all the kings of Judah resided in Jerusalem. See *Tanchuma, Kedoshim* 1, based on the verse in *Psalms* 122:5.
2. Berachos 30a.
3. *Taanis* 30b.
4. The Sages (*Tannis* 16a and Tosefos) also found in the word Moriah the root מורא (fear), implying that Jerusalem causes the nations to stand in trepidation of its grandeur.
5. *Mishneh Torah, Hilchos Sanhedrin*, 2:7–8; *Maamarim* 1:1.
6. *Zohar Chadash, parshas Noach*. See *Tannis* 5a.
7. *Eretz Yisrael*, p. 74.
8. *Tuv Yerushalayim*, p. 15b.
9. This paragraph is based on *Har HaKodesh*, pp. 32–34.
10. *Shevuos* 16a.
11. *Kaftor v'Ferach*, chap. 41; *Radvaz*, vol. 2, no. 633.
12. *Zohar* I:186a.
13. The Rambam, *Mishneh Torah, Hilchos Beis HaBechirah* 6:14. However, see the Ravad there, who disputes this point.
14. *Har HaKodesh*, pp. 40–41.

Table I

Rishon l'Tzyon

(Sephardic Chief Rav of Yerushalayim)

Rishon l'Tzyon	***Years***	***Known as***
Rav Moshe Galante	1672 – 1689	HaRav HaMagen הרב המגן
Rav Moshe Chaviv	1690 – 1696	Get Pashut גט פשוט
Rav Avraham Yitzchaki	1715 – 1729	
Rav Binyamin Maali	1729 – 1731	
Rav Eliezer Nachum	1731 – 1745	Chazon Nachum חזון נחום
Rav Nisim Mizrachi	1745 – 1749	
Rav Yisrael Yaakov Elgazi	1749 – 1756	Kehillos Yaakov קהילות יעקב
Rav Raphael Meyuchas	1756 – 1771	Pri HaAdamah פרי האדמה
Rav Yom Tov Elgazi	1771 – 1802	Hilchos Yom Tov הלכות יום טוב
Rav Yosef Meyuchas	1802 – 1806	Shaar HaMayim שער המים
Rav Mordechai HaLevi	1806	HaRav HaMelitz הרב המליץ
Rav Yaakov Iyash	1806 – 1817	
Rav Yaakov Korel	1817 – 1818	
Rav Yosef Chazon	1818 – 1820	Chekrei Lev חקרי לב
Rav Yom Tov Danon	1820 – 1823	
Rav Moshe Sozin	1824 – 1836	
Rav Moshe Yona Navon	1836 – 1841	
Rav Yehudah Navon	1841 – 1842	
Rav Avraham Chaim Gagin	1842 – 1848	HaRav Agan הרב אג״ן
*Rav Yitzchak Kobo	1848 – 1854	
*Rav Chaim Nisim Abulafia	1854 – 1861	HaRav Chana הרב חנ״א
*Rav David Chazon	1861 – 1869	Chad Bedara חד בדרא
*Rav Avraham Ashkenazi	1869 – 1880	
*Rav Meir Panijel	1880 – 1892	HaMarpah המרפ״א
*Rav Yaakov Shaul Elyashar	1892 – 1906	Yisa Bracha ישׂ״א ברכה
* Rav Yaakov Meir	1906 – 1907	
* Rav Eliyahu Moshe Panijel	1907 – 1908	
Rav Nachman Betito	1908 – 1909	
Rav Moshe Pranko	1909 – 1911	
Rav Nisim Danon	1911 – 1914	
Rav Chaim Moshe Elyashar	1915 – 1918	

*Also called *Chacham Bashi*

Table 2

Development of Jerusalem Suburbs

(Based on *Yerushalayim Shechunos Saviv La*)
A Partial Listing
Census of 1938: Jewish Population: 75,000 (*Vaad HaKehillah*)
Old City: Jewish Population: (about) 16,000

	Suburb	***Year Founded***	***Named after or Founded by***	***Type of Residents***	***Pop. in 1938***
1.	**Mishkenos Sha'ananim**	1855	"My people shall dwell in a peaceful habitation, a secure dwelling" (*Isa.* 32:18)	poor Ashkenazim, Sephardim	2,000
2.	**Machane Yisrael**	1866		Moroccan	
3.	**Nachalas Shiva**	1869	The seven founders		3,500
4.	**Meah Shearim**	1874	"A hundredfold" (*Gen.* 26:12)	Ashkenazim	3,700
5.	**Even Yisrael**	1875	"The Stone of Israel" (*Gen.* 49:24)	Ashkenazim, Sephardim	450
6.	**Mishkenos Yisrael**	1877	"How goodly are your tents, Yaakov, and your tabernacles, Yisrael" (*Num.* 24:5)	Ashkenazim, Sephardim, Yemenites	
7.	**Beis David**	1877	R. David Reiss	poor	
8.	**Beis Yaakov**	1879	"All the souls of the House of Yaakov...were seventy" (*Genesis* 46:27)	Ashkenazim, Sephardim	200
9.	**Kiyrat Ne'emana (Battei Nisan Beck)**	1879	"The faithful City" (*Isa.* 1:21)	Chassidim, Sephardim	
10.	**Mizkeret Moshe**	1882	Sir Moses Montefiore	Ashkenazim	700
11.	**Ohel Moshe**	1885	Sir Moses Montefiore	Sephardim	500
12.	**Shaarei Moshe (Battei Wittenberg)**	1885	R. Moshe Wittenberg	Ashkenazim	
13.	**Beis Yisrael**	1885		Ashkenazim, Sephardim	7,000
14.	**Kefar Shiloach**	1887		Yemenites	
15.	**Kerem**	1886		Ashkenazim, Sephardim	1,300

	Suburb	*Year Founded*	*Named after or Founded by*	*Type of Residents*	*Pop. in 1938*
16.	**Machane Yehudah**	1887	Yehudah Navon	Ashkenazim, Sephardim	600
17.	**Sukkas Shalom**	1888	Shalom Konestarim	Ashkenazim, Sephardim, Yemenites	400
18.	**Shaar Hapina**	1889		Yemenites, Ashkenazim, Sephardim	1,000
19.	**Shaarei Tzedek**	1889	"Gates of righteousness" (*Psalms* 119:19)	Sephardim, Yemenites, Persian	300
20.	**Nachalat Shimon**	1891	Shimon HaTzaddik	Sephardim, Yemenites	200
21.	**Shaarei Yerushalayim**	1891	First suburb when entering Jerusalem; Yitzchak Lipkin	Sephardim	400
22.	**Battei Ungarin (Nachalas Tzvi)**	1892	R. Tzvi Razsadorfer	Ashkenazim	1,700
23.	**Battei Vilna (Beis Avraham)**	1892	R. Avraham Zabrodasky	Ashkenazim	1,300
24.	**Battei Horodna (Damascus Eliezer)**	1892	R. Eliezer Kahana	Ashkenazim	
25.	**Battei Volhylin (Battei Hornstein)**	1892	R. Dov Hornstein	Ashkenazim	
26.	**Shevet Achim**	1892	"How pleasant for brothers to dwell together" (*Psalms* 133:1)	Persians, Sephardim, Yemenites	
27.	**Agudas Shlomo (Battei Milner)**	1892	Shlomo Milner	Ashkenazim	200
28.	**Bucharim (Rechovos)**	1893	"He called the name of it Rechovos" (*Gen.* 26:22)	Buchari, Persians	4,500
29.	**Nachalat Tzyon**	1893	Tzyon	Persians, Sephardim	
30.	**Knesses Yisrael** **— 1** **— 2** **— 3**	 1893 1908 1926	Talmudic expression	Ashkenazim	2,200
31.	**Battei Minsk**	1894		Ashkenazim	
32.	**Yemin Moshe**	1895	Sir Moses Montefiore	Sephardim, Ashkenazim	
33.	**Shaarei Simcha**	1895	Rav Simcha Sofer	Russians	
34.	**Even Yehoshua (Battei Holfman)**	1895	Yehoshua Holfman	Ashkenazim	500

	Suburb	*Year Founded*	*Named after or Founded by*	*Type of Residents*	*Pop. in 1938*
35.	**Battei Warsaw (Nachalat Yaakov)**	1896	Yaakov Tennvarsal	Ashkenazim	1,000
36.	**Chatzer Strauss**	1896	Rav Shmuel Strauss	Ashkenazim	
37.	**Chatzer HaRav m'Lublin**	1902	Rav Shneur Zalman	Chabad	350
38.	**Battei Broide**	1902	Rav Yaakov Yosef Broide	Perushim	200
39.	**Battei Varner (Ohel Moshe)**	1902	Legacy of M.A. Zilberman	Ashkenazim	
40.	**Battei Neitin**	1902	Menachem Neitin	Ashkenazim	300
41.	**Zichron Moshe**	1906	Sir Moses Montefiore	Ashkenazim, Sephardim	3,200
42.	**Battei Hornstein**	1908	R. David Hornstein	Ashkenazim	200
	Yagia Kipaim	1908	Agudas Baalei Malacha	Ashkenazim	1,200
43.	**Achva**	1908	Agudas Achva	Ashkenazim	1,000
44.	**Battei Ziberbergen**	1908	Kollel Ziberbergen	Ashkenazim	150
45.	**Givat Shaul**	1908	Rav Yaakov Shaul Elyshar	Yemenites, Sephardim, Ashkenazim	1,100
46.	**Shaarei Chesed**	1908		Ashkenazim	500
47.	**Battei Rand**	1910	Rav Mendel Rand	Ashkenazim	
	Rochama	1921		Ashkenazim, Sephardim	2,000
48.	**Rechavia**	1921		Ashkenazim	3,200
	Romema	1921	"The right hand of Hashem is exalted" (*Psalms* 118:16)		500
49.	**Beit HaKerem**	1921		Ashkenazim	800
50.	**Talpiot**	1922	"Your neck is like the tower of David built with turrets" (*Songs* 4:4)	Ashkenazim	400
51.	**Bayit Vegan**	1922		Ashkenazim, Sephardim	500
52.	**Nachalat Achim**	1922	C. S. Iraki	Yemenites, Sephardim	2,000
53.	**Geula**	1925	Amdorsky	Ashkenazim	2,000
54.	**Kiryat Moshe**	1928	Sir Moses Montefiore	Ashkenazim, Sephardim	400
55.	**Mekor Baruch**	1924	"Let your fountain be blessed" (*Prov.* 5:18)	Ashkenazim, Sephardim	2,500
56.	**Ramat Rachel**	1926		Ashkenazim	250
57.	**Kiryat Shmuel**	1926	Rav Shmuel Salant	Ashkenazim	400
58.	**Sanhedria**	1926	Agudat Nachalat Bayit	Ashkenazim, Yemenites	380
60.	**Etz Chaim**	1928	Wolfson	Ashkenazim	

	Suburb	*Year Founded*	*Named after or Founded by*	*Type of Residents*	*Pop. in 1938*
61.	**Yaffe Nof**	1929		Ashkenazim	
62.	**Shuk Machane Yehudah**	1930			4,500
63.	**Kerem Avraham**	1930	Chevrat Ezrat Nidachim (London)		3,500
64.	**Tel Arza**	1931		Ashkenazim, Sephardim	500
65.	**Shechunot Paggi**	1946	Poalei Agudas Yisrael	Ashkenazim	*
66.	**Katamon**	1948			*
67.	**Ein Kerem**	1949			*
68.	**Kiryat HaYovel**	1954			*
69.	**Givat Mordechai**	1955			*
70.	**Kiryat Sanz**	1963	Chassidei Sanz		*
71.	**Mattersdorf**	1963	Mattersdorfer Rebbe		*
72.	**Ramat Eshkol**	1969	Levi Eshkol		*
73.	**Maalot Dafna**	1970			*
74.	**French Hill**	1970			*
75.	**Ramot**	1971			*
76.	**Gilo**	1972			*
77.	**Neve Yaakov**	1972			*
78.	**Har Nof**	1984		mixed	*
79.	**Ramat Shlomo**	1995	Rav Shlomo Zalman Auerbach	Ashkenazim, Chassidim, Sephardim	*

* Since 1948 there has not been a census made of each neighborhood.

Table 3

Chassidic Dynasties in Jerusalem

(based on: *Toldos HaChassidus b'Eretz Yisrael*)

Dynasty	Year Began	Moved to Eretz Yisrael	Location in Jerusalem	Rebbes in Eretz Yisrael (until given year)
Alexander	1848	1925	Beis Yisrael, Knesses 1956: Bnei Brak	Rebbe Yisrael Nisan Copperstock Rebbe Yehudah Moshe Danziger (1973) Rebbe Avraham Menachem Danziger (*shlita*)
Amshinov	1840s	1954	Bayit Vegan	Rebbe Yerachmiel Yehudah Meir Kalish (1976) Rebbe Yaakov Arie Yeshaya Milikovsky (*shlita*)
Belz	1843	1944	Agrippas, Kiryat Belz	Rebbe Aharon Rokeach (1955) Rebbe Yisachar Dov Rokeach (*shlita*)
Biala	1900	1947	Geula, Unsdorf	Rebbe Yechiel Yehoshua Rabinowitz (1982) Rebbe Benzion Rabinowitz (*shlita*)
Boston	1915	1980	Har Nof	Rebbe Pinchas David Horowitz (1940) Rebbe Levi Yitzchak Horowitz (*shlita*)
Boyan	1890s	1940	Geula	Rebbe Yisrael Friedman (1951) Rebbe Mordechai Shlomo Friedman (1971) Rebbe Nachum Dov Broyer (*shlita*)
Ger	1820s	1940	Geula	Rebbe Avraham Mordechai Alter (1948) Rebbe Yisrael Alter (1976) Rebbe Simcha Bonim Alter (1992) Rebbe Pinchas Menachem Alter (1996) Rebbe Yaakov Arie Alter (*shlita*)
Dushinsky	1910	1936	Shmuel HaNavi Street	Rebbe Yosef Tzvi Dushinsky (1948) Rebbe Yisrael Moshe Dushinsky (*shlita*)

Dynasty	***Year Began***	***Moved to Eretz Yisrael***	***Location in Jerusalem***	***Rebbes in Eretz Yisrael (until given year)***
Kapishtniz	1900	1975	Ezras Torah	Rebbe Yitzchak Meir Palintenstein (*shlita*)
Karlin-Stolin	1777	1870s	Old City, Beis Yisrael	Rebbe Yochanan Perlow (1955) Rebbe Baruch Meir Yaakov Shochet (*shlita*)
Komarna	1800	1940	Meah Shearim	Rebbe Chaim Yaakov Safrin (1969) Rebbe Shalom Safrin (1997) Rebbe Shlomo Safrin (*shlita*)
Lelov	1820	1850	Old City, Meah Shearim, Bnei Brak	Rebbe Moshe Biderman (1850) Rebbe Elazar Menachem Biderman (1883) Rebbe David Biderman (1918) Rebbe Shimon Nasan Nata Biderman (1929) Rebbe Moshe Mordechai Biderman (1987) Rebbe Avraham Biderman (*shlita*) Rebbe Shimon Nasan Nata Biderman (*shlita*)
Mattersdorf	1920s	1945	Meah Shearim	Rebbe Yisrael Tousig (1967) Rebbe Bonim Yoel Tousig (*shlita*)
Rachmistrivka	1820s	1906	Geula	Rebbe Nachum Twersky (1936) Rebbe Avraham Dov Twersky (1945) Rebbe David Twersky (1950) Rebbe Yochanan Twersky (1982) Rebbe Yisrael Mordechai Twersky (*shlita*)
Sefinka	1871	1945	Meah Shearim	Rebbe Yosef Meir Kahana (1978) Rebbe Mordechai David Kahana (*shlita*)
Shomrei Emunim	1939	1939	Meah Shearim	Rebbe Aharon Rot (1946) Rebbe Avraham Chaim Rot (*shlita*)
Slonim	1830s	1899	Meah Shearim	Rebbe Avraham Weinberg (1981) Rebbe Shalom Noach Borsovsky (*shlita*)
Sochotshov	1870s	1924	Bayit Vegan	Rebbe Chanuch Henich Burnstein (1965) Rebbe Menachem Shlomo Burnstein (1977) Rebbe Shmuel Yitzchak Burnstein (*shlita*)
Toldos Aharon	1939	1939	Meah Shearim	Rebbe Aharon Rot (1945) Rebbe Avraham Yitzchak Kahn (1996) Rebbe David Kahn (*shlita*)

Dynasty	***Year Began***	***Moved to Eretz Yisrael***	***Location in Jerusalem***	***Rebbes in Eretz Yisrael (until given year)***
Tolnah	1900	1953	Bayit Vegan	Rebbe Yochanan Twersky (1998) Rebbe Yitzchak Menachem Weinberg (*shlita*)
Trisk	1840	1980	Unsdorf	Rebbe Moshe Mordechai Eichenstein (*shlita*)
Zweille	1820	1928	Beis Yisrael	Rebbe Shlomo Goldman (1945) Rebbe Gedaliah Moshe Goldman (1949) Rebbe Mordechai Goldman (1979) Rebbe Avraham Goldman (*shlita*)

Chassidic dynasties which only have a shetibel: Bubov, Chabad, Breslov, Kalev, Klausenberg (Sanz), Nadvorna, Sadigora, Satmar, Chernobel, Strikov, and Vishnitz.

Heroes of Jerusalem

Abulafia, Rav Chaim (1660–1744): Born in Hebron; studied in Jerusalem under Rav Moshe Galante. Close comrade of Pri Chadash. Rav in Izmir, Turkey, for many years. In 1740 agreed to rebuild Jewish community of Tiberias. Close to Rav Chaim Attar. Wrote *Etz Chaim, Mikrei Kodesh*, etc.

Abulafia, Rav Chaim Nisim (died, 28 Shevat, 1861): Rav in Tiberias, Safed, and Damascus. Rishon l'Tzyon from 1854.

Abulafia, Rav Yedidiah: Disciple of Rav Avraham Sharabi, injured in 1824 when Jerusalem was attacked. Great kabbalist.

Adani, Rav Shlomo (1567–c. 1630): Born in Yemen, grew up in Safed and Jerusalem where he studied under Rav Chaim Vital and Rav Bezalel Ashkenazi. Wrote commentary on Mishnah, *Meleches Shlomo*, published 1886 by Ram brothers of Vilna.

Aharon Moshe, Rav (1775–7 Tamuz, 1847): Chassid who came to Jerusalem in 1839. Backed publication of *Chibas Yerushalayim*, to which he wrote an approbation.

Alter, Rebbe Avraham Mordechai (1865–6 Sivan, 1948): Gerrer Rebbe who came at the outbreak of WW II and established the Ger dynasty in Jerusalem. Author of *Imrei Emes.*

Alter, Rebbe Menachem (1926–16 Adar, 1996): Gerrer Rebbe from 1992 to 1996.

Alter, Rebbe Simcha Bonim (1898–7 Tamuz, 1992): Gerrer Rebbe from 1976 to 1992.

Alter, Rebbe Yaakov Aryeh (*shlita*): Present Gerrer Rebbe.

Alter, Rebbe Yisrael (1894–2 Adar, 1976): Son of Rebbe Avraham Mordechai Alter of Ger. Rebbe from 1948 to 1976, during which time Ger Chassidim grew dramatically. Influential in Agudas Yisrael.

Amigo, Rav Avraham (1610–1683): Rav in Jerusalem. Opposed Shabbetai Tzvi and his movement.

Amram, Rav Yaakov (first half of 17th century): Scholar and doctor in Jerusalem. Suffered greatly under despot Mohammed Farouk (1625–1626).

Amsterdam, Rav Naftali (1832–6 Adar, 1916): Came in 1906, known as a *mussar* leader.

Ari Zal: See *Luria, Rav Yitzchak*

Asher, Rav Chaim Avraham (died, 12 Av, 1772): *Dayan* and kabbalist, died in famine.

Ashkenazi, Rav Avraham (1811–9 Shevat, 1880): Rishon l'Tzyon from 1869.

Ashkenazi, Rav Bezalel (c. 1530–1596): Rav in Egypt during time of Radvaz. Famous for *Shitah Mekubetzes* on Shas. Rav of Jerusalem 1588–1596.

Ashkenazi, Rav Mordechai (died, 1702): Disciple of Rav Regivo. Wrote commentary to the *Zohar, Eshel Avraham.* Died suddenly soon after arrival in Jerusalem with his mentor.

Atiyah, Rav Ezra (1881–19 Iyar, 1970): Rosh Yeshivah of Porat Yosef Yeshivah from 1925 to 1970.

Attar, Rav Chaim (1696–15 Tamuz, 1743): Born in Morocco, moved to Eretz Yisrael (1741), after publishing (among other works) commentary on Torah called *Ohr HaChaim*. Recognized as a great sage, he strove to teach Torah. Baal Shem Tov even tried to journey to Eretz Yisrael to meet him. His influence has not waned at all over the generations.

Auerbach, Rav Chaim Leib (1883–28 Elul, 1954): Rosh Yeshivah Shaar HaShamayim, kabbalist, father of Rav Shlomo Zalman.

Auerbach, Rav Meir (died, 8 Iyar, 1878):

Rav of Kalish, author of *Imrei Binah.* Immigrated in 1860, became Rav of Jerusalem, leader of the *yishuv.*

Auerbach, Rav Shlomo Zalman (1910–20 Adar I, 1995): *Gadol HaDor*, Rosh Yeshivah of Kol Torah Yeshivah.

*Azariah, Rav Menachem (*17th century): Italian kabbalist. Author of *Eser Maamaros* and disseminator of teachings of Rav Moshe Cordovero.

Azulai, Rav Avraham (17th century): Kabbalist Grandfather of Chida. Known for his righteousness.

Azulai, Rav Chaim Yosef David (1724–11 Adar, 1806): Born in Jerusalem into the illustrious Azulai family; child prodigy. Studied under his uncle, Rav Yona Navon, Rav Chaim Attar, and Rav Shalom Sharabi. Close companion of Rav Yom Tov Elgazi. In 1753, went to Diaspora as a *shaliach* and spent rest of his life in *chutz laAretz* (except for 1758–1764). Wrote dozens of books on every aspect of Torah, including *Avodas HaKodesh*, *Shem HaGedolim*, and *Birkei Yosef.*

Azulai, Rav Yitzchak (1696–1759): Father of Chida. *Dayan* in Jerusalem.

Baal Shem Tov (1695–6 Sivan, 1760): Founder of Chassidus; attempted to visit Eretz Yisrael around 1740 to meet Ohr HaChaim.

Bachbot, Rav Shalom (1831–1915): Moroccan tzaddik and *chacham.* Know as wonder-worker.

Baharan, Rav Nachum of Shadik (died, 12 Cheshvan, 1865): One of Levi brothers, tzaddik and communal leader of Perushim.

Baharan, Rav Shlomo Zalman (1845–25 Adar I, 1910): One of founders of Meah Shearim and other neighborhoods.

Bardaky, Rav Shlomo: Son of Rav Yeshaya Bardaky; *chazan* at Churvah Synagogue.

Bardaky, Rav Yeshaya (died, 18 Cheshvan, 1862): Son-in-law of Rav Yisrael of Shklov; leader in *yishuv*, Rav of Sukkas Shalom Synagogue.

Beck, Rav Nisan (1813–8 Kislev, 1890): Son of Rav Yisrael Beck, communal leader of the Chassidim, builder of Tiferes Yisrael Synagogue and suburb near Damascus Gate, Battei Rav Nisan Beck.

Beck, Rav Yisrael (died, 1791–29 Cheshvan, 1874): First publisher in Jerusalem (1841), previously in Safed (1830) where he published *Pe'as HaShulchan*; communal leader.

Ben-Shimon, Rav David (1826–18 Kislev, 1879): First Rav of Moroccan community in Jerusalem. Dynamic leader who loved his people.

Ben-Shimon, Rav Raphael Aharon 1847–10 Cheshvan, 1928): Rav of Egypt (1890–1921), son of Rav David Ben-Shimon. Tzaddik in his own right, wrote *Shaar HaMifkad, Nahar Mitzrayim* (Halachah), etc.

Bengis, Rav Zelig Reuven (1864–7 Sivan, 1953): Came in 1937 as head rabbi of Eidah Charedis; Rosh Yeshivah Ohel Moshe; author of *Liflagos Reuven* (on Shas in seven volumes).

Berav, Rav Yaakov (1480–30 Nisan, 1546): *Gadol HaDor.* Rav in Morocco, Cairo, and Safed. Lived in Jerusalem for a short time in early 1520s. Most famous for reintroducing ordination in Safed. Buried in Safed in a cave near the grave of Rav Yosef Karo.

Beril, Rav Yechiel (1836–4 Cheshvan, 1887): publisher of *HaLevanan* journal.

Berlin, Rav Chaim (1832–13 Tishre, 1913): son of Netziv, came to Jerusalem (1902) and refused Rav Salant's offer to replace him as Rav of Jerusalem. Head of Central Committee.

Berlin, Rav Tzvi (died, 4 Av, 1872): Came in 1853, built up *yishuv*, especially Battei Machse.

Betito, Rav Nachman (1846–15 Elul, 1915): Asked to fill in as Rishon l'Tzyon from 1909 to 1911. Rav of Moroccan community (1900–1915).

Biderman, Rebbe David (14 Tishre, 1843–5 Elul, 1918): Son of Rebbe Elazar Mendel, continued and expanded Lelover Chassidus.

Biderman, Rebbe Elazar Mendel (1827–16 Adar, 1883): Son of Rebbe Moshe, continued Lelover dynasty in Jerusalem.

Biderman, Rebbe Moshe (1777–13 Teves, 1851): Lelover Rebbe who brought first Chassidic dynasty to Jerusalem. Died a few days after his arrival.

Binyamin of Toledo (died c. 1173): Spanish traveler of Europe and the Middle East. His journal, *Masa'os Rav Binyamin*, is considered earliest record of Jewish communities he visited.

Biton, Rav Yitzchak (first half of 17th century): Rav in Jerusalem in the time of Rav Shmuel Garmizan. His son, Rav Chaim Avraham, sat on *beis din* of Rav Moshe Galante.

Blazar, Rav Yitzchak (1837–11 Av, 1907): Disciple of Rav Yisrael Salanter, Rav of Petersburg, author of *Pri Yitzchak* and *Ohr Yisrael*. Came to Jerusalem in 1904.

Blumenthal, Rav Yaakov (died, 12 Cheshvan, 1915): Disciple of Rav Diskin, communal leader and a head of Diskin Orphanage.

Blumenthal, Rav Yosef (19th century): Patron of the *yishuv*; sent money for the poor (distributed by Rav Yosef Schwartz), then opened school for poor called *Doresh Tzyon*.

Braverman, Rav Zerach (died, 6 Shevat, 1938): Came to Jerusalem, studied privately with Rav Yehoshua Leib Diskin. Rosh Yeshivah Meah Shearim and mentor of Rav Benzion Yadler.

Burnstein, Rebbe Avraham (died, 1910): Rebbe of Sochotshov, author of *Avnei Nezer* and *Aglei Tal*.

Burnstein, Rebbe Chanuch Heinich (died, 26 Elul, 1965): Rebbe of Sochotshov from 1942–1965.

Burnstein, Rebbe David (1876–8 Kislev, 1942): Rebbe of Sochotshov from 1926–1942.

Burnstein, Rebbe Menachem Shlomo (died: 1969): Rebbe of Sochotshov from 1965–1969.

Burnstein, Rebbe Shmuel: Present Rebbe of Sochotshov.

Chagiz, Rav Moshe (1672–1744): Fighter for truth, fought against Shabbetai Tzvi movement and its leader Nechemiah Chivon. Prolific writer. Also published the works of his father (*Hilchos Ketanos*) and his grandfather, Rav Moshe Galante.

Chananiah, Rav Avraham (mid-17th century): Kabbalist and *talmid chacham*. Close to Mabit and Rav Sharaf of Constantinople. Wrote *Beis (*or *Bris) Avraham*. Son-in-law was Rav Moshe HaNazir HaLevi, author of *Yadei Moshe*. Died in plague in 1665; buried in Hebron.

Charlap, Rav Yaakov Moshe (1882–7 Kislev, 1951): *Dayan* and Rav of Shaarei Chesed and Rechavia. Rosh Yeshivah of Merkaz HaRav; wrote *Beis Zevul* (Halachah).

Chatam Sofer: See *Sofer, Rav Moshe*.

Chavilio, Rav David (died, 9 Av, 1661): Left Safed with his mentor, Rav Binyamin HaLevi (*talmid* of the Ari Zal), to settle in Jerusalem. Both left for *chutz laAretz*. Chida reported that he had a Heavenly *maggid*. Died in Izmir. His son, Rav Yehudah Chavilio, became Rav of Hebron.

Chavilio, Rav Yitzchak: Brother of Rav David Chavilio. Lived in Jerusalem during reign of terror of Farouk.

Chaviv, Rav Levi (c. 1480–c. 1542): Rav of Jerusalem in second quarter of 16th century. Son of author of *Ein Yaakov*, recognized in Salonika as one of the *gedolim* before coming to Eretz Yisrael. Instrumental in opposing *semichah d'oraysa*, which *rabbanim* of Safed reinstated (1538).

Chaviv, Rav Moshe (1654–1696): Rav of Jerusalem (1690s). Strove for betterment of community.

Chazan, Rav Benzion (died, 12 Cheshvan, 1951): Rav at Porat Yosef Yeshivah.

Chazan, Rav Chaim (early 18th century): Disciple of Rav Avraham Revigo. Wrote *Shnos Chaim, drashos* on Torah (1693).

Died in Mir on *shelichus* for Jerusalem *yishuv*.

Chazan, Rav David (1 Cheshvan, 1790–5 Shevat, 1869): Rishon l'Tzyon from 1861, author of *Nediv Lev*.

Chazan, Rav Yosef (1741–23 Cheshvan, 1820): From Izmir, Turkey. Rav in Egypt and Hebron, and finally Rishon l'Tzyon in 1818. Wrote *Chakrei Lev* (Halachah), and *Mearkei Lev (drash)*. His son, Rav David Chazan, became Rishon l'Tzyon (1861), and grandson, Rav Chaim Palagi, was one of *gedolim* of Izmir.

Chida: See *Azulai, Rav Chaim Yosef David.*

Chivon, Rav Aharon (first half of 17th century): Scholar. His son, Rav Moshe Chivon, was Rav and kabbalist, author of commentary on *Zohar*.

Chuzin, Rav Zadkah (died, 29 Shevat, 1961): Rav in Baghdad, came in 1926 and built Shemesh Tzedakah Synagogue; famous *mohel*.

Cohen, Dr. Albert (died, 1 Nisan, 1877): Sent by James Rothschild in 1854 to set up a variety of institutions. Strived to better the lot of poor people.

Cohen, Rav Michel (1834–3 Elul, 1914): One of original seven of Nachalas Shiva, publisher of *Ariel* and *Chavatzeles* (1870–1873).

Cohen, Rav Shlomo (died, 8 Tamuz, 1827): Kabbalist, expounder of mystical writing of Ari Zal. Wrote *Yafeh Sha'ah*.

Conforti, Rav David (1617–1690): Author of *Korei HaDoros*. Scholar who studied with *gedolim* in Constantinople, Egypt, and Eretz Yisrael. Studied with Rav Yaakov Tzemach and Rav Azariah Zeevi.

Cordovero, Rav Gedaliah (died, 1620s): Son of Ramak. Jewish communal leader of Jerusalem in first quarter of 17th century. Published some of his father's works on Kabbalah.

Costro, Rav David: Lived in Jerusalem during first quarter of 17th century. Studied Kabbalah and purchased important manuscript of Rav Moshe Cordovero from his son.

Coyanca, Rav Benzion Avraham (21 Nisan, 1867–16 Cheshvan, 1936): Published *Ma'asef* (1896–1914); Rosh Yeshivah Tiferes Jerusalem.

D'Lyon, Rav Moshe (13th century): Discovered *Zohar* in a Galilean cave and had it published.

Danon, Rav Nisim (1874–15 Shevat, 1920): Last Sephardic Chief Rav of Jerusalem during Turkish reign.

Danon, Rav Yom Tov (died, 8 Av, 1823): Rishon l'Tzyon from 1820–1823.

Danziger, Rebbe Yehudah Moshe (died, 23 Adar I, 1973): Rebbe of Alexander; officially *Admor* from 1947.

DeHaan, Dr. Yaakov Yisrael (1881–29 Sivan, 1924): Educated as diplomat, came to Eretz Yisrael 1920. Activist for Orthodox *yishuv* in Jerusalem. Assassinated.

Dessler, Rav Eliyahu (1891–24 Teves, 1954): Famous author (*Miktav m'Eliyahu*); came to Eretz Yisrael, 1950, to become *mashgiach* of Ponevitch Yeshivah.

Deweik, Rav Chaim Shaul (1858–4 Teves, 1932): Kabbalist, came in 1890.

Diskin, Rav Yehoshua Leib (1818–29 Teves, 1898): Rav of Brisk; came in 1878. His influence was felt in every sphere.

Diskin, Rav Yitzchak Yerucham (22 Shevat, 1839–29 Shevat, 1925): Son of Rav Yehoshua Leib; came in 1908, headed Diskin Orphanage; led *yishuv* along with Rav Zonnenfeld.

Dushinsky, Rav Yosef Tzvi (1867–14 Tishre, 1948): Rav of Galanta and Hust, Hungary, and Head of Eidah Chareidis (1933–1948) after death of Rav Zonnenfeld.

Eisenstein, Rav Avraham (1803–6 Elul, 1886): *Dayan* of Perushim *beis din* in Safed and Jerusalem.

Elbachari, Rav Emanuel: Scholar in Jerusalem during years of terror (1625–1626).

Elfandari, Rav Shlomo Eliezer (1815–22 Iyar, 1930): Known as Sabba Kaddisha. Rosh Yeshivah in Constantinople and

Chacham Bashi in Damascus. Came to Eretz Yisrael 1909. Came to Jerusalem, 1925; wrote responsa.

Elgazi, Rav Shlomo the Elder (died, c. 1740 in Egypt): One of most prominent disciples of Pri Chadash. Later became Chief Rabbi of Egypt for forty-five years.

Elgazi, Rav Yaakov (died, 1793): Only son of Rav Yom Tov Elgazi; murdered by Arabs. Left small children orphaned.

Elgazi, Rav Yisrael Yaakov (died, 6 Tamuz, 1756): Emigrated from Izmir early 1730s. Rishon l'Tzyon (1749–1756), kabbalist at Beis El Yeshivah; father of Rav Yom Tov Elgazi; author of *Kehillos Yaakov*, etc.

Elgazi, Rav Yom Tov (1727–2 Adar, 1802): Rishon l'Tzyon (1776–1802), head of Beis El Yeshivah after death of Rav Sharabi. Author of *Hilchos Yom Tov, Simchas Yom Tov*, etc. Buried near Rav Sharabi on Mount of Olives.

Elmaliach, Rav Yosef (died, 1854): Rav of Mogador, Morocco; moved to Jerusalem with his family at end of his life.

Elyashar, Rav Chaim Moshe (1845–4 Shevat, 1924): Son of Rav Yaakov Shaul Elyashar; helped his father during term of Rishon l'Tzyon and published his father's writings.

Elyashar, Rav Yaakov (end of 18th century): Son of Chaim Yerucham of Vilna, grandson of Rav Yaakov of Vilna; native Jerusalemite. Went on *shelichus* with Chida; eventually went to Persia where he was instrumental in annulling decree against Jews.

Elyashar, Rav Yaakov Shaul (23 Sivan, 1817–28 Tamuz, 1906): Rishon l'Tzyon from 1893, great communal leader.

Elyashiv, Rav Shlomo (1841–27 Adar, 1926): Kabbalist; grandfather of Rav Yosef Shalom Elyashiv, *shlita*.

Elyashiv, Rav Yosef Shalom (*shlita*): One of the great halachic authorities of this generation.

Entebbe, Rav Yaakov (died, 20 Tishre, 1846): Chacham Bashi of Damascus; imprisoned along with others in great blood libel, 1840; saved through efforts of Sir Montefiore. Spent last years in Jerusalem, aiding Ashkenazim as well as Sephardim.

Ephraim, Rav (1616–13 Sivan 1678): Rav in Vilna. Father-in-law of Chacham Tzvi. Fled Vilna, 1648, due to Cossack massacres. Rav in Prague, Wein, and Auben. Accepted post as Rav of Jerusalem in 1678, but died before he could come. Author of *Shaar Ephraim* (Halachah), and *Machane Ephraim* (*drashos*).

Epstein, Rav Moshe Mordechai (1866–10 Kislev, 1934): Rosh Yeshivah Knesset Yisrael (Hebron); wrote *Levush Mordechai.* Founder of Hadera.

Ezriel, Rav (died, 1782): Rav of Shklov. Disciple of Vilna Gaon; one of first leaders of Chazon Tzyon movement to build a *yishuv* in Eretz Yisrael. Visited Jerusalem, 1772. Grandfather of Rav Yisrael of Shklov.

Feibish, Rav Uri (Ohr) Shraga (died, c. 1670): Ashkenazic Rav of Jerusalem, mid-17th century. Studied under Rav Meir of Lublin.

Ferira, Rav Yaakov (died, end of 17th century): Philanthropist from Amsterdam. Supported yeshivah in Hebron, 1659. In 1691, he asked Rav Chizkiah Silva (author of *Pri Chadash*), to become Rosh Yeshivah of a new yeshivah, Beis Yaakov Ferira, in Jerusalem. In his will, left endowment fund for continual support of yeshivah, which lasted two hundred years and had hundreds of students.

Finkel, Rav Binyamin Beinush (1913–18 Shevat, 1990): Son of Rav Yehudah Finkel, became Rosh Yeshivah, 1965.

Finkel, Rav Chaim Zev (1906–18 Elul, 1965): Founder of Heichal HaTorah Yeshivah, Tel Aviv, and *mashgiach* at Mir Yeshivah, Jerusalem.

Finkel, Rav Eliezer Yehudah (1877–19 Tamuz, 1965): Rosh Yeshivah of Mir; after WW II, built yeshivah in Jerusalem. Wrote *Divrei Eliezer*.

Finn, James (died, 1863): British consul, Jerusalem, 1845–1863. Opened "Industrial Plantation" called Abraham's Vineyard, for sole purpose of hiring Jews.

Fish, Rav Ephraim (died, 1596): First Ashkenazic Rav of Jerusalem. Came in 1566. Grandfather of *Shaar Ephraim*.

Frank, Rav Tzvi Pesach (1873–21 Kislev, 1960): Came in 1893, *dayan* on *beis din* of Rav Salant; joined Rabbinate, 1921; became Rav of Jerusalem, 1936. Author of *Har Tzvi*, etc.

Friedman, Rebbe Mordechai Shlomo (1990–5 Adar, 1971): Boyaner Rebbe, built dynasty in Jerusalem after WW II.

Friedman, Rebbe Yisrael (1796–1850): Ruzhiner Rebbe; loved Eretz Yisrael; helped support *yishuv*, bought plot of Tiferes Yisrael Synagogue which was named after him.

Frumkin, Rav Aryeh Leib (1848–8 Sivan, 1916): Author of *Toldos Chachmei Jerusalem*.

Frumkin, Rav Yisrael Dov (1851–14 Iyar, 1914): Publisher of *Chavatzeles*, helped Yemenites settle in Shiloach.

Frust, Rav Avraham (1842–28 Kislev, 1896): One of founders of Meah Shearim; called father of community.

Gad, Rav Baruch: 17th-century scholar. Spent years as fund-raiser for Jerusalem community. While lost in Arabian desert, he came across the ten Lost Tribes.

Gagin, Rav Avraham (1787–21 Iyar, 1848): Rishon l'Tzyon, first Chacham Bashi of Jerusalem, 1842, strove to make peace; wrote *Chukei Chaim*.

Galante, Rav Moshe (Rav HaMagen) (1620–21 Shevat, 1689): *Gadol HaDor*, first Rishon l'Tzyon of Jerusalem. Rosh Yeshivah Beis Yaakov, 1674–1689. Pri Chadash was one of his disciples. Wrote *Elaf HaMagen* (Halachah), by which he became known as Rav HaMagen, *Korban Chagigah* (*drashos*), and *Zevach Hashelamim (Shas)*.

Galante, Rav Moshe the Elder (16th century): Rav of Safed. Received *semichah* from Rav Yosef Karo at age twenty-two. Lived during height of Safed's Torah golden age. His grandson was first Rishon l'Tzyon in Jerusalem, Rav HaMagen.

Gaon, Rav Yitzchak (first half of 17th century): Wealthy leader and scholar in Jerusalem. Tried to help during two-year tyranny of Farouk. Later opened yeshivah; studied Kabbalah with Rav Yaakov Tzemach.

Garmizan, Rav Shmuel (mid-17th century): Rav in Jerusalem.

Gedaliah, Rav from Poland (early 18th century): Disciple of Rav Yehudah HaChassid. Wrote pamphlet, *Sha'alu Shalom Yerushalayim*, about first years in Jerusalem.

Goldman, Rebbe Avraham (*shlita*): Present Rebbe of Zweille, son of Rebbe Mordechai.

Goldman, Rebbe Gedaliah Moshe (1887–24 Cheshvan, 1949): Son of Rebbe Shlomo; came in 1936.

Goldman, Rebbe Mordechai (1905–28 Shevat, 1979): Rebbe of Zweille, son of Rebbe Gedaliah Moshe.

Goldman, Rebbe Shlomo (1869–26 Iyar, 1945): Rebbe of Zweille from 1900. Came in 1925; known for his prayers for sick and needy.

Guta, Rav Nasan (died, 1648 in Egypt, reburied in Jerusalem): Son of Rav Zerachiah Guta, disciple of Mabit.

Gutmacher, Rav Eliyahu (1796–1874): Rav of Graidiz; met Rav Kalisher, 1860, and helped establish religious settlements in Eretz Yisrael; Sdei Eliyahu is named after him.

HaChassid, Rav Yehudah (died, 6 Cheshvan, 1700): Great leader and scholar; spent years fasting and in *teshuvah*. 1699, immigrated to Eretz Yisrael with over 1,000 followers, but died soon afterwards.

Hadaya, Rav Ovadiah (1890– 20 Shevat, 1969): *Dayan* on the Rabbinate, author, head of Beis El Yeshivah.

HaKohen, Rav Moshe of Prague (early 18th century): Ashkenazic Rosh Beis Din in Jerusalem at turn of 18th century.

HaKohen, Rav Yonasan (13th century): One of Baalei Tosefos who immigrated to Eretz Yisrael in 1211. Led *kehillah*.

HaLevi, Rav Avraham (first half of 16th century): Exiled from Spain in 1498, traveled for years along Mediterranean basin to Egypt. Came to Jerusalem with Rav Sholal, 1514. Early kabbalist; published works on Kabbalah.

HaLevi, Rav Mordechai (died, 1808): Author of *Maamar Mordechai*. Rishon l'Tzyon for one year.

HaLevi, Rav Naftali Hertz (1852–14 Sivan, 1902): Rav of Jaffa, disciple of Rav Diskin; published Gra siddur with commentary.

HaLevi, Rav Shalom Yitzchak (1891–1973): Chief Rabbi of Yemenites in Eretz Yisrael.

HaLevi, Rav Yehudah (died, 1140): Author of *Kuzari*; great poet and *chacham*, disciple of Rif. Lived in Spain until almost the end of his life when he came to Eretz Yisrael.

Hoffman, Rav Moshe Yosef (1843–1 Nisan, 1928): *Dayan* of Pappa; came in 1906. Taught in Chasam Sofer Yeshivah.

Horowitz, Rav Chaim (died, 1843): Descendant of Shelah, immigrated to Safed, 1817; moved to Jerusalem, 1826. Wrote popular book about Eretz Yisrael, *Chibas Yerushalayim*.

Horowitz, Rav Shaul Chaim (died, 3 Teves, 1916): Came in 1883; Rav of Meah Shearim, opened Pri Etz Hadar (cheder), Meah Shearim Yeshivah.

Horowitz, Rav Yeshaya (the Shelah) (1560–11 Nisan, 1530): One of great leaders of European Jewry. His *Shnei Luchos HaBris* became a classic for all Jewish scholars. Came in 1622; settled in Jerusalem, finished *Shelah*. Chief Rabbi for four years until Farouk terrorized the city. Fled for his life, resettled in Safed and Tiberias; buried next to Rabban Yochanan ben Zakkai.

Horowitz, Rebbe Levi Yitzchak (*shlita*): Second Bostoner Rebbe; built Chassidic community in Har Nof, Jerusalem, where he lives half the year.

Horowitz, Rebbe Pinchas David (1876–8 Kislev, 1941): First Rebbe of Boston; native Jerusalemite, forced to travel to America from Greece during WW I.

Houminer, Rav Shmuel (1913– 19 Sivan, 1977): Jerusalemite tzaddik and prolific writer.

Hurwitz, Rav Avraham Simcha (1848–15 Adar I, 1915): Rebbe of Barniv, lived in Jerusalem 1909–1916.

Iyash, Rav Yaakov (died, 26 Teves, 1816): Son of Rav Yehudah Iyash. Rishon l'Tzyon from 1808. Headed Chaim v'Chesed Yeshivah.

Iyash, Rav Yehudah: Author of *Shevet Yehudah* (Halachah); immigrated to Jerusalem with family.

Kahanov, Rav Moshe Nechemiah (died, 2 Sivan, 1886): Immigrated in 1867 and became Rosh Yeshivah of Etz Chaim. Dynamic leader and teacher. Helped build the suburbs. Wrote *Sha'alu Shalom Yerushalayim* and *Chukas Olam*.

*Kahn, Rebbe Avraham Yitzchak (*1914–27 Kislev, 1996): First rebbe of Toldos Aharon.

Kalish, Rebbe Shimon Shalom (died 19 Av, 1946): Rebbe of Amshinov; came in 1930s on a visit.

Kalish, Rebbe Yerachmiel Yehudah Meir (1901–26 Iyar, 1976): Rebbe of Amshinov; came in 1946.

Kalisher, Rav Tzvi Hirsch (1795–1874): Rav of Toren. Leader of movement to build settlements in Eretz Yisrael. Wrote *Drishas Tzyon*, 1862.

Katz, Rav Moshe (early 18th century): Member of Rav Yehudah HaChassid's aliyah, 1700. Wrote *Mateh Moshe*.

Kilezkin, Rav Eliyahu (1852–16 Iyar, 1932): Gaon of Lublin, came in 1925, taught in Ohel Moshe Yeshivah.

Kitover, Rav Gershon (died, 25 Adar I, 1761): Brother-in-law of Baal Shem Tov. Lived in Eretz Yisrael from 1747 (or 1743), in Safed, Hebron, and finally Jerusalem. Studied in Beis El Yeshivah with Rav Sharabi.

Kobo, Rav Yitzchak (1770–24 Av, 1854): Rishon l'Tzyon and Chacham Bashi 1848–1854.

Kohen, Rav Moshe of Prague (died, 1718): Head of Ashkenazic community of Jerusalem first decades of 18th century. *Shaliach* to Europe for many years.

Kohen, Rav Shimon: Official Sheik al-Yehud during reign of terror (1625–1626).

Kohen, Rav Yitzchak (end of 17th century): Disciple of *Pri Chadash*. Wrote *Battei Kehunah*.

Kook, Rav Avraham Yitzchak (1865–3 Elul, 1935): First Chief Rabbi of Eretz Yisrael, served earlier as Rav of Jaffa and London; wrote *Oros*, etc.

Kook, Rav Tzvi Yehudah (1891–14 Adar, 1982): Son of Rav Avraham Kook, Rosh Yeshivah Merkaz HaRav from 1951.

Korel, Rav Yaakov (died, 25 Shevat, 1818): Rishon l'Tzyon for one year. Wrote *Zimras HaAretz*.

Kornel, Rav Nachman Nasan (mid-19th century): Moved to Jerusalem from Safed after earthquake of 1837; wrote *Teshuvos HaGaonim*.

Kotna, Rav Moshe Yehudah Leib (died, 3 Shevat, 1865): Rav of Kotna. Author of *Zayis Ra'anan*; came around 1857; taught in Etz Chaim Yeshivah.

Lehren, Tzvi and Akiva (19th century): Philanthropists of Amsterdam, aided *yishuv* enormously.

Levi, Rav Asher Lemil, (died, 8 Kislev, 1850): Rav of Galin. One of Levi brothers; *dayan* in 1840s for Perushim; married daughter of Rav Moshe Rivlin.

Levi, Rav Nachum, Rav of Shadik (died, 12 Cheshvan, 1865): Came in 1840s with two brothers, *rav* and leader of *yishuv*. Descendants named Baharan after initials of his name.

Levi, Rav Yaakov Leib (died, 11 Elul, 1889): *Dayan* and head of Kollel Warsaw; kabbalist; married daughter of Rav Moshe Rivlin.

Levin, Rav Aryeh (1885–9 Nisan, 1969): Disciple of Rav Kook, known as "father of the prisoners" during Mandate period.

Linchner, Rav Alexander (1908 – 4 Sivan, 1997): Founded and head of Boys Town.

Loewe, Dr. Eliezer (1809–1888): Personal secretary of Sir Moses Montefiore for nearly fifty years. Suffered in Druse attack on Safed, 1838; stood behind all of Montefiore's beliefs.

London, Dr.: Director of Rothschild Hospital, 1866–1875.

Lunz, Rav Avraham (1854–1918): Writer and publisher of *Yerushalayim*, *Luach Eretz Yisrael*, etc.

Lunzano, Rav Menachem (end of 16th century): Scholar, poet, author of *Shetei Yados* on a variety of Torah topics.

Luria, Rav Shemarya (mid-19th century): Wealthy and influential, lived in Jerusalem for two years (1834–1836); did utmost for *yishuv*. Rav Hillel Rivlin was his father-in-law.

Luria, Rav Yitzchak: (1534–1572): Born in Jerusalem, orphaned as a child, grew up in Egypt. Studied with Rav Bezalel Ashkenazi; moved to Safed, 1570, where he initiated Rav Chaim Vital into secret world of Kabbalah received from Eliyahu the Prophet.

Maali, Rav Binyamin (died, 1731): *Dayan* and Rishon l'Tzyon (1729–1731). Many years a *rav* in Egypt.

Maharit: See *Tarani, Rav Yosef.*

Maimonides, Rav Moshe (14 Nisan, 1133–20 Teves, 1205): Known as Rambam. Born in Cordova, Spain, where he began his commentary to Mishnah. Left around 1165, passed through Eretz Yisrael, eventually settled in Egypt, became Sultan's private physician. Spent ten years (1170–1180) writing *Yad HaChazakah*, also *Sefer HaMitzvos* and *Guide to the Perplexed*.

Majar, Rav Avraham (died, 28 Kislev, 1839): Son of Rav David; kabbalist at Beis El, leader of yeshivah after death of Rav Avraham Mizrachi, 1827.

Majar, Rav David (died, 20 Adar, 1800): Kabbalist, disciple of Rav Sharabi; wrote *Chasdei David* (Kabbalah).

Malki, Rav Raphael Mordechai (lived in Jerusalem 1673–1704): Scholar and physician, father-in-law of Rav Chizkiah Silva (Pri Chadash) and Rav Moshe Chagiz. Wrote on medicine, astronomy, etc. His sons, Rav Ezra and Rav Moshe Malki, were rabbis in Safed.

Malko, Rav Yosef: Rav in Safed, he left there to settle in Jerusalem during second half of 17th century.

Mandelbaum, Rav Simcha (1860–5 Iyar, 1930): The Mandelbaum crossing between east-west Jerusalem is named after the house he built nearby.

Medini, Rav Chaim Chizkiyahu (1835–25 Kislev, 1908): Born in Jerusalem, spent most of his life in Diaspora; returned to become Rav of Hebron. Wrote *Sdei Chemed.*

Meir, Rav Yaakov (1856–9 Sivan, 1939): Rishon l'Tzyon and first Sephardic Chief Rabbi.

Meltzer, Rav Issar Zalman (1870–10 Kislev, 1953): Known as the genius of Volozhin, opened yeshivah in Slutzk; came in 1925; Rosh Yeshivah Etz Chaim; wrote *Even HaEzel* on Rambam.

Menachem Mendel, Rav (died, 1 Adar, 1827): From Shklov. Leading disciple of Vilna Gaon, publisher of most of Gaon's writings, tireless leader of Perushim in Jerusalem.

Meyuchas, Rav Avraham: (1708–29 Kislev, 1768): Born and died in Jerusalem. Author of *Sdei HaAretz* (Halachah), *Diglo Ahavah* (Kabbalah), etc. Brother of Rav Raphael, who became Rishon l'Tzyon.

Meyuchas, Rav Moshe (died, 1720s): Grandfather of Rav Raphael and Rav Avraham Meyuchas. Known as the Parnas; arrested for opposing the wicked ruler in 1723. Saved through *shelichus* of his grandson.

Meyuchas, Rav Moshe Mordechai Yosef (1738–13 Tishre, 1805): Son of Rav Raphael and son-in-law of Rav Yom Tov Elgazi. Rishon l'Tzyon from 1802. Wrote *Birchos Mayim* (on *Shulchan Aruch*) and *Shaar HaMayim (*Halachah*).*

Meyuchas, Rav Raphael (1705–1771): Born in Jerusalem, studied in Beis Yaakov Yeshivah and later in Ohr HaChaim Yeshivah. Rishon l'Tzyon from 1756 until his death. Wrote *Pri Adamah* on the Rambam and *Mizbeach Adamah*, among others.

Minzburg, Rav Yisrael Zev (Velvel) (1873–17 Adar II, 1962): Head of Chassidic *beis din* from 1937; in 1948 surrendered Old City and thereby saved 2,000 Jews; forced to leave all his manuscripts in Old City.

Mizrachi, Rav Nisim (c. 1685–4 Tamuz, 1749): *Dayan* and Rishon l'Tzyon, mid-1740s, impoverished most of his life. Wrote *Admas Kodesh* (responsa, 1742).

Mizrachi, Rav Yisrael Meir (died 1748): Studied in Beis Yaakov Yeshivah, wrote *Pri HaAretz* (Halachah) and *Tiferes Yisrael* (*drash*). Together with his brother, Rav Nisim (later Rishon l'Tzyon), called *Neros HaMizrachim.*

Montefiore, Sir Moses (1784–16 Av 1885): Benefactor of *yishuv* and Eretz Yisrael. Came seven times between 1827–1875, each time with concrete ideas to improve Jews' lot. Built monument over Tomb of Rachel, and the additional rows of stone to the Western Wall; started Jewish farms, and gave generously to new suburbs.

Munzon, Rav Shimon (1842– 14 Cheshvan, 1905): Head beadle of Churvah Synagogue for over thirty years.

Musayoff, Rav Shlomo (1852–8 Nisan, 1922): Came in 1890; helped build Bucharim Quarter. Supported *kollel* and consecrated much of his property for synagogues.

Mushkin, Rav Yechiel Michel (1865–1947): Came as child, studied in Etz Chaim and Toras Chaim yeshivos; Rosh Yeshivah Meah Shearim.

Muzafi, Rav Yaakov (1900–13 Sivan, 1983):

Born in Baghdad where he studied under Rav Agassi; became a leading Sephardic halachic authority in Jerusalem after immigrating in 1951.

Nachmanides, Rav Moshe (c. 1200–1270): Known as Ramban; one of great Rishonim; prolific writer. At end of his life immigrated to Eretz Yisrael where he wrote his famous commentary to Torah.

Nachum, Rav Eliezer (died, c. 1745): Rishon l'Tzyon (1731–1745). Wrote *Chazon Nachum* on Mishnah. Opened Talmud Torah. Rishon l'Tzyon from 1732 until his death.

Najara, Rav Moshe (mid-17th century): Son of Rav Yisrael Najara, and Rav of Gaza.

Narel, Rav Tuvia (1653–1729): Child prodigy, received *semichah* at age fifteen. Studied medicine in Frankfurt and Padova, Italy, receiving admiration of gentile leaders. His work, *Maaseh Tuvia,* 1707, discussed Hashem in physical world, medicine, and childbirth. Came to Jerusalem, 1718.

Nasan Nata, Rav (died, 22 Tishre, 1846): Son of Rav Menachem Mendel of Shklov, leader of Perushim and Churvah Shul, worked for good of *yishuv*, on *anshei gevardiah.*

Nasan Nata, Rav (early 18th century): Rav of Hagni. Joined Rav Yehudah HaChassid and came on aliyah with him, 1700. Wrote *Meoros Nasan* (on Kabbalah) with newly found companion, Rav Yaakov of Vilna. Worked to save Ashkenazic community from debts.

Nasan, Rav Avraham (late 17th century): Lived in Egypt. In 1690s, when Rav Moshe Chagiz was in Egypt, they became friends. Offered to open a yeshivah in Jerusalem, but plan never eventuated.

Navon, Rav Binyamin Mordechai (died, 1851): Sephardic Rav and stepfather of Rav Yaakov Shaul Elyashar.

Navon, Rav Yehudah (died, 1842): Rishon l'Tzyon (1836–1842).

Neiman, Dr.: First director of Rothschild hospital (1854–1864).

Nisim, Rav Yitzchak (1895–9 Av, 1982): Sephardic Chief Rabbi, 1955–1973.

Orenstein, Rav Yaakov (1859–22 Sivan, 1908): HaGaon HaYerushalmi; taught in Ohel Moshe Yeshivah; disciple of Rav Diskin.

Orenstein, Rav Yeshaya (1836–19 Cheshvan, 1909): Disciple of Rav of Kotna, builder of new city, founder of Ohel Moshe Yeshivah.

Orenstein, Rav Yitzchak (died, 18 Iyar, 1948): Rav of Kosel; killed during Arab bombing of Old City.

Ovadiah of Bartenora (c. 1465–1500? 1510? 1530?): Born in Italy, immigrated to Eretz Yisrael, 1488. Settled in Jerusalem, where he completed commentaries to Mishnah and Chumash. Buried near Shiloach pools.

Panijel, Rav Eliyahu Moshe (1850–29 Teves, 1919): Rishon l'Tzyon, 1907–1909, author of *Toras Moshe.*

Panijel, Rav Raphael Meir (1805–14 Teves 1892): Rishon l'Tzyon (1880–1892).

Paparish, Rav Meir (died, Adar, 1662): Came to Jerusalem from Europe, studied Kabbalah under Rav Yaakov Tzemach. Organized voluminous writings of Rav Chaim Vital. Wrote works on Kabbalah, the most popular being *Ohr Tzaddikim.* Buried on Mount of Olives.

Pappo, Rav Yehudah (died, 13 Sivan, 1873): Son of Rav Eliezer Pappo, who wrote *Pelei Yoetz.* Lived in Jerusalem and Hebron, scholar and businessman.

Parchi, Rav Chaim (died, 1819): From illustrious philanthropic family of Damascus. High-ranking minister in Akko, helped *yishuv* in Safed and Jews in general. Assassinated.

Parchi, Rav Ishtori (1280–c. 1330): French scholar, settled in Eretz Yisrael, 1313. Wrote masterpiece on Eretz Yisrael, *Kaftor v'Ferach.*

Parchi, Rav Yitzchak (1782–3 Iyar, 1853): Born and raised in Jerusalem. Disciple of Rav Yom Tov Elgazi; sat on *beis din* with Rav Gagin. Wrote *Tuv Yerushalayim,*

Matok m'Devash, etc.

Pardes, Rav Eliyahu (1893–11 Nisan, 1972): Sephardic Rav of Jerusalem from 1960 to 1972.

Pardo, Rav Aharon (last half of 17th century): Communal leader during 1670s and 1680s. Worked hand in hand with Rav Moshe Galante.

Pardo, Rav David (1719–12 Sivan, 1792): Immigrated from Italy, 1782. Rosh Yeshivah Chesed l'Avraham; author of ten books, including *Maskil l'David, Mizmor l'David*, and *Shoshanim l'David.*

Partzovitz, Rav Nachum (1913–18 Cheshvan, 1985): One of leading rabbis of Mir Yeshivah.

Perlo, Rav Yerucham Fishel (1846–30 Shevat, 1934): Spent 40 years writing commentary to *Sefer Mitzvos Gedolos;* came in 1927.

Perlow, Rebbe Yochanan (1900–21 Kislev, 1956): Rebbe of Lutzk (of Karlin dynasty), survived WW II; grandfather of Rebbe Baruch of Karlin-Stolin.

Philip, Rav Yaakov: Ashkenazic scholar, lived in Safed for years, moved to Jerusalem, 1630s. Tried to mediate between the two communities on issue of *chalukah.*

Porush, Rav Naftali Hirsch (died, 19 Cheshvan, 1865): Known as a tzaddik, came to Jerusalem in 1857. Father of Porush family.

Prague, Rav Avraham Yitzchak (1869–24 Teves, 1924): Head teacher at Talmud Torah Shomrei HaChomos.

Prague, Rav Yitzchak (died, 11 Shevat, 1880): Disciple of Chasam Sofer, principal of Doresh Tzyon School.

Pranko, Rav Moshe (1837–1 Teves, 1918): Filled in as Rishon l'Tzyon, 1909–1911.

Rabinovitch, Rav Eliyahu David (1843–3 Adar, 1905): Rav of Mir and Ponevitch. Came in 1901 to help Rav Salant officiate and thereby inherit post of Rav of Jerusalem, but died in 1905 before Rav Salant.

Radvaz: See *Zimra, Rav David*

Ralbach: See *Chaviv, Rav Levi*

Ralbag, Rav Eliezer Dan (1833–1895): Jerusalemite, studied under Rav Salant and Rav of Kotna; gave *shiur* in Etz Chaim Yeshivah before becoming Rosh Yeshivah in 1886.

Rambam: See *Maimonides, Rav Moshe*

Ramban: See *Nachmanides, Rav Moshe*

Rappaport, Rav Yitzchak (died, 17 Tamuz, 1755): Rishon l'Tzyon from 1749 until death. Born in Jerusalem (studied under the Pri Chadash), Rav in Izmir, Turkey, for many years, until he returned. Author of *Battei Kehunah.*

Rashash: See *Sharabi, Rav Shalom*

Revigo, Rav Avraham (died, 29 Kislev, 1713): Born in Modena, Italy; inherited vast wealth from his father. Studied Kabbalah under Rav Binyamin HaKohen and Rav Moshe Zechos, opened yeshivah and propagated study of *niglah* and *nistar*. In 1702, immigrated to Jerusalem and opened yeshivah. Spent his last year as a *shaliach* for the city.

Riki, Rav Emanuel Chai (1688–2 Adar, 1742): Great kabbalist and *rav*, author of *Mishnas Chassidim* (Kabbalah). Spent about four years in Jerusalem.

Rivlin, Rav Binyamin (died, 1812): One of founders of Chazon Tzyon Movement in Shklov, which began influx of Perushim to Eretz Yisrael in 1809. Died en route to Eretz Yisrael.

Rivlin, Rav Hillel (1758–9 Sivan, 1838): Disciple of Vilna Gaon, one of first Perushim to move to Jerusalem, leader of *yishuv*, author of *Kol HaTor*. Father of Rav Moshe the *maggid*, grandfather of Rav Yosef Yoel Rivlin.

Rivlin, Rav Moshe (died, 28 Elul, 1846): A *maggid*, son of Rav Hillel Rivlin; came in 1840 to lead *yishuv*.

Rokeach, Rebbe Aharon (1880–21 Av, 1957): *Admor* of Belz Chassidim from 1927; came in 1944, built up dynasty after Holocaust.

Rokeach, Rebbe Mordechai (1902–1949): Came in 1944 with his brother Rebbe Aharon Rokeach, *Admor* of Belz. Father of present *Admor* of Belz, Rebbe Yisachar Dov Rokeach.

Rokeach, Rebbe Yisachar Dov (*shlita*): Present Rebbe of Belz.

Rot, Rebbe Aharon (18??–6 Nisan, 1947): First Rebbe of Shomrei Emunim Chassidim.

Rot, Rebbe Avraham Chaim (*shlita*): Present Rebbe of Shomrei Emunim Chassidim.

Rothschild, Baron Alphonse (1827–1905): Son of Baron James Rothschild.

Rothschild, Baron Edmond (1845–1934): Philanthropist, built up many places in Eretz Yisrael.

Rothschild, Baron James (Yaakov): (1792–1868): Philanthropist from Paris built first Jewish hospital in Jerusalem, among other charities.

Rotsigel, Dr. Binyamin (died, 1 Adar, 1866): Director of Rothschild Hospital (1864–1866); labored to save Jewish lives during plague of 1865; died from malaria.

Rubi, Rav Raphael Yosef (died, 27 Sivan, 1791): Scholar during second half of 18th century. Author of *Derech HaMelech* on the Rambam.

Rubin, Rav Mordechai Leib (1871–3 Tamuz, 1929): Came in 1891, *dayan* and Rav of Yemin Moshe from 1909.

Salant, Rav Binyamin Beinish (1839–19 Tishre, 1900): Son of Rav Shmuel Salant, *rav* and organizer of Jewish settlements.

Salant, Rav Shmuel (1816–29 Av, 1909): Rav of Jerusalem from 1841 to 1909. One of the great *gedolim* and leaders of *yishuv*.

Salomon, Rav Yoel Moshe (1838–12 Cheshvan, 1913): Builder of new suburbs, publisher of *Yehudah v'Yerushalayim*, founder of Petach Tikva.

Sarna, Rav Yechezkel (28 Shevat, 1890–6 Elul, 1969): Rosh Yeshivah of Hebron Yeshivah (Slobodke), which moved to Jerusalem after riots of 1929.

Sasson, Yechezkel Reuven (died, in 1840s): Sephardic philanthropist, donated half the sum to build Churvah Synagogue.

Schwartz, Dr.: Director of Rothschild Hospital, 1875–1888.

Schwartz, Rav Yosef (1804–9 Shevat, 1865): First modern topographer of Eretz Yisrael, author of *Tevuos HaAretz*, builder of *yishuv*. Came to Jerusalem in 1833.

Schwester Selma (1884–3 Adar, 1984): Head nurse at Shaarei Zedek Hospital for over sixty years.

Shag, Rav Avraham (1801–29 Adar, 1876): Rav of Steldrof, Austria; mentor of Rav Zonnenfeld; came to Jerusalem, 1873; active in communal affairs.

Shalom, Yosef (*yartzeit:* 18 Av): Philanthropist from Calcutta, India; built Porat Yosef Yeshivah in Old City.

Shapiro, Rav Benzion (1873–13 Shevat, 1947): Son of Rav Tzvi Michel Shapiro; great kabbalist.

Shapiro, Rav Chaim Yaakov (died, 21 Sivan, 1908): Rosh Beis Din of Perushim at beginning of 20th century. Rav Tzvi Pesach Frank was his grandson-in-law.

Shapiro, Rav Nasan: From Cracow; Rav of Ashkenazic community of Jerusalem in mid-17th century. Traveled as *shaliach* several times. Wrote books on Kabbalah, including *Tuv HaAretz, Matzos Shemorim*, and *Meoros Nasan*.

Shapiro, Rav Tzvi Michel (1841–12 Elul, 1906): Disciple of Rav of Kotna and Rav Diskin. Author of *Tikun Chatzos*.

Sharabi, Rav Avraham Mizrachi (1774–25 Kislev, 1826): Grandson of Rav Shalom Sharabi, Rosh Yeshivah Beis El from 1802, known as wonder-worker for Jewish people.

Sharabi, Rav Shalom (1712–10 Shevat, 1770): Leading kabbalist of his times, author of deepest kabbalist works since the Ari Zal.

Shlesinger, Rav Akiva Yosef (died, 1 Iyar, 1922): Author of *Lev HaIvri*, fought against secular schools.

Shmulevitz, Rav Chaim (1902–3 Teves, 1979): Son-in-law of Rav Yehudah Finkel, Rosh Yeshivah of Mir from 1965 to 1979; famed for his weekly talks.

Shneur Zalman, Rav (1830–5, Nisan, 1902):

Rav of Lublin (1868–1892), came in 1892; taught Torah, led Chassidic community. Wrote *Toras Chaim* (Halachah and *drash*).

Shneur Zalman, Rav: (1745–24 Teves, 1812): First Lubavitcher Rebbe. Disciple of *Maggid* of Mezeritch; set off for Eretz Yisrael with Rav Menachem Mendel of Vitebst, 1777, but returned in middle of journey. Helped send money for *yishuv*; author of *Tanya*.

Shnitzer, Rav Mordechai (died, 11 Cheshvan, 1865): Scholar and master craftsman. Helped establish Bikur Cholim Hospital.

Shochet, Rebbe Baruch (*shlita*): Present Rebbe of Karlin-Stolin.

Sholal, Rav Yitzchak (died, 1 Kislev, 1524): Great scholar and leader; last of Egyptian *naggidim*; moved to Jerusalem around 1514, where he supported two yeshivos.

Shushan, Rav David (first half of 16th century): Rosh Yeshivah and physician during leadership of the *naggid*, Rav Yitzchak Sholal. When Rav Chaviv came to Jerusalem, he stepped down in order that Rav Chaviv should be Rav of Jerusalem.

Shuvaks, Rav David (died, 1926): Rav of Chassidim after Lubliner Rav died in 1902.

Sid, Rav Shmuel (died, 1645): Rav in Jerusalem during reign of terror (1625–1626) when he was imprisoned. Escaped to Constantinople to petition Sultan to stop Farouk's unlawful reign.

Silva, Rav Chizkiah (1657– 28 Kislev, 1696): Born in Italy, came to Jerusalem around 1676. Studied under Rav Moshe Galante. Author of great halachic work, *Pri Chadash*. Opened yeshivah in Jerusalem, Beis Yaakov Ferira. Buried at foot of Mount of Olives.

Sofer, Rav Moshe (1762–1839): Known as Chasam Sofer, *Gadol HaDor*, Rav of Pressburg; strengthened *yishuv*, sent disciples to Eretz Yisrael.

Sofer, Rav Yaakov Chaim (1870–9 Sivan, 1939): Kabbalist from Baghdad; came in 1904; wrote *Kaf HaChaim* (Halachah).

Soloveitchik, Rav Yitzchak Zev (1886–9 Tishre, 1959): Replaced father, Rav Chaim Soloveitchik, as Rav of Brisk in 1918. Came in 1941 and settled in Zichron Moshe neighborhood of Jerusalem.

Soloveitchik, Rav Yosef Dov Ber (died, 2 Adar, 1981): Son of Rav Yitzchak Zev; became Rosh Yeshivah in 1959.

Sorotzkin, Rav Zalman (1881–1966): Came in 1940; active in Agudas Yisrael, started Vaad HaYeshivos and Chinuch Atzmai. Wrote *Aznaim LaTorah*.

Stern, Rav Moshe Aharon (1925– 8 Adar, 1998): prominent *baal mussar*.

Sternhartz, Rav Avraham (1862–19 Elul, 1955): Rav of Uman, helped reestablish Breslov Chassidus in Eretz Yisrael.

Strauss, Nathan (1848–1931): Philanthropist, aided *yishuv*. In 1910, bought building near Kosel for scholars, called Beis Strauss.

Sozin, Rav Moshe (died, 28 Kislev, 1835): Rishon l'Tzyon from 1824, close companion of Rav Menachem Mendel of Shklov.

Tarani, Rav Yosef (Maharit) (1568–1639): His father, the Mabit, died when he was twelve years old. Traveled from Safed to Egypt and Istanbul, where he became Rosh Yeshivah and *Av Beis Din*. Later returned to Safed.

Tardiola, Rav Shmuel (died, 19 Cheshvan, 1643): Scholar and communal leader. He and his son, Rav David Tardiola, were sought by despot, Mohammed Farouk, in 1625. The son was arrested and tortured.

Tefilinsky, Rav Nasanel (Sofer) (1866–27 Adar, 1918): Greatest expert on *gassos* tefillin, which revolutionized making of tefillin.

Tuketzinsky, Rav Yechiel Michel (1872–8 Nisan, 1955): Mashgiach of Etz Chaim Yeshivah, author of *Gesher HaChaim, Ir HaKodesh v'HaMikdash, etc.*

Turjaman, Rav Moshe (mid-19th century): Moroccan Jew, attempted to strengthen the community.

Tuvo, Rav Elazar (died, 22 Adar I, 1886):

Rosh Yeshivah of Moroccan Yeshivah. Rav of Moroccan *kehillah,* 1880–1886. Wrote *Pedukas Elazar* (Halachah).

Twersky, Rebbe Avraham Dov (died, 29 Av, 1945): Rebbe of Rachmistrivka.

Twersky, Rebbe David (died, 13 Tamuz, 1950): Rebbe of Rachmistrivka.

Twersky, Rebbe Mordechai (died, 18 Iyar, 1920): Rebbe of Rachmistrivka; came in 1906; murdered in riots of 1920.

Twersky, Rebbe Nachum (died, 28 Shevat, 1936): Rebbe of Rachmistrivka, brother of Rebbe Mordechai; came in 1926.

Twersky, Rebbe Yisrael Mordechai (*shlita*): Present Rebbe of Rachmistrivka.

Twersky, Rebbe Yochanan (died, 20 Kislev, 1982): Rebbe of Rachmistrivka, built up dynasty greatly.

Tzemach, Rav Yaakov (1575–1665): Kabbalist and Sephardic Rav of Jerusalem between 1642–1665. Toiled to publish writings of Rav Chaim Vital. Due to him, many writings of Ari Zal were organized and published.

Uziel, Rav Benzion Meir (1880–24 Elul, 1953): Chief Rabbi, 1939–1953, and Rav Sephardi of Jaffa from 1912. Wrote *Mishpatei Uziel* on Halachah.

Valero, Chaim Aharon (1845–1923): Banker, funded many worthy projects.

Vega, Yaakov and Yisrael (17th century): Philanthropists from Livorno, Italy; supported Rav Yaakov Chagiz's Yeshivah, Beis Yaakov, which opened in 1658. Left endowment fund for yeshivah, but embezzlement of money forced yeshivah to close, early 1690s.

Vilna Gaon (1720–19 Tishre, 1797): *Gadol HaDor*, inspired disciples to settle in Eretz Yisrael after two futile attempts ended in failure. Perushim were his disciples.

Vital, Rav Chaim (1543–30 Nisan, 1620): One of greatest kabbalists of all time. Disciple of Rav Moshe Alshich and Rav Yitzchak Luria. Ari Zal commanded that only Rav Vital expound the concepts of Kabbalah, which he did in eight-volume *Shemona Shaarim.* Died and buried in Damascus.

Vital, Rav Shmuel (first half of 17th century): Only son of great kabbalist, Rav Chaim Vital. Spent most of his life in Damascus and Egypt, preparing his father's manuscript for publication. Kabbalist in his own right, published commentary to Siddur, *Chemdas Yisrael.* Rav Yaakov Tzemach was among his disciples.

Wallach, Dr. Moshe (1867–7 Nisan, 1957): Founder and head doctor of Shaarei Zedek Hospital. His humanitarianism was legendary.

Wallenstein, Rav Moshe Nachum (1841–23 Adar, 1922): Head of Kollel Shomrei HaChomos (from 1879), *dayan* on *beis din* of Rav Diskin and Rav Salant.

Wittenberg, Rav Moshe (died, 17 Nisan, 1899): Philanthropist, built courtyard in Moslem Quarter, and a housing project for poor near Meah Shearim called *Shaarei Moshe.*

Yaakov, Rav from Vilna (beginning of 18th century): Coauthored *Meoros Nasan.* Went on *shelichus* to try and save Ashkenazic community in the time of Rav Yehudah HaChassid. Father of Rav Chaim Yerucham, who suffered from debts of Ashkenazic community, and was even imprisoned. Died on *shelichus* in 1748. Grandfather of Rav Yaakov Elyashar.

Yadler, Rav Benzion (8 Kislev, 1871–16 Av, 1962): The *Yerushalmi Maggid,* traveled throughout Eretz Yisrael to speak; attended Agudas Yisrael Convention, 1924.

Yadler, Rav Yitzchak Zev (died, 12 Sivan, 1917): Father of the *Yerushalmi Maggid,* Rav Benzion Yadler.

Yeshaya, Rav (early 18th century): Son-in-law of Rav Yehudah HaChassid. Tried to keep the group together after sudden death of their leader in 1700.

Yevush, Rav Moshe (late 1600s): Philanthropist from Constantinople. Son of Rav Yom Tov Yevush. Supported Rav Moshe Chaviv, responsible for sending him to Jerusalem.

Yisrael, Rav of Shklov (died, 9 Sivan, 1839):

Disciple of Vilna Gaon, Perushim leader in Safed (1809–1837), author of *Pe'as HaShulchan* (Halachah). Built Sukkas Shalom Synagogue in Jerusalem.

Yitzchak bar Shmuel (13th century): Disciple of Ramban, came to Eretz Yisrael with his mentor. Later wrote *Meiros Einayim*, elucidating hidden aspects of Ramban's commentary.

Yitzchaki, Rav Avraham (1661–13 Sivan, 1729): Studied under Rav HaMagen; mentor of Rav Moshe Chagiz and Rav Yitzchak Azulai (father of Chida). In 1715, became Rishon l'Tzyon and head of *beis din*. Died in 1729, buried next to Prophet Zechariah.

Yitzchaki, Rav David (late 1600s): Son-in-law of Rav Avraham Azulai, and father of Rav Avraham and Rav Yitzchak Yitzchaki. Buried next to the *Pri Chadash* on Mount of Olives.

Yosef Zundel, Rav from Salant (1 Tishre 1785–3 Cheshvan, 1865): One of closest disciples of Rav Chaim of Volohzin, *gedol b'Torah* who always hid his greatness and strove to perfect human character; mentor of Rav Yisrael Salanter and Rav Yaakov Sapir; father-in-law of Rav Shmuel Salant; Rav in Jerusalem (1837–1865).

Zakas, Rav Mordechai (1906–6 Adar, 1993): Son-in-law of Rav Charlap; Rosh Yeshivah Beis Zevul.

Zarchi, Rav Shimon (died, 9 Elul, 1860): *Rav* in Russia, immigrated in 1840, founded Etz Chaim Yeshivah.

Zimra, Rav David (c. 1462–c. 1573): One of leading rabbis of 16th century. Known as Radvaz, *rav* in Fez, Cairo, Jerusalem, and Safed. Rav Bezalel Ashkenazi was among his *talmidim*. Wrote *Teshuvos*, *Mizudos David* on the *Taryag Mitzvos*, *Michtam l'David*, and *Yakar Tiferes*.

Zonnenfeld, Rav Avraham Aharon (1878–1912): Eldest son of Rav Yosef Chaim Zonnenfeld, published *Ohr Torah* (1897–1900).

Zonnenfeld, Rav Yosef Chaim (1851–19 Adar II, 1932): Rav of Jerusalem, came in 1873 with mentor, Rav Shag; disciple of Rav Diskin; backbone of *yishuv* through one of its most difficult transitions (1910–1933).

Zoref, Rav Mordechai (died, 9 Cheshvan, 1865): Son of Rav Shlomo Zalman Zoref, father of Rav Yoel Moshe Salomon. Helped father redeem Churvah Synagogue; opened weaving factory.

Zoref, Rav Shlomo Zalman (1785–1837): A leader of Perushim in Jerusalem, traveled to Turkey and Russia for *yishuv*. Known as peacemaker.

Zukerman, Rav Shemarya: Came in 1834 to bolster *yishuv*. Influential in many circles.

Zukerman, Rav Shmuel (1840–6 Adar II, 1929): Apprenticed at Beck Press. Bought the press in 1875 and published numerous books, including his Torah journal, *Torah MiTzyon*.

Bibliography

Achar HeAsef. Jerusalem, 1971.
Azulai, Rav Chaim Yosef David. *Shem HaGedolim*. Warsaw, 1888.
Bachbot, Rav Aharon. *Rabbeinu Chaim Abulafia*. Jerusalem, 1987.
Ben Avraham, Rav N. *Sippurim Yerushalmim* (vols. 1–2). Jerusalem, 1995.
Ben-Arieh, Yehoshua. *Jerusalem in the 19th Century* (2 vols.). Jerusalem, 1984.
Ben-Arieh, Yehoshua. *The Rediscovery of the Holy Land in the Nineteenth Century*. Jerusalem, 1979.
Ben-Shimon, Rav David. *Shaar HaChatzer*. Jerusalem, 1862.
Benvenisti, Meron. *The Crusaders in the Holy Land*. Jerusalem, 1970.
Blau, Rav Moshe. *Al Chomosaich Yerushalayim*. Bnei Brak, 1967.
Carlbach, Rav Eli Chaim. *Yad Ohr HaChaim v'Toldosav*. Jerusalem, 1981.
Chagiz, Rav Moshe. *Elei HaMitzvos*. Jerusalem, 1964.
Chagiz, Rav Moshe. *Elei Masei*. Jerusalem, 1932.
Chagiz, Rav Moshe. *Sefas Emes*. Vilna, 1876.
Chagiz, Rav Yaakov. *Zichron l'Bnei Yisrael*. Warsaw, 1909.
Chaviv, Rav Levi (Ralbach). *Responsa*.
Chaviv, Rav Levi. *Kuntras HaSemichah*.
Chen, Rav Yaakov. *Aliyos Eliyahu*. Tel Aviv, 1975.
Chorvos Yerushalayim. Venice, 1627.
Choshen, Meir. *Statistical Yearbook of Jerusalem*. no. 14 (1996). Jerusalem, 1997.
Collection. *B'yemei HaBinayim*. Jerusalem, 1979.
Collins, Larry, and Lapierre, Dominique. *O Jerusalem!* New York, 1972.
Cortefor, Rav David. *Korei HaDoros*. Petrokov, 1894.
Dayan, Rav Shlomo. *Chachmei HaMaarav*. Jerusalem, 1992.
Eisenstein, Rav Yehudah David. *Otzar Masa'os*. Jerusalem, 1969.
Elmalich, Rav Avraham. *Nasi'im b'Yisrael*. Jerusalem, 1993.
Emden, Rav Yaakov. *Zos Toras HaKina'os*.
Finn, James. *Stirring Times* (2 vols.). London, 1878.
Finn, Mrs. *Reminiscences of Mrs. Finn*. London, 1929.
Friedman, Menachem. *Chevrah v'Daas*. Jerusalem, 1978.
Frieman, Rav Nachum Dov. *Sefer HaZichron HaYerushalmi*. Jerusalem, 1913.
Frumkin, Rav Arie Leib. *Toldos Chachmei Yerushalayim* (4 vols.). Jerusalem, 1929.
Galis, Rav Yaakov. *Enziklopedia l'Toldos Chachmei Eretz Yisrael* (3 vols.). Jerusalem, 1978.
Galis, Rav Yaakov. *M'Gedolei Yerushalayim*. Jerusalem, 1967.
Galis, Rav Yaakov. *Shechunos b'Yerushalayim*. Jerusalem, 1973.
Gaon, Rav David Moshe. *Yehudi HaMizrach b'Eretz Yisrael*. Jerusalem, 1938.
Gartenhoiz, Rav Elazar Lipa. *Eshel HaGedolim*. New York, 1958.
Gedaliah, Rav. *Sha'alu Shalom Yerushalayim*. Berlin, 1716.

Gefner, Rav Yaakov Shalom. *Ohr HaGalil*. Jerusalem, 1976.
Gerlitz, Rav Menachem Mendel. *Marah d'Arah Yisrael*. Jerusalem, 1975.
Getz, Rav Menachem. *Bein Yerushalayim v'Hagolah*. Jerusalem, 1981.
Getz, Rav Menachem. *Kach Nifrazu HaChomos*. Jerusalem, 1981.
Goldstein, Rav Moshe. *Masa'os Yerushalayim*. Munkatsh, 1931.
Goldstein, Rav Yosef. *Mekomos HaKedoshim*. Jerusalem, 1978.
Greyavsky, Rav Pinchas. *Beis HaDefus HaIvri HaRishon b'Yerushalayim*. Jerusalem, 1939.
Greyavsky, Rav Pinchas. *L'Chovavim HaRishonim*. Jerusalem, 1927.
Greyavsky, Rav Pinchas. *MiGinzei Kedem*. Jerusalem, 1977.
Greyavsky, Rav Pinchas. *MiGinzei Yerushalayim*. Jerusalem, 1928.
Greyavsky, Rav Pinchas. *Sefer HaYishuv*. Jerusalem, 1939.
Grozovsky, Rav Reuven. *Biyos HaZeman*. Bnei Brak, 1988.
Halachmi, Rav David. *Chachmei Yisrael*. Bnei Brak, 1980.
Halachmi, Rav Meir. *Toldos HaChassidus b'Eretz Yisrael* (vols. 1–2). Jerusalem, 1996–1997.
Hamburger, Rav Binyamin Shlomo. *Mashichei HaSheker u'Mitnagdeihem*. Bnei Brak, 1989.
Har-el, Menashe. *This Is Jerusalem*. Jerusalem, 1977.
Heller, Rav Avraham Zeide. *HaRav HaManhig v'HaRofeh*. Safed, 1989.
Helprin, Rav Yechiel. *Seder HaDoros*. Warsaw, 1867.
Horovitz, Rav Elazar. *Mosad HaYesod*. Jerusalem, 1958.
Horovitz, Rav Yeshaya HaLevi. *Eden Tzyon*. Jerusalem, 1957.
Horowitz, Rav Chaim HaLevi. *Chibas Yerushalayim*. Jerusalem, 1964.
Kahana, Rav Tzvi. *Meah Shearim*. Jerusalem, 1984.
Kahanov, Rav Moshe Nechemiah. *Sha'alu Shalom Yerushalayim*. Jerusalem, 1969.
Kark, Ruth. *Jerusalem Neighborhoods*. Jerusalem, 1991.
Kassin, Rav Yaakov. *Pri Etz HaGan*. Jerusalem, 1931.
Kitov, Rav Eliyahu. *HaPoteach Shaar*. Jerusalem, 1956.
Kluger, Rav Binyamin. *Min HaMakor* (vols. 1–5). Jerusalem, 1987.
Kluger, Rav Binyamin. *Yerushalayim Sechunos Saviv La*. Jerusalem, 1979.
Kol Sinai (vols. 1–5). Jerusalem, 1962–1964.
Kroyanker, David. *Adrikalos b'Yerushalayim*. Jerusalem, 1983.
Landau, Rav Bezalel. *HaYishuv HaChassidi b'Yerushalayim. Machanaim:* Jerusalem, 1961.
Lipshitz, Rav Aryeh Lebush. *Yesod l'Kra*. Jerusalem, 1967.
Loewe, Dr. Eliezer. *Diaries of Sir Moses and Lady Montefiore*. London, 1890.
Lopian, Rav Eliyahu. *Lev Eliyahu*. Jerusalem, 1975.
Lunz, Rav Avraham. *HaChalukah*. Jerusalem (2nd ed.), 1912.
Lunz, Rav Avraham. *Luach Eretz Yisrael* (vols. 1–18). Jerusalem, 1895.
Lunz, Rav Avraham. *Netivos Tzyon v'Yerushalayim*. Jerusalem, 1876.
Maasef "Tzyon." Jerusalem, 1926–1935.
Malki, Rav Raphael Mordechai. *Likutim* (2 vols.). Jerusalem, 1923.
Mandelbaum, Dr. Simcha. *Esara Doros b'Eretz Yisrael*. Jerusalem, 1995.
Margolios, Rav Reuven. *Toldos HaOhr HaChaim HaKadosh*. Jerusalem, 1926.
Menachem Mendel, Rav Shneur Zalman bar. *Zichron Yerushalayim*. Jerusalem, 1876.
Meyuchas, Rav Avraham. *S'dei HaAretz*. Livorno, 1741.
Montefiore, Sir Moses. *Moshe v'Yerushalayim*. Warsaw, 1879.
Mushkovitz, Rav Tzvi. *Chayei HaRashash*. Jerusalem, 1969.
Muzafi, Rav Salomon. *Sifsei Tzaddikim*. Jerusalem, 1981.
Parchi, Rav Ishtori. *Kaftor v'Ferach*. Jerusalem, 1897.
Parchi, Rav Yitzchak. *Tuv Yerushalayim*. Jerusalem, 1843.
Parparish, Rav Meir. *Ohr Tzaddikim*. Vilna, 1889.
Phillips, John. *A Will to Survive*. New York, 1977.
Porush, Rav Eliyahu. *Zichronos Rishonos*. Jerusalem, 1963.

Porush, Rav Gershon. *B'Ohalei Torah*. Jerusalem, 1997.
Porush, Rav Gershon. *Ti'or*. Jerusalem, 1994.
Rabinovich, Avraham. The Battle for Jerusalem. New York, 1972.
Raz, Rav Simcha. *A Tzaddik in Our Time*. Jerusalem, 1977.
Reiser, Rav Menachem Mendel. *Shaarei Yerushalayim*. Jerusalem, 1871.
Reznick, Rav Leibel. *The Holy Temple Revisited*. New York, 1990.
Rimon, Amnon. *Yerushalayim HaChazuya*. Jerusalem, 1987.
Rivlin, Rav C. *Chazon Tzyon*. Jerusalem, 1946.
Rivlin, Rav Eliezer. *HaTzaddik Rav Yosef Zundel miSalant*. Jerusalem, 1927.
Rivlin, Rav Eliezer. *Tachilas Yishuv HaAshkenazim*. Jerusalem, 1928.
Rivlin, Rav Hillel. *Kol HaTor*. Bnei Brak, 1969.
Rivlin, Rav Shlomo Zalman. *HaMaggid Doresh Tzyon*. Jerusalem, 1960.
Rivlin, Rav Shlomo Zalman. *Midrash Shlomo*. Jerusalem, 1953.
Rivlin, Rav Yosef Yoel. *Reshis HaYishuv Chutz l'Chomas Yerushalayim*. Jerusalem, 1939.
Rivlin, Yaakov Moshe. *Reshis HaYishuv HaYehudi m'Chutz LaChomos*. Jerusalem, 1978.
Rosenthal, Rav Shabbetai. *Masuah l'Dor*. Jerusalem, 1971.
Rozen, Mina. *HaKehillah HaYehudis b'Yerushalayim b'Meah ha-17*. Tel Aviv, 1985.
Sasson, Rav Avraham HaLevi. *Maasei HaTzaddikim*. Jerusalem, 1889.
Schmelz, Uziel. *Population of Jerusalem*. Jerusalem, 1988.
Selma, Schwester. *My Life and Experiences at Shaarei Zeddek*. Jerusalem, 1980.
Shafar, Rav Shaul. *Har HaBayis*. Jerusalem, 1972.
Shapiro, Rav Moshe Nachum. *Har HaKodesh*. Jerusalem, 1971.
Sheinberger, Rav Yosef. *Amud Aish*. Jerusalem, 1950.
Schwartz, Rav Yoel. *Rabbeinu HaGadol*. Jerusalem, 1995.
Schwartz, Rav Yoel. *Tzyon Beis Chaiyeinu*. Jerusalem, 1980.
Schwartz, Rav Yosef. *Tevuos HaAretz*. Jerusalem, 1900.
Stern, Rav Avraham. *Melitzei Eish*. New York, 1975.
Stern, Rav Yechiel Michel. *Gedolei HaDoros*. Jerusalem, 1996.
Surasky, Rav Aharon. *Dimuyos Hod*. Jerusalem, 1978.
Surasky, Rav Aharon. *Ohros miMizrach*. Bnei Brak, 1974.
Surasky, Rav Aharon. *V'Zos LaYehudah*. Jerusalem, 1996.
Tennenbaum, Rav Moshe. *Masa'os Moshe*. Salavaki, 1925.
Tukatzinsky, Rav Nisan Aharon. *HaAretz l'Givuloseya*. Jerusalem, 1970.
Tukatzinsky, Rav Yechiel Michel. *Iyr HaKodesh v'HaMikdash*. Jerusalem, 1970.
Tukatzinsky, Rav Yechiel Michel. *Sefer Eretz Yisrael*. Jerusalem, 1970.
Varner, D. *Tzaddik Yesod Olam*. Jerusalem, 1985.
Wallach, Rav Shalom Meir. *Shosheles Boston*. Jerusalem, 1994.
Waxman, Rav Chaim Moshe. *Eretz Yisrael*. Jerusalem, 1963.
Weinman, Rav Tzvi. *M'Ktovitz ad Hei B'Iyar*. Jerusalem, 1989.
Weinstock, Rav Yitzchak Shmuel. *Bonei Yerushalayim*. Jerusalem, 1976.
Weiss, Rav Shraga. *Chachmei HaSephardim b'Eretz Yisrael*. Jerusalem, 1981.
Yaari, Rav Avraham. *Sheluchei Eretz Yisrael*. Jerusalem, 1977.
Yadler, Rav Benzion. *Betuv Yerushalayim*. Jerusalem, 1994.
Yehudah, Rav Yitzchak Yechezkel. *HaKosel HaMaaravi*. Jerusalem, 1968.
Yeshivas Mir – Yerushalayim. Jerusalem, 1994.
Yudelovitch, Rav David. *Kovetz Ma'amarim*. Tel Aviv, 1936.
Zachariah, Rav Shabbetai. *Battim u'Mosdos Yehuda'im b'Rovah HaMuslami b'Yerushalayim HaAtika*. Jerusalem, 1985.
Ziling, Rav Yehudah. *Yalkut Eretz Yisrael*. Vilna, 1891.
Zonnenfeld, Rav Shlomo Zalman. *Guardian of Jerusalem*. New York, 1986.

Glossary

(plural endings are given in parentheses)

Acharonim: Later Authorities
agunah (-os): woman unable to remarry because husband's death cannot be substantiated.
aliyah: immigration to Eretz Yisrael
anshei gevardiah: lit. "men of strength;" name of private Jewish patrol force used in the 19th century
aron kodesh: Holy Ark
avodah: service
baal(-ei) teshuvah: repentant
bachur (-im): young, unmarried man
battei: houses of
beis din: Jewish court of law
beis midrash: house of study
bimah: table upon which the *sefer Torah* is read
bris milah: circumcision ceremony
chacham (-im): Torah scholar
Chacham Bashi: Leading Wise Man
Chacham: spiritual Sephardic leader
chachmei: Torah scholars
challah (-los): loaves of sweet bread eaten on Shabbos and Yom Tov
chalukah: funds received from Diaspora for the Jewish communities in Eretz Yisrael
chametz: leavened bread
chareidi: Orthodox
chatzer: courtyard
Chazal: Talmudic Sages
cheder: talmud Torah
chelev: forbidden animal fats
cherem: ban, excommunication
chiddush (-im): novel interpretation
chilul Hashem: desecration of the Name of God
cholent: hot dish served Shabbos morning, usually made with beans, potatoes, and meat
Chumash: Five Books of Moses
churvah: destroyed place
chutz laAretz: outside of Israel, i.e., Diaspora
darshan (-im): a sermon by a rabbi
dayan (-im): rabbinic judge
dir (Arabic): courtyard
drash (-os): Torah discourse
Eretz Yisrael: Land of Israel
firman: imperial decree
gabbai: treasurer of synagogue
gadol (gedolei) hador: spiritual leader of the generation
gadol b'Torah: great in Torah
galus: exile
Gan Eden: Garden of Eden
gaon (-im): one of the highest distinctions given to a Torah scholar
gedolim: Torah sages
Gemara: explanation of the Mishnah
geula: redemption
grush (-im): Turkish currency used in the 17th century. 400 grush could buy a house in Yerushalayim.
halachah: law
hamam: Arab bathhouse
Hashem: God
hashkafah: view of life
haskamah: approbation of a book
heimish: friendly
hesger: talmud Torah
Jelebi: highest post a Jew could have in Egyptian court
k'vitel: note given to a Chassidic Rebbe
Kabbalah: Jewish mysticism
kadi (Arabic): title of highest Turkish judge; replaced every year with a new one from the capital city of Constantinople
kares: excommunication
kedushah: holiness
kehillah (-os): congregation
kever: grave, tomb
kipa: skullcap
kollel: yeshivah for married men
Kyach: abb. of *Kol Yisrael Chaverim* ("All Israel are Brothers"), used as name of secular

French school system called Alliance Israelite Universelle.
lashon hara: slander
levaya: funeral procession
likutim: compendium
maamar: imperial decree; also called a *firman*
Maariv: evening prayer service
maggid: eloquent speaker
Mashiach: Messiah
matzah shemurah: matzah guarded from time of harvest
melachah: work
menorah: candelabra
migdal: tower
mikve (mikvaos): immersion pool
Minchah: afternoon prayer service
minhag (-im): custom
mishmeres (-os): watch
Mishnah HaGadol: second in command
Mishnah: Oral Law
mitzvah: commandment
mussar: ethical self-perfection
naggid: Jewish spiritual leader in Egypt
nasi: leader of the Jewish community
niglah: revealed aspects of the Torah
nistar: mystical side of the Torah
nusach: version
parnas: Jewish communal leader
parnasah: livelihood
parshah: weekly portion of the Torah read on Shabbos
parshiyos: parchments placed inside tefillin
pasha (Arabic): Turkish mayor-governor
Perushim: disciples of the Vilna Gaon
Pesach: Passover
pesak: halachic decision
peshat: simple meaning
petirah: death, passing away
pita (-os): flat, round bread
posek (poskim): halachic authority
rabbanim: rabbis
rabbeinu: our master
rial: Egyptian currency
Rishon l'Tzyon: leader of Sephardic community
Rishonim: Early Authorities (11th–15th centuries)
Rosh (Av) Beis Din: head of the rabbinic court
Rosh Yeshivah: head of the yeshivah
roshei tevos: initial letters of Hebrew words
sefer (sefarim): book
sefer Torah: Torah scroll
segulah: good omen
seraf: angel
sh'tar pasharah: compromise agreement
Shabbos: Sabbath
Shacharis: morning prayer service
shaliach (shelichim): emissary; specifically, fund-raiser for Jewish community in Eretz Yisrael who traveled to Diaspora
Shas: the entire Talmud
shechitah: ritual slaughter
Sheik al-Yehud (Arabic): Jewish lay leader
shelichus: mission abroad from the *yishuv*
shemitah: Sabbatical year
shetibel (-blach): small shul
shidduch: marital match
shlita: abbr. of, "may he live a long and productive life, amen."
shmuessen: talks on ethical themes
shochet (shochatim): Jewish butcher
shuk: market place
siddur: prayer book
slichos: prayers of supplication
sofer (sofrim): scribe who writes *sefer Torah*, tefillin, and mezuza
takanah (-os): regulation, rule
talmid (-im): student of Torah
talmid chacham: Torah scholar
talmud Torah: elementary school, *cheder*
Tanach: Five Books of Moses, Prophets, and Writings
Tanna: Talmudic Sage
Tehillim: Book of Psalms
tevel: untithed produce
tikun: rectification
tzaddik (-im): righteous man
tzitzis: four cornered garment
wakf: a Moslem consecrated place or religious institution
yartzeit: anniversary of date of death
Yerushalayim: Jerusalem
yeshivah (-os): place for studying Torah; in earlier times it only included married men
yiras shamayim: fear of Heaven
yishuv: settlement
Yom Tov: one of the three Festivals

Index

— A —

Abba Shaul, Rav Benzion, 459
Abbasid Caliphate, 5
Abdullah Pasha, 176-177
Abuchatzera, Rav Yisrael, 223
Abulafia, Rav Chaim Nisim, 217, 219
Abulafia, Rav Chaim, 103, 127
Abulafia, Rav Yedidiah, 136, 177, 237
Adani, Rav Shlomo, 33-34
Aderes. *See* Rabinovitch-Te'umim
Aga, Ibrahim, 56-62
Aga, Ottman, 58-62, 88-91
Agudas Yisrael Convention, 406, 447
Agudas Yisrael, 409, 448-449, 451, 465, 518, 524
Aharon Moshe, Rav from Brody, 228, 265-266
Aharon, Rebbe of Karlin, 229
Ahuhav, Rav Yitzchak, 85
Akko, 6, 7, 9, 12, 163, 165, 172, 175-177, 187, 192
Akrish, Rav Yitzchak, 462
Al-Mu'azzan, 6
al-Sharaf, 124
Aleppo, 52
Alexander Dynasty, 472
Alexander, Bishop Michael, 194
Alexandria, 182, 183
Ali, Mohammed, 182, 185, 187
Allenby, General, 391, 408, 423
Alliance Israelite Universelle (Kyach), 326, 340, 445
Alshich, Rav Moshe, 30, 31
Alter, Rav Avraham Mordechai, 448-449, 472, 474, 480-481, 525
Alter, Rebbe Pinchas M., 525
Alter, Rebbe Simcha, 525
Alter, Rebbe Yisrael, 472, 525
Amalek, 170, 355
Amalric, 5, 7
Amigo, Rav Avraham, 75
Amram, Rav Yaakov ibn, 60, 89
Amshinov Dynasty, 471-472
Amsterdam Aid Fund, 407
Amsterdam, xxi, 71, 84, 213, 254
anshei gevardiah, 174, 199-200, 215, 365
Anshin, Rav Shmuel, 345
Archa, Rav Eliezer ibn, 92
Archduke Maximilian, 272
archeological digs, 244-249
Ari Zal. *See* Luria, Rav Yitzchak
Armenian Quarter, 512
Arrub Springs, xvii
Asher, Dr. Asher, 308
Asher, Rav Avraham, 140
Ashkelon, 5, 6, 7
Ashkenazi, Nasan, 73-76, 96
Ashkenazi, Rav Avraham, 217, 334, 360
Ashkenazi, Rav Bezalel, x, 30, 32-33, 43
Ashkenazi, Rav Mordechai, 115
Atiyah, Rav Ezra, 458-459, 556
Attar, Rav Chaim, x, 125, 138, 144, 153-155, 223; grave of, 95, 473; met Rav Riki, 126; in Jerusalem, 126-132; met Rav Abulafia, 127; on Yom Kippur, 129; in Karaite Synagogue, 129-130; death, 130-131; after death, 131-132; on Hoshanah Rabbah, 156
Auerbach, Rav Chaim Leib, 402, 541
Auerbach, Rav Meir, x, 174, 226, 234, 256-257, 275, 290, 295, 298, 300, 310, 317, 327-328, 334, 360, 364, 366, 445
Auerbach, Rav Moshe, 407
Auerbach, Rav Shlomo Zalman, 402, 464, 522-523, 541, 544, 558-559
Avraham's Vineyard, 253-254
Avraham, ben Avraham, 186
Avraham, Rav Shimshon of France, 9
Avraham, Rebbe of Kalisk, 228
Avritch, Rav Avraham Dov, 189, 191
Azulai, Rav Avraham, 66, 73, 80
Azulai, Rav Chaim Yosef David (Chida), x, xxi, 69, 86, 126, 129, 135-136, 141, 144, 223, 418, 559-561

— B —

Baal HaTanya, 230
Baal Shem Tov, 133
Baalei Tosefos, xix, 6, 8, 16, 444
Babba Sali. *See* Abuchatzera, Rav Yisrael
Bachbot, Rav Shalom, 270-271
Badahav, Rav Yitzchak, 417-418
Baharan, Rav Nachum of Shadik, 258
Baharan, Rav Zalman, 301, 339, 376-377
Baldwin I, 5
Balfour Declaration, 434-435, 455, 465
Balfour, Lord Arthur James, 434
Balian of Ibelin, 5
Bar Kochba, 436
Barcelona, 12
Barclay Gate, 248
Barclay, J.J., 245-246
Bardaky, Rav Shlomo, 257

Bardaky, Rav Yeshaya, xxv, 175, 186, 193, 214, 235, 237-238, 242, 256-257, 271-272
Bartenora, Rav Ovadiah, x, 3, 11, 15, 25, 39; letter, 17-18; commentary to the Mishnah, 18; grave of, 19; wrote about Cave of Prophets, 333
Baruch, Rav from Pinsk, 205-206
Baruch, Rav of Jerusalem, 13
Baruch, Yom Tov, 138
Barzani, Moshe, 495
Basan, Rav Zalman, 286
Batelman, Rav David, 498-499
Battei Broide, 385-386
Battei Kehunah, 139
Battei Machse, 254-256, 301, 411, 420, 427, 444, 482, 490
Battei Milner, 342-343
Battei Neitin, 385-386
Battei Nisan Beck, 304
Battei Rand, 346
Battei Ungarin, 342, 345, 484, 543
Battei Warsaw, 341
Battei Wittenberg, 343, 348
Battei Yehudah Touro, 284-286
Battle for Jerusalem, 530-533, 566-567
Battle of Akko, 6, 187
Battle of Ein Harod, 7
Battle of el-Alamein, 473
Battle of Hattin, 5
Baybars (Mamluk king), 7
Bayit Vegan, 454, 471-472, 539
Becher, Nisim, 326
Beck, Rav Nisan, 228, 259-260, 277-278, 306
Beck, Rav Yisrael, 183-184, 219-220, 228, 230, 259, 291, 317, 319
Bedouin, xiv-xv, 151, 184, 198-200, 203-204, 252, 262, 284, 286, 294-295, 302, 304, 362
Beira (Gan Montefiore), 226, 252, 367-368
Beirut, 172
Beis David, 174, 243, 296, 389
Beis HaMussar, 389
Beis Iksa, 175, 184
Beis Lapletos, 539
Beis Rothschild, 514
Beis Shean, 13
Beis Strauss, 392-393
Beis Yaakov, 304, 306
Beis Yisrael, 339-340, 401, 402, 472, 490-491, 543
Belz Dynasty, 526
Ben Ish Chai, 274, 458
Ben-Gurion, David, 555-556
Ben-Shimon, Rav David, xix, 223-227, 267-268, 287, 367, 483
Ben-Shimon, Rav Raphael, 225, 483
Ben-Yehudah, Eliezer, 318-319, 356
Berav, Rav Yaakov, 25, 27, 28-30, 223
Beril, Rav Yechiel, 316-317
Berlin Institute, 328-329
Berlin, Rav Chaim, 327, 389, 399-400, 405, 414
Berlin, Rav Naftali Tzvi, 445-446
Berlin, Rav Tzvi, 255
Berman, Rab Abba, 535
Berman, Yehoshua, 302
Bernadotte, Count Folke, 509
Bernstein, Rav Fishel, 443
Beruit, 7, 182, 457
Biderman, Rebbe David, 229-230, 263, 341, 419-420, 468, 470
Biderman, Rebbe Elazar Mendel, 229, 467
Biderman, Rebbe Moshe Mordechai, 230
Biderman, Rebbe Moshe, 228-229
Biderman, Rebbe Shimon Nata Nasan, 230, 470
Binyamin David, Rav from Vilna, 233
Binyamin, Rav from Toledo, 7-8, 38
Biton, Rav Yitzchak, 69
Blau, Rav Moshe, 349, 425-426, 464
Blau, Rav Yitzchak Shlomo, 326
Blazar, Rav Yitzchak, 388, 413-414
blood libel, 46-48, 211, 216, 264-265, 314, 351
Blumenthal Orphanage, 393, 539
Blumenthal, Rav Yaakov, 324
Blumenthal, Yosef, 238
Bodko, Yosef, 403
Bola, Rav Moshe, 138
Bolshevik Revolution, 433
Bonei Yerushalayim, 288-289
Boston Dynasty, 470-471
Boyan Dynasty, 526
Boys Town, 539-540
Bratrand, Madame, 245
Braverman, Rav Zerach, 378-379, 400, 406
Breslov Chassidus, 348, 528-529
Brim, Rav Chaim, 520
British, 436
Broide, Rav Yaakov Yosef, 385-386
Brovender, Rav Chaim, 536
Broyer, Rebbe Nachum, 526
Bucharim, 341-342, 447
Bukspan, Rav, 464
Bull, Odd, 530
Burma Road, 508
Burnstein, Rebbe Avraham, 471
Burnstein, Rebbe Chanuch, 471
Burnstein, Rebbe David, 471

— C —

Cailingold, Esther, 552-553
Cairo, 16-17, 72, 118, 140, 150, 186
Cave of the Prophets, 333-334
Cave of Zedekiah, 245-247
Cenacle, 23
Chabad, 230; shul, 340
Chacham Bashi, 216-218
Chacham Tzvi, 81, 112-113
Chagiz, Rav Moshe, 39, 80, 82, 116
Chagiz, Rav Yaakov, xii, 68, 69-72, 75-77, 79, 80, 82
Chagiz, Yosef, 453
Chaim Nachum, Rav, 297, 406
Chaim, Rav of Volozhin, 207
Chaiyun, Rav Gedaliah, 132, 133-134, 138
Chakrei Lev, 167
chalukah, xx-xxii, 63-64, 173-174, 221, 223, 309, 326
Chananiah, Rav Avraham, 75
Charlap, Rav Yaakov Moshe, 389, 403, 418
Chasam Sofer, 140, 176, 190-191

Chaselvitzer, Rav, 311
Chasman, Rav Leib, 541
Chassidic community, 228, 230
Chassidim, 174, 183, 227-228
Chatzer Strauss, 386-388
Chavatzeles, 291, 316-317, 333, 341
Chavilio, Rav David, 92
Chavilio, Rav Yitzchak, 58
Chaviv, Rav Levi, 25-26, 29-30, 52
Chaviv, Rav Moshe, 82-83
Chazan, Rav Benzion, 513-514
Chazan, Rav David, 167, 277
Chazan, Rav Yosef, 167, 171, 361
Chazon Ish, 459, 491-492, 522, 558-559
Chazon Tzyon movement, 168, 192
Chefetz, Rav Leib, 329
cherem, 237, 325-326
Chesed L'Avraham, 73
Chevras Ahavas Shalom, 135
Chevras Shaarei Chesed, 373
Chevras Shulei Dagim, 252
Chida. *See* Azulai, Rav Chaim Yosef David
Chinuch Atzmai, 524
Chmielnicki, 67
Chofetz Chaim, 421
Chorvos Yerushalayim, 63
Chovavei Tzyon movement, 445-446
Christianni, Pablo, 9
Churchill, Sir Winston, 437
Churvah. *See* Synagogue, Churvah
Chuzin, Rav Zadkah, 461
Citadel of David, 6, 7, 60, 62, 117, 352
Clarendon, Lord, 283
Clock Tower, 384, 394
Cohen, Dr. Albert, 242
Cohen, Rav Aharon, 554
Cohen, Rav Michel, 257, 289, 291-293, 316-318, 327
Cohen, Rav Nasanel, 426
Conforti, Rav David, 67
Conki, Avraham, 72
Constantinople, xxv, 21, 22, 71, 72, 117, 123, 139-140, 143, 144, 151, 172, 212, 239, 319, 370, 397, 462
Cordovero, Rav Gedaliah, 35-36
Cordovero, Rav Moshe, 28, 31, 35
Costro, Rav David, 35-36
Council of Clermont, 4
Coyanca, Rav Benzion, 273-274, 320
Crimean War, 247
Crusaders, 3, 4
Cunningham, Sir Alan, 436, 477, 511
Cyrus, 169
Czar Nicholas I, 259

— D —

Dahar al-Amar, 127
Damascus Gate, 245-246, 255, 304, 345, 348, 390, 423
Damascus, 5, 6, 10, 13, 46, 52, 58, 65, 80, 90, 101, 176, 179, 213
Danon, Rav Nisim, 397
Danziger, Rebbe Yehudah, 472
Darwinism, 433
Day of Judgment, 102
Dayan, Rav Aryeh Leib, 339
DeHaan, Dr. Yaakov, 450-452
Deir Yassin, 476
DeSaulcy, 244, 247
deshen, 332
Dessler, Rav Eliyahu, 538
Deutsch, Rav Yitzchak, 237
Deweik, Rav Chaim Shaul, 469, 491
Diskin Orphanage, 324, 327-329, 348, 379, 392 405, 460, 539, 541
Diskin, Rav Yehoshua Leib, 19, 229, 320-326, 346, 348, 352, 379-380, 390, 398, 405, 409-410, 460
Diskin, Rav Yitzchak Yerucham, 405, 440, 444
d'Lyon, Rav Moshe, 9
Dome of the Rock, 517
Dormition Abbey, 356
Doron, Rav Bakshi, 541
Dosa, Rabbi Chaninah ben, 98, 270
drought: of 1748, 133; of 1829, 180
Druse, 182-183, 191-192
Dushinsky, Rav Yosef Tzvi, 463-464, 503-504

— E —

earthquake, 6, 136-137, 139, 170, 174, 186, 188-192, 228, 254, 345, 454
Edessa, 5
Eidah Chareidis, 518
Eiger, Rav Akiva, 444
Ein Kerem, 282
ein rogel, xvii
Ein Yaakov, 25
Eisen, Rav Shalom, 386
Eisenstein, Rav Avraham, 256, 276-277
Elbachari, Rav Emanuel, 95
Elef HaMagen, 79
Elfandari, Rav Shlomo Eliezer, 462, 491
Elgazi, Rav Shlomo the Elder, 80, 86
Elgazi, Rav Yaakov, 144
Elgazi, Rav Yisrael Yaakov, 139-140
Elgazi, Rav Yom Tov, 126, 132, 135, 140, 144-145, 164, 166, 179
Eliezrov, Rav 464
Elimelech, Rav Yosef, 225
Elindaf, Rav Avraham, 349
Elishberg, Rav Mordechai, 446
Eliyahu HaNavi, 202
Eliyahu, Rav Mordechai, 541, 560-561
Elkalai, Rav Yehudah, 446
Elmoshnino, Rav Yosef, 93
Elyashar, Rav Chaim Moshe, 443
Elyashar, Rav Yaakov Shaul, 217, 319, 333, 335, 355, 380, 396, 415-417
Elyashiv, Rav Shlomo, 542
Elyashiv, Rav Yosef Shalom, 542-543, 558
Emden, Rav Yaakov, 120
Emperor Franz Joseph, 261, 277-278, 351, 428-430
Emperor Frederick II, 6
Emperor Wilhelm II, 352-357
Entebbe, Rav Yaakov, 213, 220
epidemics, 16
eruv, 356, 398

Ettlinger, Rav Yaakov, 255, 315, 444
Etz Chaim (commentary to Mishnah), 69
Etz Chaim (Kabbalah), 67
Even HaEzel, 459, 554-555
Even Yisrael, 304
Ezra, the Scribe, 169
Ezras Nidachim Society, 349
Ezriel, Rav (disciple of Vilna Gaon), 168
Ezriel, Rav Aharon, 136
Ezriel, Rav Avigdor, 143

— F —

Falk, Mrs. Devorah, 214
famine, 105-106
Farouk, Mohammed, 56-63, 88, 143
Fatah, 545
Fatimids, 4-5
Feinstein, Meir, 495
Feinstein, Rav Moshe, 519, 541
Feivish, Rav Uri Shraga, 68, 81
Ferira, Rav Yaakov, 85-86, 138
Finkel, Rav Beinush, 520-521, 562, 565-566
Finkel, Rav Chaim Zev, 562-563
Finkel, Rav Eliezer, 519-520, 562-563
Finkel, Rav Nasan Tzvi, 562
Finn, James, 130, 250, 253-254, 269-270, 332
Finn, Mrs., 263
firman, 171, 216, 219, 239, 289, 314, 397
Fish, Rav Ephraim, xii, 31, 33, 35
Forbes, Mr., 351
France, 7
Franciscans, 23
Frank, Rav Tzvi Pesach, 422-423, 435, 443, 459, 462-465, 473
Frankel, Ludwig, 236-237
Freidus, Rav Sender, 425
Friedman, Rav David, 326, 444
Friedman, Rebbe Avraham, 259
Friedman, Rebbe Mordechai, 526
Friedman, Rebbe Yisrael, xxi, 228, 259
Frumkin, Rav Aryeh Leib, 360-361
Frumkin, Rav Yisrael Dov, 317, 327, 333, 349
Furst, Rav Avraham, 302

— G —

Gabbai, Rav Shem Tov, 138
Gad, Rav Baruch, 68-69
Gagin, Rav Avraham, 136, 214, 218-220, 396
Galante, Rav Moshe the Elder, 28, 79
Galante, Rav Moshe, xxi, 67, 71, 79-83, 98-102, 106-107
Galloway, Mr., 351
Gan Montefiore. *See* Beira
Gaon, Rav Yitzchak, 60, 67, 89
Garmizan, Rav Shmuel, 75, 80
Gaza, 7, 73, 74, 88, 97, 180
Gedaliah, Rav, 114, 149
Gelbstein, Rav Hillel Moshe, 230, 331
Genghis Khan, 6
German Orphanage, 327
Gerrer Dynasty, 472-473, 525
Gershon, Rabbeinu, 68
Get Pashut, 82
Geula (neighborhood), 253, 321, 461, 524
Geyoni, Kasan, 118-119
Gezer, 5
Gilriran, Shimon, 140
Girls Town, 539
Givat Mordechai, 461
Givat Pinchas, 336, 471
Givat Shaul, 282, 302, 329, 392, 460
Givat Yerushalayim, 282
Godfrey of Bouillon, 5
Goldman, Rebbe Avraham, 470
Goldman, Rebbe Mordechai, 469
Goldman, Rebbe Shlomo, 469, 493-494, 500-501
Goldman, Rebbe, Gedaliah, 470
Goldman, Rebbe, Moshe, 469
Golomav, Rav, 406
goral haGra, 199
Goyatos, Rav Yitzchak, 192
Graetz, Heinrich, 327
Graf, Rav Moshe, 306
Grave of Yosef HaTzaddik, 384
Great Assembly, 334
Greinerman, Rav Chaim, 520
Grodzensky, Rav Chaim Ozer, 398, 464-465, 524
Groner, Dov, 495
Guta, Rav Nasan, 69

— H —

HaBavli, Rav Boaz, 349
HaChassid, Rav Avraham, 39
HaChassid, Rav Yehudah, xix, xxiv, 86, 111-115, 149, 228, 239, 444
Hadaya, Rav Ovadiah, 523
Haganah, 457, 476, 494, 515
Haifa, 192, 267, 475, 507
Haj Amin, 455
HaKohen, Rav Ephraim, 81
HaKohen, Rav Moshe, 118
HaKohen, Rav Nasan (*naggid* of Cairo), 17
HaKohen, Rav Yehudah Leib, 81
HaKohen, Rav Yitzchak, 86
HaKohen, Rav Yonasan of Lunil, 9
Halberstam, Rav Yechezkel (Shiniver Rav), 131, 229-230
HaLevanon, 244, 257, 316-317
HaLevi, Mr. Avraham of London, 333
HaLevi, Rav Avraham (Rav of Cairo), 86, 118
HaLevi, Rav Avraham, 23
HaLevi, Rav Binyamin, 92
HaLevi, Rav Mordechai, 166
HaLevi, Rav Moshe, 396-397
HaLevi, Rav Naftali Hertz, 320, 446
HaLevi, Rav Shalom Yitzchak, 350
HaLevi, Rav Yehudah (author of *Kuzari*), 8
HaLevi, Rav Yoel, 89-90
Halprin, Rav Zalman, 493-494
Hamid Gate, 385
Hamun, Rav Moshe, 21
HaNavi, Eliyahu, 42-43
Har HaMenuchos, 557, 559
Har Nof, 471, 533, 569-572
HaTzvi, 318, 320
Hebrew language, 324, 439, 441, 522-523
Hebrew University, 516

Hebron, xvi, xx, 7, 9, 16, 33, 63, 74-75, 85, 88, 97, 118, 144, 183, 229, 310, 344, 467, 507
Heller, Rav Shmuel, 188, 328
Heller, Rav Yom Tov, 33
Heritage House, 537
Herman, Rav Yaakov Yosef, 550-551
Herodian, xvi, 546-547
Hertz-Lemel, Mrs., 238
Hertzberg, Dr., 324, 328
Herzl, Theodore, 352-356, 482
Herzog, Rav Yitzchak, 463, 473, 558
Hilchos Yom Tov, 140
Hildescheimer, Rav Ezriel, 328
Hillel the Elder, 165
Hillel the Elder, Rav, 27
Hillel the Younger, Rav, 27-28
Hirsch, Rav Yisrael Chaim, 501-502
Hirshenson, Chaim, 328
Hivon, Rav Aharon, 81
Holy Sepulcher, 95
Horowitz, Rav Chaim, 220, 228
Horowitz, Rav Moshe Shmekel, 230
Horowitz, Rav Naftali Chaim, 230, 346
Horowitz, Rav Yeshaya, 51-54, 89-90, 470
Horowitz, Rebbe Levi Yitzchak, 471
Horowitz, Rebbe Pinchas David, 336, 470-471
Hoshanah Rabbah, 62, 156
Hospitals
— Austrian, 348
— Bikur Cholim, 243, 266, 389, 407, 427, 454, 485, 534
— Christian, 242
— Ezras Nashim, 392
— Hadassah, 516, 533-534
— Misgav Ledach, 243, 397, 552
— Mount Scopus, 476
— Rothschild, 242-243, 258, 278, 389
— Shaarei Zedek, 243, 304, 390-392, 398, 408, 451, 389, 485-489, 531, 534, 568-569
Houminer, Rav Shlomo, 304
Houminer, Rav Shmuel, 386, 566-567
Hurwitz, Rav Avraham Simcha, 469
Husseini, Abdul Khader, 476, 509
Husyatin, Rebbe Yisrael of, 473

— I —

Ibn Ezra, 11
Ibrahim Pasha, 182-184, 187
Imrei Binah, 234
Institute for the Blind, 440
intifadah, 545
Irgun, 457, 476, 494
Iyash, Rav Yaakov, 166
Iyash, Rav Yehudah, 131
Izmir, Turkey, 72, 182

— J —

Jaffa Gate, xvii, 15, 250, 261, 292, 307, 332, 352, 384, 394, 408, 425, 437
Jaffa, 180, 198, 226, 351, 367, 385, 440
Jamil Pasha, 408, 421, 425
Jerusalem Corridor, 530
Jessey, Henry, 68
Jewish Agency, 450, 455, 503
Jewish Press, 315-318
Jewish Quarter, xxv, 125, 157, 216, 234-235, 239, 254, 259, 275, 278, 281, 286, 293, 380, 390, 509-517, 533, 537, 550
Joint. *See* American Jewish Relief Fund, 408
Joseph, Dov, 476

— K —

Kaf HaChaim, 402, 481
Kaftor v'Ferach, 13, 23, 332
Kahanneman, Rav Yosef, 472, 519
Kahanov, Rav Nechemiah, xviii, xxi, 235, 276, 311, 327, 377
Kahn, Rebbe Avraham, 529
Kalba Savua, 198, 244
Kalish, Rebbe Shimon Shalom, 471-472
Kalish, Rebbe Yerachmiel, 471-472
Kalisher, Rav Tzvi, 444-445
Kalonimos, Rav, 46-48
Kamundo, Count Avraham, 216
Karlin-Pinsk, 340
Karlin-Stolin Dynasty, 526-527
Karo, Rav Yosef, 15, 24, 26-27, 28, 30, 31, 73, 79, 85
Kastel, 509
Katamon, 509, 526
Kefar Moshe, 252
Kerem Cadcod, 364
Kerem, 321
Ketav Sofer, 356
khubeiza, 509
kiddush hachodesh, 25
Kidron Valley, xvi, 18, 96, 132, 264, 380
kimcha d'pischa, 370
King Abdullah, 509
King David Hotel, 437, 457
King David, 38-39, 63, 577-578
King Farouk, 507
King Guy of Lusignan, 5
King Hezekiah, 32, 44
King Hussein of Jordan, 530
King Hussein of Transjordan, 451
King Philip II Augustus, 6
King Richard the Lion-Heart, 6
King Solomon, 39, 332, 577, 582
King Zedekiah, 246
Kiryat Belz, 526
Kiryat HaYeled, 539
Kiryat Moshe, 461
Kiryat Yearim, 165
Kitover, Rav Gershon, 120, 132-133, 135, 154-155, 228
Kleyeras, Rav Moshe, 403, 470
Knesses Yisrael, 343
Kobner, Rav Chaim, 291
Kobo, Rav Yitzchak, 217
Kol HaTor, 174, 193
Kol Nidrei, 129
Kollek, Teddy, 533, 543-544, 570
Kollel America, 221
Kollel Minsk, 373
Kollel Ungarin, 484
Kollel Warsaw, 221, 231, 345
Komarner Rebbe, 143
Kook, Rav Avraham Yitzchak, 275, 296, 403-404, 406, 434, 443-444, 446-449, 455-457, 461, 466, 482, 494
Kook, Rav Yehudah Tzvi, 461
Korei HaDoros, 67
Korel, Rav Yaakov, 166

Kornel, Rav Nachman Nasan, 188
Kosel, 24; discovery of, xxii, 39-41; forbidden entry, 58; prayers by, xxiii, 106, 164, 175, 229, 282, 474, 500, 578; writing note, 153; finding note; 550-551; crying at, 178; attempt to buy houses nearby, 186, 230, 330-331; poor at, 223; dream of, 228; approaching, 229, 573-576; study at, 230; benches at, 231; answered at, 263; streets to, 344; Herzl's visit, 356; lamps, 394; Arab claim to Wall, 455; visitors, 462; 40 days straight, 500-501; 1948 loss of, 510; regained in 1967, 532; *birkas kohanim*, 538; rabbanim at, 564-565; size, 582; builder, 582-583
Kotler, Rav Aharon, 519
Kotzk Chassidim, 230
Kreiger, Yosef, 326, 368-370
Krosz, Delisia, 483
Kunshatat, Rav Baruch, 521

— L —

Ladino, xi, 84, 115, 251, 319
Lag b'Omer, xxvi, 214, 334, 388, 513, 530
Landau, Rav Menachem Mendel, 449
Laniado, Rav Shlomo, 458
Lapoliansky, Rav Uri, 538, 572-573
Latrun, 507-508
League of Nations, 433
Lebanon, 7
Lehren, Akiva, 186, 193
Lehren, Tzvi Hirsch, 206, 213
Lemel School, 236-238
Lemil, Rav Asher, 214
Lev l'Achim, 538
Levi, Rav Yaakov Leib, 191
Levi, Rav Yaakov, 398
Levine, Rav Aryeh, 466-467, 475, 494-498
Levush, 65
Levy, David, 570
Levy, Shmuel, 386, 393
libraries
— Tiferes Yerushalayim, 327;
— Etz Chaim Yeshivah, 327
Linchner, Rav Alexander, 539-540
Linchner, Rav Moshe, 539
Lion's Gate, 531
Livorno (Leghorn), 69, 82, 83, 125, 126
locust plague of 1745, 133
Loewe, Dr. Eliezer, 283-284, 294, 310, 312-314, 368
London blitz, 550
London, 226
London, Dr., 243
Lopian, Rav Eliyahu, 569
Lord Napery, 239
Loytas, Rav Yehudah Aryeh, 306
Lumzar, Rav Leib, 291, 315
Lunzano, Rav Menachem, 34-35
Luria, Rav Shemarya, 180, 184-186, 213
Luria, Rav Yitzchak (Ari Zal), 26-27, 30, 31-32, 42-44, 65, 67, 191
Luria, Rav Yosef, 198
Lyon, Rav Benzion, 299, 302

— M —

Ma'ali, Rav Binyamin, 123
maaser, 13, 399, 445, 464
Mabit. *See* Tarani, Rav Moshe
Machane Yehudah, 393-394, 487
Machane Yisrael, 287
Machpelah, xxii, 10, 72
Maharal of Prague, 258
Maharit. *See* Tarani, Rav Yosef, 34
Maimonides, Rav Moshe (Rambam), 8, 69, 126
Majar, Rav Avraham, 136
Majar, Rav David, 135, 138
Malach, Chaim, 112
Malachi Hotel, 488
Malbim, 314
Malki, Rav Mordechai, xvi, 83, 86, 113, 116
Malki Zeddek, 580
Malko, Rav Yaakov, 86
Malko, Rav Yosef, 77, 81, 92
Mamillah Pool, xvii-xviii, 287
Mamluk, xxiv, 7, 13, 20-21
Mandate period, 453, 540, 546
Mandelbaum Gate, 516, 553
Mandelbaum, Rav Simcha, 553-555
Mandelbaum, Rav Yechezkiah, 339
Mani, Rav Eliyahu, 328
Mann, Rav Yaakov, 390-391
Marcus, David, 508
Margolios, Rav Asher Zelig, 340, 491-493, 503
Markus, Rav Baruch, 403
Marranos, 20, 29, 65
Marxism, 433
Mashiach's House, 342
Mashiach, 41, 170, 174, 179, 193-194, 206, 213, 229, 345, 545, 577, 582
Maskil l'David, 143
Meah Shearim, 258, 297-304, 339, 364-365, 366, 377, 456, 498, 503, 529, 555, 566, 569
Mecca, 176, 200
Medini, Rav Chaim Chizkiyahu, 462
Megillah, 26
Meir, Rav Yaakov, 275, 341, 392, 396, 443-444, 470
Meleches Shlomo, 33
Meltzer, Rav Issar Zalman, 459, 556-557, 566
Menachem Mendel, of Lubavitch, 230
Menachem Mendel, of Vitebsk, 228
Menachem Mendel, Rav from Shklov, xxiv, 120, 170, 175, 177-179, 193, 196, 198, 200-201, 361
Mendel, Rebbe of Kotzk, 230
Mendelowitch, Rav Shraga, 519, 539
Meron, 127, 165, 183, 191, 335
Messiah, false, 24
Meyuchas, Rav Avraham, 121, 132
Meyuchas, Rav Mordechai Yosef, 140, 164, 166
Meyuchas, Rav Moshe, 122
Meyuchas, Rav Raphael, 122-123, 129, 132, 138, 138, 150-152
Michlin, Rav Chaim Michel,

415-417
Midrash HaAgunah, 344-345
Migdal David. *See* Citadel of David
Mikve Yisrael, 353, 445
mikve, xix, 9, 185, 193, 230, 284, 300, 500
Milchamos, 9
Milikovsky, Rebbe Yaakov, 472
Minzburg, Rav Velvel, 462, 468, 513-515
Mishkenos Moshe, 314
Mishkenos Sha'ananim, 282-286, 293
Mishkenos, 494
mishmeros, 41-42
Misnagdim, 231
missionaries, 194, 220, 242-243, 253, 369
Mizkeres Moshe, 236, 313, 343
Mizrachi movement, 446, 450, 465
Mizrachi, Rav Nisim, 123, 132
Mizrachi, Rav Yisrael Meir, 132
Mizrachi, Rav Yisrael, 126
Moghrabi Quarter, 330
Mohliver, Rav Shmuel, 445
molad, 13
Mongols, 6, 7
Montague, Sir Shmuel, 308, 312
Montague-Asher Report, 309-310
Montefiore Testimonial Fund, 307-308, 313-314, 325, 390
Montefiore, Lady Judith, 202
Montefiore, Leonard, 202, 220
Montefiore, Sir Moses: to build waterduct, xvii; first visit, 180; his dream, 201-203; in Constantinople, 213; with Rav Gagin, 220; sixth visit, 225-226; sent money, 239; plan for Jews, 251-252; help in plague of 1865, 258; buys land, 283-286; windmill, 285, 340; sixth visit, 286; building neighborhoods, 288-289; seventh visit, 294; retirement, 308; last visit, 310-312; death, 313-314, built Tomb of Rachel, 336; to build railroad, 351; at Gan Montefiore, 367-368
Montefiore, Yosef Sebag, 340
Mordechai, Yona, 570
Morishkas, x-xi, xx, 115, 222
Moroccan community, 222-227
Moroccan Quarter, 223
Moshe Yehudah Leib, Rav of Kotna, 235, 257
Moslem Quarter, 40, 93, 124, 230, 286, 329, 344, 346, 348, 423, 511, 545
Moss, Rav Shimon, 377
Motza, 368-370
Mount Moriah, 578-579
Mount of Olives, 11, 38-39, 48, 86, 95, 131, 142-143, 176, 178, 192, 197, 225, 247, 265, 299, 350, 356, 360, 363, 380-381, 428, 473, 517
Mount Scopus, 437, 516
Mount Tabor, 165
Mount Zion, xvii, 22, 106, 149, 283, 293, 355, 510, 517, 581
movie house, 479
muchtar, 489, 512
Mufti, 157
Munzon, Rav Avraham, 337-338
Musayoff, Rav Shlomo, 341
Musrara, 388, 468, 516
Muzafi, Rav Yaakov, 461

— N —

Nachalas Shiva, 282, 288-295, 297, 303, 359, 361-362, 390, 437
Nachalas Yisrael, 336
Nachmanides, Rav Moshe (Ramban), 3, 9; letter, 10-11; seal, 12
Nachum, Rav Eliezer, 124, 132
Nahar, Rav Menachem, 89
Najara, Rav Moshe, 73
Najara, Rav Yisrael, 185
Nakib, 116-117
Napoleon, 145, 163-166
Narel, Rav Tuvia, 120-121
Narkiss, Uri, 533
Nasan Nata, Rav (son of Menachem Mendel), 176, 179, 183, 186, 193, 200, 214
Nasan Nata, Rav, 111-112, 116
Nasan, Rav Avraham, 82
Nasser, President, 530
Natenson, Nechemiah, 446
Navon, Rav Binyamin, 190
Navon, Rav Yehudah, 138, 218
Navon, Rav Yona, 126, 131, 132-133, 138
Navon, Yosef (of Beis Strauss), 391
Navon, Yosef, 351
Nehemiah, 185
Neiman, Dr., 242
Neiman, Rav Aryeh, 179
Neitin, Rav Menachem, 385
Neturei Carta, 518
Netziv, 399
Neuwirth, Rav Yehoshua, 523
Neve Sha'anan, 453
New Gate, 383
Ninio, Rav Yaakov, 143
Nisim, Rav Yitzchak, 541, 559
Notre Dame, 383, 517
Nur al-Din, 5

— O —

Ohel Moshe, 314
Ohr HaChaim (sefer), 126, 129
Ohr HaChaim. *See* Attar, Rav Chaim
Omar al-Khattab, 40
Operation Kedem, 510
Operation Nachshon, 476
Ophel, 546
Orenstein, Rav Yaakov, 319-320, 326
Orenstein, Rav Yitzchak, 511-512
Orthodox City Council, 443-444
Oslo Agreement, 545
Ottoman Empire, 7; conquest of Middle East, 20; life under, 21; as governing body, 54-56; reaction to Shabbetai Tzvi, 76; controlling the empire, 140; loses Middle East, 182; annulled debt of Ashkenazim, 185; regained power, 211-212; Crimean War, 247; against publications, 317-318; decline, 384

— P —

Pach, Rav Zundel, 302
Palai, Rav Yehudah, 569-572
Palestine Exploration Fund, 249
Palmach, 494

Panijel, Rav Eliyahu Moshe, 396-397, 443
Panijel, Rav Meir, 217, 351, 396
Paparish, Rav Meir, 66
Pappo, Rav Yehudah, 223-224
Parchi, Chaim, 164, 176, 179
Parchi, Raphael, 179
Parchi, Rav Ishtori, 13-15, 23
Parchi, Rav Yitzchak, 141, 192, 220
Pardes, Rav Eliyahu, 454
Pardo, Rav Aharon, 80
Pardo, Rav David, x, 138, 143-144
Parsiz, Zalman, 393
Partition Plan, 475-476, 511
Partzovitz, Rav Nachum, 560, 564
Passover, 94, 200-201
Pe'as HaShulchan, 170, 183
Pe'ilim, 538
Peel Plan, 464-465
Peel, Lord Earl, 464
Perlow, Rebbe Elimelech, 527
Perlow, Rebbe Moshe, 527
Perlow, Rebbe Yisrael, 527
Perlow, Rebbe Yochanan, 527
Perushim, 168, 185, 192, 196, 232, 239
Petach Tikva, 291, 424
Pezemano, Mr. Yozef, 238
Philip, Rav Yaakov, 64
Pines, Yechiel, 307, 313, 325-327, 389
Pinto, David, 138
Pinto, Rav Yeshaya, 92
plague, 24, 170, 175
Polansky, Rav Shimshon Aharon, 339, 381, 490-491
Pool of Amygdalon, xvii
Pope Urban II, 4
Porush, Rav Gershon, 419
Porush, Rav Menachem, 543
Porush, Rav Naftali Tzvi, 258, 387-389
Porush, Rav Naftali, 453
Porush, Rav Shlomo Zalman, 372-375
Prague, Rav Avraham Aharon, 441
Prague, Rav Yitzchak, 239, 361
Pri Chadash, 83-84, 104
Prince Arnat of Karak, 5
Purim, Shushan, 25-26

— Q —

Queen Helena, 244
Queen Sada, 244

— R —

Rabbinate Office, 443
Rabinovitch-Te'umim, Rav Eliyahu David, 236, 398-400, 446
Rachmistrivka Dynasty, 468-469
Radvaz. *See* Zimra, Rav David
railroad, 351, 385, 436
Ralbach. *See* Chaviv, Rav Levi
Ralbag, Rav Eliezer Dan, 235-236, 363
Ramat Eshkol, 533
Ramla, 7, 61, 88, 165
Ramot, 533, 571
Rand, Rav Mendel, 346
Rappaport, Rav Yitzchak, 139
Rashash. *See* Sharabi, Rav Shalom
Rechavia, 453
Reform movement, 315, 324, 327, 329, 403
Refson, Rav David, 536
Reines, Rav Yitzchak, 446
Reiss, Rav David, 235, 295, 385
Reuveni, David, 24
Revigo, Rav Avraham, 115-116
Riki, Rav Emanuel Chai, 125-126, 127, 130
Riots: of 1921, 455; of 1929, 346, 455-457; of 1936, 345, 457, 464
Rivlin, Rav Eliyahu Yosef, 230
Rivlin, Rav Binyamin, 168
Rivlin, Rav Eliezer, 361
Rivlin, Rav Eliyahu, 214
Rivlin, Rav Hillel, 168, 170-171, 174, 175, 179-180, 184, 192-193, 214, 292
Rivlin, Rav Moshe (*maggid*), 191, 192, 196, 212-215, 218, 250, 264-265, 290, 362
Rivlin, Rav Yitzchak, 335
Rivlin, Rav Yosef Yoel, 258
Rivlin, Rav Yosef, 276, 282, 288-292, 298, 301, 303, 339, 361-366, 371
Rivlin, Zalman, 360
Robinson's Arch, 248
Robinson, Edward, 192, 244, 247
Rockefeller Museum, 437, 531
Rokeach, Rebbe Aharon, 526
Rokeach, Rebbe Yisachar Dov, 435, 526
Rom, Rav Yona, 443
Rommel, Erwin, 473
Rosenthal, Rav Yitzchak, 464
Rosnis, Rav Yehudah, 122
Rot, Rebbe Aharon, 529
Rothschild, Baron Alphonse, 240, 243
Rothschild, Baron Edmond, 242, 330-331, 350
Rothschild, Baron James, 241-242
Rothschild, Baron Lionel, 238
Rothschild, Baron Wolf, 320
Rotsigel, Dr., 258
Roza, Rav Chaim, 135
Rubi, Rav Raphael Yosef, 143
Russian Compound, 293, 426, 437, 494-495
Russian Revolution, 342
Russian-Japanese War, 396
Russnak, Moshe, 513-514

— S —

Sabbatical year, 25
Sacks, Rav Menachem, 422
Safed, xvi, xx, 7, 25, 26, 29, 30, 31, 44, 52, 61, 63, 64, 65, 79, 92-93, 118, 120, 127, 139, 165, 170, 174, 176, 183, 188-189, 227, 230, 254, 256, 344, 403, 467, 507
Saladin, 5-6
Salant, Rav Binyamin Beinish, 290, 359-360
Salant, Rav Shmuel, x, xxi, 174, 213, 226, 229, 232-236, 240, 291, 295, 297, 306, 310, 312, 317, 319, 322, 327, 352, 355, 359-360, 366, 371-374, 389-390, 397, 401, 405, 410, 417, 446, 463
Salanter, Rav Yisrael, 187, 206, 213
Salomon, Rav Yoel Moshe, 257, 288-292, 315, 317-318
Samaritans, 409
Sambatiyon River, 205-206

Samuel the Prophet. *See* Tomb of Shmuel HaNavi
Samuels, Sir Herbert, 436, 465
Sandel, Theodore, 391
Sanhedria, 453
Sanhedrin, 76, 205, 578
Sanjak (pasha), 68
Sarna, Rav Chezel, 555-556
Sasson, Yechezkel Reuven, 239
Schiller, Rav Nata, 536
Schools
— Doresh Tzyon, 238-239, 311
— Eveline Rothschild, 238
— Lemel, 238, 322
— Bezalel, 403
Schwadron, Rav Shalom, 500-501, 538, 541-542, 556-557
Schwadron, Rav Yitzchak, 556-557
Schwartz, Dr., 243
Schwartz, Rav Yosef, 185, 220, 257, 272
Schweitzer, Dr. Albert, 485
Schwester Selma, 485-488
Scott, Colonel, 467
Second Wave, 395, 447
Seer of Lublin, 228, 263
Siege of Akko, 165
Selim I, 20
Seljuk, 4
semichah, 27-30, 79
Seminaries
— Eyat, 536
— Neve Yerushalayim, 536
Sennacherib, 32, 44
Sh'nei Luchos Habris, 51
Sha'alu Shalom Yerushalayim, 114-115
Shaar Ephraim, 81
Shaar HaChatzer, 223-224, 268
Shaar HaPinah, 349
Shaarei Chesed, 388-389, 403, 418, 423-424, 497, 523, 542
Shaarei Yerushalayim, xxv, 244, 332
Shabbetai Tzvi, 72-78, 80, 96-98, 112, 120
Shabbetai, Rav Uri, 232
Shag, Rav Avraham, 255, 323, 327
Shalom, Yosef, 458
Shaltiel, David, 509
Shapiro, Rav Chaim Elazar, 421, 461-462
Shapiro, Rav Chaim Yaakov, 463
Shapiro, Rav Moshe, 392, 411-413
Shapiro, Rav Nasan, 67-69
Shapiro, Rav Shlomo Zalman, 201
Shapiro, Rav Shmuel, 528
Shapiro, Rav Tzvi Michel, 235, 320
Shapiro, Rav Yudel, 520
Sharabi, Rav Avraham Mizrachi, 171, 177, 179, 218
Sharabi, Rav Shalom, 125, 132, 134, 141, 144, 156-158
Shatz, Prof. Boris, 403
Shechem, 10, 188
Sheik al-Yehud, xiii, 17, 35
Sheik Nimar, 411-412
Sheikh Jarrah, 387, 476
Sheinbaum, Rav Yisrael Chaim, 302
Sheinberg, Rav Pinchas, 535
Sheinker, Rav Shmuel, 419-420
Shelah. *See* Horowitz, Rav Yeshaya
shemitah, 13, 30, 54, 326, 445, 447, 464
Shemonah Shaarim, 31
shetibel, Ohel Moshe, 231
Shevat Achim, 339
Shevut Ami,
Shi'ites, 4-5
Shiloach Spring, 19, 32, 44-45
Shiloach, 282
Shimon HaTzaddik, 334. *See also* Tomb of Shimon HaTzaddik.
Shiriz, Rav Chaim, 90
Shitah Mekubetzes, 30, 33
Shlesinger, Rav Akiva, 229, 356
Shlesinger, Rav Yechiel, 521
Shmuel, Rav Yitzchak of Akko, 9
Shmulevitz, Rav Chaim, 520, 563-564
Shneider, Rav Shmuel, 413
Shneur Zalman, Rav of Lublin, 346, 352, 377-378, 380, 468, 470
Shneur Zalman, Rebbe of Lubavitch, 166
Shochet, Rebbe Baruch, 527
Sholal, Rav Yitzchak (*naggid* of Cairo), 14, 23-24, 25, 26, 41-32
Shomrei HaChomos, 345-346
Shpitzer, Rav Shmuel, 388
Shub, Rav Eliezer, 246
Shulchan Aruch, 104
Shushan, Rav David, 23
Shuster, Rav Meir, 537
Shuvaks, Rav David Lippman, 443, 468
Sid, Rav Shmuel ibn, 58, 62, 92
Silva, Rav Chizkiah, 83-86, 103-104, 116, 125, 129, 139
Simcha Zissel, Rav of Kelm, 386-388
Simchas Torah, 102
Simol, Rav Yaakov, 367
Single Gate, 248
Sipin, Abu, 32, 44-46
Sirilio, Rav Shlomo, 30
Sirkish, Rav Yoel (Bach), 54
Six-Day War, 520, 530, 534, 539, 545, 555, 567-568
Smith, Admiral William, 165
snowstorm, 143-144, 147-148, 479-480
Sochotshov Dynasty, 471
Sofer, Rav Shimon, 444
Sofer, Rav Yaakov Chaim, 402, 481
Sokolov, Nachum, 434
Solomon's Pools, xvi, 258, 436
Soloveitchik, Rav David, 521
Soloveitchik, Rav Dov Ber, 521
Soloveitchik, Rav Meir, 521
Soloveitchik, Rav Yitzchak Zev (Velvel), 519, 521, 543, 565, 567
Sorotzkin, Rav Zalman, 524-525
Sozin, Rav Moshe, 171, 179, 201
Spanish Expulsion, 20, 25, 28
Spector, Rav Yitzchak Elchanan, 444, 446
Statement of Policy, 465
Stern, Rav Moshe Aharon, 550-552
Sternhartz, Rav Avraham, 528
Stoller, Feivish, 373-375
Storrs, Sir Ronald, 436-437
Stratford, Lord, 283
Strauss, Nathan, 386-388, 391-392, 408
Strauss, Shmuel, 388-389
Suez Canal, 261-262

Sukkos, 10, 177
Suleiman the Magnificent, Sultan, 20-22, 39, 332
Sultan's Pool, xvii, 15
Sultan Abdul Hamid I, 140
Sultan Abdul Hamid II, 319, 355, 383-384, 397
Sultan Al-Kamil (Egyptian), 6
Sultan Mohammed (Mamluk), 15
Sultan Mohammed II, 166, 211
Sultan Abdul Majid, 211-212
sundial, 411-412
Sunnites, 4-5
Synagogues
— Bannai, 28
— Bas Aiyn, 189
— Beis Menachem, 230
— Beis Yaakov, 340, 374-375
— Churvah, xii; height, xxv; 78-79; destruction, 119-120; claim to, 171; building permit, 185; 201, 207; built, 239-242; 259; heart of *yishuv*, 260; 291; death in, 321; fight in, 326, 328; beadle of, 337; eulogy of Rav Diskin, 380; Yerushalayim Maggid speaks, 401; sundial, 411; destroyed in 1948, 513
— Eliyahu HaNavi, xi, 78, 158
— Karaite, 120-130
— Khal Tzyon, 190
— Khal Yerei'im, 346, 543
— Menachem Tzyon, 179, 185-186, 193, 207, 214, 234-235, 337, 359
— Ohel Shmuel, 341
— Ohel Yaakov, 390
— Ohr HaChaim, 170, 512
— Rabban Yochanan ben Zakkai, xi, xiii, 46, 78, 171, 277
— Ramban, 11, 16, 17, 78
— Shaarei Tzyon, 235
— Shemesh Tzadakah, 461
— Shoshanim l'David, 480
— Sukkas Shalom, 187, 193, 257
— Tefillah l'Moshe, 348
—Tiferes Yisrael, xxv, 259-262, 277-278, 468, 513-514
— Tzuf Devash, 227, 287
— Zoharei Chamah, 393, 413

— T —

Tach v'Tat, 67
Talok, Rav Mordechai, 138
Talpiot, 453
Tam, Rav, 21
Tamari, Dov, 498
Tarani, Rav Moshe, 28
Tarani, Rav Yosef, 34, 36, 184
Tardiola, Rav David, 57
Tardiola, Rav Shmuel, 57, 62
Tarinksy, Rav Moshe, 89
Tatars, 7
Tefer, Rav Moshe Leib, 295
Tefilinsky, Rav Nasanel, 420-421
Teitelbaum, Rav Yoel, 502-503, 519
Tel Aviv, 230
Tell, Abdullah, 509, 513, 515
Temple Mount, xvi, xxii, 44-45, 75, 124, 125, 142, 149, 230, 247, 278, 344-346, 356, 392, 412, 517, 547, 578-579
Temple, First, 44, 577
Temple, Second, x, xvi, 3, 169, 185, 222, 517, 577-578
Temple, Third, 547, 577
Ten Tribes, 205
Tennvarzal, Yaakov, 341
terumah, 13, 399-400, 445
Tevil, Mrs., 424
Tevuos HaAretz, 185
Tiberias, xx, 7, 22, 61, 63, 127, 165, 176, 188, 227, 467, 507
tikun chatzos, 156
Tisha b'Av, 77, 106, 178, 455
Titanic, 392
Tobler, Mr., 247-248
Toldos Aharon Dynasty, 529
Toldos Chachmei Yerushalayim, 360-361
Tombs
— of King David, 22-23, 106, 247, 331-332
— of Rachel, 106, 178, 230, 314, 336-338, 487
— of Shimon HaTzaddik, 106-107, 184, 230, 244-245, 332, 334
— of Shmuel HaNavi, xxvi, 80, 97, 149-150, 175, 184, 334-336, 471
— of the Kings, 198, 244-245
— of Zechariah, 95-96, 265-266
Touro, Judah, 282-283, 340
Treber, Feibel, 294, 306
Truman, President, 476
Tuketzinsky, Rav Nisan, 460
Tuketzinsky, Rav Yechiel Michel, 393, 459-460
Turjeman, Rav Moshe, 223
Turjeman, Rav Yaakov, 223
Turnheim, Rav Nasanel, 543
Tuv Yerushalayim, 141, 220
Tuvo, Rav Elazar, 225
Twersky, Rebbe Avraham Dov, 468
Twersky, Rebbe David, 468
Twersky, Rebbe Mordechai, 455, 468
Twersky, Rebbe Nachum, 468
Twersky, Rebbe Yisrael Mordechai, 469
Twersky, Rebbe Yochanan, 468
Tyre, 6
Tyropean Way, 546
Tzadkah, Rav Yehudah, 459
Tzemach, Rav Avraham, 67
Tzemach, Rav Yaakov, x, 65-67, 69, 75

— U —

U-Thant, 530
Uganda, 434
United Nations, 465, 475, 507, 511, 530
Uri, Rav of Starelsik, 264
Uziel, Rav Benzion, 540, 543

— V —

Vaad HaKlali, 174, 176, 296
Vaad HaYeshivos, 524-525
Valley of Ayalon, 508
Valley of Hinnom, xvii, 517
Valley of Jehoshafat, 11, 107
Vega brothers, 69, 82
Villavsky, Rav Yaakov David, 459
Vilna Gaon, 168-171, 174, 177-178, 193, 205, 212, 281, 297-298, 362, 444, 564
Vineyard of Cadcod, 298-299, 364
Vital, Rav Chaim, 26, 30, 31-32, 35, 44-46, 66, 73
Vital, Rav Shmuel, 65-66

— W —

Wailing Wall, *See* Kosel
Wallace, General, 368-369
Wallach, Dr. Moshe, 243, 389-391, 418-419, 462, 485-489
War of Independence, xvi, 507-515, 517, 551, 555
Warren, Sir Charles, 249
Wasserman, Rav Simcha, 535
Wein, Rav David, 472
Weinbach, Rav Mendel, 536
Weingarten, Rav Mordechai, 512-513, 515
Weinberg, Rav Noach, 536
Weissberg, Rav Yosele, 568-569
Weizmann, Dr. Chaim, 434, 439-443, 455
Well of Yoab, 147
Wertheimer, Rav Shimshon, xxi
Western Wall, *See* Kosel
White Paper, 465-466
Wilson's Arch, 248
Wilson, Charles, 248
windmill, 283-284
Winegrad, Rav Yitzchak, 380
Wittenberg, Rav Moshe, 329, 385
Wolbe, Rav Shlomo, 564
Wohl, Mr. Morris, 461
World War I, 392, 405-406, 433-434
World War II, 473-475
Wosner, Rav Shmuel, 542

— Y —

Yaakov, Rav from Vilna, 116, 118
Yad Ezra, 538
Yad Sarah, 538, 571
Yadler, Mrs., 371-372
Yadler, Rav Benzion, 344, 399-401, 403-404, 406
Yadler, Rav Yitzchak Zev, 400
Yanitshiri, 166
Yebrov, Rav Alter, 503
Yehodioff, Elisha, 342
Yehudiah, 184
Yellin, David, 356
Yellin, Yehoshua, 291, 327
Yemenite community, 222, 349-350
Yemin Moshe, 340-341, 401, 417
Yeshivos
— Aish HaTorah, 536
— Avnei Nezer, 471
— Beis El (Midrash Chassidim), 133, 141, 143, 144, 157, 171, 179, 218, 237, 454, 523-524
— Beis HaTalmud, 542
— Beis Yaakov (Ferira), xii, 85, 86, 125, 132, 138-139
— Beis Yaakov (Vega), xii, 69, 73, 78, 82, 93
— Brisk, 521
— Chaim v'Chesed, 166
— Chaverim Makshivim, 125
— Chayei Olam, 231, 348, 404, 454, 469
— Chesed l'Avraham, 138, 143
— Damascus Eliezer, 138
— Degal Torah, 400
— Diaspora, 536
— Dushinsky, 332
— Etz Chaim, xviii, 234-236, 255, 257, 276, 290, 311, 318, 327, 377, 390, 440, 459-460, 566
— Gedolas Mordechai, 138
— Hebron, 461, 541
— Heichal HaTorah, 563
— Iyun HaTalmud, 535
— Kedushas Yom Tov, 138
— Knesses Yisrael, 127, 131, 138, 154
— Kol Torah, 521-523, 541, 558
— Kol Yaakov, 536
— Machane Yisrael, 537
— Magen Avraham, 138
— Meah Shearim, 400, 406
— Meor Einayim, 469
— Merkaz HaRav, 461
— Mir, 340, 520-521, 561-565
— Nachalas Moshe, 536
— Navardok, 524
— Neve Shalom, 138
— Ohalei Shem, 542
— Ohel Moshe, 321, 380
— Ohr Baruch, 536
— Ohr Chadash, 388
— Ohr HaChaim, 537
— Porat Yosef, 458-459, 481, 535-536
— Shaar HaShamayim, 402-403, 454
— Shapells, 536
— Shoshanim l'David, 402
— Slobodke, 456, 461
— Talmud Torah Yeshivah, 78, 139, 158
— Tiferes Tzvi, 542
— Tiferes Yisrael, 526
— Toldos Yitzchak, 218
— Torah Ohr, 535
— Toras Chaim, 404, 457
— Volozhin, 446
— Zion, 78
Yevush, Rav Moshe, 82-83
Yisrael, Rav from Shklov, xxi, 170, 174-176, 186, 192-193, 205, 256, 361
Yitzchak, Rav Yechiel, 8-9
Yitzchaki, Rav Avraham, 86, 120-122, 132
Yitzchaki, Rav David, 80, 81
Yom Kippur, 10, 217
Yosef, Rav from Laida, 183
Yosef, Rav Ovadiah, 458, 541
Yosef, Rav Raphael, 72-73, 78
Yosuf Pasha, 122
yovel, 13
Yudelevitch, Rav Shabbetai, 538

— Z —

Zaddok, Rav, 350
Zadkah, Rav Yehudah, 480-481
Zamiro, Nasan, 370-371
Zarchi, Rav Shimon, 235
Zaya, Rav Yosef, 30
Zechariah, the Prophet, 265
Zechos, Rav Moshe, 66
Zeitlin, Rav Zalman Leib, 198
Zengi, 5
Zichron Moshe, 389, 542-543
Zichron Tuvia, 320, 373
Zichron Yaakov, 403
Zimra, Rav David, 30-31, 223, 230
Zion and Jerusalem, 581-582
Zion Gate, 242, 293, 380, 513, 515
Zionism, 356, 395, 409, 434, 439-441, 517
Zionist Congress, 353, 409, 434
Zlatnik, Rav Michel, 400
Zohar, 9, 35, 71, 115, 206, 580
Zonnenfeld, Rav Shmuel Binyamin, 427
Zonnenfeld, Rav Yosef Chaim, x, 235, 239; in Battei Machse,

255; attacked, 275; 319; disciple of Rav Diskin, 320; reviews Pines' book, 325; 329, 339, 352; at visit of Emperor Wilhelm II, 355; with Dr. Wallach, 391; refuses leadership, 397-398, 410; reaching out campaign, 403-404, 447; during WW I, 407; with Rav Moshe Shapiro, 412; with son-in-law, 419-420; death of son, 427-428; eulogizes Emperor Franz Joseph, 428-430; reaction to Balfour Declaration, 436; on Hebrew, 440; meets Weizmann, 441-442; as Rav of Jerusalem, 444; with Rav Kook, 447-448; at new Diskin Orphanage, 460; meets Rebbe Shapiro, 462; death, 463; in snowstorm, 470-480; meets Zionists, 482; *levaya* of woman, 483; with Rav Polansky, 490-491

Zoref, Rav Mordechai, 252

Zoref, Rav Shlomo Zalman, 171, 185-186, 188, 192

Zukerman, Gavriel, 294

Zukerman, Rav Shemarya, 180

Zukerman, Rav Shmuel, 319

Zundel, Rav Yosef of Salant, 187, 206-207, 213-214, 232, 258, 297

Zwebner, Rav Yisachar Ber, 323, 328

Zweille Dynasty, 469-470

Zweille, 340